Ancient Inca
Alan L. Kolata

Ancient Central China
Rowan K. Flad, Pochan Chen

The Colonial Caribbean
James A. Delle

Ancient Teotihuacan
George L. Cowgill

Early Medieval Britain
Pam J. Crabtree

Ancient Greece: Social Structure and Evolution
David B. Small

Ancient Gordion

Lisa Kealhofer
Santa Clara University

Peter Grave
University of New England

Mary M. Voigt
College of William & Mary

CAMBRIDGE
UNIVERSITY PRESS

University Printing House, Cambridge CB2 8BS, United Kingdom

One Liberty Plaza, 20th Floor, New York, NY 10006, USA

477 Williamstown Road, Port Melbourne, VIC 3207, Australia

314–321, 3rd Floor, Plot 3, Splendor Forum, Jasola District Centre, New Delhi – 110025, India

103 Penang Road, #05–06/07, Visioncrest Commercial, Singapore 238467

Cambridge University Press is part of the University of Cambridge.

It furthers the University's mission by disseminating knowledge in the pursuit of education, learning, and research at the highest international levels of excellence.

www.cambridge.org
Information on this title: www.cambridge.org/9781108490313
DOI: 10.1017/9781108780681

© Cambridge University Press 2022

This publication is in copyright. Subject to statutory exception and to the provisions of relevant collective licensing agreements, no reproduction of any part may take place without the written permission of Cambridge University Press.

First published 2022

Printed in the United Kingdom by TJ Books Limited, Padstow Cornwall

A catalogue record for this publication is available from the British Library.

Library of Congress Cataloging-in-Publication Data

Names: Kealhofer, Lisa, author. | Grave, Peter, author. | Voigt, Mary M., author.
Title: Ancient Gordion / Lisa Kealhofer, Santa Clara University, California, Peter Grave, University of New England, Australia, Mary M. Voigt, College of William and Mary, Virginia.
Other titles: Crafting ceramics and community in Iron Age Anatolia
Description: Cambridge ; New York, NY : Cambridge University Press, 2022. | Series: Case studies in early societies | Includes bibliographical references and index.
Identifiers: LCCN 2022001131 (print) | LCCN 2022001132 (ebook) | ISBN 9781108490313 (hardback) | ISBN 9781108748391 (paperback) | ISBN 9781108780681 (epub)
Subjects: LCSH: Gordion (Extinct city) | Phrygians–Antiquities. | Pottery, Ancient–Turkey–Gordion (Extinct city) | Excavations (Archaeology)–Turkey–Gordion (Extinct city) | Turkey–Antiquities. | BISAC: SOCIAL SCIENCE / Archaeology
Classification: LCC DS156.G6 K43 2022 (print) | LCC DS156.G6 (ebook) | DDC 939/.26–dc23/eng/20220112
LC record available at https://lccn.loc.gov/2022001131
LC ebook record available at https://lccn.loc.gov/2022001132

ISBN 978-1-108-49031-3 Hardback
ISBN 978-1-108-74839-1 Paperback

Cambridge University Press has no responsibility for the persistence or accuracy of URLs for external or third-party internet websites referred to in this publication and does not guarantee that any content on such websites is, or will remain, accurate or appropriate.

Contents

Acknowledgments		*page* x
List of Abbreviations		xii

1 Introduction: Iron Age Ceramics and Phrygian Gordion   1
    Groups and Identity in Archaeology   2
    The Site of Gordion and Its History   5
    The Gordion Sequence   7
    The Ceramic Assemblage   9
    Issues in Anatolian Ceramics   10
    Structure of the Book   11

2 Inventing Identity: Group Formation over the Longue Durée   12
    How and Why Archaeologists Study Groups   12
    Technology, Groups and Materiality   15
    Groups, Interaction and Style   17
    The Archaeology of Group Formation and Daily Practices   21
    Conclusion   28

3 Contextualizing the Ceramic Assemblage   29
    A Short History of Archaeology at Gordion   29
    Archaeological Contexts at Gordion   31
    Ceramic Collections   48
    The Ceramic Samples Analyzed for This Study   50
    Ceramic Perspectives on Gordion   54

4 Identifying Gordion's Groups   55
    Introduction   55
    Previous Approaches to Gordion Ceramics   56
    Chronology   57
    Field Methodology   58
    The NAA Dataset   62
    Multivariate Characterization   67
    General Patterns in the Larger Dataset   69
    Compositional Clusters and Cultural Groups   81
    Ceramics, Archaeology and Groups   82
    Conclusions   85

viii   Contents

5   The Late Bronze Age Community at Gordion:
    The Late Bronze Age YHSS 10-8 ?1500–1150 BCE   86
      Introduction   86
      Historical and Archaeological Background: Central Anatolia   89
      Late Bronze Age Ceramics in Anatolia   93
      ?1500–1150 BCE (YHSS 10-8): Bronze Age Gordion   98
      Overview of the Bronze Age Ceramic Assemblage at Gordion (YHSS 10-8)   103
      NAA Ceramic Assemblage   116
      Production, Consumption and Distribution   123
      Conclusions   133

6   Reconstituting Community in the Early Iron Age:
    The Early Iron Age YHSS 7 1150–900 BCE   136
      Introduction   136
      Transforming Identities: From Collapse to Community in Anatolia   137
      1150–900 BCE (YHSS7): Gordion EIA Excavations   139
      Overview of EIA Ceramics at Gordion   142
      NAA Ceramic Assemblage   148
      Production, Consumption and Distribution   159
      Conclusions   170

7   New Identities, New Communities: The Early Phrygian
    Period YHSS 6 900–800 BCE   171
      Introduction   171
      Transforming Identities: Emergent Communities in Central Anatolia   173
      900–800 BCE (YHSS 6): Gordion Excavations   174
      Overview of Early Phrygian Ceramics   184
      NAA Ceramic Assemblage   193
      Production, Consumption and Distribution   210
      Discussion: Transforming Identities   224
      Conclusions   226

8   Enacting Power: The Middle Phrygian Period YHSS 5
    800–540 BCE   227
      Introduction   227
      Middle Phrygian Gordion in Historical Context   228
      800–540 BCE (YHSS 5): Middle Phrygian Archaeology at Gordion   230
      Overview of Middle Phrygian Ceramics   246
      NAA Ceramic Assemblage   252
      Production, Consumption and Distribution   282
      Conclusions: Power, Identity and Group Formation   297

9   Identities in Flux: The Late Phrygian Period YHSS 4
    540–330 BCE   301
      Introduction   301
      Ca. 540–330 BCE: Achaemenid Central Anatolia   302
      Achaemenid (Late Phrygian YHSS 4) Gordion: The Excavations   304
      Overview of Late Phrygian Ceramics   318
      NAA Ceramic Assemblage   321
      Production, Consumption and Distribution   334
      Conclusions: Groups in Flux   353

10 Conclusion: The Dynamics of Groups and Power at Gordion	355
Social Groups at Gordion	355
Groups and the Dynamics of Iron Age Economies	367
Concluding Thoughts	371
Appendix: Turkish Abstract	373
References	380
Index	409

The colour plate section can be found between pages 210 and 211

Acknowledgments

All modern archaeological research at Gordion (1950–present) has been sponsored and supported by the University of Pennsylvania Museum of Archaeology and Anthropology. The College of William & Mary was a co-sponsor from 1991 to 2002, and the Royal Ontario Museum co-sponsored work carried out between 1994 and 2002. Excavation and survey at Gordion since 1988 have been supported by grants to Mary Voigt from the National Endowment for the Humanities (NEH, a US federal agency), the National Geographic Society, the Tanberg Trust, the Kress Foundation and the IBM Foundation, and by gifts from generous private donors. Additional funding for the excavation came from grants made to T. Cuyler Young, Jr. by the Social Science and Humanities Research Council of Canada and the Royal Ontario Museum. The Gordion Regional Survey was funded by grants to Lisa Kealhofer by the National Science Foundation (BCS-9903149). Support for the preparation of digital images used in this volume was provided by the 1984 Foundation. Voigt's research at Gordion was made possible and inspired by Robert H. Dyson, Keith DeVries, G. Kenneth Sams, T. Cuyler Young, Charles K. Williams, II and Brian Rose. She thanks them, along with the large and talented team of site supervisors and local workers whose labor on the R. S. Young and Voigt excavations produced the foundation on which our research for this book rests.

This international collaborative project, originating in the Anatolian Iron Age Ceramics Project (AIA), would not have been possible without the financial support of the National Science Foundation (grants BCS-9903149, 0410220, 0513403) and the Australian Research Council (grants DP0558992, DP190102089). We are indebted to the generosity of many ceramicists working at Gordion over the last two decades who have made their expertise available for this work. Many of them have also aided us in the production of this book: Carolyn Aslan, Keith DeVries, Gül Gürtekin-Demir, Robert C. Henrickson, Kathleen Lynch, G. Kenneth Sams and Galya Toteva (now Bacheva). We are particularly grateful to Gordion archivist Gareth Darbyshire for his

Acknowledgments

generosity and patience over the course of our many queries, as well as sharing his extensive knowledge of the site.

The AIA project involved close collaboration with colleague and friend Ben Marsh, whose unfailing humor and geographic expertise contributed substantially to this endeavor. We would also like to thank Janet Jones for sharing in the first season of the "weird pottery tour." Both Ben Marsh and Naomi Miller generously read and provided insightful and engaging comments on earlier drafts of this manuscript. We thank Dr. G. Bike Yazıcıoğlu-Santamaria for the Turkish translation of the abstract (see Appendix 1) and Dr. Ayşe Gürsan-Salzmann for her editorial assistance. Many illustrators have contributed to the plans and artifact drawings presented here, including Carrie Alblinger, Ardeth Anderson, Denise Hoffman, Kimberly Leaman Insua, Sondra Jarvis and Kimberly Newman, and we thank all of them. Most of the site and artifact photographs used here were taken by Laura Foos, whose endless patience and talent are gratefully acknowledged. Neutron Activation Analysis (NAA) underpins much of our project and we thank James Blackman, National Institute of Standards and Technology, Washington, DC, for generously providing his time in discussions of the YHP (Yassıhöyük Pottery) NAA dataset, and Steve Simpson from Maxxam Labs, Ontario, Canada, who facilitated the NAA program for AIA. Finally, we acknowledge the strong support of this project by the previous director of the Gordion Project, Ken Sams, and thank C. Brian Rose, current director for his encouragement and generosity in sharing archaeological perspectives on the site. We are most thankful to the Turkish Ministry of Culture and Tourism for permission to work at Gordion, and the generosity of staff at the Museum of Anatolian Civilizations in Ankara for their advice and support.

Abbreviations

AIA	Anatolian Iron Age Project (Kealhofer and Grave, umbrella project for this study)
BRH	Burned Reed House (LTS YHSS 7A)
CBH	Late Bronze Age house (LTS YHSS 8)
CC	Clay Cut building (Terrace Complex YHSS 6A)
CKD	Early Iron Age house (LTS YHSS 7B)
CM	Citadel Mound (includes EM and WM)
CV	Coefficient of variation
DFA	Discriminant function analysis
DL	Destruction Level (ca. 800 BCE, YHSS 6A)
EBA	Early Bronze Age
EIA	Early Iron Age
EIAH	Early Iron Age Handmade
EM	Eastern Mound
EP	Early Phrygian
EPB	Early Phrygian Building (gate) (YHSS 6B)
GRS	Gordion Regional Survey
HCA	Hierarchical Cluster Analysis
KDE	Kernel Density Estimation
KH	Küçük Höyük
LBA	Late Bronze Age
LIA	Late Iron Age
LP	Late Phrygian
LT	Lower Town
LTS	Lower Trench Sounding
MIA	Middle Iron Age
MBA	Middle Bronze Age
MMV	Mary M. Voigt
MP	Middle Phrygian
NAA	Neutron Activation Analysis
NCA	North Central Anatolian (applied to Bronze Age assemblages)
NIST	US National Institute of Standards and Technology

List of Abbreviations

NWZ	Northwest Zone (Western Mound)
OM	Off Mound
OT	Outer Town
PAP	Post and Poros structure (YHSS 6B)
PCA	Principal component analysis
PGH	Polychrome Gatehouse (YHSS 6A)
RLW	Red Lustrous Wheelmade
RSY	Rodney S. Young
SRM	Standard reference materials
Str.	Structure
SWZ	Southwest Zone (Western Mound)
TB	Terrace Building (Terrace Complex YHSS 6A)
UTS	Upper Trench Sounding
WM	Western Mound
YHP	Yassıhöyük Pottery (Robert Henrickson's pottery catalog)
YHSS	Yassıhöyük Stratigraphic Sequence

1 Introduction
Iron Age Ceramics and Phrygian Gordion

Archaeologists have long grappled with understanding the nature of transformations in human societies. Some of these transformations are seen as "revolutionary," including the development of tools, the creation of imagery, the domestication of plants and animals, and the rise of urban and state-level societies. While the complexity and diversity of these reconfigurations has become more apparent with every new study, social group restructuring is crucial to each. Cultural transformations may share characteristics, but the organization and workings of social groups appear specific to each threshold of change. From this perspective, we argue that fundamental societal transformations are more intimately entangled with innovations in group formation – new modes of kin definition, religious groupings, political organizations and manipulation of ancient social media – than driven by technological innovation.

One of the most dynamic periods of ancient economic, political and technological transformation is the Iron Age of the Middle East (~1150–550 BCE). Paradoxically, this period emerged out of Late Bronze Age palace economies arguably co-dependently linked through a fragile "world system" and consequently leading to a region-wide collapse (Frank 1993). A general defining feature of the Iron Age is the rapid and widespread adoption of new, more socially integrative and robust economies and technologies. After an initial, short "Dark Age," Iron Age innovations radically departed from prior cultural trajectories with ultimately longer lasting impacts (e.g. invention of money, political and military reorganization and expansion, monotheism). The Iron Age metamorphosed from many local competing polities into newly formed and competing empires. However, the emergence of new types of Iron Age groups and mechanisms for group formation, as well as new types of power structures, remain relatively poorly understood.

This book is an exploration of Iron Age group formation at the central Anatolian settlement of Gordion, over 1,000 years from the late second millennium into the first millennium BCE. While occupation of this site extends back at least to the Early Bronze Age (EBA), it is during the Iron

Age (ca. 1150–540 BCE) that it achieves its greatest prominence as an urban center and as capital of the Phrygians, a major political force in central Anatolia in the Middle Iron Age (MIA; Fig. 1.1). With a long history of excavations that are ongoing, and against the background of an extraordinarily dynamic period of cultural transformation in the ancient Middle East, Gordion provides one of our best archaeological windows on the development and negotiation of Iron Age group identities.

Group creation is an active and culturally innovative phenomenon consisting of new forms of social practices, material culture and the synergistic interplay between the two. Here we focus on ceramics as a proxy for both the practices and material culture of identity formation. Unlike many other artifact classes, ceramics span elite and quotidian use as an important medium for both domestic and public activities throughout the first millennium BCE. They provide the material evidence of practices needed to study the process of group formation and maintenance over time. They also embed the social relations of production, and as plastic, disposable media, their distribution reveals the actions that constitute group definition (e.g. domestic activities, feasting, socializing).

Groups and Identity in Archaeology

How groups are formed, how they practice and what happens to them over time have been abiding research themes for both anthropology and archaeology (e.g. Binford 1967; Lewis 1963; Redfield 1947, 1953, 1955). Groups are created as people share activities, materials and language, to name a few (Appadurai 1988). The strength and longevity of a group can be linked to the extent and type of things shared: kinship and proximity can lead to lasting group bonds – or enmities (Barth 1956). A critical element for group cohesion is ongoing, regular "practice," constituting the group through interaction and negotiation.

The formation and development of groups is particularly critical in constituting complex societies. Groups exist at every scale, from playground gangs to national political parties. They also have highly variable "lives" – from short-term political action groups to institutions that span decades or centuries, such as the Catholic Church. However, archaeologists have tended to focus on a subset of groups related to particular activities or practices: political (ruling elites, factions, etc.), domestic (households, families) and economic (trade and exchange, production and consumption). Given that a rich panoply of groups exists outside this comparatively narrow range of often formalized activities, and can also play a critical role in the development of social networks and political

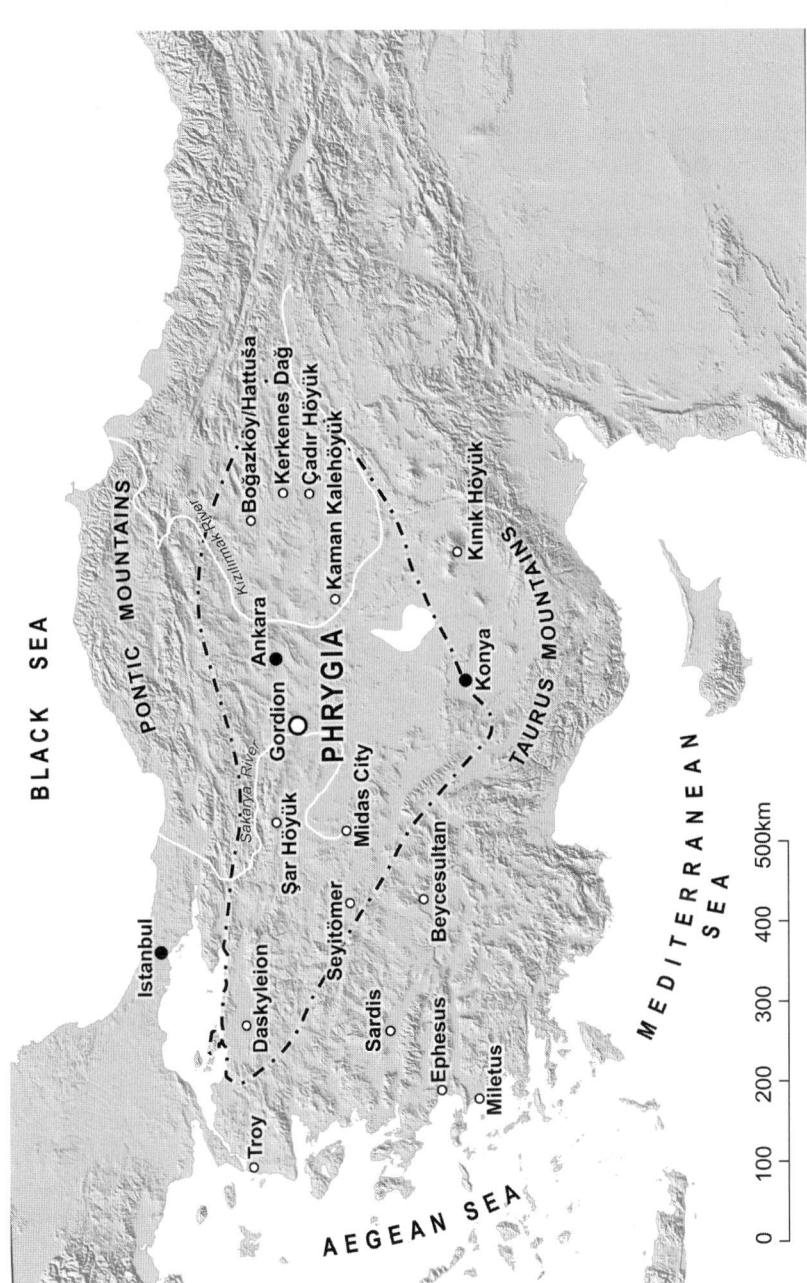

Fig. 1.1 Map of Turkey with key sites and hypothesized boundaries of Phrygia (K. Newman, after Rose 2017).

and/or economic practices, we seek to extend our analysis beyond the range of groups conventionally considered by archaeologists.

Since the 1980s, through the works of Bourdieu (1973, 1977, 1990), Foucault (1977, 1982) and Giddens (1984), archaeologists have become interested in the role of individuals, agency, practice and the dialectics of structure and process. "Identity" was a critical focus, in particular how gender, age, ethnicity, religion and status are defined, entangled, contested and malleable (Garcia et al. 2005; Insoll 2007; Meskell 2007; Shennan 2003; Thomas 1991). At the same time, attempts to redress the overly prescriptive and formalized character of conventional hierarchical typologies of groups (band, tribe, chiefdom, state; e.g. Pauketat 2007), sought more meaningful groups through daily practice in "communities" (Yaeger and Canuto 2000), however volatile (Isbell 2000).

Archaeologists have further elaborated the idea of "communities" as a productive approach for understanding group formation and dynamics. Mac Sweeney (2011:21) defined communities as a "conscious mental construct, built both on and through social practice and lived experience, which is itself facilitated by residential proximity and regular direct interaction." Isbell (2000:249), noting some of the tensions between geographic and social communities, elaborated the idea of an *imagined community*: "recogniz[ing] that correspondence between a socially interacting group, a bounded territory, economy, politics, reproductive pool, intergenerational education, desires and sentiments, *can exist only in an ideal model, not in the real world* [emphasis added]."

Arguably, most behaviors have either direct or indirect material manifestations. For archaeology, Isbell (2000:249), building on (Soja 1989), suggested that materials or goods must also be understood as "the means, medium, and outcome of social reproduction." From this perspective, the creation and use of materials constructs social relationships – with groups produced through shared processes that promote group identification (whether through similarity or difference; Preucel 2000). Material culture, therefore, is not simply a passive proxy for behavior, but plays an active role in the creation of identities at all scales, for individuals, groups and communities.

Ceramics, in both production and use, represent one means by which groups in the past were constituted. While solitary individuals can produce ceramics – gathering clay, fuel and water, constructing pots, drying and firing them – most production includes at least the cooperation of a family unit. Ceramic use, likewise, involves shared cooking, meals, goods and infrastructure/investment. More broadly, ceramic use establishes larger groups not only through shared forms and styles, but also through patterns of usage and disposal as a reflection of culinary practices (e.g. shared actions/solidarity of meal production, etiquette/table manners of food consumption, types of food and drink consumed). This is particularly evident for group events. During the Bronze and Iron Ages in Anatolia, feasting and religious ritual, as well as payments of allotted goods (beer, grain, etc.) were practiced using ceramics. Ceramic styles and forms were often emblematic of particular groups across a range of scales. As a plastic, additive technology that enables a wide range of decorative and formal choice, ceramics can also provide relatively fine-grained differentiation of social identities and relationships.

Finally, because most ceramics are relatively fragile they also have a relatively short life span, a characteristic that is particularly useful for tracking quite dynamic changes in group identity and formation over archaeologically short periods (years as opposed to decades).

The Site of Gordion and Its History

Excavated remains from the site of Gordion (modern Yassıhöyük) are the focus of this book (Fig. 1.2). Gordion is identified as the capital of Phrygia, an Iron Age polity of central Anatolia, best known through Greek records and legends referring to King Midas (e.g. Herodotus). The site was first proposed as the Phrygian capital in the 1890s by the Körte brothers on the basis of historical texts that located Gordion on the banks of the Sangarios (Sakarya) River (Sams 1995). The brothers excavated burial tumuli surrounding the site as well test trenches on the site itself (G. Körte and A. Körte 1904). Investigations resumed in 1950, under the direction of Rodney Young from the University of Pennsylvania Museum, who also excavated both nearby tumuli and areas of the Citadel Mound. Following his accidental death in 1974, fieldwork at Gordion halted, and the focus then shifted to analysis under Project Director Keith DeVries. With publication of Young's work underway, fieldwork resumed in 1988 under Mary Voigt's direction. Her aims were to establish a clear stratigraphic sequence, gain an understanding of nonelite activities and identify settlement areas beyond the Citadel Mound (Voigt 1997, 2009, 2011, 2013). Since then, excavation and site conservation have continued under the direction of Brian Rose, and a Gordion regional survey was completed by Kealhofer (Kealhofer 2005a; Kealhofer and Marsh 2019; Marsh and Kealhofer 2014; Rose 2012a, 2017; Rose and Darbyshire 2011).

Our understanding of the scale of Phrygian power and influence derives from both historical and archaeological data. DeVries (2011b), Roller (2011) and Sams (2011a) summarize the historical record, including Assyrian and Greek sources that mention the Phrygians or King

Fig. 1.2 Map of Gordion showing the location of Citadel Mound, Lower and Outer Towns, some tumuli, and Sakarya River (ancient and modern courses).
Excavated tumuli are labelled, and unexcavated tumuli are indicated by black dots (see also Fig. 3.6).
Source: Pizzorno and Darbyshire, image no. CIAG-0/1 courtesy of University of Pennsylvania Museum, Gordion Archives.

Midas. Most of the documents date to the eighth or seventh century BCE, when Phrygia seems to have been at the height of its power and influence. At that time, Phrygia was "in league" with the kings of Tabal, a region somewhere near the modern capital of Konya, contesting Assyrian intrusions into Anatolia. Sams (2011a) suggests that the Phrygians eventually paid tribute to the Assyrians, garnering support against raiders (the Kimmerians) who ranged throughout Anatolia and into Assyrian territory in the seventh century BCE. In the west, Greek references to Midas or Phrygians include marriages between ruling families (Roller 2011), reinforcing the prominence of the Phrygians in central Anatolian affairs during the first half of the first millennium BCE.

Archaeological data on the scale of Phrygian power are somewhat more challenging. There is little evidence for boundaries or borders of a Phrygian polity (Roller 2011; van Dongen 2014). Based on the distribution of Phrygian inscriptions, DeVries (2000) mapped a territory for the Phrygians that encompassed most of inland western Anatolia south to the Lake District, west of Konya (Fig. 1.1). The distribution of a distinctive type of stepped altar has also been used as a proxy for the extent of Phrygian political control (Roller 2011). From the distribution of grey ware ceramics found during Todd's survey of Nigde, near Kırşehir, Summers (1994) further suggested that Phrygian influence extended into the east – an inference confirmed by excavation at the site of Kerkenes, which is clearly a Phrygian settlement within the Halys River [Kızılırmak] bend (Summers 2018).

While both archaeological and historical data document Phrygia, the dynamic processes through which groups crafted a new Phrygian identity and community evident for Iron Age Gordion have yet to be explored.

The Gordion Sequence

Occupation at Gordion extends back into the Early Bronze Age, but our focus here is on the better documented Iron Age sequence, dating from the end of the Bronze Age through to the Early Hellenistic Period (1150–330 BCE; Table 1.1). We begin with the Late Bronze Age (LBA), 1500–1150 BCE, to set the stage for the sequence of cultural transformations during the Iron Age. Late Bronze Age Gordion was a small town likely subject to Hittite rule (based on both ceramics and epigraphic data; Gunter 1991, 2006). Following the collapse of the Hittite Empire in the twelfth century BCE, archaeologists have identified a relatively short period in the Early Iron Age (EIA) during which material culture and domestic life at Gordion changed substantially. By 900 BCE an entirely new polity emerged with Gordion as its capital.

Table 1.1. *The Yassıhöyük Stratigraphic Sequence or YHSS: YHSS phases, dates and regional periodization.*

YHSS phase	YHSS dates	Gordion phases	Regional phases
0	1920s	Modern	Modern
1	Late twelfth to early fourteenth century CE	Medieval	Medieval
2	First to fifth century CE	Roman	Roman
3	330 to first century BCE	Hellenistic	Hellenistic
4	540–330 BCE	Late Phrygian	Achaemenid
5	800–540 BCE	Middle Phrygian	Middle–Late Iron Age
6 DL	800 (–825) BCE	Destruction Level	Destruction Level
6	900–800 BCE	Early Phrygian	Middle Iron Age
7	1150–900 BCE	Early Iron Age	Early Iron Age
8–9	1400–1150 BCE	Late Bronze Age	Late Bronze Age
10	?1500–1400 BCE	Late Bronze Age	Late Bronze Age

Note that YHSS phases are only assigned for levels excavated under Voigt's direction.

This Early Phrygian period of political and community development continued with a monumental rebuild and urban expansion during the early Middle Phrygian period (mostly after 800 BCE), and a political and cultural transformation with Lydian (late Middle Phrygian) and subsequently Persian control during the Late Phrygian period. Early Hellenistic Gordion continued as a thriving center. Subsequent Galatian and Roman occupations appear to have been less substantial in population and scale.

Gordion's Late Bronze–Iron Age archaeological sequence extends over approximately 1,000 years and provides an unparalleled perspective on political (group) formation and transformation for central Anatolia. In addition to the emergence of Phrygian identity, new neighboring groups increasingly engaged with the Phrygians from the eighth century BCE. In every phase, groups at Gordion drew upon both local and exotic practices to create new types of organization as well as styles. Even after the Lydian and Persian conquests, Phrygian identity continued to be recrafted, using novel combinations of traditional elements such as tumuli and ceramics, while at the same time expanding engagement with the eastern Mediterranean world. Here we explore the ongoing creation of cultural identity and community at Gordion over a highly dynamic period of political, social and economic transformations using the lens of elite and utilitarian ceramic production, consumption and distribution.

The Ceramic Assemblage

Archaeological explorations of Gordion provide two parallel excavation sequences for evaluating how ceramics expressed group formation. One sequence is derived from Rodney Young's excavations in the core elite areas of the Citadel Mound; the other was produced by Mary Voigt's later excavations, which included both elite and non-elite areas of the settlement (Voigt 1997, 2013). While comparing assemblages excavated by different strategies and with different goals presents methodological challenges, the potential for evaluating the development of group identities within both elite and non-elite contexts over the course of the first millennium BCE provides a unique opportunity.

The quantity of ceramics uncovered by ongoing archaeological activity in the Middle East represents a vast and diverse resource. Earlier excavation projects, faced with storage limitations, commonly employed highly selective sampling largely focused on decorated or elite wares, and disposed of the majority of the remaining assemblage. Much of what was discarded was assumed to be either non-diagnostic or redundant. More recently, however, a shift in strategies to more expansive sampling includes capturing a representative range of both stylistic and technological types, as archaeologists realized the negative impacts of small or selective sampling on the robustness of interpretations and conclusions. The archaeological ceramic samples at Gordion follow this trajectory. Ceramics retained from Young's excavations (1950–1973) are a relatively small selection of decorated or unusual wares curated as a study collection and held in a small depot attached to the Gordion Museum in the village of Yassıhöyük. The ceramic assemblage from Voigt's excavations includes a much more complete and representative sample from every excavation context (see Henrickson references in the next paragraph), with a selection stored in the museum and the majority held in a recently constructed purpose-built depot in the Gordion excavation compound.

The ceramics used in the present study comprise just under 1,600 samples. They include about 680 samples from the collection of study ceramics from Young's excavations, spanning the Early Iron Age to the Hellenistic period and housed at the Gordion Museum, as well as about 900 samples from the Voigt excavations. Robert Henrickson studied the ceramics from the Voigt excavations (Henrickson 1993, 1994, 1995, 2002; Henrickson and Blackman 1996; Henrickson and Voigt 1998; Henrickson et al. 2002) and selected a relatively large and representative sequence of samples from well dated contexts for geochemical characterization (identified by the abbreviation YHP – "Yassıhöyük Pottery").

Ceramics dating from the Late Bronze Age to the Late Phrygian period from his collection (n = 705) are included here (the Hellenistic and Roman component is beyond the scope of the present study). In addition, our own work included an additional sample (n = 180) from the later phases of Voigt's excavations.

Both the Young and Voigt sets of samples have been studied formally and to some extent stylistically, and all have also been compositionally analyzed with Neutron Activation Analysis (NAA) at two different facilities: Becquerel Canada for the Anatolian Iron Age Project (AIA) samples and the National Institute of Standards and Technology (NIST) for the Henrickson YHP samples. The combination of stylistic, contextual and compositional analyses allow us to assess group formation from several complementary but independent perspectives and compare these perspectives over time. Studies of ceramic technology done by Henrickson define the scale of groups producing the ceramics and the types of technological styles in use. Identification of forms and changes in style, in relation to find and/or use contexts, define the changing patterns of consumption contexts in both elite and non-elite contexts. And finally, the compositional data from each period allows us to empirically evaluate the scale and diversity of local (clay) resource use, exchange of ceramics, and the relationship between exchange and emulation over time, all of which play into group interaction and the processes of group formation.

Issues in Anatolian Ceramics

Ceramics play a prominent role in the archaeology of the larger region to establish and correlate chronological frameworks both locally and regionally. Ceramic forms are also used to identify cultural practices: food consumption, exchange (as containers and as valuables), provisioning (food and other good storage), household patterns (through differences in consumption, production and disposal) and interaction (through visible signaling with styles, and through intergenerational transmission of learning).

In Anatolia, ceramic studies have focused on three main areas: establishing cultural and chronological frameworks for sites and regions (e.g. Hnila 2012; Mellaart 1955; Mellaart and Murray 1995; Schoop 2009, 2011; Summers 1994), understanding production technologies (e.g. Henrickson 1994, 2002, 2005) and distribution (e.g. Braekmans et al. 2011; Kibaroğlu et al. 2011; Neyt et al. 2012). Unlike work in ceramic-producing regions elsewhere (e.g. D. E. Arnold 1985; P. J. Arnold et al. 1993; Longacre et al. 1988; Rice 2015; Stark 2003; Van der Leeuw 1977), relatively few studies in this region have explored the social and behavioral facets of ceramic production, exchange and use (however, see Grave et al. 2016; Knappett 2011).

Within the broad scope of ceramic analyses in the region, a series of critical issues can be identified for ceramics during the millennium under consideration. For example, what is the cultural significance of the rapid diversification of styles and forms of ceramics in this period, and the frequent inclusion of stylistic or formal elements from distant regions or times? Genz (2000) notes a strong similarity between Early Iron Age and Early Bronze Age decorative styles in central Anatolia (cf. Summers 2013). The integration of local with exotic and chronologically distant elements appears to expand significantly during the seventh and sixth century BCE. At sites across the region, provincial versions of high styles ("Lydianizing," "Atticizing") make their first appearance (Berlin and Lynch 2002; Gürtekin-Demir 2002, 2007). These patterns raise questions about the pattern of exchange and emulation of ceramic styles over space and time, and particularly questions about the significance of stylistic and formal emulation. Emulation clearly reflects the transmission of ideas between groups. However, this transmission is not a passive diffusion of elements over space, but an active acquisition by individuals and groups of specific ideas and technologies in the form of styles and goods, a key component of group formation.

Structure of the Book

Chapter 2 introduces the ideas that underwrite this study, particularly in relation to group formation and ceramic studies. In the subsequent chapter we describe the nature of the archaeology and the ceramic datasets that are the basis for exploring group formation. The character of the long-term excavations at Gordion, as well as the nature of the sample of excavated areas, play an important role in shaping our understanding of those who lived at Gordion over the first millennium BCE. Chapter 4 explains the methods we use. The next chapters look at the evidence for group formation and group dynamics, beginning in the Late Bronze Age and ending after the Late Phrygian period (ca. 330 BCE), making use of production, distribution and consumption data. We conclude with a discussion relating the ceramic evidence for group formation over time to what we know about the political history of Gordion and Phrygia. The daily practices of groups, both elite and non-elite, as seen from ceramic data, provide a counternarrative to top-down perspectives for understanding how political regimes were created and experienced during this transformative period.

2 Inventing Identity
Group Formation over the Longue Durée

For over a millennium (1500–330 BCE), the inhabitants of Gordion repeatedly created novel social and political identities. The formation of the Iron Age Phrygian polity produced some of the most striking of these in the aftermath of the Late Bronze Age (LBA) Hittite collapse. Subsequently, identities were reshaped through Lydian, then Persian entanglements. Under each of these political regimes, local communities experimented with new and distinctive patterns of political and social formation under regime-specific economic strategies.

This chapter sets the stage for evaluating the changing identities of communities at Gordion in the late second to first millennium BCE. By drawing together a range of perspectives on the formation of groups and group identities, we show how such processes can be understood in terms of material culture and spatial patterning. Groups are created through shared action and repeated, regularized communication; the acts of communicating create material patterns – both intentional and unintentional. Over time, these repeated group actions, as cultural reproduction, produce configurations of decision-making that create styles, or distinctive ways of doing. In order to address the relatively wide range of types of group formation and dynamics over time at Gordion, we identify and evaluate the contexts and materialities that provide evidence for the changing nature of group practices. Of interest here is how these processes constituted groups. In the case of political group formation, aggrandizers or elites create or adopt (typically exotic) symbols of power and ways of doing from a field of contemporary and past political contexts. Given our focus on ceramics, we outline how others have used ceramic evidence to address comparable issues.

How and Why Archaeologists Study Groups

How people formed groups and created new political identities over time involves innovation, hybridization, selection and emulation, each of which can have clear material correlates. Inherent in these processes is the restructuring of practices and relations of power. Archaeologists have used many different approaches to study groups in the past. Here we explore those that shaped our approach to groups in Iron Age Gordion.

Understanding the processes by which groups are established, shaped or disenfranchised is a foundational project of social science; these processes include elements that are both generalizable (related to group size, types of resources, type of event) and historically contingent. The definition of group(s) in which identity formation takes place is elemental for both anthropology and archaeology. At different scales, groups can encompass a wide variety of forms, for example "cultures," "communities," "ethnicities," "political factions" and "age-based groups" (e.g. Barth 1969; Bowser 2000; Lyons and Clark 2008). Identifying such groups in ancient societies based on material cultural patterns involves significant challenges. While there is also considerable variability in how archaeologists define groups, they are largely reliant on either distinctive items of material culture that are emblematic of groups or spatial patterns of activities that reveal group practices (e.g. R. B. Campbell 2009). At the household scale, for example, archaeologists focus on functional and economic differences in order to construct domestic social identities (Blanton 1994; Kent 1993; Pluckhahn 2010; Wilk and Rathje 1982).

While the formation of political groups has been a focus within archaeology and anthropology for over a century (Childe 1925; L. H. Morgan 1877), not until the second half of the twentieth century did anthropologists work to systematize typologies of political groups (i.e. bands, tribes, chiefdoms and states) (Fried 1967; Service 1975; A. T. Smith 2003). A major criticism of these political "types" relates to their relatively static, descriptive character, as "vessels" that hold culture (Pauketat 2007).

In an attempt to move beyond such static typologies, others have turned to political practices and to distinguishing political ideology from political economy (Khatchadourian 2012; Osborne 2013; A. T. Smith 2011; Yoffee 2005). For example, rather than address how things might reflect economic relationships, Khatchadourian explores Achaemenid power through political theory and "the work of things in reproducing power" (Khatchadourian 2016: introduction). However, by merging hierarchical patterning across disparate types of groups (gender-, age- or language-based, for example), this approach masks the diversity of pathways through which power may be practiced. A more nuanced alternative has emerged over the last two decades, as archaeologists have shifted strategies to emphasize the dialectical nature of group identities, examining "communities" as continuously constructed, contested, maintained or transformed (R. B. Campbell 2009). In this context, perspectives informed by theories of practice treat group identity as more ephemeral, situationally constituted and often fluid (Barth 1956; Bourdieu 1990; Ortner 2006; Pauketat 2001).

Communities of practice experience day-to-day shifts in performance that serve to reshape groups over time. Changes in relationships, within or between groups and to their resources, can also have significant recursive effects on group salience and practice. Abrupt changes such as immigration/emigration, catastrophic events (e.g. warfare, disease, earthquakes, fires), or more gradual hegemonic changes in religious or political power, can lead not only to the formation of new groups but also to their disintegration. Groups can also resume after periods of dormancy, when their interaction (or shared action) becomes salient again.

Archaeological explorations of community emerged along with interest in the role of the *individual* and *agency* (Dobres 2000; Lyons and Clark 2008). Balancing the importance of *individuals* and subalterns against groups and elites has led to a body of "biographies" and histories emphasizing contingency and meaning (Fowles 2005; Gosden and Marshall 1999). Typically, archaeological access to individuals relies on burial contexts, depictions and historical data; for most other archaeological contexts, patterns of multiple individuals' behavior cannot be resolved beyond that of the group (e.g. households). Individuals usually belong to multiple discrete or overlapping types of groups, but groups serve specific functions and have distinctive temporal practices with patterned archaeological signatures. In other words, an individual's identity is commonly dependent on the group identity that is situationally triggered.

Investigating *agency* requires specific approaches to data that can be challenging when using legacy datasets such as that from Gordion (see Chapter 3; Dobres and Robb 2005). We view the creation of material culture as combining active decision-making with more passive imitative learning, as highlighted by Tehrani and Riede (2008).

Our research theme of group formation runs counter to a focus on the individual and agency (e.g. R. B. Campbell 2009; Knappett 2011; Schortman 2014). We also reject the applicability of network analysis in this context; while it can offer a useful interpretative framework to link individual agents, two requirements limit its usefulness here. First, it requires a regional dataset against which to set a network frame of reference. Second, it commonly focuses on elite individuals as the most archaeologically visible aggrandizing agents. Since our focus is on Gordion and its immediate environs, we lack the regional scale and depth of data to support a network approach. Even with access to such data, our interest is in the social processes that created groups across the society rather than individual agents or elites. As Adam Smith (2011) has argued, power simultaneously involves bottom-up and top-down processes between leaders and subjects. Stepping back and looking archaeologically at the types of groups and their activities potentially provides a more nuanced and complex picture of how a society negotiated power under different regimes in the past. This involves the identification of groups as well as their different scales and materialities (i.e. their intersectional *patterning*). Rather than seeking only one group – a political group or a household – we seek to layer these different groups to archaeologically define a society's structure (and structuration; Giddens 1984).

Recently, archaeologists of complex societies have also adopted a transactional "collective action" framework to investigate how elites or rulers negotiate power in relation to their populace. First articulated by Levi (1988), who posited that rulers who relied more on internal revenue (tribute, taxes, labor) were also commonly forced to cede more agency to their populaces to negotiate benefits, this approach has been subsequently elaborated (e.g. Blanton and Fargher 2008; DeMarrais and Earle 2017). Carballo and Feinman (2016) articulated examples of collective action in relation to the construction of infrastructure, such as irrigation systems, transport systems and marketplaces (see also Blanton and Fargher 2008). DeMarrais and Earle (2017) suggest that to understand the organizational frameworks of power in premodern societies it is critical to wed bottom-up with top-down approaches to identify parallel processes (i.e. collective action with political economy; see M. E. Smith 2011, also Mann 1986). Our approach shares an interest in using the evidence of collective action to interrogate the ongoing creation of power at Gordion. However, to reconstruct how power was engaged at different times at Gordion we need to go further, looking beyond collective action negotiated directly with the ruler or elites, to evaluating group "collective actions" across the range of potential scales, from household to community.

Technology, Groups and Materiality

Conceptually, our point of departure is that the dialectical nature of material culture both produces and transforms social, political and economic relationships (Appadurai 1988; Dobres and Robb 2005). Pfaffenberger provides a complementary perspective presenting technology and technological systems as a "total social phenomenon" in Mauss' (1967) sense (Pfaffenberger 1988, 1992). The creation of relationships through technologies – the production, distribution and use of material culture – also works to form new groups or communities of different sizes and scales (e.g. work groups, domestic groups, social groups; Khatchadourian 2016; Pfaffenberger 1988:249; Schortman and Urban 2004). While related to the social process of structuration (i.e. repeated human actions creating social structures that in turn shape actions; Giddens 1979), this material corollary has only relatively recently been operationalized as an archaeological tool (e.g. Hicks and Beaudry 2010; Mac Sweeney 2011; Mullins 2011).

One challenge is that situationally defined group dynamics can be highly fluid but archaeologists can only access them through the medium of material culture, a static but multi-semic medium that rarely directly replicates group behavior. These challenges are further compounded by the relatively fixed physical spaces where individuals participate in group activities (e.g. houses, temples, markets, plazas); also, the artifacts and their relationships within these spaces can conflate the practices of individual groups. The difficulty of archaeologically teasing out the actions of specific groups forces us to focus on those group practices – such as the consolidation of power – that create durable patterning of artifacts or other types of material culture (e.g. Lechtman 1993).

We argue that understanding the creation and practices of political groups in the past requires an evaluation not only of the emblematic, direct manifestations of political power (pyramids, city walls, palaces) but also of the structures and practices of the multiplicity of groups in a society through which power is enacted. In other words, while the palace provides a good indicator of the power of an elite ruler, the patterns of agricultural production and craft activities, as well as the distribution of their products, provide more critical measures of how power was constructed, transacted and practiced by groups as collective action.

To set potential archaeological parameters on the types of groups involved, we "reverse engineer" interpretation: moving from artifacts, their distribution and context (particularly evidence of production, along with patterns of consumption and disposal; Stahl et al. 2008) to group dynamics. This is best achieved by using the widest range of contexts (production, consumption or use, etc.) to identify the many lives and meanings of artifacts, and the range of ways that any particular type of artifact is involved in group creation(s). Here, the material cultural characterization of groups includes group scale and size, status (members), the contexts in which the group is activated, and more contingent attributes of group membership. To establish these parameters we rely on generalized assumptions about practices of power in the past informed by comparative evaluation of the range and types of groups in different kinds of societies, and relationships between group size, diversity and type of social complexity.

Groups, Interaction and Style

Identifying groups archaeologically inherently engages a study of style. New groups create their own styles, combining elements from multiple sources. Archaeologists use style for different types of interpretive work: to distinguish *time* through the seriation of stylistic change, to track the *creation of identity* by stylistic choice at different scales, and to identify *patterns of interaction* based on shared styles (Odess 1998). As Hegmon (1992) notes, there are almost as many approaches to the study of style in archaeology as there are archaeologists. While archaeological tools that use style to discriminate time are well-developed, attempts to recognize identities and interaction based on shared styles are more problematic (Conkey and Hastorf 1990).

Beginning in the late 1970s, "style" became a much-debated topic, as its meaning and usefulness for archaeology came under closer scrutiny (Conkey and Hastorf 1990; Dunnell 1978; Hegmon 1992, 1998; Lipo 2001; Plog 1983; Sackett 1977; Stark 1998; Wiessner 1989). Since then, archaeological discussions of style have shifted perspectives substantially. As Hegmon (1998:264) notes: "Anglo-American archaeological thought about material culture can be summed up in two phrases: 'style as function' (Wobst 1977) and 'technology as style'" (Lechtman 1977). Wobst's (1977) classic article suggested that style serves several functions: making interactions more predictable by providing people with information about participants; reinforcing social differences by identifying status or rank; and maintaining social boundaries by differentiating groups through visual differences. Styles perform both emically and etically, although the character and content of emic and etic styles are typically divergent.

Technological style, or "ways of doing," reflects choices manifested at each stage of production, and is informed by specific social, economic and political relationships (Pfaffenberger 1988). As Dobres and Hoffman (1994) note, both the process of production and the technological products are part of a society's *habitus*. In the 1990s, increased interest in agency and the individual shifted perspectives on technological style. Ingold (1993) suggested a focus on technique – something practiced by individuals – rather than technology, which archaeologists often disembody and objectify. However, his emphasis on the role of the individual works well for very specific types and volumes of material culture (e.g. identifying the "hand" of an Attic pot painter) but less well for the relatively anonymous makers of mass-produced, utilitarian wares.

In the past, discussions of the theoretical implications of style were often linked to debates about Darwinian processes, where the individual acts as information carrier (Dunnell 1978). More recently, evolutionary approaches related to style have turned to discussions of cultural transmission. Conventionally, archaeological explanations for the wholesale or partial transmission or adoption of style between groups invoked terms such as "emulation" or "diffusion." These approaches have been displaced by the idea of "cultural transmission," or how culture is transferred across space and time, usually by individuals (Eerkens and Lipo 2007; Stark et al. 2008).

However, work in the 1980s–1990s was more concerned with the selective use of the multiple types and diverse roles that style can play (see following sections). If style is defined as a way of doing, then style creation involves purposeful choices. "Ways of doing" happen at every scale, from individual practice to the nation-state. Here, we focus on style in relation to group formation, particularly in contexts where groups are materialized as both *identity* and *interaction*. Our interest here is in the action of groups at Gordion, and how they created new cultural frames during the millennium from the fourteenth to fourth centuries BCE (i.e. intentional selection, adoption and melding of elements from broader regional political and social cultures).

Style as Identity (or "Information")

Wiessner (1990:107) defined style as "a form of non-verbal communication through doing something in a certain way that communicates information about relative identity" (see also H. Burke 2012). Context and visibility are therefore critical for both the performance and the interpretation of identities through style (Rice 2015:402). The identification of meaningful patterning of variation (information) relevant to specific identity/identities of interest (Sackett 1990) remains an abiding archaeological challenge, given the potentially large range of active and passive choices made in the production of a style.

Styles have been used to identify different types of cultural groups. Early interpretations of *artifact styles* (including ceramic styles) equated them with specific (often) "ethnic" groups (Jones 1997; Lyons and Clark 2008). David and colleagues (1988) have even argued somewhat perversely, based on ethnographic work in Cameroon, that "pots are people," demonstrating the symbolic relationships between pots and the human body. However, direct relationships between pots/people/ethnic groups have more often been treated as highly problematic static and reductionist formulation (Kramer 1985; Rice 1987, 1996). Such a static equation reduces the informational potential in stylistic variability of ceramic assemblages, and ignores the multiple types of identity that are created through *styles of ceramic production, distribution, use and disposal* (Arthur 2006), which we seek to address in this book.

Ethnographic and ethnoarchaeological studies make it clear that shared styles rarely correspond to clear ethnic or bounded cultural groups (Hodder 1982; Stark 1998). Like most aspects of material culture, style can convey multiple, disparate messages in the same object, and can reflect identities in many different ways, ranging from individual expressions to group affiliation, status and world view. Shared technologies, including both emulation and exchange, may reflect different types of interaction. In place of the "pots are people" approach that statically ties a style to a cultural or ethnic group, addressing how and why style choices are shared within and between groups provides a more productive and dynamic alternative.

Styles of consumption can define aspects of both individual and corporate identity. While a consumption style is most evident for artifacts used in public arenas such as feasting, it can also be relevant in smaller-scale domestic contexts. Items used in the household production of food and meals play a central role in reproducing relationships within family and friends (e.g. Hellenistic table sets; Rotroff 2006) or larger groups (e.g. Greek symposia; Lynch 2011). We can ask, then, how changes in styles of producing and consuming meals reflect shifts in personal relationships and group identity or identities.

Lechtman's pioneering work on technological style (1984, 1993) provides an alternative framework for understanding style in relation to group identity as the social and political relations of technology (Hegmon 1998). Lemonnier (1992) argues that stages in the production of objects involve choices that both shape, and are shaped by, social processes (learning and group formation). Studying the relationship between choices and social processes can reveal how social groups, labor relations and power are constructed. Identifying the role of different styles of production (Pfaffenberger 1992) can reveal how those social relations functioned during both production and consumption (i.e. groups).

Style as Interaction

Style and social interaction are intimately linked, but interpreting the meaning of a given style in terms of a specific type of interaction is challenging at best, even when not parsing emic from etic meanings. While styles are defined by choices people make either explicitly, as intentional expressions of identity, or implicitly in conveying unintentional facets of identity, both communicate identity as *components* of interaction. The assumption that more stylistic similarity between assemblages reflects greater interaction between groups is what underwrites equating shared styles with evidence of interaction (Hodder 1982; Odess 1998). Beyond this, however, lies an extensive range of materialized styles and diverse human behaviors. Groups may share styles in one context or material (e.g. ceramic tableware) but not share others (e.g. clothing).

Ceramics and Style

Ceramics embed many different types of style: technological and decorative as well as formal and material. Ostensibly, a more objective archaeological measure of interaction equates spatial with social space, and uses design elements to identify interaction within and between groups, variously quantifying stylistic similarities to estimate interaction distances (Rice 2015:354). However, this approach faces fundamental methodological challenges involving the definition of appropriate design elements and sampling scale, and establishing meaningful typologies. Hardin, among others, argues that design structures, rather than elements, are more indicative of group membership and community interaction (Friedrich 1970; Hardin 1991; Washburn 2003).

We aim to link the range of ceramic styles (i.e. technology, motifs/design and shapes/forms) to group/identity formation and to different scales of identity, in particular the broader reach of political identity. While most work at a broad scale has been concerned with parameters for identifying ethnic groups, archaeologists have also been creative in tapping into aspects of ceramics as evidence of political praxis, particularly public "performance." For example, in Achaemenid provinces, specific forms such as "tulip" bowls are associated with feasting and political ritual (Dusinberre 2013; Petrie et al. 2008). Regional studies continue to identify pottery styles with ethnically, culturally or politically coherent groups (Hegmon 1998). Examples from the American southwest include "Hohokam" or "Puebloan." In the Mediterranean, Mycenaean pottery is seen as delineating Mycenaean political influence, while the geographic extent of *terra sigillata* is treated as a territorial proxy of Roman hegemony (Glatz 2009; Parkinson et al. 2013; Witcher 2000).

Hegmon's alternative approach for the southwest United States identified several style patterns as significant for group formation at different scales within and between societies. She suggests that "stylistic distinctions ... result in a greater degree of stylistic diversity; thus analyses of diversity or stylistic variability may reveal the existence of intrasocietal boundaries or distinctions" (Hegmon 1992:527). Therefore, the development of stylistic boundaries – or changes in the distribution of styles over time – can be interpreted in terms of social group dynamics (Hegmon 1992:528).

The production, distribution, use and disposal of material culture all provide different contexts for the formation of groups in these societies. For example, where and how various forms of *terra sigillata* were produced, distributed, used or disposed of relates to the construction of different groups within the same society, and within contemporary interacting societies.

The Archaeology of Group Formation and Daily Practices

Here we review archaeological approaches to group formation. In particular, we focus on styles and group formation in relation to production, consumption and distribution and how these may inform our questions at Gordion.

Group Formation and Production

During the twentieth century archaeologists progressively elaborated ways of studying production as a measure of how ancient societies organized power, an approach first proposed by Childe (1942, 1951). In the 1980s and 1990s more systematic work evaluated the relationships between the organization of labor, craft production and type of political organization. Early seminal studies on ceramics (Rice 1984, 1987) and craft production (Costin 1993, 2007; Costin and Hagstrum 1995) created a framework for understanding how different types of ceramic production could reflect different types of political and social organization. Costin (1991:8) proposed four variables critical for defining production systems: *context* (nature of control of production and distribution); *regional patterning*; *production scale* (and who constitutes them); and *intensity* (part- to full-time; see also Earle 1981; Peacock 1982; Van der Leeuw 1977). Each of these variables had a set of operational parameters to characterize group formation in relation to different types of production systems and consistent with political organization.

Ethnoarchaeological work since the 1980s has primarily been concerned with the social dimensions of ceramic production in the context of domestic groups. In particular, it has often focused on how artifact patterning relates to the organization of production (e.g. Neupert 2000; Stark 1992). While useful for understanding synchronic patterns, particularly in relation to household production, ethnoarchaeology offers more limited insight into the dynamics of production over time, and has yet to address relationships between ceramic production and political organization.

For Lechtman, production is a techno-ideological phenomenon where variations in production organization are treated as "styles" of production (Lechtman 1984, 1993, 1996). Her pivotal work reinforced the close relationship that exists between styles of technology – ways of producing things and relations of production – and specific ideologies and practices of power. Using cloth and metal production in the Andes, she illustrated the ideological links between the ways these craft technologies were practiced and how the state organized labor (Lechtman 1993). In this case, Inkan control over labor created unique groups within Andean societies. Work by Lemonnier (1993) and Pfaffenberger (1993) explored similar ideas in different contexts, to further articulate social frameworks of technology and production.

Schortman and Urban (2004) developed these themes by integrating functionalist studies of political economy and craft production in relation to ideological, meaning-based studies of power. As they note, authority differentials situated in ideology and world view are reflected in the production of power and political economy. They conclude that ancient political economies were elaborate, contingent and messy, where separations between elite and commoner or attached and unattached production are rarely clear. They suggest that most ancient economies were multiscalar, multicentric, involving multiple groups of elites, and operationally combined hierarchical and heterarchical principles. Within such economies individuals could simultaneously compete as members of groups or on their own for access to power and resources.

The relationships between group formation and production have thus been increasingly recognized as highly fluid and malleable. Individuals often mark or display membership in multiple groups, although their performance will vary depending on context (see also Goodenough 1965). Over longer time frames, group membership can alter in relation to shifts in power, resources and world view. This fluidity doesn't undercut the importance of groups, but serves notice that groups did not operate as reified constructs with lock-step behaviors. We expect to see different types of groups operating at the same time, with overlapping membership. The extent to which groups formed in production contexts and the potential for overlap with other groups in a society is therefore an issue that has to be addressed through other group formation contexts (e.g. consumption and distribution). This diversity and inherent messiness is informative of the organization and practices of complex social formations.

Group Formation and Consumption

Growth in the size and complexity of societies is reflected in the range and diversity of consumption contexts (social and spatial), commensurate with the size and number of groups with which an individual can engage. Groups consume or use goods in a wide range of contexts, from domestic or household to formulaic rituals. Feasting, in particular, provides a nearly universal context for politically charged consumption (Bray 2003; Dietler and Hayden 2010; Hayden and Villeneuve 2011).

During the second half of the twentieth century a translational interplay between economists, sociologists, cultural anthropologists and archaeologists greatly enhanced our understanding of the relationship between group formation and consumption in both breadth and time depth.

Throughout the twentieth century, economists drove most studies of consumption, with an almost exclusive focus on utilitarian behavior. Anthropologists' recognition of the importance of conspicuous consumption stimulated study of consumption and its importance for understanding social functions, structures and relationships (Appadurai 1988; Bourdieu 1984; Douglas and Isherwood 1979; Friedman 1994; Veblen 1899 [2007]). Friedman (1994:17) argued for the study of consumption strategies to be folded into the larger framework of studies of social reproduction, as defining in some measure the social context of practice: "[S]ocial projects are the bases for understanding the practice of consumption, and they are, by definition, projects for self-definition, whether they are voluntarily or socially determined" (Friedman 1994:16).

By the late twentieth century, sociologists began to study class formation in relationship to consumption. Here we generalize beyond class, viewing social classes as but one type of group. In Bourdieu's view (1984), classes competitively define themselves in relation to each other, based on specific lifestyles and unconscious practices of taste, consumption and identity ("habitus"). Bourdieu's understanding of consumption and identity formation is highly selective (i.e. the accumulation of either cultural or economic capital is the driving rationale for consuming; Friedman 1994). Even though he defined "habitus" as a mechanism of identity formation, the social significance of entanglements between conscious/active and unconscious/passive consumption choices had not yet been recognized. Nonetheless, Bourdieu's work illustrates a characteristic that subsequent studies have also identified: that group formation and associated patterns of consumption are highly *relational*.

Consumption patterns in colonial contexts have often been interpreted as emulation or passive acculturation in the past. More recent work, such as Friedman's (1994) case study of the Congo highlights the active selection and configuration of material culture (see also M. Roberts 1994). Given the variability and complexity of motivations, cultural content and historical structures (see also Campbell 1994), the Congolese actively appropriate "the West" to produce success as part of a local social project of identity creation.

Whether economic or anthropological, most studies of consumption remain focused on the Modern Period, and more specifically on the nineteenth and twentieth centuries (Friedman 1994). This "Modern era" bias reflects a Marxist perspective in these disciplines: originally producers and consumers were one and the same; only the increased disenfranchisement of producers from the fruits of their labor, through wage-based labor, allowed the creation of commodities and the growth of consumerism (Friedman 1994).

Despite the growing breadth of consumption studies in the late 1980s and 1990s, within anthropology a more narrow preoccupation continued to be with how goods were delivered to individuals or on how individual agency assigned meaning to things (Mullins 2011:134). Within archaeology, studies of consumption were also largely viewed as most appropriate for historical archaeology as a "Modern era" area of enquiry. This approach was used to frame issues of culture contact or acculturation and hybridization in colonial encounters, and even more specifically indigenous peoples' rather than colonizers' contexts of consumption (Brown 1979; Farnsworth 1987; Hoover 1989). Outside historical archaeology, and with few exceptions (D. Miller 1995), archaeologists paid surprisingly little attention to patterns of consumption and remained focused on production, use and disposal of artifacts. Only since the late 1990s have archaeologists begun to directly address the material cultural patterning of premodern consumption (Mills 2016; Mullins 2011). Archaeological articulation of the material links between consumption and identity typically focus on questions of status, where specific types of elite consumption are linked to attempts to create and mark social difference through both goods and practices (Card 2013; Clunas 1991; Cordell 2014; Costin and Earle 1989; Greenwood 1980; Shackel and Little 1992).

A recent review addressed the role of consumption in identity construction: consumption "revolves around the acquisition of things to confirm, display, accent, mask, and imagine who we are and who we wish to be" (Mullins 2011:135). While following Bourdieu's use of "habitus" (consumption as a largely uninflected and *nonreflective* process of identity formation), Mullins acknowledged the tension between (non-reflective) structural processes and (active) consumer agency. Mullins goes even further to suggest studies of this tension are where archaeology could contribute most to understanding consumption.

Much of the anthropological study of consumption is tied to how individuals or families produce their identities. Here we adopt the perspective that consumption strategies – like production strategies – are fundamental to practicing and producing *all social groups*. We expand on current uses of consumption and identity to address the ways in which style is implicated. Consumption includes the day-to-day use of goods for shaping identity. If patterned "ways of doing" are styles, then arguably so are patterns of use and consumption of food (from recipes to production and presentation), of housing and so forth. One of the fundamental types of consumption is the "sociality" of food (Miracle and Milner 2002). Studies of food consumption often focus on either status (e.g. meat consumption) or feasting (with special/symbolic dishes, alcohol; Dietler and Hayden 2010; Hayden 2009; Hayden and Villeneuve 2011; Kuijt 2009; Lynch 2011; Mills 2004). However, food consumption events, be they domestic or public, are also highly structured "styles of doing" that play a key role in group maintenance and creation (e.g. dinner parties, funerary feasts).

Group Formation and Resource Distribution

The scale and intensity with which people distribute resources and goods is closely related to the organizational scale and size of groups in a society: the number and diversity of groups largely governs opportunities for resource use and redistribution. How resources are redistributed by groups is in turn tied to natural constraints (e.g. geology and climate) and on the ease of transport (rivers, roads, slope). Linkages between group formation and the expansion of resource use and redistribution can also be driven by major episodic events (e.g. construction of public monuments, warfare and mortuary practices). At the same time as elites extract or (re)distribute resources for political aggrandizement, they can also craft or co-opt new symbols and ideologies to constitute groups through shared activities (e.g. feasting, construction, combat; Schortman 2014).

Historically, archaeologists focused on how elites extract resources and enact power have favored a political-economic approach (Costin 1993; D'Altroy and Earle 1985; Earle 2011; Hirth 1996). To address how elites mobilize resources to support their political power, Hirth (1996) identified four strategies commonly used in combination: elite redistribution; interregional exchange; world system linkages; and tribute-mobilization systems. *Elite redistribution* requires mobilizing resource(s) as well as distributing them both to non-elites and other elites. One of the best known internal redistribution systems is feasting, in which multiple types of resources in addition to food are typically mobilized. Redistribution often acts at several different levels, from community to region. Hirth suggests that prestige goods distribution acts in similar ways to expand supporters. *Interregional exchange*, as a second form of distribution, involves exchanges between trading partners or interacting institutions of neighboring polities. This type of exchange establishes alliances that can mediate risk, allow access to luxury items and/or locally unavailable goods. It can also serve as means for elites to gain specialized knowledge, and independent control over luxury goods to expend on political influence. A third strategy, *world-system linkages*, invokes a large-scale matrix of interaction and interdependence among multiple polities. The extent to which it structures any individual polity, or the institutional framework of the polity, is variable, but elites usually find ways to exploit and direct resource flows. The last strategy, *resource mobilization*, is the collection by elites of goods (taxes or tribute) from individuals or groups in society. This type is often embedded in socioreligious obligations, public works or military support.

In addition to identifying strategies for resource extraction, Hirth (1996) suggests four principles of political economy. Of these, the "accumulation principle" directly addresses how elites justify their accumulation of surplus: for example, collecting food or goods to mitigate cyclical shortfalls and risk or to accumulate for societal benefit, while self-servingly redirecting at least a portion of community resources and garnering greater power over time.

While conceptually useful, a political economy framework faces two potential shortcomings. First, top-down elite extraction misses bottom-up engagement (including negotiation and resistance). As noted, recent elaboration of collective action seeks to build out this perspective. Second, the creation of a (static) typology of strategies assumes power is already in place and "fixed," making it difficult to identify the dynamics of elite group formation. Typologies inherently mask the processes by which groups create, maintain or modulate power relationships.

Increasingly archaeologists recognize that power is enacted by multiple competing groups within any society (Schortman 2014; Schortman and Urban 1992; A. T. Smith 2011). This shift in focus from exchange systems that require a regional framework and relatively abstract groups to the dynamics of local-scale relationships highlights the importance of understanding group formation processes. This shift also demands a closer reading of the linkages between resource distribution and how different groups mobilized resources, particularly when groups become politically salient. Again, collective action approaches suggest that when leaders invest heavily in local resource mobilization, subalterns gain more political agency (Blanton and Fargher 2008).

Other shortcomings of the political economy approach include the implicit discounting of both the role of historical processes and the importance of the continuous construction of identities within a society, and more specifically within a community (Pauketat 2007). However, an emphasis on the importance of daily practices and identity construction also lacks two critical parameters. As the scale and population increase in urbanized societies, the articulation of larger numbers of people requires not only a larger sense of "community" or "nation" as the community becomes idealized, but also a means of integrating smaller groups of practice within this wider context. In larger, more complex societies, communities cross-cut the society and operate at multiple scales. Secondly, an argument that polities integrate migrants and diverse groups through political-ritual actions such as monumental construction (e.g. Pauketat 2007) can equally be treated as a political-economic imperative: the *redistribution* of people and their labor (Hirth 1996; see the section "Group Formation and Resource Distribution"). Integrating these two approaches allows us to assess both top-down and bottom-up group strategies, while at the same time seeking to identify tensions between disparate groups in a polity.

Other recent perspectives also focus on individuals, networks and agency to evaluate resource distribution and power (Brughmans 2010; R. B. Campbell 2009; Knappett 2011; Schortman 2014). These approaches highlight the operational complexity of power in ancient societies, with material patterning doing the work of establishing and defining networks of authority. They illustrate alternatives to static typologies of complexity that, until recently, have remained embedded in archaeological thinking. At the same time, however, to understand how and why groups form and function, which we argue is critical for understanding any scale of societal complexity, we need to move beyond individuals within networks.

Groups and Cultural Transmission

Cultural or information transmission approaches intersect studies of style and distribution and are an important component in understanding group formation and maintenance. Groups formed through the ongoing sharing of information and experiences rely on specific contexts and types of transmission. However, not all information transmissions are salient to group formation. Therefore, we selectively make use of approaches to cultural transmission (Eerkens and Lipo 2007) that highlight the importance of context, content and mode of transmission in shaping group formation.

Conclusion

Group formation is a "relational" and potentially politically charged process, as groups establish identities vis-à-vis other groups. Not all groups, however, are overtly competitive: work units, age sets and support groups, among others, can share goals without competing. This is not to say that such groups cannot be politically mobilized. While acknowledging that not all groups are equally salient – either in the past or for our purposes – in all cases, groups act as subsets of a larger society, interacting and exchanging goods, ideas and members.

Our study of groups and group formation in Iron Age communities at Gordion involves two comparative strategies. We evaluate practices within a single period to provide insight into the multiple interacting groups of practitioners. We also compare practices over time to understand how groups and their practices changed through periods of political and economic transformation. By identifying changes in the layering of group identities and their content we aim to generate new insights into the practices of power.

In the following chapters we explore group dynamics period by period, from the Late Bronze Age political collapse to the Achaemenid or Late Phrygian period. We use styles of production, consumption/use and distribution to identify groups and group formation. We focus, in particular, on patterns of ceramics consumption to provide evidence of how individuals and groups constructed identities. Consumption of particular forms, such as drinking cups, the contexts of consumption (e.g. feasting or domestic, elite or non-elite) and distribution of consumption, or where these activities occur, provide intersecting lines of tangible evidence for how practices created groups and power. Similarly, with ceramic distribution (differentiating between source context and use context), patterns of direct exchange vs. learning and emulation reveal how groups crafted new identities and established relationships. Styles of technology and production document the scale and organization of work groups in relation to political power. Notwithstanding our focus on ceramics as a ubiquitous materialization of group formation and maintenance, we are mindful that they are only one "materiality"; they may represent multiscalar and multicentric economies, but they do not represent all of those in practice during any period. We draw upon the extant archaeological record at Gordion to expand our understanding of other materialities of group creation and practice.

3 Contextualizing the Ceramic Assemblage

In this chapter we review and contextualize the ceramic assemblages from Gordion sampled for this study. Over the course of more than 50 years of excavation, different teams with diverse sampling and curation strategies and rationales collected archaeological ceramics from this site. These varying practices have directly impacted the character of our sampling regime. To clarify the similarities and difference between the assemblages sampled, we begin with a short overview of excavations and artifact curation at Gordion. We outline how and what criteria we used to sample each of the curated ceramic assemblages. One of our goals was to define the local resources available to potters by comparing the geochemistry of ceramics to the geochemistry of potential local resources, distributed over the widely varying geomorphological and geological landscape that surrounds the site. This chapter therefore also outlines our sediment sampling strategies. The final section of this chapter highlights the methodological issues inherent in both the sample and in sampling (sample size relationships and bias), and the means we used to redress these issues.

A Short History of Archaeology at Gordion

The archaeological site called Yassıhöyük (flat-topped mound) was "discovered" by engineers during the construction of the Istanbul to Ankara section of the Berlin to Baghdad railroad. The large mound was first proposed as the Phrygian capital Gordion in the 1890s by the philologist Alfred Körte on the basis of historical texts that located it on the banks of the Sangarios (Sakarya) River (A. Körte 1897; Sams 1995). In 1900 Alfred and his archaeologist brother Gustav set out to provide physical confirmation of this text-based argument, excavating on Yassıhöyük as well as at some of the larger burial tumuli surrounding the site (G. Körte and A. Körte 1904). Their work uncovered the remains of rich burials in the tumuli and large-scale architecture on the mound, and their identification of Yassıhöyük as Gordion has never been seriously challenged. Today, the site we recognize as the ancient settlement of Gordion consists of three main topographical parts: Yassıhöyük itself, also called the Citadel Mound, combining two separate mounds merged in Hellenistic times; the walled Lower Town, extending between the Citadel and fortresses to the north (Kuş Tepe) and south (Küçük Höyük); and the Outer Town, between the Citadel and the northwestern section of the fortification system (Fig. 1.2; Plate 1). Both surface and geophysical survey indicate that the settlement extended beyond the fortification walls, at least during the Middle Phrygian period (Rose 2017:fig. 9; Voigt 2013:fig. 3).

Following the initial work of the Körte brothers, Gordion was not archaeologically investigated further until after World War II with the arrival of Rodney Young from the University of Pennsylvania. He began a new archaeological campaign at the site that extended from 1950 until his death in 1974 (Sams 2005). Looking for evidence of King Midas, he excavated on the central mound as well as in 31 of the more than 100 adjacent tumuli. The largest tumulus (MM) that Young investigated preserved an intact burial. Once thought to be the tomb of King Midas, construction of MM and its central burial chamber is now dated to a generation before that ruler's death (i.e. as the tomb of a politically significant aged male, perhaps Midas' father Gordias; Liebhart 2010).

On the Citadel Mound, Young's excavations exposed a long series of occupations from the Early Bronze Age (EBA) through to the Medieval period. One of his most significant discoveries was the Destruction Level (DL) in the elite core of Gordion, encompassing a series of burnt structures with their extensive durable contents preserved *in situ*. Although Young associated this level with Midas (late eighth century to early seventh century BCE), subsequent radiocarbon and tree-ring dating places the Destruction Level event considerably earlier (ca. 800 BCE), at the end of the Early Phrygian period (DeVries et al. 2003; Rose and Darbyshire 2011; Voigt 2009). While he recovered the extensive, but badly disturbed (robbed for building materials), foundations of the elite eastern quarter rebuilt during the Middle Phrygian period, he paid minimal attention to both this and later equally disturbed levels. As a result, most excavated contexts for the Middle and Late Phrygian periods remained poorly understood, with dates for these contexts based primarily on Attic ceramic imports. After Young's death, excavation was halted while study seasons on the Gordion material continued under the direction of Keith DeVries, who had excavated with Young and was interested in the broader history of the settlement (DeVries 1990).

In 1988, the University of Pennsylvania resumed fieldwork and site conservation at Gordion under the supervision of project director G. Kenneth Sams, with a new program of excavations directed by Mary M. Voigt. Voigt's initial goal (1988–1989) was to establish a clear chronological sequence based on stratigraphy for all periods of occupation on the Citadel Mound. Two soundings, the Upper Trench Sounding (UTS) and the Lower Trench Sounding (LTS) adjacent to the Rodney Young trenches (Fig. 3.1a), allowed ceramicist Robert Henrickson to establish a local ceramic sequence; collection of plant and animal remains from these soundings also enabled reconstruction of the changing domestic economy (N. F. Miller 2010; Voigt et al. 1997; Zeder and Arter 1994). Having established a ceramic sequence, Voigt moved to excavate settlement areas on the still little known western part of the Citadel Mound (CM), and in the Lower and Outer Town areas surrounding the central mound. Her primary goal from 1993 to 2002 was to gain an understanding of non-elite activities across the site (Fig. 1.2; Voigt 1997, 2011). Surface surveys conducted initially by William M. Sumner, and later by Lisa Kealhofer, established a regional context for Gordion, and geomorphological research by Ben Marsh revealed changes in the topography of the alluvial plain around Gordion as well as on the surrounding slopes (Kealhofer 2005b; Kealhofer and Marsh 2019; Marsh 1999, 2005; Marsh and Kealhofer 2014).

In 2012, Sams and Voigt ended their active field research at Gordion, as C. Brian Rose took up the role of project director. Rose initiated new excavations, focused primarily on understanding the fortification system on the Citadel Mound (Rose 2017). He also initiated an intensive program of geophysical survey over the entire area of the settlement to define the extent and topography of the Lower and Outer Towns.

Archaeological Contexts at Gordion

The contexts recovered over the Young and Voigt excavations by multiple teams determined the character of the ceramic assemblage available for analysis (Table 3.1). Initially, Bronze Age contexts were established from relatively small soundings in the Citadel Mound made by Young and Machteld Mellink. The largest excavated areas with Bronze Age strata were on what proved to be a central high mound, located on the modern east bank of the Sakarya River; within the excavated area were domestic structures with storage pits. The high mound has been estimated to have been ca. 1–1.5 ha in area during the Early Bronze Age (EBA), rising at least 10–12 m above the third-millennium BCE

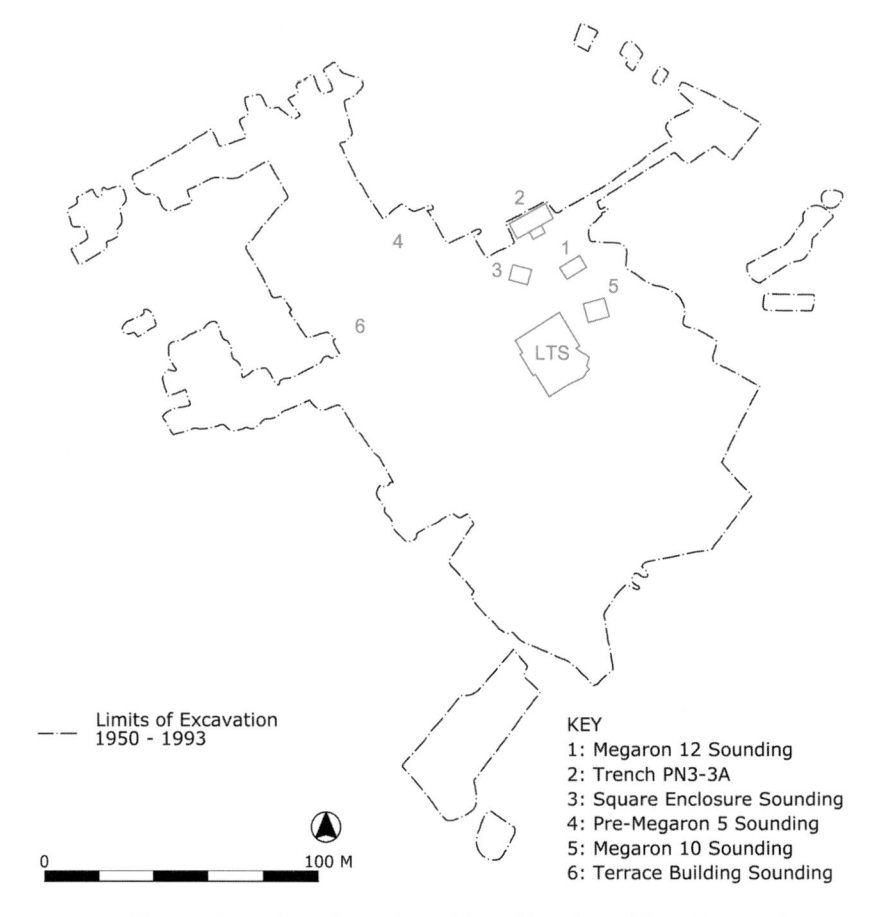

Fig. 3.1 Location of trenches with prehistoric and Late Bronze Age YHSS 10-8 deposits.
(a) Main Excavation Area on the Eastern Mound with Young, Voigt and Rose soundings. YHSS 8 Late Bronze Age remains were found in Area 1 (Megaron 12 or NCT Sounding), Area 5 (Megaron 10 or NT Sounding) and the Lower Trench Sounding (LTS).

floodplain. To the south of the high mound was a lower mound – the EBA lower town (Gunter 1991:109–110, plans 11–12; Rose 2017:155–157, fig. 17–18; Voigt 2013:173–179).

Limited areas of Late Bronze Age strata were excavated by Young and later Voigt (YHSS phases 10-8, 1600?–1150 BCE) (Fig. 3.1a–c). Bronze Age ceramic types were poorly defined for this region, so associated levels were assigned to both the MBA and LBA (Gunter 1991). More

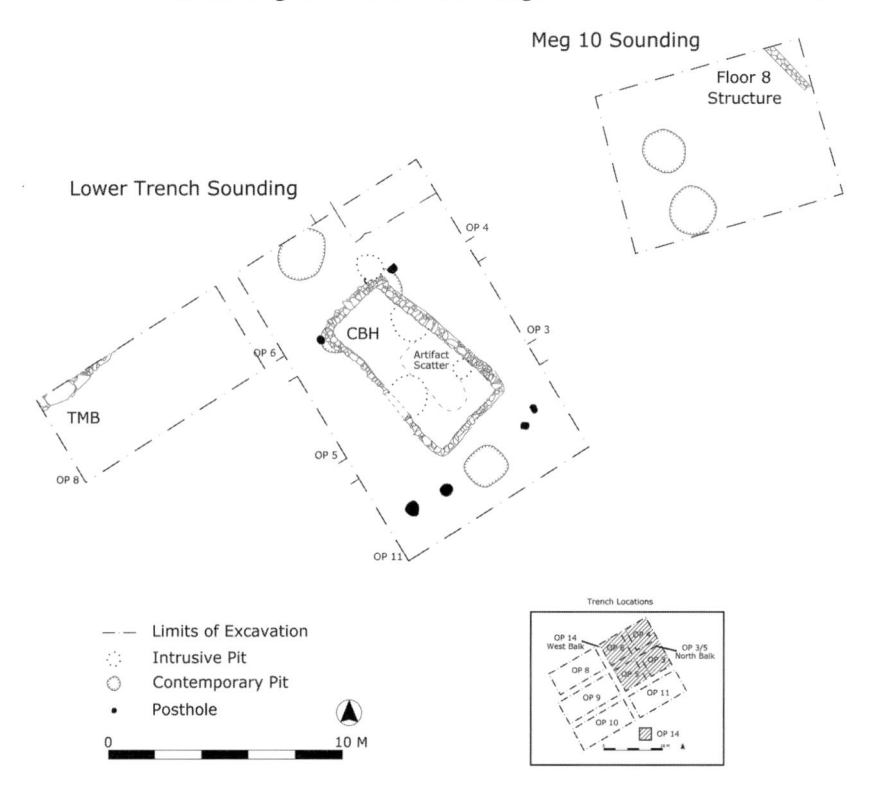

Fig. 3.1 (*cont.*) (b) Plan of Late Bronze Age YHSS 8-9 architecture in the Lower Trench and Megaron 10 Soundings.

recent ceramic comparisons suggest that two phases of the LBA were represented in the strata. For the earliest LBA we have a ceramic sample, but no coherent architecture, and can say little more than that the settlement extended over the EBA lower town mound (Gunter 1991; Voigt 2013). More extensive later LBA exposures provided a firmer ceramic sequence (Gunter 1991; Sams 1994; Voigt 2013). A larger building with a stone, mud and wooden superstructure and a stone-lined basement represents a late LBA residential/domestic structure (Fig. 3.1b). All of this evidence comes from the LBA lower town, which produced ceramics and glyptic evidence. These indicate that during the LBA Gordion was affiliated with, or perhaps incorporated into, the Hittite Empire. If there was evidence of a Hittite administrative presence, it would likely have been in a nonresidential area, on the highest part of the settlement mound. This must remain speculative as archaeological

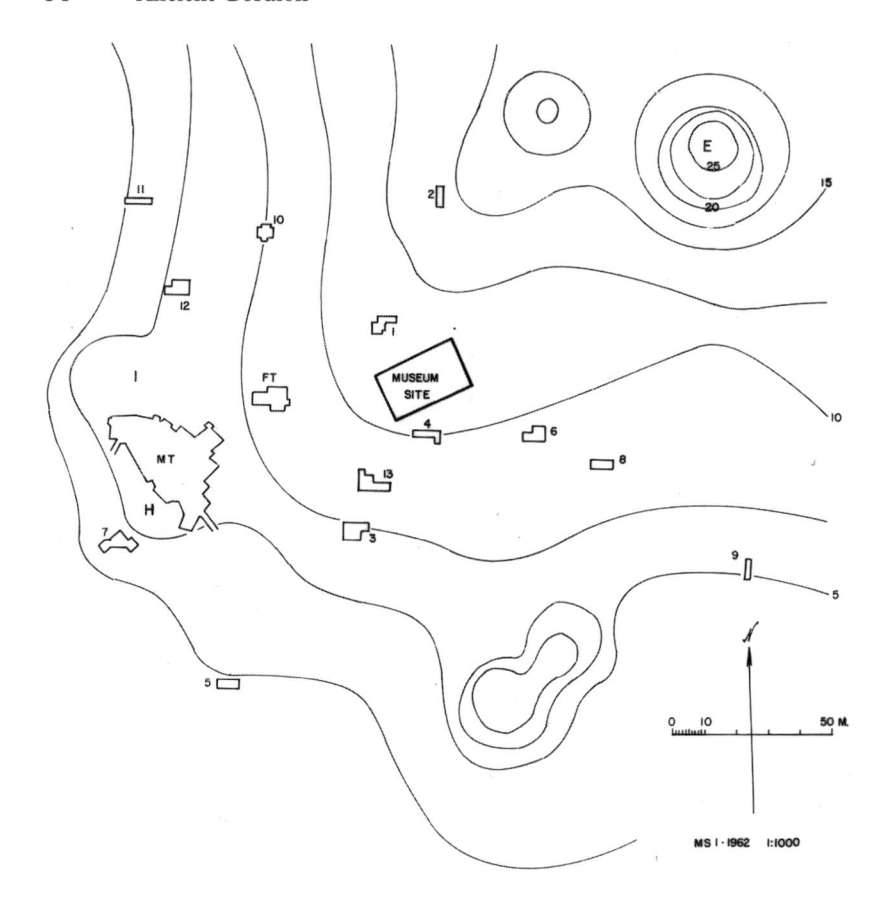

Fig. 3.1 (*cont.*) (c) The "Common Cemetery" excavation trenches on the Northeast Ridge, 1951–1962. Bronze Age burials in zone 7 (see Fig. 1.2 for location of the Northeast Ridge).
Sources: *3.1*a C. Alblinger; *3.1b* D. Hoffman, S. Jarvis and C. Alblinger; *3.1c* image no. 76583 Plan 1962-33, J. S. Last: Plan 8; all courtesy University of Pennsylvania Museum, Gordion Project Archives.

evidence recovered by Mellink and Young indicates that in Early Phrygian times (YHSS 6B) the Bronze Age mound was truncated to provide a broader area for elite and administrative structures (Voigt 2013). Destruction of what should have been the central and highest part of the prehistoric settlement would have removed any potential architectural evidence for LBA elite or religious structures.

Archaeological evidence for the earliest Iron Age (YHSS 7 1150–900 BCE) is more abundant, and shows a change in virtually all aspects of

Table 3.1. *Size of excavated area by YHSS phase: R. S. Young and M. M. Voigt excavations 1950–2002.*

YHSS phase	Phase name	Size of area excavated	Location of excavated areas
–	**Early Bronze Age**	ca. 136 m^2	1950–1965: Main Excavation Area EM Meg 10, 12/NCT, TrPN-3/3A
–	**Middle–Late Bronze Age**	ca. 60 m^2	1950–1965: Main Excavation Area EM Meg 10, 12/NCT
YHSS 10	**Late Bronze Age**	10 m^2	1988–1989: Lower Trench Sounding EM Operation 14
		ca. 105 m^2	1950–1965: Main Excavation Area EM Meg 10, 12/NCT
YHSS 9-8		126 m^2	1988–1989: Lower Trench Sounding EM Operations 14, 11
YHSS 7	**Early Iron Age**	135 m^2	1950–1965: Main Excavation Area EM Meg 10, 12/NCT
		270 m^2	1988–1989: Lower Trench Sounding EM All Operations
YHSS 6	**Early Phrygian**	ca. 3000 m^2	1950–1972: Main Excavation Area EM EPB, Meg 10, 12/NCT and adjacent trenches
YHSS 6B		370 m^2	1989–1993: Lower Trench Sounding EM All Operations, plus 15, 18, 19
YHSS 6A		ca. 2 ha	1950–1972: Main Excavation Area EM
		75 m^2	1988–1989: Upper Trench Sounding EM Operation 1
		3.6 m^2	1993: WM SW Zone Operation 12
YHSS 5	**Middle Phrygian**	ca. 2 ha	1950–1972: Main Excavation Area EM
		100 m^2	1988–1989: Upper Trench Sounding EM Operations 1-2
		ca. 1290 m^2	1950: WM SW Zone South Trench
		85 m^2	1989–1996: WM SW Zone Operations 12, 17
		ca. 160 m^2	1994–2002: WM NW Zone Operations 29, 30, 36
		?	1951–1961: Southern Lower Town Fortifications
		115 m^2	1993–1995: Southern Lower Town Area A
		260 m^2	1994–1995: Southern Lower Town Area B
		800 m^2	1950–1953: Northeast Ridge Houses beneath tumuli
		20 m^2	1993: Outer Town Operation 22

Table 3.1. (cont.)

YHSS phase	Phase name	Size of area excavated	Location of excavated areas
YHSS 4	**Late Phrygian**	ca. 2 ha	1950–1972: Main Excavation Area EM
		150 m²	1988–1989: Upper Trench Sounding EM Operations 1, 2, 7
		ca. 1290 m²	1950: WM South Trench
		110 m²	1993–1995: WM SW Zone Operation 17
		185 m²	1994–2002: WM NW Z Operations 30E, 29, 34, 36
		150 m²	1993–1995: Southern Lower Town Area A
		310 m²	1993–1995: Southern Lower Town Area B
		15 m²	1994–1995: Outer Town Operation 32

Key sources: Codella and Voigt in press; Gunter 1991; Voigt 1994, 2013; Voigt and Young 1999; Gordion Archives NBK 117)

Contextualizing the Ceramic Assemblage 37

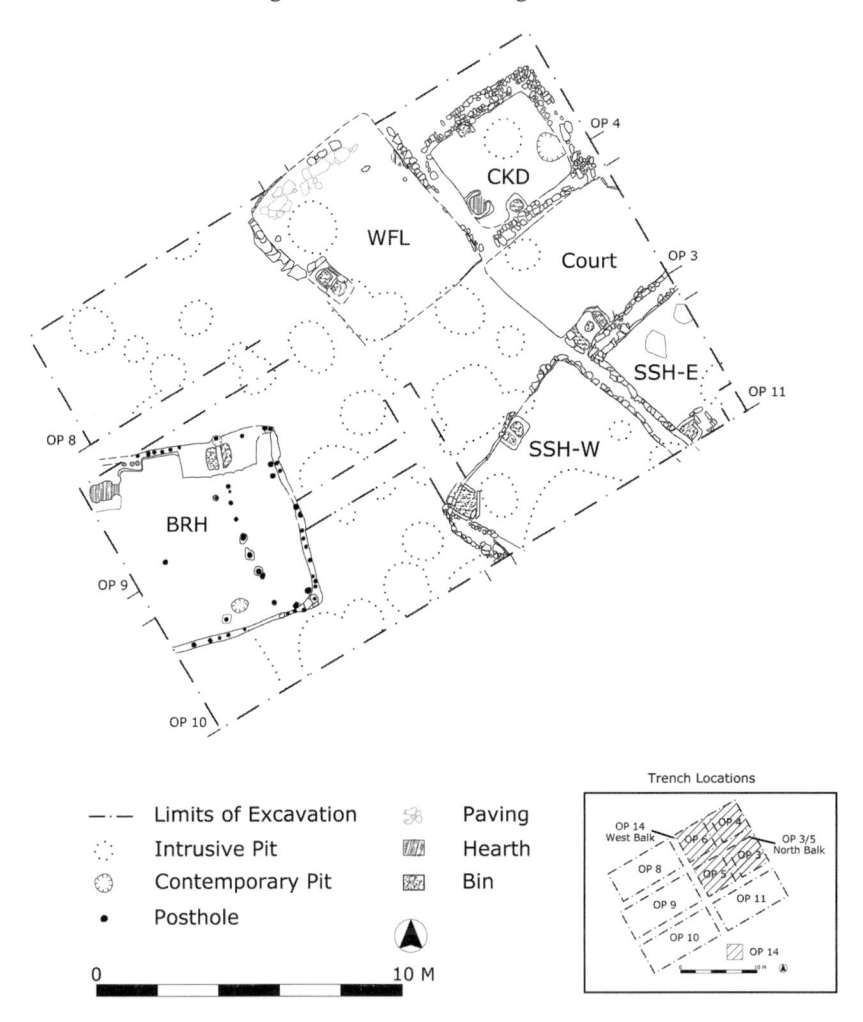

Fig. 3.2 YHSS 7 Early Iron Age Lower Trench Sounding – structures excavated by Young and Voigt.
(a) Houses in the LTS dated to YHSS 7B (to north) and initial 7A (to south).

material culture from that of the LBA. Two EIA phases can be distinguished based on stratigraphy and ceramics (YHSS 7B and 7A), but there is also evidence of continuity across the phases of this period. Small semisubterranean houses with walls of packed mud or wattle and daub are separated by courtyards with ovens and large storage pits (Fig. 3.2 a and b). Again, we assume that the central part of the EIA settlement

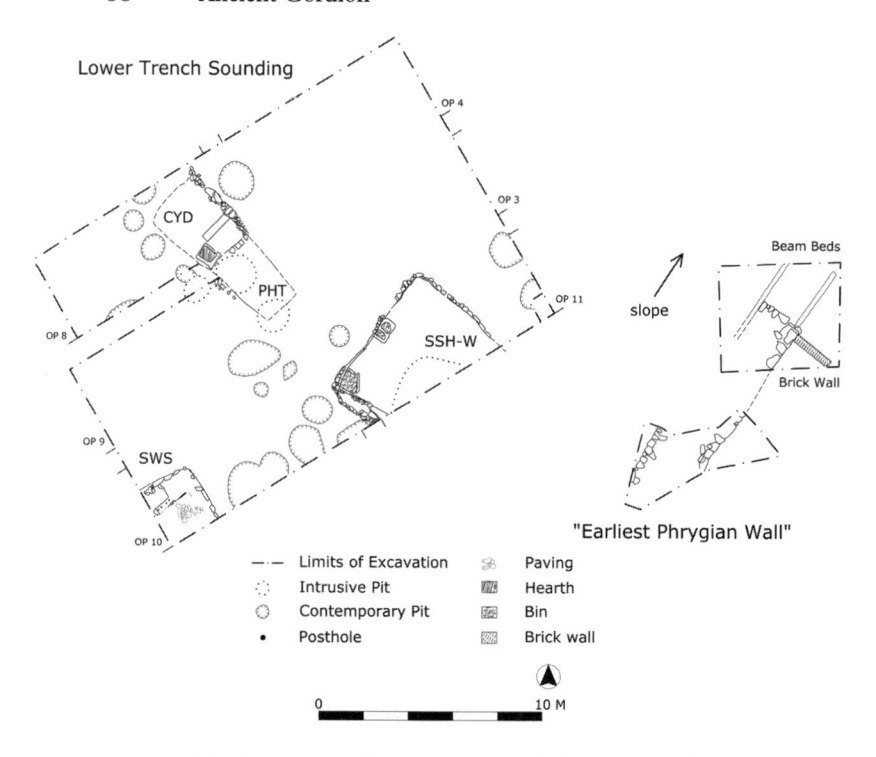

Fig. 3.2 (*cont.*) (b) Structures and pits dated to the final stage of Early Iron Age 7A. The "Earliest Phrygian Wall," excavated and named by Rodney Young, is tentatively identified as the initial fortification wall of Iron Age Gordion.
Sources: Voigt *3.2a* D. Hoffman, S. Jarvis, and C. Alblinger; *3.2b* C. Alblinger and C. K. Williams II; courtesy University of Pennsylvania Museum, Gordion Project Archives).

within the excavated area may have been destroyed in the early ninth century BCE. Thus it is possible that the apparent uniformity of houses and domestic equipment in the twelfth to tenth centuries reflects sampling bias rather than a measure of the larger domestic settlement of that period.

Following the small-scale, domestic occupation of YHSS 7, the settlement was rapidly built up and reorganized (Kealhofer et al. 2019). The Early Phrygian (EP) period (YHSS 6 900–800 BCE) began with the construction of substantial fortifications enclosing a formal layout with white stone buildings set around a courtyard (Fig. 3.3a; Voigt 2013). At the end of YHSS 6B these buildings were dismantled and replaced with a new fortification system (Fig. 3.3b; YHSS 6A). A massive wall and glacis enclosed each of two mounds separated by a wide, open area (Rose 2017;

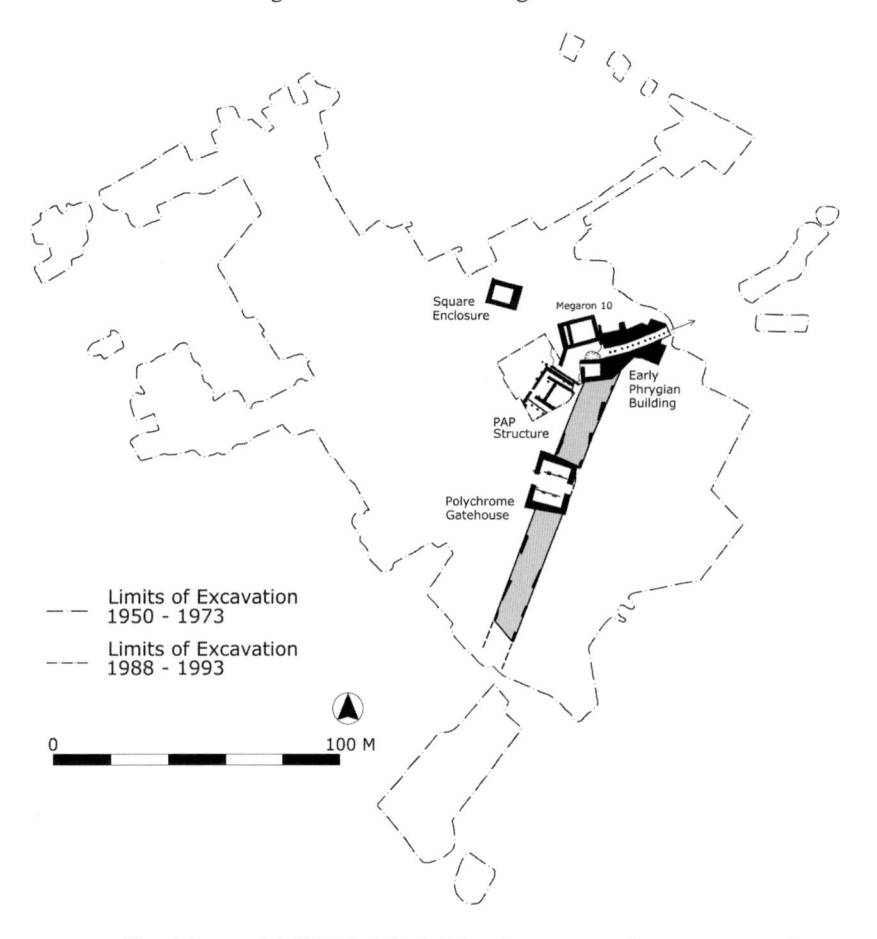

Fig. 3.3 a and b YHSS 6 Early Phrygian excavated structures on the Eastern Mound.
(a) Early Phrygian 6B was a fortified settlement with stone-built monumental structures set around an earth-packed court. This plan shows the second construction phase within 6B. At this time, there were two entrances through the citadel wall: the newly constructed Polychrome Gate House, and the previous gate or Early Phrygian building (EPB), which had been roofed and turned into a sally port. The irregular outline of the EPB reflects limits of excavation, and the fills to north and south of the gate passage extend an unknown distance. The court is surrounded by four buildings: the PAP structure, Megaron 10 and the Square Enclosure and the proposed WWS Structure (along the western side of the court (see Fig. 7.4).

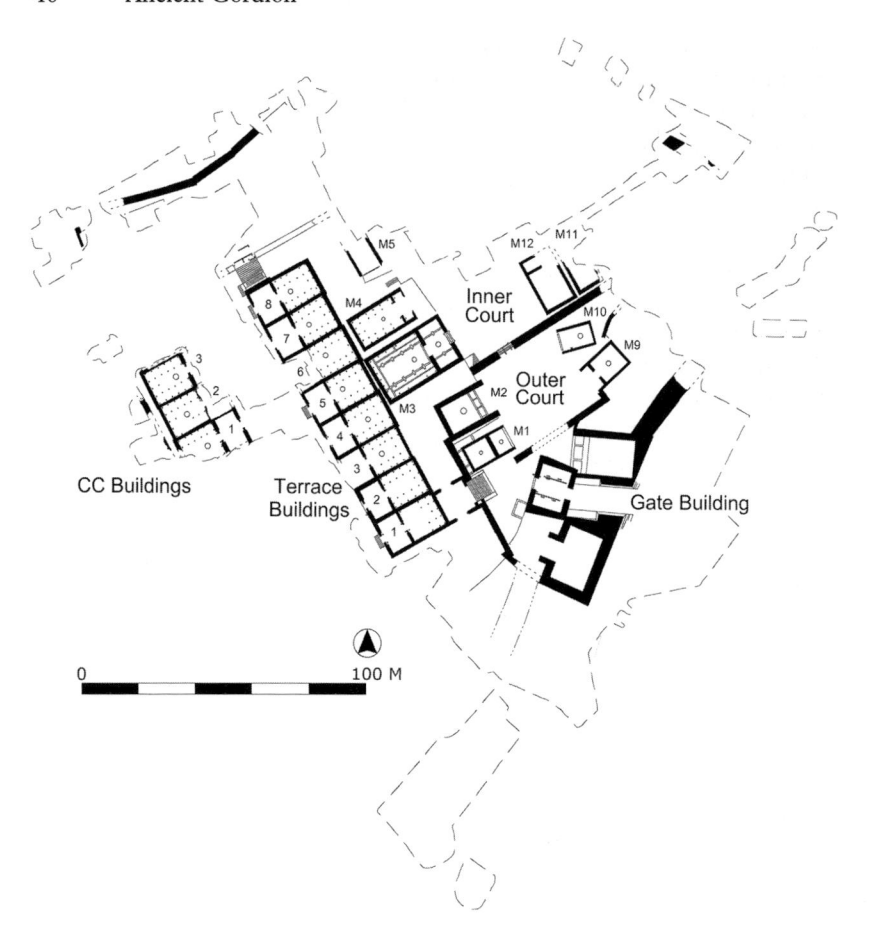

Fig. 3.3 (*cont.*) (b) Early Phrygian YHSS 6A:2 plan of the elite area on the Eastern Mound, after it had been considerably enlarged by the addition of the Terrace Complex in the late ninth century BCE. When Gordion burnt ca. 800 BCE the East Gate and the Outer Court had been greatly altered by a new construction project (see Fig. 7.6).
Sources: *3.3a* D. Hoffman, S. Jarvis and C. Alblinger using plans by R. S. Young, C. K. Williams, A. Trik and J. Shaw; *3.3b* W. Cummer, W. Remsen, D. Hoffman, S. Jarvis and C. Alblinger; courtesy University of Pennsylvania Museum, Gordion Project Archives.

Rose and Gürsan-Salzman 2017, 2018). Of these two enclosed mounds, the slightly lower mound to the west (WM) is known only from a single sounding (Voigt 2013). The majority of the evidence for the EP comes from the Eastern Mound (EM), an elite area that was mostly destroyed by fire ca. 800 BCE while in the process of being remodeled. This fire event is preserved in the "Destruction Level." Inside the walls that surrounded the Eastern Mound were multiple two-roomed buildings ("megarons"). These buildings, arranged around two adjacent courtyards, had an inner larger room often with a central hearth, and a smaller outer room that served as a reception area or porch. Those in the Outer Court, just inside a massive gate structure, were empty at the time of the fire, while two of the excavated structures in the Inner Court appear to have been still in use and furnished. Located on a terrace to the southwest of the two courts were two additional rows of large attached megarons (known as the Terrace and Clay Cut [CC] buildings), destroyed with their contents *in situ*, providing evidence of a variety of activities (spinning, weaving, food and drink production, storage; B. Burke 2005; Morgan 2018; Sams 1997).

It is clear that the megarons around the YHSS 6A Outer and Inner Courts served residential and administrative functions. However, the presence of multiple structures of similar size, with varying levels of elaboration and equipment, are difficult to interpret in relation to the organization of power in the EP period. Young believed that the largest structure, Megaron 3, was a possible "royal" residence. In contrast, DeVries suggested Megaron 3 was a temporary storage area at the time of the fire, and that the partially completed Megaron 4 was the new palace. Morgan (2018), on the other hand, argued that the architecture and associated activities are more consistent with corporate power strategies than as a palatial residence of an individual elite leader.

During the Middle Phrygian (MP) phase (YHSS 5, ca. 800–540 BCE), the settlement achieved its maximum extent (ca. 1 km^2), with clear differences in status across the site marked by architectural scale and construction methods. After the Destruction Level at the end of the ninth century BCE, the major rebuilding project on the Eastern Mound, initiated in the EP period, was renewed and expanded (Voigt 2011, 2012b, 2013). Three to five meters of clay fill were laid above the ruined Eastern Mound and on what had originally been a low-lying area of settlement to the south. The result was two high mounds separated by an open space, covering the area of the EP citadel. Structures with deep rubble foundations and dressed stone walls were built on both mounds, and a fortification wall with a multicolored stone glacis was built around the perimeter unifying the central area of the settlement. The structures on the Eastern Mound largely copied the EP layout (Fig. 3.4). Although none of the MP buildings were found with their contents *in situ*, the functions of each of the new MP structures are likely to have replicated that of their EP predecessors.

During the MP Gordion became a significant urban center, with a Lower Town to the north and south of the central mound protected by

Fig. 3.4 YHSS 5 Middle Phrygian plan, rebuilt elite area on the Eastern Mound.
Located just inside the East Gate in the walled Outer Court are Buildings C, D, E, F and G; in the Inner Court are Buildings H, M, O (with South Cellar), Q, and P; a row of similar structures leads to the northeast of the NCT Building. Separated from both courts by a heavy wall were the two rows of buildings that make up the Middle Phrygian Terrace Complex. Along the edge of the East Mound to the northwest is the PPB, made up of small, cell-like rooms and thought to be a storage facility. Note that the megarons directly above the EP YHSS 6A:2 Terrace complex are free-standing in YHSS 5.
Source: W. Cummer, W. Remsen, D. Hoffman and C. Alblinger; courtesy University of Pennsylvania Museum, Gordion Project Archives.

new massive outer walls anchored by tall fortresses; to the northwest the Outer Town was protected by earthen walls (Voigt 2013). In the southern part of the Lower Town, more fill was used to support two distinct kinds of architecture. To the east was an area with large stone structures with rubble foundations similar to buildings on the Citadel Mound, and to the west were small, mud brick houses (Codella and Voigt in press; Voigt and Young 1999). Geophysical survey indicates that an open area ran between these two mounds (Rose 2017:fig. 9), emphasizing likely differences in the social and economic roles of these two neighborhoods. However, several phases of post-urban sedimentation built up in this area (Marsh 1999:fig. 3), leaving open the question of how the area covered by the sediments was originally used. In the Outer Town the only excavated structure is semisubterranean, perhaps attached to a mud brick structure built at surface level (Voigt and Young 1999). With limited archaeological soundings in the Lower and Outer Towns, estimates of the occupational density of this area remain uncertain.

By the late MP period, late seventh century BCE, Phrygian power declined as Lydian influence gained strength across the region. On the Eastern Mound, some structures were modified but maintained, and in the early sixth century BCE some of the stone buildings were given new tile roofs in Lydian style (Codella and Voigt in press; Glendinning 2005; Rose 2018). On the Western Mound (WM), more substantial changes during the MP included the abandonment of the large stone structures, and their replacement by smaller domestic houses (Codella and Voigt in press). A large dump of pottery and other artifacts dated to the end of the MP indicates both prosperity and access to luxury goods (Dusinberre et al. 2019).

The Middle Phrygian period ended with the Persian siege of Lydian Gordion that left the remains of an earthen siege ramp on the outside of a fortress wall protecting the southern Lower Town (see Fig. 8.5 in Chapter 8); remains of another fortress and siege mound have been documented by geo-prospection at the northern end of the northern Lower Town (Rose 2017). Following the siege, Gordion was incorporated into the Achaemenid Empire that extended control over much of Anatolia. The Late Phrygian (YHSS 4 540–330 BCE) settlement continued as an urban center, with Late Phrygian (LP) occupation documented for all parts of the site (Fig. 3.5a). Maintenance of a new elite quarter, smaller than in the preceding MP phase, can be seen in early LP remodeling of buildings around the Outer Court on the Eastern Mound, as well as the addition of a few new structures (Fig. 3.5b; Fields 2010; Rose 2018; Voigt 2013). These included the large "Mosaic Building" on

44   Ancient Gordion

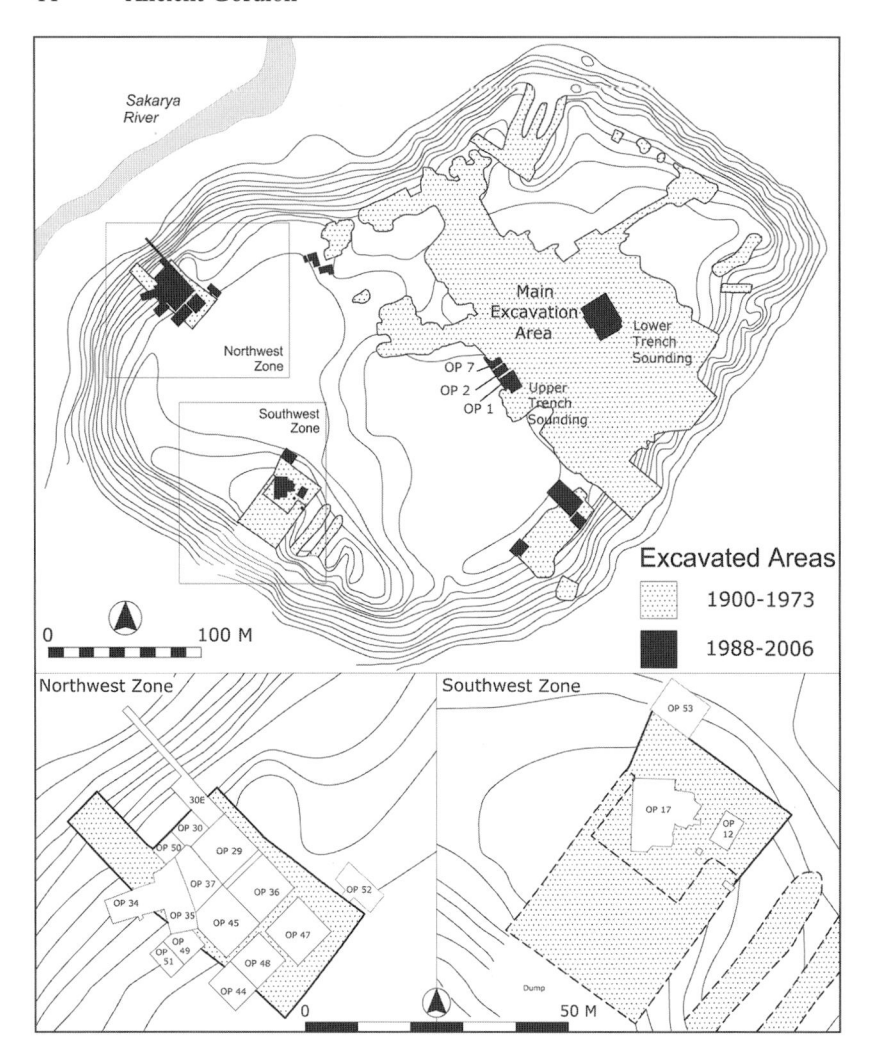

Fig. 3.5 Location of all excavation units on the Citadel Mound.
(a) Plan showing all excavated areas on the Citadel Mound (top). Box insets show detailed operation plans for the two sectors on the Western Mound (Northwest and Southwest Zones).

the southern edge of the mound, and a small semisubterranean structure with elaborate wall paintings set between MP buildings C and G.

Significant change in the political organization of Gordion is evident in the early fifth century BCE, when small semisubterranean structures

Fig. 3.5 (*cont.*) (b) Late Phrygian YHSS 4 formal architecture on the Eastern Mound included both remodeled and new structures, here shown in relationship to the MP building plan. Only one of the many small pithouses ("cellars") cut into MP buildings across the entire EM is shown.

Middle and Late Phrygian (YHSS 5 and 4) contexts have been excavated across the entire Main Excavation Area (except the LTS), in Ops 30, 29 and 36 in the Northwest Zone and Ops 12 and 17 in the Southwest Zone; LP deposits were excavated in the Mosaic Trench along the southeastern edge of the mound.

Sources: *3.5a*. D. Hoffman, S. Jarvis, B. Burke, and C. Alblinger; *3.5b*. E. Dusinberre (2019) with permission from *Anatolian Studies*, courtesy University of Pennsylvania Museum, Gordion Project Archives.

Fig. 3.6 Map of the major topographic zones within Gordion, showing the location of the Citadel Mound and the Lower and Outer Towns. Lower and Outer Town trenches excavated 1993–1995, with additional settlement areas identified by intensive surface survey and coring.
Source: S. Jarvis, courtesy University of Pennsylvania Museum, Gordion Project Archives.

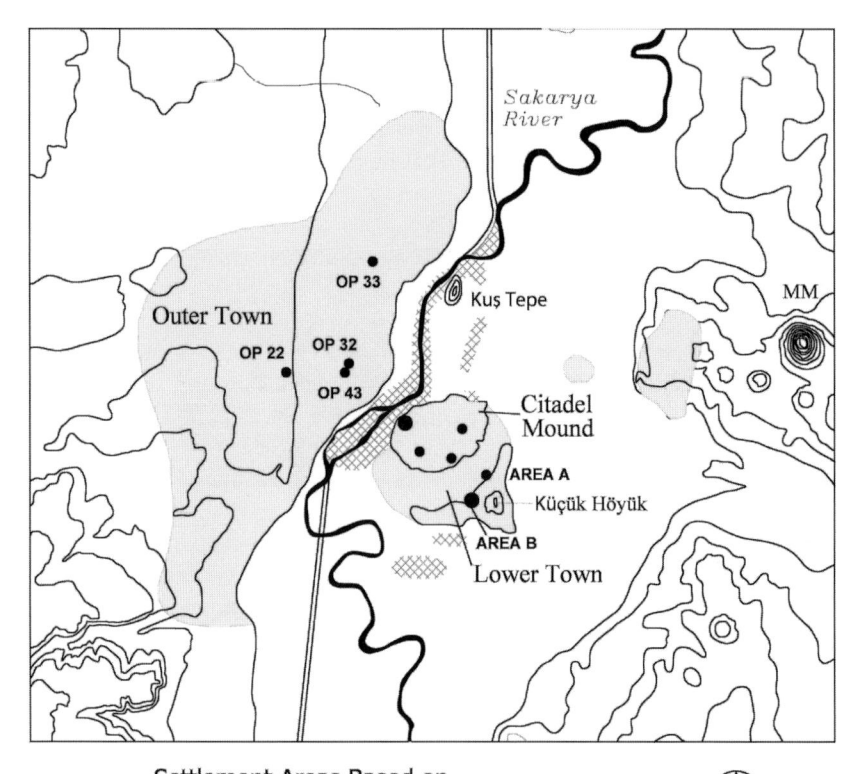

were built above the MP Terrace and Clay Cut service buildings. By the end of the LP most of the Eastern Mound was covered by such structures as well as metallurgical workshops (Voigt 2013). On the Western Mound two distinct architectural zones have been excavated (Fig. 3.5a). To the northwest during the early LP large stone structures were built, but by the end of the period only small structures were in use (Voigt 2013; Voigt and Young 1999). Two areas within the NW Zone have evidence of activities involving high temperatures that were not part of ordinary domestic practice (sloping floors with burning that were repeatedly replastered and an area with multiple hearths and cinder-like debris), and apparently used for an as yet indeterminate type of production (Voigt 2013:fig. 44). The Southwest Zone on the Western Mound had a more domestic trajectory, with well-constructed semisubterranean houses present throughout the LP (Voigt and Young 1999). Excavations beyond the Citadel Mound, in the southern Lower and Outer Towns, revealed semisubterranean houses that varied in size and interior fittings (Fig. 3.6; and see Figs. 9.5–9.6 in Chapter 9; Rademakers et al. 2018; Voigt 2011). The Late Phrygian city may not have been as politically significant as in previous phases, but it still extended over an area ca. 1 sq. km, as a densely occupied and apparently cosmopolitan hub for the production and consumption of diverse Lydian, Attic, Persian and Phrygian style goods, with stone, bone, antler, ivory and metallurgical workshops and many ceramic imports.

Alexander's conquest of the region in the late fourth century BCE marked the commencement of a series of culturally distinct occupation phases from the Hellenistic (YHSS 3) to Medieval (YHSS 1) periods. By the Early Hellenistic phase, the density and extent of habitation at Gordion was greatly reduced. During this phase, the area between the Eastern and Western Mounds was infilled, creating the single mound we see today, and the fortification system was abandoned. Excavations produced largely domestic structures, though with increasingly Greek affinities (coinage, inscriptions), and Hellenistic cosmopolitan practices (Stewart 2010; Wells 2012). By the mid-third century BCE Galatian immigrants settled in what remained a prosperous town with a new, walled elite quarter on the northwestern part of the Citadel Mound (Voigt 2012a). In the first to fourth centuries CE a Roman military outpost occupied the western part of the Citadel Mound, providing protection for an adjacent Roman road (Goldman and Voigt 2014). The site was briefly occupied in Byzantine times, and after a period of abandonment that began in the seventh century CE, a provincial Selçuk–Early Ottoman period town was established on the Citadel Mound.

Ceramic Collections

The largely first millennium BCE development of this settlement has rendered radiocarbon dating less useful for refining its absolute chronology (due to the long calibration "plateau" from ca. 800 to 300 BCE). More reliance has been placed on combined stratigraphic and ceramic stylistic sequences to provide relative chronologies for this period. The prominent role of ceramics at Gordion is also reflected in the number and diversity of typological, technological and archaeometric specialists who have worked at the site since 1950. Since the renewed phase of excavations in 1988 these include G. K. Sams, R. C. Henrickson, K. Devries, K. Lynch, M. Lawall, S. Stewart, G. Schaus, G. Gurtekin-Demir, G. Bacheva (previously G. Toteva), A. Goldman, C. Aslan and G. Günata, as well as authors Grave and Kealhofer.

Beyond the primary importance of excavation contexts, a study of Gordion ceramics must contend with the impact that changes in excavation and curation strategies have had on the composition of the curated archaeological assemblage. Young's ambitious and extensive excavation program primarily targeted understanding the major architectural developments of the site. As a result, he exposed large areas of the site in any given excavation season. The logistical demands of this approach involved earth-moving operations on a scale that required the construction of a movable railroad to redeposit large volumes of excavated material around the perimeter of the mound.

Young's excavation strategy also produced large quantities of artifacts. In contrast to his excavation program, artifact collection strategies remained modest. Emphasis was placed on retaining exotic, significant or intact artifacts, i.e. a very small and nonrepresentative portion of the overall excavated assemblage including coins and complete objects. For ceramics, intact pots and highly diagnostic sherds were "registered" and curated. A card catalog enumerated and described these (www.penn.museum/sites/gordion/gordion-archive/). Selected individual diagnostic sherds were sorted by style and organized in cabinets with labeled drawers. When particularly significant contexts were encountered, a selection of sherds was assembled in a "context" bag (linked to field notebook descriptions) as a study collection. Sherds not considered to be diagnostic (i.e. the vast majority, including most "coarse" pottery), were discarded in excavation dumps. It is difficult to accurately estimate the volume of material discarded, but given the size of the extant ceramic collection from the Young period relative to that from more recent excavations, we presume it to have been extremely large. Ceramic information (e.g. ware counts, vessel profiles) was recorded at times in excavators' field notebooks, and excavators often included comments on location and quantities of material, although the amount of information varied by excavator (Sams 1994). With the opening of the Gordion Museum, a small selection of restored pots was permanently displayed in groups by period.

An exception to this collection strategy was the ceramic assemblage from the ca. 800 BCE Destruction Level. Relatively *in situ* EP material from the Eastern Mound included whole pots (usually burned and primarily from Megaron 3 in the Inner Court and the service buildings on the terrace). Much of it was curated, creating a more coherent assemblage than most others from Young's Gordion excavations. Sams (1994:2) notes: "The culminating stratigraphic phase of the Early Phrygian period, hereafter the Destruction Level, has yielded an estimated three thousand vessels in excavation." And in footnote 8 (Sams 1994):

The figure is based on excavators' accounts of the quantities within an individual unit. Overall, considerably fewer than half of the vessels retrieved were actually kept. Slightly over 1200 items of pottery from the level have been inventoried, of which about 860 are included by entry or reference in the Catalogue (410–1035).

Following Young's premature death in 1974, researchers focused on publishing aspects of this excavated material, in relation to specific contexts, periods or artifact types – e.g. *The Three Great Early Tumuli* (Young 1981), *The Bronze Age* (Gunter 1991) and *The Early Phrygian Pottery* (Sams 1994). When excavations resumed in 1988 under Voigt's direction, a new approach was taken to excavation, documentation, sampling and curation strategies.

Analysis and publication of periods later than EP were adversely affected by Young's treatment of ceramics, especially the privileging of imports. The date of any piece of pottery was attributed on the basis of style or assumed date of manufacture. The date or period of deposition (i.e. excavated contexts), was not taken into account, and the dates of architecture and other deposits were assigned based on attributed periods of pottery production. This effectively undermined the reliability of the Gordion chronology as constructed by Young. Given the amount of pitting and churning, especially in MP and later deposits, using the attributed period of production of ceramics to date deposits resulted in a somewhat confusing combination of decreasing age estimates for phases that were in fact much earlier, as well as attributing early dates to phases that were much later. For example, Lydian and Attic sherds used to date Middle Phrygian architecture resulted in Young's initial attribution of the MP construction (800–540 BCE) to the Persians (540–330 BCE), while Medieval contexts were incorrectly assigned Hellenistic dates. By the mid-1980s these chronological issues were clearly evident to then director, DeVries, and led to his recognition and support of the need for new excavations.

To clarify stratigraphic relationships and chronology, Voigt commenced excavations in 1988 with a pilot phase of deep soundings in, and adjacent to, Young's original excavations. Subsequent excavations on and around the Citadel Mound provided a broader sample of activities across the periods of occupation (see Table 1.1). Voigt's recovery strategies included sieving for most units (which ironically resulted in enhanced recovery of small fragments of Attic imports). All diagnostic sherds (both plain and decorated) from an excavation unit were washed, sorted, labeled and bagged for storage in a depot within the Gordion excavation compound. Any relatively intact object was identified as a "small find" and curated in the storage depot at the museum at Gordion, or if deemed sufficiently worthy, the Museum of Anatolian Civilizations in Ankara. Non-diagnostic sherds were at least counted and often weighed before being discarded. Ceramics of possible west or east Greek origin were curated separately for study by ceramic specialists Keith DeVries, and subsequently Kathleen Lynch and Mark Lawall.

The systematic excavation, sampling and recording strategies of the 1990s and 2000s were significant departures from earlier work, and produced a much larger, more representative and trackable collection of diagnostic material in relation to the volume and types of material recovered. Recording and storage of the Voigt sample was based on depositional units, another significant departure from Young's approach. Because of the degree to which deposits from many periods were disturbed by stone robbing and pitting, depositional units included sherds with widely varying attributed periods of production. This is especially obvious for contexts with Attic imported ceramics, where it is now clear that individual sherds provide a substantially later date than the rest of the ceramic sample from that context. Henrickson produced a depositional phasing that more closely corresponded to the period of production by focusing on the entire sample from excavated contexts. These had first been placed in stratigraphic order by the excavators, and this resulted in a technologically coherent ceramic sequence for local wares reflecting changes in distinctive types of fabric, surface finish and vessel form over time.

The Ceramic Samples Analyzed for This Study

There are three sets of ceramic data from Gordion integrated in this study of ceramic production and exchange. The different strategies, undertaken at different times, from the 1990s through to 2008, are described here.

1990s: The Yassıhöyük Pottery (YHP) Assemblage

After studying Gordion ceramics from Voigt's 1988–1989 excavations, Henrickson sampled ceramics from each period for more intensive compositional analysis. This sample was generally chosen to represent the entire range of most common forms and styles for each period, unlike the ceramics curated during the Rodney Young excavations, which emphasized the unusual and exotic. Henrickson's sample, labeled YHP, includes 781 sherds from the YHSS sequence 10-2 (Late Bronze Age to Roman periods; the Hellenistic [YHSS 3] and Roman [YHSS 2] components of YHP are not included in this study). Parts of this sequence have been published (e.g. Henrickson and Blackman 1996).

Henrickson collaborated with James Blackman at the Smithsonian Institution for a program of elemental analysis using NAA to understand local resource use over time. In addition to the MMV ceramic sample, he selected a few additional samples from contexts excavated by Rodney Young's team to augment phases not as well represented in the Voigt soundings (e.g. Mellink's LP excavations on Küçük Höyük).

The YHP ceramic assemblage overall has the best chronological control of any at Gordion. While a few individual contexts from the Young sample are distinctive and securely dated (e.g. the Destruction Level; the Middle Hellenistic abandonment), the 1988–1989 sequence provides new and more reliable dates for most ceramic samples collected. In addition, Henrickson's analysis of the ceramic production techniques for the YHSS phases provides another critical technological dimension to the ceramic data (Henrickson 1993, 1994, 1995, 2001, 2002, 2005; Henrickson and Blackman 1996; Henrickson and Voigt 1998; Henrickson et al. 2002).

2003–2008: Anatolian Iron Age (AIA) Ceramics Project (Grave and Kealhofer) – Gordion

In 2003, the AIA project began a pilot study at three sites in western Turkey, as a baseline for studying large-scale regional patterns of trade and exchange after the collapse of the Hittite Empire. Gordion was one of these sites. Over the course of three years (2003–2005) AIA collected sherds from both ongoing Voigt excavations and unregistered study material from Young's excavations, particularly Late Phrygian, Hellenistic and Roman period deposits. The AIA analyses of much of this material were compared with previously published Gordion NAA results (Grave et al. 2009; Henrickson and Blackman 1996). In 2008, AIA returned to apply a larger and more systematic sampling regime of the Gordion ceramic assemblage.

1950s–1970s: The Eski Depot Assemblage

As noted, Young's excavations produced a comparatively modest, highly selective sample of diagnostic sherds and vessels that were registered and curated in a storage area, now associated with the Gordion Museum in Yassıhöyük village. This storage area, the "Eski Depot," included mainly study collections, with examples of the range of excavated metals, ceramics, glass and other materials. As this material was also an officially registered museum collection, it was initially available for visual inspection but not for other forms of investigation. In 2008, however, this policy changed. Staff from the Museum of Anatolian Civilizations in Ankara reinventoried the Eski Depot collections, accessioning some materials for the Ankara Museum and allowing the remaining Eski Depot collections to be sampled for geochemical analysis.

In 2008, therefore, AIA returned to Gordion to collect a larger sample of the Young study collection. AIA sampled more than 500 sherds for NAA from the Eski Depot collection, spanning the Early Iron (YHSS 7) to Hellenistic periods (YHSS 3). As the collection was organized to associate particular ceramic styles in separate cabinet drawers, the AIA strategy was to sample every distinct stylistic type and form by drawer. The main goal of the sampling was to provide geochemical characterization of the Early Phrygian corpus that had been published by Sams (1994), and to further identify both exotic and regional production within this corpus. Earlier and later materials were included in order to evaluate how production and exchange changed over time. Additional samples were also chosen to collaboratively facilitate the research of other site ceramicists studying Attic/Greek, Lydian (e.g. Gürtekin-Demir 2021), and Late Phrygian ceramic types (Bacheva 2018). Results for the Hellenistic and Roman period ceramics sampled during this process are beyond the scope of the present work.

1996–2001: The Gordion Regional Survey (GRS) Sediments

In 1996, Kealhofer commenced a settlement survey (the Gordion Regional Survey – GRS), in a 20 × 20 km region centered on the site of Gordion. In the process of evaluating changing patterns of land use, the survey identified 11 prehistoric to Late Classical sites in the region (Kealhofer 2005b; Kealhofer and Marsh 2019; Marsh and Kealhofer 2014). Over the course of five years, more than 100 sediment samples, multiple sediment cores, and ca. 10,000 sherds were collected. In 2008, in tandem with sampling Eski Depot ceramics, AIA also sampled 1,109 of the GRS ceramics from those 11 sites. While the results of the AIA NAA characterization study of the survey ceramics are not presented here (see Kealhofer and Marsh 2019; Marsh and Kealhofer 2014), NAA results for the GRS sediments are included to define local geochemical profiles and identify locally produced ceramics.

Summary of Ceramic Collections

The Late Bronze to Late Phrygian ceramic sample for this study derives from both Young and Voigt's excavations to which we add an additional 72 sediment samples (Table 3.2). Nearly half of our total assemblage is made up of Henrickson's YHP collection (n = 733) largely representing Voigt's 1988–1989 stratigraphic sequence on the Eastern Mound; however, he also included 72 samples from the Young collection in this YHP collection. The main focus of AIA sampling was on the Young study collection (Table 3.2). AIA samples also included sherds chosen from Voigt's excavations (n = 182), but focused on excavation zones (the Western Mound, Lower Town and Outer Town) beyond the Eastern Mound.

As geochemical studies go, our total ceramic sample population might be considered a large dataset; but when broken down as a chronologically and contextually stratified sample of ceramics from any period of excavations or survey, individual sample lots are relatively modest. Because local production dominates the assemblage, and Henrickson specifically focused on local ceramics, we have likely captured the geochemical extent of local production (within the constraints of excavation contexts).

Table 3.2. *Samples taken and analyzed in this study ("Sampled" column denotes total sample taken in the field; "NAA data" denotes samples that have compositional data. Reference soil samples were taken to define local resource zones geochemically; see Fig. 4.2).*

	Sampled	NAA data
Henrickson YHP samples	733	705
AIA MMV ceramic samples	182	179
AIA RSY ceramic samples	680	677
Total	1,595	1,561
Reference samples (soils)	77	72

All ceramics sampled are included in assemblage descriptions. Only samples with NAA data are included in compositional component of analyses.

However, the extent to which we captured the full range of exotic ceramics transported to Gordion is more difficult to evaluate. Interpretations must be tempered by archaeological contexts (elite vs. domestic, floors vs. trash or industrial deposits), and the volume of material recovered for any particular period or phase (Table 3.1). The Voigt excavations provide a solid longitudinal sample for Gordion, particularly from the Late Bronze Age through to the Roman period, with a few broader windows on domestic and industrial contexts in the later periods, while the Young excavations better document elite areas of the site during the Early Phrygian period.

Defining the Baseline for Identifying Local Ceramics

In addition to the sediments collected during the Gordion Regional Survey, sediment and clay samples were collected from both the surface and site stratigraphic layers, and from the surrounding area, to better resolve the potential geochemical range of local production. Clay samples from the site and immediately adjacent floodplain were collected by Henrickson and Marsh, while Marsh later collected additional clay and brick samples from the larger survey region (during the AIA project). These sample datasets and their analyses are discussed further in Chapter 4.

Ceramic Perspectives on Gordion

Despite efforts by most archaeologists to gain representative samples of the past societies that they study, this is rarely achievable even with complete site excavation given the biases inherent in patterns of discard and preservation. The datasets that are interpreted through the remainder of this volume are certainly not a "sample" in any statistically representative sense. However, the scale of analyses (AIA and YHP), and Voigt's strategies of systematic collection for all occupation phases at the site and to a certain extent across space nonetheless provide us with critical insights into an ancient community's changing way of life over time that few other sites can match. In subsequent chapters, the specific sampling contexts for the period under consideration are considered, as each phase provides different opportunities for analysis.

4 Identifying Gordion's Groups

Introduction

One of the most fundamental steps in answering questions about societies in the past is linking interpretative or theoretical issues to the data. In this chapter we explain how we use the Gordion archaeological ceramic assemblage to help understand the operation of groups and communities in the past. While we focus on quantitative approaches to ceramic compositional data and clustering protocols, we also make use of multiple lines of evidence, such as "legacy" ceramic data and contextual evidence. Together we view these through the lens of daily practices of producing, distributing and consuming goods, using them to inform and guide our reconstruction of groups and group dynamics at Gordion over time.

Our ability to reconstruct groups and the extent to which they can be interpreted as culturally meaningful entities at Gordion involves two critical elements. The first, as discussed in Chapter 3, centers on the role excavation strategies have had in shaping the ceramic assemblages available. In this chapter we discuss the second element: the role of analytical (geochemical) methods in identifying both analytical clusters and how they relate to cultural groups.

A challenge for identifying cultural entities in the past is the extent to which they are materialized in the archaeological record (e.g. Hodder 1982), the fluidity of identities over time and the changing character of archaeological markers that can also vary with context. Here we explore how we link the theoretical discussions of groups (Chapter 2) to the data we have (Chapter 3). Since a "top-down" approach connecting high-end theory to data cannot be convincingly made in one step, we employ the concept of "empirical theory" to scaffold our data and ultimately address larger interpretative issues (Merton 1968; M. E. Smith 2011). As discussed in Chapter 2, a long history of work on ceramics has steadily moved away from "pots as people" – where stylistic and formal types are equated with discrete cultures – to aspects of the manufacture, distribution and consumption of pots informing us about social identities and group behavior (Bowser 2000; Eckert et al. 2015; Gosselain 2000; Rice 2015).

The following sections outline our methods for identifying groups based on multiple ceramic datasets (composition, technology and style). We begin with a description of the field methodology used for NAA sample selection. Following a discussion of the control procedures used to ensure the accuracy and precision of our NAA data, we introduce our analytical protocols for defining analytical clusters, identifying local vs. nonlocal production, and how we interpret clusters as culturally meaningful. Just as pots are not people, analytical clusters are not cultural groups. Our initial focus is on the analysis and interpretation of compositional data for the initial creation of "object clusters" (Cowgill 1982). The archaeological robustness and coherence of these clusters is then evaluated through the incorporation of our own technological, typological and stylistic data as well as that generated by previous analysts (Robert Henrickson for technology, G. Kenneth Sams, Keith DeVries and others for specific formal and stylistic analyses). Finally, we outline additional nonquantitative criteria, such as observations about ceramic technology, styles and forms for cross-checking the coherence and integrity of clusters. This combined approach is adopted in order to evaluate geochemically based clusters more robustly in relation to potential cultural groups. In subsequent chapters, relevant archaeological data are also used to further contextualize these groups and their dynamics over time.

Previous Approaches to Gordion Ceramics

A number of studies have focused on different aspects of the Gordion ceramic assemblage. The first systematic attempt to describe and categorize Phrygian ceramics was undertaken for the Rodney Young (RSY) assemblage by Sams, who compiled a comprehensive catalogue of the complex range of Early Phrygian ceramic types (Sams 1994). He visually distinguished production techniques (handmade/wheelmade) and fabrics, but principally concentrated on defining a typology of styles (forms, decorative treatments, decorative elements). Sams equated the distinctive styles of Early Phrygian ceramics with cultural identity in terms of both influences and invention (Sams 1974, 1988). He used stylistic uniformity and change to define cultural groups and the way that they changed over time. This work remains a definitive reference that paved the way for other studies of ceramic styles and influences at Gordion (e.g. changes in ceramic styles during the Achaemenid occupation; Toteva 2007).

Moving away from conventional stylistic comparisons, Henrickson produced the first systematic evaluation of the technology of ceramic production at Gordion from the LBA to the Hellenistic period (Henrickson 1993, 1994, 2001, 2002, 2005; Henrickson and Blackman 1996; Henrickson and Voigt 1998; Henrickson et al. 2002). This work combined two complementary agent-based approaches to understand the economic and technological underpinnings of ceramic production (Lechtman 1977; Van der Leeuw 1977). The first involved treating the organization of ceramic production as a series of deliberate performative acts, each of which was potentially discoverable. The second was a focus on the economy governing potters' decisions as a function of the amount of labor involved. Through this combined approach Henrickson developed a technological understanding of ceramic production and chronology at Gordion. The skills of local potters and the materials they chose to use were treated as reflecting a historically and geographically contingent repertoire, especially evident in his discussion of the production of Hellenistic roof tiles (Henrickson and Blackman 1999), and in intersite comparisons (Henrickson 1995).

Rather than using typological uniformity to create ceramic groups, Henrickson treated contemporary assemblages as polythetic, context-specific sets. He focused on the range of technological styles and differences in the economic logic of decision-making for ceramic production. Part of his approach involved defining both potential resource availability and limitations for the Gordion potters. In this context, he undertook a collaboration with James Blackman at the National Institute of Standards and Technology (NIST) for a program of geochemical analysis by Neutron Activation Analysis (NAA). One outcome of this work was a comparison of changes in resource use between two periods of large-scale ceramic production at the site – the LBA and EP (Henrickson and Blackman 1996). They found that while evidence for large-scale production was comparable (volume of production, use of fast wheel, uniformity in forms), there were also substantial differences in the resources used during each period that required further exploration. Henrickson's work provides a crucial component of the current study, adding to it both previously unpublished ceramic compositional data and his interpretations and analyses of Gordion pottery production.

Chronology

Control over time is a critical element in understanding group processes. We evaluate this dimension by combining stratigraphic and contextual analysis with radiocarbon determinations where relevant. Our period of interest (ca. 1500–330 BCE) falls into two radiocarbon phases. In the first, from 1500 to 800 BCE, calibrated radiocarbon resolution ranges from medium to high (i.e. <20-year calibrated range error). However, the second phase, from 800 to 300 BCE, represents a region of the calibration curve with a single extended "plateau," and very poor resolution (ca. 400–500-year calibrated age ranges). As a result, chronological sequencing of this phase is entirely reliant on stratigraphic relationships, with cross-correlation of well-dated material to establish relative chronology. In some cases, imports (typically Greek ceramics) from historically dated sites provide absolute date ranges. While our understanding of the rate of change documented by stratigraphy during the first phase (LBA to EP) is relatively tight, and absolutely controlled through a radiocarbon chronological framework, the rate of change during the second phase (MP to LP) is less certain, and reliant on approximations of deposition rates across a diversity of stratigraphic contexts, many of which have been badly disturbed or lack diagnostic "index fossils."

Field Methodology

Ceramic Samples

The ceramic datasets used in this study include both local and nonlocal ceramics predominantly from excavations on the Citadel Mound. Other excavation areas sampled less intensively include the southern Lower Town, Outer Town, Northeast Ridge and tumuli (Fig. 1.2). In Chapter 3 we noted that the respective composition of each dataset inherently reflects substantial differences in sampling strategies, in terms of both original excavation techniques and the rationale behind the creation of each assemblage. The ceramic data combine two sets from the excavations of Young (RSY) (1950–1973), and Voigt (MMV) (1988–2006). The NAA dataset combines two different NAA collection protocols, one undertaken by Henrickson (YHP) in the 1990s focused mainly on the MMV 1988–1989 stratigraphic units, and including some RSY materials, and the other undertaken by AIA, mainly focusing on RSY material, but including some MMV samples. Here we describe the AIA sampling protocol.

Sherds selected from collections stored at Gordion were registered and labeled with project prefix and numeric identifier prior to being inventoried (i.e. photographed, briefly described with any associated data recorded). At this stage, initial documentation included basic information (e.g. excavation registration number where available, provenience to

Fig. 4.1 Example of AIA sample recording and documentation methodology: scaled digital photographs of sample AIA 6226e left (exterior) – with blue background stripped away for publication; and right (interior).
AIA#: 6226, Site: Gordion, Context Info Drawer in Depot: C3.2, Gordion inventory no. 7462-P-2937 Ware Form: a tan lebes? (small cauldron); Form size: m; Texture: slightly sandy; Description: Brown on buff – lines, wavy lines, and circles; Period: YHSS 6A EP – Destruction Level; Compositional designation: Group L01 – nonlocal = Bonn NAA variant "Miletos A" (see Plate 5; Table 4.5) (courtesy of AIA project).

the extent available, as well as whatever associated descriptive and contextual information had been recorded by excavators or analysts). Scaled photos of both sides of each sherd were taken prior to sampling, along with profile photographs where appropriate for unusual forms (Fig. 4.1). A small sample (ca. 0.5–5 g in size, constrained by both the size and surface treatment of the original sherd) was removed with a water-cooled diamond band saw, dried, bagged and labeled with registration information. Following authorization for shipment by the Turkish Ministry of Culture and the Ankara Museum of Anatolian Civilization authorities, the officially sealed sample box was sent to a preparation facility at the University of New England, Australia.

At this facility, incoming samples were checked against registration details before processing. Subsequently, samples were cleaned in a heated (30°C) ultrasonic bath of deionized water for 15 minutes to remove surficial debris and soluble salts. Typically, ~1 g of sample was then removed for further processing and analysis. While relatively large, this sample size offered the advantage of reducing measurement biases due to sample heterogeneity, whose effects increase with smaller sample quantities, a particular concern for samples with larger clastics (i.e. sediments and coarse earthenware ceramics). After drying, sample surfaces were mechanically removed using a variable speed drill and tungsten carbide burr, placed in an acetate envelope and then crushed using a hydraulic press. The powdered sample was then stored in 5 mm plastic vials identified with the sample registration number. Sample batches were sent, along with their registration summary, to a commercial NAA laboratory in Ontario, Canada. Following irradiation and measurement at the McMaster University research reactor, the mildly radioactive samples were then stored in a dedicated containment facility in Ontario.

Sediment Samples

As geochemical variation between resources tends to be more dominant than variation introduced by cultural modification (Neff et al. 1989), compositional distinctions were expected to be primarily geospatial in character. The geology of the region around Gordion is shaped by Neogene intrusive basalts uplifting earlier Miocene lakebed deposits (marls; Bingöl 1989). The igneous intrusions produced some metamorphic interfaces, as well as some localized, hydrothermally created chert sources. Subsequent Pleistocene and Holocene erosion and alluviation has created valley deposits and eroded hillslopes with exposed basalts and marls. Basalt-derived "red" and marl-derived "white" clays are both common near Gordion and represent potentially compositionally distinct resource zones.

Typically, sediment samples were collected from surface deposits, occasionally road cuts or natural sections and, less commonly, sediment cores (see Chapter 3). Following preliminary sieving to remove rock clasts >0.5 mm and organic debris, samples were processed (detailed in the following paragraphs) for NAA.

As a reference baseline for identifying the local resource area (which may include natural or artificial mixes from different locations) we collected broadly across the region (a 20×20 km area centered on Gordion; Fig. 4.2). This collection strategy combined samples from cores taken during the Gordion Regional Survey (GRS) project by Kealhofer with 55 "grab" samples collected by Kealhofer and Marsh during the course of soil mapping for the Gordion survey region. A few additional samples were collected by Marsh during the AIA project.

On the basis of ethnoarchaeological work by D. E. Arnold and colleagues (1999:63), premodern potters (i.e. pre-automobile transport) usually mined clays located at a distance from ca. 1 km up to a maximum of 7 km radius from their production area. The scale of our regional sampling program serves two purposes in providing a larger geographic

Identifying Gordion's Groups 61

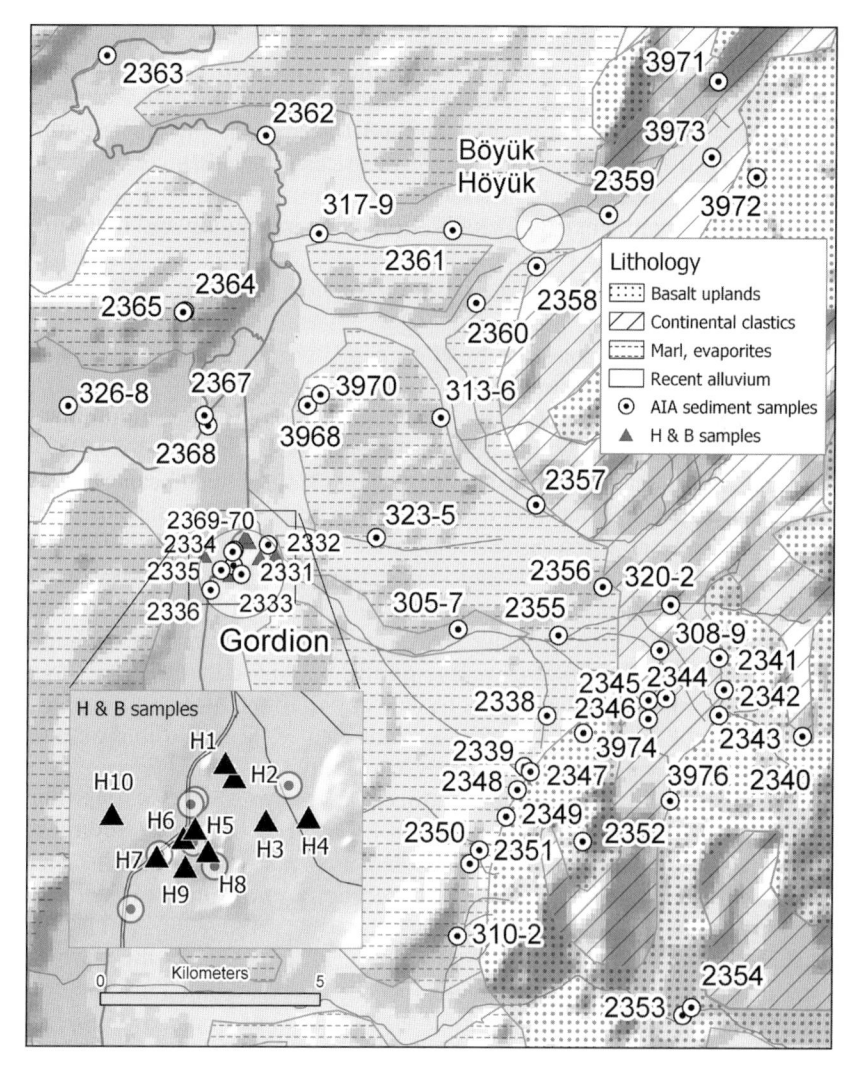

Fig. 4.2 Generalized lithology of the Gordion catchment showing AIA numbered sampling locations, and Hendrickson and Blackman (1996) (inset) sample locations ("H&B" in inset and legend).
Source: Ben Marsh, courtesy of the Gordion Regional Survey and AIA.

frame than local potters were likely to have exploited. First, it provides a baseline for evaluating the compositional scope and range of the regional geology in relation to the compositional profile of local production. Second, where ceramics are not typologically clear imports, this geochemical sediment profile of the broader catchment enables non-matching compositional profiles to be more readily identified as potential signatures of more distant regional production locales (>7 km radius).

Henrickson and Blackman also sampled 15 sediment and clay samples from within a 1 km radius of the site (Henrickson and Blackman 1996). Based on their publication, the same region and general locations were captured in the more extensive AIA sediment program (see Fig. 4.2 inset).

The NAA Dataset

The ceramic sample collected by Henrickson was collated in a database that lacked photographs or drawings, and was later subsampled for NAA at the National Institute of Standards and Technology, Washington DC. The total ceramic dataset includes 1,595 ceramic samples and 72 (of 77 original) sediment samples (see Chapter 3). Of the original sample only 1,561 have NAA results (856 from AIA; 705 from YHP), due to analytically unviable sample weights for a small subset of samples. However, other metadata generated for these samples (e.g. descriptions of fabric or decoration) are used where appropriate in this study.

In addition to the two primary NAA datasets for Gordion (i.e. AIA and Henrickson and Blackman), we use published AIA datasets from other sites in central and western Anatolia as comparators to evaluate potential origins for the Gordion data that are not clearly local. To this we add published legacy data from another NAA facility (the "Bonn dataset") for roughly contemporary ceramics produced at western Anatolian sites. The NAA Bonn dataset produced by Hans Mommsen of Bonn University, working with ceramicist Michael Kerschner, is particularly useful. They generated compositional data for a limited range of diagnostic decorative types of tradewares from the Archaic to Classical period (?750–450 BCE), each a distinctive product of an East Greek center along the western Anatolian coast (n = 179; Akürgal et al. 2002). The typological distinctiveness of the subsets of this sample also enabled Mommsen to apply a "ceramic dilution factor" or "best relative fit." This method is designed to correct geochemical variations introduced by small differences in the amount of quartz present that are thought to adversely impact (or variably dilute) what would otherwise be a highly homogenous composition from a single production center (Sterba et al. 2009). For comparing AIA and Bonn data it is useful to establish the reliability of intercomparability between NAA facilities through analysis of a shared standard. Previously we have published our experimental results for the Bonn pottery standard (Grave et al. 2013) which showed good to excellent reproducibility between the Bonn and McMasters NAA facilities.

NAA Datasets from Comparator Sites and Studies

The AIA NAA datasets from our previously published work includes sites in east-central (Çadır Höyük, Kaman Kalehöyük), west-central (Seyitömer, Eskişehir regional survey around Şar Höyük) and western areas of Anatolia (Sardis; Fig. 1.1; Grave and Kealhofer 2006; Grave et al. 2012, 2016; Kealhofer et al. 2008, 2010, 2013). As described for Gordion, sediment samples were also taken at our comparator sites to assist in distinguishing probable local from nonlocal production (Fig. 4.3). An exception is the site of Seyitömer, where sediment sampling was not feasible due to its location within a large open-cut lignite mine. The total geographic range of our comparator sites extends over 500 km from east to west across central Anatolia. Lacking firm typological constraints, such as those used in more focused studies like that of Mommsen and Kerschner, our approach is necessarily probabilistic. We identify general distance decay trends in the data for the purposes of establishing potential origins for the nonlocal component of the Gordion ceramic dataset. Together, these NAA datasets enable identification of (a) the relation between ceramics and sediments to build a spatial picture of the dynamics of local resource use over time; (b) the range and types of local and regional production at Gordion over time; and (c) the range, potential provenience and timing for at least some of the imported ceramics at the site.

Geochemical Data Accuracy and Precision: NIST Standard Reference Materials (SRM) Results

The AIA experimental dataset involved a protracted period of measurement (over several years), and a large number of NAA irradiation/counting sessions. To establish the accuracy and precision of results for ceramic compositional "unknowns," the AIA program of analysis included replicates of three NIST Standard Reference Materials (SRM) with certified/measured elemental concentrations (SRM679 – Ohio brick clay; SRM2711 – Montana contaminated soil; and SRM1633b – coal fly ash) (Table 4.1). These SRMs were selected to provide either matrices approximately comparable to ceramics (brick clay) or compositions that contained less common trace elements potentially present in "unknown" samples (Montana contaminated soil, coal fly ash). The NIST standards were routinely included in NAA sample batches over the course of the project, ultimately producing a relatively large time-series of experimental SRM data ($n = 231$). Through this procedure we empirically established *accuracy*, expressed as the mean percentage recovery of experimental to certified/published values, and *precision*, expressed as the coefficient of variation (CV) for the replicate

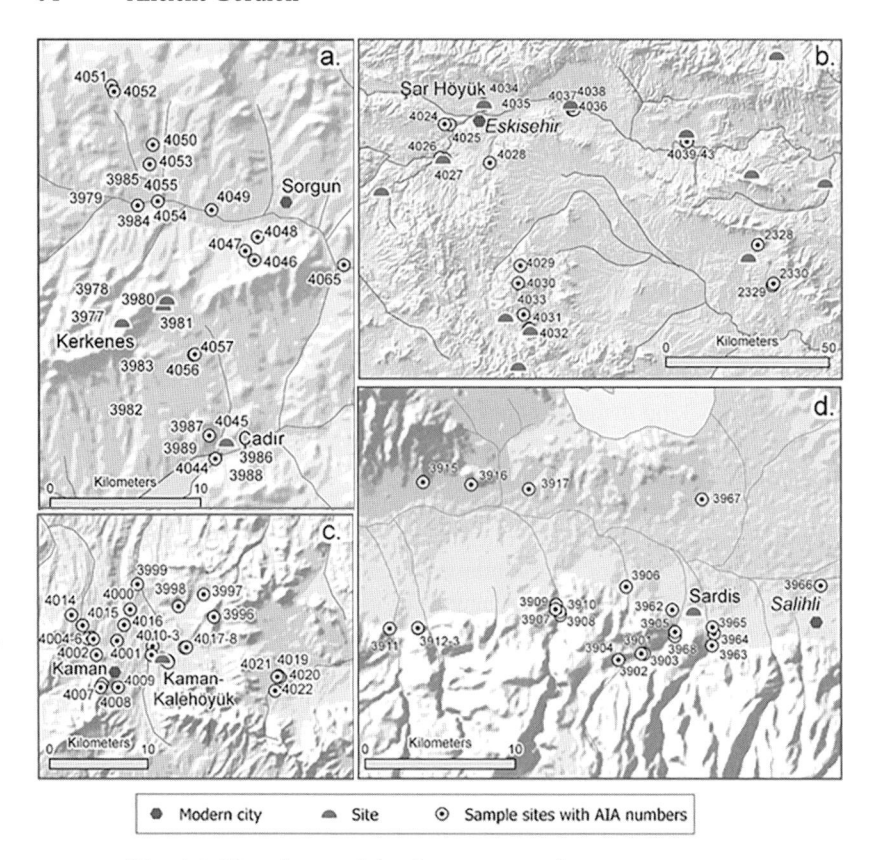

Fig. 4.3 Elevation models of comparator sites.
Clockwise from top Kerkenes, Şar Höyuk-Eskişehir, Sardis, and Kaman Kalehöyuk, with sediment sample locales identified.
Source: Ben Marsh, courtesy of the AIA project.

experimental results. In Table 4.1 the certified/published values for the three NIST SRMs are compared to our experimental results. The data show our experimental level of measurement accuracy averages >95% with CVs (precision) generally <10%, and provides a high level of confidence in the reliability of experimental NAA results our extended measurement time frame.

The SRM results can also be used to highlight NAA detection characteristics for different elements. The detection limit or measurement sensitivity – in other words when the amount of an element present is too small to measure – reflects a general relationship between measurement precision and counts. Statistically, as an elemental detection limit is

Table 4.1. *Establishing data quality of AIA NAA measurements used in this study. Comparison of experimental percentage recoveries and coefficients of variation (CVs) with certified/published values for three NIST Standard Reference Materials (SRMs).*

	\multicolumn{3}{c	}{NIST (Standard Reference Materials)}						
	\multicolumn{3}{c	}{SRM1633b (n = 80)}	\multicolumn{3}{c	}{SRM679 (n = 87)}	\multicolumn{3}{c}{SRM2711 (n = 86)}
	Cert/pub	% recovery	CV	Cert/pub	% recovery	CV	Cert/pub	% recovery	CV
As	136.2	96.56	2.16	–	–	–	–	–	–
Ba	709	95.10	9.66	432.2	102.28	13.18	726	96.63	7.70
Br	2.9	95.62	34.14	–	–	–	5	98.45	12.88
Ca%	1.51	109.00	36.31	0.1628	–	–	2.88	94.17	25.42
Ce	190	96.22	2.35	105	95.93	4.81	69	103.49	3.67
Co	50	98.64	2.73	26	98.75	7.31	10	100.62	6.45
Cr	198.2	102.51	2.96	109.7	96.76	6.93	47	101.52	5.20
Cs	11	96.48	6.64	9.6	99.31	6.58	6.1	106.14	6.06
Eu	4.1	95.96	6.30	1.9	91.49	9.50	1.1	95.73	12.14
Fe%	7.78	100.92	2.51	9.05	99.03	7.72	2.89	99.91	2.68
Hf	6.8	99.69	5.24	4.6	90.56	14.84	7.3	107.19	5.58
K%	1.95	69.26	55.39	2.433	88.45	29.19	2.45	104.29	16.70
La	94	93.82	2.32	–	–	–	40	93.67	2.50
Lu	1.2	86.74	6.60	–	–	–	–	–	–
Na%	0.201	100.33	4.45	0.1304	108.88	73.03	1.14	97.65	2.93

Table 4.1. (cont.)

NIST (Standard Reference Materials)

	SRM1633b (n = 80)			SRM679 (n = 87)			SRM2711 (n = 86)		
	Cert/pub	% recovery	CV	Cert/pub	% recovery	CV	Cert/pub	% recovery	CV
Nd	85	93.83	11.97	–	–	–	31	103.01	13.94
Rb	140	96.80	6.09	190	94.09	7.82	110	99.89	7.00
Sb	6	84.97	3.37	–	–	–	–	–	–
Sc	41	98.76	3.21	22.5	99.15	7.16	9	102.03	3.60
Sm	20	92.09	1.91	–	–	–	5.9	101.30	2.09
Sr	1041	99.94	12.83	73.4	–	–	245.3	–	–
Ta	1.8	109.06	26.91	–	–	–	2.47	57.03	29.03
Tb	2.6	105.54	11.08	–	–	–	–	–	–
Th	25.7	98.02	2.88	14	98.86	4.36	14	96.54	3.84
U	8.79	101.42	8.76	–	–	–	2.6	108.05	15.21
Yb	7.6	94.85	5.08	–	–	–	2.7	107.39	6.24
Zn	210	86.15	19.25	150	75.44	27.09	350.4	97.58	5.53
% recovery avg.		96.08			95.64			98.56	

approached, an increase in the CV corresponds to increasingly unreliable measurement. For NAA, elements with large nuclear cross-sections (Fisher 1989) provide better counting targets with lower detection limits and measurement error (< ca. 2–6.5%), compared to elements with smaller cross-sections. Exceptions are elements that may not have a particularly large cross-section but are present in high abundance (e.g. Fe), which can also produce reliable measurement statistics. The range of elements and different concentrations of the same elements in the three NIST standards enabled us to empirically determine element detection limits. Using CVs as a check on measurement quality, we could establish the minimum element concentrations before measurement quality started to degrade. This enabled us to confirm that, in general, our experimental NAA dataset for the larger ceramic and sediment sample was analytically reliable and well above the detection limits for most elements.

Multivariate Characterization

A central goal of elemental characterization of ceramics and sediments is to identify patterns of relationships (i.e. within and between compositional clusters) that are both compositionally coherent and archaeologically (culturally) meaningful. In the first phase of this process, we adopt a nested combination of multivariate analytical techniques for establishing robust analytical clusters (Glascock et al. 2004).

Analytically, we are interested in defining relationships between elemental behavior (positive or negative correlations, independence) and ceramic clusters. These relationships are necessarily fewer than the total number of elements of a dataset. Preliminary multivariate evaluation using conventional Principal Component Analysis (PCA) effectively captures the relationships between samples (eigenvalues) in relation to NAA elements (eigenvectors), and reduces them to components orthogonally organized from greatest to least descriptive power (i.e. percentage of variability described by each successive component; orthogonal – not otherwise captured by a preceding component). Typically, for a dataset with meaningful (nonrandom) internal structure, the first three components of a PCA will account for at least ~50 of overall variability, effectively capturing the most salient compositional features of the assemblage. This characteristic of PCA – reduction of compositional complexity to a relatively small number of components – enables 2D and 3D graphic projections of these components for visual identification of analytical groups in terms of diversity, range and distribution in PCA space. Note that, as a nonparametric procedure, PCA involves no *a priori* assumptions by the analyst about sample group membership.

Choice of software was based on the need for comparatively powerful, multiscalar integration between different analytical procedures; a commercial software package provided this (JMP Professional versions 14 and 15; Sall et al. 2017). For example, the software allowed the determination of preliminary compositional clusters through a graphic, three-dimensional and dynamic (rotatable) projection using the first three components of a PCA. This enabled an effective and relatively rapid visual identification of the most salient features of the dataset. Subsequently, these features can be classified and tagged using Hierarchical Cluster Analysis and dynamically adjustable cluster thresholds to best fit visually defined analytical groups (Neff 1993).

Compositional Clusters and Data Density

Meaningful parsing into clusters of a large compositional dataset that is assumed to combine evidence of both local and nonlocal production, and also involves multiple chronological phases, presents a substantial challenge for the type of fine-grained analysis required here. Kernel Density Estimation (KDE) provides a robust (reproducible) means to first identify and isolate large-scale structures in this type of geochemical dataset (Baxter et al. 1997; Beardah 1999; Spencer et al. 2017). A scatterplot of the dataset using the first two components of a PCA provides the basis for a KDE transformation of the scatterplot into a density contour map (Plate 2). A projection using the two component scores for the X/Y axes, in conjunction with the density quantile for the Z axis, results in a three-dimensional topography of the dataset structure. KDE-identified regions with the highest relative densities of data points of this PCA/KDE topographic map are filtered using 1σ (68%) confidence threshold. These high-density zones are then used to define the cores of compositional clusters.

Using the initial cluster assignment at the 1σ threshold to seed cluster identification, a combination of Hierarchical Cluster Analysis (HCA) and parametric Discriminant Function Analysis (DFA), enables expansion of these seed clusters through predictive, iterative refinement of cluster membership. The resultant analytical clusters are again evaluated in terms of archaeological contexts and typological coherence or diversity, with particular attention to potential outliers. When finalized, analytical clusters are tabulated and summarized as elemental averages and coefficients of variation. These finalized clusters form the basis for integrating the NAA compositional data with other archaeological datasets. The extent to which these clusters also equate with local/regional/nonlocal resource zones can then be evaluated through a comparison with sediment results.

General Patterns in the Larger Dataset

Initial multivariate analysis of the NAA dataset ($n = 1,633$) included ceramics from AIA ($n = 856$), YHP ($n = 705$) and sediment samples ($n = 72$). This first analysis highlights the structured character of the dataset with the first three principal components accounting for almost 70% of overall variation. A scatterplot of the first two components (36.2% × 12.5%) shows its structure to be defined by both irregular distribution and highly variable density (Plate 2).

Using the combination of a plot of samples on the first two components from a PCA of this dataset, a KDE of the sample distribution and iterative cluster membership as described, we identify 13 major discrete clusters (labeled A–M) in the dataset (Plate 3; Table 4.2). The greatest concentration of samples occurs in a distinctive high-density region of the plot with a varying but continuous distribution moving from high Ca/ low Fe in the lower left-hand corner (group A) to decreased Ca and elevated Fe at the top (group B) that together capture the majority of our sample data (~960 samples or ~60%). The remaining clusters (C–M) define sample clusters in varying, but generally decreasing sizes, dispersed along the first component/x axis. Iterative evaluation of each of these major clusters, where compositional similarities were compared to typological and contextual data, enables us to identify a range of compositional subgroups (e.g. A1, A2). In general, the number of subgroups identified was sample-size dependent (i.e. proportional to the size of the group; Fig. 4.4). In some cases subgroups were identified that were both compositionally distinct and period-specific. For a worked example of the procedure see *Defining Subgroups: Clusters L and M*.

Defining Local Provenience Using Sediments

The AIA strategy for understanding geochemical "local" was based on extended sediment sampling of the geological "envelope" surrounding a site. As ancient clay beds are rarely identifiable, we first evaluate the diversity of source lithology in a region (in this case Neogene basalts and older marls), and sample each geological facies, as well as depositional sediment mixes present in lowland areas. The range of geochemistries present in a local region then defines the potential geochemical "envelope" of locally available clay sources.

To identify the geochemical envelope that represents local production we begin by combining the NAA results for the Gordion ceramics with the 72 sediment results (excluding outliers) (Plate 3). While we aimed to sample most if not all of the major lithofacies present around the site,

Table 4.2. Gordion NAA dataset summary statistics (Avg = average; CV = coefficient of variation) for 13 major groups. Cluster A local; Clusters B–D local/regional, clusters E–M nonlocal (see Table 4.3).

Cluster	A (n = 538) Avg.	A CV	B (n = 420) Avg.	B CV	C (n = 207) Avg.	C CV	D (n = 54) Avg.	D CV	E (n = 117) Avg.	E CV	F (n = 157) Avg.	F CV	G (n = 32) Avg.	G CV
As	54.3	91.7	40.4	92.8	40.8	90.9	28.1	100.8	40.5	85.3	35.5	69.3	42.3	105.3
Ba	328.5	43.6	356.7	48.9	505.0	35.1	648.9	36.0	542.7	36.5	541.0	29.7	635.7	27.4
Ca%	9.9	37.9	5.9	40.2	5.5	59.3	3.7	115.9	4.1	63.3	2.6	83.5	2.6	82.5
Ce	44.7	17.4	56.5	16.9	66.9	14.1	84.0	13.1	80.3	9.3	89.9	10.4	101.0	7.2
Co	21.8	28.4	35.5	51.3	19.0	27.0	13.1	39.8	23.3	32.7	28.8	40.4	29.9	49.2
Cr	272.6	49.8	337.6	45.3	165.4	51.1	79.0	41.5	165.1	37.4	219.9	32.2	190.7	47.7
Cs	7.1	44.4	7.1	47.0	8.7	76.9	7.1	57.5	11.5	83.0	14.2	121.9	16.7	88.4
Eu	0.9	18.7	1.3	18.5	1.2	13.9	1.2	14.6	1.3	12.0	1.4	14.1	1.6	13.3
Fe%	3.9	18.8	5.6	15.5	4.1	12.3	3.2	14.1	4.7	11.0	5.3	11.6	5.4	9.5
Hf	3.4	19.3	4.2	31.8	4.7	16.4	5.9	21.6	5.6	16.3	6.0	20.4	5.8	24.3
K%	2.1	27.6	2.2	30.5	2.5	24.2	2.6	20.5	2.7	24.8	2.8	25.3	3.0	31.1
La	24.6	18.0	29.9	17.7	36.9	13.2	48.5	14.3	42.6	11.2	46.8	10.1	53.3	9.1
Lu	0.2	20.4	0.3	19.6	0.3	20.3	0.3	29.1	0.4	12.0	0.5	12.3	0.5	11.4
Na%	1.0	36.5	1.1	31.2	1.2	41.2	1.7	32.3	0.9	40.7	1.0	29.3	0.8	34.2
Rb	69.9	27.1	90.7	33.9	101.4	26.6	111.4	22.9	129.0	18.3	148.4	21.8	163.1	23.8
Sb	1.0	57.3	1.4	76.5	1.3	91.0	0.9	68.6	1.4	93.9	1.3	77.1	2.2	71.3
Sc	13.2	24.9	19.8	19.0	13.8	15.1	9.2	15.9	16.9	13.8	18.9	12.3	18.8	11.6
Sm	3.9	13.7	5.1	13.2	5.2	11.4	5.4	14.2	6.5	8.0	7.2	7.2	8.2	7.3
Ta	0.8	46.2	1.3	72.7	1.1	44.3	1.2	41.0	1.4	56.4	1.6	71.4	2.0	76.4
Tb	0.4	65.3	0.7	53.4	0.6	50.3	0.6	31.2	0.7	54.3	0.9	40.9	1.1	30.9
Th	7.8	22.2	9.3	27.6	12.1	20.0	17.3	20.3	15.0	16.2	15.8	13.8	18.6	13.0
U	2.0	101.4	1.9	86.0	2.6	104.9	2.9	74.2	3.4	56.6	2.3	67.8	2.9	43.9
Yb	1.7	15.0	2.3	15.5	2.1	17.2	2.0	21.1	2.8	11.4	3.1	10.4	3.3	13.0
Zn	84.2	30.4	115.0	32.3	94.1	24.7	80.2	36.3	112.5	25.2	121.9	26.3	118.3	26.0

Cluster	H (n = 21) Avg.	H CV	I (n = 7) Avg.	I CV	J (n = 14) Avg.	J CV	K (n = 8) Avg.	K CV	L (n = 50) Avg.	L CV	M (n = 2) Avg.	M CV
As	33.0	47.9	28.5	58.5	29.8	42.8	28.1	68.4	48.4	92.1	47.5	10.4
Ba	741.7	18.7	603.0	30.9	664.6	31.4	763.8	41.4	707.9	26.7	705.0	9.0
Ca%	2.7	50.4	2.9	58.5	1.7	86.5	3.3	56.9	4.0	45.1	2.9	2.5
Ce	94.3	6.3	106.3	5.6	116.4	14.4	74.1	14.5	108.4	10.1	121.5	5.2
Co	29.4	13.4	23.6	16.1	36.6	79.8	89.3	68.9	18.8	28.8	7.5	9.4
Cr	188.8	42.0	134.6	7.6	188.7	37.5	275.9	50.7	126.6	33.1	34.0	12.5
Cs	21.7	32.1	17.0	26.1	17.5	57.8	9.7	41.9	16.4	50.0	59.0	0.7
Eu	1.8	12.5	1.7	5.3	2.1	13.9	1.4	26.3	1.5	17.7	1.0	19.0
Fe%	6.8	6.4	5.6	2.8	6.1	18.9	6.7	16.6	4.7	10.6	3.0	5.9
Hf	4.8	30.2	6.0	9.8	6.4	25.3	7.4	94.6	6.6	16.8	7.6	1.9
K%	3.2	26.1	3.6	30.1	3.1	28.2	3.3	29.2	3.5	23.4	5.6	5.1
La	48.5	8.5	56.7	4.6	59.7	15.1	37.3	11.4	57.0	10.0	70.5	5.7
Lu	0.5	7.7	0.5	3.2	0.6	20.4	0.4	13.2	0.5	19.9	0.4	0.0
Na%	1.1	16.2	0.7	29.1	1.0	22.9	1.2	47.7	0.7	46.3	0.8	4.3
Rb	153.1	16.1	180.1	11.0	166.7	16.0	123.5	22.3	179.2	17.8	490.0	5.8
Sb	5.2	30.2	2.8	33.8	3.5	65.1	0.6	115.9	2.7	34.5	2.4	3.0
Sc	23.3	9.3	21.5	3.3	21.0	8.5	27.5	25.9	16.6	12.4	5.3	2.7
Sm	8.9	5.4	9.1	4.8	10.3	17.5	6.5	17.8	8.8	6.1	6.2	7.4
Ta	1.2	71.8	2.1	35.3	2.7	101.0	10.1	121.6	1.7	47.3	2.1	17.2
Tb	1.1	37.7	1.3	22.9	1.6	18.5	1.0	44.0	1.1	35.6	0.0	0.0
Th	14.9	7.4	20.9	4.8	19.7	20.3	12.0	10.9	23.2	13.1	43.1	5.1
U	2.6	45.1	3.1	47.5	2.8	54.0	1.9	68.5	5.8	103.7	5.0	4.3
Yb	3.5	7.4	3.5	5.8	4.3	23.2	3.1	13.2	3.5	16.4	2.5	0.0
Zn	149.0	24.5	120.1	15.0	139.5	17.8	132.5	28.8	105.5	30.1	99.0	14

72   Ancient Gordion

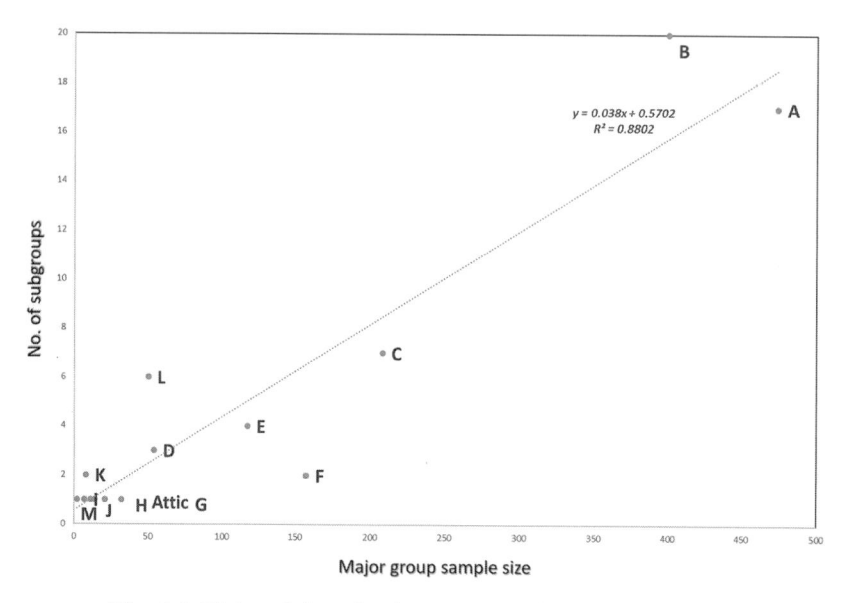

Fig. 4.4 Biplot of size of major groups and number of subgroups identified in the Gordion NAA dataset showing strong sample size effect.

ranging from evaporate basin marls to basalt-capped ridges, in multivariate space the majority of sediment samples nonetheless fall within the cluster-A envelope. The comparison enables us to unequivocally confirm cluster A as reflecting the major local Gordion resource for ceramic production across all periods represented. Some sediment samples, adjacent to cluster A (lower left of Plate 3), have few ceramic matches, and evidently represent resources that while potentially available were not suitable for potting. A smaller number of sediment samples, dispersed in an area adjacent to cluster B, are from a small number of samples of upland clastic and basalt facies several kilometers to the east and north east of the site (see Fig. 4.2). They represent geologies also apparently unsuitable (or too distant) for local potters.

The Null Hypothesis and Evaluating Alternative Scenarios

We can evaluate different potential scenarios related to source use by comparing the compositional and typological characteristics of the ceramic assemblage in relation to archaeological contexts and over time. Any patterning present (compositional, typological, contextual alone or in some combination) then requires evaluation first in terms of a null hypothesis (i.e. local resources were potentially equally available to Gordion potters at any given time). A test expectation can then be formalized where, allowing for sample size effects and sampling biases, local resource use should be equally represented regardless of period or other criteria. When these conditions are not met, then alternative scenarios need to be evaluated that better fit the data (e.g. in the case of evidence for highly variable, discrete use of resources over time, the potential for multiple groups, different levels of technical expertise, differential access to resources between contemporary groups, differences in clay properties, or over time).

Identifying Regional/Nonlocal Ceramics

In the "provenance hypothesis" (Tite 2008) elemental profiles of nonlocal tradewares are defined by their origins in diverse geographic regions, and are presumed to involve highly specialized production and elaboration. As a result, compositional groups for imported ceramics should tend to be highly discrete and distinct in multivariate space, increasing overall compositional patterning in terms of diversity and scale.

While the provenance hypothesis underpins compositional approaches to ceramic characterization, a caveat is required especially in a dataset of the size and complexity of this study. Where suspected nonlocal ceramics and groups show little or no compositional difference (i.e. multivariate intermingling or overlap) with the profile for local resource zones, care is required in evaluating other noncompositional criteria, such as typologies, to distinguish likely local from nonlocal results.

As noted, to identify potential regional and nonlocal ceramics in our sample, and more specifically to establish their likely provenance where possible, we rely on comparisons with our previously published AIA NAA sets for several comparator sites across the region as well as the Mommsen (Bonn) NAA reference dataset (described earlier). The Bonn west Anatolian dataset ($n = 179$) was originally classified into 12 compositional groups that correlated with specific ceramic types, localities and resource variants (e.g. "Miletos A"). Where a specific locality was not identified a more general type/variant designation was used (e.g. "Northern Ionian E," "F1," "F2"), and in one case an unidentified origin was simply tagged as a separate compositional group (e.g. "J").

To establish broad linkages between the Gordion dataset and our comparator datasets we compare projections of the first two components of a PCA of the Gordion data with those of each of the other site datasets. We use our cluster identifications (A–M) for the Gordion dataset to seed a supervised Discriminant Function classification of each of the comparator datasets. The multivariate comparison shows the Bonn results occupy highly discrete regions largely overlapping our clusters E–L

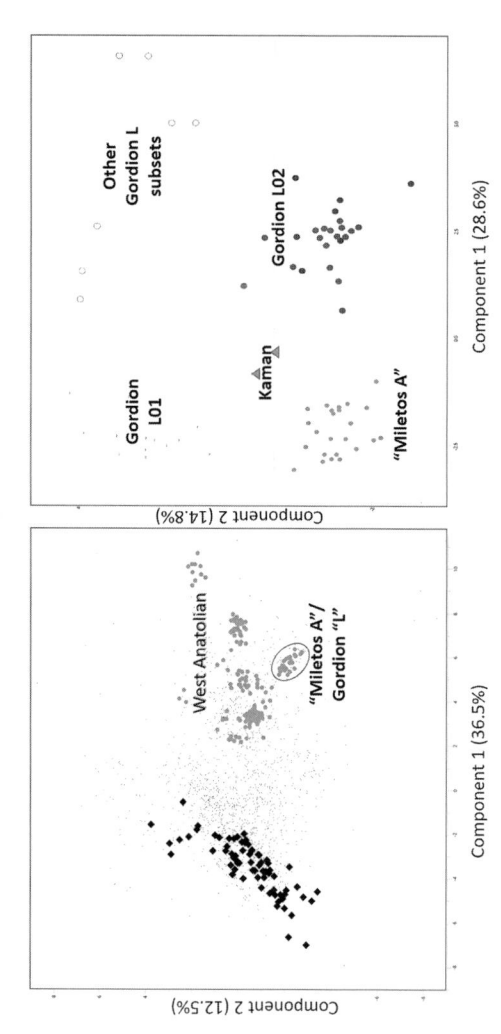

Fig. 4.5 Biplots of first two principal components of NAA results for Gordion ceramics and sediments overlaid with: *left*: Bonn NAA results for ceramics from several production centers in West Anatolia with position of "Miletos A" overlapping Gordion cluster L indicated (Akurgal et al. 2002); *right*: Principal Component Analysis of Gordion cluster L showing similarities for two Kaman samples with the subset of Gordion samples (L01) that most closely approximate the West Anatolian "Miletos A" compositional profile (i.e. minor compositional differences indicated by separation along the second component (15%). Larger differences are indicated by separation of the Gordion Group L02 subset along the first component (~28%), cf. Table 4.5.

(Fig. 4.5). Note that the relatively tightly packed and highly discrete appearance of the Bonn groups appears to reflect their postanalysis treatment by "dilution factor" reduction of compositional range. Nonetheless, the comparison highlights several regions where overlap between the west Anatolian groups and Gordion samples offers potential to identify a specific production origin or more general provenance.

With the exception of the Bonn NAA dataset for western Anatolia, the data from our other comparator sites tend not to present discrete groups. Rather they occupy and overlap the Gordion data in different areas of the component plot as a more generalized reflection of the potential geological resources underlying the compositional range of these samples (Plate 4). The results of this comparison are presented in Table 4.3.

Geospatial Trends in the NAA Dataset as Derived from Comparator Site Matching

Here, we summarize the broad geographic trends evident in our comparator results. To compensate for the large differences in sample size between the Gordion and comparator sites, raw counts of group distribution are converted to site percentages (Table 4.4). Sites are organized in geographic order from east to west with results analyzed in a clustering procedure that reorders groups to optimize "within and between" correlations. In Table 4.4 the results of this clustering procedure are presented both numerically and as a density map to graphically highlight a distance decay signal in relation to Gordion measured as the difference in percentage cluster values compared across sites. This enables us to identify clusters of groups in terms of strength of correlations and direction (central east or west) and ranked as primary (concentrated in fewer groups) or secondary (dispersed over more clusters).

Through this process we identified four discrete geospatial trends: Central (cluster A), Central West I (clusters B/K) and II (clusters F/L); Central East (clusters C/D/E/M) and West (clusters G/H/J/I). Note the Central West pattern suggests systematic regional differences within this cluster. Cluster L and particularly F are most strongly represented at Seyitömer and at twice the percentage of either Eskişehir or Gordion, indicating a west Anatolian, but non-Sardian, origin. For the other pair of clusters in this set, B and K, the pattern suggests a regional origin in the Eskişehir/Gordion catchments.

An example of a first-ranked distance decay cluster is the "Central" cluster, A, that is most heavily represented at Gordion, then in lower proportions at Kaman Kalehöyük and Eskişehir, but is almost totally

Table 4.3. Summary table of compositional cluster assignment for all ceramic samples from Gordion and AIA comparator sites (see Plate 4) with geographic region designators (E = East, CE = Central East, CW = Central West, W = West) (top left) and Bonn west Anatolian NAA data (top right). Assignments based on a Discriminant Function Analysis of NAA results using Gordion clusters (A–M) to seed identifications in comparator group datasets sorted by most to least abundant for each section of clusters. Lower left of table shows groups that received general cluster assignment but proved specific to a site (e.g. Eski 1, Group L specific to Çadır Höyük = LCad) or type (e.g. Attic).

NAA clusters	W Sardis	CW Seyitmer	CW Eskibehir	C Gordion	CE Kaman	E Çadır	N Ionia E	N Ionia B/C	Miletos D	S Ionia	?	Ephesus?	N Ionia F1	N Ionia F2	Aeolis	Miletos A	Ephesus H	Σ
B	5	32	135	400	37	35												644
A	3	11	15	474	56	5												564
C	16	7	48	208	62	40												381
D	2	1	31	54	46	42												176
E	20	29	81	117	79	50	9	12	2									399
F	22	43	61	157	15	3		40	5	6								353
G	40	17	5	32	12	4			5		1							136
H	64	19	4	21	3	1						9	5	7				115
L	2	12	20	50	2	–					1			2		24		110
K	1	7	57	8	1	1												76
I	17	6	1	7	1	2					1				5			39
J	27	7	1	14	–	–												49
M	–	–	–	3	3	26												32
Σ = 2,974	219	191	459	1,545	317	209												
LKam					77													77
Eski_1			68															68
Aeolis G				6											35			41
LCad						34												34
Attic			11	11														22
Ephesos H				1													10	11
Σ = 3,148	219	202	527	1563	394	243	9	52	12	6	3	9	5	9	40	24	10	3327

76

Table 4.4. Geospatial trends in main compositional groups: comparator sites compared to Gordion with group membership converted to percentages (rows). Two-way cluster analysis (cluster dendrogram bottom), used to optimize comparisons across sites for each group based on relative densities (columns), showing general trends in cluster density/site/geographic region (e.g. dominance of clusters I–G at Sardis with a pattern of distance decay from west to central and east).

	13	12	11	10	9	8	7	6	5	4	3	2	1
		West				Central East			Cent W II		Central West		Central
	I	J	H	G	M	E	D	C	L	F	K	B	A
Çadır	0.96	0.00	0.48	1.91	12.44	23.92	20.10	19.14	0.00	1.44	0.48	16.75	2.39
Kaman	0.32	0.00	0.95	3.79	0.95	24.92	14.51	19.56	0.63	4.73	0.32	11.67	17.67
Gordion	0.45	0.91	1.36	2.07	0.19	7.57	3.50	13.46	3.24	10.16	0.52	25.89	30.68
Eskişehir	0.22	0.22	0.87	1.09	0.00	17.65	6.75	10.46	4.36	13.29	12.42	29.41	3.27
Seyitömer	3.14	3.66	9.95	8.90	0.00	15.18	0.52	3.66	6.28	22.51	3.66	16.75	5.76
Sardis	7.76	12.33	29.22	18.26	0.00	9.13	0.91	7.31	0.91	10.05	0.46	2.28	1.37

absent from Sardis. Next is a pair of "Central West" clusters, B and K, that are best represented at Eskişehir. B is quite widespread in central Anatolia and most common at Gordion and Eskişehir, but virtually absent at Sardis. A third cluster combination, "Central West II," F and L, appears to reflect a shift further west and is most abundant at Seyitömer with an apparent distance decay distribution that now includes Sardis but does not extend as far east as Çadır Höyük. The "Central East" set combines clusters C, D, E and M with the greatest concentrations at Çadır and Kaman and is then variably distributed at the remaining sites. Finally, the "Central West II" set of G/H/J/I also appears to conform to a distance decay curve with the majority representing a western Anatolian Sardis origin, followed by Seyitömer in proportions between a third and a half of the Sardis percentage. This same set of clusters is also fully represented at Gordion, although a small proportion of the total Gordion sample.

Defining Subgroups: Clusters L and M

One of the best defined of the nonlocal compositional clusters, L, isolated a number of Gordion decorated ceramics that, while typologically varied, include a relatively large number of vessels with brown on buff decoration in predominantly Protogeometric styles (i.e. concentric, multiple brush-drawn circles) and designs (e.g. wavy line, concentric circles and pendent semicircles, geometric meander patterns; Papadopoulos et al. 1998). In the PCA of the full dataset, the Group L region of the plot appears to have samples from all comparator sites. However, a PCA (Fig. 4.5, right) of only the subset of samples that occupy this general space excludes many general cluster L members, from both Gordion and comparator sites, but distinguishes two coherent compositional and typological subsets, a "wavy line" group (L01; Plate 5) and a Lydianizing group (L02). At this finer scale, the Bonn west Anatolian "Miletos A" and a pair of Kaman samples match L01, occupying the same compositional space on the first component (28% variation). The separation between these clusters on the second component (15% variation), hence relatively minor compositional differences, may reflect alone or in combination: technological treatments; the effect of "dilution factor" calculations for the Bonn cluster; or minor differences in resource use. The second subgroup, clearly distanced on the first component, consists of the Lydianizing group (L02; Plate 6).

The potential for identifying a geographic origin for the Gordion L01 and L02 subsets was evaluated by comparing both measurement accuracy (group means) and precision (group coefficients of variation – CVs; Table 4.5) for the Gordion, Miletus and Kaman samples. A range

Table 4.5. *Comparison of NAA results for Bonn "Miletos A" with the subset of Gordion and Kaman Kalehöyük cluster L results that most closely approximate "Miletos A" in a PCA (see Plate 5) expressed as averages (accuracy) and coefficients of variation (precision) and mean element % recovery – elements outside ~80–120% band highlighted.*

	W Anatolian		Cluster L groups (Gordion, Kaman)						% recovery of Miletos A			Element sensitivity as (t)race/%
	Miletos A (n = 24)		Gordion L01 (n = 14)		Gordion L02 (n = 24)		Kaman (n = 2)		Gordion L01 (n = 14)	Gordion L02 (n = 24)	Kaman (n = 2)	
	Avg.	CV	Avg.	CV	Avg.	CV	Avg.	CV	± %	± %		
As	16.9	32.7	60.7	82.3	30.1	84.9	89.5	26.1	359.0	177.7	529.1	t<100
Ba	520.5	11.4	552.9	9.3	810.6	20.0	620.0	2.3	106.2	155.7	119.1	t>500
Ca%	4.7	27.5	4.4	20.1	3.5	57.5	4.6	9.2	93.5	75.2	97.9	%<5
Ce	105.8	2.8	99.1	4.1	108.8	5.7	96.5	2.2	93.6	102.9	91.2	t<100
Co	20.0	11.1	16.1	34.7	21.3	23.1	16.5	4.3	80.6	106.5	82.4	t<20
Cr	140.6	20.5	105.6	5.5	137.1	17.7	118.5	0.6	75.2	97.5	84.3	t<150
Cs	11.8	2.7	17.9	15.2	11.9	31.6	11.0	0.0	152.4	101.5	93.5	t<20
Eu	1.5	3.1	1.2	9.7	1.7	6.9	1.5	9.4	83.9	113.7	103.0	t<2
Fe%	4.4	4.2	4.2	3.8	4.8	6.1	3.9	0.5	96.0	110.3	89.1	%<5
Hf	5.7	9.9	5.7	6.2	6.8	10.9	6.9	2.0	99.4	118.7	121.3	t<10
K%	3.5	4.6	4.2	11.3	3.2	20.4	4.9	8.7	119.4	92.1	139.5	%<5
La	50.6	3.1	51.4	3.4	58.7	6.9	49.3	1.3	101.5	115.9	97.3	t<50
Lu	0.5	5.6	0.6	7.0	0.5	16.6	0.6	0.0	111.3	95.8	104.5	t<60
Na%	1.1	16.9	0.4	61.5	0.8	18.5	0.7	0.9	37.7	73.0	66.8	%<2
Rb	219.5	4.8	215.0	8.3	166.5	10.3	190.0	7.4	97.9	75.8	86.5	t<220
Sb	1.6	10.9	3.4	10.6	2.4	26.1	1.2	6.1	217.4	152.7	74.0	t<5
Sc	14.2	3.9	15.3	4.8	17.6	6.4	19.8	0.7	107.4	123.5	139.2	t<20
Sm	8.0	4.8	8.9	3.6	8.6	4.4	8.2	1.3	110.7	107.9	102.2	t<10
Ta	1.6	3.3	1.5	59.0	1.7	33.9	1.7	25.0	95.9	111.0	109.7	t<2
Tb	1.2	5.6	1.2	38.6	1.2	14.0	1.3	10.9	98.2	99.5	107.1	t<2
Th	25.8	3.8	25.2	9.1	21.9	7.8	21.6	0.7	97.8	85.1	83.9	t<25
U	4.4	6.2	5.7	89.3	4.4	24.9	3.8	22.3	128.6	99.9	86.2	t<10
Yb	4.2	4.2	4.0	4.6	3.4	11.7	3.5	4.0	95.5	80.2	83.1	t<5
Zn	81.1	4.8	83.6	11.5	102.7	21.2	105.5	19.4	103.0	126.6	130.0	t<100

of +/− 20% of 100% was set as a measure of goodness of fit and contrasted with measurement sensitivity for both major (%) and trace elements (i.e. elements counted between <2 and >500 ppm). In terms of accuracy, the mean values for 17 of 24 elements in the 80–120% range for both "Miletos A" and the Kaman pair of samples indicate good correspondence between these datasets. Comparison of precision was less conclusive. We note that results for the Kaman pair of samples would be expected to have the least variance compared to the larger Gordion group. This is reflected in Table 4.5, where 17 elements have less than half of the percentage variance of the Gordion group. The Bonn "Miletos A" group, with an even larger number of samples, shows a pattern comparable to the Kaman pair with 11 elements less than 50% of the Gordion range. We attribute this comparatively anomalous pattern to the use of the post-analysis "dilution factor" correction to enhance measurement precision for the "Miletos A" group. Similar matches between most of the other west Anatolian clusters enables a potential provenance for the Gordion subsets of other gross groupings to be explored if not assigned.

With relatively high typological diversity, comparison of the Gordion nonlocal sample to the Bonn west Anatolian typologically driven clusters flags a range of potential highly specific (e.g. "Miletos A") as well as more general west Anatolian provenances (e.g. "Ionian"). However, a large number of the Gordion samples remain unmatched to the Mommsen west Anatolian compositional profiles. Group M is one example. As evident in its outlying position in the PCA of the full dataset (Plate 3), group M is the most compositionally distinct cluster, and is made up of three finely decorated sherds in bichrome and geometric designs (Plate 7 a–c). In combination, these features highlight the nonlocal character of group M and raise the question of a likely region of origin in Anatolia. The position of this cluster in the whole-assemblage plot indicates a potential regional origin in east-central Anatolia. Three samples from the site of Kaman Kalehöyük, east of Gordion, approximate cluster M compositionally, and to some extent stylistically, with polychrome decoration but lacking the same level of decorative detail (Plate 7 d–f). A more compelling case for a central-east origin of this group comes from a comparatively large, and more typologically diverse, but relatively finely decorated range of samples from the more easterly site of Çadır Höyük that are a close compositional match (Plate 7 g–k). Following the procedures outlined for groups L01 and L02, comparison of the relative accuracy of these matches with Gordion cluster M shows the Çadır dataset to be the stronger match of the two with recoveries for 17 elements in the 80–110% band (Table 4.6).

Identifying Gordon's Groups

Table 4.6. *Comparison of NAA results for Gordion cluster M, with matching sample compositions from Çadır Höyük and Kaman Kalehöyük expressed as averages (accuracy) and coefficients of variation (precision) and mean element percentage recovery – elements outside 80–120% band highlighted. See Plate 7 for Cluster M ceramic samples.*

	Cluster M Gordion (n = 2) Avg.	CV	Cluster M groups Çadır (n = 17) Avg.	CV	Kaman (n = 3) Avg.	CV	Cluster M % recovery Çadır % recov.	Kaman % recov.
As	47.5	10.4	48.4	28.0	88.3	32.7	101.8	186.0
Ba	705.0	9.0	697.1	16.6	610.0	28.0	98.9	86.5
Ca%	2.9	2.5	4.7	46.0	3.1	49.1	164.9	107.6
Ce	121.5	5.2	118.2	9.8	133.7	9.4	97.3	110.0
Co	7.5	9.4	7.9	17.3	10.7	21.7	105.1	142.2
Cr	34.0	12.5	30.1	59.0	73.0	49.5	88.4	214.7
Cs	59.0	0.7	53.8	17.5	24.3	52.2	91.1	41.2
Eu	1.0	19.0	1.3	14.6	1.0	29.2	134.0	105.8
Fe%	3.0	5.9	2.7	7.7	3.1	15.0	90.8	104.2
Hf	7.6	1.9	6.5	7.8	7.9	16.0	85.1	104.4
K%	5.6	5.1	6.7	22.2	5.5	10.4	120.2	97.6
La	70.5	5.7	68.9	9.3	78.8	18.2	97.8	111.9
Lu	0.4	0.0	0.4	6.9	0.4	7.6	95.0	85.4
Na%	0.8	4.3	0.7	13.3	1.2	41.7	84.0	143.4
Rb	490.0	5.8	457.6	20.7	303.3	11.6	93.4	61.9
Sb	2.4	3.0	4.1	63.2	5.3	60.5	172.7	225.5
Sc	5.3	2.7	5.4	22.5	8.7	37.6	101.9	164.2
Sm	6.2	7.4	5.9	9.4	5.1	14.9	95.2	82.5
Ta	2.1	17.2	2.5	19.5	1.7	33.8	123.7	84.6
Tb	–	–	0.6	51.6	0.5	–	–	–
Th	43.1	5.1	45.8	11.5	62.0	17.0	106.3	144.1
U	5.0	4.3	5.6	39.5	10.1	48.0	113.5	204.0
Yb	2.5	0.0	2.5	11.1	2.0	17.3	101.4	81.3
Zn	99.0	1.4	106.3	15.3	119.3	17.6	107.4	120.5

Compositional Clusters and Cultural Groups

The protocol described in this chapter thus far outlines our analytical methodology for systematic identification and definition of geochemical clusters and intra- and interrelationships. The challenge is to then translate these clusters and relationships into culturally meaningful groups. A number of operational, noncontroversial, assumptions are required to make these links. First, geochemical clusters are assumed to represent some combination of specific clay (re)source(s), and cultural modification (adding or removing ingredients) that reflect technological preferences (ceramic "recipes," customary or constrained resource zones). Second, for interpreting local and nonlocal period-specific assemblages of ceramics, we assume geographically separated, culturally coherent groups of people selected and processed the geological resource(s) used. This raises two possibilities of particular relevance for local production. If only one clay source was available or used at one settlement, then regardless of number of groups involved, the ceramic assemblage would reflect a single compositional profile, with variations contingent on recipe and degree of processing. A more complex scenario arises for multiple local resources (i.e. within a 1–7 km catchment) with distinct geochemical profiles. If all potters in the settlement had equal access to the full range of potential resources at any given time, then little group-specific patterning should be apparent (the null hypothesis described earlier). Alternatively, if compositional differences within a contemporary assemblage reflect distinct source or compositional choices of different contemporary groups, then this should result in discernible patterning in the data.

Interpretation of the NAA datasets (Gordion "local, local/regional and nonlocal") involves different strategies in light of basic differences in the character of the sample. For Gordion "local," the generally continuous character of the compositional distribution is differentiated by regions of varying density with density "hot spots" defining the most heavily used resources. Making use of our null hypothesis, that all local resources were potentially available to Gordion potters at any given time, allowing for sample size effects, local resources should be equally represented regardless of period or other criteria. Where this is not the case then other factors need to be considered such as the influence of changing technology (e.g. open-fired/kiln-fired; handmade/wheel-thrown) on resource selection and level of processing.

Elemental profiles of tradewares are defined by a combination of their origins in diverse geographic regions, and their generally highly specialized character of production and stylistic and formal elaboration.

Ceramics, Archaeology and Groups

Compositional patterning first allows us to identify clusters in relation to potential resources. However, understanding these clusters in culturally meaningful ways requires articulating their material characteristics, and their contexts and distribution in relation to social, political, ritual and economic behavior (e.g. potential relationships of specific social groups with specific statuses, exchange patterns, styles, forms and/or social contexts).

We make use of two other approaches to ceramics to triangulate the identity of groups at ancient Gordion. Both of these approaches are based on previous work on ceramics at Gordion, highlighted at the beginning of this chapter. The first approach uses technological style and *chaîne opératoire* to characterize groups involved at various stages of ceramic production. Henrickson's contributions allow this categorization. The second approach looks at styles of ceramic decoration and form as markers of identity, making use of the work of Sams, DeVries and others. As discussed in Chapter 2, the contextual, and multivalent fluidity of identity makes this is a more complex task (e.g. Hodder 1982; Meskell 2007). Interpreting styles and forms in terms of group identity, therefore, requires careful contextual and scalar evaluation.

The daily practices of people include basic behaviors surrounding the production, distribution and consumption of goods. While commonly framed as economic, these behaviors also effectively embed political and ritual actions in social contexts. Building on the discrete data of individual ceramics and ceramic assemblages, we evaluate the archaeology of each period in terms of production, distribution and consumption, focusing specifically on identifying the evidence for different types of groups in each of these contexts. For example, identifying what kinds of groups are consuming (using) ceramics. Conversely, identifying what kinds of ceramics and where they are used informs us about the organization of the community. This approach draws upon archaeological perspectives on ancient economies in complex societies, particularly those of Hirth (1996), M. E. Smith (2004) and McAnany and Wells (2008). Layering evidence for groups based on production, consumption and interaction or distribution allows a "thicker" description of group formation and dynamics over the course of the Iron Age.

Groups and the Organization of Ceramic Production

Ceramicists have focused in particular on production contexts. Here, we make use of a more elaborated understanding of ceramic production in our discussion and analyses. Rice (2015:356) outlines 13 key (but non-exclusive) categories for evaluating the organization of production in relation to specialization. Of these, six can be applied, at least in some cases, to our data: skill level; technology investment; kinds and quantities of output; uniformity of output; investment in infrastructure and tools; the location, number and spatial proximity of producers and consumers. While these categories relate to aspects of production, we are particularly interested in the more challenging task of identifying and characterizing them in terms of interacting production groups. For example, uniformity of output as a measure of forming control can be directly related to high output (mass production) or to high skill levels of experienced potters

(Longacre 1999; Longacre et al. 1988). Therefore, by itself uniformity is not a clear delineator of one or the other. Nevertheless, we consider each of these variables to provide a basis for inferences about group composition and scale in production.

Scale of Ceramic Production

Estimating scale of production is a key factor in assessing the relative importance of individuals and groups in a particular industry. At the domestic scale of production, individuals and sometimes additional members of their households control all stages of clay acquisition, processing and ceramic production. This usually means that domestic ceramic production is a relatively small-scale, seasonal or intermittent activity, as production is scheduled into a wider group of household activities. In more complex preindustrial societies, ceramics are often produced under multiple types of organizing conditions which may cooccur in a community. For example, sometimes a single form is mass-produced for local specialized consumption (e.g. Aegean LBA cups or Mesopotamian bevel rim bowls (Berg 2004; Blackman et al. 1993). In other cases, forms are produced for elite ritual and widely traded (e.g. LBA Red Lustrous Ware; Kozal 2003) or produced by workshops for consumption in both elite and commoner contexts (P. J. Arnold et al. 1993; Nichols et al. 2002).

Workshops?

Understanding the nature of the economy in early complex societies often centers on evaluating the ways in which production and distribution are organized, as well as the relationships between what is produced as opposed to what is distributed. For early complex societies, distinguishing when and in what contexts, as well as for what items, workshop production emerged has been seen central to understanding the underlying political economy (Costin 2020). Over the last few decades archaeologists have explored the relationships between social group size and composition in relation to production output. These relationships are often framed in terms of household production, workshop production and industrial production. Costin (2020) has recently discussed challenges in identifying workshops and workshop production. She suggests that archaeologists should be cautious about identifying workshops using only indirect evidence (i.e. without the actual workshop *places* identified archaeologically). Similarly, specialized production is frequently managed within households in complex societies. While we have one small kiln, no ceramic workshops have been identified at Gordion. We are particularly cognizant that an equation cannot be made between a unique composition and a workshop, as often multiple resources are accessed by multiple groups (Hirth 2008). We therefore focus at a more general level, looking for evidence of interaction among potters based on shared styles of production and decoration to identify work groups.

Conclusions

In this chapter we have outlined the methods underlying the analytical component of this study for differentiating local from nonlocal wares, establishing different local resource zones, proveniencing imported wares using legacy NAA datasets (where possible) and constructing discrete compositional groups, either through density partitioning of local resource zone profiles or as multivariately defined subsets of clusters. We used two cases (L01 and M) to show how we could propose and compositionally validate relatively precise origins for some subsets of clusters. For the majority of samples we demonstrate broader geospatial trends in our dataset through comparison with NAA datasets from other sites and regions in eastern, central and western Anatolia. In the following chapters we evaluate these compositional groups in relation to the dynamics of cultural group formation and the development of Phrygian identity over the course of the Iron Age at Gordion.

One of the key features of our dataset is its longitudinal character. While we evaluate the types of social groups that are materialized for each period in subsequent chapters, the potential to compare and contrast group behavior over time makes it possible to relate group dynamics to other longitudinal datasets (environmental, historical, etc.). This provides a foundation for identifying correlations and potential causal dynamics in Gordion's communities through the Iron Age. In each of the following chapters, we integrate the multiple types of ceramic data with other lines of evidence from Gordion to elaborate what we can say about the operation of groups in the community over time.

5 The Late Bronze Age Community at Gordion
The Late Bronze Age YHSS 10–8 ?1500–1150 BCE

Introduction

Late Bronze Age Gordion, while well west of the Hittite political core, nonetheless seems to have been incorporated into its social and political sphere (Glatz 2011; Gunter 1991). Beginning in the Middle Bronze Age (MBA), Hittite influence enveloped agricultural communities across central Anatolia. Hittite texts document the nature of this relationship with provincial towns used as centers for collecting and redistributing goods, including agricultural land and products, as well as managing military armament (Imparati 2002). This undoubtedly created new tensions for local groups caught between their established social and economic relationships and those imposed by the Hittites. Hittite texts also hint at a complex negotiation between local power structures, interest groups and the state, the terms of which likely also created opportunities for local factions that could apparently levy "duties" for specific infractions. In other instances, central administrators directed local communities and their leaders to actively resist corrupt oversight, such as the potential for excess resource collection by local Hittite officials (Imparati 2002:100).

Here we address two related questions. First, what can we say about the formation of groups in Late Bronze Age Gordion (YHSS phases 10-8) based on the ceramic assemblage? Second, what can we say about group formation at Gordion, specifically in relationship to Hittite oversight from the geographically distant capital at Hattuša (modern Boğazköy)?

Archaeological evidence for the LBA community at Gordion comes from a limited number of soundings: excavation of a domestic complex on the Citadel Mound and of a Bronze Age cemetery on the adjacent Northeast Ridge (Gunter 1991; Mellink 1956; Voigt 2013; see Figs. 1.2, 3.1a–c, 5.1). As noted in Chapter 3, remodeling of the top of the mound in the Early Phrygian period removed any potential evidence of central LBA administrative buildings from the high mound, leaving only the

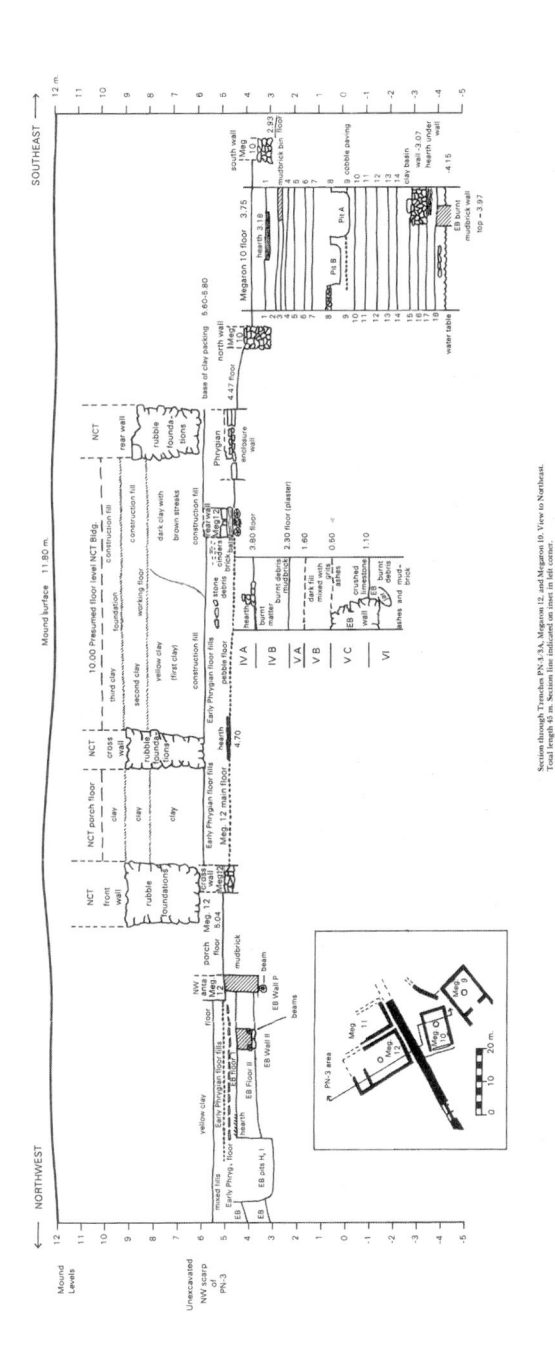

Fig. 5.1 Late Bronze Age excavations at Gordion, selected mound and LTS sections.
(a) Northwest–southeast section through trenches PN-3/3A, Megaron 12, and Megaron 10. Test units excavated under R. S. Young's direction, reconstructed by M. J. Mellink. Absolute level for LBA deposits is generally below +2 on the depth axis. Inset shows the location of these soundings within Early Phrygian/6A structures (see also Fig. 3.1a).

Fig. 5.1 (cont.) (b) Early Iron Age–Late Bronze Age stratigraphic section from M. M. Voigt Lower Trench Sounding (Op 14 north baulk). Deposits labeled with phase numbers in the Yassıhöyük Stratigraphic Sequence (YHSS).
Sources: 5.1a image no. AG1991-Plan 11; 5.1b image no. 89-1065:12, L. Foos; both courtesy University of Pennsylvania Museum, Gordion Project Archives.

lower town to provide any traces of an LBA settlement. Test excavations on the mound uncovered occupation debris suggesting a continuously occupied settlement from at least the late EBA (III) to the end of the Bronze Age (see Table 1.1). While excavations were limited in area, the data provide insights into the nature of ceramic production, use and exchange, as well as the scale, organization and identity of groups forming the LBA community at Gordion.

In this chapter we examine the LBA community at Gordion through comparison of the local ceramic sequence to the wider central Anatolian LBA ceramic evidence, focusing in particular on traditions at the Hittite capital of Hattuša. After situating Gordion within this broader context, we explore the identities of LBA groups at Gordion as expressed through their ceramics and artifact assemblages. Developments identified here for the LBA also provide a foundation for studying the trajectories of subsequent political and economic groups at the site. We argue that the shaping and reshaping of communities over the course of the LBA was critical for how they ultimately responded to the collapse of the Hittite polity, as well as how Phrygian power emerged at the end of the tenth century BCE.

Historical and Archaeological Background: Central Anatolia

As LBA Gordion appears to have been at least under Hittite influence, if not actual administration (Glatz 2009), an overview of LBA archaeology in north-central Anatolia is necessary to contextualize the community at Gordion within its larger social and political sphere (Fig. 5.2a–b; Glatz 2011; Seeher 2011). Mellink (1956), Glatz (2011) and others have questioned using "Hittite" as a label for LBA material culture across the region as it assumes relationships between production and political power that are currently themselves the subject of critical evaluation and problematization. Glatz suggests "north-central Anatolian" or NCA as an alternative name for the material assemblage of the Middle and Late Bronze Age of the north-central Anatolian plateau (Glatz 2009, 2011). Accepting this critique, we distinguish "Hittite" as referring to the polity and the state apparatus from the material culture found in the Hittite heartland and adopt NCA or NCA-style for this and related assemblages. It should be noted, however, that NCA-type assemblages stretch beyond north-central Anatolia, through south-central Anatolia and into the Mediterranean littoral (see discussion following).

The Hittite heartland and its capital, Hattuša, were located within the bend of the Kızılırmak River (Fig. 1.1). However, Hittite political

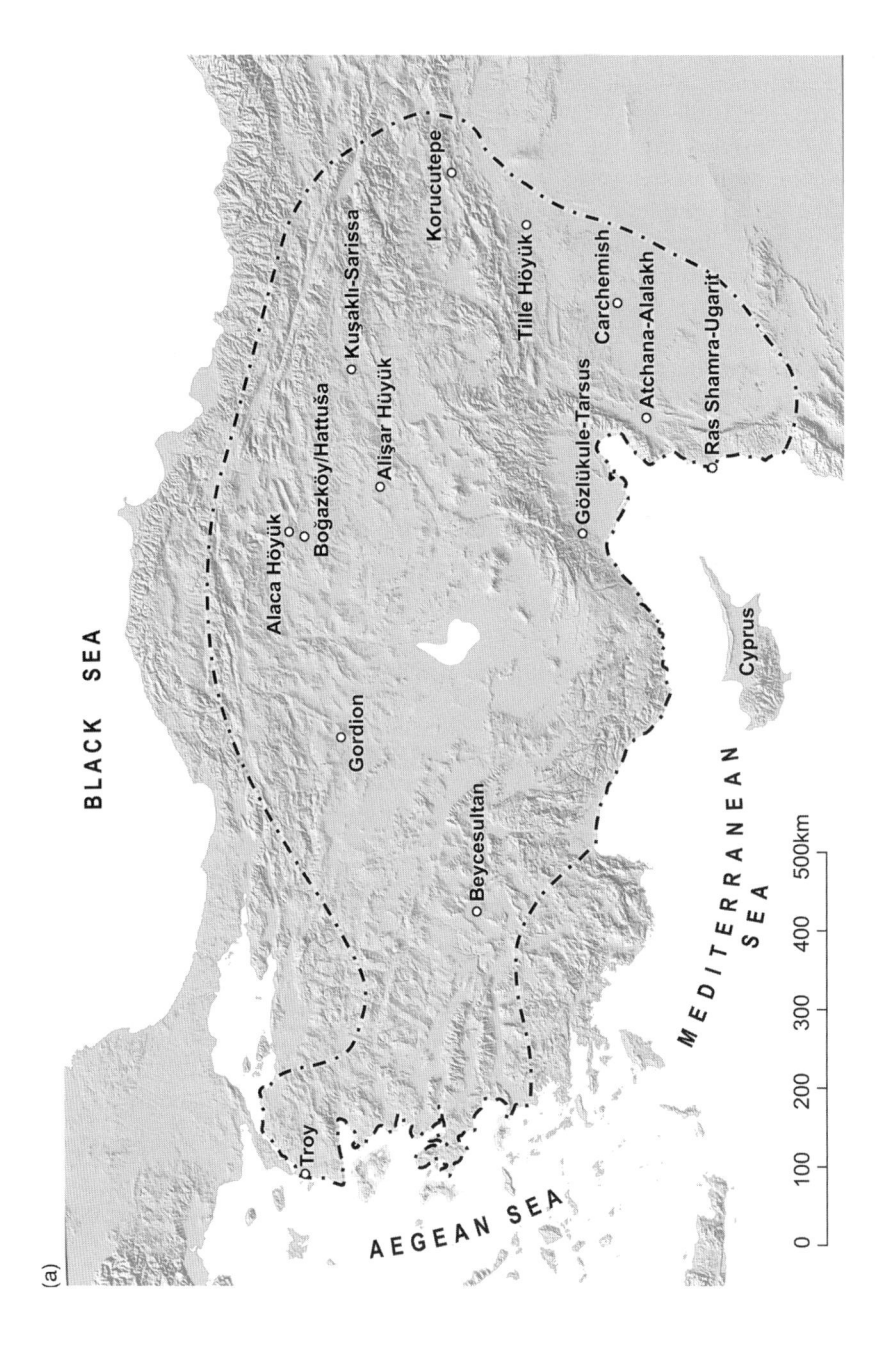

Fig. 5.2 Maps of Hittite influence based on texts and material culture distribution. (a) Map of Hittite influence at its maximum extent in the Late Bronze Age based on fourteenth to thirteenth century BCE textual sources.

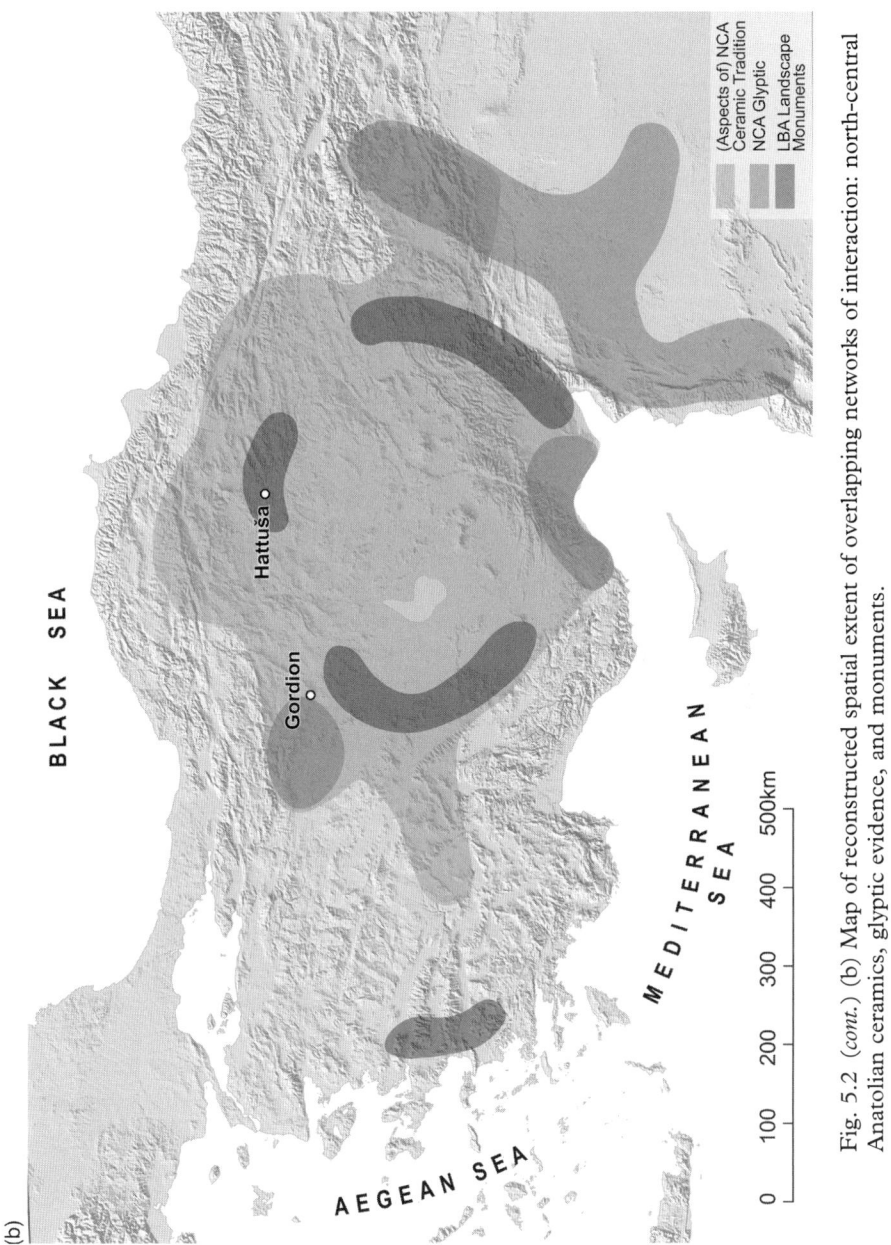

Fig. 5.2 (*cont.*) (b) Map of reconstructed spatial extent of overlapping networks of interaction: north-central Anatolian ceramics, glyptic evidence, and monuments.
Source: K. Newman, adapted from Glatz 2009 with permission from *Journal of Anthropological Archaeology*, Elsevier; 5.2a figure 1; 5.2b figure 9.

influence and control extended somewhat variably over a large swath of inland Anatolia, west and south to the mountain ranges that separate the interior from the coasts (Fig. 5.2a). The dynamic, though at times ephemeral, character of Hittite political expansion means that definitions and evidence of Hittite political boundaries typically vary by period and type (Helft 2010; Seeher 2011:376–377). Dates for the beginning of the Hittite Empire period, for example, vary between textual (ca. 1350 BCE) and cultural material evidence (ca. 1400 BCE).

The chronology of Hittite hegemony also remains contentious and contingent on which perspective or framework is favored (Seeher 2011:378–379): archaeological (i.e. two stage – Old and New Kingdom/Empire period) or historical (i.e. three stage – Old, Middle, New Kingdom). Historical data from the capital suggest the emergence of a state-level apparatus just after 1650 BCE. The Late or Empire period began ca. 1400–1350 BCE, lasting until the final collapse ca. 1200/1180 BCE. During this roughly 200-year phase the distribution of both NCA-style artifacts and landscape monuments reached their maximum extent.

Beyond a constrained set of textual references (cult and festival texts, political and diplomatic correspondence, a few administrative and land deed texts; Cammarosano 2018; Van den Hout 2011), little is known about the organization of Hittite political and economic systems or how these developed or were articulated over time and space. Based on textual data, rulers deployed a variety of strategies to exercise power. Texts record military advances, both west and south, and coercive control over local populations, in some cases involving the forced resettlement of entire communities. The king often installed relatives as local rulers or administrators. Incorporation of local deities into the Hittite pantheon served to both ritually integrate but also to subjugate local communities. Multiple positions of bureaucratic power are identified in Hittite texts, although the organization and management of any individual position remains unclear. Competition between family members, factions and other elite administrators was periodically politically destabilizing (Van den Hout 2011). During the Empire period these strategies culminated in the centralization of power and the adoption of divine kingship.

Relative to the geographic extent and complexity of the Hittite Empire, only limited archaeological evidence is available to potentially address questions of Hittite political or economic practice (Glatz 2011:878, 882; Matsumura and Weeden 2017). Hittite influence included population resettlement, wide dissemination of Hittite monuments and seals, and the local adoption of a relatively uniform, utilitarian, plain pottery assemblages (Glatz 2009, 2011). Recent work in three spheres is clarifying these dynamics: refinements of both ceramic and radiocarbon chronologies (Bouthillier et al. 2014; Schoop and Seeher 2006; Schoop et al. 2009; Seeher 2006); analysis of agricultural regimes and food storage (Fairbairn and Omura 2005; Müller-Karpe 2009); and comparative studies of NCA and NCA-style material culture across Anatolia and the northern Levant (Glatz 2009, 2011; Matsumura and Weeden 2017). Collectively, this work is providing new ways to evaluate Hittite population and economic dynamics, and more nuanced models of regional differences in how the Hittites negotiated control and influence, and how local communities engaged with Hittite ideology and hegemony.

Iconic NCA material culture includes the red-burnished beaked jugs of the Old Kingdom, Red Lustrous Wheelmade (RLW) ware primarily of the Empire period, monumental stone sculpture and water management structures (e.g. the Eflatunpınar Monument near Beyşehir), early use of iron (Old Kingdom), seal impressions and bullae (predominantly from the Empire period), and the creation of what was to become the most ubiquitous ceramic marker of Hittite occupation: monochrome "Standard" or "Drab" ware (Glatz 2011; Schoop 2009, 2011; Seeher 2011).

Late Bronze Age Ceramics in Anatolia

The relationships between ceramic production, consumption and distribution at Gordion and contemporaneous settlements are key to interpreting Gordion's LBA community and its relationship to communities in the larger region. LBA ceramics in central and western Anatolia are relatively well studied (Akça et al. 2009; Ertem and Demirci 1999; Gates 2001, 2007; Glatz 2009; Glatz and Matthews 2005; Gunter 1991, 2006; Mielke 2006, 2007, 2016; Müller-Karpe 1988; Postgate 2007; Schoop 2003, 2009, 2011). Much of this work focused on defining formal ceramic characteristics (e.g. Schoop, Mielke, Müller-Karpe, Orthmann) and establishing links between LBA sites and Hattuša's ceramic traditions (Gates, Glatz, Henrickson). The relatively uniform, utilitarian range of forms and styles for the bulk of NCA ceramics (Fig. 5.3) is belied by museum displays of the elaborated exceptions such as the relatively rare, highly decorative Old Kingdom red-burnished beaked jugs (Schoop 2011). The greatest diversity of NCA forms is found at the Hittite capital Hattuša (modern Boğazköy), while typically, smaller LBA sites like Gordion and Kilise Tepe have a more limited range (Bouthillier et al. 2014; Henrickson 2002).

Schoop (2011) characterized the pottery at Boğazköy as generally homogenous buff ware, with grit or sand inclusions and few fabric variants (cooking ware excluded), and with little attention paid to finishing (Schoop 2003, 2006). The range of forms (e.g. Schoop 2011:figs.

94 Ancient Gordion

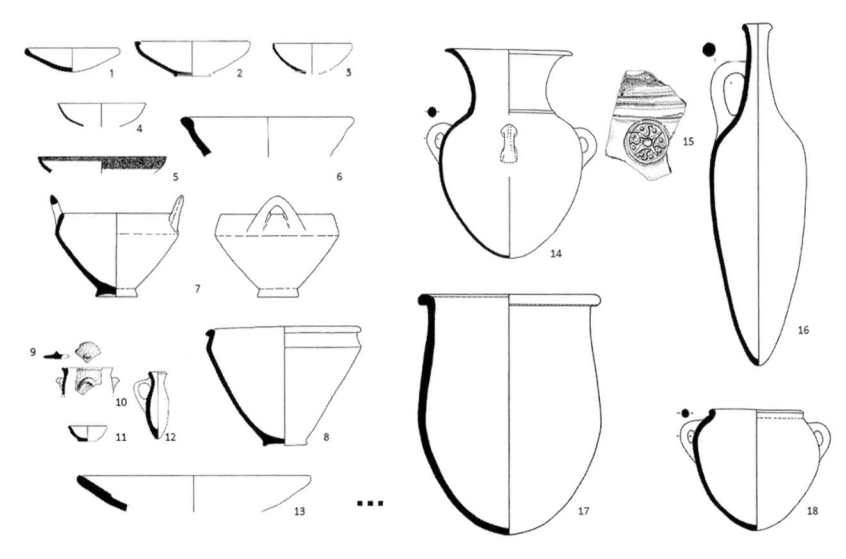

Fig. 5.3 Examples from Boğazköy of Late Bronze Age ceramic types (all courtesy of Ulf Schoop). Flat bowl variants (1-6), deep bowls (7-8), small pot and lid (9-10), 'votive' vessels (11-12), baking plate (13). Scale 1:5. Multi-purpose pots (14, 17), 'signe royal' (15), storage jar (16), cooking pot (18). Scale 1:9 (14, 16-18), 1:3 (15).

1–4) includes bowls, shallow bowls/plates, jars, baking plates, pots, cooking pots, storage jars, jugs, lentoid flasks and small vessels, with some changes in form frequency over time (e.g. the decline in medium-sized bowls during the Empire period; Schoop 2011). Overall, red or white slipped vessels, some of which are burnished, already comprising only a small percentage of the assemblage in the Old Kingdom, become rare late in the LBA, and particularly by the Empire period. In terms of production, the fast wheel, introduced quite early in the Hittite core area (ca. 1900 BCE), continued in use until the end of the LBA. With a few exceptions (e.g. baking plates) vessels were wheelmade. In some cases, multiple forming techniques were used for a single vessel type (e.g. when producing bases; Mielke 2016).

Boğazköy's pottery is most often undecorated. Figurative reliefs, usually of humans in procession with tribute or offerings, are occasionally used to decorate some vessels at a few sites (Schoop 2011:fig. 6.1–2). In addition, a small number of vessels were elaborated with plastic modeling, typically of animals, such as bulls' heads, or more rarely gods. Simple painted designs (triangles, zigzags, etc.), usually in red or brown, are equally rare, as is incised decoration, but when present, motifs are similar to painted designs. By the end of the LBA painted decoration is marginally more frequent in the southeastern extent of the NCA range (Schoop 2011:259). Slips, common in the early phases, decline in abundance and in the size of the area slipped by the Empire period (Müller-Karpe 1988; Schoop 2011). Relatively rare "Gold" ware has a golden micaceous finish (typically poorly preserved), apparently applied to provide a metallic appearance.

Only a few styles of pottery are recognizable imports into the Hittite region. These include Mycenaean and Cypriot wares, most notably Red Lustrous Wheelmade ware (Fig. 5.4). Forms in an apparent nonlocal fabric, "Weisston," provide limited evidence for regional exchange. All imports are uncommon to rare and, with the exception of RLW, generally tend to feature more in coastal sites (Schoop 2011:263). The use of RLW in Hittite ritual and elite practices is suggested by the single most abundant source in central Anatolia: an LBA temple dump in the Southern Ponds area of the Hittite capital (Schoop 2011).

While there are very few discontinuities in the development of potting traditions from the Karum period (twentieth to eighteenth century BCE) onward, assemblage composition nonetheless shifts over time. Schoop hypothesized that these shifts reflect the changing role of pottery, moving from more carefully decorated, elaborated and high-fired prestige goods to plain relatively low-fired "Standard Ware" (Schoop 2011:265). Müller-Karpe (2000) goes further, linking a decline in production standards to the erosion of state control and the beginning of Hittite collapse toward the end of the Empire period.

Current NCA ceramic analytical issues focus on the internal patterning of variation within and between archaeological sites across the region under Hittite influence (Bouthillier et al. 2014; Gates 2011; Gunter 2006). Regional studies (Bouthillier et al. 2014; Henrickson 2002) suggest strong similarities among LBA ceramic assemblages. However, in the absence of systematic comparative analysis of large contemporary Late Bronze Age assemblages, our understanding of the actual extent of uniformity and/or standardization in forms, fabric (types) and production techniques remains ill-defined.

Hittite Hegemony and Ceramics

Despite substantial gaps in the evidence, the distribution of NCA "Standard Ware" has been linked to Hittite political control (Gates 2001, 2007; Glatz 2009; Postgate 2007). Postgate (2007) proposed that the distinctive forms at Kilise Tepe in Cilicia (particularly undecorated plates and "internal rim" bowls) are so similar to those at

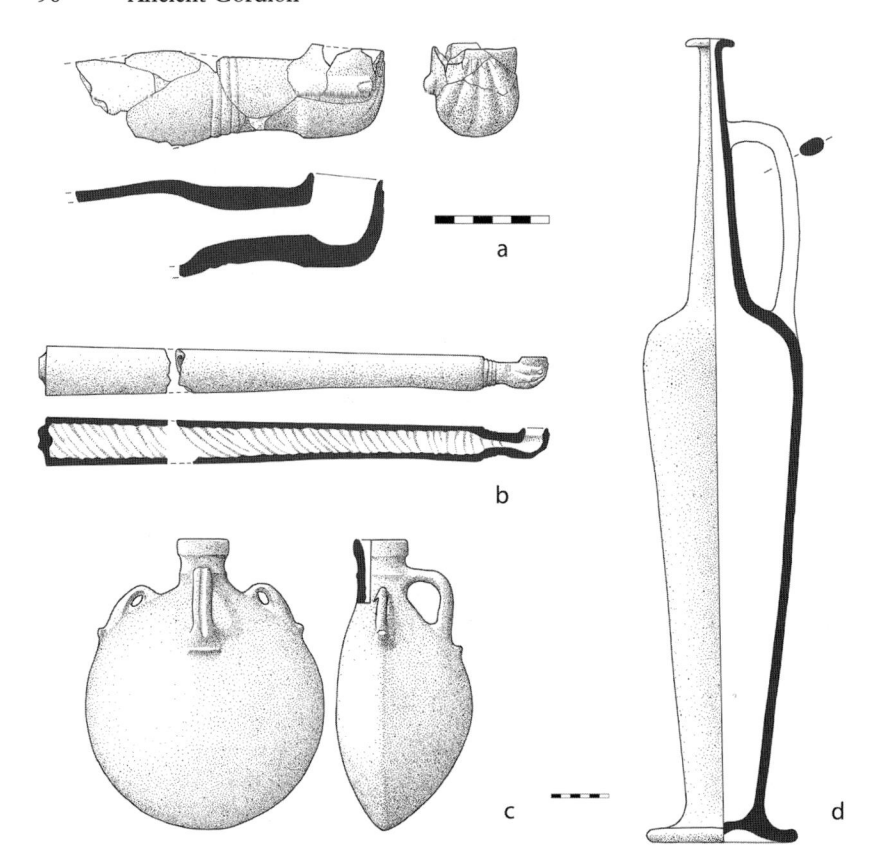

Fig. 5.4 Late Bronze Age Red Lustrous Wheelmade ware, typical forms.
(a) Hand-and-bowl fragment of an arm-shaped vessel (Boğazköy, Southern Ponds).
(b) Arm-shaped vessel (Ayios Iakovos, Cyprus).
(c) Lentoid flask from Cyprus.
(d) Spindle bottle (Boğazköy, Upper City).
Source: Grave et al. 2014:fig. 2, with permission from *Antiquity*.

Boğazköy that they must represent Hittite administrative control at Kilise. He went further to suggest that such assemblages, where identified elsewhere in Anatolia, equally represent Hittite control, citing Gordion in the west, Kinet Höyük in the south and Tille Höyük in the east, as well as at sites in between (Gates 2011; Henrickson 2002; Postgate 2007; Summers 1993).

Adoption and promotion of a "standardization scenario" for these LBA ceramic assemblages led Postgate to query how and why it occurred over this region. At most sites with NCA ceramics, including Kilise and Gordion, LBA potters made use of local clays (Henrickson and Blackman 1996; Postgate 2007). However, standardized NCA forms made of local fabrics present interpretive challenges where shape templates, rather than actual products, were transmitted. Gates (2001:141) solved this by proposing a mechanism whereby state-controlled workshops employed potters to make pots to specific standards for local distribution. Postgate suggested an alternative "administrative" model, where a few Hittite supervisors managed local production.

Schoop (2011) maintained that a regional LBA Hittite standardization scenario is more apparent than real. Rather than providing evidence of some form of hegemonic control, he argued that both composition and vessel sizes of LBA assemblages vary regionally and, with the accumulation of more archaeological evidence, such scenarios remain speculative at best. Basic questions remain unanswered about the scale of production at any particular site (however see Glatz 2016b), the extent of exchange of LBA ceramics within the Hittite region, and the means by which apparent similarities and/or standards were achieved (e.g. transmission or coercion). For example, at Kilise Tepe, from ca. 1350/the early fourteenth century BCE (end of Level III), Postgate noted an increased abundance of ceramics associated with a western Cilician local ceramic sphere ("Cilician Red Painted Ware") and changes in jar forms (often handmade), both of which occurred well in advance of the final Hittite collapse. Subsequent excavations (Bouthillier et al. 2014) support the variability in the LBA ceramic assemblage at Kilise and clarify the dates of the LBA phases at the site. Glatz's more detailed comparison of LBA pottery at Kilise and Boğazköy (in Bouthillier et al. 2014) also identifies greater variability in forms and decoration that is not consistent with the "standardization" scenario. In a study of LBII monochrome ware ceramics at Tarsus, Karacic (2014) also proposes a more complex set of relationships between local groups and the Hittites than is suggested by a top-down "state control mechanism." Together, the ceramic data underscore the nature of interactions between the Hittite center and Cilicia as contingent and negotiated, rather than centralized by either administrative or economic control over the production of NCA-style ceramics. This appears to be the case for centers across the LBA Hittite Empire, where local potter-introduced variations appear, in varying degrees, to have uniquely identified their communities in relation to the Hittite koine.

In a wider, regional-level analysis seeking to define the practices of Hittite power in different regions of Anatolia, Glatz (2009) compared overlapping spatial distributions of four different domains of NCA material culture across eight sites to characterize Hittite hegemony: ceramics, settlement patterns, Hittite administrative technology and Hittite monuments (Fig. 5.2b). Beyond basic shapes and surface treatments the ceramic assemblages included disparate NCA forms. Even when relaxing comparative criteria to focus on types rather than metrics, Glatz observed considerable regional and temporal variability both in forms and decoration.

While Glatz's work (2009, 2011) suggests differential patterns of interaction between the Hittites and local communities and polities across the larger region, the timing and chronological development of these relationships remains uncertain. For southern Anatolian sites, previous interpretations that posited a significant increase in Hittite influence during the Empire period relied on the conventional Boğazköy ceramic chronology (Gates 2011). Schoop's detailed reassessment of the Boğazköy ceramic sequence and chronology, employing new radiocarbon dates, now places this development significantly earlier, with consequences for interpreting the timing of Hittite influence at other Anatolian LBA sites including Gordion (Schoop 2006; Schoop and Seeher 2006).

Nevertheless, the overlaps in Glatz's (2009) artifact distribution map firmly place Gordion in the core western NCA realm, and well within the sphere of Hittite political hegemony (Fig. 5.2b). Based on this model, it appears likely that LBA elites at Gordion would have been actively engaged in negotiating identities within that larger political milieu.

?1500–1150 BCE (YHSS 10–8): Bronze Age Gordion

Excavations on the Citadel Mound suggest that occupation began at least by the Early Bronze Age (EBA III), although very little of this phase has been excavated (Gunter 1991). Limited test trenching in the 1960s (PN-3/3A, Megaron 12/NCT, Megaron 10/NT) focused on the northeastern part of Young's Main Excavation Area (Fig. 3.1a; Voigt and Kealhofer in press). In 1988–1989 the Lower Trench Sounding (Fig. 5.5), also laid out within the Main Excavation Area, uncovered enough, together with Young's evidence, to hypothesize the extent of the Late Bronze Age occupation of the mound. Three Bronze Age chronological units were identified in the LTS: YHSS 10–8. Pottery and subsequent radiocarbon dates link YHSS 9 and 8 to the late LBA (fourteenth to twelfth century BCE), with YHSS 10 dated to an earlier mid millennium phase (seventeenth to sixteenth century BCE) based on seals and seal impressions. Stratigraphically, an eroded surface between YHSS 10 and 9 suggests a break in occupation in this part of the site. Ceramic parallels suggest

Fig. 5.5 Lower Trench Sounding on the Eastern Mound. View of the LTS, set within standing architecture of the Early Phrygian Destruction Level 6A:3, looking south east.

Source: Image no. 93-1002:03, M. Daniels; courtesy University of Pennsylvania Museum, Gordion Project Archives.

a slightly later date for YHSS 10: sixteenth to fifteenth century BCE (Schoop personal communication). Following Yakar (2011), our chronological frame for the LBA is ca. sixteenth century BCE to ca. 1200 BCE, placing YHSS 10 at the beginning of the LBA. Without substantial differences in material culture, YHSS 9 and 8, though stratigraphically distinct, are treated here as a single chronological unit.

In addition to occupation on the Citadel Mound, excavations on the Northeast Ridge encountered a ca. 600 square meter cemetery, primarily composed of pithos (n = 42 of 55) and cist burials, and an EBA cist burial under Tumulus F (see Figs. 1.2, 3.1c; Gunter 1991; Mellink 1956). The chronology of the cemetery remains poorly defined, but Gunter (1991:7) suggests an early to mid second millennium BCE use, potentially including late MBA burials. If so, it predates the LBA Citadel Mound evidence discussed here.

?1500–1150 BCE (YHSS 10-8) Late Bronze Age Gordion Excavations

Only a small area of the LBA settlement has been excavated, lying at an absolute level well below that of nearby houses dated to the EBA (Voigt 2013). Comparisons of levels across the site suggest that during the EBA a central high mound existed north of the Lower Trench Sounding. It seems likely that the LBA settlement also had a central high mound subsequently truncated in Early Phrygian times (YHSS 6B; Fig. 5.6). The 1988–1989 excavations encountered an LBA residential area interpreted as part of a Bronze Age lower town that extended to the south and west (Mellink in Gunter 1991:109–110; Voigt 2013:173–179, 182; see also Rose 2017:155–156). A hypothesized LBA citadel, potentially removed by Early Phrygian leveling activity, would likely have been an area used by ruling elites (Mielke 2011a).

Voigt's 1988–1989 sounding (ca. 300 m^2) uncovered a semisubterranean building with a deep stone foundation and a superstructure apparently of wood (CBH Structure) (Fig. 5.7a and b). Large cylindrical pits in adjacent open areas were used for the storage of organics, probably cereals (Fig. 5.7a and b). Additional LBA structures were uncovered during Young's excavations, but not recognized as such at the time, including part of a partial semisubterranean building and possibly a mudbrick building. Based on the depth of deposits in both the Voigt and Young soundings, the duration of the LBA settlement appears to have been lengthy. While we have no direct evidence for the size of the Bronze Age settlement, a sounding on the western part of the Citadel Mound exposed an Early Phrygian surface that lies far above the present

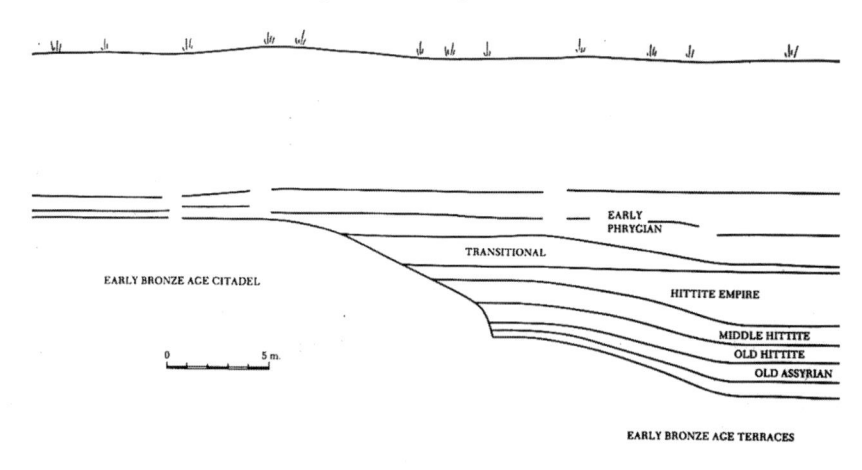

Fig. 5.6 Schematic section of the Bronze and Early Iron Age mound at Gordion by M. J. Mellink, based on the Rodney Young deep soundings (see Fig. 5.1a). As shown, the high Early Bronze Age mound to the left was truncated in Early Phrygian/6B times, possibly removing LBA deposits. The Lower Trench Sounding explored the part of the early mound shown to the right.
Source: Gunter 1991: Plan 12; courtesy University of Pennsylvania Museum, Gordion Project Archives.

plain level and 8–10 m above the mid second millennium BCE plain. With such deep deposits predating the Middle Iron Age, at least some of this extensive cultural accumulation is likely to be of Bronze Age origin (Voigt 2013:179–184).

Late Bronze Age artifacts provide some limited evidence of connections between Gordion and the Hittite Empire. Four Hittite-style seals and a bulla were found in post-Bronze Age deposits by Young, and a Hittite-style stamp and two stamped sherds were found in Bronze Age deposits in the Lower Trench Sounding (Figs. 5.8 and 5.9a). A seal impression bearing a Hittite name was also found on an NCA-style vessel recovered from fill inside the YHSS 8 house (Fig. 5.9b) (Dusinberre 2005:20–21, 37–41, figs. 17–24).

In sum, while the excavated area of LBA Gordion is relatively small, both ceramic and glyptic evidence indicate NCA and Hittite connections. In the surrounding region, the Gordion Regional Survey identified a sharp decline in the number of LBA sites relative to the MBA. When combined with a suggested increase in the extent of LBA Gordion (i.e. in lower town), this pattern is consistent with urban consolidation and/or

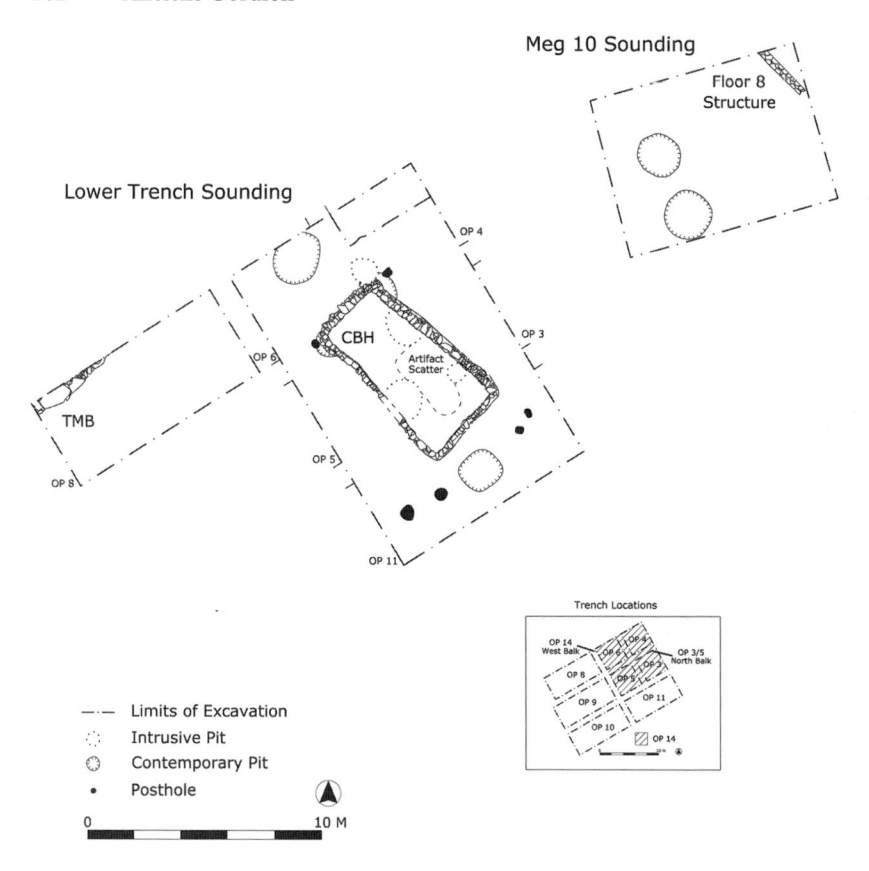

Fig. 5.7 YHSS 8 Late Bronze Age house, the CBH Structure in the Lower Trench Sounding.
(a) Plan of CBH Structure in the Lower Trench Sounding with contemporary pits and a Late Bronze Age structure with pits in the nearby Megaron 10 Sounding.

regional outmigration (Kealhofer 2005b). The location and size of Gordion puts it well within the parameters typical of Hittite settlements (5–18 ha, located on a crossroads; Mielke 2011b).

Glatz (2009) notes that a key strategy of Hittite political control was the practice of resettling outlying populations within the Hittite heartland. This strategy may also have impacted the LBA settlement pattern around Gordion (see also Mielke 2017). Additional evidence for this pattern is seen in other LBA settlements across the western region, suggesting occupation at the major centers at the same time as a reduction in the number of smaller LBA sites (Weeden et al. 2017).

Fig 5.7 YHSS 8 Late Bronze Age house (*cont.*) (b) The CBH Structure with walls cut into earlier LBA deposits. The trenches excavated below the house floor (foreground and right) removed YHSS 9 trash deposits. *Sources*: 5.7a D. Hoffman, S. Jarvis, C. Alblinger; 5.7b image no. 89-1060:36, L. Foos; courtesy University of Pennsylvania Museum, Gordion Project Archives.

Overview of the Bronze Age Ceramic Assemblage at Gordion (YHSS 10-8)

Both Gunter and Henrickson have published on Late Bronze Age Gordion ceramics, and more recently Aslan and Günata have been restudying the LBA pottery. Gunter and Mellink studied Bronze Age deposits and finds excavated at Gordion from the late 1950s to early 1960s (Gunter 1991; Mellink 1956), and Henrickson worked on the ceramic assemblages excavated during the Voigt sounding in 1988–1989 (Henrickson 1993, 2002; Henrickson and Blackman 1996). Henrickson attributed YHSS 10 ceramics to the MBA, and YHSS 9-8 to the LBA, based on ceramic parallels. Revision of the date for YHSS 10 to the late sixteenth to early fifteenth century BCE now likely places it in the early LBA. Gunter, working with a less detailed stratigraphic sequence, noted trends over time but could not fully differentiate MBA and LBA ceramics.

104 Ancient Gordion

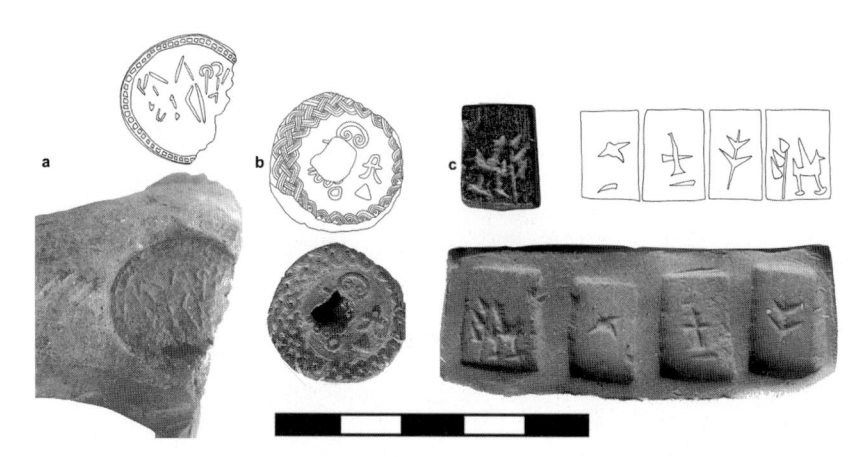

Fig. 5.8 Bronze Age seals and sealings from Young's excavations, all recovered from post-LBA contexts.
(a) Handle with impression of Hittite stamp seal, seal diameter 2.2 cm (Gordion inventory no. 8326-SS-223; Dusinberre 2005 Cat. no. 5; photograph R619-24, drawing image no. ERMD Cat. 5).
(b) Conical clay bulla with Hittite seal on base, diameter 2.1 cm (Gordion inventory no. 7804-SS-209; Dusinberre 2005 Cat. no. 10; photograph R610-29, drawing image no. ERMD Cat. 10).
(c) Four-sided bead seal with hole, slightly worn, 1.4 cm tall (Gordion inventory no. 10437-SS-260; Dusinberre 2005 Cat. no. 4; photograph R734-37, drawing image no. ERMD Cat. 4).
Source: Drawings by E.R.M. Dusinberre 2005; photos and drawings courtesy University of Pennsylvania Museum, Gordion Project Archives

The approaches of these two ceramicists were also quite different, with Henrickson focusing on production (technological styles), and Gunter on more conventional formal description of the excavated assemblages. Henrickson (2002) broadly characterized the Gordion LBA ceramic assemblage as notably standardized and simple (Figs. 5.10 and 5.11) with respect to the range of forms, decoration and production sequences (Table 5.1). While Henrickson concentrated on the LBA ceramics recovered during Voigt's excavations, Gunter (1991) detailed the longer sequence of Bronze Age ceramics found in both Young's soundings on the mound and the Bronze Age cemetery located within the adjacent present-day village of Yassıhöyük. The difference between the Middle and Late Bronze Age ceramic assemblage is characterized by Gunter as a gradual "drift" in decoration and shape, with few period-specific forms. Bowl forms, both shallow and hemispherical, showed the greatest change.

Fig. 5.9 Late Bronze Age glyptic evidence from Voigt's excavations, all recovered from LBA deposits.
(a) YHSS 9 stamp impressions and stamp (YHSF 89-530, 563, 531).

Fabrics
Both Henrickson and Gunter defined the Bronze Age wares using the same descriptive parameters (i.e. temper, inclusions and surface treatment). Henrickson's data descriptions often include additional "texture" data that is similar to the way that fabric is used here. Where possible, we distinguish surface treatment from fabric to compare and contrast patterns of production over time.

Gunter (1991:28–29) identified seven different wheelmade wares for the Middle and Late Bronze Age: buff, buff and orange, red-slipped, buff-slipped "enamel" wares (white); painted wares; cooking pot ware; and buff or orange micaceous wares. However, as the same fabric is often used to make different "wares," which are only differentiated by their surface treatment, characterizing this assemblage in terms of wares rather than fabrics can overestimate assemblage variability. The difference between the MBA and LBA assemblages is seen in a decrease in red slipping and an increase in grit in the fabric. To avoid confusion between Gunter's typology and descriptions of the composition of the paste (i.e. fabric in our vocabulary), her "units" are relabeled here as "ceramic groups."

Fig 5.9 (*cont.*) (b) Personal name in Hittite hieroglyphs on the rim of a large jar from the YHSS 8 CBH Structure (YHSF 88-157).
Sources: image nos. *5.9a.* 90-1016:022; *5.9b.*90-1011:020, L. Foos; courtesy University of Pennsylvania Museum, Gordion Project Archives.

Gunter noted that while most ceramic groups have the same fabric (all but the micaceous groups), the amount of "grit" inclusions appears to increase over time. Finer versions of this fabric have less visible temper. The buff-slipped "enamel ware" group has a fine fabric with few visible inclusions that may parallel production of the white-slipped wares from Boğazköy (Schoop 2009, 2011). Cooking pots with a distinctive, gritty, coarse fabric (>5 mm inclusions), can be self-slipped ("cooking pot ware"; Gunter 1991:29). The buff or orange micaceous ware with a surface mica concentration occurs in low frequency (potentially a local variant of Hittite Gold Wash ware?), and Gunter (1991:30) suggests early examples of this group were potentially imported, although she does not elaborate in terms of fabric differences.

Henrickson recognized a larger range of YHSS 10 fabrics (early LBA), with medium-fine and medium-coarse wares most common, in addition to the more basic fine, cooking and "common" ware categories. He also identified two possible fabrics used for cooking in YHSS 10. For the later LBA (YHSS 9-8), Henrickson (2002) identified only three ceramic

Fig. 5.10 Late Bronze Age YHSS 8 pottery.
This group of pots was found nested together in a small pit that had been dug into wall collapse inside the CBH Structure; dated to the end of the LBA occupation at Gordion (a) front row, YH 22300 small bowl, YH 22776 large bowl; back row YH 22299 bowl, YH 22451 deep bowl, YH 22777 small pinched bowl.

groups or "wares" based on differences in fabric (Table 5.1). "Common" ware (white, buff, brown) accounts for nearly 90% of the ceramic assemblage. The YHSS 9-8 pottery had a "medium-sized grit temper with a dense paste." The fine ware had no grit, and cooking ware had more – particularly organic – temper. The three YHSS 9-8 groups (buff common, buff fine and cooking ware) suggest production of more homogenized, if often somewhat coarser fabrics.

Both ceramicists confirm differences in surface treatment and inclusions that highlight systematic changes in ceramic production during the LBA (YHSS 10-8), notwithstanding differences that appear to largely reflect Gunter's conflation of MBA and LBA phases.

Forms

Vessel shapes reveal multiple types of information about function, from food consumption and production to storage, each of which tells us about contemporary cultural group practices. The YHSS 9-8 ceramic assemblage has a relatively limited range of identified forms: several types

108   Ancient Gordion

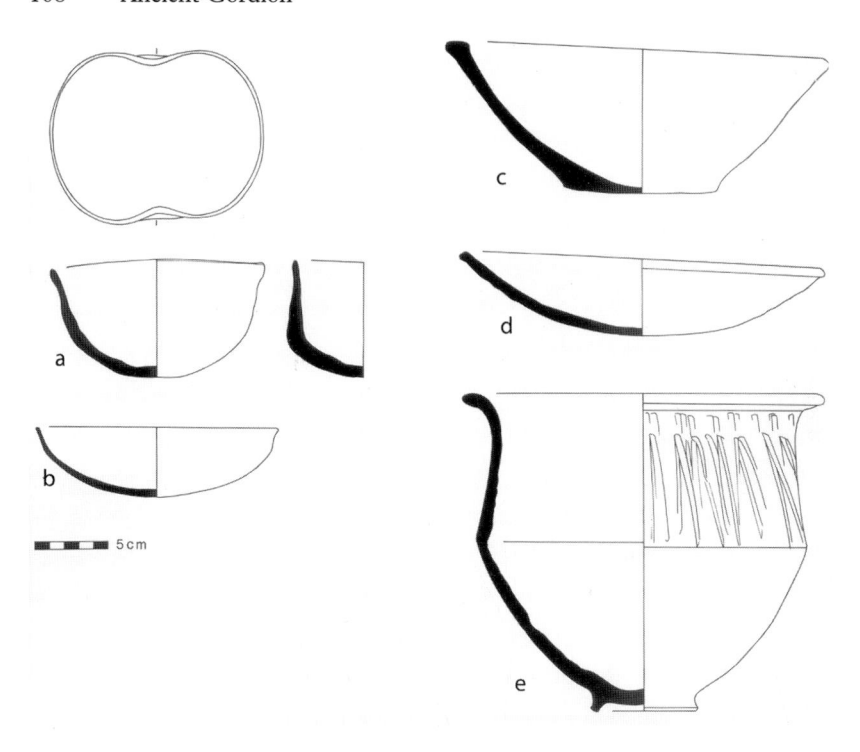

Fig 5.10 (*cont.*) (b) Drawings of same pots.
Sources: *5.10a* image no. 90-1007:031, L. Foos; *5.10b* image no. 90-1007:31, D. Hoffman; courtesy University of Pennsylvania Museum, Gordion Project Archives.

of bowls, plates, cooking pots and jars (Figs. 5.10 and 5.11; Table 5.1). Bowls include small fine ware, shallow conical bowls (a few with distinctive raised decoration: "welts") and medium round-based and conical bowls. Two main types of jars were represented: small to medium thin-walled jars and larger tapered cylindrical and point-based "torpedo" jars, along with jars with handles typical of pitchers and jugs. Pitchers are distinguished by having opposing spouts and handles. Cooking pots are typically wide-mouthed vessels with rounded bases and variable rim profiles. The largest vessels include "vats" or "bathtubs" and large storage jars or pithoi. Zoomorphic vessels are also present (Gunter 1991:30–37; Henrickson 2002:125–128).

For Gunter (1991), typical LBA bowls were shallow, with either inverted or carinated rims, which generally became shallower over time, modified by both shoulder angle (carination) and rim treatment. Within these larger

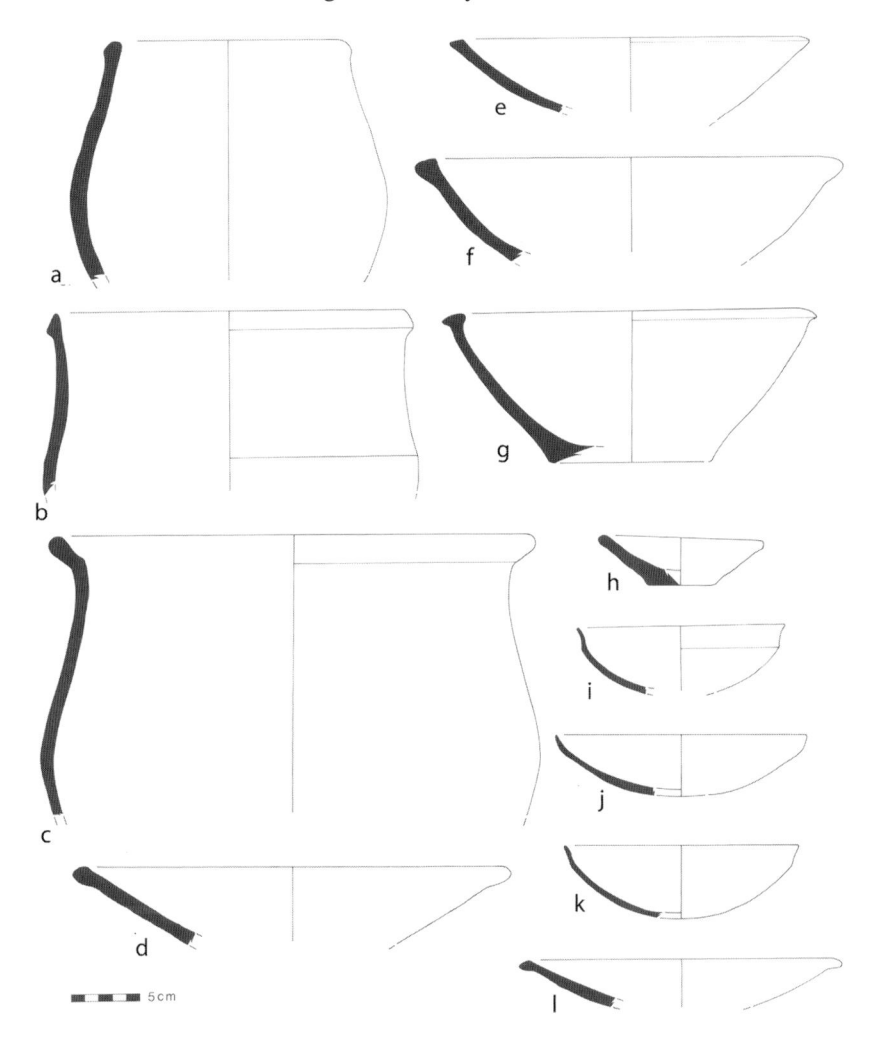

Fig. 5.11 Late Bronze Age YHSS 9-8 pottery, selected bowl, pot and jar forms.
(a) Bowls a–c: YH 22271.2, 23209.1, 31683.3; d–l YH 29960.18, 20310.4, 20219.5, 23169.19, 31684.9, 22960.12, 29993.4, 19962.2, 29960.4.

groupings, carination varied considerably (angled to vertical) and in the thickness and shape of the rim ("bullnose" to thickened, "overhanging" or simple). With the exception of a few possible ring and pedestal bases, the paucity of discrete bases suggests most vessels had rounded bottoms.

110   Ancient Gordion

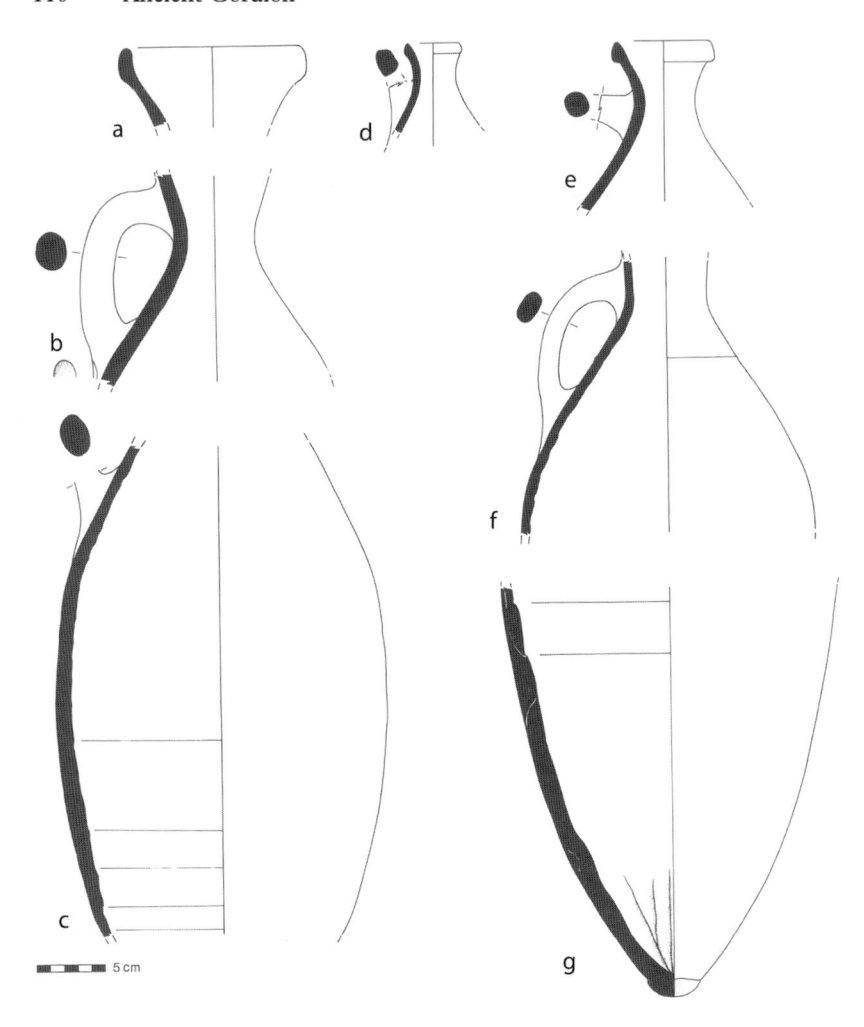

Fig. 5.11 (*cont.*) (b) Jars a–g: YH29960.20, 33189.4, 32732.5, 23189.4, 23201.1, 23169.8, 23834.1.
Sources: R. Henrickson and D. Hoffman; courtesy University of Pennsylvania Museum, Gordion Project Archives.

Decorative Styles and Finishes

Decoration potentially signifies identity, whether individual, family, household, gender, kin group or class. Typical LBA finishes involved smoothing, with the limited evidence for slipping decreasing over time. In some cases wet-smoothing resulted in "self-slipping." More elaborate

Table 5.1. *YHSS 10-8 Late Bronze Age ceramic forms, finishes, fabric, production techniques summarized from Gunter (1991) and Henrickson (1993).*

Form	Finish	Fabric	Forming techniques	Firing temperature	Change over time	Comments
Bowls: shallow bowls, carinated bowls, conical bowls, round and flat-based bowls (sizes: small and medium)	Red slips, self slips, burnishing all rare; MBA painted or incised geometric shapes (e.g. triangles), some fine welt decoration	Fine for smaller bowls, common for remainder	Fast wheel-thrown; conical bowls and flat-based bowls, hand-coiled, finished on tournette	800–1000 °C – kiln	Hemispherical becomes increasingly shallow, carination decreases, slips decrease	
Plates/platters: small (22–35 cm – lids?), large 38–60 cm	Large occasional red slip	Common to coarse	Hand formed	800–1000 °C – kiln	Only found in the LBA (?)	
Jars: variable, globular, cylindrical, conical; with and without shoulder; highly variable rim treatment (everted, thickened, wedged, incurved etc.)	Smoothed or slipped	Common	Small: fast wheelthrown; large: hand formed, finished on tournette, constructed in slabs or with coils	800–1000 °C – kiln	Rim forms simplify over time	Vessel forms cluster in size: interpreted as standardization (Henrickson 2002:128)
Jugs: round and trefoil rims, some with strainers	Smoothed or slipped	Common	Small: fast wheelthrown; large: hand-formed coils, finished on tournette	800–1000 °C – kiln		MBA beaked forms decrease by LBA

111

Table 5.1. (cont.)

Form	Finish	Fabric	Forming techniques	Firing temperature	Change over time	Comments
Cooking pots – bag shape, open mouth	Interior smoothed	Cooking ware (medium grit)	Hand-coiled, bases molded?	600–700° C – bonfire		
Lentoid flask (upcast in EIA contexts)	Smoothed or slipped	Common	Molded?	800–1,000 °C – kiln		
Pithoi: hole mouth and rim-thickened forms		Coarse	Hand-formed slabs smoothed	800–1,000 °C – kiln		
Vats/large storage vessel	Smoothed	Coarse	Coiled and/or pulled			
Small vessels (votive cups, small pots) rare	Smoothed or slipped	Fine	Wheel-thrown and coiled	800–1,000 °C – kiln		

decoration is rare and includes red slip or painted bands, a few with geometric "net" designs (Gunter 1991). "Gold wash" and white slips are uncommon. Burnishing is also rare and casually executed (unlike MBA burnishing). Cooking pot interiors were more carefully finished than their exteriors, suggesting that, at least in this case, finishing was functional (i.e. to seal the porous inner surface).

Production Sequences

Vessels commonly embed evidence of production techniques that can be tied to group organization and scale. LBA potters were familiar with a variety of forming techniques, including the fast wheel, turntable and hand forming by coiling or slabs (Henrickson 2002). Small vessels (<20 cm diameter) were thrown on the wheel, while larger vessels often show evidence of hand forming. Turntables were then used to smooth irregular surfaces of these larger handmade vessels. Rim shapes were formed by rounding or were slightly everted with some reinforcing thickening, and became more simplified over time.

Smaller wheel-thrown vessels, such as most small and medium bowls, were first dried "leather-hard" then trimmed to shape on a turntable and smoothed prior to firing. Medium conical bowls were hand-coiled then smoothed on a turntable. Small to medium jars were also wheel-thrown. Larger conical jars, however, were constructed in stages from separate pieces. The main body of the pot was coiled, and perhaps the neck/rim section as well. The pieces were joined on a turntable and smoothed and scraped. Handles were added, and then the final step was to fashion the base into a point (either by pinching or by adding additional clay). Very large vessels appear to have been made primarily by coiling, and finished on a turntable. Slab construction was used in some instances for the base of large jars. Cooking pots were primarily handmade by coiling, although the base portion in some cases looks molded.

Refiring experiments suggest firing temperatures of 800–1,000°C were attained for common and fine buff ware, indicating the use of kilns and controlled (oxidizing) atmospheres (Henrickson and Blackman 1996). In contrast, cooking pots were fired at lower temperatures (<700°C), consistent with open firing.

Comparisons between Boğazköy and Gordion (Form, Style, Production)

Interpreting and understanding LBA ceramic production, style and distribution at Gordion requires comparisons with both earlier and wider regional ceramic practices. In this section, we compare previous work on LBA ceramics with the LBA ceramic assemblage at the principal

Hittite type-site, the capital Hattuša, adjacent to the modern village of Boğazköy.

Comparing published assemblages of LBA ceramics from different sites, while challenging, can provide insights into relationships between settlements as well as differences in their economies. Here we compare Gordion's LBA ceramic sequences to those of Boğazköy, focusing primarily on Schoop's recent work. Müller-Karpe, and later Parzinger and Sanz, published Boğazköy's ceramic corpus (Müller-Karpe 1988; Parzinger and Sanz 1992). However, the complexity of typologies presented in these studies makes it difficult, if not impossible, to align with the LBA ceramic descriptions presented by Henrickson (Henrickson 2002; Henrickson and Blackman 1996). We instead rely on Schoop's more recent work (Schoop 2009, 2011), which classified forms and fabrics into general categories more readily comparable to those described for Gordion.

Two problems are encountered in comparing LBA Boğazköy and Gordion: the first stems from the difference in the size of the excavated sample and the variety of contexts: abundant for the former compared to the latter. Most LBA ceramic forms at Gordion were reconstructed from rim and base fragments, with period-specific typologies further complicated by Gunter's conflation of LBA and MBA forms; in contrast, the LBA assemblage sequence Schoop studied at Boğazköy was selected from chronologically controlled contexts and included nearly complete vessel shapes and rims, with attributes that distinguish the MBA sequence (Schoop 2009, 2011). Differences in descriptive terminology further complicate comparisons between the Gordion and Boğazköy assemblages. The second problem relates to correlating site chronologies, both absolute and relative, especially for YHSS 10 at Gordion.

In general, both the forms and decoration of the two assemblages look similar. At both sites hemispherical bowls became shallower, with rounder bottoms over time. Decoration (usually red slips and/or burnishing) also decreased over time at both sites. Carinated bowls change substantially at Boğazköy from the MBA to the LBA, while at Gordion this shift is less pronounced. The proportion of carinated bowls decreased from the MBA into the LBA, with rims becoming increasingly simplified over time. At Gordion, rims for small, fine bowls are vertical and thin, while rims on larger bowls are often thickened. At Boğazköy, rim shapes shifted over time, and were sometimes form-specific (from incurved, to shallower and thickened, to more pointed; Schoop 2011:243–245). At Gordion, "inverted rims" (rim thickening protrudes toward both the interior and exterior) remained common through to the end of the LBA. Shallow bowls or plates are common at both sites, but are more frequent in both coarse and fine micaceous slip versions in the later LBA phases at Gordion.

At Boğazköy, cooking pots were wheelthrown, typically globular, holemouth, or with externally strengthened rims, and often had handles. A handmade cooking vessel type, "baking plate," is the largest of the cooking ware forms (up to ~80 cm diameter?). Most often they are made of a cooking pot fabric, also used in the wheelthrown cooking pots. The size of baking plates decreased over time and some late Hittite versions were produced in "Standard Ware." Similar large, coarse plates are restricted to the later LBA levels at Gordion and are possibly slightly smaller (60 cm; Gunter 1991:46). At Büyükkaya, a sector within Boğazköy, a baking plate was apparently installed as the base for a small moveable oven (Seeher 1995:figs. 12–13, 612).

Other jars and pots have highly variable rim forms (straight, everted, constricted) at Boğazköy. Some of these, deeper forms, appear related to beer consumption based on finds from a brewery in another Hittite urban centre, Kuşaklı (Müller-Karpe 2000:328–333). Schoop specifically identifies a funnel-shaped form, which seems to be similar to cylindrical flared-neck forms from Gordion (Gunter 1991:33). Jars in the later LBA levels at Gordion often have everted rims, with some evidence of round and flat bases, as well as ridges for cover lids (Gunter 1991:42–43).

Jugs are present in all Gordion LBA levels; both jugs and pitchers include trefoil rim types, and some jugs have strainer spouts. Gunter suggests jugs become more abundant over time. At Boğazköy, beaked jugs (mainly restricted to nondomestic assemblages), were most abundant in the MBA and become rare by the LBA. Lentoid flasks, always in fine ware and burnished, occur throughout the LBA sequence at Boğazköy; the few that occur at Gordion are from EIA contexts, presumably LBA residuals upcast during digging out pits for houses and storage. Large jars with handles are common in domestic contexts, with thickened rims that became more angular over time (as with the bowls). As at Gordion, conical bases are typical of both storage jars and jugs. At Boğazköy, few pithoi have been found *in situ*, but pithos sherds from official storage buildings appear to be much larger than those from domestic contexts. Pithoi decrease in household contexts through the LBA. At Gordion, pithoi include both hole-mouth and thickened-rim forms, and were commonly reused as burial containers in the BA cemetery (as at Boğazköy during the Old Kingdom; Seeher 2011:388).

Schoop (2011) describes a variety of types of small vessels with S-shaped profiles, including cups, beakers, small pots or flasks and votive cups (small conical bowls and juglets). Similar types are also present at Gordion, but it is unclear if the full range of forms is represented.

In sum, in the absence of comprehensive datasets, the forms found in the LBA ceramic assemblages at Gordion nonetheless look very similar to those of Boğazköy; so too do the trajectories of change in form and decoration. Assemblages at both sites show decreasing attention to surface treatment and red slipping, along with a simplification of forms and rim shapes. The extent to which the frequency of certain forms varies at both sites remains uncertain. Similarly, the variability in vessel sizes and rim treatments is difficult to compare. The diversity of the formal descriptions of the Boğazköy assemblage, in particular, seems to belie claims of a limited number of simple forms (Parzinger and Sanz 1992; Schoop 2011). While there do appear to be some basic shape templates, the range and variability of rim forms, sizes and shapes remains large.

One of the potentially most significant differences between Gordion and Boğazköy seems to be technological. With few exceptions, most of the LBA ceramics from Boğazköy were wheelmade (Müller-Karpe 1988:163; Schoop 2011). At Gordion only smaller vessels were wheelmade (Henrickson 2002), with larger vessels finished on a slow wheel or turntable. This difference in ceramic production between the two sites is evidence of both different scales of production. organization and potentially different skill sets (Henrickson 2002; Schoop 2011). Form size may also be significant, as in the differences in baking plate dimensions.

NAA Ceramic Assemblage

The Sample

Geochemical data contribute several different types of information for understanding change over time and the practices of different cultural groups (e.g. changing resource use, provenience, differentiation of techniques, recipes). The Bronze Age assemblage analyzed here was collected by Henrickson as part of a larger study of Gordion ceramic technology. This section discusses the results of the Neutron Activation Analysis of the YHP assemblage.

Henrickson sampled 161 sherds for NAA from MMV LBA excavation contexts: YHSS 10 ($n = 53$) and YHSS 9-8 ($n = 108$). All of the YHSS 10 samples were drawn from the Lower Trench Sounding Operation 14, while the YHSS 9-8 samples included LTS Operations 3 (1988) and 14 (1989) (Figs. 5.1b, 5.5). Henrickson and Blackman (1996) published the LBA NIST NAA results. Published results for NIST standards (Grave et al. 2013) along with replicate analysis of a subset of Henrickson's YHP

Table 5.2. *YHSS 10-8 Late Bronze Age assemblage used for NAA: ceramic form by YHSS phase (counts and totals).*

Form	10	9-8	Total
Body	6	81	87
Body-cooking	0	10	10
Bowl	9	1	10
Jar	33	14	47
Jar/pot	0	1	1
Pot	3	1	4
Pot – small	3	0	3
Total	54	108	162

Note that there are no NAA results for one YHSS 10 sample ($n = 161$ for NAA data).

assemblage established interlaboratory data comparability, and confirmed the consistency of results between the NIST and our Ontario NAA facilities. We incorporate the full NIST NAA results for the LBA Gordion ceramics here. While MBA and LBA ceramics can be difficult to differentiate from the Young (RSY) excavations (Gunter 1991), the stratigraphic levels from the Voigt excavations were better defined. This makes it possible to compare changes in fabrics and compositional data within the smaller subset of better contextualized Bronze Age material.

Turkish government guidelines for archaeologists in the late 1980s and early 1990s permitted only the export of typologically nondiagnostic sherds. As a result, Henrickson's sample included visually distinctive fabric types, but few identifiable forms or decorative treatments (e.g. Table 5.2). None of the latest LBA YHSS 9-8 samples were decorated, while ca. 25% of the earliest YHSS 10 samples were red-slipped or painted. As noted, Henrickson identified nine different ceramic groups or wares for YHSS 10, and only three for YHSS 9-8. In YHSS 10, the assemblage included a range of wares: ca. 15% common ware, 15% fine ware, just over half medium-fine ware and ca. 15% coarse ware. In YHSS 9-8 a little under 10% was fine ware, and ca. 10% was cooking ware, with the majority being common ware. This latter pattern appears similar to that of the Hittite Empire period at Boğazköy (Schoop personal comment)

LBA Results (see Chapter 4 for Methodology)

The number of NAA groups identified is strongly influenced by sample size (i.e. the larger the sample size the larger the number of groups;

e.g. Grave et al. 2013). In this case, the YHSS 9-8 sample ($n = 108$) is just over twice as large as the YHSS 10 sample ($n = 53$), so we would expect a proportional increase in the number of NAA groups (i.e. by a factor of two; Table 5.3). However, while the number of groups did increase, it was only half of what was expected. As described in Chapter 4, compositional cluster A represents local production and clusters B–D local/regional production. Subgroups of clusters C, D and E also overlap with sediment compositions from Kaman Kalehöyük and Çadır Höyük (see Table 4.4). The outlying cluster M most closely matches samples from Çadır Höyük. The remainder of the clusters, F–L (except K), match west Anatolian sources, including those from coastal East Greek sites and Lydia.

The combined LBA assemblage is notably local in character, with 94% of it matching local and local/regional sources. During all the LBA phases, local group A is dominant, with local/regional B subgroups remaining secondary (Table 5.3). Over time, however, resource use changes at both larger and smaller scales. In YHSS 9-8 local/regional clusters B and C became more important sources, and samples are more evenly distributed across a larger array of recipes or sources. Again, this may in part be a function of sample size and excavation area sampled. The very small percentage of nonlocal samples is equally split between eastern and western Anatolian sources in both phases.

NAA: Wares, Decoration and Forms

In YHSS 10 medium-fine fabrics were dominant, with common, medium-coarse and fine fabrics each contributing about 15% of the assemblage. Common and fine to medium-fine fabrics had different recipes (Table 5.4a and b). For example, medium-fine and common fabrics matched cluster A; most fine fabrics matched local/regional cluster B; whereas medium-coarse fabrics, represented only in YHSS 10, are distributed across a wider range of sources.

During YHSS 9-8, fabric heterogeneity decreased along with an overall shift in resource use (Table 5.4b). Despite an increase in the uniformity of forms and visual fabrics, common wares (ca. 90% of YHSS 9-8 ceramics) are represented in over 15 compositional groups. While cluster A is still most abundant, other subgroups of A as well as cluster C are better represented than previously, suggesting a shift in production, sources or both. Fine wares become relatively rare (<10% of YHSS 10 assemblage), but are distributed across multiple clusters, with limited evidence for a preferred source or recipe. Cooking ware fabric, first appearing in this phase, was made from specific subgroups of local A and local/regional cluster C, as potential evidence of specialization, source preference or some combination of both.

Table 5.3. *YHSS 10-8 Late Bronze Age NAA ceramic sample distribution by YHSS phase with number of NAA groups in right-hand column. Cluster A local, clusters B–D local/regional, clusters E–G nonlocal.*

(a) Counts

	A	A1	A2	A6	A_ol2	B	B1	B2	B4	B7	B9	B13	B15	C	C1	C2	D	D1	E	E1	F	G	Total	#groups
10	28	0	0	0	0	0	0	3	0	10	1	1	2	2	1	0	2	1	0	1	0	1	53	12
9-8	35	5	1	6	1	25	5	1	1	0	0	4	0	13	2	1	0	1	4	1	2	0	108	17
Total	63	5	1	6	1	25	5	4	1	10	1	5	2	15	3	1	2	2	4	2	2	1	161	22
%	39	3	1	4	1	16	3	2	1	6	1	3	1	9	2	1	1	1	2	1	1	1	100	

(b) Percentages

%	A	A1	A2	A6	A_ol2	B	B1	B2	B4	B7	B9	B13	B15	C	C1	C2	D	D1	E	E1	F	G	Total
10	53	0	0	0	0	0	0	6	0	19	2	2	4	4	2	0	4	2	0	2	0	2	100
9-8	32	5	1	6	1	23	5	1	1	0	0	4	0	12	2	1	0	1	4	1	2	0	100

119

Table 5.4. YHSS 10-8 Late Bronze Age fabric types by NAA group (counts). Fabric percentages in right-hand columns. Cluster A local, clusters B–D local/regional, clusters E–G nonlocal.

(a) YHSS10

	A	B2	B7	B9	B13	B15	C	C1	D	D1	E1	G	Total	%
Medium-fine	20	0	5	0	0	1	1	0	0	0	1	1	29	55
Common	6	0	0	0	1	0	0	1	0	0	0	0	8	15
Fine	2	0	5	0	0	1	0	0	0	0	0	0	8	15
Medium-coarse	0	3	0	1	0	0	1	0	2	1	0	0	8	15
Total	28	3	10	1	1	2	2	1	2	1	1	1	53	
%	53	6	19	2	2	4	4	2	4	2	2	2		100

(b) YHSS 9-8 (number of NAA groups tabulated in right column)

	A	A1	A2	A6	A_ol2	B	B1	B2	B4	B13	C	C1	C2	D1	E	E1	F	Total	%	# groups
Common	31	1	1	6	1	23	5	0	1	4	8	2	1	0	3	1	2	90	83	15
Cooking	1	4	0	0	0	0	0	1	0	0	4	0	0	0	0	0	0	10	9	4
Fine	3	0	0	0	0	2	0	0	0	0	1	0	0	1	1	0	0	8	7	5
Total	35	5	1	6	1	25	5	1	1	4	13	2	1	1	4	1	2	108	100	17
%	32	5	1	6	1	23	5	1	1	4	12	2	1	1	4	1	2	100		

Table 5.5. *YHSS 10 Late Bronze Age. Decoration by NAA group. (YHSS 9-8 sample undecorated). Cluster A local, clusters B–D local/regional, clusters E–G nonlocal groups.*

	A	B2	B7	B9	B13	B15	C	C1	D	D1	E1	G	Total	%
None	18	3	9	1	1	0	2	1	2	1	0	1	39	74
Red paint	1	0	0	0	0	0	0	0	0	0	0	0	1	2
Red slip	9	0	1	0	0	2	0	0	0	0	1	0	13	25
Total	28	3	10	1	1	2	2	1	2	1	1	1	53	100

The limited use of decoration constrains interpretation of decorative styles. During YHSS 10 the only decoration present is red paint and slip, with a small amount of burnishing (Table 5.5); the YHSS 9-8 assemblage is undecorated. Red slips are most common on bowls and small pots. Most decorated samples are locally produced, group A, with a few local/regional examples (B subgroups) and one import (E1). The YHSS 10 undecorated sample is almost equally split between local and local/regional supply, with one exotic match with western Anatolia (group G).

Despite the overall dominance of local group A in both phases of the LBA (Table 5.3), individual forms have quite disparate distributions. Jars are best represented in both phases (Table 5.2); in YHSS 10 they are equally distributed between local A and local/regional clusters B and C, while in YHSS 9-8 local/regional B becomes much more common (Table 5.6). In YHSS 10, on the other hand, bowls are strongly matched with local group A.

Summary

While forms and styles vary between YHSS 10 and YHSS 9-8, there is continuity in the two main sources used, local cluster A and local/regional cluster B. Within the local catchment multiple new sources or recipes were adopted in YHSS 9-8. The general range of nonlocal sources is also similar in both periods, but once again, preferences for specific sources and recipes shifted.

The overall abundance of fine ware decreases, and the preferential use of local/regional group B sources in YHSS 10 for fine wares is no longer evident in the YHSS 9-8 bowl sample. The increased frequency of C subgroups, potentially including regional matches further east (see Table 4.4), is consonant with strengthening ties among north-central Anatolian communities during the Hittite Empire period. The introduction of special cooking fabrics in YHSS 9-8 includes equal preference for both local and local/regional sources. The YHSS 9-8 uniformity in fabric

Table 5.6. *YHSS 10-8 Late Bronze Age. Forms by NAA group (in percent). Forms are sorted by abundance, with the most abundant forms at the top of each table (see Table 5.1). Cluster A local, clusters B–D local/regional, clusters E–G nonlocal groups.*

(a) YHSS 10 (%)

	A	B2	B7	B9	B13	B15	C	C1	D	D1	E1	G	Total
Jar	44	9	16	3	3	3	6	3	6	3	0	3	100
Bowl	67	0	22	0	0	11	0	0	0	0	0	0	100
Body	83	0	0	0	0	0	0	0	0	0	17	0	100
Pot	33	0	67	0	0	0	0	0	0	0	0	0	100
Pot – small	67	0	33	0	0	0	0	0	0	0	0	0	100

(b) YHSS 9-8 (%)

	A	A1	A2	A6	A_ol2	B	B1	B2	B4	B13	C	C1	C2	D1	E	E1	F	Total
Body	41	1	1	7	1	23	0	0	1	2	10	2	1	1	4	1	1	100
Jar	7	0	0	0	0	29	36	0	0	14	7	0	0	0	0	0	7	100
Body cooking	10	40	0	0	0	0	0	10	0	0	40	0	0	0	0	0	0	100
Bowl	0	0	0	0	0	100	0	0	0	0	0	0	0	0	0	0	0	100
Jar/pot	0	0	0	0	0	100	0	0	0	0	0	0	0	0	0	0	0	100
Pot	0	0	0	0	0	0	0	0	0	0	0	0	0	0	100	0	0	100

and simplicity in forms is only partially mirrored in the compositional clusters. Specialization is suggested with the development of specific cooking fabrics. However, while some sources or recipes dominate, the use of multiple sources for each form suggests production by multiple groups. In both periods, the relatively large number of local/regional jar sources suggest goods were moving around the local region, and this increased during YHSS 9-8. The distribution of sources also changed.

If work groups were specializing in particular forms or wares, we might expect to see stronger correlations between fabrics and compositional groups. However, YHSS 9-8 common-ware fabrics, as noted, occur across multiple local, local/regional and exotic compositional clusters. Medium-coarse fabrics in YHSS 10 show a similar diversity.

Production, Consumption and Distribution

To draw inferences about the nature and behavior of LBA groups at Gordion, we integrate both ceramic and nonceramic data, through the perspectives of production, consumption and distribution.

Group Formation and Production

Nonceramic Evidence for Production and Group Formation

Evidence for LBA production at Gordion is restricted to domestic structures (YHSS 9-8), and food, ceramics, and lithics from domestic and mortuary (YHSS 10) contexts. A few pieces of slag and possible ore (YHSS 9-8) may indicate metalworking. Most of this evidence currently points to household-scale production. However, a few key indicators suggest the presence of larger groups, as well as larger spheres of integration and interaction.

People built houses from materials obtained well beyond the site's immediate catchment. Two types of houses, mudbrick (YHSS 9) and stone with wood (YHSS 8) required different resources and organization. The semisubterranean house in YHSS 8 included both stone and wood in its superstructure, based on postholes at each end of the stone foundations. Juniper, pine and oak are the most abundant local arboreal species, with juniper and pine the most abundant charcoal found on site in the LBA. Pine and juniper wood suitable for construction were located some distance away from the site (15–50 km), suggesting coordination of labor in timber harvesting, transport, seasoning and processing (N. F. Miller 2010). Interaction with communities and groups adjacent, and likely controlling access, to these sources may also be inferred.

As food production is one of the core activities in preindustrial societies, the balance of subsistence vs. surplus production is a key element in the creation of group differentiation and the maintenance of different types of groups. Not surprisingly, in this limited domestic context subsistence food production is primarily household-based. Surplus production involves individuals and groups in the more complex logistics of redistribution, management and storage. LBA Gordion has thus far produced little direct evidence of surplus production. Evidence for food preparation and storage includes cylindrical pits of various sizes associated with houses in both the LTS and Young's Megaron 10 sounding. Groundstone tools including grinding slabs, handstones, and pounding stones were associated with the only well-documented house (CBH) and nearby storage pits (Voigt 1994). A range of flint/chert blades and bladelets indicate an ongoing reliance on the production of lithic tools in the LBA, likely related to food production and processing (harvesting, threshing, butchering, etc.). Specific sources for these lithics have not been identified, but a chert outcrop is located ~5 km east of Gordion, and debitage from tool production is common in household deposits.

The subsistence economy of LBA Gordion integrated pastoralism and dry farming (N. F. Miller et al. 2009), probably involving cooperation of an extended family or household for activities such as moving herds. Particular activities within the annual agricultural cycle (e.g. harvesting, threshing, etc.), were probably undertaken by groups within the community. Currently, there is no clear evidence that local Bronze Age farmers irrigated their fields, although water control at this time is known from other regions in Anatolia (e.g. Müller-Karpe 2009).

While the source of most carbonized seed remains recovered on site appears to be secondary (i.e. from animal dung used as fuel), seed type and proportion can still be used to infer patterns of local land use (N. F. Miller 2010). In the LBA, barley dominates the assemblage, with wheat a close second (bread wheat, emmer and einkorn). Minor components included bitter vetch and lentils. N. F. Miller (2010:64) notes that barley may have been used to provision animals as well as people. Sheep and goat dominated the pastoral economy, with cattle a distant third (N. F. Miller et al. 2009).

Hittite texts describe tribute imposed on rural settlements. Foods in particular were required as Hittite cult offerings and for seasonal and annual festivals (Cammarosano 2018). Agricultural surpluses would be one form of potential tribute from regional LBA sites such as Gordion, along with providing labor or goods such as textiles. However, the limited LBA excavations recovered no large storage areas or grain silos, present at some Hittite sites (Fairbairn and Omura 2005; Müller-Karpe

2009). Storage pits and sherds from pithoi found within the Gordion house suggest domestic storage of local crops and goods (Gunter 1991; Voigt 2013).

As noted earlier, LBA settlement dynamics in the area around Gordion include a decrease in the number of small villages compared to the MBA. Land use beyond a 5 km radius of Gordion also appears to have changed significantly, becoming more strongly pastoral, potentially an adaptation to drought in the LBA (N. Roberts et al. 2016). On the other hand, it is possible that subsequent large-scale Phrygian earthmoving within and around the town, and Iron Age land use more generally, adversely impacted LBA deposits in the immediate environs of the site (see Chapters 7 and 8). Subsequent erosion and alluviation may also have played a role in further obscuring the record (Marsh and Kealhofer 2014).

While other artifacts recovered from the Lower Trench and Megaron 10 Soundings relate to production, none suggest a scale of production beyond the household or small workshop. A bone awl may have been used for working leather or heavy textiles. Both worked antler and bone, and bone bosses, both partial and complete, indicate production of objects for status/identity differentiation (Fig. 5.12). Spindle whorls of terracotta and stone and a single terracotta loom weight document household textile production, and recovery of a needle suggests domestic mending or making clothing. The frequency of other artifacts (e.g. metal pins and points), for which we have little evidence of manufacture (e.g. slag fragments), are still abundant enough to suggest local production.

Ceramic Production and Groups

We use categories defined by Costin (1991) and Rice (2015) to organize our discussion of ceramic production (see discussion in Chapter 4).

<u>Scale of production</u> From the analysis of LBA pottery (summarized above), Henrickson (1993, 2002) argued that the forms, level of standardization (uniformity and simplicity of the pottery forms and decoration) and production techniques (the use of the potter's wheel as well as kiln firing) indicate the operation of large-scale, specialist workshops for mass production.

<u>Uniformity of output</u> Henrickson characterization of the YHSS 9-8 assemblage as standardized and mass-produced appears to be mainly based on the relative simplicity of forms, lack of decoration and uniformity of the visual fabric. As yet, no metric studies have evaluated the extent to which individual forms were standard(ized) in size or shape (e.g. Roux 2003). Compared with assemblages both before and after the last phase of the LBA, NCA ceramics appear relatively uniform (Glatz 2016a).

126   Ancient Gordion

Fig. 5.12 Late Bronze Age YHSS 8 bone bosses and unfinished products. One of the finished pieces was found on the floor of the CBH Structure, as were two of the unfinished blanks; the rest of the bosses and blanks along with the bone tool came from storage pits located near the CBH Structure.
(a) Finished products: YHSF 89-248, 89-269, 88-140.

(b) Blanks retaining thin ridges from manufacture on lathe, and bone tool with chipped tip: YHSF 89-274, 277, 419, 433, 455.
Source: Image nos. 89-1076:004, 89-1074:004, L. Foos, courtesy University of Pennsylvania Museum, Gordion Project Archives.

Kinds and quantities of output Henrickson speculates that the scale of production, at odds with purely local needs, may reflect pressures to supply a larger region. However, as local NCA ceramics were rare in the surrounding region surveyed by the Gordion Regional Survey, any such surpluses, if they existed, must have been exported to more distant populations.

Location, number and spatial proximity of producers and consumers The NAA compositional data supports a scenario for the emergence of multiple local pottery work groups during the LBA, consistent with the interpretation of larger-scale production exceeding local needs (Henrickson and Blackman 1996). Additionally, the presence of jars from the wider region also suggests integration with, and operation of, an extended regional economy by this time.

Production location/numbers/spatial proximity The limited area of BA excavations at Gordion provides no direct evidence of ceramic production. Henrickson and Blackman (1996) analyzed 62 clay samples from in and around the site (1 km radius) and concluded that the LBA ceramics were made predominantly from adjacent, relatively homogenous, alluvial clays. Our NAA sediment data support this conclusion and also indicate that much of the assemblage studied was local. Workshop facilities and/or kilns may well have been located on the periphery of the settlement to facilitate movement of raw materials (clay, temper, fuel) and provide space to store both vessels in production and materials. Keeping smoke from industrial activity out of the settlement would be another advantage to a peripheral, downwind location. If so, specialized groups within the community with specific resource requirements may also have been spatially segregated.

Skill level A relatively simple, undecorated ceramic assemblage with few forms appears undemanding in terms of expertise. However, while little time was invested in producing individual vessels, the creation of some wheel-thrown vessels, as well as uniform vessel types and sizes suggests a level of technical proficiency that required development and cultural transmission. Similarly, producing uniform kiln-fired products also involves a separate, specialized pyrotechnological skill base. If a reflection of full-time rather than part-time specialists, this would also demand group interdependence and a reliance on exchanges to meet subsistence and other resource needs. Coordinating production within and between communities also would have facilitated group formation both in the settlement and across the wider catchment.

Technological investment LBA ceramics document investment in a variety of installations and tools: fast wheel, tournette and kilns. Storage and processing areas were also required, as well as fuel acquisition, and distribution networks (roads) both within and between settlements.

Current evidence suggests that all NCA settlements across Anatolia produced ceramics.

Summary: Producing Groups
Most of the archaeological evidence from LBA Gordion indicates that production occurred in household and/or extended family groups. The restricted scale of excavations undoubtedly hampers our understanding of production scale and specialization. The probable loss of the highest part of the settlement also leaves open the question of elite occupation as well as the likely operation of larger-scale production groups. However, both the scale and type of ceramic production provide key indications that Gordion was not a small or isolated rural community during the LBA. Local production of a large range of NCA Standard Ware – distinct from YHSS 10 local production – demonstrates some level of integration into the wider political economy of the Hittite Empire. A notable feature of this assemblage is the general absence of elite styles or forms. While specialization is commonly linked to increases in societal complexity and hierarchy, and the local production style of NCA ceramics suggests specialization, this contrasts with the otherwise limited range of products and the domestic consumption contexts.

The specialized production of ceramics – and inferred specialized production groups – undoubtedly transformed the social and economic fabric of the community. The production of administrative seals and bullae suggests another specialist group, as well as likely linkages between groups at LBA Gordion with those at other Hittite centers. Promotion of interdependence between groups would have created a new social environment for both social and political networking. This environment would have also been where daily practices of power were most manifest.

If we compare Gordion YHSS 9-8 agricultural production data with other LBA settlements, particularly Boğazköy, both the crop seeds and animal bones suggest a comparable set of agricultural strategies. At Boğazköy, barley remains were even more dominant. They occur in food storage contexts, associated with beer production, and in burnt dung (Dörfler et al. 2011), evidence that barley was produced both as a comestible (eaten, fermented) and as animal feed. The quantity of sheep and goat bone increases at both sites, but to a greater extent at Gordion than at Boğazköy. Caprine herding, relative to cattle husbandry, increased during the Empire period at both Gordion (YHSS 9-8) and Boğazköy. However, cattle were more common at Boğazköy than at Gordion. Dörfler notes that sheep were particularly important for Hittite religious sacrifices and this might be one reason for their relative prominence at Gordion in this period (Zeder and Arter 1994:112).

Bones from game animals are few, although red deer are found at both sites, suggesting hunting was of limited economic importance, although may well have had other significance. Thus, within the broad data constraints, Gordion's agricultural economy looks like a lower elevation, more temperate version of the core Hittite rural economy.

Group Formation and Consumption

Nonceramic Evidence for Consumption

Consumption patterns can be used to define group activities that take place in contexts where people are likely to gather to use or consume goods, including food and drink. In contrast to the highly indirect evidence for production during the Late Bronze Age (based on the use of individual artifacts and their distribution to make inferences about production, e.g. spindle whorls and textile production), evidence for consumption is mostly derived from relatively unambiguous archaeological contexts.

Gordion's LBA contexts provide evidence primarily of domestic and/or household consumption, with limited evidence for public, elite or religious consumption. The activities and consumption patterns represented in the domestic contexts include mainly fuel and food, and storage areas/pits to a more limited extent.

Trash deposits and house excavations produced evidence for a rich diversity of animal remains, and some plants (N. F. Miller 2010; Zeder and Arter 1994). The overall pattern of animal consumption most closely matched that of the Early Phrygian period. Sheep and goat dominate the faunal assemblage, with sheep the more common of the two (Fig. 5.13). Cattle and pig use was also higher in YHSS 10 and 9 relative to subsequent phases, but may have declined through the LBA. More beef and pork was consumed only during the Middle Phrygian YHSS 5 period, when Gordion was the urban capital of the Phrygian polity (Zeder and Arter 1994:fig. 3). Other minor contributors to the diet during YHSS 10-8 include fish, shellfish, tortoise, hare, deer and birds, with the greatest fish consumption in YHSS 9-8. It is tempting to link sociopolitical status – integration within a larger state and/or urban environment – to this consumption pattern. However, changes in climate (drought) and pasture composition complicate our understanding of the shifting balance of sheep/goat pastoralism (see discussions of LBA drought; Kaniewski et al. 2015; N. Roberts et al. 2016).

Evidence for the consumption of possible exotic items during the LBA is limited (a small number of glass/frit beads, two fine bronze points, finger rings). These artifacts appear to mark individual identity, if not status differences. In the absence of a LBA elite quarter, the presence of bullae

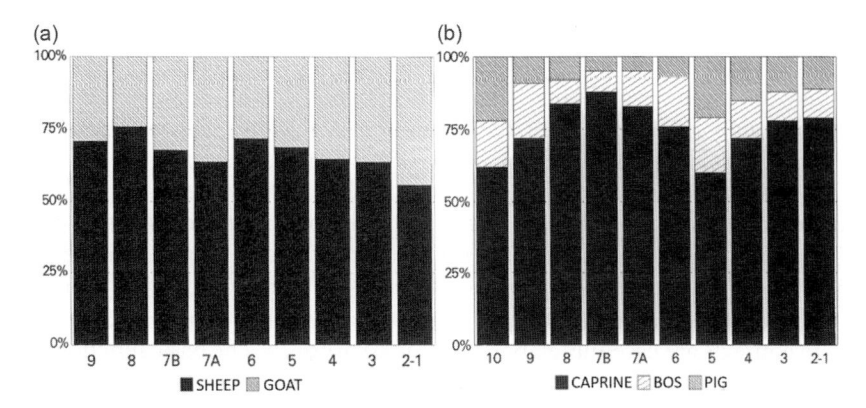

Fig. 5.13 Faunal remains by YHSS phase from LBA YHSS 9 – Roman YHSS 2-11.
(a) Proportion of sheep to goats.
(b) Proportion of major meat contributors: caprines, *Bos* sp. and pig.
Percentages based on number of bones.
Source: After Zeder and Arter 1994:figs. 5, 3; courtesy Penn Museum, Gordion Project Archives, by permission of *Paleorient*.

and pots with Hittite seal impressions on the rim and shoulder (i.e. highly visible) – of non-specified likely origin, but recovered from the LBA domestic contexts – has been cited to suggest the potential presence of Hittite administrators in the local community (Dusinberre 2005). However, use of personal names rather than titles makes this link less conclusive.

Ceramics and Consumption

Ceramics contribute two types of information related to consumption. First, as containers for goods or food, they are proxies for patterns of consumption of other types of more ephemeral goods. Second, through use and display, ceramics are "consumed" in their own right as markers of status and identity, ideology and interaction.

Looking first at ceramics as vessels for food and storing goods, large conical-based jars and pithoi, as well as abundant sherd disks likely used as lids for storage jars, demonstrate significant storage capacity at the household level, as do nearby pits. The relatively wide range of storage jar forms and sizes, suggesting product or use diversity, and jars from multiple nonlocal sources may also indicate the consumption of nonlocal goods. Otherwise, ceramic forms give little indication of specific types of storage or consumption.

The YHSS 9-8 LBA ceramics at Gordion, like those at Boğazköy, reveal very little "activity specialization" in patterns of use. Bowls (hemispheric to shallow forms), cooking pots, baking plates, jugs and jars reflect a functional range of vessels for household activities, with limited formal variation within types. This uniformity, including overall size ranges, has implications for patterns of behavior in relation to more coherent and constrained practices of consumption.

The relative uniformity and limited decoration of the ceramics suggests their limited potential as a medium for local identity formation and/or status differentiation. This is particularly evident in comparisons with the ceramic assemblage from the subsequent Early Phrygian YHSS 6 period where consumption vessels (jugs, craters, cups/bowls) recovered from elite contexts are carefully elaborated (see Chapter 7). The basic functionality of the LBA ceramic assemblage indicates very little household, individual or social display. No other archaeological materials suggest potential alternatives for these roles, although textiles might be expected to have played a key role in status and identity display. At a larger scale, however, the congruence of the NCA assemblage style at Gordion with those across central Anatolia does seem to reflect a coherent, region-wide approach to identity creation and group formation. The significant shift in fabrics and forms in YHSS 9-8 does suggest Hittite hegemony played some role in local production and consumption patterns.

NAA Data and Consumption

Henrickson and Blackman (1996) identified the production and consumption of ceramics in the LBA as primarily local, with ca. 15% of their study assemblage identified as "exotic." Making use of a wider geological sample, the AIA NAA study identified a slightly smaller percentage of nonlocal ceramics in the LBA assemblage (YHSS 9-8 44% local [A], ca. 50% local/regional [B–D], and 6–7% exotic [E–F]). Cooking pots and jars were most often from local/regional sources.

Despite a highly localized pattern of consumption for most other materials in this assemblage, the production of NCA styles and forms, as well as the exchange of these across the region, provides strong evidence for integration into a Hittite political economy. Extensive textual evidence documents Hittite regional strategies that involved provision of services related to transportation, religious festivals and/or feasting (e.g. Cammarosano 2018). It seems likely that ceramics were also integrated into the consumption practices of this ritual economy.

Summary: Groups and Consumption

The limited scale of LBA excavations constrains a broader understanding of LBA consumption, particularly in relation to group formation beyond the household. The patterns of food consumption suggest a somewhat hierarchical and generally well-provisioned settlement, with greater reliance on sheep, cows and pigs relative to most other periods. Patterns of lithic and food consumption also suggest a heightened level of household self-reliance with a wide inventory of tools and storage facilities. Ceramic consumption, on the other hand, indicates interdependence, with multiple workgroups and some exchange of goods, particularly within the local area. The shift from highly variable and decorated YHSS 10 ceramics to uniform, simplified, undecorated YHSS 9-8 ceramics suggests purposeful downplaying of local individual or group differentiation and reinforcement of a wider, more regionally scaled identity.

Based on vessels and animal bone, foodways and consumption patterns shifted during YHSS 10-8. However, the limited scale of these data hinders greater certainty over potential relationships to ritual or political economic change during the LBA.

Group Formation and Distribution

Distribution can be divided into the circulation of goods and ideas (emulation). As noted, we have limited direct evidence for the distribution of goods, other than ceramics, into or out of Gordion during the LBA. Seals and sealings, however, are tantalizing evidence of a wider distribution system.

Two aspects of the distribution of ceramics are important here. First, local resource use shifts from a limited range of local (cluster A) sources in YHSS 10 to a larger, different set of sources/recipes during YHSS 9-8. Creation of a specific cooking pot fabric is one element of this specialization. Second, in both phases of the LBA ca. a third of the ceramics, mostly jars, are from a disparate set of subgroups of local/regional cluster B sources. Within cluster B, resource use shifts substantially between phases (group B vs. B7), suggesting significant shifts in exchange and/or source use during the LBA. The increased use of local/regional group C sources highlights this change as well. A few compositionally matched exotic ceramics are also present in both phases from both east-central and western Anatolia. Unsurprisingly, this combination suggests that Gordion participated in the communication routes between east and west at this time. Marginally more abundant YHSS 9-8 imports from the east may indicate increased interaction with the core Hittite area at this time (i.e. Empire period).

There is also substantial evidence for emulation. Glatz's (2009) discussion of the distribution of NCA material culture provides a context for interpreting the Gordion assemblage. "Standard Ware" ceramics and

Hittite seals constitute two of the most ubiquitous elements of NCA, a pattern that suggests not only the transmission of ideas but also shared behaviors that link groups across central Anatolia. The adoption – or implementation – of a widespread material culture, deeply embedded in household food production and socialization, may have been an active strategy for social unification during the LBA. While evidence of changing behaviors across the MBA/LBA/EIA transitions at Gordion remains generally inadequate, relatively large changes in subsistence and household organization occurred during the LBA/EIA transition. These suggest that external political or ritual engagement may have played a major role in maintaining group identities and practices during the LBA.

The restricted evidence for economic and administrative ties to the Hittites (a handful of seals and seal impressions, and one conical bulla; Dusinberre 2005), indicate not only some level of local literacy, but also group interaction well beyond the confines of the local LBA community.

Conclusions

Although a limited sample, LBA domestic household ceramics provide unique insights into community and group formation at Gordion at this time. While LBA ceramics at Gordion fall within the wider NCA tradition and are similar to those found at Boğazköy, technological comparisons and geochemical results highlight distinctive, site-specific patterns.

If we return to the debate about "Standard Ware" ceramics, and the extent of oversight by state administrators, the data from Gordion suggest yet another pattern of interaction. The use of the wheel at Gordion, restricted to smaller vessels, represents a separate production tradition both in technology and scale, from that practiced at Hattuša. Differences in some forms, such as the baking plates, are also evident. Contrary to the "standardization hypothesis," these differences indicate that potters were not obligated to produce goods in the same ways that they were produced in the capital, as claimed for other regions under Hittite hegemony (Gates 2001; Postgate 2007). Variation in vessel forms may also represent local differences in foodways and group scale. Nevertheless, remarkable typological similarities still underscore the strength of ties between Gordion and NCA communities within the Hittite core area. The precise nature of these ties, as political or economic strategies, remains unclear, but may likely have encompassed a range of integrating actions and policies.

The formal and stylistic characteristics of assemblages at both Gordion and Boğazköy show fairly subtle but steady and continuous change in the overall ceramic assemblage through the LBA, as production becomes more cursory and less attention is paid to surface finishes and embellishment. The compositional data, however, provide a different picture with changes in clay types and sources suggesting shifts in the organization of production at Gordion from the beginning of YHSS 9-8. Production evidence reveals specialization, in both fabric geochemistry and the ceramic technologies. Consumption evidence suggests a regional interaction sphere, likely of goods transported in jars. These changes may reflect fundamental shifts in the relationship between Gordion and the Hittite core at this time.

How do we interpret these data in light of group formation and community? The material evidence documents not only domestic groups, but also a variety of other types of groups. Production groups, particularly associated with ceramics, potentially include additional larger-than-domestic-scale practices (i.e. herding and farming, construction and other types of craft production). While consumption evidence is limited, the distribution of styles indicates networks and communities integrated well beyond the household. The pattern of regional ceramic distribution indicates facilitation of transport and some surplus production, by some administrative group(s). The strong similarities in ceramics between Gordion and Boğazköy are quite different from the regional variation evident in Cilician LBA sites (Bouthillier et al. 2014), and it seems likely that the practices of power and the nature of interactions were very different at Gordion as well. At the macro-scale the material record provides scant evidence for how these relationships changed over time. Nonetheless, compositional data are consistent with substantial strengthening of Hittite influence and control in the LBA, particularly during the Empire period (YHSS 9-8). The administrative evidence during the LBA throughout the Empire (potters marks, seals, bullae, etc.) seems to support this scenario. While there is no extant evidence that Gordion was a major Hittite center at any stage, or had any substantial ritual or political functions, the evidence for such a high level of interaction and consilience in a small regional center on the western frontier remains striking.

Recent dating of the LBA/EIA transition at Gordion provides new insight into the nature and timing of political relationships at the end of the Bronze Age. Within a generation of the collapse of Hattuša, a new and distinctive phase of material culture emerges at Gordion, the Early Iron Age YHSS 7 (Kealhofer et al. 2019). The sequence at Gordion diverges from contemporary trajectories of change in Cilicia and around Kilise Tepe, where it looks as if Hittite power contracted prior to the final collapse of the Empire, with local groups retrenched in what was apparently a very volatile landscape. In contrast, continuity elsewhere in local regimes suggests more resilient community power structures (d'Alfonso 2020).

One of the key issues introduced in Chapter 2 was the importance of understanding not only group formation but also the layering of contemporary, overlapping and intersecting groups, and how these patterns changed over time. While the LBA data from Gordion clearly cannot present an archaeologically comprehensive perspective on all the groups interacting, the current incommensurate patterning (e.g. agricultural vs. ceramic) suggests a dynamic beyond what would be expected if strictly economic factors were in play. If Gordion were incorporated into the Hittite economic sphere, one might expect demands on surplus agricultural production to support the state's cult or religious practices. As yet, the only possible evidence of this are changes in the proportion of domestic economic taxa (i.e. an elevated presence of sheep). The ceramic assemblage, however, reveals a scale and intensity of production and local distribution that sits unconformably beside this domestic-scale scenario. The apparently standardized character of these ceramics is also inconsistent with what appears to be an otherwise locally focused economy. The NCA ceramics at Gordion, and their unique technological style, suggest unusual relationships beyond the local community which challenge a strictly economic interpretation. The presence of Hittite-style seals and sealings, as well as regional ceramics, even in the very small areas excavated, appears to be evidence for the development of wider-scale interaction (and the formation of alliances?) with other NCA communities from YHSS 10 to YHSS 8. This elaboration of specific types of groups highlights the multiscalar organization of the LBA community at Gordion, in stark contrast to the subsequent EIA period.

6 Reconstituting Community in the Early Iron Age
The Early Iron Age YHSS 7 1150–900 BCE

Introduction

The early twelfth century BCE collapse of the Hittite Empire transformed cultural landscapes across Anatolia (Sams 2011a). These changes have variously been interpreted as the disruptive result of incoming groups, drought, local responses to a volatile political environment, either by themselves or in combination (Genz 2011; Kaniewski et al. 2015; Voigt 2011). In some regions, sites were abandoned or destroyed, while in others community organization was substantially altered. Gordion was occupied continuously through this transition, but the Early Iron Age (EIA YHSS 7) community's material culture and social organization is marked by profound changes across a variety of spheres (i.e. ceramics, foodways, and house and storage structures).

The excavated EIA settlement included domestic structures of more or less similar construction, form, size and contents, suggesting a community in which the household was a primary social and economic unit. This reconstruction is, however, based on a sector of the EIA settlement that does not include the central high mound, levelled in the Early Phrygian period, but that likely existed during BA and EIA times. In some ways, our limited archaeological window makes the substantial shifts we see within the EIA community even more significant, with evidence of group creation beyond the domestic scale during this phase.

Over the course of 250 years (1150–900 BCE) the EIA inhabitants of Gordion redefined or established new groups. By the late tenth century BCE the emergence of an integrated Early Phrygian community in turn initiated entirely new and more complex social and political configurations markedly different from their Bronze Age or EIA predecessors (Voigt 2011, 2013; Voigt and Kealhofer in press). In this chapter, we explore the materialization of group dynamics during the EIA (YHSS 7) phase and suggest that changes in ceramic production presage the rapidly emergent complexity of the subsequent EP period (YHSS 6).

Transforming Identities: From Collapse to Community in Anatolia

The Early Iron Age represents one of the most enigmatic archaeological phases in Anatolian prehistory, in part because it has been overshadowed by two more dominant fields of archaeological research. In inland Anatolia archaeologists have typically focused on periods of emerging sociopolitical complexity (i.e. the Bronze Age). In contrast, coastal zones have received greatest archaeological attention from Classical archaeologists due to the historically attested mid first millennium BCE sites that are contemporary with, or directly affected by, Greek colonization. Between these two sets of interests, Iron Age dynamics in both regions have often been ignored. Beyond Gordion, interest in Iron Age developments of the interior, in the areas that became Phrygia and Urartu, is comparatively recent (Çilingiroğlu and French 1991, 1994; d'Alfonso 2012; Smith 2006; Zimansky 2011).

A second challenge for EIA archaeology in central Anatolia is the nature of the archaeological record itself. EIA settlements across the region (e.g. Gordion, Kaman Kalehöyük and Büyükkale at Boğazköy) were heavily churned by Iron Age domestic practices: excavation of storage pits and construction of semisubterranean habitations that can render EIA archaeology taphonomically complex and difficult to interpret (Kealhofer and Grave 2011).

Further complicating our understanding of the LBA–EIA transition is a growing recognition that the collapse of the Hittite Empire impacted regions across Anatolia in disparate ways (see Fig. 7.1; Sams 2011a). To the southeast, city-states in northern Syria and southern Anatolia developed along very different political and economic trajectories, while still maintaining linguistic and symbolic links to LBA Hittite ideology and imagery until the ninth century BCE (e.g. d'Alfonso 2020; Manuelli 2012; Mora and d'Alfonso 2012; Porter 2016). Although smaller in scale than the Hittite Empire, these centers were prominent in the political landscape of the larger region of the Levant and south-central Anatolia during the EIA. Coastal centers bore the brunt of changes in power relations, with inland Levantine sites seemingly more insulated from LBA/EIA discontinuities (Porter 2016).

In eastern Anatolia, the collapse of the Hittite core left little material trace, and archaeologists struggle to differentiate LBA from EIA cultures (Khatchadourian 2011). In the Van region, sites dating to the earliest Iron Age have yet to be securely identified. While textual evidence portrays the Urartian kings as emergent, powerful agents of political expansion in the mid ninth century BCE, archaeological evidence presents a less definitive picture due to a combination of competing dating frameworks and the complex political affiliations of the period (A. T. Smith 2003). Urartian hilltop fortress sites also often sit somewhat unconformably within a landscape of lowland centers with different ceramic traditions. Further west in the area near Erzurum, while chronology remains problematic, the LBA/IA transition appears more pronounced (e.g. major changes in ceramics), with greater evidence for the impact of Hittite collapse on local societies (Sagona 1999).

For the Black Sea region of Anatolia, as in eastern Turkey, the effects of Hittite collapse and the extent of Early Iron Age settlement remain obscure (Bauer and Doonan 2012). Survey around Sinop suggests some continuity in occupation from the Bronze Age through the EIA (Doonan 2010). Later first millennium BCE colonial Greek sites around Sinop and along the western coast of Anatolia are better documented.

In west-central and western Anatolia political change at the start of the Iron Age is quite distinct (see Fig. 1.1). Recent excavations at Sardis have identified, for the first time, LBA and EIA occupation at the site. Dates suggest the city had monumental elements by the ninth century BCE (Cahill 2020), much earlier than previously accepted. To the far west, along the Anatolian Aegean coast, it seems likely that late Mycenaean–Hittite interactions and disruptions were strong catalysts for coastal community transformation. Only recently have archaeologists begun to explore these coastal EIA settlements (Aytaçlar 2004; Hnila 2012; Vaessen 2014). Multifaceted interactions between Greek colonists and local societies in the harbor towns and adjacent river valleys of the coast in the late second millennium BCE produced several "East Greek" alliances (Aeolis, Ionia, and Dorian Hexapolis; Greaves 2011; Sams 2011a). East Greek cities, including Miletus and Ephesus, as well as Mediterranean coastal towns such as Side, are best known from their mid first millennium BCE remains. However, in many cases these cities also had local LBA precursors (Greaves 2011; Niemeier 2005). The processes by which coastal groups interacted and progressively defined and refined new identities remain largely unexplored, with a few recent exceptions at Troy and at other sites in western Anatolia such as Beycesultan (Aslan et al. 2014; Mac Sweeney 2011).

The evidence for the BA–IA transition in Central Anatolia remains controversial. In a 2011 summary of Iron Age archaeology in this area, Genz pointed out that for this region only Gordion and Boğazköy have a long stratigraphic sequence that is both "well excavated and adequately published" (Genz 2011:333). At these sites there are significant cultural transformations, with new Iron Age settlements made up of relatively independent households, and no evidence of large-scale administrative structures. Since 2011, excavations further east at Kınık and Çadır

Höyük have provided new evidence for the LBA–EIA transition that is different from that documented to the north and west (d'Alfonso 2020; Steadman et al. 2019). At both sites there are elements of continuity in the form of large-scale architecture, but also an apparent rejection of Hittite symbols of power. While there is a major disruptive burning event at Çadır during the LBA, evidence suggests occupation was more or less continuous, with Iron Age fortification walls built directly over those of the LBA. At Kınık the LBA fortifications were also rebuilt and large silos for grain storage were constructed in the EIA, indicating the operation of a complex administrative system at this time (Castellano 2018; d'Alfonso 2020).

At Gordion, little time elapsed between the latest LBA strata and the earliest EIA structures. While there is no evidence of a terminal destruction event, rapid change apparent in virtually every aspect of material culture, has been interpreted as evidence for an in-migration of people. This interpretation is data-driven, and takes into account the need to explain when and how a group of people speaking a Balkan language came to live at Gordion before 800 BCE (Henrickson and Voigt 1998; Sams 1988, 1995; Voigt and Henrickson 2000a, 2000b).

In contrast, abandonment of the Hittite capital of Hattuša at the end of the LBA was followed by small-scale and patchy Early Iron Age reoccupation. Rather than invasion or migration, this transformation has been argued to reflect local community adjustment to the rapid dissolution of Hittite political authority and economic institutions (Genz 2003). Genz extends his explanation of events after the Hittite collapse to Gordion, concluding that there is "so far no unequivocal proof of the Phrygian migration ... in the archaeological record" (Genz 2011:360). From our perspective, this line of argument disregards the substantial differences in process and sequence between Boğazköy and the broader shifts in material culture at Gordion, instead focusing more narrowly on ceramic change. Whether due to migrations or *in situ* economic and political transformation, there is little doubt that the contracted scale of political organization produced a vastly more diverse and fragmented social and political landscape during the early Iron Age across much of central Anatolia.

1150–900 BCE (YHSS 7): Gordion EIA Excavations

Until 1988, archaeologists at Gordion concentrated on the substantial monumental remains associated with the Early Phrygian polity, directing less attention to LBA and EIA contexts and processes of cultural transformation. Excavation strategies reflect this bias with constraints placed on the size and location of LBA and EIA excavation units on the Eastern Mound in order to maintain the integrity of Early Phrygian YHSS

6 monumental architecture. Voigt's excavations, remaining within these spatial confines, provided more detail on the prehistoric sequence, as well as on subsequent periods at Gordion elsewhere on the mound (Rose 2012a; Sams 2011a, 2012; Voigt 1994, 2011, 2012b, 2013). This work is briefly summarized here to provide context for interpreting the ceramic assemblages.

EIA Gordion (YHSS 7)

The total excavated area of EIA Gordion is ca. 400 m^2: 135 m^2 cleared by Young over multiple, discontinuous trenches and 270 m^2 cleared by Voigt in a single area (see Figs. 3.1a, 3.2; Voigt 2002:190–191). The Early Iron Age chronology includes two subphases, YHSS 7B and 7A, defined by changes in stratigraphy, architecture, and other aspects of material culture.

Excavations by both Young and Voigt revealed relatively modest domestic structures dated to YHSS 7B (ca. 1150–950 BCE), that extended over an area at least 100 m long on the Eastern Mound (Kealhofer et al. 2019; Voigt 2013; Voigt and Kealhofer in press). As noted earlier, the excavated area appears to reveal houses located at the foot of a (posited) higher mound. Houses were typically one-room semisubterranean structures, cut 30–50 cm below the ground level (Fig. 6.1a). Walls were made of mud, occasionally mud bricks or mud-coated reeds; the house pits were lined with mud plaster, and in some cases vertical stone slabs were set at the base of walls. Common household features include ovens, hearths, bins, pits and handmade ceramics (Voigt 2011). Because the style of these buildings (both construction techniques and plan), as well as most other aspects of material culture, were very different from that of the LBA, Voigt proposed that these changes were introduced by a new in-migrating group. Later evidence for adoption of a Greek-related Phrygian language at the site suggests these new groups may have been a first wave of Phrygian-speaking migrants from the west (Henrickson and Voigt 1998; Obrador-Cursach 2019; Voigt and Henrickson 2000a).

The second stratigraphically defined subphase of the EIA, YHSS 7A (ca. 950–900 BCE), also contained new material cultural patterns. While still retaining elements of pithouse construction, a well-preserved structure (the "Burned Reed House" – BRH) used more wood in the superstructure and added an internal subdivision (two spaces separated by a relatively flimsy partition supported by posts; Fig. 6.1b). The BRH contained both a well-preserved oven with a chimney or a flue and an elaborate double bin, features that have no parallels in any of the earlier 7B houses. Associated ceramics are wheelmade buff wares in an

Reconstituting Community in the Early Iron Age

Fig. 6.1 Excavation of Early Iron Age YHSS 7 deposits.
(a) The YHSS 7B CKD structure from the northwest.

(b) The YHSS 7A BRH structure from the southeast.
Sources: *6.1a–b* image no. 89-1025:08, 89-1065:16; L. Foos; courtesy University of Pennsylvania Museum, Gordion Project Archives.

expanded range of forms. Other, later 7A houses, more similar to those of 7B in plan and construction, produced ceramics that included a mix of handmade and wheelmade wares (e.g. the SSH structure). The small size of this sample limits conclusions about whether or not the diversity in housing and ceramics within 7B and 7A represents variation within a single tradition.

Overview of EIA Ceramics at Gordion

EIA ceramics were excavated under two different regimes and analyzed by different scholars (see Chapter 3). As mentioned earlier, one of the general challenges for determining the chronology and distribution of EIA materials relates to the stratigraphic impact of EIA pits and construction of semisubterranean houses. By cutting into earlier EIA and LBA levels, the pits often mixed excavated LBA sediments and pottery in EIA contexts. Sams (1988, 1994) notes that much of the EIA pottery excavated during the Young excavations was recovered from Early Phrygian fills in a fragmentary state, making it difficult either to date the ceramics or to understand vessel forms (see also Chapter 7). The Henrickson team, using material excavated in 1988–1989, paid careful attention to pottery joins and focused on relatively complete or reconstructed vessels as opposed to isolated sherds (Henrickson 1993, 1994). In combination with an improved understanding of the stratigraphy, this method has enabled us to better differentiate *in situ* EIA deposits from disturbed contexts and assemblages.

The most obvious change in the ceramic assemblage from the LBA to the EIA is the adoption of handmade, reduction-fired ceramics (Early Iron Age handmade [EIAH]) in the earliest phase, 7B (Fig. 6.2). Within both the Voigt and Young excavations, LBA buff wheelmade wares continue to be found in YHSS 7B. Henrickson (1994:107) argued that LBA NCA-style buff ware was no longer being made in the earliest EIA phase, based on the absence of joins between (upcast) LBA sherds and the presence of complete or restorable EIA handmade vessels from the same contexts. Nevertheless, during 7B EIA handmade pottery represents a small but regular component of most excavated contexts (ca. 5%, with only one context that approached 50%; Aslan personal communication 2020). EIAH forms continue into the EP period, before virtually disappearing after the earliest subphases of EP YHSS 6B.

EIAH fabrics are described as "poorly refined and prepared" (Sams 1994), with "abundant coarse grit temper" (Henrickson 1994:107). Firing temperatures appear to have been relatively low, likely in the 600–700°C range (reflected in a "soft" or friable fabric), and commonly

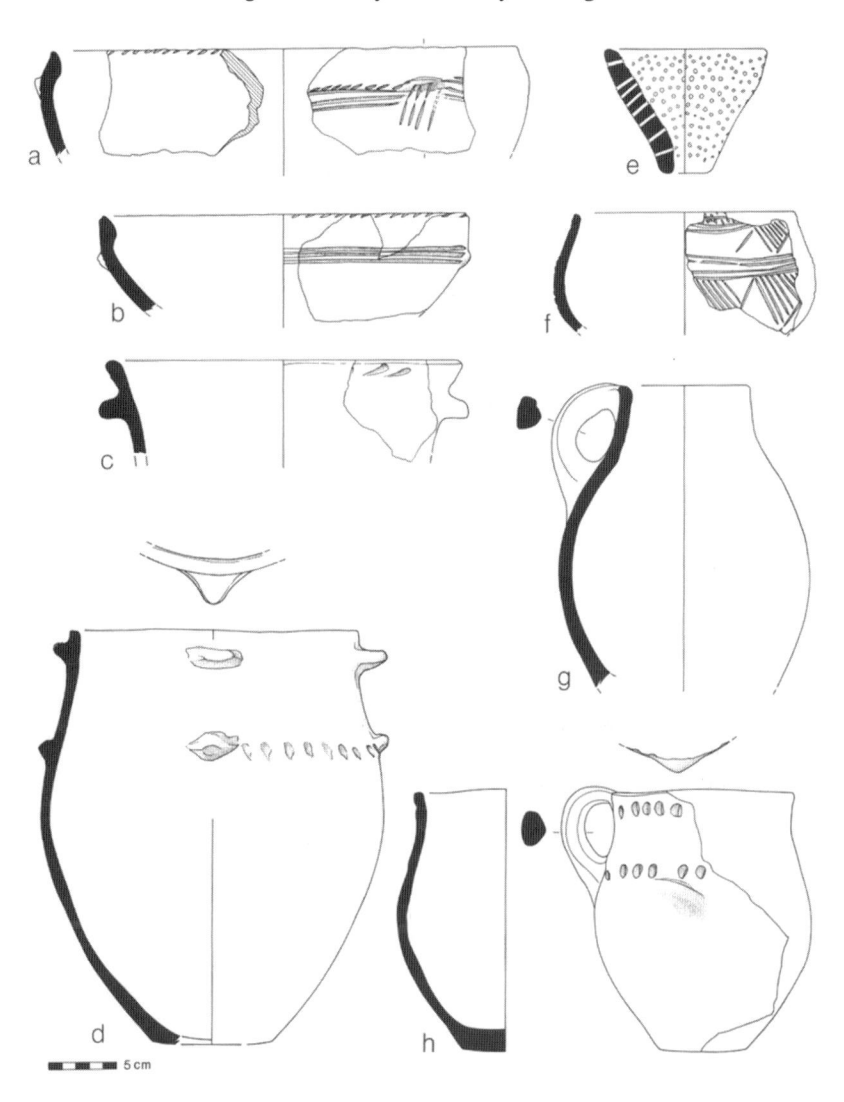

Reconstituting Community in the Early Iron Age 143

Fig. 6.2 Early Iron Age handmade pottery from YHSS 7B.
(a) Vessel profiles, illustrating decorative elements: incising (a, b, f: YH22494, 23155, 21286); impressing (d, h: YH 31661, 28479); lug handles (a, c, d; YH 22494, 23247, 31661), strap handles (g, h: YH 21543, 28479); and strainer (e, YH 23526).

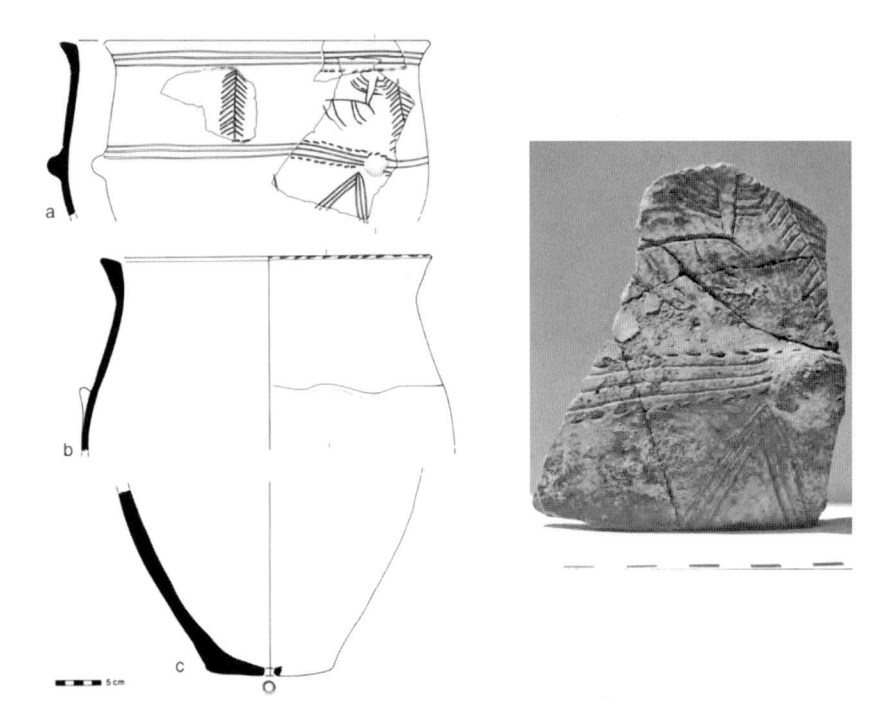

Fig 6.2 (*cont.*) (b) *Top*: Large vessel with incised deer and vegetation (drawing a. and photo right: YH29401); *center*: large jar with incised rim and lug on shoulder (b: YH 20569.9); *bottom*: large jar with hole drilled in base, found on the floor of the CKD structure (c: YH 29391).
Sources: *6.2a–b* D. Hoffman; *6.2b* image no. 90-1008:13, L. Foos; courtesy University of Pennsylvania Museum, Gordion Project Archives.

took place in an oxygen-depleted (reducing) atmosphere. The assemblage includes a wide range of oxidation/reduction effects producing a mix of grey, black, variegated and buff colors reflecting relatively limited control over firing conditions. Closed vessels tended to have oxidized interiors and reduced exterior surfaces, typical of open-air dung firing where vessels are placed at the base of the fire (Sillar 2000). Henrickson (2010) describes forming techniques as pinching, coiling and molding, with secondary forming including paddle-beating to thin and reshape walls (particularly evident for larger vessels).

As the name implies, EIA buff wheelmade pottery is oxidized (buff to orange; Fig. 6.3). While the earliest examples from the BRH were reoxidized in a destructive burning event, all other examples are also buff. Firing temperatures tend to be higher than for EIAH, suggesting

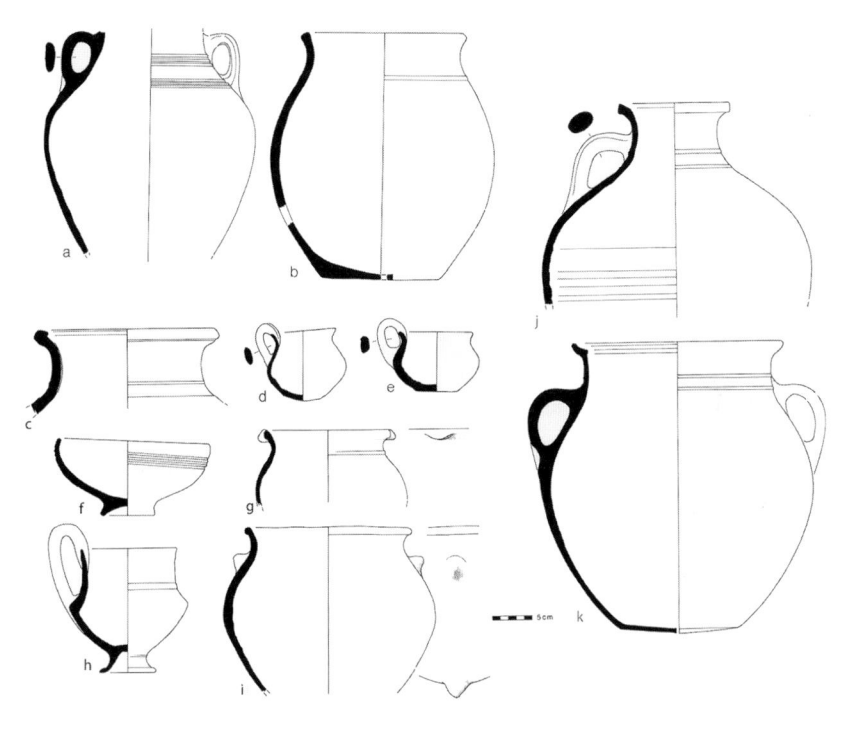

Fig. 6.3 Early Iron Age buff ware from the floor of the BRH structure (YHSS 7A).
(a) a. jar (YH 34305): b. pot with hole in base (YH 33375); c. jar (YH33387); d.–e. and h. juglets (YH 30414, 32457, 33376); f. bowl (YH 30719); g. small pot (YH 33368); i. pot (YH 34309); j. jar (YH 33324.6); k. pot (YH 34307).

kiln firing. Forming techniques included use of the potter's wheel for both throwing and finishing small forms, with hand forming for larger vessels; surface finishing included a range of simple techniques from smoothing or self-slipping to limited burnishing and more rarely, application of micaceous slip or wash (Henrickson 2010).

The cultural significance of the EIAH ceramic assemblage is the subject of ongoing discussion with respect to its bearing on the population at Gordion after the Hittite collapse and the potential origin(s) of both the handmade and the wheelmade wares. Sams (1988, 1994:20) interpreted the Gordion EIA handmade ceramics as derived from a larger, generalized Balkan handmade tradition (Late Halladic III), found in Greece and also at Troy VIIb (twelfth to eleventh century BCE), but specific parallels in vessel form and ornament are rare (Aslan and Günata 2016). Sams

Fig 6.3 (*cont.*) (b) YHSS 7 EIA buff ware: Set of tableware found next to the oven in the BRH structure. Bowl and juglets (from the left: juglet YH 32457, bowl YH 30719, juglet (taller) YH 30414, and juglet/ pedestalled cup YH 33376).
Note the greater standardization of forms in comparison to EIA handmade vessels shown on Fig. 6.2.
Sources: *6.3a* D. Hoffman; *6.3b* image no. 89-102:15, L. Foos; courtesy University of Pennsylvania Museum, Gordion Project Archives.

(1994:21, 23–26, 175–178) also identified some parallels between EIA handmade and earlier LBA forms. More recently, the body of evidence has grown for cultural change and population movement in northeastern Anatolia at the end of the LBA. At Troy, the appearance of handmade ceramics with comparanda in the Balkans (Aslan and Günata 2016), along with evidence for change in "an entire constellation of cultural features" between Troy VIIb1 and VII b2, is now seen as support for a migration from the north into Troy (Aslan and Hnila 2015:191). In addition, however, it is clear that local groups remained in the region, interacting and engaging with new ideas and people (Aslan et al. 2014; Grave et al. 2013).

Shared ceramic attributes between Gordion and the Balkans are limited (lugs, simple impressed and incised decoration), and many of the forms and decorative styles known from Troy are also absent at Gordion. Aslan and Günata (2016) identify some similarities in ceramics and architecture (orthostats) between Gordion and Troy to argue that Gordion was part of a twelfth century BCE interaction sphere that extended to Thrace and the Balkans. Key to this reevaluation are the results of surveys carried out by Turkish scholars in Thrace (Aydıngün and Aydıngün 2013). Based on the distribution of two loosely defined handmade ceramic groups, they suggest that immigrant populations followed multiple routes east and south out of the Balkans; the route to Troy came across the Dardanelles, while the route to Gordion crossed the Bosphorus (Aydıngün and Aydıngün 2013:66). Linguistic links between the Balkans and Gordion support comparably scaled interaction as well (Roller 2011). As already noted, others have argued that, rather than a disruption in local populations *per se*, production of EIA handmade wares at sites across western Anatolia reflects a broader socioeconomic shift related to region-wide political and economic disruption at this time (Genz 2005; Small 1990). Of course, these processes are not mutually exclusive.

The EIA handmade ceramic tradition at Gordion makes the apparent sudden appearance of EIA wheelmade buff pottery in the BRH structure problematic. Stratigraphically, the BRH marks the beginning of YHSS 7A based on a series of breaks in material culture, many of which remain unique to that structure (Voigt 1994:267–270; pl. 25.3.3–4.2). In more recent work, Henrickson identified parallels in production methods between EIA buff and LBA buff ware and considers the two wares "related in some way" (Henrickson 2010; Fig. 5.11). More concrete evidence is provided by Aslan and Günata's reanalysis of Gordion ceramics, isolating a few wheelmade sherds tentatively identified as "EIA/EP buff ware, not LBA" (Aslan 2013). Based on this evidence, we suggest that wheel-throwing stayed in the cultural repertoire of potters living and working in the Gordion region during the earliest phases of the EIA. If supported by more detailed study, these rare finds would be our first evidence that wheelmade buff ware continued to be produced and used somewhere in the local catchment during YHSS 7B. It becomes increasingly visible at Gordion during 7A when both EIA handmade and EIA buff are represented by complete pots as well as sherds.

Forms

The combination of relative simplicity and highly variable dimensions of EIA handmade pottery at Gordion challenges attempts at finer-grained typological classification. Henrickson characterized the forms recovered from the Voigt excavations as few in number but highly variable (Henrickson 1993, 1994). Identifiable tablewares, in general, are rare in 7B (Sams 1994), with some difference between handmade and wheelmade products. However, EIAH bowls are common during both 7B and 7A (Fig. 6.2a). Most of the sample of EIA buff wheelmade was found in the BRH structure (including tableware: two small cups, a stemmed cup and a single bowl; Fig. 6.3b). More striking is a difference in the production of storage vessels, with large and medium-sized jars that are rare during 7B, but common in the 7A BRH buff assemblage.

Working with the RSY assemblage, Sams' classification of vessel forms emphasized continuity between EIA handmade and Early Phrygian forms. EIA handmade sherds (along with large quantities of LBA sherds) are found in fills and pits dated to early YHSS 6B (Early Phrygian) and a few handmade types continued as late as the ca. 800 BCE 6A Destruction Level (i.e. basin, amphora, utility pots and spouted jugs; Sams 1994:175–178). EIA buff ware forms appear to be very similar to those used in the EP period (Chapter 7), and some of the forms found on the floor of the BRH (e.g. ledge rim jars, pedestaled goblets) are virtually identical to Early Phrygian 6A Destruction Level forms of a century or so later (i.e. 825–800 BCE) (described in Chapter 7, the section "Overview of Early Phrygian Ceramics"; Figs. 6.3 and 7.7).

Decorative Styles

Unlike LBA ceramics, EIA handmade pottery is frequently decorated (Table 6.1, Fig. 6.2a–b). The general range of surface treatments includes incision (most common in the sample analyzed by Sams 1994:26), impression and applied decoration. Surfaces were often slipped, while smaller vessels were more commonly polished or burnished, although the extent of surface burnishing is highly variable. Open-mouthed vessels were finished in the interior as well as exterior. Rims, a common focal point for decoration, were often notched, nicked or ribbed. These decorative techniques also have parallels in EIA northwest Anatolia (i.e. Troy VIIb2, Hnila 2012).

In contrast, decoration of EIA buff or wheelmade forms is rare but typically includes raised bands and sets of parallel incised lines on vessel bodies (e.g. Henrickson and Voigt 1998:figs. 15–16). Modeled decoration of rims is absent. Patterned incision and raised bands continue into the Early Phrygian period, and remain one of the principal types of non-paint embellishment on wheelmade forms other than bowls (Sams 1994:28).

NAA Ceramic Assemblage

The Sample

The EIA compositional data set totals 118 EIA samples (of 122 collected), combining results from the two excavated assemblages: the

Table 6.1. *YHSS 7 Early Iron Age pottery decoration and fabrics: NAA assemblage.*

(a) Pottery surface treatments by EIA phase for the NAA sample studied here (YHSS 7B to 7A, with "7all" representing mixed contexts with EIA pottery).

	7B	7A	7 all	Total
No decoration	6	71	5	82
Slipped burnished	12	5	14	31
Slipped	1	0	4	5
Incised – buff	0	0	2	2
Burnished	0	0	1	1
Incised – handmade	0	0	1	1
Total	19	76	27	122

(b) Handmade and wheelmade buff ware ("common") by YHSS 7 subphase.

	7B	7A	7 other	Total
Buff common	3	49	3	55
Common; burned	0	5	0	5
Hearth tray fragment	1	0	0	1
Early handmade all	15	22	24	61
Total	19	76	27	122

majority from Voigt's excavations ($n = 114$), supplemented by a few more from the Young study collection ($n = 4$ EIAH). The compositional data from the Voigt excavations for this period are from analyses carried out at NIST under the direction of Blackman on typical samples selected by Henrickson (Henrickson and Blackman 1996), with a sample cross-validated with AIA analyses. The compositional data from the Young pottery were generated by the AIA project (see Chapter 4). To evaluate change in resource use/recipes over time we compare the EIA compositional data with NAA data from the Late Bronze Age (Chapter 5).

EIA NAA Results (n = 118 of 122 total sample)

The sample distribution of EIA ceramics was equally split between common Early Iron Age buff wheelmade and Early Iron Age handmade wares (Table 6.1b). Just over half are gritty to sandy fabrics (as in the LBA), with the balance as coarse pastes (none are fine ware). In the EIA handmade assemblage, ca. 90% are reduction fired (grey or black), or fired in a variable atmosphere (range of fabric oxidation effects).

Table 6.2. *YHSS 7 Early Iron Age pottery: NAA assemblage*

Compositional groups (top) and phases (left) represented (counts). "7 combined" includes sherds from mixed YHSS 7 contexts (see also Fig. 6.5). Percentages and number of NAA groups by phase.

	A	A1	A3	A4	A5	A10	B	B1	B2	B_ol2	B_ol3	C	C1	D	D1	D2	E	E1	E2	E_ol1	F	F1	J	L	total	%	# groups
7 combined	2	3	0	4	1	0	3	0	0	0	1	6	1	1	0	1	0	0	0	1	1	0	0	0	25	21	12
7B	2	3	0	0	0	1	0	2	1	1	0	4	0	1	1	2	0	0	0	0	0	0	0	0	18	15	10
7A	7	1	1	10	12	0	17	0	0	0	0	8	3	2	0	0	4	2	2	0	2	1	1	2	75	64	16
Total	11	7	1	14	13	1	20	2	1	1	1	18	4	4	1	3	4	2	2	1	3	1	1	2	118	100	24
%	9	6	1	12	11	1	17	2	1	1	1	15	3	3	1	3	3	2	2	1	3	1	1	2	100		

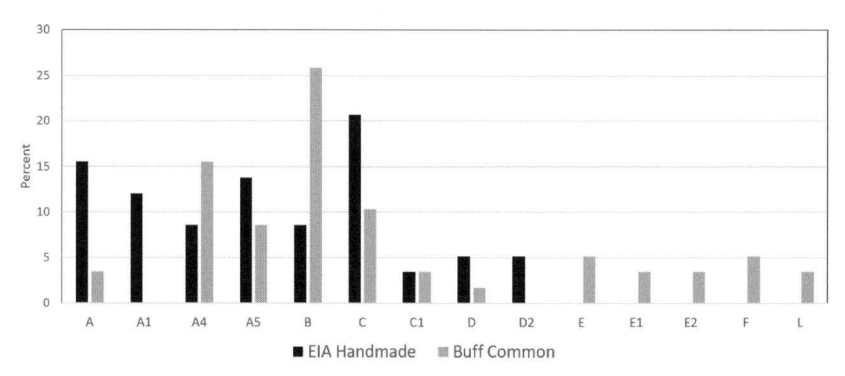

Fig. 6.4 EIA YHSS 7: percentage of EIA handmade vs. EIA buff ware in each compositional group (>2%).

Given its relatively modest size, the EIA sample is surprisingly compositionally diverse (i.e. 24 NAA groups, including 9 singletons). Forty percent are accounted for in local cluster A subgroups (Table 6.2), with an additional 22% in local/regional cluster B. The remaining local/regional clusters C and D make up a quarter of the sample and include a significant percentage of EIA handmade samples (Fig. 6.4). Nonlocal groups comprise ca. 15% of the assemblage and include both east-central (E) and western Anatolian matches (F, J and L).

By phase, the sample is dominantly 7A (67%). Compositional diversity by phase appears to be directly related to sample size, with 7A slightly less diverse than 7B (Fig. 6.5a). The YHSS 7A assemblage includes a mix of handmade and wheelmade wares, while the 7B assemblage is dominated by handmade wares. The most common local/regional sources are typical of both phases, but subgroup sources or recipes shift from 7B to 7A, particularly within local cluster A and local/regional cluster B (Fig. 6.5b).

Handmade vs. Wheelmade

The comparable size of the EIA handmade (EIAH) and EIA buff wheelmade ware sub-assemblages enables direct comparison of their compositional makeup (Fig. 6.4). As handmade pottery likely represents household production, we might expect greater compositional diversity, but from resources within the local catchment. In contrast, the composition of EIA buff ware, thought to have been made in workshops, would be expected to exhibit less diversity. In terms of production origins, EIAH matches only local and local/regional sources. Somewhat surprisingly, geochemical diversity is only marginally less for the buff wheelmade wares, and they generally share the same compositional clusters, although preferences shift substantially (more A, A1 and C in 7B, more other

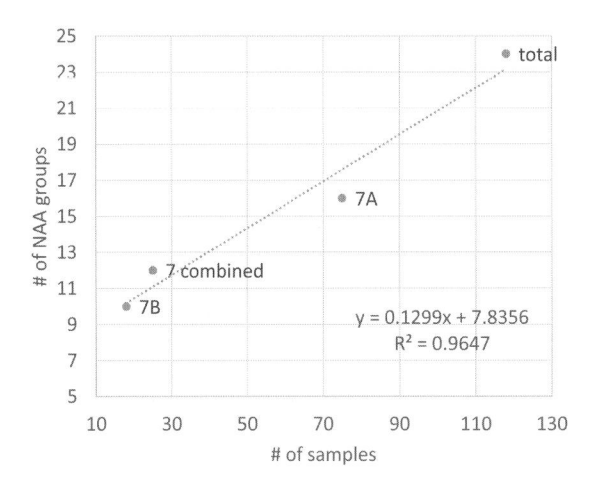

Fig. 6.5 Comparisons of EIA NAA groups in YHSS 7A and 7B.
(a) Graph of YHSS 7. Number samples counts (x-axis) by number of NAA groups (y-axis). Note strong linear relationship between sample size and number of NAA groups, with 7A only slightly underrepresented in number of NAA groups.

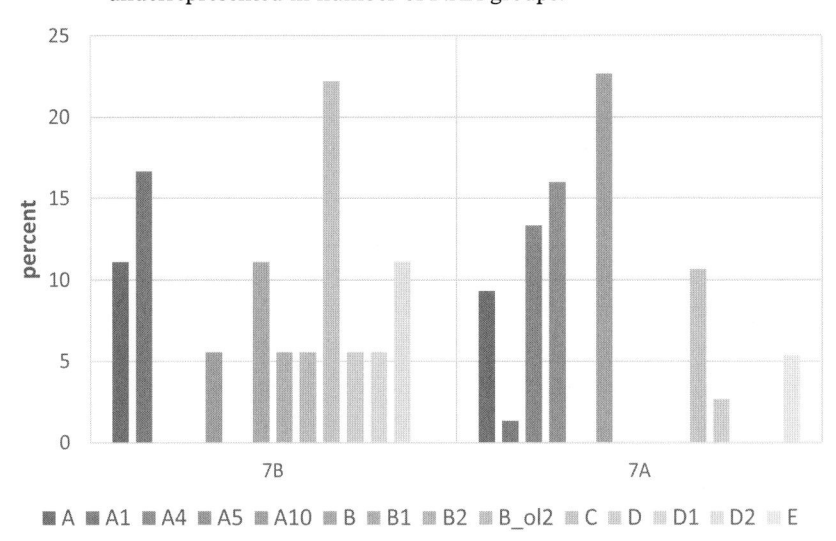

(b) Graph of main groups in percentages found in phases 7A and 7B. Resource use changes over time and is more concentrated in 7A.

A subgroups and B subgroups in 7A; Fig. 6.6). The most parsimonious interpretation of these compositional profiles is that they reflect shifts in resource use rather than changes in the organization of production. Notably, only the buff ware sub-assemblage included nonlocal sources.

Forms

The relatively small-sized sherds and simplicity of the forms in the EIA NAA sample limit any detailed identification or comparisons. Just over half the assemblage is composed of nondiagnostic body sherds. Most of the remaining sample could be distinguished as either bowls, jars, pots or large pots (Table 6.3). Henrickson used the term "pots" in his (YHP) database, referring to wide-mouth, open forms, but not necessarily implying only cooking pots (Fig. 6.2a *h*). "Pots" in a variety of sizes dominate the assemblage, with various size jars the next most common forms. The variety of forms that could suggest additional types of consumption (e.g. cups, trays, craters) are rare.

The small number of identifiable EIA forms compromises our ability to establish relationships between particular forms and compositional groups. Predictably, the number of compositional groups increases with the sample size of any particular form.

While overall sample sizes are not large, source preferences appear somewhat different for jars and pots. Pots are split equally between local A and C subgroups, while local/regional cluster B is the most common source for jars (Fig. 6.6), with the largest diagnostic form group, pots,

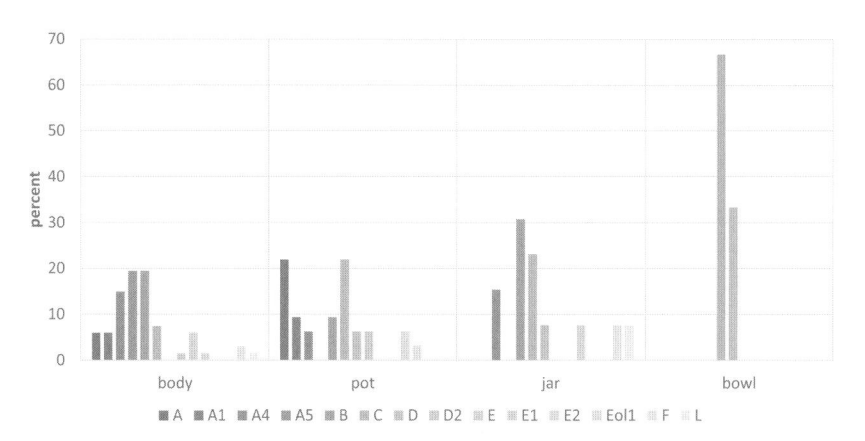

Fig. 6.6 Early Iron Age YHSS 7 NAA assemblage: forms by compositional group. Data are in percent (only forms with >5% of the assemblage are included).

Table 6.3. *YHSS 7 Early Iron Age pottery: NAA assemblage. Forms in relation to compositional groups.*

(a) Raw counts and total percentage per form.

	A	A1	A3	A4	A5	A10	B	B1	B2	B_ol2	B_ol3	C	C1	D	D1	D2	E	E1	E2	E_ol1	F	F1	J	L	Total	%
body	4	4	1	10	13	1	13	1	1	0	0	5	2	0	1	1	4	1	0	0	2	1	1	1	67	57
pot	7	3	0	2	0	0	3	1	0	0	1	7	1	2	0	2	0	0	2	1	0	0	0	0	32	27
jar	0	0	0	2	0	0	4	0	0	0	0	3	0	1	0	0	0	1	0	0	1	0	0	1	13	11
bowl	0	0	0	0	0	0	0	0	0	0	0	2	0	1	0	0	0	0	0	0	0	0	0	0	3	3
crater	0	0	0	0	0	0	0	0	0	0	0	1	0	0	0	0	0	0	0	0	0	0	0	0	1	1
cup	0	0	0	0	0	0	0	0	0	1	0	0	1	0	0	0	0	0	0	0	0	0	0	0	1	1
hearth tray	0	0	0	0	0	0	0	0	0	0	0	0	0	0	0	0	0	0	0	0	0	0	0	0	1	1
Total	11	7	1	14	13	1	20	2	1	1	1	18	4	4	1	3	4	2	2	1	3	1	1	2	118	100
%	9	6	1	12	11	1	17	2	1	1	1	15	3	3	1	3	3	2	2	1	3	1	1	2	100	

(b) Percentage for forms $n > 1$, number of NAA groups per form category.

%	A	A1	A3	A4	A5	A10	B	B1	B2	B_ol2	B_ol3	C	C1	D	D1	D2	E	E1	E2	E_ol1	F	F1	J	L	Total	# NAA groups
body	6	6	1	15	19	1	19	1	1	0	0	7	3	0	1	1	6	1	0	0	3	1	1	1	100	19
pot	22	9	0	6	0	0	9	3	0	0	3	22	3	6	0	6	0	0	6	3	0	0	0	0	100	12
jar	0	0	0	15	0	0	31	0	0	0	0	23	0	8	0	0	0	8	0	0	8	0	0	8	100	7
bowl	0	0	0	0	0	0	0	0	0	0	0	67	0	33	0	0	0	0	0	0	0	0	0	0	100	2

showing the greatest compositional diversity. The correlation between fabric types, forms and compositional groups suggests the potters are making function-informed choices (i.e. cooking vs. storage vs. tableware) in relation to sources and their processing.

Both pots and jars include E sources (east-central Anatolia), but jars also match west Anatolian sources F and L. The nonlocal and local/regional compositions of jars may indicate either that household members brought in jars from diverse locations outside the immediate area, or (less likely), individual households sourced the clay for their pots from a diverse range of more distant sources. Potentially, this represents the import of goods within jars from different locations as well.

Decoration

Just over 70% of the sherds in the NAA assemblage are undecorated ($n = 82$) (Table 6.4a). Of the remainder, burnished slips are the most common decoration (ca. 25%), with incising and combinations of incising, slipping and burnishing each under 5%. Decoration is much more

Table 6.4. *YHSS 7 Early Iron Age pottery: NAA assemblage.*

(a) The distribution of EIA forms in relation to the most common decorative styles (note that four of these samples are not included in the NAA dataset).

	Body	Pot	Jar	Bowl	Crater	Cup	Hearth tray	Total
None	63	4	14	0	0	0	1	82
Slipped burnished	4	24	0	3	0	0	0	31
Slipped	0	5	0	0	0	0	0	5
Incised – handmade	0	2	0	0	1	0	0	3
Burnished	0	0	0	0	0	1	0	1
Total	67	35	14	3	1	1	1	122

(b) The distribution of decoration by YHSS 7 phase.

	7B	7A	7 all	Total
None	6	71	5	82
Slipped burnished	12	5	14	31
Slipped	1	0	4	5
Incised – handmade	0	0	3	3
Burnished	0	0	1	1
Total	19	76	27	122

common on 7B samples than on those of 7A (Table 6.4b). While all bowls and most pots in the sample were decorated, jar sherds were not.

Establishing relationships between decoration and compositional groups (or sources) is further challenged by the limited size of the decorated sample. The compositional diversity of the undecorated sherds is surprising. Compositional differences between decorated and undecorated sherds suggests that there are also real preferential differences between sources for decorated vs. undecorated vessels. While slipped and burnished pots (7B) are most frequently local (A and A1), they are also relatively common from local/regional sources in C and D (Table 6.5). Undecorated sherds are more common from different local A subgroups, as well as local/regional cluster B and nonlocal cluster E. The distribution of decoration between compositional groups is linked to the specific form: pots and bowls are slipped and burnished, jars are undecorated (Table 6.4a). This suggests that "pots" in this assemblage likely include both utility and tablewares.

Summary

EIA potters used more diverse clay sources or recipes for both buff and handmade wares than potters in the LBA, despite the smaller size of the EIA sample (Figs. 6.7 and 6.8). There are clear overlaps in sources used, but the LBA is notable for a restricted range of compositional groups focused on local cluster A sources. In this case, given the differences in production scale and technology, we suggest these source differences are linked to the significant shift in the organization of production rather than a change in source use. Greater overall EIA diversity in clay sources is consistent with increased emphasis, or reliance, on household rather than workgroup-type production with EIA households drawing from a wider region.

EIA nonlocal compositional diversity is greater than in the LBA, while the general pattern of local/regional source use is very similar in both periods. On the other hand, the range of local/regional sources is higher in the LBA. While local/regional connections are denser and more significant in the LBA, a more geographically extensive network is apparent in the EIA.

EIA buff ware presents something of an apparent contradiction. Fast-wheel technology would suggest workshop production and more restricted use of sources. Yet the compositional variation of this ware (sample size vs. number of groups) is similar to that of handmade wares, suggesting a comparable scale of household production with multiple production locations and sources (see however Glatz's (2016a) discussion of "fast-wheel" ceramic production in the Bronze Age).

Table 6.5. *YHSS 7 Early Iron Age pottery: NAA assemblage. Decoration distributed across compositional groups. Note the incised samples are not from local cluster A.*

	A	A1	A3	A4	A5	A10	B	B1	B2	B$_{ol2}$	B$_{ol3}$	C	C1	D	D1	D2	E	E1	E2	E$_{ol1}$	F	F1	J	L	Total	%
None	4	2	1	12	13	1	17	1	1	1	0	8	3	1	1	0	4	2	2	0	3	1	1	2	81	69
Slipped burnished	7	4	0	2	0	0	1	1	0	0	1	7	0	3	0	3	0	0	0	1	0	0	0	0	30	25
Incised – handmade	0	0	0	0	0	0	1	0	0	0	0	2	0	0	0	0	0	0	0	0	0	0	0	0	3	3
Slipped	0	1	0	0	0	0	1	0	0	0	0	1	0	0	0	0	0	0	0	0	0	0	1	0	3	3
Burnished	0	0	0	0	0	0	0	0	0	0	0	0	1	0	0	0	0	0	0	0	0	0	0	0	1	1
Total	11	7	1	14	13	1	20	2	1	1	1	18	4	4	1	3	4	2	2	1	3	1	1	2	118	100
%	9	6	1	12	11	1	17	2	1	1	1	15	3	3	1	3	3	2	2	1	3	1	1	2	100	

158   Ancient Gordion

Compositional Evidence for Changing Resource Use over Time
Patterns of production in the LBA and EIA reveal changing resource geographies. In the LBA, sources are predominantly local and include a local/regional source (cluster B). However, in the latest LBA phase, 9-8, another regional source (cluster C) is introduced, and remains important through the Middle Phrygian period. By the EIA more complex patterns of local and regional production emerge, with shifts in both local and regional sources (for example, cluster B becomes more important in 7A, as it was in the latest LBA). For wheelmade ceramics produced throughout the EIA, source diversity changes marginally, although local production is more common, while specific source configurations and/or work groups shift markedly within local cluster A (Fig. 6.7). The diversity of regional sources found during 7B also decreases in 7A, when resource acquisition becomes more focused (Figs. 6.5b and 6.7). In sum, these complex changing patterns of resource use and modification suggest a rapidly shifting network of interaction and group alliances, accompanied by changes in vessel types, use, production and production relationships.

The pattern and nature of clay sources and fabric recipes changed substantially both during the LBA and through the EIA (YHSS 10-7; Fig. 6.7). In all of these phases, local ceramic production is common, but after YHSS 10 local production (cluster A) accounts for less than half of the assemblage, and generally declines through the EIA. In the LBA, specialized production appears with specific fabrics and compositions

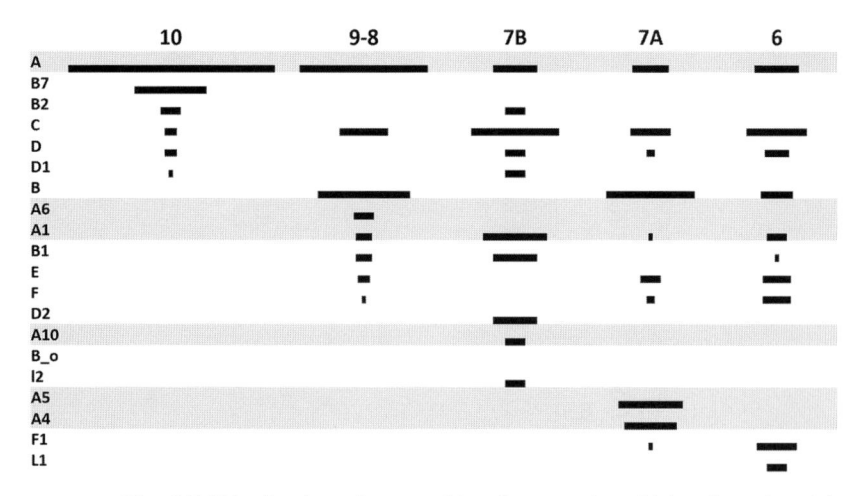

Fig. 6.7 Distribution of compositional groups (*y*-axis) by phase (*x*-axis) from LBA YHSS 10 to Early Phrygian YHSS 6.
Note substantial changes in resource use over time. Local A groups highlighted in grey. Data are percent (NAA groups >5%)

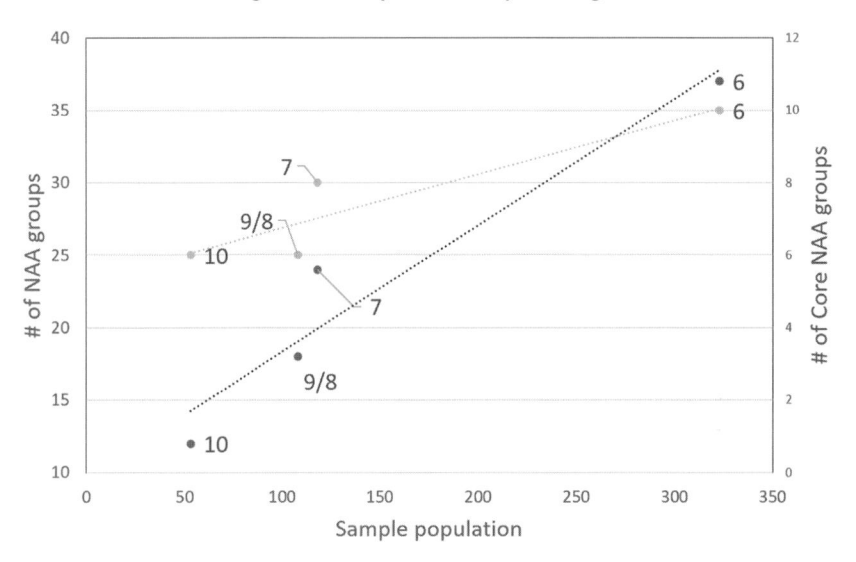

Fig. 6.8 Comparison of sample size by phase (YHSS 10-6) to number of compositional groups (number of cluster letter groups right vertical axis [A-M]; all cluster subgroups left vertical axis).

Note that YHSS 9/8 has fewer core compositional clusters than trendline suggests might be expected and YHSS7 has more.

related to particular forms, as suggested by Henrickson's (1993) work (Table 5.6b). A marginal reduction in sources in LBA 9-8 also supports this scenario, as does the subsequent increase in the number of clusters in the EIA, YHSS 7 (Fig. 6.8). On the other hand, cluster B, important throughout the LBA, remains prominent in the EIA 7B. However, the diversity of B subgroups present in both the LBA and 7B collapses to only a single B subgroup in 7A (even with a larger sample size for this phase). This suggests a complex shift in both vessel types and preferred sources.

Production, Consumption and Distribution

Group Formation and Production

Nonceramic Evidence for Production

Communities are shaped by the scale and functions of their social groups. During the EIA, social groups appear to have been primarily small-scale, functionally domestic and self-reliant (Voigt and Henrickson 2000a), with household units producing and processing most of their own food, clothing and other goods. While limited in extent, the EIA excavated area encompassed a number of production contexts for household food processing, storage (pits) and meal production (cooking). Meal production equipment included bins and ovens made of stone and clay and grinding stones, as well as a highly variable assemblage of ceramic vessels (see next section). Foods produced included cereals and lentils, as well as meat (and likely dairy products) from sheep and goats (N. F. Miller et al. 2009; Zeder and Arter 1994).

Generally, plant crops did not change dramatically over the Gordion sequence, but EIA households produced the highest sheep and (particularly) goat remains of any phase, although hunting was well represented by abundant deer bone (Fig. 5.13). This agricultural and economic focus may reflect a variety of factors: as a response to increased risk of drought and a closer integration of economic and social spheres.

Identification of a pyrotechnic feature and small pieces of slag suggest that household groups also engaged in small-scale metal working/production. A range of small metal items, both iron (e.g. nails) and copper or bronze (rings, points) are distributed throughout both phases of the EIA and could have been produced locally. However, with no known ore sources in the immediate region, metal (re)working might be more likely than primary production. Where identifiable, most iron objects were utilitarian, while most copper/bronze objects were ornaments (rings, pins).

Both loom weights and spindle whorls found in 7B and 7A indicate ongoing household production of textiles. Beyond what is discussed later, there are few clear changes in production activities from EIA 7B to 7A. The only potential evidence that points to larger-scale organization is in agricultural/herding practices and potentially lithic acquisition (if lithic sources were exploited outside the site catchment). Evidence from soundings by Young for the "earliest Phrygian wall" dating to 7A may provide additional evidence of greater organizational scale (see discussion in Chapter 7, Early Phrygian Gordion and Fig. 3.2b).

Ceramic Production and Groups

Potters in the EIA produced both handmade and wheelmade vessels. They used a limited range of hand forming methods (coiled, slab-built and possibly molded; Henrickson 1993:table 1, 1994:101–102). Henrickson characterized the energy expended per vessel for handmade wares as "moderate to high," noting this is typical of household level production of goods on an *ad hoc* basis. Furthermore, ethnographic examples show this type of production can involve multiple household members and be gender-structured (D. E. Arnold 2008). The complexity of ceramic production, involving multiple activities (clay acquisition, preparation, forming, firing) and scheduling, would have further integrated household members and communities through shared knowledge and cooperation related to requisite resource acquisition, production and firing.

Shifts to more standardized forms and techniques (including fast wheel for smaller wares) suggests producers of EIA buff ware may have been organized in work groups (Henrickson 1994). While there is some evidence for the production of buff wheelmade pottery in 7B, it is not until phase 7A that wheelmade ceramic production increases, reflecting the likely expansion of group organization. Buff ware production would have reshaped daily activities and practices, including elaboration of material culture (wheel, kiln, etc.), and involved new behaviors, production techniques and spatial organization. The production of EIA buff ware didn't immediately replace handmade ceramics in 7A, supplying evidence to suggest the presence of multiple means of organizing labor, including work groups and household production.

Scale of production Most production in the EIA appears to be characterized by relatively self-sufficient household-scale groups. Exchanges with other households undoubtedly occurred, as individuals and groups negotiated marriage/kin, labor and goods. Whether or not buff ware production represented part- or full-time specialization, production groups likely also included non-household members (or extended household members), and opportunities for group formation beyond the household. Thus, during the course of the EIA we have evidence for changes and expansion in group formation.

For EIA handmade wares, considerable effort was expended per vessel despite a typologically limited, but dimensionally highly variable, range of forms (Henrickson 1994). Wheel throwing and reduced variability within forms is linked not only to larger scales of production, but to a decrease in effort expended per vessel.

Uniformity of production The increase in wheelmade buff ware contributed to an overall increase in more uniform vessel shapes. This is true not only of forms but of firing conditions: both the increase in temperature and the control of temperature created a more uniform buff ware assemblage, alongside the continued, more variable production of handmade wares.

Kinds and quantities of output The variability in handmade forms makes the types of outputs more difficult to access; however, somewhat surprisingly, there appears to be a relatively wide range of forms even within the EIAH assemblage. This is reflected in Sams identifying EP form precursors in the EIAH assemblage. By 7A EIA buff ware production included more formalized types, including jugs, jars and pots, types often associated with communal serving of beverages and food. Formal diversity is relatively high, particularly in comparison with NCA LBA assemblages.

Quantities of output are more difficult to define, although use of the wheel suggests that output increased in 7A.

Location, number and spatial proximity of producers and consumers Without evidence for kilns or pottery production areas, we rely on reference compositional data to infer the potential number and location of production groups. EIA handmade includes a greater reliance, in terms of overall abundance, on local clay sources (50% cluster A). EIA buff production included a larger range of production groups from local/regional sources and includes use/consumption of vessels from western Anatolian sources. Compared with EIA handmade wares, buff ware production includes a similar number of local sources or recipes, but they are distributed quite differently. Differences in production location (sources) and organization (abundance of use) in 7A (Fig. 6.5b) appear to signal changes in social and economic organization, at least among some groups in the settlement.

Production skill A range of potter skill levels are evident in the EIA. The highly variable handmade forms of the EIA are consistent with nonspecialist skills (Voigt and Henrickson 2000a:table 17.2). However, a relatively large amount of time was invested in finishing some vessels (e.g. burnishing). In contrast, the more uniform fabrics, forms and decoration of the buff ware suggest skilled workshop-based potters, higher outputs and a lower per unit amount of time (Roux 2003).

If the buff ware was produced in workshops, work group establishment and expansion would likely have led to differences in cultural transmission, with more skills-focused apprenticeship and peer-to-peer learning of innovations allowing production to adapt to new demands. Greater uniformity might also reflect an increase in specialization and a need for community integration. The addition of socially crosscutting workshop groups to domestic household groups also likely created new patterns of interaction and opportunities for aggrandizement. The organizational requirements of buff ware production and its continued diversity presages the pattern of group organization and elaboration evident in the architectural features of the subsequent EP period (YHSS 6B).

Technological investment As noted earlier, there is no direct evidence for infrastructural investment (e.g. installations) in ceramic production for the EIA period. During the 7B EIA, domestic production within the confines of the house or adjacent courtyard areas would have required little additional infrastructure. Based on ethnographic data, open firing areas may have been situated just outside the settled area (Bernardini 2000; LaViolette 2000).

Infrastructure to support workshop production of wheelmade wares would have required a potters' wheel and tournette(s), work areas including drying areas, and kilns. Storage for fuel, clay and temper would also require additional space. Given the space and resourcing required, and the new levels of environmental impact, it seems likely such infrastructure would have been at the periphery of the settlement or beyond.

Kiln construction, use, maintenance and repair involves substantial expertise, both in understanding the relationships between design and construction, thermal dynamics, fuel type and packing, as well as in the effective control of firing intensity, kiln atmosphere and duration (Rice 2015). Unlike household-scale levels of production and open firing for handmade wares, kiln operation generally extends beyond individual households to service a wider range of producers, workshops and users (Rice 2015).

The creation of new spaces and places change social interactions in multiple ways (Bowser 2004; Rodman 1992). Broadly, the expansion of infrastructure and internal specialization both in the creation of buff ware pottery and the likely creation of workgroups within workshops over time, would have increased pressures on group differentiation. This would also be expected to result in differences in status and identity for production group members.

Summary: Producing Groups

In the earlier EIA phase (7B), creation of new production and user relationships focused within households is suggested by both an increase in the variety of clay sources and recipes and the changing pattern of resource use compared to the LBA. The archaeological data indirectly attest to the formation and expansion of discrete, more specialized ceramic production groups during the subsequent 7A phase.

The elaboration and differentiation of groups in the EIA, in terms of both production and sources, are also consistent with the emergence of new practices of power and ideologies. Although there is some limited evidence for external stimulus (late tenth century BCE, see section "Group Formation and Distribution"), this process seems largely contingent on emergent local dynamics. As yet the evidence for EIA extralocal dynamics remains limited to the ceramic sphere, where the appearance of buff ware ceramic production seems technologically more sophisticated than the household contexts in which it appears, foreshadowing developments in subsequent EP traditions.

Group Formation and Consumption

Nonceramic Consumption Evidence

Of particular interest at this juncture is evidence for group consumption in contexts beyond the household. For both phases of the EIA, individual households are the dominant identifiable groups. The sequential and singular nature of the YHSS 7 houses and associated assemblages makes it difficult to disentangle interhousehold variation from broader patterns or sequential developments. For example, differences in house form and materials may represent differential access to resources and expertise, ethnic or family affiliations, or changes over time in use. The relatively small excavated sample limits interpretations of the variability evident between these households in terms of differences in status or hierarchy.

One particular 7B feature, a pit with a single deposition of multiple sheep and goat skeletons along with large amounts of charcoal, provides a tantalizing window on group consumption or feasting practices (Fig. 6.9). Associated with the skeletons are two small bowls that could be used for drinking and a strainer, the latter form often associated with the consumption of beer, which may have a floating residue of barley. The presence of EIAH one-handled pots in 7B (WFL structure) and the use of a handmade pot with the same form and decoration in the EP period (TB3; Sams 1994:fig. 5, cat. no. 411) provides some support for the ongoing importance of these consumption practices.

Another unique feature of the EIA period is the abundance of horses in both subphases relative to all other phases at the site (Zeder and Arter 1994). This, in combination with the dominance of goats and sheep, suggests a highly mobile community likely making use of resources from a wider region than at other times.

A few items in the assemblage suggest the presence of groups which crosscut households. For example, bone gaming pieces (sheep or goat astragals) from outdoor contexts are present in both phases, perhaps representing social groups interacting within the community. Similarly, small figurines and tokens (showing little wear) may document shared group belief systems and practices that extended outside the family or household. Glass beads and copper/bronze rings, as personal decoration, indicate signaling in a larger social milieu.

The current EIA nonceramic evidence suggests groups used or consumed most goods at the household scale, including storage and consumption of food, fuel and construction materials (N. F. Miller et al. 2009). However, a variety of other types of social groups undoubtedly created different social networks across the community.

Ceramics and Consumption

EIA handmade ceramics found at Gordion are entirely domestic in character and relate to cooking, storage and food consumption. There is little sign of the kinds of social or status display in relation to either food preparation or consumption that are seen in later periods. No specialized forms were used. The frequency of decoration on EIA

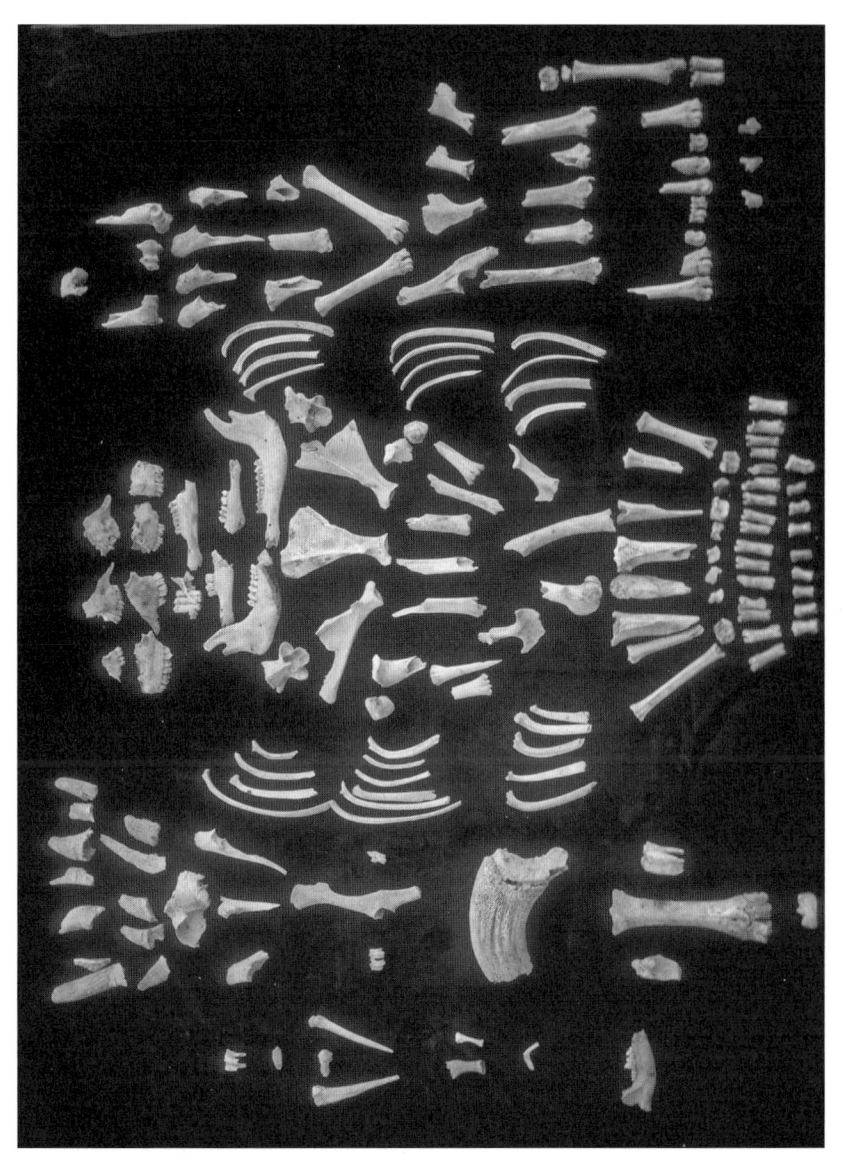

Fig. 6.9 YHSS 7B bone assemblage from the "party pit" (YHSS 730.02).
Source: Image no. 88-1024:22, L. Foos; courtesy University of Pennsylvania Museum, Gordion Project Archives.

handmade ceramics, with burnishing, incised designs and impressions, may be functional (surface roughening or sealing) as well as serving to mark family, gendered identities or kin relationships within the larger community or region.

In contrast, the EIA buff ware is evidence of a very different pattern of consumption. The limited decoration and more standardized forms suggest that household identities, marked through individualized styles, were less important where buff ware was in use. They come in new forms, specifically related to drinking, group/display and possibly feasting (e.g. smaller goblets/juglets, open pots (craters) and larger jugs and jars).

Summary: Groups and Consumption

The EIA community at Gordion was evidently relatively small, but potentially drawn from disparate origins. Nonetheless, during the course of this phase, it appears to have prefigured some of the usage patterns of the EP 6 community. The expanded use of more standardized wheelmade ceramics in a wider range of forms, particularly associated with food and drink, signals the creation of novel social contexts and ways of defining identities. The evidence for social differentiation in this setting also suggests that these practices began within family groups throughout the community. Together these changes reveal that by EIA 7A, the community was beginning to adopt new behaviors and statuses that moved beyond the scale of household or family. However, continued use of handmade ceramics alongside wheelmade buff ware suggests the persistence of variable practices and identities within the community through the late EIA period.

Group Formation and Distribution

Nonceramic Evidence of Distribution

The range of origins evident in goods and materials reinforces the importance of household relationships for distribution within the EIA community at Gordion. With the exception of some ceramics, most common EIA household goods were produced either on site or in the immediate region. Building materials, such as pine, represent some of the most distantly acquired material (ca. 30 km + N. F. Miller 2010). Other possible imported goods or materials might include metal or metal ore and glass beads, Similarly, while the grazing range of sheep and goat pastoralism at that time is unknown, comparison with modern pastoral practices in the region suggests they were also likely herded across a local, albeit relatively large, catchment to find pasture and springs and perhaps taken even longer distances during the dry summers. Even so, cultural activities that typically require larger groups, including material acquisition or processing, and perhaps ritual and marriage/rites of passage, likely provided opportunities for bigger groups to coalesce on a temporary or cyclical basis.

Ceramics, Distribution and Group Formation
EIA daily practices (foodways, ceramic production, household organization) continuously changed from the collapse of the Hittite Empire through the following ca. 280 years. Because the handmade EIA ceramic tradition represents a clear departure from the wheelmade buff ware production of the preceding LBA, its relatively sudden appearance (along with other key changes) has been used to argue for in-migration. As discussed previously, the Balkan region, specifically Thrace, provides the closest and earliest technological and stylistic parallels (e.g. dark, handmade, lugs, incised decoration). These similarities are seen as part of the cultural package brought with the migration of Indo-European groups from the Balkans into western and central Anatolia. The compositional data show that just over a third of the EIA handmade ceramics were locally produced in the immediate environs of Gordion (local cluster A), and all but one of the remainder produced from local/regional sources (clusters B–D). One example appears to match with east-central Anatolian sources, but is a compositional outlier. Similar patterns are seen in western Turkey, where EIA handmade wares were also locally produced at Troy (Grave et al. 2013).

The 7A buff ware, while technologically very different, was locally produced in smaller numbers and drawn from different local sub-sources but also included a significantly larger exotic component (ca. 25%). The transition from mainly local production in the LBA (cluster A), to production from sources across the region, and eventually to an even larger network by the last phase of the EIA, highlights significant changes in social and economic relationships. Regional networks and interactions appear to have played an increasingly critical role in defining new groups and shaping the EIA community; the extension of these to the west suggests rapid consolidation of social and political networks across western Anatolia by the end of the tenth century. An increase again in local production in 7A also signals the emergence of new groups and shifts in group organization within the community.

<u>Forms</u> As noted, the limited range of EIA 7B ceramics as well as their contexts constrain interpretations of the extent of exchange in different forms of vessels. Even though relatively small, the 7B sample includes all of the local and local/regional source clusters present in the

larger YHSS 7 assemblage. Pot forms in particular had a wide source network (Fig. 6.6). As open vessels, it seems probable that pots were transported for their own value or meaning, rather than as containers for other goods.

The 7A sample is larger 7B but with fewer identifiable forms. The small sample of jars, predominantly sourced from local/regional sources, includes a few local cluster A products, with a few nonlocal sources as well, including western Anatolia. Pots, on the other hand, were mostly local, with two samples potentially from east-central Anatolian sources.

The shift in the relationship between forms and sources across the two phases, as well as the overall expansion of source geography in 7A highlights important changes in patterns of distribution. Imported jars suggest the possibility of other imported goods as well. Similarly, the distribution of variability across household contexts highlights the prominent role EIA households played in the larger regional economy.

Decoration The highly localized and individualized character of decoration on EIA handmade pottery suggests that the use of decoration was less related to strategies of group formation, and more driven by household scales of production, reflecting the preferences of individual producers and their families. Nearly twice as much of the decorated sample (all 7B) is from local/regional sources compared with local cluster A. This distribution pattern suggests that decoration or finishing styles played an important role in articulating households during 7B (as seen with pots). For the undecorated sample, local and local regional sources are approximately evenly split, though with a relatively large nonlocal component (ca. 18%). The absence of decoration on EIA buff ware, predominant in the 7A assemblage, appears to signal a significant change in the mechanisms and venues for marking family identities.

Summary: Distribution and Group Formation

The distributional evidence for group formation reveals a shift from earlier LBA communities dominated by local workshop production to household groups engaged in more extended and diverse local/regional interaction networks (Fig. 6.7). Over the course of the EIA both the abundance of local products and the diversity of local sources expanded (cluster A), while the diversity and abundance of local/regional sources decreased. This shift to more focused use of local resources, however, went hand in hand with a sharp increase in nonlocal source use. These changes appear to reflect new strategies for both local and larger regional networks as groups consolidated power at the end of the EIA. This consolidation can be seen in the extension of relationships as far as coastal western Anatolia.

Discussion: Transforming Identities

Most of the material evidence we have from EIA Gordion points to groups organized primarily at a household scale, with some indications these patterns were changing toward the end of this phase. Two types of ceramic evidence reveal a more extended interaction sphere: the stylistic similarities with handmade ceramics from Thrace and western Anatolian sites, and the compositional evidence for transport of vessels into Gordion. How evidence from the (subsequently demolished) high mound or apex of the site would change this interpretation must remain speculative. The similarities with western ceramic styles may indicate migration, exchange and/or emulative interaction. The adoption of more standardized wheelmade ware provides evidence for an increase in the scale and nature of group elaboration and complexity at Gordion. Changes in production and distribution suggest the elaboration of both local and extended group interactions were critical for the subsequent emergence of the Phrygian polity.

With the scale of production significantly reoriented, from workshop to household and back to work groups (LBA–EIA), we also see shifts in the symbolic marking of vessels associated with food preparation and consumption. While we lack direct evidence to suggest that ceramic production was directly controlled by officials or elites during the Hittite period, the speed with which the technology shifted with the adoption of EIA handmade suggests a rapid reorganization of what had been a relatively focused organization of pottery workshops.

Following the limited evidence for redistribution beyond the local and local/regional settlements in the LBA, the EIA represents a new phase of expansion of both local and extra-regional production and organization. Similarly, while the same general core local clay resources were used throughout these phases, specific source or recipe preferences shifted significantly. Work groups, and possibly workshops, resurfaced with the expanded production of EIA buff ware (Henrickson 1994), but their organizational structures (as in the LBA) remain obscure. Differences in both ceramic outputs and source diversity, though, underscore substantial operational contrasts between LBA and EIA working groups.

Unlike the following Early Phrygian YHSS 6 phase, we have no direct evidence to suggest hierarchies or elites existed during the EIA. Nonetheless, changes in patterns of ceramic production, distribution and consumption during this phase appear to have laid the foundation for group elaboration and new contexts for practices of power. These subsequently shaped social and political differentiation in the EP period.

Conclusions

In this chapter we have argued that EIA changes in material culture are likely to represent transformation of community identity, with the incorporation of new groups with disparate traditions and practices (Pauketat 2007). Previous interpretations of both the ceramics and the patterning of other material remains at Gordion have suggested at least one influx of new groups into the settlement after the collapse of the Hittite political center at the end of the LBA (early to mid twelfth century BCE). While many of the alterations that occurred could reflect economic downsizing of production and exchange spheres, shifts in the organization of houses and storage also suggest major changes in what are typically highly conservative cultural patterns. Much of the material culture showed limited change during the EIA, but evidence of ongoing reorganization in ceramic production and distribution signals rapid and complex social and economic shifts. Changing behaviors suggesting group formation are also evident in both food deposits and items reflecting emergent social practices. While some of these are already apparent in 7B, they rapidly coalesce in 7A (950–900 BCE).

Accepting the argument for the in-migration of new groups at EIA Gordion, the complexity of material patterning suggests this is not simply a replacement of population or a reorganization after political collapse. Generalized continuities in animal and plant use, as well as in ceramic technologies, forms and sources, indicate cultural continuity across the LBA political and economic boundary from YHSS 9-8 into the EIA 7B (N. F. Miller 2010; N. F. Miller et al. 2009; Sams 1994; Zeder and Arter 1994). Increases in (deer) hunting and a shift toward more sheep/goat pastoralism, along with the sharp increase in the use of horses, nonetheless indicate significant reorganization and likely spatial expansion of food acquisition and management.

The contexts of ceramic practices reveal how different emergent Phrygian sociopolitical structures were from those of the Hittites. Fairly rapid and continuous cultural change is evident in the ceramics from the LBA 9-8 through EIA 7B to 7A, specifically in sources and distribution. The reorganization of ceramic distribution and production across the region also suggests group formation well beyond the domestic scale. Diversification of specific forms related to food points to new consumption practices, and new contexts for the production of social identity. The creation of new socially crosscutting groups set the stage for layering of more complex, overlapping identities and practices of power that distinguish the subsequent Early Phrygian period.

7 New Identities, New Communities
The Early Phrygian Period YHSS 6 900–800 BCE

Introduction

Over the course of the ninth century BCE Phrygia emerged as an influential power in central Anatolia (Fig. 7.1). At the Phrygian capital of Gordion, groups created entirely new social and political configurations, elaborating and displaying status in ways that contrasted sharply with their Bronze Age and EIA predecessors. The territorial extent of Phrygia has been defined using multiple lines of evidence. Material evidence for the range of Phrygian influence includes strong ceramic parallels with pottery at sites to the southeast (Bahar 1999; Osborne 2020), as well as the distribution of monuments and inscriptions at least as far west as Daskyleion (DeVries 2000). Historical data for the Halys River (modern Kızılırmak) area in the east suggest the presence of a complex political palimpsest of multiple competing polities (Sams 2011a). By the late seventh century BCE both ceramics and Phrygian inscriptions at the fortified hilltop site of Kerkenes indicate Phrygian influence extended at least this far east (Summers 2018), but we know little about the ninth and eighth centuries BCE in this area. However, geographic delineation of Phrygia has not advanced understanding of the organization and practices of Phrygian power, arguably major drivers of political expansion at this time. In this chapter, we consider the Phrygian capital Gordion and the daily practices of local groups as a foundation for addressing Phrygian practices of power.

The interval from the LBA to the Early Phrygian period was a dynamic phase of cultural transformation across central Anatolia. As discussed in Chapter 6, at Gordion it involved initiation of group reconfiguration beginning in the Early Iron Age (YHSS 7B, mid twelfth century BCE), with a relatively fast tempo of change in domestic and subsistence practices, and the formation of new group identities and the introduction of new technologies. After this initial transition at the beginning of the EIA, there is little evidence for significant change in complexity across central and western Anatolia until the last decades of the tenth century BCE

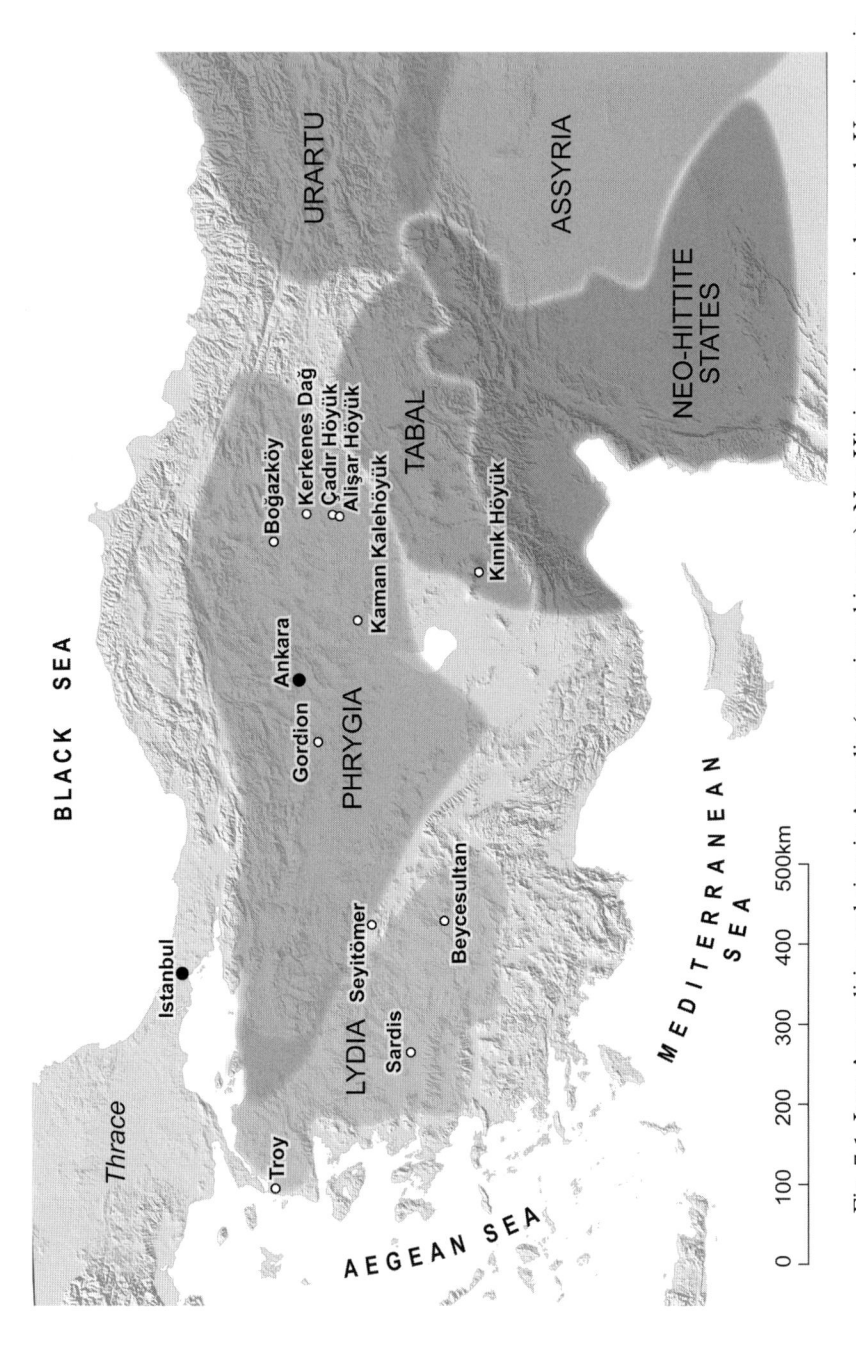

Fig. 7.1 Iron Age polities and sites in Anatolia (mentioned in text): Neo-Hittite city states in the south, Urartians in the east, Phrygia in the central west, Lydia in the west, and Tabal in the central east.
Source: K. Newman, based on Pauly online Anatolia tenth to seventh century BCE, Brill.

(YHSS 7A, end of EIA), when the distinctive features of the Early Phrygian polity began to emerge. The adoption of two key strategies appears to have been particularly significant for EP development. One of these involved the coordination of groups for large-scale public works in the development of a ritual economy, and the other, intimately linked, was the adoption of costly signaling through conspicuous consumption (Conolly 2017). The intensified investment both in building projects and in the production of prestige goods signaled the emergence of new groups and forms of status in the ninth century BCE. Here, we explore how ceramic production, consumption and distribution help explain the creation of these new identities.

Transforming Identities: Emergent Communities in Central Anatolia

Our understanding of the Middle Iron Age (ca. 900–?700 BCE) in central Turkey is constructed from disparate archaeological evidence at a handful of sites. Without an absolute dating framework site-specific sequences and phasing make coherent inter-site comparisons challenging (Kealhofer and Grave 2011; Summers 2008). Using a broad regional chronology, at Gordion the Early Iron Age (ca. 1200–900 BCE) is followed by the Early Phrygian period, the first phase of the Middle Iron Age (see Table 1.1).

Across the region, communities both grew and elaborated new political frameworks. One example is the increasing investment in display and defense, with the construction of fortification walls at many sites. To the east of Gordion, Boğazköy, Kaman Kalehöyük, Alişar Höyük, Cadır Höyük and Kınık all preserve evidence of MIA occupation (d'Alfonso 2020; Genz 2011; Matsumura 2008; Omura 2011; Ross 2010; Steadman et al. 2017). At Boğazköy, a MIA settlement expanded from the EIA village on Büyükkaya. During the MIA and Late Iron Age (LIA), construction took place in two areas (a hilltop "Southern Fortress" and the "Northwest Slope"), and included public buildings and fortifications (Genz 2007, 2011). A contemporary cemetery also provides evidence of differences in economic status between burials. Southwest of Boğazköy, at Kaman Kalehöyük, MIA levels (IIc1) include storage rooms, possibly constructed as basements below domestic living areas (Omura 2011). The two phases within the MIA at Kaman Kalehöyük appear to show a shift in ceramics from Alişar IV "Silhouette" style to Middle Phrygian black polished and grey wares. This change might also indicate a shift in regional interaction during Phrygian political expansion. Southeast of Boğazköy, at Çadır Höyük, excavations on two portions of the mound exposed Iron Age occupation, on the top of the mound (LIA), and a fortification wall in a step trench (EIA and MIA; Ross 2010; Steadman and McMahon 2017; Steadman et al. 2017). With few exceptions, ceramics were wheelmade, and include a range of decoration influenced by silhouette styles and, later, grey ware. Recent work at sites further to the southeast reveals strong continuity from the LBA through to the MIA (d'Alfonso 2020; Osborne 2020), and in some cases show links to Phrygia based on ceramic parallels (painted buff ware and grey ware; Osborne 2020).

To the west of Gordion, a full sequence of Iron Age ceramic styles has been found at several coastal sites (Old Smyrna, Miletus and Ephesus), suggesting continuous occupation from the LBA to the MIA (Greaves 2011:509). With the exception of work at Troy and a handful of other sites in western Anatolia (Aslan et al. 2014; Mac Sweeney 2011), few archaeological investigations have explored how coastal groups interacted or created new identities (Aytaçlar 2004; Hnila 2012; Vaessen 2014). At Sardis, recent excavation of exceptionally deep trenches have recovered, for the first time, evidence of MIA walls and an occupation sequence extending into the Bronze Age (Cahill 2018, 2020).

900–800 BCE (YHSS 6): Gordion Excavations

The formative phase of the Early Phrygian period at Gordion (YHSS 6B) includes the construction of the first monumental architecture and fortifications (see Fig. 3.3a). The following 6A phase ended with a fiery conflagration in the elite quarter – the "Destruction Level" (6A DL). DL architecture and artifacts, though charred and fragmented, were preserved *in situ* by rapid burial under 4–5m of clay fill, laid down as the city was rebuilt in Middle Phrygian YHSS 5. *In situ* preservation and conservation of terminal 6A DL architecture on the Eastern Mound has curtailed excavation of earlier 6B remains in this area of the site (Voigt 2012b, 2013). In addition to the Citadel Mound settlement, six tumuli have been dated to the EP period (G, W, X, Y, Q, S; see Fig. 1.2; Rose and Darbyshire 2011:fig. 7.10).

Early Phrygian Gordion YHSS 6

We know little about the form or size of the Early Phrygian 6B settlement, but during 6A Gordion consisted of two separate occupation mounds surrounded by a single fortification system with at least two gates (Rose 2017). Recent excavation and geophysical survey have explored the gap between the mounds, but its dimensions and purpose remain poorly understood. At the beginning of the Hellenistic period this gap was infilled to form the single flat-topped Citadel Mound that we see today. The Early Phrygian phases on the two mounds produced very different occupation evidence. On the Eastern Mound, monumental architecture and finds indicate elite occupation (Voigt 2013). A very small area excavated on the Western Mound (a 2.5 × 1.7 m unit), produced a surface littered with trash and a large hearth in what seems to have been a domestic area. Our knowledge of Gordion's EP community is, therefore, largely based on the elite quarter on the Eastern Mound, supplemented by six tumulus burials, only one of them intact (Tumulus W; Liebhart et al. 2016:table 1).

The total excavated area for EP Gordion varies substantially by phase: the 6B excavations uncovered 3,370 m^2, while the area of the 6A excavations was over 20,000 m^2 (see Fig. 3.3a and b; Table 3.1; Voigt 2002). As yet, there is no evidence of people living on the floodplain adjacent to the Eastern Mound (unlike during the subsequent Middle Phrygian period). If settlement was confined to the walled citadel, the town would have already been sizable, extending over ca. 13 ha. However, the EP construction of the elite quarter on the Eastern Mound, consisting of a series of megarons as well as large open courtyards, would have taken up a large part of the walled area, leaving only limited space for a non-elite resident population on the Western Mound. Voigt (2013) has estimated the maximum population within the citadel walls as no more than a few thousand people.

Recent study of the EP contexts at Gordion has defined multiple construction subphases for the Early Phrygian citadel. These provide a relatively secure framework for the ceramic sequence and at the same time allow us to trace increasing inputs of materials and labor. While representing only a small portion of the townscape, the evidence for ongoing monumental construction suggests the transformation of political and economic power through the tenth to early ninth century BCE was also continuous.

This transformation is well-documented in the history of Gordion's Iron Age fortification system. The modest beginnings of a fortified settlement are found in the final phase of the EIA 7A (see Fig. 3.2b). In the late tenth century BCE over half of the area within the LTS was open, cut by a multitude of bell-shaped storage pits, most evident to the west of three houses. The largest of these houses, SSH-W, contained nearly complete vessels of both EIAH and EIA buff. The smaller(?) SWS structure lies just within the excavated area and is noteworthy because of its different orientation (the same as that of later formal architecture during 6A), and the absence of features characteristic of YHSS 7 houses. In an area to the east of the LTS, Rodney Young, while investigating the 6B fortification wall, found a segment of a sandstone wall 2.65 m thick

Fig. 7.2 Early Phrygian 6B Buildings in the Outer Court, East Mound. (a) LTS, Operation 8, southwest baulk showing ramp. The earthen ramp and the white stone construction debris resting on the ramp slope up from right to left (northwest to southeast). The surface around the trench with scattered paving stones and traces of burning dates to the YHSS 6A.3 DL. When the paving was laid at the start of 6A, the top of the 6B ramp was cut away.

running beneath the 6B wall. In his field notes the sandstone wall was nicknamed the "earliest Phrygian wall" and in a 1963 preliminary report he suggests that the wall was part of the initial Phrygian fortification system (Young 1964:292, pl. 86, fig. 32). More of this wall, along with additional architectural fragments, was later recovered beneath the first 6B gate, the Early Phrygian Building or EPB (Young 1966:pl. 70, fig. 17). Although the early sandstone wall cannot be linked stratigraphically to the latest 7A domestic structures, both are in the same stratigraphic position relative to the formal 6B architecture, and the alignment of Young's "earliest Phrygian wall" matches that of the SSH-W structure. It therefore seems likely that the first wall around the Gordion settlement protected a group of late EIA 7A households with little evidence of social stratification within the excavated area.

The nature of the eastern elite zone changed dramatically in Early Phrygian Phase YHSS 6B (early ninth century BCE). The earliest event

Fig. 7.2 (cont.) (b) *In situ* remains of the PAP structure. Left, floor blocks with a single wall block in place on the stone floor. A row of cuts in the floor documents wooden posts that lined the interior wall face. Immediately to the right of the preserved floor are "shadow blocks" documented by fine stone dust and chips where final trimming was done *in situ*. The empty area to the far right was excavated by R. S. Young.
Sources: 7.2a no archive number, R.H. Dyson; 7.2b 93-1044:12, M. Daniels, courtesy University of Pennsylvania Museum, Gordion Project Archives).

was the leveling of an elevated part of the Eastern Mound, allowing for the construction of an expanded monumental zone. YHSS 6B has two major construction phases, with the later phase defining a massive fortification system surrounding stone structures arranged around an open space or court, a pattern that persists throughout 6A and MP 5. At the beginning of 6B a 9.5 m-wide stone wall was constructed, with two monumental gates: the EPB, accessed from a low area to the northeast (where the Sakarya River then flowed), and the Proto-Polychrome Gate Complex with red, yellow and white walls identified beneath the later massive 6A Eastern gate (Young 1964:291, fig. 31). Inside the wall, at a slightly higher elevation, an open area of hard-packed earth was documented in the LTS. Areas of fill ca. 0.5 m deep ramp upward from this surface to the northwest (deposited above the razed prehistoric mound) and to the southwest (Fig. 7.2a). Layers of white stone debris lying on the ramps suggest the presence of elevated stone structures beyond the area excavated. To the northwest such a structure was preserved and excavated: the Square Enclosure, built with white stone blocks and wooden elements (Fig. 7.3). Given the location and orientation of the southwestern ramp and chips of white stone, the raised structure to the southwest lay beneath the 6A Megaron 2 (see Fig. 7.3 Structure WSS).

By the end of 6B, probably sometime in the second quarter of the ninth century, the initial gate (EPB) had been transformed into a narrow roofed passage suggestive of a sally port, and a new, elaborate gate of stones of different colors (the Polychrome Gatehouse) was built to the southwest (Fig. 7.3; Voigt 2013; Young 1966). Inside the fortifications, two new white stone buildings, both megarons in plan, were constructed (Megaron 10 and the PAP [Post and Poros] structure; Figs. 3.3a, 7.2b). The Square Enclosure was still in use and, if WSS was still in use (beneath the subsequent Megaron 2), the hard-packed surface of the court was surrounded by a series of stone structures. These lay at odd angles to each other on three sides of the hard-packed court, which had again been raised by a layer of fill.

With the exception of Megaron 10, all 6B EP buildings were buried under fill, demolished or renovated in the course of ongoing construction during the ninth century. Carved orthostats found in MP construction contexts but dated to 6B by a fragment found near the Post and Poros structure (Fig. 7.2b), were probably associated with the 6B (and potentially also 6A) gatehouse and/or perhaps the PAP structure (Voigt and DeVries 2011). The orthostat imagery stylistically parallels late tenth century Syro-Hittite reliefs at Zincirli and Carchemish (Sams 1989). These images not only help date this phase, but also strongly point to southeastern Anatolia as a source of political elite legitimation strategies for Gordion's emerging elites. There is, however, one important aspect of the Gordion reliefs that is striking. While they portray animals and supernatural beings (identified on the Syro-Hittite orthostats), they lack human representations (unlike the Syro-Hittite orthostats).

The following 6A phase (third quarter of the ninth century to ca. 825 BCE), with a larger excavation area, is far better documented (Fig. 3.3b). Construction during this phase included completely new and far more substantial fortifications that enclose both the Eastern and Western Mounds (Rose 2017), and a walled quarter on the Eastern Mound containing well-defined courtyards and megaron-style buildings. These megarons were built from stone, mudbrick and wood in a variety of construction styles.

YHSS 6A represents a relatively short period of time, but within this period three significant construction projects were undertaken (6A:1–3), each modifying the topography of Gordion. The first of these projects

Fig. 7.3 Balloon photo of Eastern Mound, Outer Court showing YHSS 6 structures and the Voigt Lower Trench Sounding [LTS] at the beginning of the 1989 season. In LTS Operations 8 and 9 (left), a line of white chips is visible marking the line of the "ramp" of hard clay found at the surface of these trenches (Fig. 7.2a). The ramp was constructed at the very beginning of 6B, suggesting an early building beneath Megaron 2 and/or 1 (WSS). 6B structures in white font, 6A structures in black font. LTS is italicized.

Source: Image no. Gordion 1#8m, W. and E. Meyers; courtesy University of Pennsylvania Museum, Gordion Project Archives.

began with the deposition of a deep layer of fill above the initial 6B gate (EPB), to extend the mound to the east and support the new 6A:1 fortification system (Fig. 3.3b). To the southwest, the Eastern Gate included large rooms or bastions forming the sides of a stone passageway with mud-plastered walls that led to the Polychrome Gatehouse. Excavation of one of these rooms showed it was originally constructed with rows of large storage vessels set in its floor (Young 1956). The fortification walls extending from the outside of the bastions were massive near the Eastern Gate, but much narrower in the segments excavated further away to the northeast and northwest. Inside the fortification walls and gate, the elite quarter was partitioned into two large courts surrounded by new megarons that were larger than the 6B buildings (Fig. 3.3b; DeVries 1990; Rose and Darbyshire 2011:fig 7.5). Later in the ninth century (construction phase 6A:2), two large new buildings separated by a wide street were constructed on a terrace ca. 2 m higher than the megarons, flanking the courts to the southwest. This large-scale undertaking (now referred to as the Terrace Complex) also began with the laying of fill that consisted primarily of stone rubble.

Another phase of remodeling (6A:3, the "Unfinished Project"), was interrupted by the ca. 800 BCE fire that destroyed a large part of the EM elite quarter (the "Destruction Level" – 6A DL). Commencement of the 6A:3 project appears to have prompted emptying of most of the 6A:2 megarons. Only a few in the Inner Court were left with any substantial quantity of goods. While most building functions are consequently uncertain, the overall layout of the eastern elite zone during 6A:2 suggests three different functional areas. In the second half of the ninth century, visitors would have entered this zone through the Eastern Gate, a cobble-paved passage with towering 12 m walls. Once through the Polychrome Gatehouse, visitors could have made a sharp right turn and entered the stone-paved (public?) Outer Court, which was surrounded by four large structures, three of which had pebble mosaic floors (Megarons 1, 2, 9; Fig. 3.3b). All of these Outer Court buildings had been largely or completely emptied in preparation for the 6A:3 renovations, but the substantial investment in architectural adornment and stone paving suggests an area designed for heavy traffic, and likely used for reception and administration. The visitor may have passed through a second gate into the (private/elite?) Inner Court (Voigt 2013). This area was only partially excavated, but given the overall layout of the elite quarter in 6A the Inner Court must have had a large number of structures. The two most elaborate buildings, Megarons 3 (Fig. 7.4) and 4, were likely elite residences, given the high-status goods as well as vessels for the consumption of food and drink found *in situ* (Voigt 2013).

Fig. 7.4 Eastern Mound, Early Phrygian YHSS 6A Destruction Level. Megaron 3, the largest of the Early Phrygian 6A megarons, was located in the Inner Court and destroyed in the 800 BCE fire with its contents intact.
Source: Gordion slide G-3915; courtesy University of Pennsylvania Museum, Gordion Project Archives.

The third functional area was formed by two long stone buildings located on the terrace above and to the southwest of the courts: the Terrace Building (TB) and the Clay Cut Building (CC) (B. Burke 2005; DeVries 1980; K. R. Morgan 2018). The TB was made up of eight megarons identical in size and plan; only part of three CC megarons were excavated, but these are assumed to be part of a parallel row of eight. These structures were still in use at the time of the ca. 800 BCE fire, with contents preserved *in situ* albeit burned, providing much of the extant and contextualized artifact assemblage for 6A. All of these structures contained ceramic and, less commonly, metal vessels as well as a variety of other goods. The quantity of pottery varied between rooms and buildings, but was generally relatively large: for example, TB 7 contained at least 500 vessels (Sams 1994:4). There is also abundant evidence for textile production in the form of spindle whorls, loom weights and charred textile fragments. Some of the rooms contained a disparate range of artifacts, ranging from imported ivory horse gear to heavy-duty iron

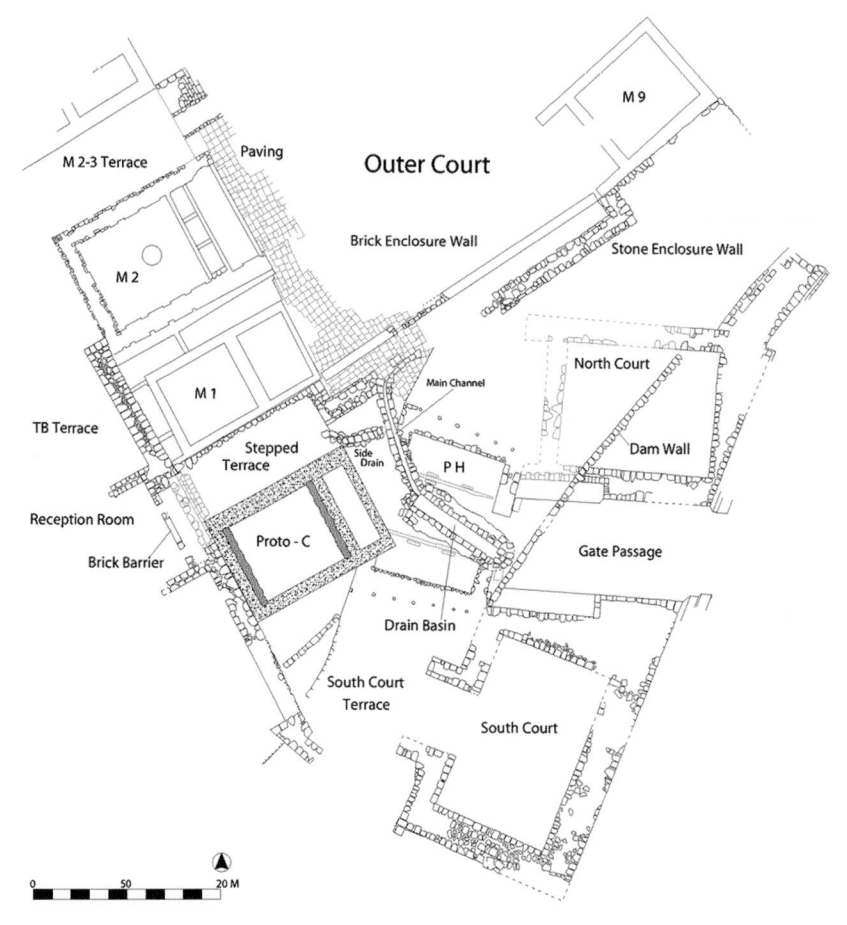

Fig. 7.5 The Early Phrygian YHSS 6A:3 Unfinished Project. Underway at the time of the ca. 800 BCE fire, the project involved building a new drainage system, construction of a new gate system, and laying fill to raise the level of the Outer Court. One new megaron was under construction, Building Proto-C.
Source: W. Cummer and C. Alblinger; courtesy University of Pennsylvania Museum, Gordion Project Archives.

tools (hoes, axes and pitchforks). This diversity may in part represent temporary storage, while the court areas were being remodeled.

Voigt (2012b) detailed the character of the 6A:3 transformation underway before the elite quarter burned (Fig. 7.5). Architectural changes were focused in the Gate Complex and the Outer Court. Rubble and earth fill was laid inside the 6A:2 gate, and a layer of clay fill inside the gate enclosed rubble foundations for one new megaron (Building Proto-C). Although details of the construction plan may have changed after the fire, there is little doubt that the earliest phase of the Middle Phrygian period (YHSS 5C) represents a completion of this 6A:3 project. The terminal date for the Early Phrygian period is conventionally linked to the Destruction Level, with the beginning of the Middle Phrygian period defined by the laying of ca. 3–5 m of fill that capped the remains of the DL. This stratigraphic break forms a readily identified archaeological boundary. However, ongoing changes in ceramics and architecture were more gradual and provide little evidence for a cultural break between the Early and Middle Phrygian periods.

Monumental tumuli on the immediate outskirts of Gordion provide mortuary evidence for the emergence of an affluent and powerful elite during the ninth century BCE (Sams and Voigt 2011; Young 1981). Six excavated tumuli have been dated to the last half of the Early Phrygian period (850–800 BCE), with the earliest, Tumulus W, dating to the mid ninth century BCE. Of these, only Tumulus W, an inhumation in a wooden chamber, remained intact (Sams and Voigt 2011; Young 1981). Liebhart and colleagues (2016) pointed out that the alignment of Tumulus W with the Early Phrygian (6A) gate passage on the Citadel Mound was a daily reminder of – and a permanent memorial to – its occupant for anyone leaving the Citadel. In general, the size of EP tumuli varied considerably, as did the decorated pottery recovered from Tumuli W, G and X. While the relationships between the work groups used for construction projects on the Citadel and those involved in building the tumuli are unclear, the comparable scale of labor and logistics involved in both cases likely represents management of similar-sized work groups to develop different aspects of the substantive and ritual economy.

The precocious growth of EP Gordion suggests that interactions between local and newly arrived groups at the start of the EIA were likely more complex than previously supposed. As outlined in Chapter 6, several lines of evidence, including both linguistic and artifactual data, link Gordion's YHSS 7 inhabitants to groups from Thrace and the Balkans. Monochrome handmade ceramics and their distinctive decorative styles are one material marker (Sams 1988). The Phrygian language, as a close relative of Greek, also indicates western origins (Ligorio and Lubotsky 2018). DeVries (1980) noted that the elite material cultural assemblage of Early Phrygian Gordion is similar to that described by Homer for the Greeks.

At the same time that groups in EP Gordion renewed links to communities in the west, the elite of the Early Phrygian period drew selectively on political (and elite) iconography of contemporary Neo-Hittite city states to the southeast. The 6B orthostats on the Eastern Mound, the early monumental gate style, as well as ivory plaques from Megaron 3, bronze omphalos bowls in Tumulus W, and ivory horse gear from TB2, all reflect north Syrian and/or Neo-Hittite styles (Sams 1988, 1995, 2012). By the end of the EP period the scale of political and economic interaction, at least among Gordion's elite, appears to have been comparable if not larger than the interaction sphere of the preceding LBA settlement.

Overview of Early Phrygian Ceramics

Early Phrygian ceramics from Gordion have been studied most extensively by Sams (1994) and Henrickson (1993, 1994). The earliest EP pottery (6B) was recovered from stratified contexts in three areas: a series of courtyard surfaces between early stone structures on the Eastern Mound; a sounding in the path leading between the EPB and the courtyard; and a large pit cut into this path (Sams 1994:plate F). Sams notes that much of the pre-Destruction Level EP pottery recovered during the Young excavations was fragmentary, making it difficult to either date or reconstruct vessel forms. The Destruction Level (6A:3), on the other hand, provided the final, largest and best preserved layer of the EP sequence on the Eastern Mound with abundant restorable vessels.

The early EP assemblage began as primarily buff ware, but over the course of YHSS 6 the proportion of grey fabrics increased to ca. 80%. Our understanding of this fabric color distribution is hampered by the exclusive focus of excavations of elite contexts and by the impact of the high temperatures of the ca. 800 BCE DL fire (ca. 1000°C) on many of these (Fig. 7.6; Henrickson 1994). A large proportion of the pottery from these burnt contexts was exposed to a strongly oxidizing environment, effectively refiring them (i.e. vessels turned to a red or buff color irrespective of the original firing conditions). EP fabrics also include a wider size range of inclusions, from "fine" fabrics to distinctive medium and coarser fabrics. Around 5–10% are fine wares (i.e. pastes with no visible inclusions), while the more typical "common" wares are tempered with "medium grit" (Henrickson 2005).

As in the LBA, EP potters produced vessel forms using specific sequences related to size: smaller vessels were wheel-thrown, often with careful secondary forming and/or finishing; larger vessels were handmade then finished on a slow wheel or tournette; and the largest storage vessels (50–80cm diameter) were coiled and smoothed (Henrickson 1993, 1994:101, 111; 2001). EP potters used finishing techniques

Fig. 7.6 Early Phrygian YHSS 6A floor deposit in the anteroom of Early Phrygian Terrace Building 2, preserved *in situ* by the ca. 800 BCE fire. Most of the pottery in this part of the room consisted of common ware jars, ranging in size from large storage jars to small bowls; other artifacts included baskets, loomweights and spindle whorls, some of the latter stored in pots.

Source: Image no. 89-1051:21, L. Foos; courtesy University of Pennsylvania Museum, Gordion Project Archives.

similar to those of the EIA, including smoothing, slipping and burnishing, as well as painting, but largely abandoned EIA techniques of incision and impressed decoration, except for relatively rare handmade forms.

Both EIA handmade and later 6A EP potting traditions involved relatively low-temperature, reduction firing to produce grey wares. However, technologically EP period grey ware fabrics have a more consistent appearance, indicating more controlled firing. Johnston (1970:66–67) and Sams (1994:22) both suggest that lighter colored grey fabrics reflect somewhat higher firing temperatures. A second distinct EP pottery type, buff ware (7A-6A), was fired in an oxidizing atmosphere with a marginally higher temperature than reduction-fired equivalents. While buff ware is slightly harder than reduction-fired wares, by the end of the EP, lower-fired, grey fabrics are dominant (Henrickson and Blackman 1996).

Henrickson and Blackman (1996) compared LBA and EP production, particularly in relation to sources. They characterize production in both periods as "specialist," mass-produced and likely made in "workshops" (Henrickson 2001), but noted that a production difference between the LBA and EP was choice of clay. While sources in the immediate area around the site are mostly calcareous, and were preferred by LBA potters, potters in the EP apparently used a more diverse range of clays (Grave et al. 2009; Henrickson and Blackman 1996).

Sams also suggested the operation of multiple ceramic workshops during the EP period. The DL excavations produced instances in which EP bowls were stacked (up to 28), set on shelves or stored in wicker baskets preserved underneath the vessels (Sams 1994:4, pl. B–E). Certain rooms in the Terrace Buildings, a shed next to the gate building controlling access to the Terrace and auxiliary rooms to some of the megarons also contained ceramics stacked along the walls, mostly related to drinking and storage (Sams 1994:2–7). Based on the disposition and appearance of these vessels, Sams proposed these bowls were brought into town by outside groups (Henrickson 2005; Sams 1994:3, 6, 42–43, 187 pl. D1–2, E1). When combined with the highly specific painting styles of the painted buff ware, Sams suggested this as evidence of the operation of multiple ceramic workshops and workshop-specific styles during the EP.

The EP ceramic tradition appears to be a local Anatolian development that integrated LBA techniques on one hand, with the practices of disparate communities brought together in Early Iron Age Gordion on the other (Sams 1994). Contemporary painted wares, with decoration generically similar to the painted EP buff ware, also have strong parallels to the east in central Anatolia (Genz 2005, 2011).

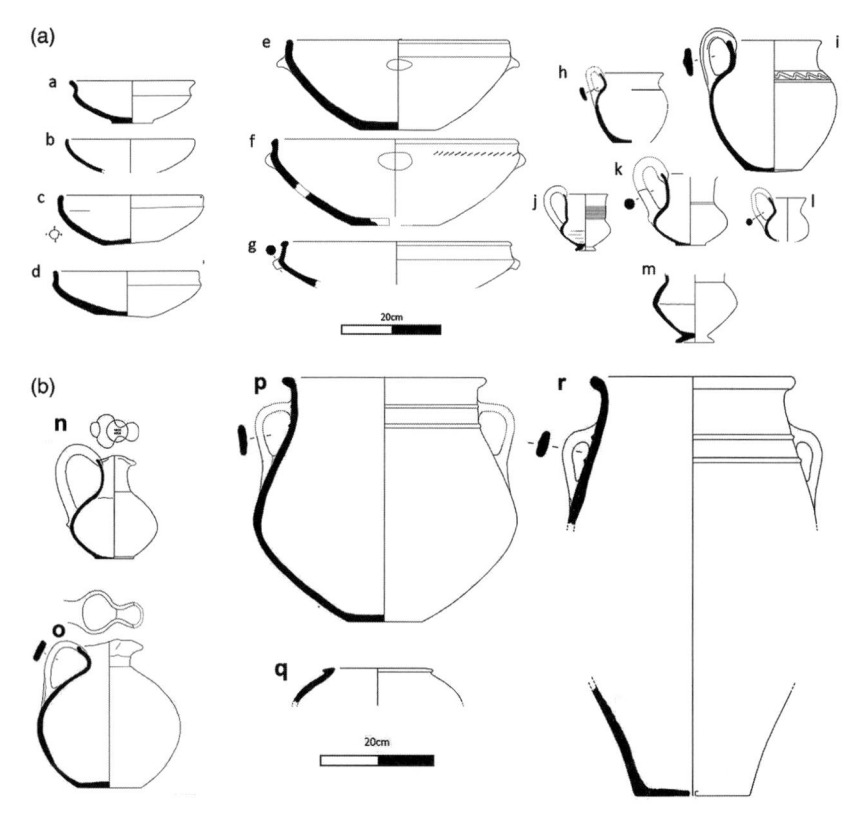

Fig. 7.7 Early Phrygian YHSS 6A common vessel forms.
(a) a–d: small and medium bowls (YH22625, 24639, 24911. 24905);
e–g: large carinated bowl and basins (YH24963, 24977, 24906); h–i:
pots (YH24637, 24901); j–l: goblets (juglets) (YH24628, 24644,
24998); m: small jar? (YH24638).
(b) n–o: trefoil jugs (YH24910, 24973); p: open storage vessel
(YH24954); q: dinos (YH24999); r: wide-mouth pot (YH24960).
Sources: D. Hoffman, K. Lehman-Insua, A. Anderson and P. Grave; courtesy
University of Pennsylvania Museum, Gordion Project Archives.

Forms

A striking difference between the LBA, EIA and EP periods is the notable increase in the number and elaboration of classes of forms during the EP (Fig. 7.7). Nine general form classes were identified for the EIA; this doubled by the Early Phrygian period, with multiple types within general classes (e.g. different formalized shapes of jugs or bowls; Table 7.1a). At the same time, variability within classes decreased (i.e. forms became more uniform).

Table 7.1. *YHSS 6 Early Phrygian pottery (based on Sams 1994).*

(a) Early Phrygian YHSS 6 ceramic forms (Sams 1994).

Bowls	Cups	Jugs	Small jars	Necked jars	Amphoras	Amphoras with 3–4 handles	Crater/wide-neck amphora	Pot	Storage jars	Cylindrical pot stands	Other
Carinated bowls	Sipping chalice	Side-spout jug		Dinos, low-necked	Small and large	(Not true amphora)	Large – some with lids	Multiple sizes	Large – common		Rhyton
Flaring-rim bowls	Kantharos/ krater	Side-spout sieve jug (3+ types)		Multiple variants	Neck handle			One-handled utility pot	Narrow neck		Pans
Plain bowls		Spouted-mouth jug			Shoulder handle				Low neck		
Bowls with articulated rims		Duofoil jug			Open mouth				Wide neck		
Bowls with perforated covers		Sieve jugs			Narrow neck				(Some similar to amphoras)		
		Round mouth Jug: large			Wide neck						
		Narrow neck jugs									
		Trefoil (multiple shapes)									
		Trefoil miniature									
		Juglet									
		Askoi									

(b) Early Phrygian YHSS 6 decorative styles after Sams (1994: 134–165).

Plastic decoration	Surface finishing	Painted styles
Incisions	Burnishing	Plain slips (including "sheen")
Patterned incisions	Polishing	Pure wavy line
Stamping (storage jars)		Partial wavy line
Skeuomorphs		Ladder
		Single circles
		Zig zag
		Chevron triangle style
		Ornate class (complex)
		Brown on buff
		Meanders (DL)
		Checkerboard patterns (including oblique and bichrome)
		Cross and lozenge
		Stippled lozenge
		X-panel
		Semicircle panel
		RARE styles: running dog, hooked lambdas, feather trees, rosettes

While a few highly decorated fine-ware forms were recovered from DL terrace buildings, the majority were utilitarian (ca. 90%; Henrickson and Blackman 1996; Young 1962). If we compare the EIA and EP phases (combined subphases), the overall percentages of several types remained similar: jars make up 13–15%, bowls 8–9%, and cups 1% (the number of sherds from unidentified forms is also comparable at just over 50% of the assemblage). Trefoil jugs were a major new form category, not found in the EIA, and were elaborated over time; "craters" (reflecting the similarity with a Greek form of large open pot used for mixing wine) also become more common, although what liquids they contained has not been evaluated. The more elaborate character of these forms may reflect their use in the 6A elite quarter where they likely played a role in social display during meals or feasting.

Sams observed some continuity in forms from the LBA (Sams 1994:26): low-necked jars are found from the LBA through to the EP; the sequence of carinated bowls, from LBA through EIA into the EP, also provides some evidence for local technological continuity; goblets (also called juglets) and ledge-rim jars continue from EIA 7A through the EP. However, other forms and styles with no local antecedents (e.g. stamping) have wide-ranging parallels that flag the likely scale and importance of regional interaction networks at this time (from the Balkans to northern Syria, and other central Anatolian sites like Alişar; Sams 1994:177).

Decorative Styles

The most common type of EP pottery was grey ware. While buff ware represents a small percentage (ca. 7–10%; Henrickson 2005), painted buff ware from elite contexts and burials includes a wide range of decorative styles from simple to highly elaborate (Fig. 7.8, Plate 8; Table 7.1b; Sams 1994). Sams (1974, 1978, 1994) details the Early Phrygian decorated pottery from the Young excavations. Table 7.1a–b summarizes general forms and decorative styles he identified. His local decorative styles included burnishing, stamping, sheen slips, bichrome and monochrome painting, incising and/or grooving, on buff and grey fabrics. EP styles were quite distinct from those of the EIA: incising becomes rare, burnishing is retained, but in combination with other decorative elements, such as stamping or skeuomorphic shapes (mimicking metal shapes and techniques like riveting). A limited range of plain slips is seen ($n = 17$) in the EP, including a micaceous "sheen slip," as

New Identities, New Communities

Fig. 7.8 Early Phrygian YHSS 6 decorated wares.
(a) Painted crater from Terrace Building 8, Early Phrygian Destruction Level [6A.3 DL]. Style identified as "Silhouette ware" or Alşar IV ware [GKS cat. 932] (Gordion inventory 9300-P-3729).

well as red slips/washes (although distinctive, all have LBA parallels at Gordion).

Painted wares have few LBA or EIA precursors in the local region (Sams 1994:134). Basic geometric elements parallel contemporary ceramics from northern Thessaly, but are also common to many contemporary traditions across the larger region from Greece to the Balkans, as well as northern Syria (Sams 1978, 1994). However, Phrygian configurations of these elements remain unique. To the east, in central Anatolia, painted wares occurred much earlier, in the EBA, and reappear in the EIA (Genz 2005).

Painted decoration is typically restricted to vessel shoulders and adjacent zones, often in panels surrounded by a limited range of geometric motifs (e.g. triangles, lozenges, zig-zags, meanders, checkerboards,

192 Ancient Gordion

Fig. 7.8 (*cont.*)(b) Side-spouted sieve jug in Brown on Buff ware from Clay Cut Building 2 (CC-2), Destruction Level (Gordion inventory no. 3525-P-1270).
Sources: *7.8a and b*: Gordion Archive image no. CIAG-4/25 and 59251; courtesy University of Pennsylvania Museum, Gordion Project Archives.

lattices, wavy lines). Elaborations of motifs are common; triangles, for example, are cross-hatched and solid, and occur in combination with chevrons. Sams (1994:155) identified a series of "styles" that combine specific motifs (e.g. "Wavy Line Style," "Chevron Triangle Style," "Fine Line Buff Ware"), as well as specific fabrics, slips, forms and contexts. These combinations distinguish Phrygian pottery from that of other Anatolian regions with similar painted traditions. Sams (1994:172) suggested these styles reflect specific workshops or "communities" of potters. Styles from other regions, such as Alişar IV "Silhouette" ware, present in small numbers in the EP continue into the MP at Gordion.

Jars and jugs are the most frequently decorated forms, often with brown painted styles (from most common to least: round mouth, trefoil [small and medium], side-spouted sieve jugs, amphoras and jars) (Fig. 7.8a and b). Only a few craters or open-mouthed forms, including mixing bowls or "dinoi," and other types of low-necked jars were painted. Jars are the form most frequently stamped. Bowls tend to have a wider range of decoration and finishes other than paint, while jugs tend to have a higher frequency of painted decoration. While EP bowls were abundant, surprisingly few are painted and they appear to be used as serving vessels (i.e. with handles and/or spouts). This further reinforces the relationship between decorative elaboration and the forms used for consumption by emergent elite groups.

In the Young excavations, painted wares first appear in substantial numbers at the beginning of 6A (in the Outer Court paving fill, Sams' EPB V [30 vessels]), and continue up to the Destruction Level, which produced ca. 200 painted vessels (Sams 1994). Their distribution in the better dated tumuli suggests that the social role of painted wares peaked between 850 and 750 BCE; thus they were still in use at the beginning of the Middle Phrygian period (ca. 800 BCE), but decreased in popularity through the later MP period (Sams 2012).

NAA Ceramic Assemblage

The Sample

As described in Chapter 4, the EP compositional data combine results from both the Young study collection and Voigt's excavations. Of the original 333 EP samples 323 provided NAA data, as 10 samples were too small to analyze. Two-thirds of the assemblage dates to 6A, and the remainder to 6B. For forms and decoration identified in this NAA assemblage see Table 7.2. We compare compositional data for the EP with data from earlier periods to evaluate changes in resource use over time. We also compare the NAA assemblage to the excavated assemblage representing all of the Gordion ceramics that Henrickson analyzed and described (summarized in the section "Overview of Early Phrygian Ceramics") so that we can assess potential sample bias in the selection of ceramics for NAA.

Table 7.2. *YHSS 6 Early Phrygian forms and decoration in the NAA sample.*

	None – grey	Brown on X	None – buff	Stamped	Black/ brown on red	Burnished	Incised	Sheen	Orange/ red various	Bichrome	Grey: various	Other	Total	%
Body	103	2	46		2		1		1	1		3	159	48
Jar		17	1	16	7	1	8		1	1		2	54	16
Bowl	2	5	4		3	7	1	4	4	1		6	37	11
Jug	1	11	2	1	1	1		4		3	4		28	8
Crater		8		1	3					1			13	4
Bowl – shallow		2			1	1					1		5	2
Jug – sieve		1	1			1		1			1		5	2
Other: closed vessel	2	11	1	3	2		1					2	22	7
Other: open vessel	1	2	4		1				2				10	3
Total	109	59	59	21	20	11	11	9	8	7	6	13	333	100
%	33	18	18	6	6	3	3	3	2	2	2	4	100	

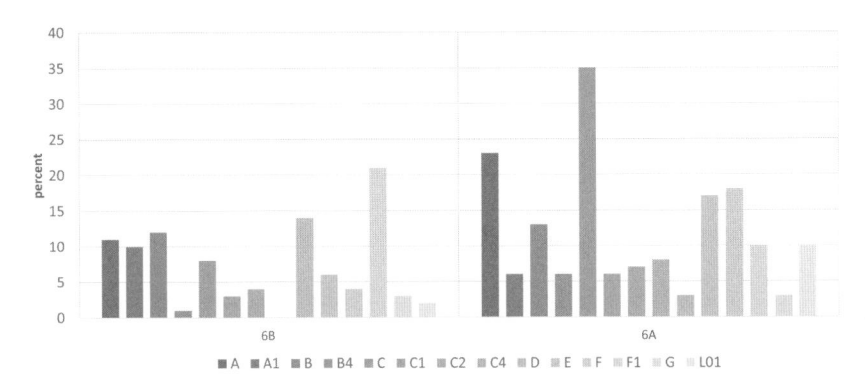

Fig. 7.9 Early Phrygian ceramic distribution across dominant compositions, showing the differences between the earlier phase YHSS 6B and later 6A distributions. Note the variation between local (A cluster), local/regional clusters (B–D), and nonlocal clusters (E–L). (6B n = 107; 6A n = 202).

Early Phrygian NAA Results (n = 323 [of total 333])

The EP NAA assemblage comprises 37 groups of which 9 are singletons that are typically compositional outliers (treated as imports *prima facie*). Local cluster A accounts for 20% of the EP sample, with another 15% from local/regional group B. Local/regional clusters C–D account for another 30%, with the remaining 35% nonlocal (see Chapter 4 for how we define local, regional and nonlocal). While the percentage of local vs. nonlocal samples is just slightly higher for 6B, the distribution of all local, regional and nonlocal sources shifts substantially between subphases (Fig. 7.9). Local cluster A and local/regional cluster C are most common in the 6A subsample, while local/regional cluster B is better represented in 6B. Similarly, nonlocal group F1 dominates 6B, while F is more common in 6A. Overall, a wider range of nonlocal clusters is represented in 6A. Some of this diversity reflects Young's preferential sampling and curation of unusual ceramics from the elite area, but we would note that sample diversity is similar for both EP phases, even though their contexts and sample sizes are very different; 6A sherds were sampled from intact elite or TB contexts, whereas 6B contexts included courtyard fills, a roadway and a single large pit.

Firing and fabrics Shifts in firing strategies during the EP period are reflected in the changing proportion of oxidized buff and reduction grey wares in the assemblage (Fig. 7.10). The NAA assemblage differs from the larger excavated assemblage analyzed by Henrickson as buff ware is marginally more common overall. In the NAA sample, grey ware is more

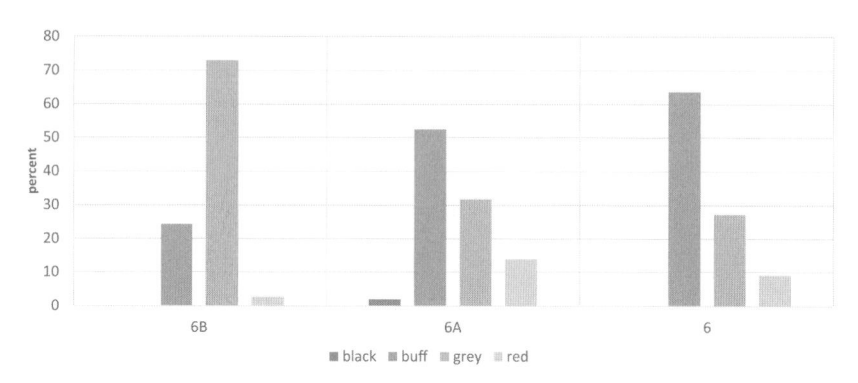

Fig. 7.10 Pottery fabric color in percentages by Early Phrygian subphase. "6" represents samples from contexts that were not phased within the EP ($n = 13$). The proportions are somewhat skewed because 6B grey includes EIA Handmade and 6A buff includes Destruction Level oxidized ceramics.

abundant in the earlier 6B phase, with oxidized wares (combined buff and red wares) more frequent in the 6A assemblage.

The diverse fabric colors of the EP assemblage reflect a mix of both different fabrics and variable firing conditions for the same fabrics (further complicated by the oxidation effects of DL burning); on the other hand, the diversity of fabric colors in the EIA seems to be primarily due to variable firing rather than to compositional differences between clay sources. In general, EP grey wares are more uniform in color than their EIA equivalents (reduction-fired).

Sample sizes for buff and grey fabrics are comparable (both ca. 140), with both distributed across a wide range of sub-cluster sources (Fig. 7.11; Table 7.3a). However, while buff ware is slightly more common in local and local/regional sources (clusters A and B–D), grey wares include a surprisingly large proportion of cluster F (west Anatolian) subsets. Red fabrics are less common, with more than half also matching coastal or west Anatolian clusters (e.g. subsets of groups F and L). Black fabrics are rare, but mostly local in YHSS 6.

The distribution of different fabrics across compositional groups shows that source preferences are evident for some types (e.g. group C for common and coarse ware). However, virtually all sources (local, local/regional, nonlocal) are represented across fabrics (Fig. 7.12). Exceptions are the medium-coarse fabrics of the small sample of cooking pots restricted to group D and nonlocal group E. Medium-fine fabrics included a large percentage of L subgroups (west Anatolian/Miletus),

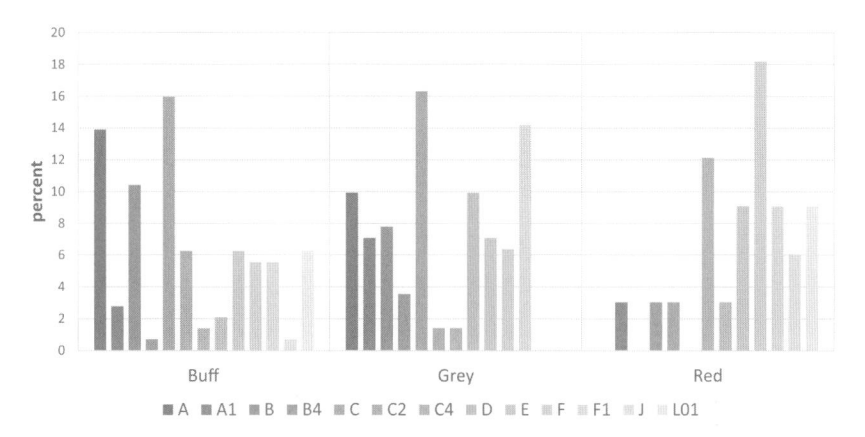

Fig. 7.11 Early Phrygian fabric colors by NAA groups. Note the diversity of sources for each fabric color, and the dominance of nonlocal sources for red fabrics (clusters E–L). Both buff and grey fabrics are made from most of the same local sources if in disparate amounts, but local/regional group C is a preferred source for both. Buff ware includes a higher percentage of local A group.

while the range of imported fine fabrics were mostly from F (Ionian) subgroups.

An overall trend from the LBA to the EP is a shift in the proportion of local, local/regional and nonlocal sources. Two significant differences characterize the Early Phrygian period. First, in comparison with the EIA, there is a substantial increase in the number of imports (from 15% to 35%; Fig. 7.13). Second, local cluster A resource use declines by 50% between the EIA and the EP, with a substantial shift within local A sources. Local/regional resource use shows a less pronounced decline (clusters B and D), with an increase in the use of cluster C sources. Given the use of most sources for most fabrics, this does not seem to be related to a purely technological shift in clay use. Our null hypothesis is that all local resource zones were equally accessible to all potters in all periods. Departures from this premise could indicate specialization in forms or styles or both. Hypothetically, the extent to which sources were "owned" or controlled could also dictate access of a work group to particular sources.

Forms Our NAA sample of the Gordion EP assemblage includes bowls, jars and pots, as in the EIA, but also more distinctive shapes (e.g. rhyton, plate, crater, pithos; Tables 7.1a and 7.2). More than twice as many forms are identifiable in the EP than in the EIA assemblage, in part due to the elaboration and increase in the uniformity of individual

Table 7.3. *YHSS 6 Early Phrygian pottery fabrics.*

(a) Early Phrygian fabric color by NAA group (in percent). Note nonlocal source groups for red fabrics (F–L subgroups).

	A	A1	A2	A8	A11	A12	A13	A_ol3	B	B1	B2	B3	B4	B8	B9	B12	B14	C	C1	C2	C4	D	D1	E	E1	E2	F	F1	G	H	I	J	K	L01	L02	L1	L2	L3	Total
Buff	14	3	1	1	1	1	1	1		10	2		1	1	1	1	1	16	3	6	1	2		6	1	1	6	6	1	1	1	6	1	1			1		100
Grey	10	7	1	1					8				4	1	1		1	16	4	1	1	10	1	7	1	1	6	14	4	1				1					100
Red	3											3	3	3				3	3			3		9			18	9	3		6		9		3	3	3		100
Black	25	50											3											25															100

(b) Fabric texture by NAA group (in percent). Note differences in local (A) coarse and finer ware sources, as well as the finer fabrics of most nonlocal sources. Cooking pot and medium coarse fabric sample sizes are small, but suggest regional and nonlocal imports for some jars and cooking vessels.

	A	A1	A2	A8	A11	A12	A13	A_ol3	B	B1	B2	B3	B4	B8	B9	B12	B14	C	C1	C2	C4	D	D1	E	E1	E2	F	F1	G	H	I	J	K	L01	L02	L1	L2	L3	Total
Common	12	6	2	1	1		1	1	7			1	3	1	1	1	1	20	4	3	3	5	1	8	1		7	10	2		1	2		10	2	1	1	1	100
Medium fine	12	1			1					11	1			1	1			6	4	4	1	6		5	1	1	10	11							2	1	1	1	100
Fine	12	2			2	2				7	2	2	2					2	5	5	5	7		7	2		7	12	5	5		2	5		9					100
Coarse	18	5								9	5		5		5		5	32	5					5		5													100
Cooking																						50		5	50														100
Medium coarse																								100															100

198

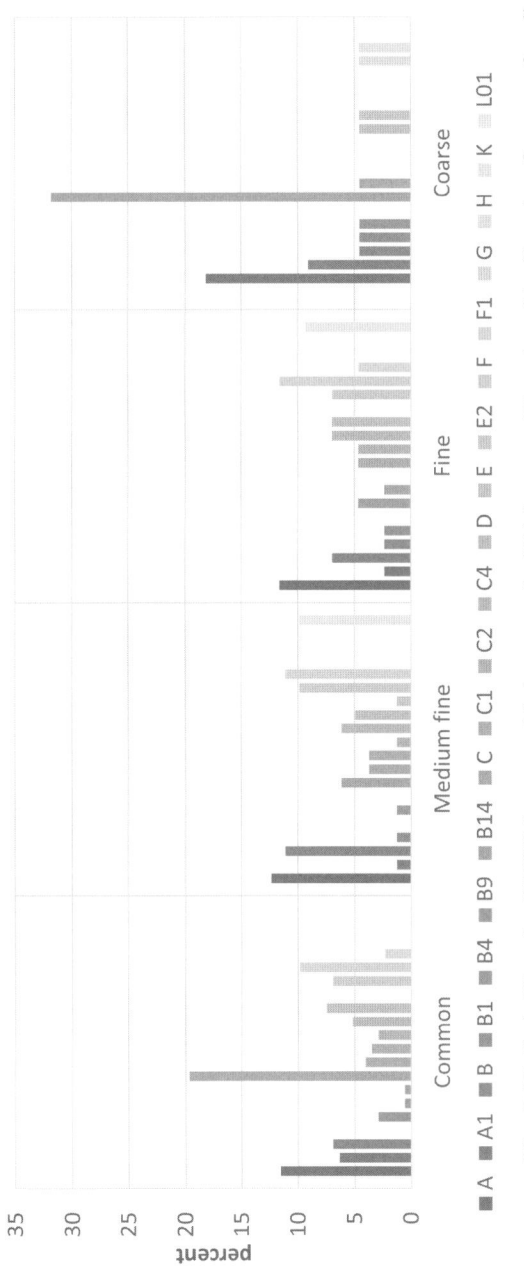

Fig. 7.12 Early Phrygian YHSS 6 pottery fabric texture by NAA group. Note the wide diversity of sources for all of the most abundant fabrics, with little relationship between source and texture. Group C is preferred for both common and coarse fabrics.

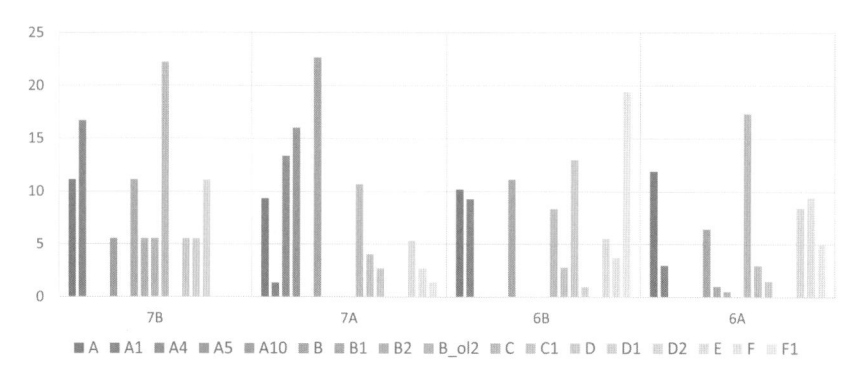

Fig. 7.13 Changing patterns of resource use from Early Iron Age 7B to Early Phrygian 6A. All phases are different from each other, particularly in the balance of local Group A cluster sources. EP YHSS 6 phases include many more exotic sources (F, F1, G, L), with a decline in local cluster A (A1–A10). [NAA groups with >5% of sample]

forms (partially a result of sampling). Just under half of the EP assemblage is composed of unidentified body sherds, with bowls (11%), jars (16%), jugs and sieve jugs (10%) and craters (4%) constituting the most abundant identifiable types (Table 7.2).

All forms show considerable compositional diversity, and a relatively high percentage of nonlocal groups: for example, the 28 jug sherds are spread across 17 different groups (Table 7.4). Jars and jugs represent a disproportionately large number of sources overall (Fig. 7.14), and particularly nonlocal sources (ca. 22%). While not as pronounced, bowls also include a larger number of nonlocal groups than the overall average. However, bowls are also the most common form in local compositional cluster A. In terms of form-specific percentages, jars and craters were the most frequent import (ca. >30% nonlocal), with bowls and jugs somewhat less frequent (15–20% nonlocal). In contrast to the source diversity for other forms, craters predominantly come from one local/regional source (C), in addition to having a relatively high frequency of Ionian (23% group F) sources. In the non-diagnostic (body sherd) sample, 18% were local, just under 50% were local/regional (B–D), with ca. 34% identified as nonlocal.

Focusing on local sources, two large A subgroups account for most local production, with six additional minor subgroups of one to three samples. With the exception of craters, local group A is used for all forms. There is no clear relationship between local A cluster sources and specific forms, except one source uniquely used for jugs with Fine

Table 7.4. YHSS 6 Early Phrygian NAA ceramic forms by NAA clusters.

	A	A1	A2	A8	A11	A12	A13	A_o13	B	B1	B2	B3	B4	B8	B9	B12	B14	C	C1	C2	C4	D	D1	E	E1	E2	F	F1	G	H	I	J	K	L01	L02	L1	L2	L3	Total	%	# of NAA groups
Body	13	10	1	1		1			9	1		1	2	3			2	28	4	3	5	14	1	11	2	1	5	24	5		1		1	4	1	1		1	149	46	25
Jar	3	4	1	1					5		1	2	1					4	3	2		3		3			10	1		1						2			54	17	22
Bowl	6	3	1			1			7									3	2	1	2			2				3			1	1		1	1				37	11	15
Jug	5				1				2	1				1	1	1		2	1	2	1			2	1	1	3	1	1	1		1		2					28	9	17
Crater										1								6	1	1							1	2						1					13	4	7
Bowl – Shallow	2								1				1																					1					5	2	4
Jug – sieve	1								1									1												1									5	2	5
Jar/jug	1								1																												1		4	1	4
Pithos													2		1									1															4	1	3
Rim	1													1				1									1												4	1	4
Closed																		1																2					3	1	2
Pot				1																														1					3	1	3
Shoulder																		1						1															3	1	3
Body Cooking																					1			1															2	1	2
Cup																			1					1															2	1	2
Other forms	3													1										2							1								7	2.2	4
Total	35	17	3	2	1	2		1	26	3	1	2	7	3	3	1	3	47	11	11	8	18	1	24	3	2	23	31	6	1	1	3	1	12	2	3	1	2	323	100	38
%	11	5	1	1	0	1		0	8	1	0	1	2	1	1	0	1	15	3	3	2	6	0	7	1	1	7	10	2	0	0	1	0	4	1	1	0	1	100		

201

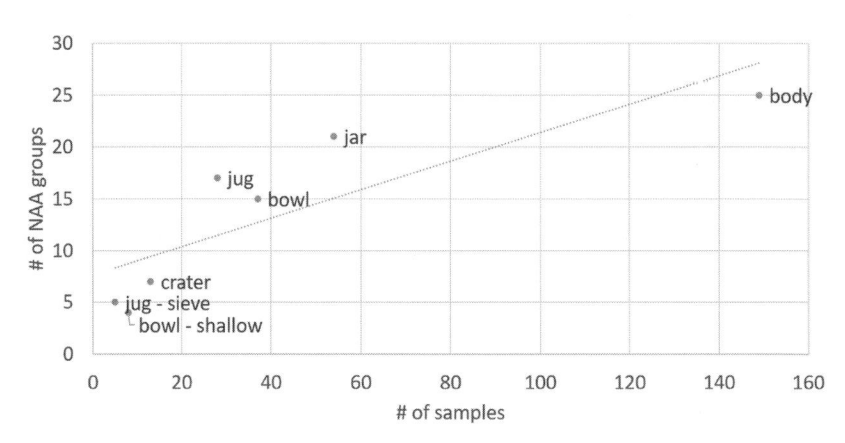

Fig. 7.14 Early Phrygian YHSS 6. Diversity in sources in relation to forms. Number of samples (*x*-axis) by number of NAA groups (*y*-axis). Note higher diversity of jars and jugs relative to bowls (above trendline).

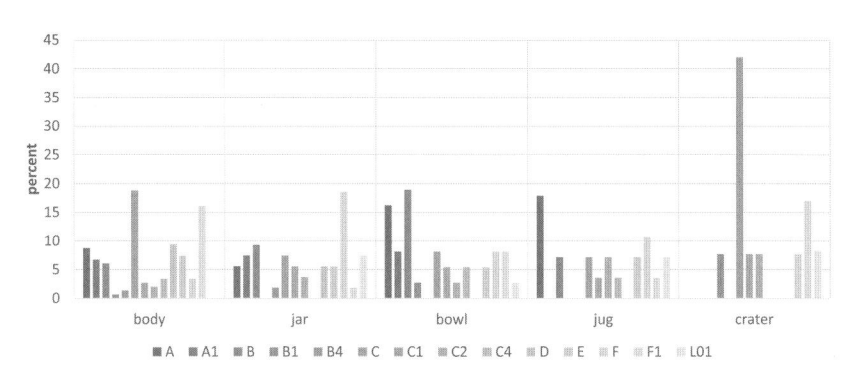

Fig. 7.15 Early Phrygian YHSS 6 forms by more common NAA groups. Note the diverse range of sources used for each form (simplified form types, and only forms with larger sample size).

Line decoration (A12). While specific sources are common to most forms (e.g. local group A and A1), each form is distributed differently between local, local/regional and nonlocal source clusters (Fig. 7.15, Table 7.4). This suggests an extension of source use beyond what was most expedient (i.e. local cluster A production). While compositional diversity is clearly enhanced by the sample selection biases inherent in the RSY study collection, it nonetheless provides a qualitative window on the extent of production and supply networks accessed by EP Gordion groups.

Decoration Just over half of the EP NAA assemblage is decorated (165 of 323), with more than twice as many decorative styles as in the EIA sample (Table 7.5). It includes painted decoration (ca. 25%), primarily brown on X (i.e. Brown on buff, ground, or white) applied in geometric designs, and a smaller number of Black (or brown) on red, stamped, burnished and incised examples. The prominence of decorated wares in our EP sample, not representative of the overall assemblage as described by Henrickson, reflects sampling biases introduced by different curation strategies (discussed in Chapter 3).

There is a general correlation between the number of compositional groups and the size of the decorative subgroup (Fig. 7.16). Exceptions that suggest different production strategies include brown on X with relatively high compositional diversity, in contrast to undecorated grey wares. Undecorated buff ware is also much more compositionally diverse than its undecorated grey ware counterparts. The most commonly imported style was Black/brown on red (ca. 95% nonlocal), with brown on X the next most frequent (Table 7.5, Fig. 7.17). Both the decorative repertoire and the sources are also unusually diverse compared to other periods and other styles, although many styles (and sources) are present at low percentages. Styles with a strong representation of local production (>25% cluster A) include burnished, incised and bichromes.

Most of the decorative categories used here combine a variety of styles, although usually in small numbers. A closer look at one of the larger decorative categories, brown on X, distinguishes a variety of treatments (brown on white, buff or ground/clay slip). Even though the samples sizes are relatively small, brown on X styles are distributed over a diverse range of sources (Fig. 7.18). Brown on white and brown on ground match more local and local/regional sources than brown on X or Black/brown on red. Nonlocal Brown on buff samples only come from west Anatolian sources, while Black/brown on red decorative types are imported from both east-central and western Anatolia. The L group, and particularly the L01 subset, first discussed in Chapter 4, is a close compositional match for ceramics identified as "Miletos A" (Akürgal et al. 2002). We discuss this match in further detail in the following section.

Sourcing nonlocal ceramics In Chapter 4, we compared the NAA geochemistry of the ceramics to sediment NAA geochemical assemblages from other sites to identify potential source matches. While very few of the production centers have been characterized, Mommsen and colleagues defined several discrete geochemical regions for western Anatolia based on typologies and find spots (Akürgal et al. 2002).

About 25% (86 of 323) of our EP NAA assemblage matches or approximates Ionian and Lydian wares to the west (Clusters F–L;

Table 7.5. YHSS 6 Early Phrygian NAA sample decorative styles by compositional group (counts). Decorative treatment percentages in the column at the right.

	A	A1	A2	A8	A11	A12	A13	A_ol3	B	B1	B2	B3	B4	B8	B9	B12	B14	C	C1	C2	C4	D	D1	E	E1	E2	F	F1	G	H	I	J	K	L01	L02	L1	L2	L3	Total	%
None – grey	11	5	1						5				2	1			2	18	3	2	1	13	1	9	2		3	20	4										103	32
None	2	3		1					6	1		1		2	1			13	1	2	4	1		8			2	2	1							1	1		55	17
Brown on X	9		1	1	2	1			5	1		1	1					6	2	6	1				1	2	5	1			1		9	1	2			2	59	18
Stamped	1							1	2				2					4	2		2						5			1									21	7
Black/brown on red	1																							2			6	5				2	3		1				20	6
Burnished	7						1			1	1																	1											11	3
Incised		5	1						1				1					1						2			1	1					1						11	3
Sheen		1														1		1			2			2			1	1											9	3
Orange/red various					1								1	1					1			1		1				2											8	2
Bichrome	2								3																					1									7	2
Grey – various									2									1	1								1												6	2
Bands									2									1																					3	1
Black – various	1	1									1							1																					3	1
Grooved/impressed	1											1																											3	1
Modeled	1																	1			1																		3	1
Streaky	1																																						1	0
Total	35	17	3	2	2	1	1	1	26	3	1	2	7	3	3	1	3	47	11	11	8	18	1	24	3	2	23	31	6	1	1	3	12	2	3	1	2	2	323	100
%	11	5	1	1	1	0	0	0	8	1	0	1	2	1	1	0	1	15	3	3	2	6	0	7	1	1	7	10	2	0	0	1	4	1	1	0	1	1	100	

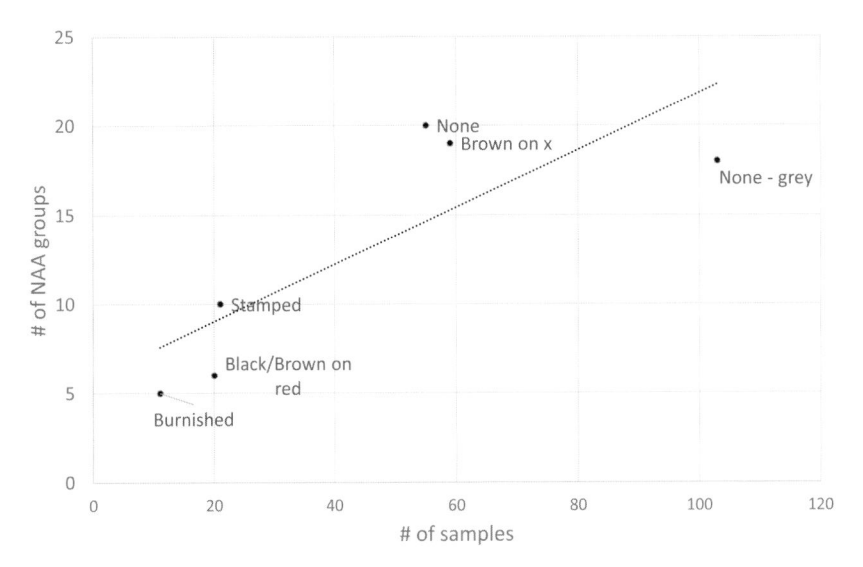

Fig. 7.16 Early Phrygian YHSS 6 pottery decoration and NAA groups. Sample size (*x*-axis) by number of NAA groups (*y*-axis). Note larger number of NAA group for brown on X decoration, and low number for undecorated grey ware.

Table 7.5). One of the more striking matches is between Mommsen's "Miletos A" group (*n* = 11) and a decoratively coherent Gordion subgroup consisting of Brown on buff Wavy Line or Partial Wavy Line decorative style (see Sams 1994). Contextually all but one of the Wavy Line decorated samples that matched "Miletos A" came from the 6A Destruction Level (one additional sample is 6B). Another well-represented nonlocal cluster, F, is found most commonly at the site of Seyitömer, to the west.

Just under 10% of the sample matches with east-central Anatolia cluster E. While the majority of subgroups within clusters B–D are local/regional, there are also matches with east-central Anatolian sites within clusters C–D (Kaman Kalehöyük and Çadır Höyük). Most of the matched samples are undecorated however, making independent typological cross-checking of groups not possible.

These compositional comparisons raise several issues. First, there are as yet very few published comparanda for the ninth century BCE from the Ionian region of western Anatolia (Aytaçlar 2004; Kahya 2002; Vaessen 2014). It is unclear what the regional pattern of settlement looks like, with some suggesting the area was depopulated (C. Aslan personal

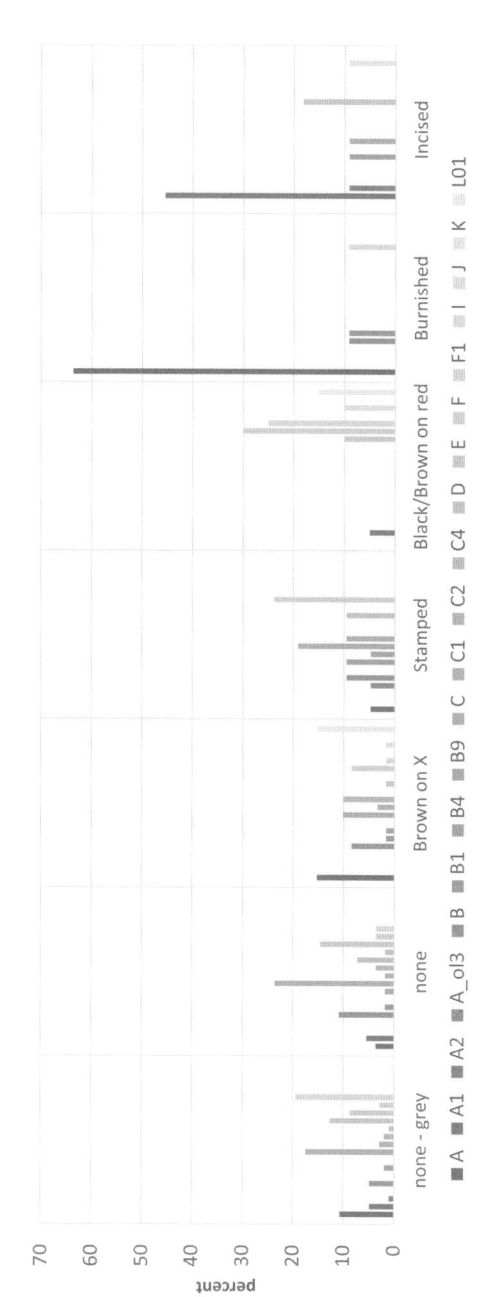

Fig. 7.17 Early Phrygian YHSS 6. Distribution of sources across pottery decorative styles. Percentage of NAA groups (>5%) by dominant decorative types. Note overall diversity in undecorated buff and grey wares, as well as nonlocal diversity of brown on X and Black/brown on red (F, J, L) styles. Incised and burnished styles are dominated by local cluster A groups.

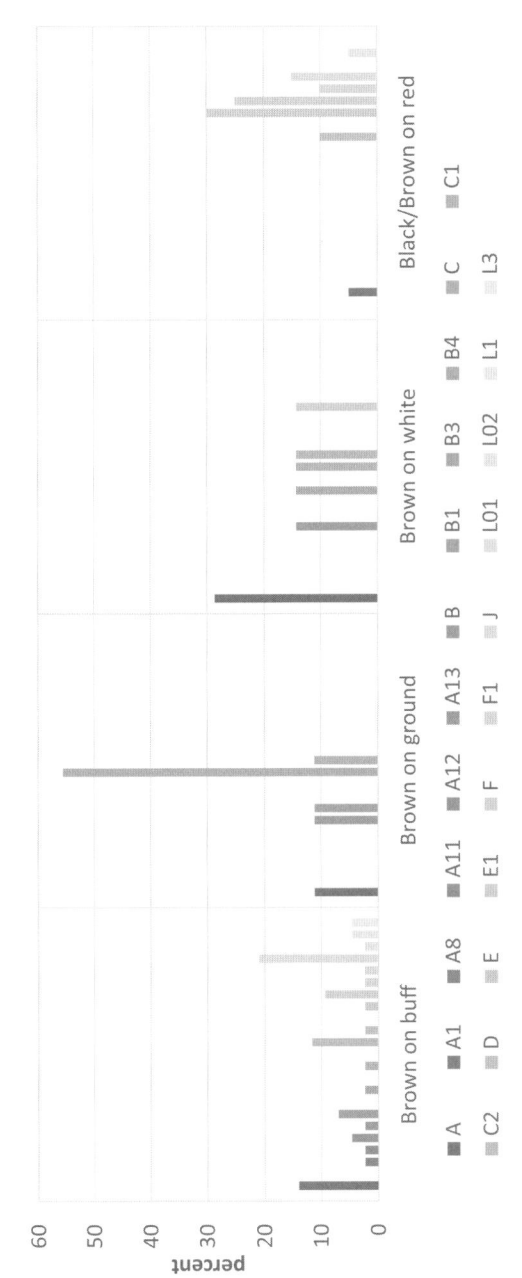

Fig. 7.18 Early Phrygian YHSS 6 brown on X styles and Black/brown on red decoration by NAA group (percent). Note diversity of Brown on buff, and the nonlocal sources for Black/brown on red. Brown on ground, on the other hand, matches mostly local and local/regional sources.

207

communication 2017). There is ongoing occupation, however, at Troy and in its environs, and it seems likely that a current absence of evidence is not evidence of absence (Aslan and Günata 2016; Aslan et al. 2014; Greaves 2011). Recent work at Sardis is also beginning to reveal evidence of LBA and EIA occupation (Cahill 2020). These tantalizing data suggest that, in addition to the clear stylistic links between EP Gordion and groups to the east and south of Gordion (e.g. Sams 1978, 1994), the Gordion elite may well have exchanged gifts and goods with elites from Ionia and the region that became Lydia. This is particularly evident in the second phase of the EP period (6A).

Second, several samples were attributed to another iconic Iron Age style, Alişar IV or "Silhouette style." The compositional data suggest this style was produced at multiple sites and widely emulated. Another style, designated as "Halys River" (in the RSY study collection) has painted geometric decoration on a flat rim of a shallow bowl. All samples matched different sources including one local example ($n = 5$). Taken together, these comparisons suggest that emulation of eastern styles (rather than direct exchange) from the Halys Bend (Kızılırmak) region formed another important component of Early Phrygian identity.

Sams (1994:155–162) attributed several styles as characteristically (early) Phrygian: for example, Wavy-Line style, Ornate class of Brown on buff, and Polychrome House style. Of these, examples of both Wavy-Line and Polychrome House style derive from western Anatolia, and mostly likely East Greek Protogeometric-period sites. Ornate Brown on buff, seen in particular on the larger craters, is from local/regional C sources. Only Fine Line Buff is local cluster A (A12).

Changing resource use over time The pattern and character of clay resource/fabric recipe use changed significantly from the LBA to the EP (Fig. 6.7). Given the large number of compositional groups ($n = 39$), comparison here focuses on those with more than five samples from the LBA to the EP. From YHSS 10 through to the EP, local use of resources changes: local group A, the primary source in the LBA, becomes much less common in the EIA and EP (Figs. 6.7 and 7.19). B cluster subgroups similarly decrease. In contrast, cluster C is much more commonly used during the EP. The shift likely reflects not only changes in technology (also related to typology), but changes in the organization of production, as well as resource distribution and use.

If we compare compositional diversity across the periods from the LBA (YHSS 10-8) to the LP (YHSS 4), the EP period is notable for its source/workshop diversity (Fig. 7.20). The diversity of local sources in

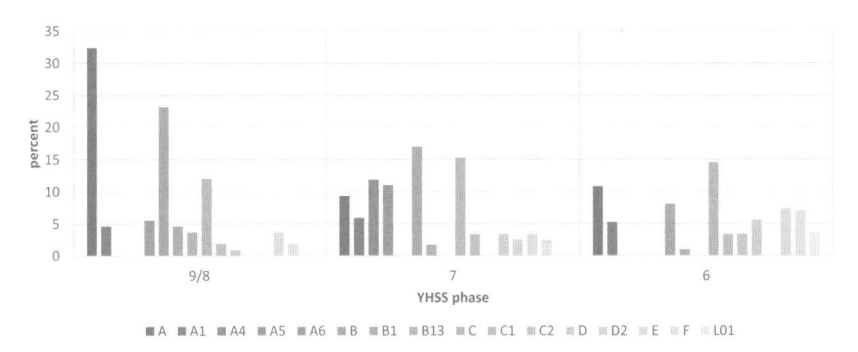

Fig. 7.19 Dominant NAA groups by YHSS phase: latest Late Bronze Age to Early Phrygian period (1400–800 BCE).

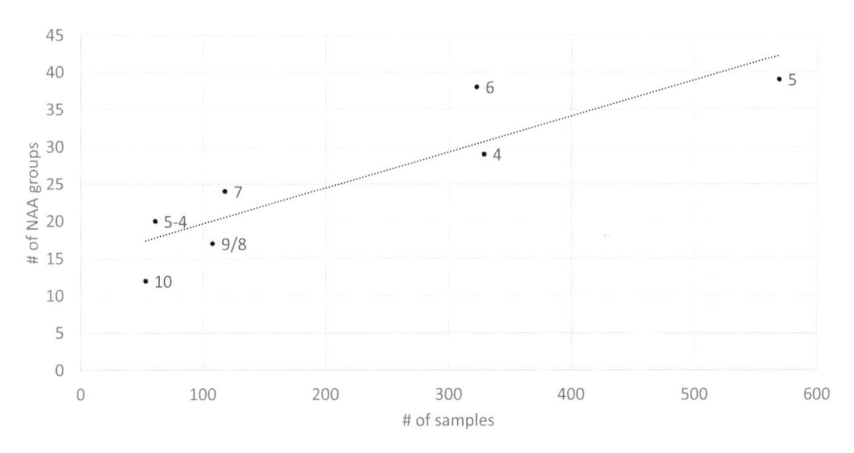

Fig. 7.20 Changing source diversity/workshop diversity over time, from the LBA (YHSS 10-8) to the LP (YHSS 4). Number of samples (x-axis) by number of compositional groups (y-axis).

the EP also suggests that sources from across the local region – or work groups in local communities – were used to produce the ceramics found at Gordion. Sams (1994) suggested this as well (as described in the section "Overview of Early Phrygian Ceramics"). This directly contrasts with the general technological uniformity observed in EP ceramics (Henrickson and Blackman 1996).

The LBA and EP also contrast sharply in geographic patterns of production. During the LBA, nearly all production was focused at Gordion. While local/regional production featured in the LBA, by the

EP period local/regional and nonlocal sources appear to increase not only in distance from Gordion, but also in diversity.

Production, Consumption and Distribution

For each period we present data on production, consumption (use) and distribution from the site and the ceramic analyses in order to better gain multiple perspectives on group formation. In the preceding chapter, most of the data from the Early Iron Age YHSS 7 pointed to household-scale groups, with some hints at larger-scale group interaction in the last decades of the tenth century BCE (7A). In this chapter, to investigate the emergence of a new polity and enhance our understanding of EP groups and group formation, we make use of Hirth's (1996) articulation of relationships between the economy and the polity (see Chapter 4). As in earlier chapters, we also use Costin's (1991) categorization of production strategies. Where available, we document evidence for these production variables as well.

Group Formation and Production

Nonceramic Production Evidence
Communities are shaped by the scale and composition of their social units, including work groups. During the Early Phrygian period construction practices were one of the key sets of activities that undoubtedly catalyzed the formation of new groups in the community, as well as the restructuring of the community. In the earliest phases of the EP (6B), the restricted and non-domestic nature of the excavated area limits our ability to directly identify production groups. It also provides very different behavioral contexts for comparison with both previous and later phases. The general scarcity of small finds in 6B levels (Voigt and Henrickson 2000a), and the apparent speed with which buildings and renovations were undertaken, makes architecture a key indicator of emergent groups in this earliest phase of the EP period. While architecture is commonly not a sensitive indicator of cultural change, the pace of renovation makes it surprisingly useful.

At Gordion, production of architecture clearly involved multiple layers of organization, and many people in different work groups – the types of groups for which there was very limited evidence in the EIA. While Young's excavation notes suggest the possibility of late 7A fortification walls, the most labor-intensive architectural undertaking was the 6B construction of a 9.5 m-thick stone fortification wall with an initial gate (EPB) built of sandstone and timber, and a later gate (Polychrome

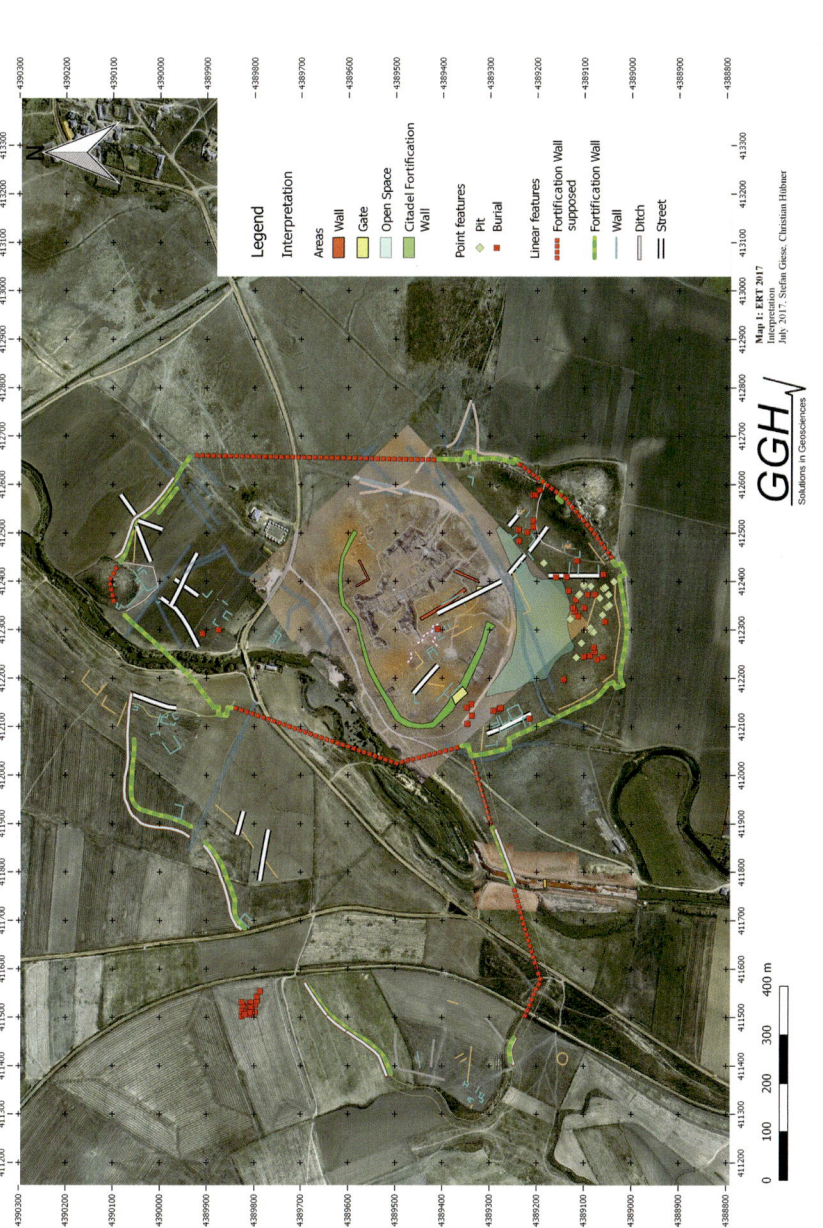

Plate 1 Geophysical survey showing subsurface remains in Lower and Outer Town. MP fortification walls highlighted. The Sakarya River currently cuts through the ancient city to the north of the Citadel Mound, but during the Middle Phrygian period it followed a course along the eastern walls of the YHSS 5 fortification system. The two fortresses that bracket the Lower Town walls are the Küçük Höyük (south) and Kuş Tepe (north).
Image no GGH-2017-Map 2, geophysical data from S. Giese and C. Hübner GGH; courtesy University of Pennsylvania Museum, Gordion Project Archives.

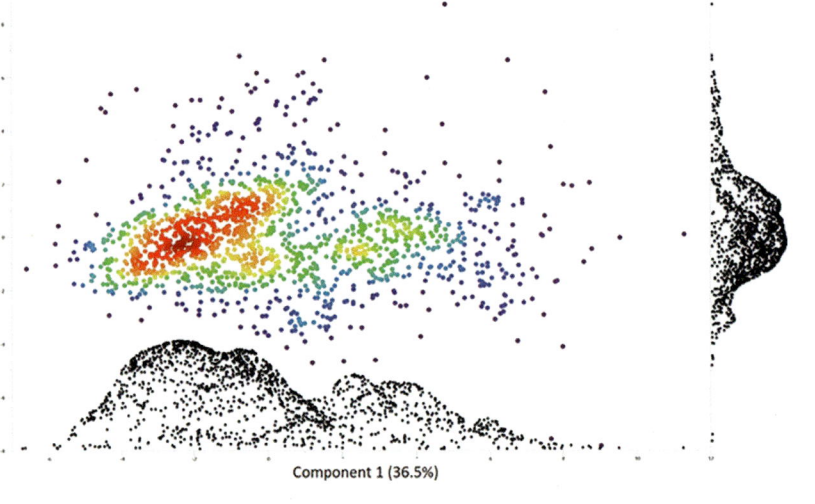

Plate 2 Kernel Density Estimate (KDE) mapping of NAA results for Gordion ceramic sample on first two principal components (~50% of total variation) color-coded by density from red (most dense) to purple (least dense), with density profiles for each component (scale: maximum = 1).

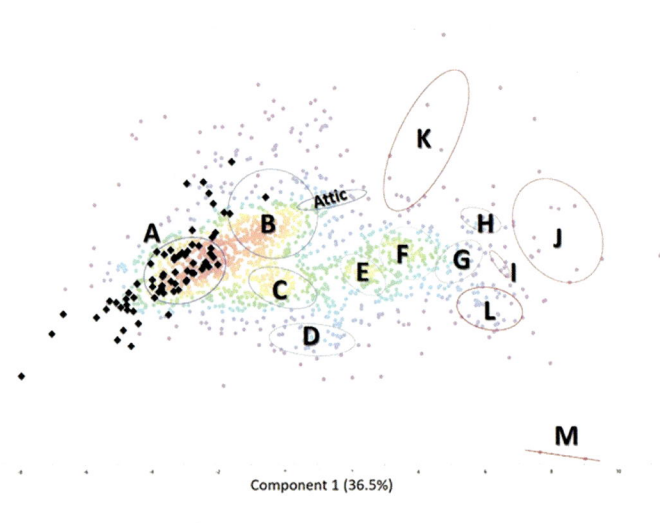

Plate 3 Cluster partitioning of the Gordion compositional profile based on Kernel Density Estimates of the first two components of a PCA (~50% of total variation) for the combined AIA and YHP NAA dataset (n = 1,561); note disposition of Gordion sediments (Fig. 4.2) – black diamonds (n = 72) - in relation to clusters A–M (ellipses 50% confidence).

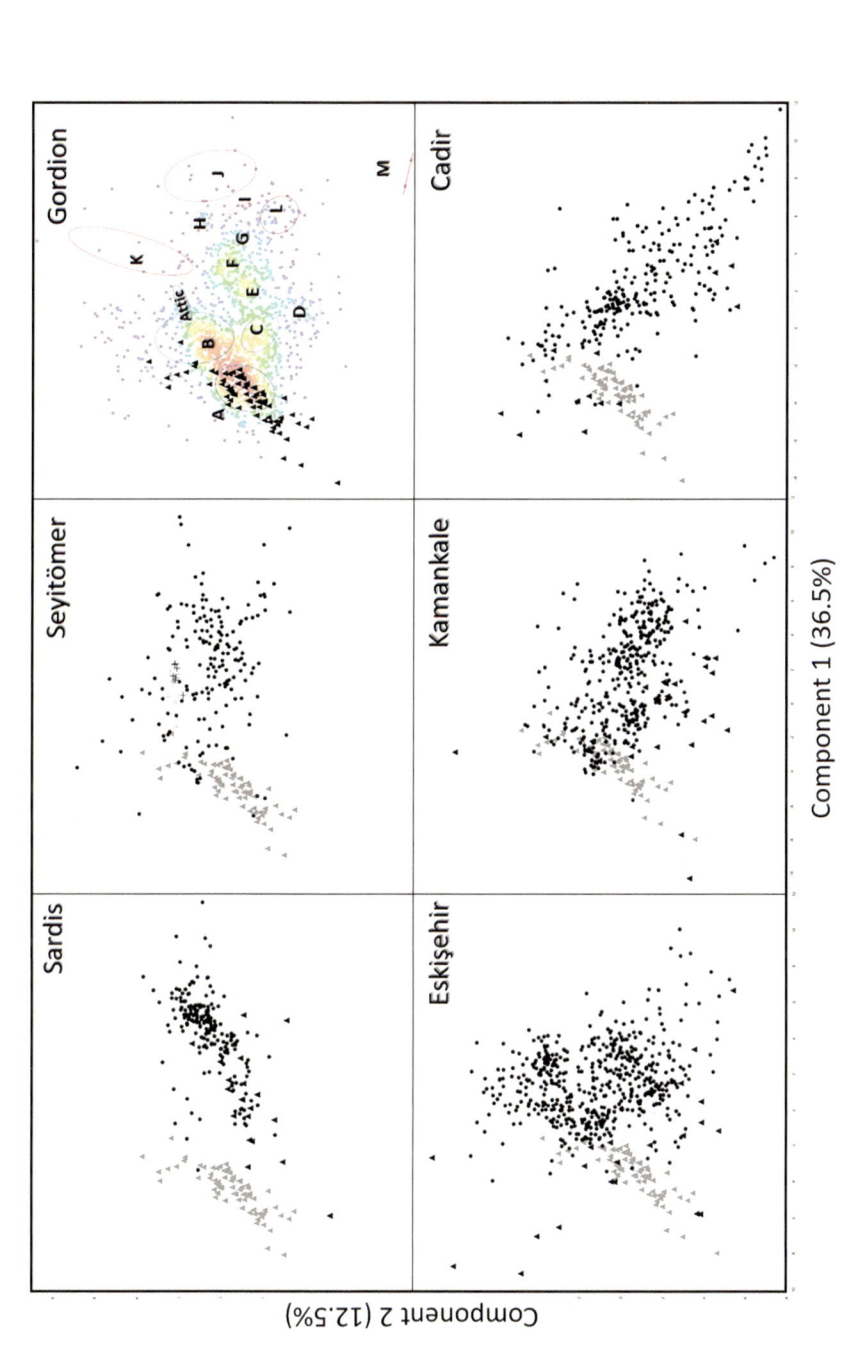

Plate 4 Biplots of first two principal components comparing NAA results for Gordion ceramic and sediment clusters (top right), dimmed for comparison with NAA results for AIA comparator site ceramics (points) and sediments (triangles).
Note original scale has been retained to facilitate comparisons; crosses in Seyitömer plot denote Attic samples.

Plate 5 Group L01 subset ($n = 14$) of Gordion samples that most closely approximate the west Anatolian "Miletos A" compositional profile with several distinctively East Greek Protogeometric types.
a = AIA 37, b = AIA 6226, c = AIA 6218, d = AIA 6221, e = AIA 6222, f = AIA 6129, g = AIA 6388, h = AIA 495, i = AIA 6233, j = AIA 6135, k = AIA 6228, l = AIA 496, m = AIA 6352, n = AIA 7019, o (Kaman Kalehöyük) = AIA 574 and AIA 58). Note that n shows interior and exterior of ceramic.

Plate 6 Group L02 subset ($n = 24$) of Gordion samples showing general typological distinctiveness (Lydianizing but not Sardis manufacture).
a–g = AIA 6405, AIA 6158, AIA 6435, AIA 296, AIA 6440, AIA 6997 and AIA 7000. Note that a and c show sherd interior and exterior.

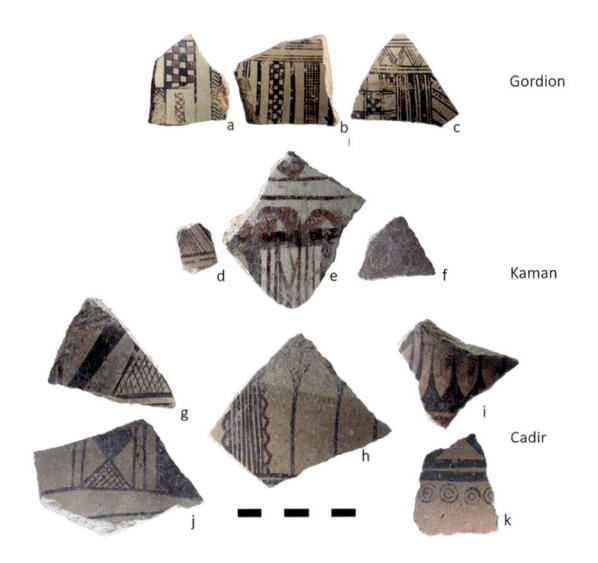

Plate 7 Cluster M samples.
Gordion (*n* = 3), Kaman Kalehöyük (*n* = 3), and Çadır examples (*n* = 17) (Gordion: *a* = AIA 6356, *b* = AIA 6355, *c* = AIA 6361; Kaman Kalehöyük: *d* = AIA 592, *e* = AIA 623, *f* = AIA 522; Çadır: *g* = AIA 696, *h* = AIA 721, *i* = AIA 695, *j* = AIA 3333, *k* = AIA 3336).

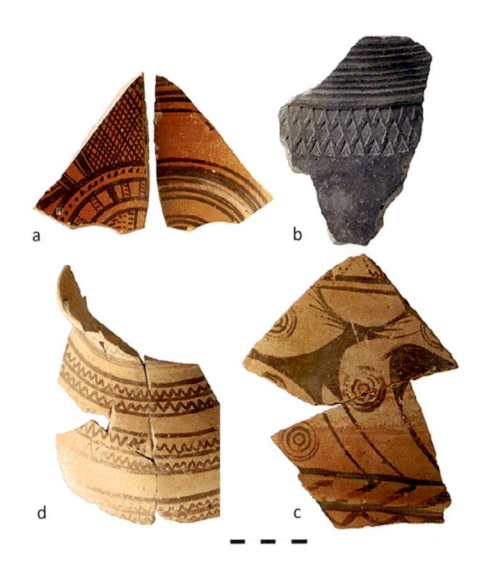

Plate 8 Early Phrygian YHSS 6 Decorated wares (Anatolian Iron Age ceramics project photographs).
a = Black/brown on red AIA 6130 (Gordion inventory no. 8279-P-3328);
b = Grey stamped AIA 6142 (Gordion inventory no. 11746-P-5002);
c = Brown on buff silhouette or Alişar IV ware AIA 6212 (Gordion inventory no. 5745-P2149a);
d = Brown on buff Wavy line AIA 6352 (Gordion inventory no 3112-P-1048a).

Plate 9 Selected Middle Phrygian fine ware decorative styles (courtesy of AIA).
a = Black/brown on red bowl AIA 6405 (Gordion inventory no. 8432-P-3398) (exterior left, interior right).
b = Black/brown on red bowl AIA 6414 (Gordion inventory no. 12617-P-5650) (exterior right, interior left).
c = Black/brown on red stemmed bowl/fruitstand AIA 6406 (Gordion inventory no. 12468-P-5570) (exterior top, interior bottom).
d = Black polished AIA 6982 (Gordion inventory no. 3695-P-1352i) (exterior left, interior right).
e = Black incised sieve jug AIA 6936 (Gordion inventory no. 4801-P-1821a) (exterior left, interior right.

Plate 10 Middle Phrygian fine ware, bichrome spouted jug from the South Cellar. Total height 28.2 cm (YHSS 5B, early seventh century. BCE). (Gordion Inventory no. 8424-P-3395).
Source: Image no. 2015_03252, G. Bieg, courtesy of the University of Pennsylvania, Gordion Archives).

Plate 11 New forms introduced during Middle Phrygian 5A
a = Lekythos from Küçük Höyük (AIA 7003; 1732 P561).
b = Lydion from Küçük Höyük (AIA 6997; 4639 P1744).
c -d. = Skyphoi; c: AIA 6399 interior (top) and exterior (bottom) [cluster B] 10984-P-4496a; d: AIA 6402 [cluster F] 11724-P-4981.
e = Pedestalled bowl/fruitstand from WM SWZ Op 17 (YH 55656).
a–d AIA sampled, reference vessels; *e* after Henrickson 2005.

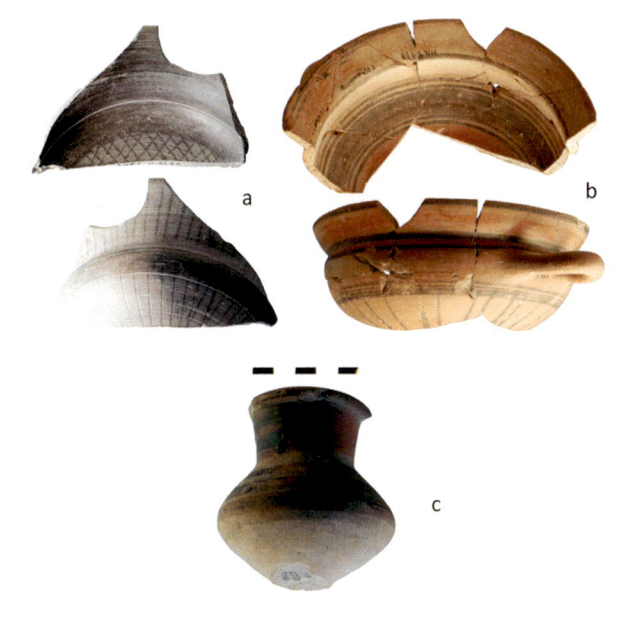

Plate 12 YHSS 4 Late Phrygian vessel forms and styles from across the settlement (courtesy AIA). Emulations of nonlocal forms.
a = Achaemenid bowl AIA 6195 Grey ware with pattern burnish decoration (top interior, bottom exterior).
b = Cup/skyphos AIA 6401 bichrome red and brown decoration (top interior, bottom exterior).
c = Lydion AIA 6999.

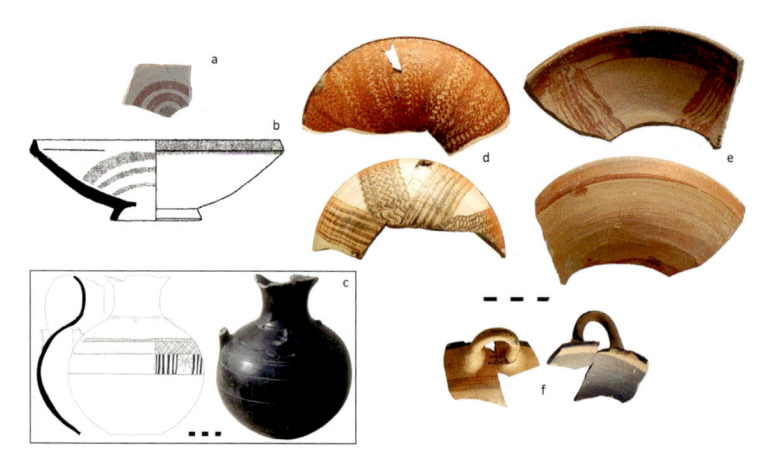

Plate 13 YHSS 4 Late Phrygian vessel forms and decorative styles from across the settlement.
a = Banded bowl (red) AIA472 (YH62910).
b = Banded bowl (red decoration) (Toteva 2007 Pl2 #23).
c = Pattern burnish, black polished trefoil jug (YHSF 89-013) from the floor of LP pithouse cut into MP I:2 [UTS], height 27cm.
d = Lydian marbleizing AIA 6191 (top interior, bottom exterior). (Gordion inventory # 3376-P-1173)
e = Gordion emulation of marbleizing AIA6193 (Gordion inventory # 10929-P-4476) (top interior, bottom exterior).
f = Gordion local glazed skyphos AIA6510 (Gordion inventory # 10959-P-4486) (left exterior, right interior).
Source: *a, d-f* AIA; *b* Galya Toteva [Bacheva]; *c* drawing D. Hoffman, photo L. Foos. University of Pennsylvania Museum, Gordion Project Archives.

Plate 14 YHSS 4 Late Phrygian metallurgical debris.
During the fourth century, the Eastern Mound became the site of small-scale metallurgical production (see Fig. 3.5b, Foundry and area of MP Building I:2). Crucibles with slag and copper prills from LP deposits in the Upper Trench Sounding (see also Rademakers et al 2018:Fig. 3).
Source: Image no. 90-1036:007, L. Foos; courtesy University of Pennsylvania Museum, Gordion Project Archives.

Gatehouse) of more durable stone selected from different outcrops around the Gordion region (Sams and Voigt 2011). The buildings inside the fortification wall used more timber and a bright white, fine-grained and soft mudstone or "poros," and one or more structures were ornamented with poros moldings and sculptures (e.g. Post and Poros structure and the Polychrome Gatehouse). These are the first buildings to make use of stone working, shaping blocks for walls. To produce architecture at this monumental scale would have minimally required a specialized labor force that included overseers, quarry workers, stone masons, builders, carpenters and sculptors along with unskilled laborers and draft animals to haul large quantities of timber and stone.

Prior to this 6B construction, a workforce flattened the top of the Eastern Mound, removing Bronze Age (and perhaps Early Iron Age) structures, potentially including public architecture and/or the remains of LBA temples. Arguably, this clearing served both a functional purpose in creating a place for monumental architecture, as well as destroying a place likely associated with LBA elites and rituals. While more destruction than construction *per se*, this work produced the foundational space enabling the expansion of the EP elite quarter.

The 6A fortifications were even more massive, a wall built of large stone blocks protected by a glacis, that apparently encircled the entire area of what would become the Citadel Mound (Rose 2017). Voigt (2013:191) suggests that the cold bond/segmented construction evident in the new northwest fortification wall (see Fig. 3.3b; DeVries 1990:fig. 10) may reflect "piecework" organization of labor, with wall segments assigned to particular (corvée?) groups. She also proposes that the wall may have been as much symbolic as functional, given weaknesses inherent in its construction. The new 6A Eastern Gate shares the same properties: massive, designed to impress, but with clear structural flaws in its northeast corner. Equally, the wooden doors used to close the entrance to the Polychrome Gatehouse, while perhaps impressive, were also a glaring functional weakness in the overall defensive architecture of the site.

In addition to new fortifications built on large quantities of earth fill above the EPB and 6B fortification walls, new works in 6A included at least 12 megarons (Inner and Outer Court, with separating wall), and the massive terrace supporting the Terrace Complex (Fig. 7.3). The substantial logistical challenges presented by the ambitious scale and timing of this undertaking, over a ca. 50–60-year period in the ninth century BCE, would have minimally involved engaging, scheduling and maintaining a committed and periodically rejuvenated labor force – as well as overseers – to acquire the timber and stone, and to transform raw materials into construction materials to build the EP citadel and elite zone.

Six excavated tumuli from the EP period provide insight into the mortuary practices of multiple elite families or kin groups with access to labor, and local and exotic trade goods (Kohler 1995; Stephens 2018). While these tumuli are highly variable in size and construction practices, none stand out with elaboration at a higher order of magnitude expected of a ruler or king, suggesting that EP elite organization lacked the apical hierarchy of the succeeding Middle Phrygian period. However, the alignment of the East Gate with Tumulus W (Liebhart et al. 2016), the largest tumulus of the period, may be evidence for emergent hierarchical rule.

Food production in the EP period remained heavily reliant on sheep and goat pastoralism. A shift toward more intensive and localized agricultural strategies, including grain production, is suggested by a modest decrease in sheep and goat, along with a commensurate increase in cattle and pigs requiring fodder crops such as barley (N. F. Miller et al. 2009). It also seems likely some water management strategies would have been used to ameliorate periodic water shortages. Environmental data attest to ninth century BCE droughts both locally and across the larger region (K. R. Morgan 2018:216: footnote 106; N. Roberts et al. 2016). Morgan (2018) argues for feasting, particularly beer production and consumption, as a regular practice in EP Gordion; if so, an expansion in grain production (and storage facilities) at this time could be expected. Our evidence for food production, the introduction of intensification strategies, and increased demand, however, provides only indirect support for group dynamics.

Archaeologically, the final 6A Destruction Level preserves the most evidence in terms of volume of material and diversity of contexts at Gordion. It reveals intertwined patterns of consumption and production (detailed in the section "Group Formation and Consumption"), particularly from the Terrace Complex. The burned Terrace Complex (i.e. Terrace Building and Clay Cut Building), with their contents intact at the time of the fire, provide a uniquely rich window on the character of EP production. Of the 11 excavated service units, nine were used for the storage and production of food, beer and textiles, and two more were used primarily for textile production and storage. Wheat and barley, along with multiple grinding stones set in benches, and ovens were common to all nine production units. A few units also contained other food types (lentils, hazelnuts), and in CC3, a single butchered calf (DeVries 1980:39). Loom weights and tools, as well as textile fragments, suggest production of multiple, generally heavier-gauge weights of cloth (B. Burke 1998, 2005). Many of the iron tools were likely related to food processing (meat) and preparation, managing cooking/ovens and perhaps woodworking; other tools may have been in storage rather than in use at the time of the fire (Darbyshire personal communication 2017). The proximity of the Terrace Complex rooms to each other and to the Inner Court megarons suggests some type of centralized management.

The scale of production and the position of the buildings in the Terrace Complex suggests these activities mainly served the occupants and guests living in the adjacent enclosed courts. DeVries (1980) estimated each service unit was supported by ca. 25 workers, totaling over 200 workers when fully staffed, based on the quantities of looms, grinding stones and other goods in each megaron. How these groups were constituted or their terms of service remains unknown. Morgan (2018) suggests that production in the Terrace Complex was likely in support of feasting at multiple scales, and served as one of the key mechanisms of Phrygian sociopolitical formation.

Goods found in the Inner and Outer Court megarons (mainly Megaron 3) also indirectly provide additional evidence of production. For example, textiles (linen or hemp and animal fiber), interpreted as clothing, wall hangings and/or part of furniture, were likely to have been locally produced (DeVries 1980; Holzman 2019). Drinking vessels, as well as cauldrons and craters, for beer and potentially wine or other fermented beverages, indicate a local origin for these beverages as well. Iron tools, some possibly large hearth furniture (rakes, tongs), were also probably forged locally given their relative frequency across 6A contexts (DeVries 1980:36). The abundance of items related to spinning and weaving in both the Terrace service buildings and elite megarons suggests multiple contexts and meanings for textile production.

Whether other items were locally produced (i.e. bronze bowls and cauldrons, glassware, ivory plaques and decorative elements) has yet to be determined. Stylistically, many of these show eastern or northern Syrian stylistic influences, as do the images on the probably still-in-use 6B orthostats as well as the graffiti on the "Doodle Stones" associated with Megaron 2 (Roller 1999).

Ongoing construction and remodeling projects of the ninth century BCE document not only the formation of a variety of work groups, but also the need to continuously acquire materials and produce furnishings. The extensiveness of construction, across a large area over a relatively short period (a few decades), would have required specialized skilled labor groups, and highlights the potential costs involved in the aggrandizing role of increasingly status-differentiated elites at Gordion. In addition, the nature of this construction work suggests a workforce that was not created *ad hoc* or seasonally, but was likely employed on a regular if not permanent basis. Support for this specialized workforce undoubtedly also involved provisioning with additional surplus resources, particularly food, reflected in the intensification of agricultural strategies.

Ceramic Production and Groups

EP household groups no longer, or rarely, produced handmade ceramics, potentially reflecting major changes in household organization, with implications for scheduling, activities and relationships. As in many societies, however, specialized household production might have continued. In a more specialized economy increased demand for production of other goods, or for labor, would have encouraged acquisition rather than household production of ceramic vessels for domestic use. Potters, now organized into at least part-time work groups, may have also been spatially and temporally separated from households, in the process defining new groups with different sets of interests and identities. This new level of ceramic diversity and elaboration in production plays out across multiple types of Early Phrygian material culture and, in some cases at least, seems to represent the intentional construction and maintenance of a distinctive identity across multiple spheres.

<u>Scale of production – production sequences</u> The EP assemblage includes few elaborated forms or surface treatments. The time and effort expended producing most vessels was low to moderate (i.e. less than for the EIAH; Henrickson 1994). More elaborated types (i.e. decorated jugs, jars and pots) are relatively uncommon and typically associated with communal serving of beverages.

In the absence of any clear relationship between sources and forms, we have little evidence of specialization in producing particular types, or even in the production of elite vs. common styles of pottery. Allowing for sample size effects, most forms (craters are the exception) were produced across the range of local sources. However, there are clear differences in source distribution (Table 7.4). This pattern is similar for fabrics, as both buff and grey fabrics are locally and regionally produced, with somewhat greater source diversity for buff ware. As noted, most red fabrics were not local (Table 7.3a).

Henrickson proposed that EP pottery was produced by a few, likely modest-sized workshops, that were spatially widely distributed (beyond the Citadel Mound; Henrickson 2010). Part-time specialization also seems likely. Mass-production first (re)appeared and expanded in this period, with a concomitant increase in uniformity (Henrickson 1994:111). Our compositional evidence for production of ceramics from numerous sources complicates this scenario, suggesting either considerable exchange or tribute, or the use of a disparate range of resources from the Gordion hinterland, a pattern at odds with streamlining of resources for mass production at this time. Changes in ceramic production, from firing to clay source use and production styles, suggest that work groups may have shared general technological traditions in vessel formation and firing, but there were also many more work groups or sources than expected in a simple local supply-and-demand scenario. This raises a further question: if forms are relatively uniform or standard (bowl types for example), yet come from both local and nonlocal sources, how was this uniformity established, extended or maintained over the wider region?

Production location/numbers/spatial proximity Despite the lack of evidence for actual pottery production locales, compositional data provide indirect evidence for number of work groups and in some measure their spatial relationships in the EP. Using the composition of soil and clay reference samples to identify local production, it is clear that EP-period production included multiple groups from local, regional and more distant areas, along with new sources of imports from groups east and west (cf. Henrickson 2001). Differences in the proportion of compositional groups also suggest changing resource preferences between the EIA and EP periods (see Figs. 6.7, 7.19).

The number of production groups in the EP is large in contrast to the LBA, which stands out as a period of relatively low resource diversity (Fig. 7.20). Given the general similarities in EP and LBA production (relatively uniform, work group production), an expectation is that compositional profiles of the two periods should also be comparable. Instead, EP diversity appears to reflect the operation of a substantially larger number of work groups across the local and regional landscape. These were potentially under the patronage of elite families or competing factions in the EP countryside. Ceramic production, therefore, was likely not under the kind of centralized management suggested by the contents of the 6A terrace buildings on the Eastern Mound.

The contrasts in this patterning related to production location are particularly apparent if we compare the grey with buff fabrics. Buff fabrics show much greater overall source diversity than grey fabrics and are more typically from local A cluster sources. Both buff and grey fabrics have a relatively high frequency of nonlocal sources, but from different sources (e.g. decorated buff pottery is spread across a range of coastal and Lydian sources, while grey fabrics are most common from source F1 (Ionian, western Anatolia).

Skill level The skill sets of potters changed substantially from the EIA through the EP. More uniform fabrics, forms and decoration of buff ware

(7A-6A) and EP grey wares suggest the operation of an increasingly restricted number of specialist work groups producing for a larger catchment. The production of buff ware from the later EIA (7A) period provides evidence of group organization and elaboration prefiguring the elaboration in architectural evidence we find at the start of the EP period (YHSS 6B).

Standardization (or relative metric homogeneity) as a measure of skill may be distinct from execution, but the two can be difficult to differentiate (Roux 2003). For example, rapid repetitive execution (as a measure of proficiency and skill) can still result in variable quality and divergent metrics. While forming evidence indicates little about variability in skill level, the painted decoration of EP buff ware provides more graphic evidence of considerable variation in ability among contemporary specialists. This suggests that at least some work groups had highly proficient painters, and likely also potters, but multiple skill levels were present. Work groups probably supported cultural transmission of skills both between generations and peer to peer, augmenting the homogeneity of forms and perhaps allowing for innovative stylistic demands of their patrons (e.g. workgroups with a few specialists, or "masters" along with apprentices).

Technological investment The elaboration of infrastructure and internal specialization over time required the formation of work groups, further contributing to group differentiation, while creating differences in status and identity for production group members.

As noted, we have little direct evidence of ceramic production for the EP period. Henrickson suggests that both buff and grey wares were produced in workshops and were likely kiln fired. If so, then technological investment, and other activities related to groups, may have taken place on the edge of town or in the surrounding countryside.

Production infrastructure likely comprised potters' wheels and tournettes, work areas (including drying area) and kilns. Storage for fuel, clay, temper and materials used in decoration would also require additional investment and space.

Kiln construction, use, maintenance and repair entails levels of experience, both in understanding the complex relationships between design and construction, thermal dynamics, fuel type and packing, as well as in the effective control of firing intensity in relation to specific clay recipe thermal behavior, kiln atmosphere, and firing duration (Rice 2015). While independent households may have operated kilns seasonally, the repertoire of locally produced fine wares appears consistent with production by specialists using kilns operated either communally or in conjunction with workshops (Rice 2015).

Summary: Producing Groups

The archaeological data for production provide compelling, if indirect, evidence for the relatively rapid formation of new and different types of production groups during the EP period; these groups in turn defined new modes and organizational structures of status and power. Early Phrygian groups planned, built and occupied a monumental fortress and megarons within it, created large-scale working and feasting areas, produced a range of material culture that included cloth and other textiles, elaborated ceramics and possibly metal goods and precious stones. Such groups operated in quite distinct social contexts: those within the elite core, those pressed into service for set outputs (corvée) and those more loosely linked to production for elites and other sectors of society. The elaboration of high-status ceramic types (and clay sources/recipes) created and reinforced distinct identities and groupings within both production and consumption contexts.

Arguably, daily practices related to production as well as work groups were one of the most critical components of the ritual economy at Gordion. Rapid elaboration and differentiation of groups beginning ca. 900 BCE crosscut kin, tribute and production, and flags the potential emergence of effective integrative ideology supporting charismatic leaders in this period. Early Phrygian power appears distributed across multiple groups, with increasingly hierarchical relations evident in the following MP period. However, the formation and practices of these work groups also likely created new tensions and contradictions within the EP community at Gordion, particularly as members negotiated their roles and relationships across different spheres.

Group Formation and Consumption

Nonceramic Consumption Evidence

Understanding group consumption contexts as they relate to Gordion's EP economy and politics provides a second perspective on group formation and practice.

While it appears that many 6B EP contexts were destroyed by later construction, several foundations and architectural remnants can be related to 6B construction phases (Voigt 1994). This includes the settlement wall, gates and elaborate buildings. Voigt (2013) suggested that those who entered the 6B gate to the elite quarter entered an open area with both residential and administrative structures. In this type of arrangement, individuals from disparate groups would have commingled to some extent. However, subsequent (6A) changes in the organization of the Inner and Outer Court increased segregation between public and private practices, further differentiating patterns and contexts of consumption.

Biological evidence from the Voigt excavations also suggests a shift in food consumption in the EP period. Remains of sheep and goat decreased relative to cattle and pig. Nearly all of the faunal remains come from the LTS within the elite quarter and appear to document beef and pork as food status markers in the EP diet (Zeder and Arter 1994). A recent analysis of bone recovered by Young from CC3 within the Terrace Complex further reinforces this interpretation: the collection included at least five cattle (three of them sub-adult), at least one large deer, three sheep, one goat and six young pigs, several of them found in pots (Slim 2020).

The pattern of fuel consumption also marks a key transition during the EP period as people shifted from burning juniper (probably including trimmings from construction timber) to (possibly) burning more distant pine, proportionately the largest component of the EP charcoal assemblage (60–80%). Subsequently, in the MP period, oak was most intensively used. Miller (2010) noted that oak and juniper form the understory of pine forests about 50 km away. When pine trees are cleared, secondary growth of oak increases, as pine trees are much slower to recover, particularly in drier areas such as those around Gordion. This pattern therefore suggests that following the decline of the closest stands of juniper and oak, more distant pine forests were then targeted during the EP period for fuel and likely other purposes, before people shifted to using secondary and understory woody species. Given the lack of pine in the immediate area, the logistics of acquisition must have involved considerable organization, labor and transport infrastructure.

The ca. 800 BCE 6A:3 Destruction Level preserves an unusually detailed picture of elite consumption at Gordion, both because it was quickly sealed by rapid burial and leveling operations, and also because of the extensive scale of excavations for this subphase. In particular, the lavish decoration of Megaron 3 (finely inlaid wood furniture and wall hangings) led DeVries and others to suggest it may have been a royal residence (DeVries 1980). Consumption of exotic items, likely from the east to southeast (northern Syria today), included ivory plaques (furniture decoration?) and ornaments, bronze bowls and cauldrons, and a small amount of gold. The rooms around the Inner Court were clearly used for the consumption of food and drink, if not larger-scale communal dining or feasting. Status markers also included relatively exotic foods, such as cornelian cherries and hazelnuts, as well as highly elaborated drinking vessels and containers. While Megaron 3 may have been a private elite residence, its location along with the range and type of goods recovered as material reinforcements of status, wealth and power suggest it may also have played a role in forms of elite status display for those admitted to the Inner Court.

Adjacent to the Outer and Inner Courts on the Eastern Mound, the Terrace Complex buildings (TB and CC) primarily preserve evidence of production, but consumption evidence forms an equally informative, if less well-represented, counterpart. The main room of TB2 had caches of jewelry, bronze figurines and fine ivory horse trappings, as well as stored bronze cauldrons (DeVries 1980). This seemingly disparate cache potentially represents items placed in temporary storage during the 6A:3 remodeling, but a longer-term use of TB2 for storage rather than food preparation is evident in the absence of grinding stones and ovens, found in 9 of the 11 TC units. In other units, a small number of goods similar to those found in the megarons, such as hazelnut shells and individual fine drinking vessels, suggest workers had access to some of the same provisions as those in the Inner Court megarons.

Morgan (2018) suggests construction of the megarons and courts created feasting and performance space for ritualized production and consumption. The evidence for feasting is strong, and Morgan (2018:199–202) cites the "charming messiness" of the highly variable assemblages in the Terrace Buildings, and to some extent the megarons around the courts, as evidence for participation in communal rituals of production and consumption to establish/reaffirm group solidarity rather than attached production in support of ruling elites. Nonetheless, given the spatial distribution of high-status goods, elites appear to have played critical roles in group formation in these contexts. Elite consumption associated with the megarons (particularly M3) was paralleled in burial practices, where the same goods, including fine furniture, multiple types of textiles and elaborate bronze and ceramic drinking and eating vessels were part of the furnishings for the deceased (e.g. Tumulus W). The evidence for feasting crosscuts multiple contexts, suggesting a complex range of practices, and groups, associated with commensal consumption. Unfortunately, the lack of non-elite EP contexts stymies our understanding of non-elite consumption.

Consumption and Ceramics

Performance of feasting – communal consumption of food and drink – serves both to integrate groups and to establish often hierarchical status relationships (Dietler and Hayden 2010; Hayden and Villeneuve 2011). The EP ceramic assemblage includes vessels appropriate for feasting. New vessel forms (i.e. tablewares such as juglets or goblets, diverse types of jugs and craters with elaborated forms and decoration; Fig. 7.8b) seem specifically designed to enhance group display and feasting. Many of these forms appear to be mimicking similar forms made of metal, as becomes even more evident in the subsequent Middle Phrygian period.

EP evidence for ceramic consumption (use) practices derives from elite contexts associated with the megarons, Terrace Buildings (primary and secondary contexts) and Tumulus W. While the nature of the vessel forms strongly implicates feasting, with an emphasis on drinking as a key component in elite practices of power, DeVries (1980) cautions that some of the vessel forms we associate with liquids (jars, jugs) were also at times used for storage of small goods (e.g. knives, spindle whorls, etc.). Both food and more durable goods were commonly found in rooms of both the Terrace Complex and megarons. The abundance of bowls and large pots or craters in mortuary contexts, however, reinforces the central performative role of drink in elite group consumption. Tumulus W and the 6A:3 Destruction Level contexts (Megaron 3) provide our strongest indication of the practice of feasting with multiple bowls, jugs and cauldrons – e.g. Sams (1994:136) notes that of ca. 200 painted vessels curated from the Destruction Level at least 20 are from M3.

Early Phrygian ceramics provide several other lines of evidence for understanding relationships between groups and consumption. While painted buff ware constitutes a relatively small component of the overall assemblage (1:15? or ca. 7%; Sams 1994), buff ware associated with drinking (e.g. round mouth, small trefoil and sieve jugs), and specifically pouring vessels, exhibit some of the most elaborate and diverse styles of painted decoration (Sams 1994:137). Styles range from simple (e.g. single or multiple wavy lines), to highly elaborate, finely rendered geometric patterns ("Ornate" ware). Among the decorated forms, few decorative patterns or arrangements are repeated (Sams 1994:134). This highly individualized approach is consistent with displays of identity of individual elites (and/or their kin). The styles also reveal links to groups both east (e.g. Alişar [IV]) and west (e.g. northern Thessaly; western Anatolia discussed further in the section "Group Formation and Distribution"), highlighting another aspect of status display. While Sams (1994:135) maintained that the strongest EP links were to the east with central Anatolia and northern Syria, EP networks were clearly wider. Stamped jars may also relate to status display through consumption of the exotic, both as vessels as containers for goods and as relatively rare decorative styles. The compositional data indicates that while a few are locally produced, most come from local/regional or west Anatolian sources.

Summary: Consuming Groups
The changing nature of consumption and the introduction of new contexts of consumption were key parts of group formation across EP

Gordion. The transition from the EIA to the EP involved a profound change in the creation and signaling of groups at Gordion. These new EP groups were discernible in many ways. Consumption of food and drink in strongly marked and elaborated places reveals at least one of the ways that these new groups formed and practiced, as evident in the buildings (and burials), their contents and the vessels themselves. Elaboration of jugs and craters for communal drinking emphasizes the significance of these activities. The elaboration of these larger vessels rather than individual cups or bowls appears to mark particular groups rather than individuals within the elite community. Uniquely decorated containers for liquid may also indicate a relationship between specific groups and vessel contents. The use of highly decorated and labor-intensive cloth/textiles, with similar decorative elements, also reveals the multiplicity of ways in which identities were constructed and practiced.

The diversity and distribution of ceramic compositional groups in the EP may reflect the patronage of individuals or families who contributed vessels and goods made at Gordion and in its neighboring communities, as well as further afield (as tribute? or part of feasting rituals) for group consumption (Grave et al. 2009). If this were so, various feasting strategies emerge as one of a suite of new strategies to gather resources and support across the region, as well as in the construction and practice of political power defining more cosmopolitan groups and networks.

Group Formation and Distribution

Nonceramic Evidence of Distribution

Here we look at the distribution of goods and materials in relation to their origin (as opposed to distribution of goods across the site). Aside from physical geospatial provenance, we are also interested in the origin of particular styles or forms (emulation). Each of these reveals different dimensions of group formation and identity.

Few of the nonceramic assemblages at Gordion have been analyzed with respect to context and association. One exception is DeVries' (1980) discussion of the parallels for many of the items found in EP elite contexts. The strongest links, in general, are with sites and styles found to the east and southeast in central Anatolia and northern Syria (e.g. decorative elements on bronze cauldrons, ivory ornaments; Roller 2008). It is likely that most of these items were brought into Gordion as finished objects rather than as raw materials. Probable sources of food provide some of the few better provenanced items. DeVries (1980) noted that the hazelnuts and cherries in Megaron 3 were both likely to have been imported from the north (closest sources: Black Sea region and the

Pontus Mountains). Bronze fibulae from the tumuli burials, stylistically identified as exotic, provide other possible evidence for regional exchange networks (Kohler 1995). While iron is common in EP contexts on the Eastern Mound, the proportion of imports versus local products has yet to be established.

In addition to imports, local emulation of elite goods from the Neo-Hittite region of north Syria suggests that EP elites selectively adopted well-developed symbols and methods as a means to legitimate local power relationships. This is particularly clear in the production of orthostats at the beginning of the EP period, using a subset of Neo-Hittite iconography to display elite status. Their use in public areas appears to support this suggestion. While the collapse of the Hittite Empire had taken place over two centuries before, we cannot dismiss those relationships of power as entirely forgotten, particularly as groups to the southeast continue many of these practices through the EIA. However, the choice to emulate arenas of feasting and face-to-face negotiations of power, rather than the highly ritualized religious and public displays of Hittite imperial power, highlight the very different character of EP elite group formation and identity (Beckman 1989, 2000).

Ceramics and Distribution

The expansion of pottery imports as well as the diversification of local sources further highlight significant changes in EP communities at Gordion.

Forms The abundance of particular imported forms (jars, jugs, craters) suggests individuals or groups brought vessels into the center, both to carry goods (in relatively small volumes based on these vessel sizes) and as consumables, supporting the idea they were organizing feasting events that brought outside elites and high-value resources into the capital. The particularly high diversity of jars (potentially conflated with jugs), also suggests that imported goods were valued as a component of the emerging ritual economy (McAnany and Wells 2008).

Different groups contributed different ceramic forms to EP Gordion. While jars and jugs come from the same nonlocal East Greek/west Anatolian sources, bowls are more often locally produced (Table 7.4). Potentially, these differences in vessel provenance reflect the nature of economic and political interaction between groups in these regions.

The diversity of local/regional and nonlocal EP vessels reinforces an interpretation that public displays of different types of identity during drinking (and eating) functioned as critical acts establishing groups within EP communities.

Decoration The evidence for both emulation and exchange during the EP period shows the emergence of new processes and contexts for group formation and group differentiation. The prevalence of stylistic emulation of other regions of Anatolia, along with actual exchange of ceramics in the EP period, reveals a rapid transformation in the type and scale of interactions among EP community groups. Two main decorative styles were most likely imported: brown on X and Black (or brown) on red, with links to groups both east and west of Gordion. Black on red decorated ceramics were imported from several sources to the west, with very little local or local/regional production (Table 7.5). Brown on X wares, on the other hand, reveal a more complex dynamic, representing a diverse set of both nonlocal and local sources (Fig. 7.18). The import of a set of Brown on buff wavy line-decorated jars/jugs and dinoi, which closely approximate the "Miletos A" compositional cluster, highlights the significance of exotic relationships on display during the consumption of drink (predominantly 6A DL). While most stamped jars matched local and local/regional sources, the import of stamped jars from a single (possibly west Anatolian) source found widely distributed across Terrace Building and megaron contexts, suggests a particular significance for these vessels, and potentially their contents. Sams (1988) suggested these stamped vessels had very close parallels with pottery in Thrace. This differential distribution of the two wares, with different functions, also suggests both distinct interaction networks and discrete meanings in consumption contexts.

Only a few of the better-represented decorative styles of the EP show evidence of emulation, specifically variants of brown on X and grey stamped. Brown on X wares include a range of styles, with both eastern and western elements and somewhat generic geometric elements (lines, wavy lines, triangles; Sams 1978). Hatched triangles and diamonds are the most common decorative elements in local cluster A. A few other samples with also appear to be emulations of mainly west Anatolian decorative styles.

Previous interpretations of EP decoration also highlight the diversity of groups likely to have produced the decorated buff ware (Henrickson 2005; Sams 1994). Yet suggestions that EP stylistic diversity marks the florescence and development of local Phrygian style implies a highly endogenous level of creativity among the craftspeople supporting EP elites. The compositional data frame a more complex picture. Most of the locally produced styles are unique (Fine Line Buff) or highly generic (hatched triangles and diamonds). The compositional data indicate active exchange with groups both locally and more broadly across western Anatolia (at least from Lydia to Ionia). This suggests that EP elites were constructing groups and fashioning their identities, not only from local creative developments in ceramic styles and forms (e.g. the elaboration of fine Brown on buff and later black-decorated wares), but also through integrating diverse types of relationships with more distant groups across the region.

Summary: Distribution and Group Formation

The EP community was composed of functionally discrete groups organized in multiple ways. Criteria for group formation were contingent and crosscutting (e.g. see labor discussion in the earlier section "Group Formation and Production"). The ceramic compositional evidence provides a new dimension beyond previous interpretations, underlining the greater range of cosmopolitan interactions of the EP groups, not only with groups in the southeast in the northern Levant/Syria, but also with less well-known Protogeometric-period communities of Ionia and western Anatolia.

Two main facets of distribution were new in the EP period. First, elites at Gordion acquired a significant number of ceramic jars and decorated tablewares from beyond the capital. Based on current matches, these came from as far afield as Ionia (Aegean coast to the west and southwest) and central Anatolia, in the vicinities of Çadır and Kaman Kalehöyük. Strong links to the west have not previously been documented for EP-period ceramics, and little is known of ninth century BCE Ionia. Second, even local EP ceramics are more compositionally diverse than LBA ceramics (relative to sample size). In this context, we suggest that diversity is not related to variability in household production (e.g. as in the EIA), but to a larger number of EP work groups, particularly those producing jars and jugs (Fig. 7.14).

Discussion: Transforming Identities

From the LBA through the EP periods, the scale of ceramic production cycled from more specialized work groups to more household production and back. The symbolic marking associated with food preparation and consumption also changed. In the LBA, there is little evidence of display or identity marking in food-related ceramics, while in the EP many new forms and styles are specifically related to drinking. These changes undoubtedly impacted gender relationships within and between families, as tasks and work groups reorganized and consumption patterns changed. While an overlapping set of local clay resources were used throughout these phases, the redistribution of LBA ceramics was limited to the local region. In contrast, EIA and EP pottery production and organization were both more expansive and diverse, with more specialized work groups reemerging by the EP (Henrickson 2005), although the underlying structures of organization and control in the EP (as in the LBA) remain uncertain.

Compositional data provide new insights into the differences in production between the LBA and EP. The limited diversity of compositional groups during the LBA (see Fig. 6.7) suggests a small number of relatively large work groups used a narrow range of local clay sources for the production of a limited array of vessel types (see Table 5.6). The contrast with the compositional diversity present in the EP is striking, where a variety of resources were exploited as multiple sources were used to produce a wide range of forms and styles (Figs. 7.15, 7.17, Tables 7.4, 7.5).

Our reference sediments allow us to define the potential range and variety of local resources. Early Phrygian production was specialized, but it was also dispersed across a broad resource landscape. While direct links to political economy are difficult to parse, the EP hierarchy looks "flatter," or more heterarchical, than LBA organization (Fig. 6.7). However, it was also more factionalized and competitive based on the multiple and diverse markers of identity in use.

Identity and marking of social relationships differ sharply between the LBA and EP. The introduction of stylistically marked interaction in the EP, as both emulation and exchange, reveals the creation of high-status identities in relation to much larger and more varied political and social fields. Also newly established in the EP is an array of specialized forms that highlight aspects of group identities in semi-public arenas. The ceramics used for these displays were made from a disparate range of sources, both local and exotic, suggesting that many groups contributed to and/or participated in these feasting and drinking events. The creation of spaces and places for group action and definition, as well as the development and consumption of material props, signals the changing ways EP elites adopted or created novel and sophisticated strategies to construct power (Khatchadourian 2016). Both the open courts and the open space between the Eastern and Western Mounds were arguably locations for such public practices.

Strong contrasts between the EP and earlier EIA communities derive in part from differences in excavation contexts (elite vs. domestic). While the EP ceramic assemblage is stylistically close to EIA buff ware, there is a marked shift from mainly buff to mainly grey (reduction-fired) ware in the EP period. This technological trend appears to parallel a political shift in how elites practiced power at this time. Potentially, local elites, who referenced external links early in their acquisition of power, redefined their styles to establish stronger local identities. Practices of power may have also begun to shift to include more exclusionary and hierarchical genres. Both of these patterns are more clearly apparent in the subsequent Middle Phrygian period.

Conclusions

Rapid expansion in the numbers and types of groups in the EP period at Gordion is visible through multiple lines of evidence. Large construction projects and architectural elaboration contribute clear arenas for group formation, performance and materialization of practices of power. The ceramic data not only provide additional lines of evidence for new types of groups and relationships across the region, but also add a new dimension to our understanding of emergent practices of Phrygian power.

As noted at the beginning of this chapter, Conolly (2017:440) recently highlighted the role of signaling strategies in relation to prestige goods for the operation of political economies. In the context of the expansion of group size and regional interaction at EP Gordion, signaling involved enhancement of status through "costly investments in technological innovation and production of prestige goods" (Plourde 2008). Feasting appears to have been one of the central ritualized activities for promoting elite interests through group integration and differentiation both at Gordion and across the larger region. Production, consumption and distribution evidence further highlights the complex practices and strategies of these EP groups.

At Gordion, group or communal practices appear deeply embedded in a complex ritual economy. Group *production* was required for the creation of the new elite core of the settlement as well as the monuments of state (e.g. tumuli, city walls), and group *consumption* was carefully and intimately situated within these monuments and spaces. The *distribution* of source materials also suggests that larger group networks, across Anatolia both east and west, played a key role in the formative processes of Phrygian power and hegemony.

The resource demands in the creation and maintenance of these strategies, and the contradictory tensions they created among emergent groups, undoubtedly contributed to the ultimate fragility of EP social structures and their transformation in the subsequent Middle Phrygian period.

8 Enacting Power
The Middle Phrygian Period YHSS 5 800–540 BCE

Introduction

From the ninth to the seventh century BCE, Phrygia was one of multiple emerging polities across Anatolia. To the east, mid ninth century BCE Urartian rulers extended their power into northern Mesopotamia (Inomata and Coben 2006). To the west, along the Aegean coast, Greek colonists established new cities and broadened their influence south and east along the Mediterranean coast (Greaves 2011). In central Anatolia, Phrygia became the dominant political force (Fig. 7.1).

When their political power was at its height, during the first half of the Middle Phrygian period (eighth century BCE), Phrygians negotiated alliances with other regional polities and sought to counter incursions by the expanding Assyrian state (and possibly other groups). In the early seventh century BCE, Lydian rulers, from their capital Sardis, began territorial expansion from the west into central Anatolia (Greenewalt 2011). Assyrian references also describe increasing raids by Kimmerians (Sams 1995). By the late seventh century, with their power waning, the Phrygian capital, Gordion, was incorporated along with much of western Anatolia into the expanding Lydian sphere. The MP period comes to an end in the mid sixth century BCE with an attack on Gordion by the Persian army as they consolidated control over much of Anatolia, including Lydian-held territory. The disparate political tensions of the 260-year period were equally critical in the ongoing production of Phrygian power and identity, as well as in its decline.

Other than the distribution of Phrygian inscriptions and monuments, and rare mentions in the records of Assyria and Greece, our understanding of how this polity functioned is almost entirely reliant on the archaeological record in and around Gordion, supplemented by a small number of contemporary sites across the larger region. The monumental scale of the urban, defensive and mortuary architecture at MP Gordion, as well as the richness of MP elite burials, provide the most tangible evidence of its considerable political power. Somewhat anomalously among contemporary polities, MP iconography lacks depictions of a ruling elite, or anthropomorphic entities more generally. A variety of archaeological data provides insight into the organization and practices of MP communities, but most of our information comes from areas beyond the Eastern Mound. This elite area of Middle Phrygian Gordion was mined for building materials in subsequent periods, leaving limited evidence *in situ*.

The Middle Phrygian period represents something of a work in progress, combining what are arguably two if not three phases of cultural and political transformation. Thus, understanding this period requires, to the extent possible, careful attention to evidence for how groups responded to a volatile political landscape. Recently defined stratigraphic subphases (5C-A) partially parallel these political changes (Codella and Voigt in press).

In this chapter we explore MP ceramic production, distribution and consumption in the context of what we know from excavation as well as from survey (the Gordion Regional Survey) in order to understand group formation and practices of power in this period. Unlike earlier phases, the abundance and diversity of MP archaeological contexts across the site provide a unique perspective on how the Phrygians constructed political identity in the rapidly changing landscapes of power across Anatolia at this time.

Middle Phrygian Gordion in Historical Context

The political landscape of the Middle Phrygian period, from the Aegean to eastern Anatolia and northern Mesopotamia, was a complex palimpsest of competing polities (see Fig. 7.1; d'Alfonso 2019, 2020; Greaves 2011). During the MP YHSS 5 phase the footprint of the Phrygian capital reached its maximum extent (ca. 1 km^2), encompassing both the Eastern and Western Mounds in the central area, as well as Lower Towns to the north and south, and an Outer Town to the northwest (see Figs. 1.2 and 3.6, Plate 1; Rose 2018; Voigt 2013). Based on its size, form and organization, the Phrygian capital had become a city at this time.

The economic and political power of the MP polity is attested to by a large-scale program of urban and monument construction that began in earnest immediately after the fire of ca. 800 BCE. Construction included two substantial stone and mudbrick fortification walls: an inner wall surrounding the Citadel Mound and an outer wall surrounding the Lower Town. The Outer Town was also enclosed by a wall and exterior ditch. In addition to these urban architectural expressions of Phrygian hegemony, we see power manifested in the proliferation of tumuli (burial mounds). Only 44 of the more than 200 tumuli in the Gordion region have been investigated archaeologically, but the majority of those date to this period (Liebhart et al. 2016). The massive scale of some of these tumuli (e.g. tumulus MM is currently preserved to a height of 54 m) exemplifies the likely scale of resources controlled by Phrygian elites in the eighth century BCE (Stephens 2018). An urban context for elite monuments is provided by excavation of both institutional and household structures across the city beyond the main excavation area on the Eastern Mound (Codella and Voigt in press; Voigt and Young 1999).

While contemporary polities were literate, there is a paucity of historical data for central Anatolia for the eighth to mid sixth century BCE. In general, the few relevant sources are extraterritorial – Greek and Assyrian accounts of central Anatolia. Classical Greek references to Midas have been linked to the late eighth century BCE Assyrian records of Mita (ruler of the Mushki; DeVries 2011b), and both highlight a wider acknowledgement of Phrygian elite influence during the MP period. Phrygian kings are described as presenting gifts to Greek sanctuaries as well as intermarrying with Greek elites (Muscarella 1989). Even today, King Midas and his golden touch, while mythical, provide a distant reflection of a charismatic Phrygian ruler.

Middle Phrygian power was not, however, unchallenged. The (Neo-)Assyrian conquest of the Neo-Hittite city states of the Early Iron Age created a new northern Mesopotamian empire and contested border region. In the early ninth century BCE, Assyrians began to push this border into central Anatolia, specifically into the territory of Tabal (Hawkins 1982:390). For the Assyrians, Phrygians were a potential threat on their northern periphery. Yet subsequent Assyrian texts, in the late eighth century BCE, report Phrygians seeking Assyrian alliances, perhaps to mitigate a threat from Tabal (Osborne 2020). Neo-Assyrian accounts also underscore the political fluidity of relationships between groups. For example, in the early seventh century BCE, the Kimmerians, at one time allies, become raiders of the Phrygian heartland (DeVries 2011b).

Following 700 BCE, in an increasingly politically tumultuous landscape, Gordion was beset by Lydian incursions and perhaps Kimmerian raiders. Both historical and archaeological data suggest Phrygian territorial authority declined at this time. By the end of the seventh century BCE, Gordion had become part of the Lydian sphere, and Lydian influence remained strong through the early sixth century BCE (Dusinberre et al. 2019; Lynch 2016). The mid sixth century BCE Persian conquest of Anatolia integrated the Phrygians with other fractious communities, formulating new relationships (Dusinberre 2013). Despite this political disruption, archaeological evidence suggests Gordion continued as an economically vibrant center up to the time of Alexander's conquest (Codella and Voigt in press).

800–540 BCE (YHSS 5): Middle Phrygian Archaeology at Gordion

The transition between the EP and the MP periods has long been defined by the "Destruction Level" identified by Rodney Young. Voigt (2007) suggests that while the ca. 800 BCE fiery conflagration on the Eastern Mound devastated much of the core elite area, it was not a substantial cultural or political break. Voigt's study of what DeVries called the "Unfinished Project" demonstrates that the fire took place in an area already undergoing extensive remodeling in the late ninth century. At the time of the fire, all but two of the megarons around the two formal courts were empty and not in use, and areas inside the EP city gate were in the process of being filled, raised, levelled and reconstructed (DeVries 1990; see discussion in Chapter 7).

After the fire, construction resumed with the levelling of the burned EP buildings and the covering of both of the ninth century central mounds with 3–5 m of fill, while still maintaining the open space between them. The organization of the rebuilt urban core, the lack of an erosion surface after the destruction and the continuity in material culture shows this MP reconstruction project happened relatively quickly, and was probably completed within a decade or two (Fig. 3.4; Voigt 2007:319; 2013). The MP fill often contains large quantities of Bronze Age material, especially in the areas where rebuilding began (in and to the north of the Early Phrygian gate). We presume this reflects the mining of sediments from occupation areas with earlier cultural debris, either at Gordion or from adjacent sites. As the project moved away from the Eastern Gate, culturally sterile clay was brought in, perhaps in part derived from the construction of water-management facilities out on the surrounding alluvial plain.

The MP period extended over more than two and a half centuries, but until recently the only deposits that had been studied carefully date to the beginning and the end of the period. While Voigt's 1988–1989 Upper Trench Sounding exposed only a small area of the MP city, a detailed study of the stratigraphic evidence, combined with information from excavation across the site in 1993–2002, identified a sequence of sub-phases (5C-5A) with distinctive assemblages of material culture including local and imported ceramics (Codella and Voigt in press). Thus, for

Fig. 8.1 Eastern Mound YHSS 5C Building C. The fill between MP Building C and EP Megaron 1 is part of the Unfinished Project construction destroyed in 800 BCE. To the left is the 6A gate with fragments of the 5C Middle Phrygian East gate left in place atop its walls. Most of the Middle Phrygian structures were removed by R. Young in order to reach the EP Destruction Level.
Source: No archive number, R. S. Young, courtesy University of Pennsylvania Museum, Gordion Project Archives.

the first time, we are able to construct a continuous occupation sequence within the MP period, from the time of the post ca. 800 BCE fire rebuilding to the Persian conquest.

On the Eastern Mound, Middle Phrygian phase YHSS 5C, immediately following the ca. 800 BCE fire, represents recommencement of the unfinished 6A construction project. Later in the eighth century, phase 5B is defined by the remodeling or replacement of some of the 5C buildings around the courts, for example the total reconstruction of Building C (Fig. 8.1) next to the entrance to the Outer Court and the remodeling of Building E (Rose 2018). New construction in 5B includes a wall with a cobble foundation cut into the clay fill found in the Upper Trench Sounding; this wall blocked the wide street that ran down the center of the 5C Terrace Complex (Codella and Voigt in press). Building the wall would have transformed the Terrace Complex into two separate zones, arguably changing the function and significance of these buildings.

During the late eighth century, or more likely early seventh century BCE, some structures were abandoned including several storage buildings (the Phrygian Persian Building [PPB] and South Cellar, see Fig. 3.4), signaling the beginning of a period of transformation in the urban core. There is little evidence of elite activities during much of the seventh century. Phase 5A covers a ca. 60-year period (600–540 BCE) when Lydian influence is evident in the form of new Lydian-style tile roofs added to structures on the EM and Lydian-style ceramics, and it ends with the Persian conquest. However, these renovations suggest that elite use of this sector continued. While this sequence was initially defined using evidence from the Main Excavation Area on the Eastern Mound, it has also been replicated and enhanced by excavations on the Western Mound [WM] in the NW and SW Zones (Fig. 3.5).

The initial or MP 5C renovation and expansion of the city involved the transport and deposition of massive amounts of earth and the construction of defensive walls that together profoundly changed the topography of the settlement. In addition to the deep layer of clay on the Eastern Mound, the Western Mound appears to have been raised to the same height, also requiring a substantial quantity of fill to achieve the same absolute level (Voigt 2007). Given the high and steep slopes created by the added fill, Voigt proposed that the WM was enclosed with a wall (Voigt 2002), an argument confirmed by geophysical survey and the excavation of a wall and glacis that encircles both mounds by Rose (see Plate 1; Rose 2017).

Encircling the Lower Town, a second line of defense was constructed in the form of a heavy wall that stood 18 m high, anchored by tall fortresses (over 50 m high) to the north and south of the Citadel Mound (Rose 2017). The northern part of the Lower Town is known primarily through geophysical survey, but the walls and fortress of the southern LT were excavated, as were smaller soundings within the walls. A layer of fill several meters deep was added in the southern LT in a semicircle inside the walls. On this raised platform buildings were separated by streets (Rose 2017; Voigt 2011). Excavations by Mellink of the fortress in the southern LT, known as the Küçük Höyük (KH) or "little mound," also revealed an associated siege ramp of Persian construction (Mellink 1959).

Most of the Outer Town that extended to the west and north of the Citadel Mound was protected by a fortification wall initially identified in satellite images by Marsh (Voigt 2013:37), and now defined in part by geophysical survey (Plate 1; Rose 2017). Middle Phrygian occupation of the Outer Town is also documented by ceramics collected during intensive surface survey and by excavation of a semisubterranean house

(Voigt and Young 1999). Both geophysical and surface survey identified settlement remains beyond the Outer Town wall, but the extent of this habitation remains undefined (Rose 2017). Other evidence outside the walls includes a kiln excavated by Mellink just beyond the southern Lower Town wall (see discussion in the section "A MP Kiln"), and on the Northeast Ridge a substantial cluster of MP houses and cemetery that were subsequently covered by tumuli (see Fig. 1.2; Anderson 2012).

The location, size and contents of MP tumuli provide several key archaeological contributions to understanding Phrygian power and elite identity. Located on high ground mostly on the east side of the city, and flanking roads leading into it, these massive artificial hills have been called "the dominant visual record of the Phrygians on the landscape at Gordion" (Liebhart et al. 2016:627), and demonstrate the affluence, affiliations and aspirations of Phrygian elites. They also allow us to closely date associated elite ceramic and artifact assemblages through dendrochronology as well as artifact styles (Dusinberre 2005; Kuniholm et al. 2011; Sams 2011b).

The regional settlement pattern around Gordion, in both number and size of sites, also suggests substantial population expansion during this period. In addition to residential complexes located near springs, ceramics from the lower terraces of the mounded site at Böyük Höyük (near modern Şabanözü, ca. 10 km north of Gordion) also appear to reflect the expansion of a large "outer town" during the MP, as at Gordion (Kealhofer 2005b). More distant Phrygian sites like the well-fortified Haci Tuğrul in the next valley east of Gordion, and possibly Kerkenes far to the east in the Kızılırmak bend, highlight the spread of MP power and influence across central Anatolia (Summers 2018; Sumner 1987).

Voigt (2011) noted the apparent enigma of the location and function of Gordion as the Phrygian capital given the high-risk, drought-prone nature of cereal-based intensive agriculture in this region, both today and in the past. Recent environmental evidence highlights the frequency of droughts during the late LBA and into the Phrygian period (MIA), increasing the risk of failure for rainfall agriculture (N. Roberts et al. 2016). However, these conditions may have actually promoted the development of new strategies, including water management and the need for coordinated logistical organization (e.g. labor, scheduling and grain storage).

The city's strategic location, at the crossroads of exchange routes extending north–south and east–west across Anatolia, may also have promoted its growth as a political center. There is some evidence (presented in Chapter 7) for an extended interaction network centered on Gordion during the EP period (e.g. ceramics and elite iconography).

However, developments in the early Middle Phrygian period present a somewhat different picture of Phrygian political economy at the height of its power, when there is increasing investment in local styles and production.

Middle Phrygian Contexts: Variation in Time and Space

Our understanding of the MP period, while more archaeologically comprehensive than other phases, is still strongly shaped by the types of contexts excavated. Unlike earlier periods, MP excavations uncovered substantial occupation in four different zones: the elite quarter (mostly disturbed) on the Eastern Mound; the Northwest and Southwest Zones (both located on the Western Mound); the southern Lower Town, including the outer fortification of Küçük Höyük; and, beyond these walls, a house in the Outer Town and a kiln area just outside the Lower Town wall (see Figs. 3.5a, 3.6). This geography allows our first comparison of activities in different sectors across the city.

However, making these comparisons involves the challenge of establishing secure chronological correlations across discontinuous excavation sectors. This begins with the Eastern Mound where some of the Middle Phrygian 5C structures remained in use until Late Phrygian YHSS 4 (fourth to fifth century BCE). The 5C rubble wall foundations are the primary evidence for the very solid-looking walls drawn on the frequently published Middle Phrygian, now YHSS 5C, plan (Fig. 3.4). The depth and massiveness of these foundations have withstood repeated "robbing" from ancient to modern times.

The shift in date of the Early Phrygian destruction to ca. 800 BCE (DeVries et al. 2003), together with new excavations and reassessment of the plans and notes from the Young excavations, has substantially changed our interpretation of the character and duration of the MP period. The Middle Phrygian period was initially assumed to be relatively short, beginning in the sixth or even fifth century BCE based on proposed links to historical narratives and the recovery of Attic imports from what have proven to be disturbed contexts (Voigt 2009). The more recent Voigt excavations found that many of the Attic sherds from the EM were deposited in pits, robber trenches and later houses cut into earlier 5C structures, but a few early (late eighth to early seventh century) imported sherds were found in undisturbed 5C-B contexts excavated by Young (DeVries 2005).

While 5C foundations provide a chronological baseline for MP buildings in the EM sector, excavation notes from the Young excavations are inadequate for correlating layers and levels between excavation units within the Eastern Mound (see Fields 2010). The small Upper Trench Sounding [UTS] opened by Voigt using more chronologically controlled excavation units was ultimately crucial for understanding the MP sequence and continuity with the EP period on the Eastern Mound (see Figs. 3.3–3.4). However, because of the limited area of the UTS excavation, it still offered only restricted scope for defining broader activity patterns. The UTS did point to remodeling that occurred inside one 5C building during 5B, suggesting it may be possible to document such change within individual structures with a detailed restudy of the Young field records, especially changes in floor plans that must reflect alteration in function. At present, however, information on these phases comes primarily from excavation in other sectors, particularly the WM and southern LT areas.

Eastern Mound

Using the new MP sequence, 5C-A, we can now recognize some of the changes that took place across the city (Codella and Voigt in press). On the Eastern Mound, excavated remains of the initial MP (5C) structures were massive and are still impressive where preserved in the area of the Eastern Gate (Voigt 2013). Middle Phrygian rubble foundations were set into the deep layer of fill as it was laid, supporting heavy stone walls made of cut blocks that were sometimes laid with different colors of stone (Fig. 8.2; Voigt 2007, 2013). Unfortunately these walls and foundations are no longer available for study. To expose features of the underlying Early Phrygian period, Young removed all vestiges of even well-preserved MP structures, with the sole exception of fragments of the Eastern Gate.

While the plan of the EM is often said to replicate the Early Phrygian layout (6A:2), there are significant differences (Rose 2018:fig. 3). Most striking – and indicative of the changing character of MP Gordion – was a strengthening of the citadel wall and its glacis, and the construction of a substantially higher, larger and more impressive East Gate, built of white stone (gypsum) and colored stone blocks. Inside the gate, buildings with a megaron layout still surrounded an Outer and Inner Court, but they were more regular in size and construction than their EP predecessors. Replacement buildings for the rows of attached megarons above the EP Terrace Complex were freestanding rather than connected (see Fig. 3.4). Assuming that the function of these new structures was the same as the old, some have suggested that the isolation of each building was a way of preventing the spread of an intense blaze like that of the Destruction Level that consumed EP structures full of stored foodstuffs and textiles.

During phase 5C three new construction projects were undertaken inside the walls on the Eastern Mound. These included: Building A, a

236 Ancient Gordion

Fig. 8.2 Contrast between Early (YHSS 6) and Middle Phrygian (YHSS 5) stone masonry on the Eastern Mound. In the foreground is a portion of the Middle Phrygian 5C gate built of large white, red, green, yellow and grey stones, while in the distance to the left is the buff-colored stone of the Early Phrygian 6A gate. The small segment of poly-colored masonry jutting up in the center of the photo is also part of the Middle Phrygian gate.
Source: No archive number, E. Wisner, courtesy University of Pennsylvania Museum, Gordion Project Archives.

row of attached megarons along the southwestern wall of the Citadel Mound, parallel to but separated from the East Gate; the PPB, a large building to the northwest of the 5C terrace complex that is mostly made up of square cells of uniform size (DeVries 1990); and lastly, semisubterranean structures referred to as "cellars": the North and South Cellars and Building I:2 Cellar (see Fig. 3.4; B. Burke 2012; Codella and Voigt in press; Rose 2018). While Building A might be a series of offices where administrative functions were carried out, most of the rooms in the PPB have no doorways and so must have been accessed from above – a typical characteristic of large-scale storage units. The ten 6 × 6 m rooms in the PPB could have stored ca. 612 m^3 of grain or other goods. This is some 40% larger than any one of the LBA grain silos at the

Hittite capital of Hattuša, which held an estimated 432 m^3 of grain each (ca. 1,800–2,400 tons).

Later during the eighth century BCE or early in YHSS 5B, a few new structures on the EM were built and others were remodeled. The largest 5B project was the reconstruction and enlargement of structures in the Outer Court: Buildings C and G to the southwest and the small, carefully maintained Building E located next to the northeastern court of the East Gate building (Rose 2018). As noted in the earlier section "Middle Phrygian Archaeology at Gordion," one of the more substantial remodeling projects was the construction of a wall across the Terrace Complex (SW–NE), splitting the complex into two sections, potentially with discrete functions. This period of renewed construction was short-lived. Later in 5B the North and South cellars to the northwest of the Inner Court were first modified and then abandoned, providing closed deposits dated to the early seventh century BCE. The PPB storage building further to the northwest was abandoned at approximately the same time (Sams in press), as was the Building I:2 cellar (which had been turned into a storage area at the beginning of 5B) (see Fig. 3.4).

The closure of these storage structures in the first half of the seventh century suggests a decline in the authority of the Phrygian rulers to control agricultural production and/or collect a surplus of staple foods or other goods as tribute. Several additional lines of evidence point to disruptions in the city. Black polished wares associated with drinking (including spouted cups with strainers that have been associated with beer consumption; Sams 1977) were recovered from early seventh century abandonment deposits in EM storage structures (South Cellar, PPB; Sams in press). In these same abandonment deposits were both Bichrome and Greek imported vessels, items of dress found in elite tombs (belts, 40 fibulae), and four ivory pieces including a stamp seal and a figurine interpreted as a priest or priestess (DeVries 2008; Dusinberre and Vassileva 2018; Sams in press; Young 1966). The abandonment of buildings related to the control of stored food and the contemporary discard of iconic ornaments and drinking/feasting vessels similar to those in the elite tumulus burials suggest that high-status people may have experienced challenges at this time. Given the evidence for political and organizational disruption within the settlement, it is perhaps not surprising that tumulus construction also ceased in the early seventh century BCE and was not resumed until the end of the seventh or early sixth century BCE (Sams and Voigt 2011:164).

At the beginning of MP 5A, Gordion underwent a revival that is closely tied to Lydian influence or sponsorship. Structures around the Inner and Outer Courts were given new tile roofs in Lydian style

(Glendinning 2005; Rose 2018). However, away from this public area, the seventh century changes in use continued on the Eastern Mound. Evidence from the Upper Trench Sounding indicates that service buildings to the west were modified and subdivided into smaller rooms (as in Building I:1 and I:2), and large pits were cut into the 5B fill in the I:2 cellar (see Fig. 3.4).

Between the Eastern and Western Mounds
New excavation of an open area between the two high mounds that Young originally considered a street has been reinterpreted as a broader open space that existed throughout the Middle and Late Phrygian periods (Rose and Gürsan-Salzman 2017, 2018:11). Excavation along the northern and southern edge of the Citadel Mound found no means of access to this open space (Rose and Gürsan-Salzman 2018). If not a thoroughfare, the core location of this open area could readily have functioned as an arena for displays or performance.

Western Mound: Northwest Zone and Southwest Zone
One of the more surprising results of research since 1988 was the recovery in the Western Mound's Northwest Zone (NWZ) of fragmentary but convincing evidence for a 5C monumental structure with rubble foundations set into a deep clay fill (Unit 1; Codella and Voigt in press). While not in use for long, construction of this building suggests that, broadly defined, the kind of activities performed in similar buildings in the EM elite zone were practiced more widely during 5C. Recent excavations have also uncovered a South Gate along the central edge of the Citadel Mound, as well as an apparent road leading upward along the southern edge of the Western Mound that presumably continues to the Middle Phrygian settlement at the top of the WM (Rose and Gürsan-Salzman 2018). The width and gradual slope of this ramp or road suggests that it was used by wheeled vehicles, carrying heavy items, perhaps agricultural products as well as construction materials.

During 5B, a small pit house was cut into the clay fill in the NWZ, using the rubble foundations of the earlier structure as wall faces, a construction technique that became common across the EM in the fifth century BCE (Codella and Voigt in press; Voigt 2007). In the final subphase of 5A, a new house was built at surface level (Fig. 8.3a and b). Composed of at least three rooms with attached outbuildings, the best-preserved phase of this house had a kitchen, a room with a pebble-paved floor, and a room with white plastered walls, all indicating skilled construction labor; attached structures included an oven and storage units (Codella and Voigt in press).

Enacting Power 239

Fig. 8.3 Middle Phrygian YHSS 5A houses on the Western Mound and in the Lower Town.
(a) Two rooms of a large WM NWZ building with heavy exterior walls robbed down to their rubble foundations, and a thin interior wall with white plastered faces. The floor of the most elaborate room (Unit 7) is paved with pebbles set in a clay base. Looking toward the northeast baulk.

The Middle Phrygian sequence in the Southwest Zone (SWZ) of the Western Mound shares some features with the NWZ. The earliest excavated structures in the SWZ are built on top of the 5C clay and are therefore dated to 5B. All but one of these structures was excavated in 1950. Both the density of walls recovered in 1950 and the stratigraphic sequence in a very small adjacent sounding carried out in 1989 indicate 5B contained several subphases, but only a small number of contemporary structures can be isolated within the maze of walls recorded in 1950 (Codella and Voigt in press). Unfortunately, the contents of the structures were not recorded during these excavations. What we do know is that at least some of these structures, likely houses, had pebble-paved floors like the 5A structure in the NWZ. A structure partially excavated in 1989 indicates household storage in large jars, presumably intended

Fig. 8.3 (*cont.*) (b) Plan of the same 5A house WM Northwest Zone (8.3a).

for cereals; pottery vessels sealed within two of the jars include a black polished spouted strainer, a set of five shallow bowls best interpreted as drinking cups, a small jar and a pitcher (Fig. 8.4; Henrickson 1994: 10.7). That this drinking set was a prized possession of a household member is supported by graffiti on the bowls and pitcher: a personal name in Phrygian script and nonalphabetic motifs.

The subsequent 5A phase in the SWZ provides a unique window on MP practices in the form of a trash deposit dumped into a square pit that was probably an abandoned (pit-)house (Dusinberre et al. 2019). The final layer in this dump contains many whole pots ranging in size from miniatures to pithoi, and includes a large number of vessels used in the

Fig. 8.3 (cont.) (c) Part of a five-roomed structure from Lower Town Area B, looking west. This 5A house was built at surface level with low cobble foundations supporting packed mud and mudbrick walls and a plaster floor; it was cut by a deep YHSS 4 Late Phrygian pithouse (lower right-hand corner).

storage, preparation and service of food and drink. Associated with these was a wide array of ornaments, weapons and horse gear. Dated by imported ceramic vessels to the mid sixth century, the deposit seems to represent the disposal of goods from one or more households, which took place about the time of the Achaemenid military conquest. The ceramics are interpreted as the possessions of a "mid-level elite household (or households)" who participated in feasting that was "probably intended to reinforce hierarchy or define a group" (Dusinberre et al. 2019:194).

Lower Town and Outer Town

Surrounding the Lower Town (see Plate 1), a fortification system was built at the start of 5C; consisting of thick walls with heavy stone foundations and a mud-brick superstructure, the walls were anchored by tall fortresses (the Küçük Höyük and Kuş Tepe; Edwards 1959; Rose and

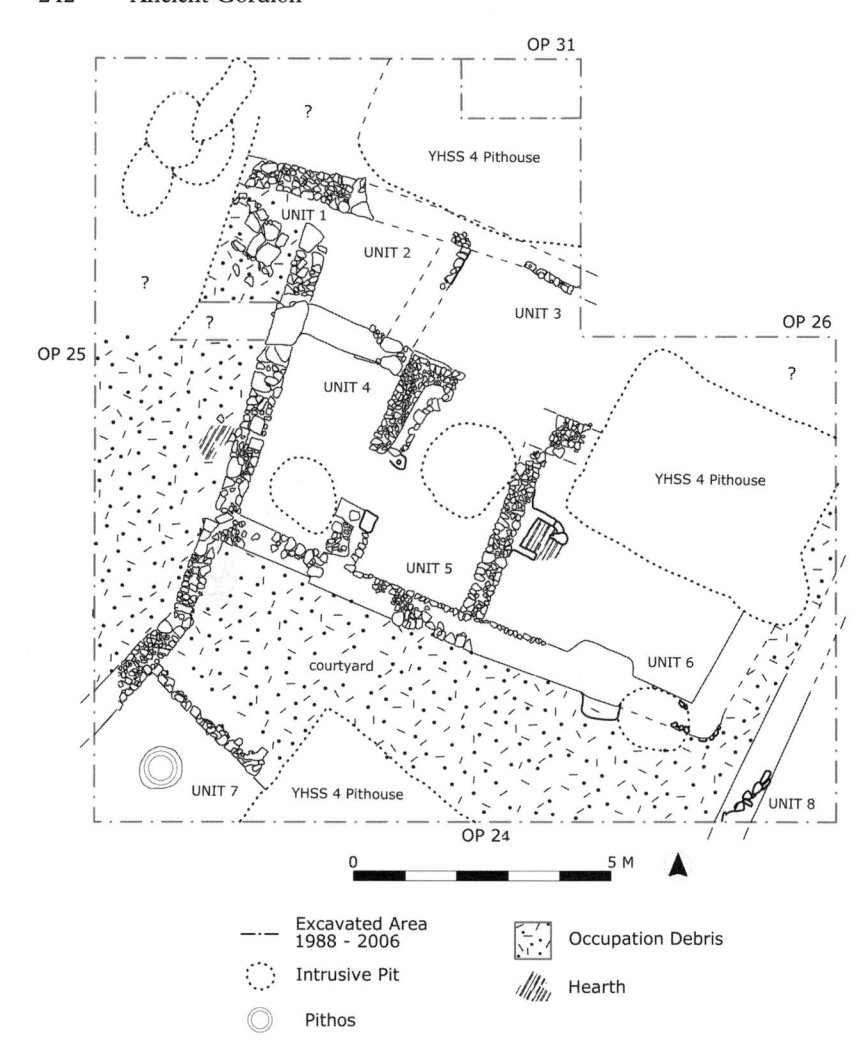

Fig. 8.3 (*cont.*) (d) Plan of house in 8.3c.
Sources: *8.3a* and *c* image nos. 02-025:34 and 95-040:32, Mary Voigt; *8.3b* and *d*. K. Codella and C. Alblinger; courtesy University of Pennsylvania Museum, Gordion Project Archives.

Darbyshire 2011). This was the primary defense perimeter until overtaken by the Persian army in ca. 540 BCE. Within this walled Lower Town, building types mirror the primary functional zones on the Citadel Mound: to the east (Area A), formal buildings with ashlar walls had rubble foundations set in fill, while to the west (Area B) were domestic

Fig. 8.4 Middle Phrygian 5B vessels from sealed contexts on the Western Mound, Southwest Zone. Black polished spouted-strainer juglet (YH32374), and in common grey ware, a set of five shallow bowls (drinking cups; left to right YH32651, 32654, 32648, 32635, 32658), a small jar (YH32649) and a pitcher (YH32652). Graffiti were incised on the bowls and pitcher, including non-alphabetic motifs and a personal name in Phrygian script (for line drawings see Fig. 8.6b).
Source: Image no. 89-1069:015, L. Foos, courtesy University of Pennsylvania Museum, Gordion Project Archives.

structures with low cobble foundations and mudbrick walls built at surface level (Fig. 8.3c and d).

The stone structures in Area A, like those on the EM, were heavily robbed, with little well-stratified or datable material. They are assigned to 5C/B based on architectural form (Codella and Voigt in press; Voigt 2013; Voigt and Young 1999). A potential indicator of the kinds of activities carried out within these buildings is a small ivory plaque depicting a kneeling warrior with sword and shield, suggesting use for military or administrative purposes (Sheftel in press:cat. no. 149).

Evidence for domestic remodeling is consistent with fluctuations in household size and organization in 5A. In Area B, evidence of domestic architecture with light stone foundations dated to 5B was recovered, but the best-preserved structures are dated to 5A. These were abandoned, probably during the Persian siege of the nearby LT fortress (Voigt and

Young 1999). One large house is unique, with rooms and open courts that represent additions and subtractions to an original single room, with room function sometimes changing in this process (Codella and Voigt in press).

The Gordion Outer Town has been defined by geophysical (Rose 2017) and intensive surface survey (Voigt 2013), but only one of four excavated areas produced Middle Phrygian material (Voigt and Young 1999: fig. 2). In Operation 22 (see Fig. 3.6) a subterranean structure was excavated, apparently associated with walls constructed at surface level in an adjacent area. The Op. 22 house had an oven and contained complete and fragmentary plain and painted pots that Sams and Henrickson viewed as typologically transitional between the EP and MP 5C (Sams and Voigt 1995; Voigt and Young 1999).

Middle Phrygian Tumuli

The earliest tumuli date to the EP period, but over half of the earthen burial mounds or tumuli explored around Gordion were constructed during the Middle Phrygian period (23 of 44 investigated). The contents of Tumulus MM (740 BCE) and the slightly earlier Tumulus P were particularly well-preserved, with intact inlaid wood furniture, textiles and metal clothing items including fibulae and belts. Tumulus MM protected a wooden chamber that held a 60–65-year-old male, laid out on textiles in a wooden coffin, with an extensive array of metal serving vessels. These are thought to be the remains of a funerary feast and included bronze and brass vessels ranging in size from large cauldrons to elaborate shallow bowls, probably drinking vessels (McGovern et al. 1999; Young 1981). Tumulus P held a child's burial pointing to the probable role of inherited status among the Phrygian elite. A wide variety of ceramic vessels were recovered from this burial, which ranged from plain serving and storage vessels to elaborate painted and black polished vessels. In contrast, only a few ceramics of a single type (small storage vessels) were deposited in Tumulus MM (Simpson and Spirydowicz 1999; Young 1981). Otherwise, most of the ceramics associated with tumuli included in this study came from construction fill, and therefore likely predate tumulus construction.

The only non-elite MP burials known are inhumations located on the Northeast Ridge near the largest tumuli. Their simplicity has been used to suggest that the people buried in them were workers involved in the construction of tumuli and their family members (Anderson 2012). No other Early or Middle Phrygian commoner cemeteries are known from Gordion (however, see Genz 2019 for Boğazköy).

Stephens' (2018) recent study of the tumuli and their importance for the Iron Age landscape illustrates the role of tumuli as visual markers along roads and as part of the networks that connected communities in the local region. The construction of mounds not used for burial, but placed in highly visible locations, tracks the ways people experienced and moved through the countryside. Tumuli clearly played multiple symbolic roles, during their construction as well as subsequently, as they were integrated into the daily use of the fields and countryside during and after the Phrygian period.

Excavation Summary
Recent work on the stratigraphic sequence of the Eastern and Western Mounds has tied together the stratigraphic sequence across the settlement (Codella and Voigt in press). These sequences document the spatial extent of MP occupation on and around the city mounds. The earliest phase (5C, early to late eighth century BCE) shows strong continuity with the EP period. The final 5A phase (ca. 600–540 BCE), however, reveals increasingly strong Lydian influences (from roof tiles to ceramics) and perhaps a Lydian presence. The Persian siege (ca. 540 BCE) marks an abrupt end to the Middle Phrygian period. This event is well-documented in the archaeological record, with a siege ramp and numerous bronze arrow points preserved in the walls of the Küçük Höyük fortress in the Lower Town (Fig. 8.5a and b).

Excavated contexts show significant differences in the status and activities of Gordion's Middle Phrygian inhabitants. The elite quarter on the Eastern Mound remains our primary source of information on the main phase of Phrygian expansion (800 to late eighth century BCE). There are, however, at least two 5C administrative (?) structures built with rubble foundations and cut stone blocks, one on the Western Mound and another in the southern Lower Town (Codella and Voigt in press; Voigt 2013). Houses that differ in form, size and degree of elaboration are found on the Western Mound and in the southern Lower and Outer Towns, with most of the excavated examples dated to the seventh to sixth century BCE (5B-5A). Residential occupation during the MP in the Outer Town is suggested by a domestic structure that apparently dates to the eighth century (5C), but there is also a monumental stone structure still visible on the surface, interpreted as part of a MP fortress (Rose 2017:146).

By the eighth century BCE, Gordion's MP archaeology materializes the capacity of Phrygian rulers to mobilize a substantial labor force for construction works in and around the Phrygian capital. Middle Phrygian buildings are notable for their distinct aesthetic in symmetry and use of materials. The city's citadel stood high above the alluvial plain and took advantage of variously colored stonework and the reflection of the Anatolian sun to impress and affirm the power of those who lived there. This visual expression of power extended to the distribution of tumuli

(a)

Fig. 8.5 Excavations on the Küçük Höyük and the Lower Town carried out by M. J. Mellink.
(a) Interior of the Middle Phrygian Küçük Höyük complex situated at the southeast corner of the Lower Town enceinte (Fig. 3.6b). The building was over 10 m wide and over 50 m long, and was at least four stories high. The rooms shown here were excavated in 1957. It was burned during the battle with the Persian army ca. 540 BCE.

over the local viewscape. The presence of large administrative or elite buildings in multiple sectors of the city suggests the development of an administrative hierarchy. However, from the early seventh to early sixth century BCE the practices of power at Gordion shifted. Clear evidence of this transformation includes changes in building functions, artifact assemblages, and elite and commoner burial practices (Anderson 2012; Lynch 2016). How these changing dynamics played out in relation to production, consumption and distribution of ceramics across the city is explored in subsequent sections.

Overview of Middle Phrygian Ceramics

Henrickson's study of MP Gordion ceramic production techniques is summarized here. While there is extensive continuity between EP and MP ceramics, a few aspects of production changed, including an increase in reduction firing at slightly lower temperatures. While there is continuity

Fig. 8.5 (*cont.*) (b) Upper part of the southwest corner of the mudbrick platform (12 m high), excavated in 1956, on top of which the Küçük Höyük building complex was constructed. The adjoining fortification walls were a similar height. YHSS5A. Preserved by a Persian siege mound built against the fortifications.
Source: *8.5a* image no. G-3061; *8.5b* G-2216; courtesy University of Pennsylvania Museum, Gordion Project Archives.

in forming traditions, he suggests potters generally paid more attention to quantity than to quality of output, with likely more mass production (Henrickson 1993:133). Recent work on a 5A assemblage from the Western Mound details the latest MP ceramics (Dusinberre et al. 2019).

Forming techniques included the potters' wheel for small to medium vessels and fine wares, tournettes for finishing, particularly for larger and/or handmade vessels, and coil hand building (e.g. globular cooking pots; Henrickson 1993:132–139). Production of specialized forms involved the most complex sequences. Fine ware vessels, particularly those with spouts or pedestals, were first thrown in separate parts then assembled on a slow wheel. A few fine wares were molded (e.g. those with raised diamonds).

Finishing methods included burnishing and polishing. Decoration varied from slipping and smoothing to molding, incising and painting (monochrome, bichrome and polychrome). Henrickson also framed vessel production in terms of expenditure of effort, with utilitarian wares ranked low and fine wares high. Many utilitarian vessels were cursorily finished, with some smoothed. Fine wares were more carefully finished, usually incised or burnished and/or painted with elaborate designs, or less commonly modeled. Some of the burnished wares (both black and grey) were made with gritty paste; polish and sintered slips were also used to create a smooth glossy finish (Henrickson et al. 2002). Cooking pots were finished on a tournette and the fabric appears coarser in the MP than the EP.

Firing techniques were predominantly kiln-fired under redox (oxygen-depleted) conditions (the dominant grey and black wares). Experimental firing suggested that lower firing temperatures, made possible by using the great fluxing capacity of calcareous clays, both reduced fuel requirements and resulted in fewer overfired wasters (Johnston 1970). Firing temperatures ranged from 700 to 900°C, but were mostly in the higher end of this range, particularly for fine wares. Most (intentionally) oxidized vessels were large, coarse wares and typically storage vessels.

Forms

In general, forms were similar to those of the EP period, with minor modifications. Typical forms include bowls, carinated bowls, globular and other jugs, ledge-rim storage jars and handmade cooking pots (Fig. 8.6a; Henrickson 1993). Forms identified as Greek or East Greek also increase through this phase, particularly in 5A (e.g. cups, bottles, plates, lydions or small vessels likely used for perfume). Jugs, and particularly juglets (Henrickson's "goblets"), on the other hand, decline in

5A. Bowl forms shift, particularly with the introduction of stemmed bowls also known as "fruitstands." Until the adoption of Greek cup forms, small bowls apparently served as cups (Figs. 8.4, 8.6b).

Decorative Styles

Decoration remains relatively rare in the MP period, with common pottery mostly undecorated grey ware. However, new styles are adopted and developed: elaborated black polished or slipped, molded vessel walls and bichrome decoration (Fig. 8.7, Plates 9, 10). While distinctive, the execution of bichrome decoration is both highly individualized and variable in quality. Elaborated black decorated wares were vehicles for a range of decorative elements, including molded and modeled surfaces, with raised diamond facets, fine ribbing, gadrooning (inverted fluting), incising, etc. These variants are labeled "black various" here (similarly for grey and red-orange various) and are uniquely Phrygian in style. In 5A pattern burnishing became common, on mainly grey ware with other color variants rare. Black decorated styles continue through the latest phases of the MP (5B and A) and into the early Late Phrygian (4) period.

Both black decorated and bichrome styles are at their most elaborated on vessels related to food consumption. The grey and black fine wares are commonly seen as skeuomorphs of metal vessels, with both shapes and surfaces mimicking small metal bowls and jugs (e.g. polished, molded), and included manufacturing details (e.g. rivets). DeVries (2008:41) also suggests some styles imitate wood carving. The limited use of these wares in elite burials in comparison to fine bronze bowls and their more frequent occurrence in consumption contexts on the EM and WM, further support their likely role as metal proxies.

One unusual feature of MP ceramics, ranging in date from 5C-B contexts (the I:2 and South Cellars) to the end of 5A (in the SWZ), is the presence of symbols or graffiti typically inscribed on the base of bowls. Frequently the symbols are geometric but occasionally they are letters and names (Fig. 8.6b; Brixhe 2004). These appear highly individualized, and marks scratched into the surface after firing strongly suggest that they relate to the user rather than the maker. This is further evidence of increasingly fine-grained markers of identity present by the mid eighth to early seventh century BCE among households across the city (Codella and Voigt in press; DeVries 2005).

A MP kiln: Excavations in and around the Küçük Höyük in 1958–1959 by Mellink uncovered a small updraft kiln just outside the Lower Town wall. Johnston (1970) reconstructed the kiln as a semisubterranean updraft type with a domed firing chamber (top missing) ca. 90 cm tall,

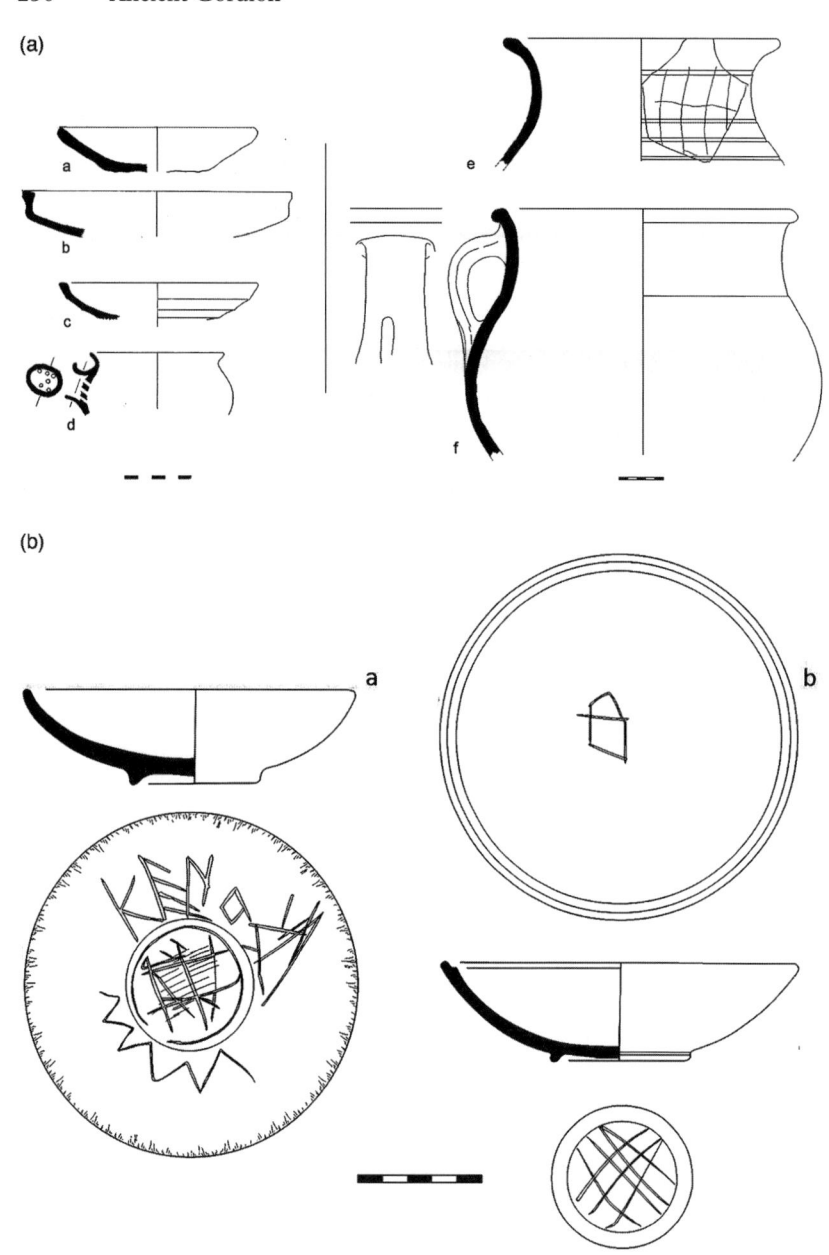

Fig. 8.6 YHSS 5 Middle Phrygian common grey ware forms.
(a) Profiles of three different bowls types (*a–c* YH: 30106-1, 30106-2, 31425-2), a strainer spouted vessel (*d* YH 32324-2), storage jar (*e* YH 32560-7), and a one-handled pot (*f* YH 30172.01).
(b) Two bowls with graffiti scratched on their bases from the Southwest Zone YHSS 5B (*a* YH 32651, *b* YH 32648); see also Fig. 8.4.
Source: D. Hoffman, R. Henrickson, P. Grave; courtesy University of Pennsylvania Museum, Gordon Project Archives.

Fig. 8.7 Fragmentary black polished vessel from the South Cellar (YHSS 5B, early seventh century BCE).
Source: Gordion inventory no. 8179-P-3282. Image no. 2015_03574, G. Bieg, courtesy of the University of Pennsylvania, Gordion Archives.

and about the same in maximum diameter. A firebox was located below the chamber, separated by a grate. A trench for feeding fuel into the firebox opened to the north as an intake for the updraft. The structure was additionally encased in packed earth to further insulate the firing chamber. Johnston (1970:193) concludes that firing temperatures within the kiln could have easily attained 800–900°C, the temperature range typical for earthenware production, and experimentally confirmed by Henrickson (1994). Johnston compares the kiln to a variety of Hittite and Neo-Hittite kilns, noting that such small single kilns were often part of larger complexes.

Kiln construction and operation require expertise, in understanding the complex relationships between design and ventilation, thermal dynamics, fuel type and packing, as well as in the effective control of firing intensity, kiln atmosphere and duration (Rice 2015). Based on ethnographic data, kiln size is influenced by several factors: the scale of production, the size of the group of people involved, the type of assemblage and the type and availability of fuel (Bernardini 2000; Blinman and Swink 1997). The volume of pottery that could be fired in a single firing provides some measure of the possible scale of production. In an evaluation of ceramic production in the southwest United States, Bernardini (2000:366) makes several points salient for Gordion. Because trench kilns around Mesa Verde came in a couple of sizes, he inferred firing group sizes at both the household and community scale. Trench-kiln firing groups were also likely different than those engaged in other stages of ceramic production (both in size and in composition). Bernardini (2000:369) also suggests that firing is one of the first stages to involve specialization in the chain of production, and as one of the riskiest production stages it is also the stage most likely to be collaborative. Ethnographically, specialization in different stages of production occurs when production scale and/or intensity increases and producers are not skilled in all stages (D. E. Arnold 1998).

While trench kilns are usually larger than the updraft kiln at Gordion, it seems likely that these general observations remain relevant. The location of kilns outside the city wall may indicate that workshops and kilns were spatially separated and represented different operational groups. While the Gordion kiln is a singular example, undoubtedly this relatively small kiln was only one of many in use at the time, given the volume of local MP pottery in the city. Without more evidence, it is not feasible to estimate the likely scale, intensity or volume of production. However, given the associated ceramic assemblage, it seems most likely that this kiln was used to fire small to medium-sized vessels (<100 (?) depending on vessel size and stacking).

The ceramic sample from the kiln area analyzed here (n = 72) is all undecorated grey wares, except for a single black polished sample; where forms were identified they are mainly jars and pots, with a few bowls. Based on the following NAA data discussion, the sample collected from this area, although mostly local and local/regional, was surprisingly varied (i.e. 17 different [NAA groups] sources/recipes).

NAA Ceramic Assemblage

The Sample and Sampling Issues

The MP ceramic sample, appropriately, is by far the largest subsample of the entire assemblage (n = 573; 566 with compositional data; Table 8.1a), with 376 samples from Young's (RSY) excavations and 197 from Voigt's (MMV) excavations. The sherds were chosen both by AIA (n = 352) and Henrickson (n = 221). Henrickson's sample comprises ca. 40% of the MP assemblage discussed here. While most of

Table 8.1. *YHSS 5 NAA sample distribution by Middle Phrygian subphases (5C-5A).*

Sample includes seven sherds with no NAA data.

(a) Column headings are samples collected by Henrickson (YHP) and AIA; these samples were drawn from excavations by Voigt (MMV) and Young (RSY).

YHSS phase	AIA	YHP	MMV	RSY	Total
5C	19	36	40	15	55
5C&B	147			147	147
5B	28	94	27	95	122
5B&A	23			23	23
5A	102	91	130	63	193
5	33			33	33
Total	352	221	197	376	573

(b) Excavation zone totals by YHSS 5 subphases. In the chapter discussion, the two West Mound zones are combined, as are all of the zones off the Mound.

	5C	5C&B	5B	5B&A	5A	5	Total
East Mound	41	144	37	21	22	33	298
West Mound SWZ	9				102		111
West Mound NWZ		1	4		23		28
Küçük Höyük		2	72	2	37		113
Lower Town					4		4
Tumuli (fill)			9		4		13
Outer Town	5						5
Northeast Ridge					1		1
Total	55	147	122	23	193	33	573

Henrickson's sample focused on MMV excavated pottery, he also sampled sherds from the 5B kiln described in the previous section (Table 8.1a). AIA sampling focused on the RSY excavated material ($n = 306$) with a small number of sherds from MMV excavations ($n = 46$) chosen because they appeared to differ from the common local types.

The MP assemblage includes sherds from more excavation areas with a greater diversity of function than any other period in our NAA ceramic sample (Table 8.1b): the Eastern Mound elite area, the NWZ and SWZ on the Western Mound, the Küçük Höyük, as well as a much smaller set of samples from the Lower and Outer Towns, tumulus fill and the MP cemetery on the Northeast ridge (Table 8.1b). The latter set of contexts, given the smaller sample sizes, is grouped together in our discussion as "off mound." The spatial spread of MP samples makes it possible to compare activities in different sectors, although comparisons are still challenged by the constraints imposed by the poor chronological resolution of the RSY assemblage as well as sample size differences.

To glean evidence of change over time, all of the MP ceramics were assigned to the phases described above. For the MMV excavations, this followed the three stratigraphic phases (5C to 5A). For the RSY excavated material, ceramic phasing was established by using publications and notebook entries to assign sherds to either 5C-B or 5B-A; only in a few contexts was it possible to associate RSY pottery with a single phase (e.g. Küçük Höyük).

The majority of the RSY MP sample studied here derives from the Eastern Mound elite zone. Tumuli and the Küçük Höyük excavations provide some additional "geography" for the Middle Phrygian RSY assemblage. The MMV sample, on the other hand, includes material from stratigraphic testing on the EM, but the majority of the sample derives from the Western Mound excavation zones (SWZ and NWZ), with a small sample from the Lower and Outer Towns (see Figs. 3.5a and 3.6). Subphase 5A provides the largest sample in these sectors.

A further issue challenges comparisons between the MMV and RSY assemblages. When Henrickson selected samples for analysis his interest was in studying local production and, for the most part, he chose sherds to represent the range of form and fabric variation, but which were generally undecorated. The RSY study collection assemblage, on the other hand, is highly skewed toward decorated and unusual forms, with few of the common domestic forms or styles. For the comparisons made here we generally focus within each assemblage (RSY or MMV) to maintain some relative consistency, particularly in relation to style/decoration. Only in the EM sub-assemblage can the RSY and MMV samples be integrated.

NAA Assemblage: Decoration and Forms

Henrickson, working with a sample that included all sherds recovered in the field, estimated that ca. 85% of the MMV MP assemblage was undecorated (Fig. 8.6a). In comparison with that repertoire (Henrickson 1994), just under one-third of the NAA assemblage is undecorated (grey and buff undecorated combined; Table 8.2) and mostly derives from Henrickson's sample. Typical decorative treatments include brown on X (which includes Brown on buff, slip/ground or white ground), bichrome painted, and black and grey variously decorated (e.g. burnished or polished, sintered slips, molded, plastic decoration; Sams in press; Plates 9, 10). This disproportionately decorated sample is likely to overemphasize elite and more exotic components of the assemblage.

Table 8.2. *YHSS 5 Middle Phrygian NAA assemblage forms and decoration (simplified). Totals and percentages for each style and form are tabulated.*

	Jar	Body	Jug	Bowl	Pot / jar	Bowl – Pot stemmed	Bowl – Cup shallow	Bowl – Crater	Bottle	Jar/ jug	Closed	Rhyton	Lydion	Amphora	Pot – small	Jug – sieve	Plate	Vessel parts	Other forms (<2)	Total	%
None – grey	11	64	4	4	24	4		1							2			2	2	114	20
Brown on X	37	4	11	6		1	2	5	3	4	2			2				1		79	14
Bichrome	27	26				6		1	3		3	1		1				1		70	12
Black – various	9	18	10			7	2	3	2		1	3	4		1	2				62	11
None	3	40	2	2	5														2	58	10
Grey – various	4	2	5	11	12	3	1	4				2							1	46	8
Orange/red various	12	1	3	2		3	1	1						3				4	3	36	6
Bands	15	3		7			6			1	1			1			1			35	6
Black/brown on red	7	1	4	8		5	2			1	1						1	1		31	5
Streaky	2			3			2	1	1		2			1				1		13	2
Burnished		7	1				1		1											10	2
Stamped	7	1					1													9	2
Black glaze	1						2													3	1
Marbleizing				1		1		1		1										3	1
Brown glaze		1					1													2	0
Grooved/impressed	1																			1	0
Incised						1														1	0
White	1																			1	0
Total	137	123	69	54	41	23	21	18	16	10	8	8	6	6	5	4	3	2	10	8	574	100
%	24	21	12	9	7	4	4	3	3	2	1	1	1	1	1	1	1	0	2	1	100

As noted, bichrome decoration first appears at Gordion in this phase. Our sample includes considerable variation in motif (geometric to figure, panel vs. encircling), in shades of brown and red on a white or slipped background (e.g. Plates 9, 10). Often the white-slipped area is a panel or zone on the vessel, with a red slip outside the panel.

Similarly, 75% of the sherds are attributed to some formal, although highly generalized, shape ("jars" = 24% of MP samples, and likely include some jugs; Table 8.2; Fig. 8.6a for examples of common ware forms). To the extent that decorated shapes might be different from undecorated shapes, the assemblage of shapes is also likely skewed. Across the general form categories, the NAA sample assemblage includes only 33% of the common ware shapes that make up at least half of the 5C MP assemblage described by Henrickson.

Middle Phrygian Results

The MP ceramics are differentially distributed among 37 NAA groups (including five singletons; Table 8.3a). These MP geochemical groups represent change over time in sources or clay recipes, both at the larger scale of YHSS phases and also within the subphases of the MP. These differences allow us to postulate a relationship between resource use, cultural choices and changes in political and economic organization. Similarly, the distribution of MP archaeology across the site allows comparisons of intra-settlement differences in behavior.

During the MP, local cluster A dominates (ca. 37%) production (Table 8.3a), with two subgroups (A2 and A3) uniquely prominent in this phase. Local/regional cluster B is also well represented. Overall ~75% of the MP sample is produced in the local region (clusters A–D). With the exception of nonlocal cluster F, most nonlocal groups decrease during this period. Group M, unique to the MP period and most closely matched to the east-central settlement of Çadır Höyük, cannot be assigned to a specific subphase. Even though the MP assemblage is not equally distributed across its three subphases, there appear to be significant shifts in the use of local resources (varying from 25–40%), particularly in 5A, as discussed below (Table 8.3a and b; Fig. 8.8). The pattern of nonlocal ceramics also shows complex changes across potential western Anatolian and Ionian sources (groups F–L; Fig. 8.8).

Decorative styles are distributed across most of the dominant local sources or recipes, with a few showing some source preference (Table 8.4a). Most styles have strong representation in local cluster A. Brown on X, banded and orange-red decorated wares also show

Table 8.3. *Middle Phrygian NAA groups by YHSS 5 phase.*

(a) Counts. Number of NAA groups per phase is summed at the right. Number of groups provides a measure of diversity.

	A	A1	A2	A3	A7	A8	B	B1	B2	B3	B4	B5	B11	B16	B_oII	C	C1	C2	C3	D	D1	E	E1	E2	F	F1	G	H	I	J	K	L01	L02	L1	L2	L4	M	Total	%	# groups
5C	14	1	1				8	1	1			1	1	1		6				3	2	2	3		3	1	5				1							55	10	18
5C&B	40	3	1				1	32	7	4	1	2	3		1	7	2	3	2	2	2	16	1	1	10	2	1		1	1		1		1	1			147	26	27
5B	35	5	31	1	1	1	13	4	3	1		2	1			11	2		4	4	4	7			12	1	1	1			1							118	21	23
5B&A	3						5	1								2	2					3			5		1		1									23	4	9
5A	73	1	7	12			20	5	3	1	2	1			1	13	3		2	4	1	5	3		13	1	1	7	1	2		4	1	1	1			190	34	29
5	8	1	2				6									1		2		1		2	1		5							1	1				3	34	6	13
Total	173	11	14	13	1	2	84	18	11	3	4	7	3	2	1	40	9	5	11	13	7	36	5	1	48	5	8	9	1	3	2	2	7	1	2	2	3	567	100	37
%	31	2	2	2	0	0	15	3	2	1	1	1	1	0	0	7	2	1	2	2	1	6	1	0	8	1	1	2	0	1	0	0	1	0	0	0	1	100		

(b) Middle Phrygian NAA groups by YHSS5: Percentages.

	A	A1	A2	A3	A7	A8	B	B1	B2	B3	B4	B5	B11	B16	B_oII	C	C1	C2	C3	D	D1	E	E1	E2	F	F1	G	H	I	J	K	L01	L02	L1	L2	L4	M	Total %
5C	25	2	2				15	2	2			2	2	2		11				5	4	4	5		5	2	9				2							100
5C&B	27	2	1				1	22	5	3	1	1	2		1	5	1	2	1	1	1	11	1	1	7	1	1		1	1		1		1	1			100
5B	30	4	3	1	1	1	11	3	3	1		2	1			9	2		3	3	3	6			10	1	1	1			1							100
5B&A	13						22	4								9	9					13			22		4		4									100
5A	38	1	4	6			11	3	2	1	1	1			1	7	2		1	2	1	3	2		7	1	1	4	1	1		2	1	1	1			100
5	24	3	6				18									3		6		3		6	3		15							3	3				9	100

257

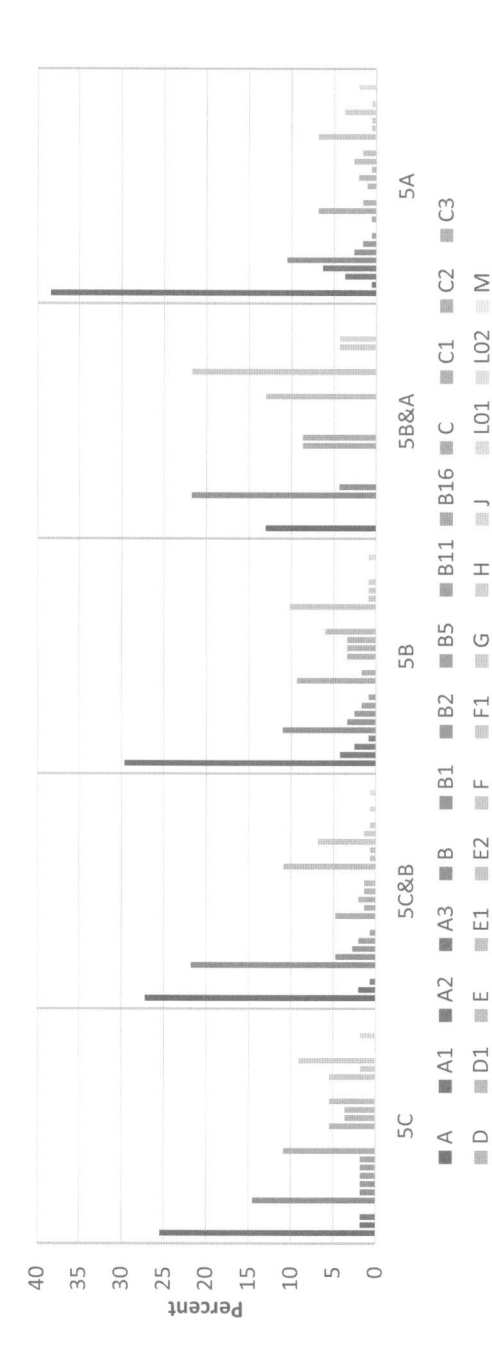

Fig. 8.8 YHSS 5 Middle Phrygian NAA groups by subphase (groups >1%). Cluster A is local, clusters B–D are local/regional, and clusters E–M are nonlocal sources.

strong local/regional production with representation in cluster B. As in the EP period, Black/brown on red is mostly nonlocal cluster F. Some decorative styles are better represented in a more limited number of recipes/sources (e.g. black various and bichromes), while others show greater than expected diversity given the size of the subsample (brown on X and Black/brown on red; Fig. 8.9a). Undecorated buff ware has more source diversity than undecorated grey ware. However, no style is exclusively linked to a single source or workshop, and no source or workshop is focused on a single style.

Most of the forms represented in the NAA sample were also represented in all of the local source clusters or recipes (Table 8.4b). As with the decorative styles, most forms are local cluster A. The exceptions are cups and craters, both of which are more common in local/regional cluster B. Jars and jugs also share a strong local/regional group representation. In terms of diversity, bowls include a more diverse set of sources, many of which are nonlocal. Jugs, to a lesser extent, are also marginally more diverse than the average (Fig. 8.9b). Group M, most closely matched to Çadır Höyük, comprises sherds of bichrome jugs. Cluster F (western Anatolia) is the most common nonlocal source shared by many forms, particularly for tablewares such as cups, stemmed bowls and jugs.

Phases and Places of the Middle Phrygian City

Here we turn to the internal dynamics of MP pottery production and consumption over space and time. The nature of our sample assemblage makes it possible to evaluate three general zones at Gordion: the Eastern Mound (the core social and political center), a combined sample from off the mounds (Outer Town, Lower Town, tumulus fill and excavations near or in the Küçük Höyük fortress) and the Western Mound.

The sectors are examined, to the extent possible, in chronological order, with the EM best representing 5C and 5C-B, off mound mostly 5B, and the WM 5A. However, all sectors include some samples from other phases. For examining change over time in each, phasing is related to the differences in excavation strategies: for the RSY assemblage, mostly EM, two subphases (5C-B, 5B-A) and for the MMV assemblage three subphases (5C to 5A, as described).

In the following discussion, we intersperse chronological summaries of subphases after the site sector where that phase is best represented. Our aim is to describe change over time as well as differences in spatial patterning.

The View from the Eastern Mound Zone (n = 298)

The elite walled precinct on the EM provides the largest single sample in the NAA ceramic assemblage, and includes samples from a storage

Table 8.4. *YHSS 5 Middle Phrygian compositional groups by decoration and form.*

(a) Surface decoration by compositional groups. Counts. Cluster A is local, clusters B–D are local/regional, and clusters E–M are nonlocal.

	A	A1	A2	A3	A7	A8	B	B1	B2	B3	B4	B5	B11	B16	B_oll	C	C1	C2	C3	D	D1	E	E1	E2	F	F1	G	H	I	J	K	L01	L02	L1	L2	L4	M	Total	%	# groups
None – grey	42	4	5			1	10	2	3	1	1	1				10	2			5	4	3	2		10	1	1					1						109	19	20
None	19	1	3		1		1	1		1	1					4		1	5	4	1	3			4	1	5	1					1					58	10	19
Brown on X	13		1	1			21	6	1		1			1		4	1	1	4	3	2		6	4	5	1			1									79	14	21
Bichrome	21	5	1			1	16	3	3		1	2				4			1		1		5		3					1							3	70	12	15
Black – various	15	1	4				8	3	1	1			1			9	1					10			7		1											62	11	13
Grey – various	22	2	4				2	1	1						1	5	3	1		2					1											1		46	8	13
Bands	5						12	2			2					1			1			2			2	1	4	1			2							35	6	12
Orange/red	12	1	2				11		2																2		2		1	1	1					1		35	6	10
Black/brown on red	4											1				1	2		1			4			10	1	1	1	1	1	1					1		30	5	14
Streaky	5																							1	2		2	1			2							13	2	6
Burnished	8															1							1															10	2	3
Stamped	5	1					1									1							1															9	2	5
Black glaze													1												1													3	1	3
Marbleizing							2					1																										3	1	2
Brown glaze								1																	1													2	0	2
Grooved/impressed	1																																					1	0	1
Incised	1																			1																		1	0	1
White																																						1	0	1
Total	173	11	14	13	1	2	84	18	11	3	4	7	3	2	1	40	9	5	11	13	7	36	5	1	48	5	8	9	1	3	2	2	7	1	2	2	3	567	100	37
%	31	2	2	2	0	0	15	3	2	1	1	1	1	0	0	7	2	1	2	2	1	6	1	0	8	1	1	2	0	1	0	0	1	0	0	0	1	100		

260

Table 8.4. (cont.)

(b) Middle Phrygian forms by compositional groups. Counts. Percentages and number of NAA groups per form in right column (compositional group percentages in Table 8.4a).

	A	A1	A2	A3	A7	A8	B	B1	B2	B3	B4	B5	B11	B16	B_oll	C	C1	C2	C3	D	D1	E	E1	E2	F	F1	G	H	I	J	K	L01	L02	L1	L2	L4	M	Total	%	#groups
Jar	36	4	3	3				29	6	5		1	3			4	2	3	1	2	1	13	1	1	9	3	2		2	1	1					1		137	24	25
Body sherd	34	4	2		1	1	1	11	2	3	1		2	1	1	14	1			3	7	8			12	1	4	1			1							120	21	23
Jug	17	1	1	1		1		15	2		1	2				3		1		2	1	7	2		10		1								1	2		70	12	18
Bowl	14		1	6				6	1				1			3	1	1							3			1	3				3				1	54	10	20
Pot/jar	21	4	1					1	1	1	1					3		2	2	2	1	3	2		1		1	3	1									40	7	13
Bowl – stemmed	13							1		1				1			1	1			1				5													21	4	5
Pot	11		1					2								5		1							1													21	4	6
Cup	2	1	1					6								3	1					1			3													18	3	8
Bowl – shallow	8							3					1			1	1									1												16	3	7
Crater	2	1						3	2					1					1						1													10	2	6
Bottle								2														1			2				1				2					8	1	5
Jar/jug	3									1							1	1				1	1					1									1	8	1	6
Closed	1		2													1						1	1		1													6	1	5
Rhyton	1								1	1	1					2																						6	1	5
Lydion								1																			2						1				1	5	1	4
Amphora	1							1	1							1																						4	1	4
Handle	1							1	1								1												1									4	1	4
Other forms	8		1					2	1				1				1		1						1		2						1					19	3	10
Total	173	11	14	13	1	2	2	84	18	11	3	4	7	3	2	1	40	9	5	11	13	7	36	5	1	48	5	8	9	13	2	2	7	1	2	2	3	567	100	37

261

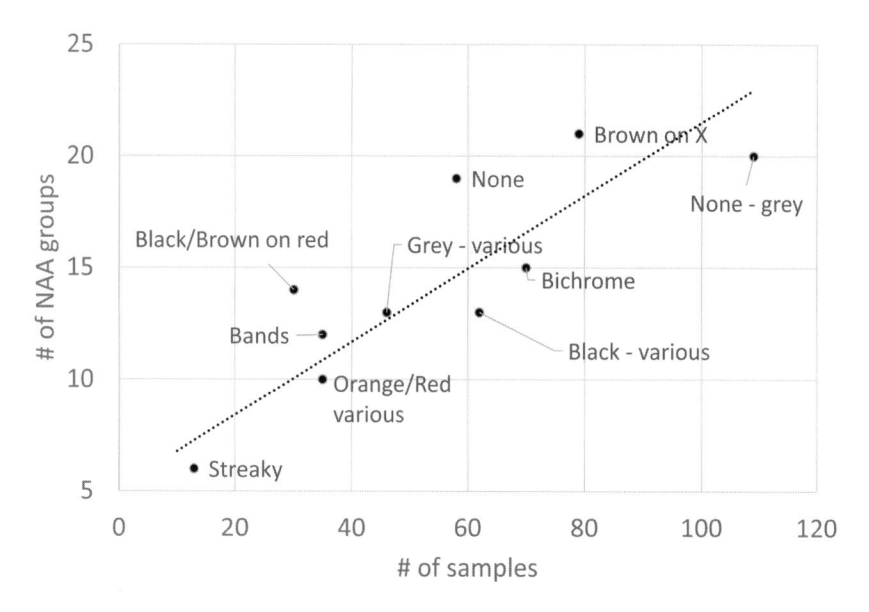

Fig. 8.9 YHSS 5 Middle Phrygian ceramics: sample size and NAA groups
(a) Number of samples/decorative style (*x*-axis) by number of compositional groups per form (*y*-axis). Graph illustrates forms with greater diversity [above trend line] and lesser group diversity [below the trend line].

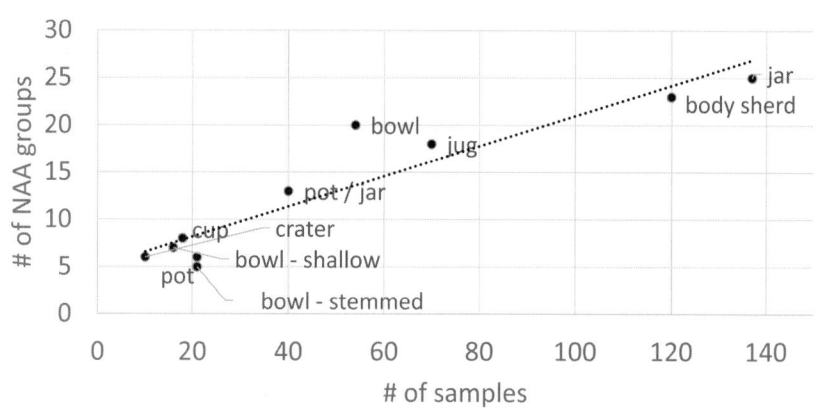

(b) Number of samples/form (*x*-axis) by number of compositional groups (*y*-axis). Bowls show more source diversity than other forms.

building (PPB), multiple megarons and the structures that were built above the Early Phrygian Terrace Complex (90% of the sample). The distribution of EM forms and styles by NAA group is presented in Tables 8.5a and b. Much of this sample is from subphases 5C-5B (75%; Table 8.1b).

Nearly 75% of the EM sub-assemblage, like the entire MP 5 assemblage, is from local or local/regional sources. Nonlocal sources include both east-central and west Anatolian matches, and a specifically Lydian matched component during 5A. West Anatolian sources comprise the largest component of the nonlocal sample (Table 8.5a), but east-central sources are well-represented.

This highly decorated MP sub-assemblage (ca. 85%) includes three main decorative schemes: brown decorated, bichromes and black variants (Table 8.5b). While all of these are predominantly from local to local/regional sources, bichromes are more often local and local/regional than brown on X and black various. Of all the decorated wares, bichromes are best-represented in the most local (sediment matched), cluster A. Brown on X, on the other hand, includes only 20% local cluster A sources.

Matches with east-central Anatolian sources are strongest for brown on X and black variants; however, bichromes include one very close imported match with Çadır Höyük (group M) also to the east (Kealhofer et al. 2010). This suggests that bichrome styles either developed locally or were emulations of east-central Anatolian styles (e.g. Kaman Kalehöyük; Grave and Kealhofer 2006).

Western Anatolian source groups (F–L) comprise just over 5% for both brown on X and bichromes, but are much more common for various black styles. Both black/brown on red and brown on X show the greatest source diversity.

A variety of other decorative styles are present, but in lower frequencies (see Table 8.5b). As in the EP period, Black/brown on red is relatively uncommon as a local cluster A product with well over half of the examples matching west Anatolian or coastal sources. Burnished and stamped styles, on the other hand, are dominated by local cluster A. Both banded and orange-red various styles include a diverse range of local/regional and west Anatolian sources.

Where forms could be identified, the majority sampled were jugs or jars (Table 8.5a). An abundance of jugs in the EM sample appears to be correlated with elaborate decoration (display). Bowls show the greatest overall source diversity, the greatest nonlocal source diversity, as well as the greatest percentage of nonlocal matches. For the distribution of forms across local vs. nonlocal groups, EM jars are more local than the

Table 8.5. *YHSS 5 Middle Phrygian Eastern Mound sub-assemblage.*

(a) Vessel forms by compositional group (counts <2 combined in "other forms"). Number of NAA groups in right-hand column.

	A	A1	A2	A7	A8	B	B1	B2	B3	B4	B5	B11	B16	C	C1	C2	C3	D	D1	E	E1	E2	F	F1	G	H	I	J	L01	L02	L2	L4	M	Total	%	#groups
Jar	24	2		1		20	4	4		2				3	2	3		1	2	7	1	1	6	2				1	1		1			88	30	20
Jug	16	1	1	1	1	14	2	1		2		1		2			2	1	1	7	2		10		1							1	2	65	22	16
Body	15	1	1	1	1	2	1		1	1	1			5	1			1	6	4	5		4	1	1	1			1					52	17	18
Bowl	3					3	1				1			3		1				3	1		2				1			2	1			24	8	14
Crater	2	1				3	2		1				1				1																	10	3	6
Bowl – shallow	3					2					1			1																				7	2	4
Jar/jug	2								1	0					1	1		1		1											1			7	2	6
Pot	4						1							1						1		1												7	2	4
Closed	1	2												1						1		1	1											6	2	5
Cup	1	1				1								1	1					1														6	2	6
Rhyton	1					1	1	1						2																				6	2	5
Bottle						2														1								1						4	1	3
Amphora	1					1	1																											3	1	3
Bowl – stemmed	0																					3												3	1	1
Other forms	4					1	1							1									1			1						1		10	3	7
Total	77	6	4	1	2	51	13	6	1	2	5	2	1	19	5	5	5	9	4	26	4	1	28	3	2	2	2	1	2	2	2	2	3	298	100	33
%	26	2	1	0	1	17	4	2	0	1	2	1	0	6	2	2	2	3	1	9	1	0	9	1	1	1	1	0	1	1	1	1	1	100		

264

Table 8.5. (cont.)

(b) Decoration by compositional group. Number of compositional groups in right-hand column (note stylistic variants are grouped together to simplify the table).

	A	A1	A2	A7	A8	B	B1	B2	B3	B4	B5	B11	B16	C	C1	C2	C3	D	D1	E	E1	E2	F	F1	G	H	I	J	L01	L02	L2	L4	M	Total	%	#groups
Brown on X	12	1				20	4	1		1	1			3	1	4	2	2		6	4	1	2	1					1		1			68	23	19
Bichrome	21	4		1		13	3	3		1	2			3			1			4		3	3			1							3	63	21	14
Black – various	13		1			8	3	1	1					4	1					7		7	7		1									47	16	11
None	7	1	1	1			1			1	1			3		1	5	4	3	3		3	3	1	1	1								35	12	16
Black/Brown on red	2										1			1	2		1			2		7	7	1			1	1	1					21	7	13
Grey – various	4					1	1							3	1	1		2		2												1		14	5	8
Bands	3					2	1			1				1				1		1		1	1				1			1				13	4	10
Orange/Red various	3	1				5		1														2	2								1			13	4	6
Burnished	5																			1														6	2	2
None – grey	2				1									1								2	2											6	2	4
Stamped	3	1				1						1										1	1											6	2	4
Other (<5)	2					1										1											1							6	2	5
Total	77	6	4	1	2	51	13	6	1	2	5	2	1	19	5	5	5	9	4	26	4	1	28	3	2	2	2	1	2	2	2	2	3	298	100	33

265

YHSS 5 assemblage average and include a wider range of local and local/regional sources. Jugs are marginally more nonlocal, and also have a relatively lower diversity of local/regional sources (Fig. 8.10). While the nonlocal sources were similar for jars, jugs and bowls, jars and jugs included an equal percentage of western and central-eastern Anatolian matches, whereas nonlocal bowls more commonly match west Anatolian sources. However, all stemmed bowls match a single non-local source, west Anatolian/Ionian group F, while all shallow bowls are local or local/regional. Unsurprisingly, larger, more difficult to transport forms (e.g. craters and rhytons) are all produced within the local to regional catchment.

Nearly all common forms and styles are distributed among local and regional clusters, with a few preferences evident for particular sources or recipes (Table 8.5b; Fig. 8.10). The sample of body sherds interestingly shows less use of local/regional group B sources than either jars or jugs, with a greater focus on local cluster A sources, presumably representing more quotidian functions.

Overall, relative to other areas of the city, EM source diversity is highest, particularly in bowl forms. While source diversity was also seen in the EP period, this shift to diversity in bowl forms flags a change from earlier EP use patterns, when jugs and jars showed greater source diversity. This subassemblage is >80% RSY, and therefore skewed strongly toward decorated or unusual samples. However, even allowing for sample biases, these data suggest that groups in the elite core area distinguished themselves through changing patterns of consumption in the MP. Even with the higher EM source diversity during the MP, local and local/regional source use is substantially more common than during the EP period.

Unlike other YHSS 5 sectors, local cluster A source use declined in EM contexts through the MP period (Fig. 8.11, Table 8.6). The adoption of new decorative styles on the Eastern Mound, particularly bichromes and black various, however, correlates with an increase in local and regional production during the eighth century (5C-B). By 5A, nonlocal sources increase for both west and east Anatolian sources in this sector.

Subphase Summary: 5C (n = 55) and 5C-B (n = 147) Combined Excavation Sectors

Both 5C and 5C-B phases are comprised of very similar percentages of local and local/regional samples. The differences in sample sizes and sampling strategies make it difficult to directly compare groupings of these two phases. Given 5C-B is a highly selective RSY sample, many more sherds are decorated and have identified forms. While not

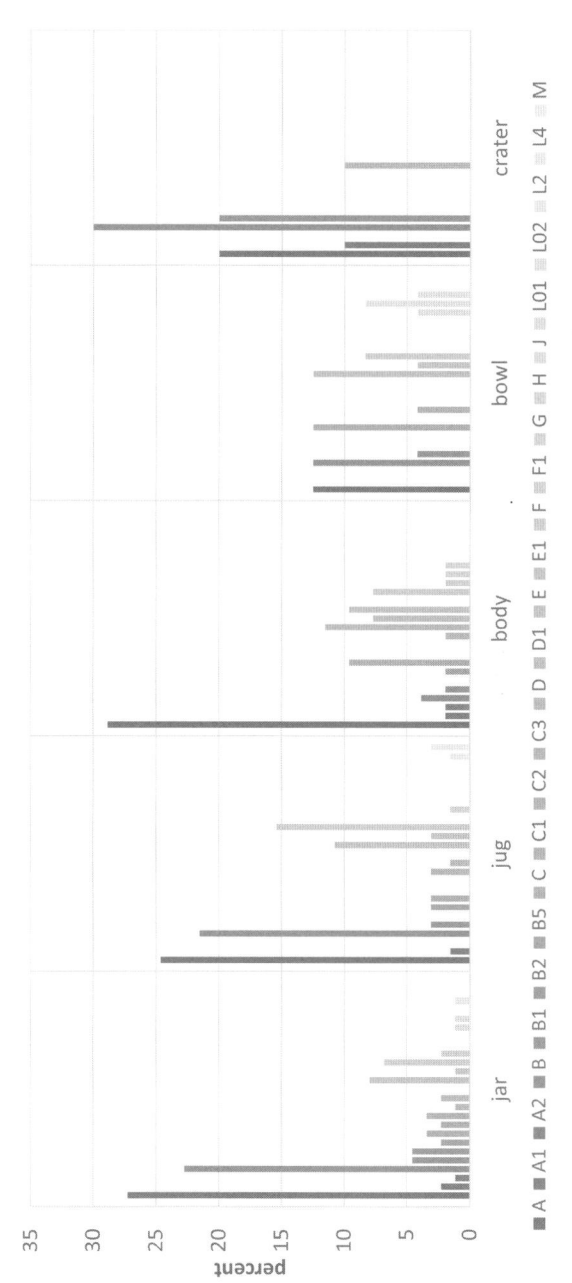

Fig. 8.10 YHSS 5 Middle Phrygian Eastern Mound: forms (with >10 sherds) by compositional groups (>2 samples).

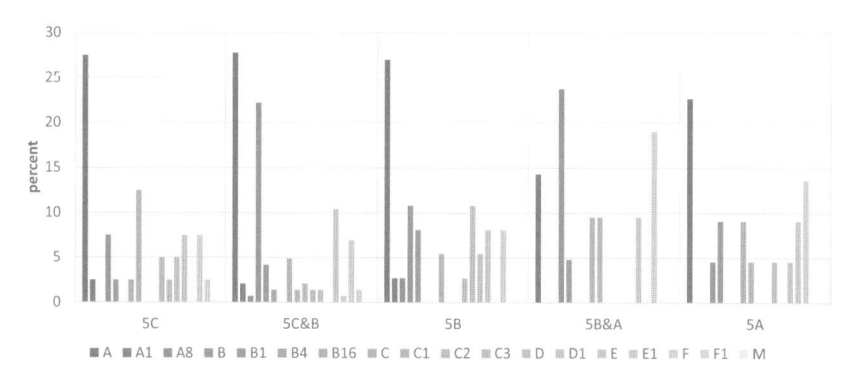

Fig. 8.11 Eastern Mound distribution of NAA groups across the MP phases (5C-5A). Note decline in use of local cluster A sources, as well as decrease in group diversity.

common, a few new forms appear, including pot and bottle types. Overall, these subphases show greater continuity with YHSS 6A in styles and forms, although with a much greater frequency of local and local/regional production.

A Ritual Economy?
In the EM elite area, feasting and food consumption contexts and beverages remain important for the materialization of both individual and group identities during the MP period. Henrickson noted that vessel forms remained relatively conservative and standardized, but new styles of decoration were also adopted (e.g. bichromes and black sintered slips). However, as in the EP period, the highly variable individualized decoration for pouring (?) and drinking vessels along with the scratching of names and geometric patterns on drinking bowls in the WM sector suggests identity signaling during the communal consumption of food and drink. Production of local styles (vs. emulations) was at its peak in the earlier 5C and 5B subphases.

Higher regional compositional diversity and frequencies in 5C-B are consistent with local elites bringing wares (and goods as tribute?) produced in the surrounding area to the capital to service feasting activities and also competitive display. The greater number of nonlocal sources for bowls suggests these may have been more commonly brought into the quarter by consumers; this pattern decreased in 5A, along with declining use of east-central Anatolian sources. More fundamentally, changes in the organization of production and resource zone patterning suggest comparable shifts in the ritual economy. The trends in the EM sector

Table 8.6. *Eastern Mound: Middle Phrygian subphases by compositional group. Most of the grouped phase samples (e.g. 5C&B) are from Young excavations, while most of the ungrouped samples are from Voigt excavations.*

	A	A1	A2	A7	A8	B	B1	B2	B3	B4	B5	B11	B16	C	C1	C2	C3	D	D1	E	E1	E2	F	F1	G	H	I	J	L01	L02	L2	L4	M	Total	%
5C	11	1	1			3	1	1		1	1	1	1	5			2	1	2	3			3	1	1				1					40	13
5C&B	40	3		1	1	32	6	4	1	2	3	1		7	2	3	2	2		15	1	1	10	2	1	1	1			1	1	1		144	48
5B	10	1		1	1	4	3				1			2	2		1	4	2	3			3		1									37	12
5B&A	3					5	1							2	2					2			4		1	1								21	7
5A	5	1				1	2	1			5			2	1			1		1	2		3							1	1			22	7
5 (not phased)	7	1	2			6				1	2	1		1		2		1		2	1		5						1	1			3	33	11
Total	76	6	4	1	2	51	13	6	1	2	5	2	1	19	5	5	5	9	4	26	4	1	28	3	2	2	1	2	2	2	2	2	3	297	100
%	26	2	1	0	1	17	4	2	0	1	2	1	0	6	2	2	2	3	1	9	1	0	9	1	1	1	0	1	1	1	1	1	1	100	

strongly contrast with both the trends in other sectors and the overall YHSS 5 assemblage.

Off the Citadel Mound (n = 137) (132 with NAA data)
The "off mound" assemblage combines several contexts with smaller sample sizes (Tables 8.1b, 8.7). All three subphases are represented, but 5B is most common (60%) and 5A comprises the majority of the remainder (33%). The largest sample ($n = 113$) is from in and around the Küçük Höyük areas excavated by Mellink. The KH sample includes two excavation locations: one directly from the fortification ($n = 41$) and one from a kiln area ("Fazli's kiln" $n = 72$) outside the Lower Town wall, just beyond the base of the Persian siege mound. In addition, a handful of samples ($n = 9$) come from the Lower Town and the Outer Town, while another small group ($n = 14$) is from tumulus fill or the adjacent MP cemetery. One sample is from the city wall.

As elsewhere during YHSS 5, close to 75% of this assemblage is local or local/regional (clusters A–D). Nearly one-third of the sub-assemblage is local cluster A, similar to the EM sub-assemblage distribution, highlighting both the cultural continuity between 5C and 5B and similarities in consumption across the city in these subphases. Western Anatolian sources from off mound contexts comprise more than 20%, higher than on the EM. While a similar range of local cluster A sources are present in both WM and off mound contexts, local cluster A is present in a much lower frequency (31% vs. 61%) in this sector, with local/regional sources more common and nonlocal sources more than twice as frequent as in WM contexts.

Just over half of this sub-assemblage has identifiable forms (Table 8.8a). Tablewares include multiple bowl types (shallow and stemmed), as well as a few other forms (plates, jugs, small pots). The

Table 8.7. *YHSS 5 Middle Phrygian Off Mound sub-assemblage sector (left) and MP YHSS subphase (top).*

	5C	5C&B	5B	5B&A	5A	Total
Küçük Höyük		2	72	2	37	113
Tumuli fill/cemetery			9		5	14
Outer Town	5					5
Lower Town	0				4	4
City wall	1					1
Total	6	2	81	2	46	137

Table 8.8. *YHSS 5 Middle Phrygian off the Citadel Mound sub-assemblage (counts and percentages).*

(a) Form by compositional group. Number of compositional groups in right-hand column.

	A	A1	A2	A3	B	B1	B2	B3	B5	B11	B16	C	C1	C3	D	D1	E	F	F1	G	H	J	K	L02	Total	%	# groups
Body	16	3	1		9	1	3	1	1			8	1	2	1	1	3	7	1	1				1	60	45.5	17
Jar	6	2	1	1	5	1	1		1							1	5	1	1	1	1	1			29	22	15
Bowl	3			1	1									1				1			1				8	6	6
Cup	1				3							1		1				3							8	6	4
Bowl – stemmed								1									1	2							4	3	3
Bottle																	1							2	3	2	2
Bowl – shallow					1						1								1						3	2	3
Jug			1		1							1													3	2	3
Pot	1				1					1															3	2	3
Pot – small	1									1				1											3	2	3
Lydion					1																			1	2	2	3
Plate	1						1																		2	2	3
Base			1																						1	1	1
Bowl – Achaemenid																							1		1	1	1
Handle	1																								1	1	1
Jar/jug																									1	1	1
Total	30	5	4	2	22	3	4	2	2	1	1	10	2	4	1	2	9	15	2	2	2	1	2	4	132	100	24
%	23	4	3	2	17	2	3	2	2	1	1	8	2	3	1	2	7	11	2	2	2	1	2	3	100		

Table 8.8. (cont.)

(b) Decoration by compositional group. Number of NAA groups in right-hand column.

	A	A1	A2	A3	B	B1	B2	B3	B5	B11	B16	C	C1	C3	D	D1	E	F	F1	G	H	J	K	L02	Total	%	# groups
None – grey	21	4	3		9	1	3	1	1			8	2	3	1	2	2	8	1	1	1			1	72	55	18
Bands	2				7	1		1										1	1		2				15	11	7
Black/nrown on red	2																2	3		1			1		9	7	5
Bichrome		1	1		3							1					1								7	5	5
Orange/red various					3		1															1	1	1	6	5	4
Black – various			1							1							3								5	4	3
Streaky	1																	1				1		2	5	4	3
Brown on X						1								1				1							4	3	4
Black glaze			1								0 1							1							3	2	3
Stamped	2																								3	2	1
Incised	1																1								1	1	1
Marbleizing							1																		1	1	1
None	1																								1	1	1
Total	30	5	4	2	22	3	4	2	2	1	1	10	2	4	1	2	9	15	2	2	2	2	2	4	132	100	24
%	23	4	3	2	17	2	3	2	2	1	1	8	2	3	1	2	7	11	2	2	2	1	2	3	100		

jars include a larger nonlocal component than the overall off mound sector (33% vs. 25%). The nonlocal component is even larger for bowls, with just under half of the bowls and cups matching nonlocal sources. Both stemmed and shallow bowls matched nonlocal west Anatolian sources. Lydions and bottles match Lydian (Sardis) sources, reflecting exchange or import rather than local emulation. Eastern sources continue to be present in these contexts.

The majority of the samples are undecorated grey ware (55%, mostly from "Fazli's kiln"). Unlike both the EM and the WM, simple band decoration and Black/brown on red are the most common decorative styles, with some bichromes, orange/red variants and black variants (Table 8.8b). Most styles are dominated by local and local/regional production, with only Black/brown on red and streaky decoration more frequently matching nonlocal sources. Brown on X, as in the WM contexts, is a very small percentage of the sample. The samples from both KH excavation areas include western Anatolian styles and forms (bands, streaky, marbleizing, orange/red; stemmed bowls, cups, bottles, jars). Somewhat surprisingly, source diversity is high, particularly within the local/regional cluster B, with a more limited range of nonlocal sources (Table 8.8b). While the "Fazli's kiln" sample is mostly local, it includes more than 13 local-to-regional sources, as well as a range of nonlocal sources that suggests the sample includes material not directly associated with this kiln (Table 8.9).

Subphase Summary: 5B (n = 118) Combined Excavation Sectors
The majority of 5B samples, ca. 60%, are from the off mound assemblage discussed in the last section (Table 8.1b). This subphase includes a larger local sample (ca. 80% local and local/regional, 40% group A) than earlier subphases (5C and 5C-B; Fig. 8.8). The nonlocal assemblage is dominated by west Anatolian sources (group F), with fewer east-central Anatolian samples. West Anatolian sourced forms include a bowl, bottle and two jar sherds. East-central Anatolian forms include jars and jugs (group E). As in 5C-B, bottles and pots are present but rare. Like the general off mound sample, most of the 5B sample is undecorated; however, in the 5B sample conservative decorative styles similar to 5C are most common (black various styles, brown on X and a few burnished examples). Similarly, only about a third of the 5B sherds are identifiable, mainly as jars and bowls. Phase 5B thus reveals strong continuity with 5C, an increasing trend toward local production, a decrease in east-central Anatolian sources and continued exchange with western Anatolia.

Table 8.9. *YHSS 5 Middle Phrygian off the Citadel Mound: Küçük Höyük sub-assemblages by NAA groups.*

	A	A1	A2	B	B1	B2	B3	B5	B11	B16
Fazli's kiln	31	6	4	10	1	4	1	1	1	
Küçük Höyük excavations	15	3	3	23	5		3	3		3

Table 8.10. *Middle Phrygian Western Mound sub-assemblage: YHSS 5 subphases by compositional groups.*

	A	A2	A3	B	B1	B2	B4	B_oll	C	C1
5C	3			2					1	
5C&B					1					
5B	2			1						
5A	61	6	11	8	1	1	2	1	10	2
Total	66	6	11	11	2	1	2	1	11	2
%	48	4	8	8	1	1	1	1	8	1

C	C1	C3	D1	E	F	F1	H	J	K	L02	Total	# groups
12	3	3	3	3	12	1				1	68	17
				8	15	3	5	3	5	8	40	15

C3	D	D1	E	E1	F	G	H	L02	L1	Total
						3				9
										1
					1					4
2	3	1	1	1	4	1	5	1	1	123
2	3	1	1	1	5	4	5	1	1	137
1	2	1	1	1	4	3	4	1	1	100

Western Mound [n = 139]

The Western Mound is known from two excavation areas, the Northwest zone (NWZ) and the Southwest zone (SWZ; Fig. 3.5a). The vast majority of the sample is from phase 5A (90%; Table 8.10), when both the NWZ and SWZ were affluent domestic contexts. The SWZ deposit is interpreted as a single depositional ("dump") event involving one or more elite households (Dusinberre et al. 2019).

The WM assemblage has a stronger local signature than either the EM or off mound sectors. It is comprised predominantly of local and local/regional clusters A–D (ca. 85%), with local cluster A making up 60% of the WM sub-assemblage. This suggests that production and supply during 5A was focused in the immediate environs of Gordion, with less regional input than in earlier phases. It may also mean preferential consumption by WM families of locally produced ceramics. A new local source or recipe was introduced (A3) and used for open vessels (e.g. bowls, pots). The relatively small nonlocal proportion (ca. 15%) is primarily Lydian and west Anatolian.

Pots, bowls and jars dominate the WM sample (>80%), with both stemmed bowls ("fruitstands") and shallow bowls common (Table 8.11a). Jars are not as abundant in 5A as earlier (ca. 15%; however, the category of pot/jar likely contributes a larger percentage of jars). Jugs, common in earlier MP groupings, are now rare (1%). Open pots and stemmed bowls are relatively new forms, and both are now more common than in earlier contexts. A handful of western Anatolian forms include a lydion (perfume container) and a lekythos (bottle); the lydion matches a local Sardis source, while the bottle matches a more general west Anatolian source. Cups, also relatively rare until 5A, are all locally or local/regionally sourced. In terms of source diversity, jars and bowls show greater variation than pots or stemmed bowls. The larger excavated sample includes a greater proportion of non-local wares (vs. this NAA sample).

Compared with other periods, the WM 5A sample is more decorated (ca. 60%), but grey undecorated ware still makes up a sizeable component of the total (23% vs. 50% in the excavated assemblage; Table 8.11b). There is a major shift in decorative repertoire in this subphase, as complex painted decoration decreases in relation grey and black decorated styles, as well as orange/red variants (43% combined). For example, brown on X styles, most common in the 5C-5B EM sample, are now relatively rare (5%). The pot/jar forms are most often not decorated, just as bowls and cups are commonly decorated (bowls as grey various, cups as a wider range of styles). However, just over half the pot sample is black decorated (pot forms include shapes similar to craters). The majority of grey decorated and black decorated wares are from the SWZ, with

Table 8.11. *YHSS 5 Middle Phrygian Western Mound sub-assemblage (counts/percentages).*

(a) Form by compositional group. Number of compositional groups in right-hand column.

	A	A2	A3	B	B1	B2	B4	B_o11	C	C1	C3	D	D1	E	E1	F	G	H	L02	L1	Total	%	# groups
Pot/jar	21	4	1	1	1	1	1		3		2	2	1			1				1	40	29	13
Bowl	8	1	5	2						1		1			1			2	1		22	16	9
Jar	6	1	2	4	1		1		1							2		1			20	15	10
Bowl – stemmed	13			1										1							14	10	2
Pot	6								4												11	8	3
Body	3		1					1	1							1	2				8	6	5
Bowl – shallow	5									1											6	4	2
Cup			1	2					1												4	3	3
Base	1			1																	2	1	2
Jug	1		1																		2	1	2
Rim	2																				2	1	1
Other forms (<2)									1							1	2	2			6	4	4
Total	66	6	11	11	2	1	2	1	11	2	2	3	1	1	1	5	4	5	1	1	137	100	20
%	48	4	8	8	1	1	1	1	8	1	1	2	1	1	1	4	3	4	1	1	100		

Table 8.11. (cont.)

(b) Decoration by compositional group. Number of compositional groups in right-hand column.

	A	A2	A3	B	B1	B2	B4	B_oll	C	C1	C3	D	D1	E	E1	F	G	H	L02	L1	Total	%	# groups
Grey – various	18	2	4	1		1		1	2	2						1					32	23	9
None – grey	19	2		1	1		1		1		2	3	1			1	4				31	23	9
None	11	2		1			1		1									2		1	22	16	8
Orange/red various	9		2	3																	16	12	4
Black – various	2		3						5												10	7	3
Bands				3									1					2	1		7	5	4
Brown on X	1		1	1	1				1							2		1			7	5	6
Streaky	3													1	1	1					6	4	4
Burnished	3								1												4	3	1
Other decorative (<2)			1	1															1	1	2	1	2
Total	66	6	11	11	2	1	2	1	11	2	2	3	1	1	1	5	4	5	1	1	137	100	20
%	48	4	8	8	1	1	1	1	8	1	1	2	1	1	1	4	3	4	1	1	100		

Enacting Power 279

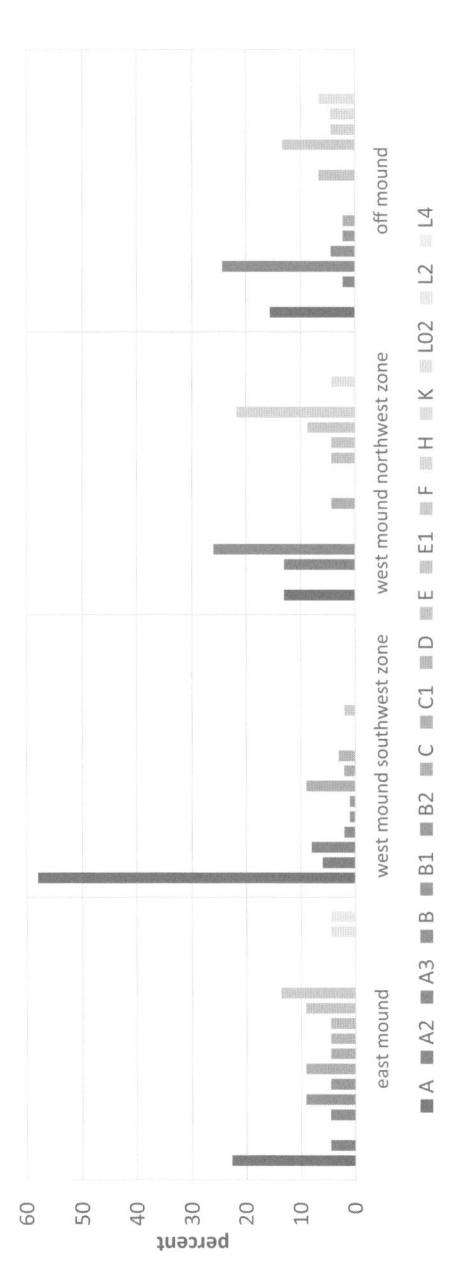

Fig. 8.12 YHSS 5A Middle Phrygian distribution of NAA groups by excavation sector. Cluster A local, clusters B–D local/regional, clusters E–L nonlocal.

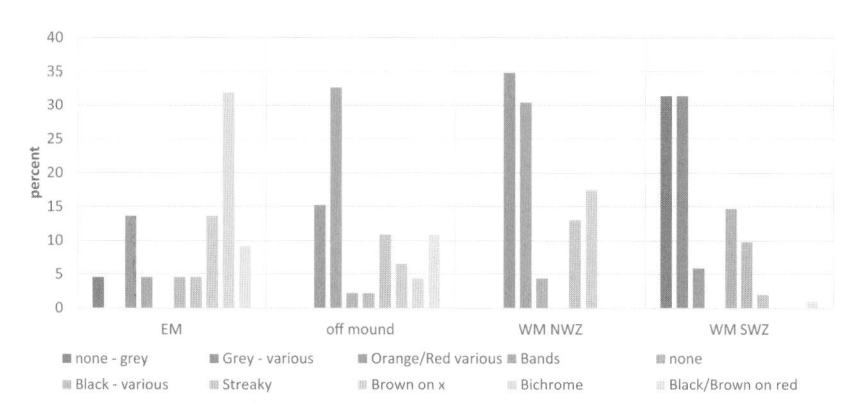

Fig. 8.13 YHSS 5A Middle Phrygian main decorative styles by excavation zone. Note sector differences.

orange/red decorated most common in the NWZ. Of these two decorative styles, nearly half are from 5C and 5B, with Brown on buff only found in these earlier subphases (with the *caveat* that sample sizes are relatively small).

Subphase Summary: 5A (n = 190) Combined Excavation Sectors
For the final MP 5A phase, substantial changes appear in the NAA assemblage. The largest portion of the 5A sample comes from WM contexts (NWZ and SWZ, ca. 75%); just over 20% is from the KH sub-assemblages, with smaller percentages from the EM, and additional off mound contexts (Table 8.1b).

As in earlier subphases, local and local/regional sources dominate but the balance shifts to the most local sources, with 50% of the sub-assemblage now from local cluster A (Fig. 8.8). The SWZ WM in particular highlights this shift. Nonlocal sources make up ca. 20% of the 5A sample, as in 5B, but mostly match west Anatolian sources (particularly groups F and H) with a smaller east-central source contribution (group E).

Another major change from earlier subphases is the clear difference in the distribution of local and local/regional sources between sectors on the site (Fig. 8.12). The contrast is particularly strong for the two WM sectors. Similarly, 5A nonlocal sources (groups E–L) vary substantially by sector, with the SWZ only 4% nonlocal, while the NWZ is more than 40% nonlocal (as is KH) (Fig. 8.12). Specific nonlocal sources are sector-distinct, and source matches with Lydia are more common (groups H and L) in the EM and KH samples. However, east-central Anatolian group E is still present, particularly in the EM sample.

In addition to source differences on the WM, the decorative palette is quite different in the NWZ and the SWZ (Fig. 8.13), suggesting a diversity of social groups in these two sectors, consistent with the differences between the architectural remains in each area. The off mound assemblage is similar stylistically to the NWZ, and both contexts, as well as the EM, include specifically Lydian sources (L groups and H group) supporting an argument for a Lydian presence in these zones.

The general patterning of 5A wares reflects a shift both in ceramic forms and in decoration to a more diverse household assemblage by the end of the MP. Jugs become a relatively small component of the assemblage, whereas pots, bowls and cups are more common than in earlier phases. The relative increase in tableware diversity, particularly in various bowl and cup forms, alongside the decrease in elaborate decoration (e.g. grey various, bands, streaky), suggests changes in the ways individual status and identity were practiced in relation to foodways.

The shift toward increasing emulation also underlines the increased role of local production in this last phase of the Middle Phrygian period. Most common decorated styles are both exchanged and locally emulated; however, undecorated grey is completely local, and bichrome and black and grey decorative variants are mostly sourced locally. Black/brown on red, mostly nonlocal in earlier phases, has both local and nonlocal sources in 5A.

Major shifts in 5A in both architecture and ceramics reflect a new interest in the elaboration of local production for household or domestic display that seems to move away from elite practices of display in highly charged communal food consumption contexts. This is most apparent in the sectors outside the EM. While 5A contextual comparisons are challenging due to the varied levels of stratigraphic resolution involved, these shifts also appear to mark changes within specific social groups in the city.

Change over Time across Sectors: Summary
Several general trends can be identified through the phases of MP 5 (Fig. 8.8). With the exception of 5B-A, local cluster A sources increase steadily. Local/regional sources, such as B and C, fluctuate over time, but decline in 5A. Similarly, nonlocal sources fluctuate but increase through 5B, including both east-central and western Anatolian sources. Nonlocal sources generally decrease in 5A, but with a greater diversity of west Anatolian, including Lydian, sources. The decorative palette and range of forms also shift through these phases. The use of jugs decreases, the proportion of pots and bowls increases, and decoration shifts from elaborately painted bichromes and variously decorated black and grey to more colorful but simply decorated red and orange styles (e.g. bands

and lines). Dusinberre and colleagues (2019) describe the 5A SWZ dump assemblage as less varied, with a more limited range of decoration than in earlier MP phases. Another broad trend is the increasing differentiation of sectors across the settlement over time, in both styles and exchange patterns, a pattern that continues in the LP period.

Production, Consumption and Distribution

We now turn to exploring these three vectors of the economy at MP Gordion, summarizing other archaeological data, where available, and using the ceramic and compositional data to provide new interpretations.

Group Formation and Production

Nonceramic Evidence for Production

Production data, from scale and resources to archaeological contexts and materials, provide insight into how different types of work groups were organized at Gordion during the MP. To understand the types of groups involved in production in any period, therefore, requires framing the salient range of production areas and products from which to infer group organization. While a basic economic activity, production is also often a key element of ritual (McAnany and Wells 2008), and is closely entangled with social practices, identity, politics and power.

Agriculture continued as a core production sphere during the Iron Age. Throughout the occupation of ancient Gordion, the topography, rainfall and vegetation regime favored pastoralism (Fig. 5.13; N. F. Miller et al. 2009; Zeder and Arter 1994). Recent palaeoenvironmental data from central Turkey suggests a dry phase continued into the MIA (N. Roberts et al. 2016). If so, then the ascendency and apogee of Phrygian political expansion occurred in a period affected by drought. This makes the MP period seemingly anomalous. On one hand it was still mainly a pastoral economy, on the other it is in this period that cattle and pigs, animals that have a high water requirement, are most common and were likely pastured close to home and fed on harvest stubble and cultivated cereals. Sheep and goats, which can use uncultivated pasture, are still proportionally important, but less so than during the EP. Wild animals, such as hares, remain minor supplements to the diet (Zeder and Arter 1994).

The increased use in the MP of cattle and pigs, as well as a shift toward greater production of wheat, has been suggested as evidence of agricultural intensification at this time (Marston 2012). In response to increased risk of drought new water management systems along the Sakarya River would have also played a role in a changing MP agricultural economy

(Marsh 2012; N. F. Miller 2010). As intensification of production postdates the formation of the Phrygian polity in the EP, it appears that political development at Gordion preceded major changes in agricultural strategies and intensification. Such patterns of agricultural intensification following initial expansion of political power are also found in other parts of the world (e.g. Kealhofer and Grave 2008; Sidky 1997).

Monumental construction is the most visible production sphere for MP Gordion. The scale and logistics of labor supply and maintenance, along with the pace of construction and infrastructure during early MP (5C), are at a peak compared to both preceding and following periods. Middle Phrygian construction projects involved movement of very large quantities of earth, quarrying and shaping of stone for foundations and walls, and the manufacture of mud bricks for their superstructures. Starting with the amount of fill that had to be moved to build up a layer 3–5 m deep over two mounds, one estimate is half a million cubic meters (Peter Kuniholm personal communication 2009). In addition, the MP community built a similar platform in the Lower Town (Voigt 2011). Walls surrounding the Lower Town (ca. 2.8 km) and Outer Town (>1 km), as well as the Lower Town fortresses (Fig. 8.5b), were also constructed at this time to protect a residential area that extended over more than 103 ha (see Plate 1; Rose 2017). The multiple types of stone used in the fortification system – glacis, wall and gates – were sourced from several quarries to create a carefully color-patterned external facade. While most of the sources of stone, including gypsum, (black) basalt, (red) sandstone, distinctive yellow and green stones and (white) siltstones, are available within a 10 km radius of Gordion (Marsh personal communication 2018), the effort to haul, quarry and cut to best display a colorful façade for the city wall represents another impressive demonstration of MP elite logistics and capacity.

In addition to elite administrative, workshop and residential(?) buildings overlooking the plain from the top of the EM (5C), monumental tumuli were erected on the surrounding landscape, with at least six built and furnished during the eighth century BCE (Rose and Darbyshire 2011). Stephens (2018:174–181, table 5, fig. 98–101) has compiled data on the labor and material resources required for their construction. He calculated the number of person-days needed for building each tumulus, highlighting the labor requirements for the late eighth century construction of tumulus MM as an order of magnitude greater (nearly 300,000 person-days) than the more common small tumuli at a few hundred person-days. The few hundred person-days needed for most of the ninth to eighth century tumuli – may be more in line with an elite cemetery than a mortuary complex reserved for rulers (Stephens 2018:175–176, 185). Stephens also noted that a likely construction time of 40–90 days for tumulus MM would require more labor than could be supplied by Gordion alone, with an estimated population of ca. 10,000 (Stephens 2018:184).

Water management infrastructure would also have involved substantial labor input and logistical expertise, whether to construct and maintain an irrigation system (N. F. Miller 2010) or to supply water to the city (Marsh 2005). While the size and sources of the labor force required to complete each of these projects remains uncertain, the scale of works suggests that a sizable number of both skilled (masons, engineers) and unskilled workers were engaged through the eighth century BCE. After reviewing a variety of potential labor arrangements, Stephens (2018: 158) concluded that corvée labor (potentially tied into work feasts) was most likely for large construction projects.

Most other direct evidence of production spheres at Gordion primarily date to either the EP (food and textiles in the TB and CC complexes) or the LP (metal production, production of stone vessels and bone/antler working). On the Eastern Mound, MP rebuilding of the Terrace Complex (above EP CC and TB), in an area that in the EP was associated with food, beer and textile production, *may* reveal the continuation of practices of production for elite and/or ritual consumption (see discussion in Chapter 6). In support of this interpretation the 5C-B I:2 cellar (Fig. 3.4), attached to one of the YHSS 5 Terrace Complex structures, had both a hearth and oven, and associated finds included weaving tools as well as cooking/serving food-related items. Other artifacts from the I:2 cellar can be related to individual identity: a bronze fibula (clothing) and sherds with graffiti in the Phrygian alphabet (Codella and Voigt in press). The MP (5B) community on the Northeast Ridge had a room ("the bakery") with many grinding stones and a large oven (Anderson 2012; Sams in press) indicating food processing beyond the domestic needs of one or two households, possibly provisioning construction groups. In the Lower Town, within a domestic context, a pyrotechnic feature and a stone mold for a small ornament imply metal-working occurred somewhere nearby (5A) (Codella and Voigt in press). On the Western Mound during 5A, metal, alabaster and horn-working evidence is present.

The presence of finely worked metal, wood and relatively rare glass products from MP tumuli points to skilled local work groups producing sophisticated, high-quality products for elite consumption (J. D. Jones 2009; Simpson and Spirydowicz 1999). Precious metals, on the other hand, are virtually nonexistent in the archaeological record, with the exception of small, likely exotic, items of lead, gold and silver from the 5A dump in the WM SWZ. For the most part craftspeople in the

MP period focused on bronze, brass, wood/cabinet crafts, textiles and perhaps glass, and the value placed on these is evident from their inclusion in the rich grave goods in the tumuli. Clothing items in the tumuli, such as fibula and belts as well as textiles, also underscore the role of local crafts for the materialization of elite identities (Sams 1995).

The spatial patterning of both production and product sources suggests multiple modes of production were practiced at Gordion, in addition to the likely drafting of a sizable body of corvée labor. The labor force required for the construction of irrigation canals and tumuli, for example, would likely have been organized differently from that required for stone-working or textile production. The domestic contexts of much of the production may argue for part-time specialization and/or household specialization as a common mode of production. Ceramic production provides yet another sphere of labor or work group organization in the MP.

Ceramic Production and Groups

We return to review the most salient variables for MP ceramic production: skill level, technology investment, kinds/quantities of output, uniformity of output, investment in places/tools, producers' location/numbers/spatial proximity and consumers' location/numbers/spatial proximity. Here we combine these variables to develop inferences about work group composition and production scale. We follow two main lines of evidence for ceramic production at MP Gordion: Henrickson's interpretation of ceramic production sequences (outlined earlier) and the compositional data.

Scale of Production: Workshops?

<u>Uniformity, Kinds and Quantities of Outputs</u> Henrickson classified MP production as "workshop" organization that involved a relatively small number of specialized potters (Henrickson 1993, 1994). He based this on the limited range of forms with similar dimensions and production sequences. Henrickson describes the production sequence as "standardized," in terms of the relative uniformity of both products and production sequences for each form (Henrickson 1993:132). Johnston (1970) also identified well-defined size categories of Phrygian jug volumes adding support for this interpretation of standardization. The complexity of production sequences also formed part of Henrickson's attribution of workshop production. For the utilitarian wares, his suggestion of "mass production" likely meant distribution beyond the site of Gordion itself. Fine ware production, while likely more limited in volume, may also have been exchanged across the region.

NAA Data

The relationships between geochemical groups and decorative types and forms enables us to develop another line of evidence to evaluate workshop production. As discussed in Chapter 4, our null hypothesis is that all sources/resource zones were equally accessible to all potters in all periods. To the extent this expectation is not met, we can evaluate if and at what stage specialization occurred. Since sample sizes are variable for each sub-assemblage, we correct for sample size by evaluating the nature of the relationship between the number of groups and the number of types, (#groups/#types) to identify the size of deviations from the expected number of forms or styles as a measure of specialization (e.g. Fig. 8.9).

Decorative styles In terms of the local source distribution, all styles were produced from multiple sources (Table 8.4a). For the local cluster A, subgroup A is the most commonly used (particularly for Black/brown on red, grey various and orange/red various). However, for several styles other local/regional sources are more frequent (brown on X and bands). Every style with a sample greater than five includes nonlocal sources. In terms of local vs. nonlocal distribution, some styles show a much greater number of nonlocal groups (Black/brown on red, brown on X, bands and streaky), while others are dominated by local production (mainly the undecorated buff ware and bichromes). In terms of sources, brown decorated undecorated, and Black/brown on red wares are the most diverse, highlighting their potential social and/or ritual value (Fig. 8.9a).

Forms The relationship between number of NAA groups and forms correlates well with sample size, although bowls and jugs, to a lesser extent, exhibit greater than average diversity (Fig. 8.9b). Jars and bowls have the greatest number of sources, with bowls representing the largest number of nonlocal sources/workshops (Fig. 8.10, Table 8.4b). This diversity seems likely to be part of the materialization of identities, as in economically rational terms the demand for bowls could have been met by a couple of workshops or sources.

The relationship between forms and sources follows a similar pattern to that discussed for style: all forms were made from multiple sources/workshops. In a few cases, a single source appears to be preferred (e.g. for stemmed bowls, pot/jar). Caveats aside, these relationships suggest there is little workshop specialization in particular ceramic forms or decoration.

Change over Time

Given the biases in our sampling regime, any evaluation of change over time has to contend with the differences between the archaeological contexts that produced our sample (sample sizes were disparate across contexts that are functionally and depositionally different). For all periods, local and local/regional production dominates (75% or more; Table 8.3b)

Despite an abundance of local samples, overall 5A also has fewer local *sources* with one contributing nearly 40% of the sample, compared to 30% or less in other phases, suggesting local resource use was more focused. This might reflect closer control over either the sources or the labor (workshops) than earlier or later periods.

Discussion
Based on Henrickson's characterization of MP ceramic production patterns, potters likely formed distinct groups or communities in MP Gordion. One might expect that different work groups would produce specific wares (utilitarian, specialized or fine) and specialize in specific types of decoration or production. However, while MP ceramics encompass a diversity of wares and decorative treatments, the NAA data indicate that the range of local and local/regional sources (or clay preparation "recipes") in use are widely represented across almost all decorative and form types, although the inventory varies somewhat by geochemical group. If compositional groups reflect specific workshops that controlled access to particular clay sources or recipes, then each workshop appears to have maintained a repertoire of MP ceramic production that extended across a wide spectrum of wares, from "mass-produced" utilitarian wares to carefully finished fine wares.

Henrickson (1993) suggested that a relatively small number of people or workshops were required to produce the type of assemblage seen in this period. The large number of sources seen in the local diversity of the NAA data indicate a different pattern. An abundance of sources seems to reflect social group elaboration in MP Gordion, rather than more economically rational behaviors (in other words, fewer work groups using fewer sources would be expected for more efficient production).

While geochemical subgroups define differences, the data do not always allow us to resolve whether these are technological (i.e. workshops), spatial or some combination of both. If sources are treated as signatures of workshops, the relatively large number of local and local/regional MP sources (21), seems to suggest little centralized control over production, and more likely represents smaller-scale economic or social groups. This situation begins to shift toward the end of the MP period, with increased output from a reduced range of local sources.

Production location/numbers/spatial proximity Beyond the excavation evidence from the small MP kiln, actual or potential ceramic workshop areas have yet to be identified. The NAA data provide indirect insight into potential production locales through the identification of compositional groups and clusters. In terms of the null hypothesis, we can interpret the MP NAA groups as representing multiple work groups producing the full range of Phrygian ceramics. The diversity of NAA sources suggests that production was widely distributed across the landscape. What is less clear is the proximity of these work groups: whether they were local, clustered in the immediate hinterland in and around Gordion, more dispersed across the region, or more likely some combination of both.

Skill level Several types of expertise are involved: resource mining and preparation, forming (particularly in relation to multipart or very large vessels), finishing (from basic surface treatments such as burnishing to culturally coded elaboration) and firing (also critical in relation to vessel size and finishing techniques, reduction firing, etc.). In the absence of direct evidence of production infrastructure (workshops or production areas – potters' wheels and tournette(s), work area(s) for clay preparation, slaking, green pottery drying area – or kilns, probably not in the same work space), it nonetheless seems likely that different groups were engaged in these activities, with some type of coordination if not integrated management (Rice 2015).

As Henrickson (1993) noted, MP ceramic technologies reflect multiple skill levels, from relatively rapidly produced domestic wares showing a basic level of competence in forming and finishing (Fig. 8.6), to the highly labor-intensive, finely shaped, slipped, polished or painted elite wares (Fig. 8.7; Plates 9, 10). The range of skill sets apparent in all of these steps, particularly forming and painting, suggests that work groups included potters with quite specific skills. The wide distribution of decorative types and forms within geochemical groups (sources or processing styles?) also suggests that each work group included people with different skill levels – combining relatively low-energy, rapid output for common use and more energy-intensive but lower output for elite ceramic production.

Given this range of expertise, and the established canonical repertoire of MP ceramics, work groups may have been relatively large, and internally stratified (e.g. from "master craftsman" to "apprentice"), to support cultural transmission of skills that was both intergenerational and peer-to-peer. This too suggests a pattern very different to a small number of workshops or a small number of people in work groups. If, as suggested earlier, the seemingly large number of work groups reflects a range of competing factional MP communities, then changes in production at the end of the MP (5A), with a notable reduction in the number of local sources used, also suggests a new political environment compared to earlier, relatively high levels of factionalism.

Technological investment For most phases at Gordion, the lack of direct evidence for production infrastructure is not unexpected given a general practice to locate these types of operation outside domestic settlement boundaries. One of the rare excavation units beyond the Citadel Mound and tumuli serendipitously uncovered the small MP (5B) updraft kiln just outside the Lower Town wall (Johnston 1970).

While seasonal household operation of kilns is well-documented ethnographically, the large and typically elaborate repertoire of locally produced fine wares in our sample suggests specialist rather than household production, where kilns would have been used regularly in conjunction with workshops or work groups' shared kilns (Rice 2015). As the ceramic assemblage associated with the MP updraft kiln represents multiple different sources or "recipes," it also appears that MP kilns at Gordion, in line with well-documented ethnographic evidence, likely serviced multiple pottery producers located around the urban core. This indicates another layer of specialization. The dimensions of the sole MP kiln suggest that, at least in this case, it could only be used for vessels at the smaller end of the size range of the Gordion repertoire. The rarity of decorated vessels in this assemblage also supports a utilitarian focus.

Producing Groups: Summary

Multiple lines of MP evidence support the presence of a diverse set of groups, organized in different ways, were involved in a wide array of disparate production contexts at Gordion at this time, particularly during the first two phases (5C-5B). The ongoing production of monumental architecture and landscape features formalized group practices and likely group relationships. In terms of ceramics, the use of many different sources, and/or many different groups, to make similar forms and styles suggests that ceramic production was firmly embedded in a ritual economy of social and political processes (i.e. beyond economic logic). This also appears to be true for the production of other items. However, while specific types of ceramics featured in communal practices of power (e.g. bowls, jugs, juglets used in feasting), it appears that there was little political or administrative oversight of ceramic production. As with the production of public monuments, ceramic production and elaboration seems to have played a different but key role in the competitive and ritual practices of a larger community, including groups across the wider region, where socially embedded production processes served the needs of the MP ritual economy.

Group Formation and Consumption

Nonceramic Evidence for Consumption

Previous research on consumption at Gordion has focused on specific materials or archaeological contexts. For example, biologically based studies of fuel, or likely meat/animals, have been used to evaluate consumption by chronological phase (N. F. Miller 2010; N. F. Miller et al. 2009) rather than at smaller scales of household or workplace, arguably more useful for understanding group behavior. In large measure, this is due to sample size constraints (N. F. Miller 2010). Few other artifact classes have the requisite sample size and distribution to make on-site, small-scale consumption studies practical. As noted earlier, robbing of stone structures and their foundations on the MP Eastern Mound, and the limited intact remains from household units elsewhere (mainly ceramics and biological remains), constrain our perspective on MP consumption. One group of artifacts was widespread – arrow and spear points made from copper and iron; however, most were found in disturbed contexts in both the Western Mound and Lower Town Area A.

MP food consumption can be inferred from production remains (discussed in the earlier section "Nonceramic Evidence for Production") or contexts where food was evidently prepared. The increased production of cattle and pigs suggests an increase in consumption or use of these animals (N. F. Miller et al. 2009). Similarly, while barley (used primarily for animal fodder and probably for beer) remains more common than wheat, the increased abundance of wheat may also indicate a shift in particular food preferences (N. F. Miller 2010).

On the EM, the only 5C-B phase living space with a wide inventory of finds is the Building I:2 cellar, with trash deposits yielding a full range of household belongings: a grinding stone, pottery vessels ranging in size from pithoi to bowls with inscribed graffiti, a set of clay loom weights, pottery whorls, jewelry (bronze fibulae, amber and frit beads, and canid tooth pendant) and iron tools. Based on this assemblage, people associated with elite institutions appear relatively prosperous (as were people in the 6A Terrace Complex). A domestic context in the SW Zone (5A) provides a distinctive deposit of household goods with a mix of animals, ceramics, personal ornaments, arrowheads and horse trappings that also suggest affluence (Codella and Voigt in press; Dusinberre et al. 2019).

A unique insight into the role of goods in the materialization of elite identity is provided by burial contexts preserved in several MP tumuli. The MM tumulus burial chamber (740 BCE; 5B) included the remains of a feast; its composition (reconstructed from vessel residues) included sheep/goat stew with lentils and a barley/wine/mead beverage (Kuniholm et al. 2011; McGovern 2000). An emphasis on drinking is confirmed by many large and small vessels associated with serving and imbibing beverages. Presumably used in the funeral feast were over 150 metal vessels (including bronze bowls), 14 items of inlaid wood furniture (tables) and coarse and fine textiles that together represent a lavish offering of high-quality, high-investment goods. As part of the mortuary ritual, the presence of fibulae (pins for clothing) provides another set of markers of identity and status.

The scale and timing of tumulus construction also reveal changes in patterns of elite consumption. Following a burst of tumulus construction in the eighth century BCE, the practice apparently tapered off in the seventh century BCE, before peaking again in the late seventh and early sixth century BCE (Liebhart et al. 2016). Later tumuli are comparatively small, and include new burial practices such as cremation. Burial goods including gold jewelry are thought to reflect the (female) gender of the interred (Kohler 1980). While an incomplete sample, this pattern highlights both renewed expressions of affluence and shifts in the meaning and associations of elite practices at the end of YHSS 5B and in 5A.

Many of the artifact classes we have discussed relate to manufacture, though the actual daily use of these reflects patterns of consumption. Both the creation and consumption of items in the public or social sphere would have been key components of the daily practices of power as part of the ritual economy. Food and textiles produced within the elite zone were presumably for elite consumption or redistribution. The abundance and rapidity of stylistic change in bronze fibulae, used to fasten clothing, highlights the ongoing importance of dress for the day-to-day production and negotiation of identity. The significance of daily use is also true of the architecture, as it established pathways for movement, control and display through the site: the elaboration and formalization of walls and buildings, including the increasing segmentation of space, in the MP period also suggests increasingly differentiated consumption practices.

Ceramics, Consumption and Group Identity
Previous studies of Gordion ceramics, typically focused on Greek imports, provide information on consumption practices (DeVries 1997; Lawall 2012; Lynch 2016; Winter 1973). Much of the focus has been on stylistically well-documented imported ceramics to establish chronology during the difficult-to-date MP and LP periods (e.g. DeVries 2005). Lynch's (2016) discussion of MP and LP Greek ceramics at Gordion noted that a small component (Euboean and Corinthian) date to the eighth century. MP amphorae attributed to Klazomenai and Lesbos (Lawall 2012) provide evidence of increasing engagement with the East Greek communities during the late seventh century, along with the consumption of imported goods from this region, usually as food stuffs (e.g. oil, wine). However, from the second quarter of the sixth century BCE (5A) the consumption of Greek imports increased notably. Most are tableware (bowls), however some containers such as lekythoi and

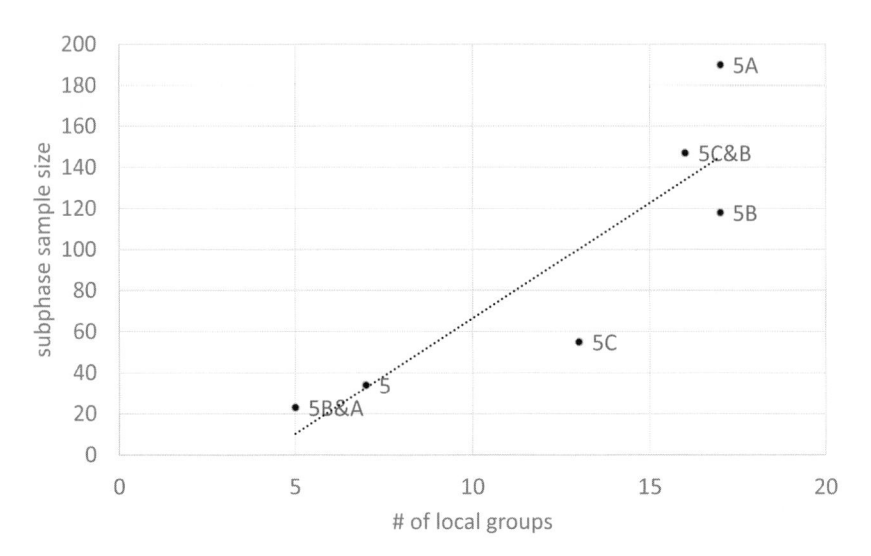

Fig. 8.14 YHSS 5 Middle Phrygian pottery: Number of NAA local groups (clusters A–D) (*x*-axis) by subphase sample population (*y*-axis). Subphases below the trendline are more diverse than those above the line, relative to sample size.

lydions suggest imported contents as well. Lynch (2016) proposes that Attic wares, imported by Lydians, were used to distinguish social identity (wine drinking) at Phrygian Gordion from 600 BCE.

Our focus here is on evaluating the changing patterns of ceramic consumption through the MP period at Gordion at the scale of archaeological context/excavation area, or sector. Beginning with the earliest MP phase (5C), sample size ($n = 55$) limits our interpretation to comparisons with the broader dataset. While multiple samples match nonlocal sources, both east and west, only a cooking vessel and storage jar were identifiable as somewhat unexpected imported forms. The diversity of local sources is generally greater for both 5C and 5B (relative to sample size; Fig. 8.14). While not a representative sample, the diverse array of local and local/regional groups among vessels related to food consumption and drinking, combined with the number of sources related to diverse brown on X styles, appears consistent with contributions by different regional groups participating in feasting activities or offered as tribute.

Combining the sample from phases 5C-B with 5B provides a larger and more varied sample from multiple sectors (Table 8.3). Eastern Mound contexts generally reflect a slightly greater consumption of east-central Anatolian ceramics, and off mound contexts include slightly more use of local cluster A and west Anatolian sources. The EM sample's abundance of decorated jugs in a new range of styles suggests that consumption of (?) beer was at least as important as in the EP period in the core elite area (with jugs rare elsewhere). The increased frequency of nonlocal bowls during the early MP over that of the EP also reveals a shift in consumption patterns, in which bowls acquired new significance. The distribution of decorated fine ware ceramics across multiple contexts and on the Northeast Ridge (Sams in press), indicates widespread elaboration of food consumption in this subphase (including beverages) along with an expansion in the arenas in which identity was being marked.

The pattern of consumption is very different in the WM 5A assemblages. In both WM zones locally produced wares dominate (Table 8.11a, b). However, the two WM contexts are substantially different. The SWZ dump deposit reveals that materially elaborated social dining was an important activity in households outside of the EM elite area; the NAA assemblage is heavily dominated by locally produced ceramics (the larger assemblage includes a small amount of Greek tablewares). While the NWZ context seems functionally similar to the SWZ, households in this zone preferentially consumed more western Anatolian wares and styles, suggesting a clear difference in identity and preferences. In 5A there appears to be a broad adoption of what had been core elite practices among households that had wealth and presumably status, but given their site locations, were probably not members of the ruling elite.

In off mound 5A contexts nonlocal ceramic consumption showed a strong west Anatolian preference from both emulative styles and forms as well as imports; potential Sardis matches, however, contribute a small percentage of this (ca. 5%). As in the NWZ, west Anatolian styles were common, but were even more strongly represented here. This preference is also seen in the forms used. Pottery not included in the NAA sample indicate that imported Greek vessels were in use during the sixth century in what are clearly non-elite households in the Lower Town.

All of the 5A zones suggest rapid social change with the emergence of new group identities in the late MP as demonstrated by the adoption of new styles, goods and contexts of consumption. However, despite the use of Lydian-style architectural elements in the EM elite core (e.g. terracotta roof tiles and ornaments), ceramic data suggest that this sector was also the most stylistically conservative. In addition, there is more evidence for use of styles and forms linked to east-central Anatolia in elite EM contexts, highlighting social and perhaps political differences among contemporary groups.

Major shifts in consumption patterns from 5C to 5A are also evident both in the way that identities and politics were negotiated in relation to food, and in the way that individual families and households crafted public identities. A new constellation of styles and goods for consumption was elaborated to create a distinctive Phrygian identity (5C-B). The fundamental character of MP Gordion reflects greater investment in local production and the creation of local styles. An emphasis in 5C-5B on pouring vessels (jugs of various types for beer consumption) and decorated drinking vessels in apparently communal/group consumption (larger serving vessels) shifted in 5A to individualized consumption with less decoratived vessels (used in household contexts), most likely used for wine as well as beer. While all three areas show evidence of elite or affluent group consumption during 5C-B, each area appears to have had distinct social groups. These differences become most pronounced during 5A (early sixth century).

Group Formation and Distribution

Nonceramic Evidence for Distribution and Groups
From the range of MP archaeological contexts available, the best evidence for distribution derives from MP tumuli and a few household contexts. It seems likely some goods moved freely across the larger region, but we currently have limited evidence to evaluate this until the final MP phase 5A. While much of the local metal assemblage appears to have been locally produced, bronze fibula and belts, bronze bowls and pouring vessels, as well as arrow points may have circulated in a larger interaction sphere. Small ivory plaques, found in several sectors (e.g. EM, LT), were undoubtedly imported, likely from the southeast. Frit or faience is also rare and potentially exotic. Burial offerings in late seventh/early sixth century tumuli include gold jewelry, also likely imported. While exotic goods were integrated into elite practices, neither the flow of exotic goods nor emulation of styles or ideas seem to have played a major role in group formation in 5C-5B MP Gordion.

Ceramic Distribution: Exchange and Emulation
Ceramic distribution can be viewed in terms of spatial distribution (where goods are found), or in terms of the diversity of apparent origins of production (geochemical provenience). The spatial distribution of forms and styles was presented above in terms of consumption. Here we focus on the provenience data. Note that the term "provenience" can conflate two parameters: the actual production location and the location of origin for particular styles or forms. Each of these reflects different aspects of group formation and identity.

Henrickson's (1993) description of Middle Phrygian ceramics focused on production styles. He suggested that MP assemblage forms and decoration were predominantly local, with little evidence of emulation or other external influences. He saw this as anomalous given that the assemblage came almost exclusively from the elite section of the city. He found few identifiable imports, with only Anatolian Red on black ware as a clear nonlocal style suggested to come from southwestern Anatolia (Plate 9 a, b, c). A few Alişar IV-style vessels, 5C-5B (see EP example in Plate 8), as well as a few Greek and East Greek ceramics were also identified from MP contexts based solely on style and visible fabric (5B-5A; DeVries 2005; Lynch 2016); similarly, two locally rare types of trade amphora were identified by Lawall (from Lesbos and Klazomenai to the west; Lawall 2012). In contrast, the NAA data (sample) suggest that nonlocal ceramics were not uncommon in EM contexts.

In 5A, nonlocal ceramics in varying abundance were recovered from all sectors of the site. In the EM sample, local ceramics declined over time as west Anatolian imports increased. In other sectors, the opposite trend occurs: local ceramics increased (particularly local cluster A) as imports generally declined. These varying proportions may signal significant differences among occupants in each sector. The strong influence of imports on local production can be gauged through the observation that most nonlocal styles were locally emulated by 5A. Somewhat surprisingly, even the sample of utilitarian wares appears to have included compositionally nonlocal ceramics.

Forms While the excavated ceramic assemblage from 5C-5B included few forms clearly identifiable as nonlocal, by the end of the seventh century BCE some groups in the city began to prefer Lydian forms and decorative styles. By the final MP 5A phase, several new ceramic types were introduced and included forms related to food consumption (e.g. plates, cups/skyphoi, stemmed bowls or "fruitstands"), as well as new forms of containers for other goods (lydions, lekythoi; Plate 11). While the majority of tablewares were locally produced, they also emulated nonlocal counterparts. In 5C nonlocal jugs were more common in EM contexts and tumuli. In 5A preferences shifted toward imported jars (to the extent they can be distinguished); however, the frequency of imports is low overall.

Although Lydian forms are relatively uncommon in our assemblage, lydions, lekythoi and some bowls appear to be mainly imported. Both lydions and lekythoi match several western Anatolian sources. Stemmed bowls were imported from western Anatolia in 5B-A, but in 5A contexts most were locally produced. The small number of stemmed bowls recovered from the KH fortress are all decorated differently from those from the SWZ and represent different sources (one local). The SWZ stemmed bowls, however, all come from a single local source (A). This distribution reinforces the suggestion that there were basic differences in the groups that occupied these areas of the town, possibly tied to function (e.g. of KH as a fortress and barracks vs. a household context).

Styles Turning to the evidence for exchange of specific decorative styles, nonlocal styles also vary by sector (Tables 8.5b, 8.8b, 8.11b; Fig. 8.13). Most decorative styles are local, but include a few nonlocal examples. Lydianizing/marbleizing styles were all locally emulated, with streaky slips ca. 40% local. While the MP assemblage includes a small number of glazed sherds (red, black, brown), all but one were produced locally. Only Black/brown on red was predominantly nonlocal (west Anatolian) until 5A but some local emulation were also present.

Styles exchanged in the local area include bichromes, brown on X, and orange/red variants (local/regional cluster B). Somewhat surprisingly, black decorated variants come from a wide range of local and nonlocal sources. Among our undecorated sample, buff ware is more likely to be exchanged than grey wares. Less surprising is the strong association of Greek forms and decoration even when locally produced, primarily during the later MP (5A).

Change over time An overarching distinguishing feature of the MP period is the steady decrease in ceramic exchange. Stylistically local decoration and locally produced emulations of both east-central (e.g. some bichromes) and west Anatolian styles dominate the MP ceramic assemblage. MP nonlocal components are proportionally smaller than in either the EP or subsequent LP. Factors that could have affected this change include a shift in patterns of consumption and identity formation to focus on the import of other goods (textiles? jewelry? glass?); an increasing technical facility for emulation along with more cursory decorative styles on ceramics (in 5A); and/or a shift in supply patterns potentially related to regionwide changes in political or economic relationships.

Local preferences for imported styles shift during the MP. In the earlier phases on the EM, brown on X and Black/brown on red are the styles most likely to be nonlocal; by the final MP phase, imported styles, while still including Black/brown on red, are dominated by banded, black various and streaky wares.

While the EP was a stylistically eclectic period, building on influences and supply from a diverse range of outside sources, earlier phases of the MP show much more selective behavior, and identity formation that is more creative, inward-looking and insular. The later MP is marked as a new phase, with a return to a more outward-looking identity formation that included emulation of western consumption practices (food and

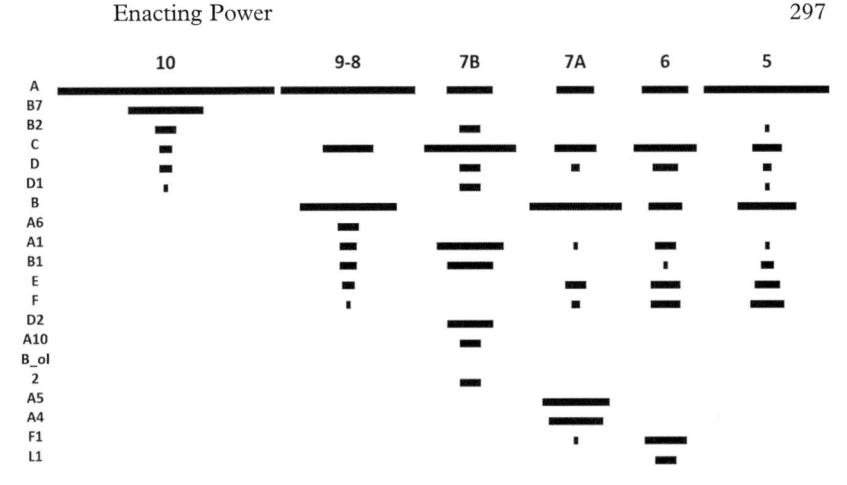

Fig. 8.15 Relative frequency of most common NAA groups [y axis] across YHSS phases [x axis]. Width of bars reflects percentages for each group. Note increased use of local group A in the Middle Phrygian period. Only NAA groups with ≥5% are included.

drink as well as value-added goods in lydions and lekythoi), along with increased imports of other goods.

Discussion

Perhaps one of the more interesting observations here relates to an underlying assumption that as complex societies develop they extend and deepen their interaction networks beyond their borders (e.g. Feinman 2004). The ceramic evidence from the MP at Gordion appears to run counter to this supposition (Fig. 8.15). Specifically, the use of ceramics in elaborated food consumption and social identity formation suggests that the diverse local production of styles and forms was intentional, ritualized practice critical to MP identity and polity formation. While elaboration of local styles appears *within* the polity during the MP, it is not until the final 5A phase, when Phrygia came under the influence of the Lydians that these patterns change substantially.

Conclusions: Power, Identity and Group Formation

The evidence presented in this chapter makes it possible to identify different types of groups that emerged and transformed during the MP period. We argue that intentional shifts in how power and ideology were performed and negotiated shaped the complexity of work and consumption relationships evident in the data.

The expansion of agricultural production during the MP as a stable base for specialization also undoubtedly played a key role in the creation of new groups of both producers and consumers, as well as generating novel contexts for group formation. While disentangling the timing in the increases in agricultural production and the expansion of Phrygian political power remains challenging, it seems likely that expanded agricultural production, as well as shifts in its management and content, occurred with the creation of larger labor groups. Certainly the presence of large storage facilities on the EM (PPB) implies the production and management of surplus. Underlying both, however, is the emergence of new practices and ideology that supported the MP ritual political economy.

Group formation in the MP was shaped by the dominance of local styles of consumption and production, intimately tied to local elite practices. During the EP, feasting involved individualized drinking vessels that were highly marked and uniquely decorated; during the MP, while feasting (or elaborated food consumption practices) appears to remain important, the stylistic ceramic repertoire becomes more homogenous (e.g. vessel size, grey wares, metal skeuomorphs). Import diversity shifted from jars and jugs in the EP to bowls in the MP. These changes in identity making during the MP within shared food consumption settings suggest the development of new strategies to negotiate power relationships. Individuals still chose to emphasize ownership of ceramic vessels used for drinking by marking a name or a symbol on the base where it could easily be viewed while imbibing.

Substantial changes occur in pottery across the MP phases, not only in styles and forms, but in the preference for particular local sources, and an overall decrease in reliance on imports. We contend that increased emphasis on local production, particularly the prominence of local cluster A, is an intentional strategy by local elites engaged in constructing a new Phrygian identity. Identity formation driven by elite factional competition was marked by uniquely Phrygian styles of consumption (food and drink practices, as well as dress). Communal food consumption, particularly feasting, drew these groups or factions into an arena where existing hierarchical relationships could be both reinforced and challenged. The simultaneous creation of internal differentiation of groups and the introduction of more uniform and homogeneous styles during MP 5C-B appear to be interwoven as the rulers sought to mitigate social and political fragmentation.

By the end of the MP (5A) the loss of political hegemony and the rise of western Anatolian influence is reflected in an expansion of emulation of western Anatolian and East Greek forms and decoration. However, while both forms and decorative styles document this shift, local production continued to increase, likely due at least in part to the disruption of regional networks in the late seventh and early sixth century BCE.

Practices of power crosscut and interlinked groups in the community through the elaboration of uniquely Phrygian monuments, including tumuli, and aspects of material culture. The performance of production remained a critical part of the ritual of power. Nevertheless, it appears clear that elite factionalism created tensions throughout the eighth century BCE. Competitive emulation between elites is visible in the landscape of tumuli surrounding the city. At the same time, eighth century elites turned their attention outward across central Anatolia, to their growing interactions with Lydia, Tabal (?) and Neo-Assyria. Their ability to do so was likely underwritten by newly formed groups, created for other purposes. The continued presence of both imported and emulated east-central Anatolian ceramics in elite contexts throughout this period highlights the ongoing importance of relationships to the east as well as to the west.

Increased specialization in production of ceramics and other goods, as well as monuments, suggests the development of a complex society that arguably had elements of both heterarchy (multiple competing production/power centers) and hierarchy (elite tumuli and high-status goods). We have no clear evidence for institutions that might represent different power centers, but we do have evidence in multiple spheres for factionalism and competition (e.g. access to labor, tumuli, modes of food consumption, etc.). Nevertheless, the ability to control labor for the production of multiple kilometers of substantial city walls, the movement of large volumes of clay and fill to elevate the city, and the construction of massive burial tumuli, all suggest hierarchical elite control during MP 5C-B. Control over labor is already evident in the large construction projects of the EP, but by the MP the scale of construction increases dramatically. For example, the size of labor force required to construct the MM tumulus (ca. 740 BCE) stands out against the background of more than 100 other smaller tumuli: more labor was required to build it than all the other tumuli combined (Stephens 2018:182). Whether work groups were recruited and managed by a few or articulated through the hands of groups or factions remains speculative. Stephens suggests work groups were populated and managed through corvée, a labor obligation to a central authority; however, from our evaluation of the organization of MP ceramic production it seems that not all crafts were integrated under close political or elite management. For MP ceramics, production appears to have been operationalized through the hands of many small groups or factions. The combination of different types of labor organization highlight the critical importance that relatively small groups, likely including households, played in the MP ritual economy.

As Voigt has noted, the location of Gordion at one of the most important crossroads in central Turkey was undoubtedly a key factor in the city's development. However, during the MP period this geographically strategic advantage somewhat paradoxically appears to have stimulated processes of centralization and concentration of resources and resource use (including infrastructural development), rather than new economic expansion (e.g. long-distance exchange).

Hirth (1996) identified four types of redistribution as fundamental in supporting political power (see also Chapter 2). Based on both the larger inventory of material culture and the ceramic sphere during the consolidation of Phrygian hegemony, two of these appear most critical in the early MP period: *elite redistribution* and *resource mobilization* (including tribute and taxation). While the evidence for elite redistribution, and elaborated identities in relation to food consumption, is perhaps strongest, we have argued that the organization of ceramic and monument production in and around Gordion reflects complex resource mobilization by multiple groups or factions. Production of ceramics by multiple groups enacted the political and social relations of the city, and arguably is critical in underwriting the production dynamics discussed earlier.

The development of multiscalar and multicentric economies described by Schortman and Urban as central to political formation (Schortman 2014; Schortman and Urban 1992) also appear to be critical features of Phrygian development. These complex economies can equally be seen as creating new mechanisms for expanding group engagement and participation. Diverse construction and production projects were vital in the ongoing (re)creation and maintenance of the Phrygian ritual economy. This does not mean, however, that Phrygian political influence remained site-bound, as both historical and archaeological evidence reveal wide-ranging Phrygian interaction across central Anatolia. While their territorial footprint is extensive, there is limited exotic evidence within the Phrygian capital of this engagement.

During the MP the Phrygians shaped and differentiated a local and unique identity – evident in their monuments, religion and ceramics – to establish a new ideology that linked diverse central Anatolian groups into a polity (Pauketat 2007). This ideology, however, appears never to have developed an explicit iconography of power, in stark contrast to that of earlier Anatolian polities (e.g. the legitimation of Hittite Empire and Neo-Hittite rulers through a divine pantheon). But the sharp differences in how power was displayed, from the Hittite Empire to the MP period, does not resolve the question as to whether this was, as argued here, intentional, or emerged through the daily practices of groups negotiating power.

9 Identities in Flux
The Late Phrygian Period YHSS 4 540–330 BCE

Introduction

Even when viewed at a distance of almost 3,000 years, the political and social upheavals of first millennium BCE Gordion are striking. The rise of Lydian influence across central Anatolia in the late MP period transformed local communities at Gordion, changing daily domestic practices and introducing new ways of enacting power. This transformation, commencing in the late seventh century BCE, was well underway at the time of the Persian conquest in the mid sixth century BCE. Evidence of the Persian military attack is still visible in the siege works built against the Lower Town fortification system and the burnt remains of the Küçük Höyük mudbrick fortress. While widespread, the impact of Persian power and organizational structures across Anatolia was treated as largely ephemeral until recently (Dusinberre 2013; Khatchadourian 2012). The impacts of a Persian administrative presence were substantial, however, not only as disruptors of the local political order, but also as stimulants for new opportunities of group formation that superseded previous social, economic and political entanglements.

The articulation of Achaemenid and local practices of power was key to the (re)configuration of community identities in places like Gordion. As an established economic and political center, the ways in which Persians enacted and negotiated top-down power, and how this was accommodated or contested in Gordion, provide critical insights into the highly fluid and opportunistic dynamics of identity formation and transformation in this period. Ceramic evidence (patterning of production organization, consumption and distribution) documents how local groups engaged with the expanded Persian political and economic spheres, particularly evident in changes to foodways.

Ca. 540–330 BCE: Achaemenid Central Anatolia

During the late seventh century BCE, Lydians based at Sardis commenced rapid political expansion eastward into central Anatolia. By the early sixth century BCE (YHSS 5A) they had occupied the Phrygian capital (Rose 2012b). Lydian expansion coincided with Persian armies moving north and west from Assyria through Anatolia, and by 542 BCE Cyrus had established Achaemenid rule across western Anatolia (Dusinberre 2013). Following this initial phase of conquest in the late sixth century BCE, Persian rulers reorganized the structure of their empire into satrapies to create more readily governed units (Dusinberre 2013). From their capitals in southwestern Iran (Persepolis and Susa), the Achaemenids (ca. 550–330 BCE) ruled over much of southwest Asia, from the Indus River in the east to Egypt in the south and Anatolia in the north (Dusinberre 2013). Throughout their reign, local revolts and incursions repeatedly tested Achaemenid authority. Rapid expansion and subsequent consolidation of such a large area relied on active engagement with local elites, coupled with an effective administrative and communication structure. Phrygia was divided by the Persians into administrative districts with boundaries that fluctuated over time (Fig. 9.1). Greater Phrygia (the southern part of eighth century Phrygia) became a minor district that was at times administered from the Achaemenid Great Satrapy of Lydia at Sardis, and at other times from Hellespontine Phrygia (northwestern Phrygia; Dusinberre 2013; Roller 2011).

Local economies in Anatolia were strongly influenced by Achaemenid modes of administration. Dusinberre (2013:35) highlights several roles for local Achaemenid administrators or satraps: collecting taxes, managing land and resources (for maintaining a tax base), managing local rulers, sustaining a standing army and keeping roads open. The most important type of income was from the land, but also extended to local products and trade, including market and poll taxes. Building on earlier road networks, the Persians expanded and consolidated a system of roads throughout Anatolia, including one connecting Phrygia and Cilicia (Fig. 9.1). They also created a royal road from Sardis to Susa (Dusinberre 2013:48). Under a well-administered satrapy, the movement of goods and valuables likely expanded. However, the extent to which this increased interaction and exchange within satrapies, between satrapies or regional centers and from these entities to Achaemenid capitals remains poorly defined.

Material evidence for an Achaemenid presence in Anatolia remains disparate (Cahill 1988; Dusinberre 2013), with much of the recent

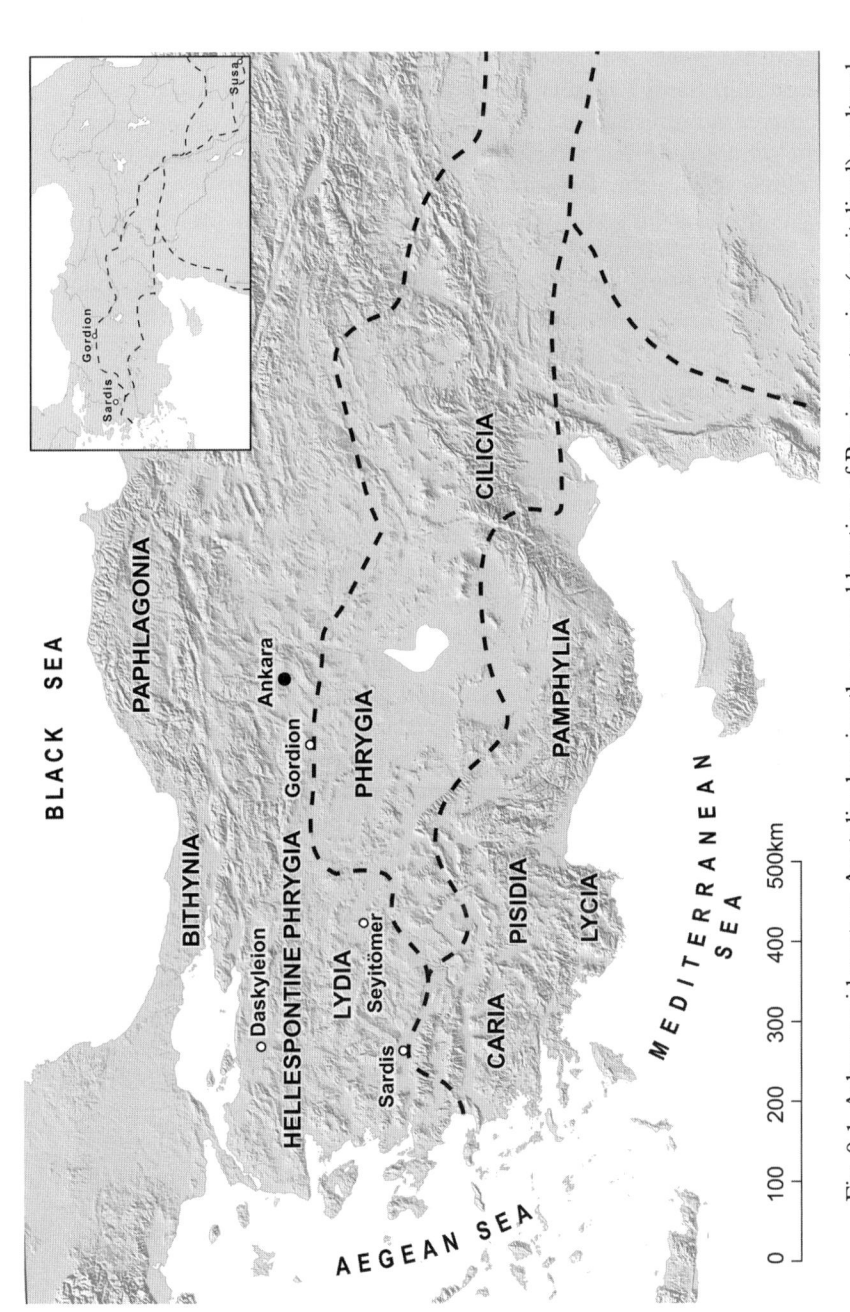

Fig. 9.1 Achaemenid western Anatolia showing the general location of Persian satrapies (capitalized), cultural regions, the modern capital of Ankara and contemporary archaeological sites mentioned in the text. The location of the Persian royal road is marked as dashed lines and also shown in the inset.
Source: K. Newman after Dusinberre 2013:30, Waters 2014.

scholarship focused on specific items (e.g. seals, coins, horse trappings, "Achaemenid bowls" both metal and ceramic), architectural features at a few sites (e.g. Sardis, Dascylium and Gordion), or mortuary features. Achaemenid administration, where known, relied heavily on appointed satraps, satrapal administrators and military hierarchy working through local elites. While the Persians were highly successful in extracting resources from groups and territories incorporated into the empire, it also seems clear that some local elites benefited from increased social, political and economic opportunities (Grave et al. 2016; Khatchadourian 2012).

Achaemenid (Late Phrygian YHSS 4) Gordion: The Excavations

Unlike the satrap of Sardis (Dusinberre 1999, 2003), Gordion was not an Achaemenid center, and there is little historical evidence for it playing a role in wider administrative affairs. Nevertheless, archaeological evidence suggests the city remained well populated with a vibrant economy through much of the period (Voigt and Young 1999). Based on intensive surface survey and multiple excavation sectors (see Figs. 3.5a and 3.6, Plate 1), the extent of the city remained about 1 square kilometer. While defensive structures had been breached in the initial Persian attack, the Eastern and Western Mounds initially retained their defensive wall and gates. The fortification wall in the southern Lower Town may no longer have been maintained but its mudbrick walls remained intact until Hellenistic times (Voigt 2013:222). While this period lacks overt architectural statements of Achaemenid identity, fifth century BCE construction of large public buildings highlights local affluence in a more geographically connected empire (Fig. 3.5b; Dusinberre 2019a, 2019b; Voigt 2013).

Defining the Achaemenid period at Gordion has been a recurring issue since 1950, when Rodney Young established a stratigraphic sequence on the EM (Voigt 2009). Stratified above Late Bronze Age or "Hittite" remains was a large building with grey pottery that he considered "Phrygian." The massive construction project above this (the remains we now call Middle Phrygian YHSS 5) had produced fragments of painted tiles that Young dated to the sixth century and tentatively attributed to the Persians (Young 1950:198). By 1953, the monumental architecture with deep rubble foundations characteristic of this "archaic level" had become "the city of Achaemenian times," complete with a building devoted to a "fire cult" (Young 1955:1–6). With ongoing excavation, his colleague G. Roger Edwards challenged this view and coined the term "Middle Phrygian" as a way to recognize continuity between the Phrygian Level (referred to as the "Kimmerian Destruction Level," here YHSS 6A:3 DL) and the subsequent "Post-Kimmerian" or Persian/ Archaic rebuilding (Edwards 1959:263–264). Later, Young attributed the rebuilding to the Lydians based on the recovery of a hoard of Lydian coins and tiles paralleled in early sixth century Sardis, and this dating of Edwards' Middle Phrygian Gordion was accepted by DeVries (1990:93–94). DeVries, who had excavated and studied the Attic imports at Gordion, also revived an idea (first suggested by Young) that damage to buildings dated by Attic pottery near the end of the fifth century BCE might have been caused by an earthquake (DeVries 1990:399–400; Young 1955:6). However, if so this event did not end the Persian occupation which continued until the arrival of Alexander in 333 BCE. DeVries considered the break in material culture that coincided with this damage substantial enough to be identified as a new chronological unit: the Late Phrygian period. This new phase was characterized by "generally shabby" structures or "cellars" that were cut into the MP stone structures, and were also badly disturbed by later Hellenistic builders (DeVries 1990:400).

Voigt set out to refine this chronological sequence when she began the Upper Trench Sounding in 1988–1989 (Fig. 3.5a). As expected, her team found heavily churned deposits and "cellars" cut into the monumental MP structures. More surprising was the early date for a deposit immediately beneath one of the better preserved cellars, provided by a nearly complete early fifth century BCE Attic lekythos. This suggested that destruction of the Middle Phrygian rebuilding had started a century earlier than first proposed by DeVries. Moreover, stratigraphic evidence placed the Middle Phrygian rebuilding soon after the 6A:3 DL fire. Even with a date of ca. 700 BCE for the fire, this evidence ruled out Persian responsibility for the MP construction project (Voigt 2007).

When Voigt published the first iteration of her new stratigraphic sequence, what was not clear from the UTS was the calendric end date for MP YHSS 5 and the beginning of Late Phrygian YHSS 4. This was due to the absence of deposits that could be clearly dated to the first half of the sixth century in the UTS (Voigt 1994:274–276; Voigt and Young 1999:note 4). Only after excavation of well-preserved strata on the Western Mound (SWZ) was a stratigraphic break between the MP and LP defined and dated by imported Greek ceramics to ca. 540 BCE (Dusinberre et al. 2019). This phasing, which places the period of Lydian influence or occupation at the end of the Middle Phrygian period (rather than its beginning), is supported by recent reanalyses of the Rodney Young material from the Outer and Inner Courts of the EM

(Dusinberre 2019a; Fields 2010; Lynch 2016; Rose 2018). As a result, the Late Phrygian phase or YHSS 4 can now be equated with the period of Achaemenid rule at Gordion, and divided into two major subphases, roughly corresponding to the fifth and fourth century BCE.

With a secure chronology based on stratigraphy, a local ceramic assemblage defined by Henrickson and associated imports identified by DeVries and Lynch, it is now possible to look at the impact of Achaemenid conquest and change. Evidence for occupation during the LP (see Table 3.1) has been identified on both the Eastern and Western Mounds (same locations as MP period excavations, Fig. 3.5a), in the southern Lower Town and Outer Town, and in three excavated tumuli (Kohler and Dusinberre 2022; Voigt 2013). We can now recognize a sequence across topographic zones that tells a consistent story.

For the period immediately following the Persian conquest (ca. 540–500 BCE), very little archaeological evidence was preserved, with the exception of several tumuli and some pits and fragmentary architectural remains in the Western Mound NWZ. However, in the early fifth century BCE construction and renovations resumed on the Eastern Mound as well as in the Western Mound NWZ. More dramatic changes in architecture and the use of space occur in the early fourth century BCE. Although it may have had some impact on people living at Gordion, a reported skirmish by a Spartan army ca. 395 BCE seems unlikely to account for these structural changes, which occur in all sectors of the site. Instead, Young and DeVries' 400 BCE earthquake hypothesis, initially based on deposits with fallen tile roofs on the EM, now appears to best fit the available contemporary evidence including wall collapse in the NWZ on the WM (Codella personal communication 2018).

One of the most interesting aspects of LP Gordion is the degree to which variation in material culture and especially in architecture can be tracked across the city. The variability identified for the Middle Phrygian period is even more pronounced in the Late Phrygian. Returning to the early fifth century architecture BCE (earliest LP) on the EM, some MP structures remained in use, but the organization and function of the EM elite zone was dramatically altered, especially in the Outer Court. These alterations signal substantial changes in the use of space, and more specifically the location of political activities.

Immediately inside the gate, the Outer Court buildings seem to have remained in use after modification: Buildings D, E and F were rebuilt, while C and G received minor remodeling in the early to mid fifth century BCE (see Fig. 3.5b; Dusinberre 2019a). The most significant LP alteration in this area was the construction of a small but elaborate building: the "Painted House" (Dusinberre 2019a:112–113, figs.

116–117; Young 1956:255–256, pl. 285, 286). Around 500 BCE, a rectangular pit was cut down into the MP clay fill between Buildings C and G. The excavated area was lined with stone to create a small one-room structure that opened onto a passage that led behind Buildings C and G. To enter from the passage, one walked down a short stairway to a landing ca. 1 m below ground level; a sharp left-hand turn led into a small vestibule with walls ornamented with small clay cones; a right-hand turn then led into the single room of the Painted House, which measured ca. 2.5 m by 3.75 m (Fig. 9.2a and b; Dusinberre 2019a:fig. 6). The walls of this room had been decorated with polychrome paintings that were recovered from the floor in small fragments. Partial reconstruction produced a large frieze depicting a ritual (?) procession of mostly women (Dusinberre 2019a; Mellink 1980). Its architectural character combined with the content of the wall paintings led Dusinberre (2019a:113) to propose a cultic or ritual function for the Painted House. However, whatever the purpose of this structure and its murals, both its secluded bent-access entrance well away from the open court and the size of this building limited its access to a very small number of people at any given time.

Although the rebuilding of several megarons and the construction of the Painted House suggest that the Outer Court retained its function as a reception and perhaps ritual area as in the earlier EP and MP periods, its communication with other parts of the eastern elite zone changed, indicating a significant shift in practice. In MP times, the Outer Court was enclosed by substantial (2.5 m-wide) walls of squared blocks with rubble fill (Young 1956:254), and one passed from the Outer Court to the Inner Court through a narrow gate. In the early fifth century most of the southwestern part of this wall was removed and the gate to the Inner Court was blocked by a new mudbrick structure built ca. 475 BCE. Because the interior walls of this building were covered with bright yellow plaster it became known as the "Yellow House" (Fig. 3.5b; Dusinberre 2019a; Fields 2010). A second major change was the dismantling of the enclosure wall to the southeast that had separated the MP version of the Terrace Complex from the Inner and Outer Courts. Here too, new LP structures were built in the early fifth century, several of them ornamented with columns (Floor S House, Room with Columns; Fig. 3.5b) (Fields 2010).

The changing character of architectural remains in the Outer and Inner Courts suggests that they no longer functioned as an integrated locus of political and administrative activities. This hypothesis is strengthened by the construction of a second new LP structure, the Mosaic Building, to the southwest of the Eastern Gate (Fig. 9.3). The

Fig. 9.2 YHSS 4 Late Phrygian Painted House on the Eastern Mound.
(a) Plan of the Painted House in 1955. Semisubterranean structure.
(b) The Painted House in 1955, looking northeast. Main room and vestibule cut down next to the foundations of Middle Phrygian Building C.
Sources: 9.2a image no. 98043, original drawing by C. Polycarpou, modified by G. Darbyshire and A. Anderson, courtesy of *Anatolian Studies*; 9.2b image no. G-1250; courtesy University of Pennsylvania Museum, Gordion Project Archives.

Fig. 9.3 YHSS 4 Late Phrygian Mosaic Building on the Eastern Mound. Mosaic Building rooms with pebble mosaic floors and paved courtyard in the distance, Looking northeast in 1952 (see Fig. 3.5b for plan and location).
Source: Image no. G-674, D. Cox and R. Young, courtesy University of Pennsylvania Museum, Gordion Project Archives.

relatively large size, tiled roof and pebble-mosaic floors of the new "Mosaic Building" makes it the most elaborate of the LP structures, and a likely candidate for housing Achaemenid administrative activity. The Mosaic Building was constructed over the southeastern part of Middle Phrygian Building A ca. 475–450 BCE (Fig. 3.5b; Dusinberre 2019a; Sams and Burke 2008; Sams et al. 2007). The four northeastern rooms of Building A remained in use, perhaps in support of activities carried out by those residing in the Mosaic Building. The layout of the Mosaic Building, with a paved court and a series of rooms that roughly follows the northeast–southwest orientation of Building A, is very different from earlier MP (and EP) megarons. Attached to its northwest façade was a colonnaded porch surrounding a mosaic floor (Fig. 9.3; Dusinberre 2019a:fig. 5). Terracotta pegs were used to create wall mosaics in this building, as well as in the Painted House and possibly in a building in the NWZ. Some of the Mosaic Building's architectural elements, including terracotta roof tiles, were reused material from late MP 5A and earlier LP buildings (Glendinning 2005). Both the Painted

House (Fig. 3.5b) and the "Room with Columns" feature introduced Persian elements similar to those in the Mosaic Building: columns, column bases, tiled roofs.

Elsewhere on the Eastern Mound, both in the area that had been the Inner Court and in the area of the Terrace Complex, Middle Phrygian buildings were abandoned and their walls were robbed in order to build new, relatively small, semisubterranean buildings or "cellars" (Fields 2010; Voigt and Young 1999). These "cellars" were rectangular pits cut into the YHSS 5 clay fill, usually next to the rubble foundations of MP walls, and often in an interior corner of a MP building. In relatively well-preserved examples within the UTS, in and above the former Terrace Complex, slabs from the walls of MP Building I:2 were set in a vertical position (technically orthostats) to provide smooth interior cellar walls (Fields 2010; Voigt and Young 1999). Adjacent to these mid fifth century cellars, and perhaps constructed slightly later, is a two-room structure cut into the clay fill between MP buildings I:2 and J that was also recorded in a RSY trench. This I:2–J structure had a large number of roof tiles collapsed onto its latest floor, dating its end to the beginning of the fourth century BCE.

By the early fourth century, the spatial function of the Inner Court and area of the Terrace Complex was substantially altered, with large areas given over to more pithouses and manufacturing (Dusinberre 2019a: fig. 5, areas with dark shading). Across this area are metalworking installations, including a "Foundry" that partially overlay Buildings C and G (Fig. 3.5b; Fields 2010). Within the UTS were numerous ashy pits with slag, crucibles and clay molds indicative of smelting and the production of bronze and (rare) silver items (Fields 2010; Rademakers et al. 2018; Voigt and Young 1999). The recovery of manufacturing debris indicates that bone, antler, ivory and stone artifacts were also produced on the Eastern Mound (Dusinberre 2019a; Zouck 1974:116).

On the Western Mound in the NWZ, a short break in building activities at the end of the MP was followed in the early fifth century BCE by the construction of a large, but poorly preserved, mudbrick structure (Voigt and Young 1999:fig. 30). This was replaced by a building with stone foundations that were subsequently robbed out, leaving only a few large slabs set in a very shallow foundation trench (Fig. 9.4a). The main room was partially paved with stone and an attached room had a row of hearths (Fig. 9.4b; Voigt and Young 1999). A military function for this structure has been proposed based on its strategic viewshed, military use of the same location during the Roman period, and the recovery of specific items related to the military (bronze arrowheads, armor, etc.; Goldman and Voigt 2014). A silver *siglos* (Achaemenid coin minted at

Fig. 9.4 YHSS 4 Late Phrygian Western Mound, Northwest Zone structures.
(a) In the Northwest Zone, buildings with heavy stone walls set in shallow foundations were constructed in the later fifth century BCE. The walls of the building shown here were almost entirely robbed, but the floor is intact, partially paved and partly of packed earth. To the left was a small room that had a line of hearths along one wall.

(b) Room with line of hearths. While there was no identifiable manufacturing debris, the room was filled with a coarse, friable, orange deposit when it was abandoned.
Source: *9.4a–b* image nos. 97-1005:7, 20 M. Voigt; courtesy University of Pennsylvania, Gordon Project Archives.

Sardis ca. 450–425 BCE: Dusinberre 2013; Kenneth Harl personal communication 2008) from the NWZ provides tantalizing, albeit scant, potential evidence of military pay. The overall importance of the WM NWZ during the LP is also suggested by the recovery of an unusual number of small clay cones of the type used in mosaics in both the Painted House and the Mosaic Building. While such cones were found across a range of LP contexts, they occur in far greater numbers in the NWZ than in either of the two EM contexts near structures with intact cone wall ornaments (in Operation 39 next to the Mosaic Building and in the UTS).

During the fifth century BCE most buildings in the NWZ were built on the ground surface, frequently with ashlar blocks. However, subsequently a single "cellar" was cut into a deposit of fallen rock suggesting earthquake collapse, dating the cellar to the second phase of YHSS 4 (Codella personal communication 2018). This small structure was built next to a large feature consisting of steeply sloped plaster surfaces with heavy burning. Used throughout the LP period, these surfaces appear to be some kind of industrial installation, although no manufacturing debris was found in the very limited excavation area (Voigt 2013).

The Western Mound SWZ contained relatively well-preserved LP pithouses, as well as trash and collapse layers rich in artifacts. The deposits in this trench span the period of Achaemenid occupation at Gordion and provide a good contrast both in architecture and in material culture with the WM NWZ. The best preserved buildings were partially or wholly subterranean and date to the late fifth to late fourth century BCE, their remains sealed by an Early Hellenistic (YHSS 3B) house (Voigt 2013; Voigt and Young 1999). The plans of these two SWZ LP houses are structurally quite different (Figs. 9.5 and 9.6a, b). The late fifth century TOH structure was built inside a rectangular pit, with walls made of stones varying in size and a pair of large postholes that would have supported the roof. The later LPH structure was in use during the second half of the fourth century. It is small, deep and subrectangular in plan, made by cutting a pit with slightly battered sides that were then rock-lined. A thin mudbrick wall divided it into two rooms, and the upper external walls were also mudbrick. In one corner was a carefully built hearth with high sides (Fig. 9.6; Voigt and Young 1999:fig. 27).

LP remains in the Lower Town were also mostly domestic, semisubterranean one-room structures, except for a possible kiln in Area A. Occupation appears to be continuous through the LP, with "wattle and daub"-type domestic structures built on cobble foundations (Voigt and Young 1999). In general these structures are relatively modest, with the exception of a large house from Area B (the DLW

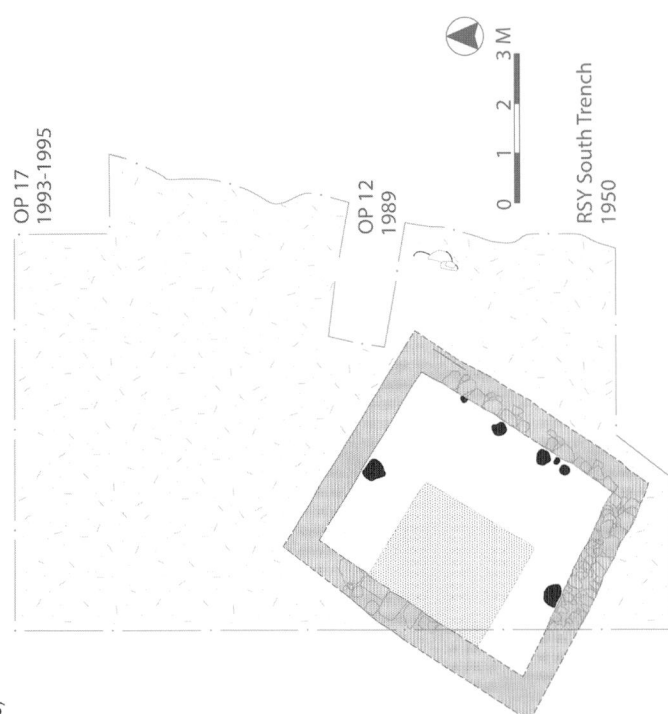

Fig. 9.5 YHSS 4 Late Phrygian house on the Western Mound Southwest Zone (SWZ).
(a) Well-constructed late fifth century BCE pithouse (TOH structure) with plaster floor preserved to west; to the east (foreground), the floor was disturbed by a later house pit. The walls are mostly robbed, but are preserved in the western corner of the trench (background). Inside the room were postholes that would have supported the roof. Looking southwest. Sloping area to the south/left was excavated in the 1950s.
(b) Plan of the building in Fig. 9.5a showing excavation boundaries.
Figs. 9.5 and 9.6 reveal the variability in housing in the Late Phrygian period.
Sources: 9.5a image no. 95–1039:26, M. Voigt; *9.5b* S. Jarvis; courtesy University of Pennsylvania Museum, Gordion Project Archives.

314   Ancient Gordion

Fig. 9.6 YHSS 4 Late Phrygian houses on the WM and in the Lower Town.
(a) Western Mound Southwest Zone (SWZ) LPH pithouse with hearth and mud plastered walls, looking southwest. Note very different plan and construction than pithouse illustrated in Fig. 9.5. The test pit next to the hearth reached an earlier floor in this house.
(b) Plan of pithouse in Fig. 9.6a showing excavation boundaries.

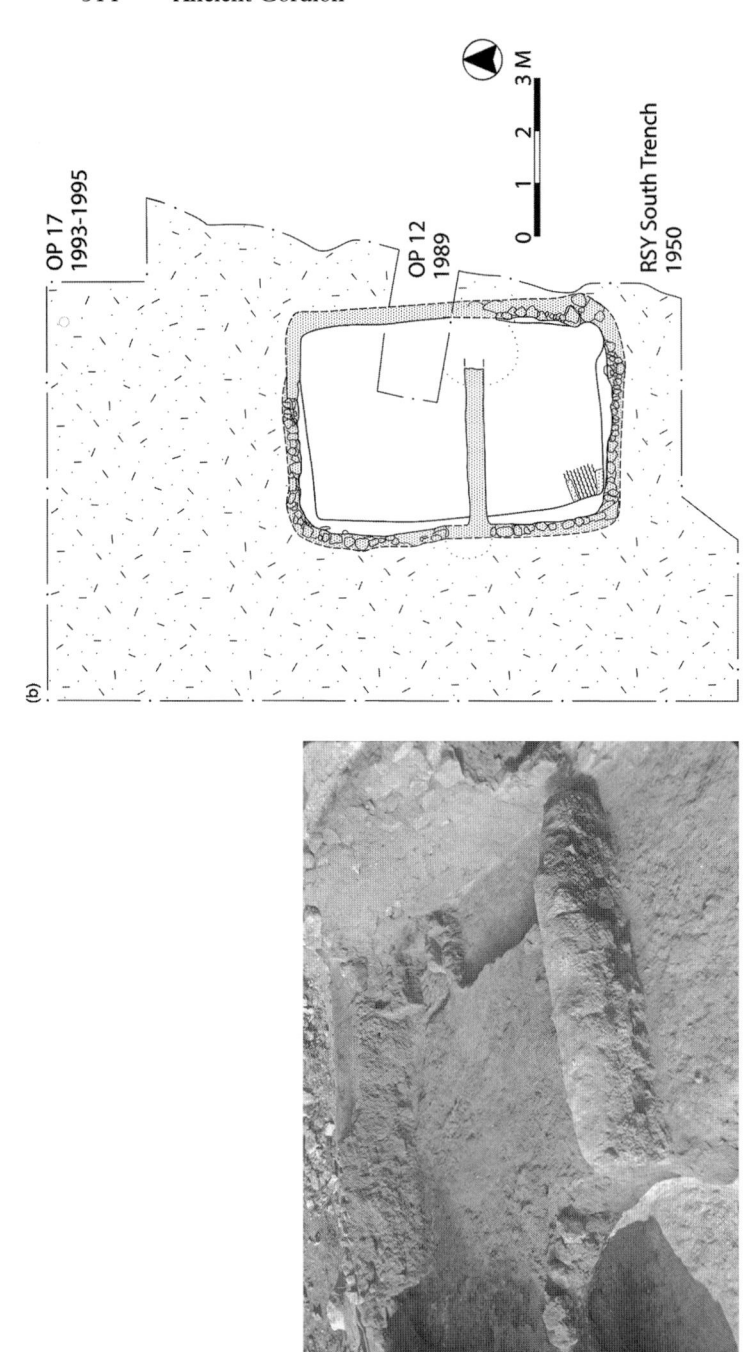

(c)

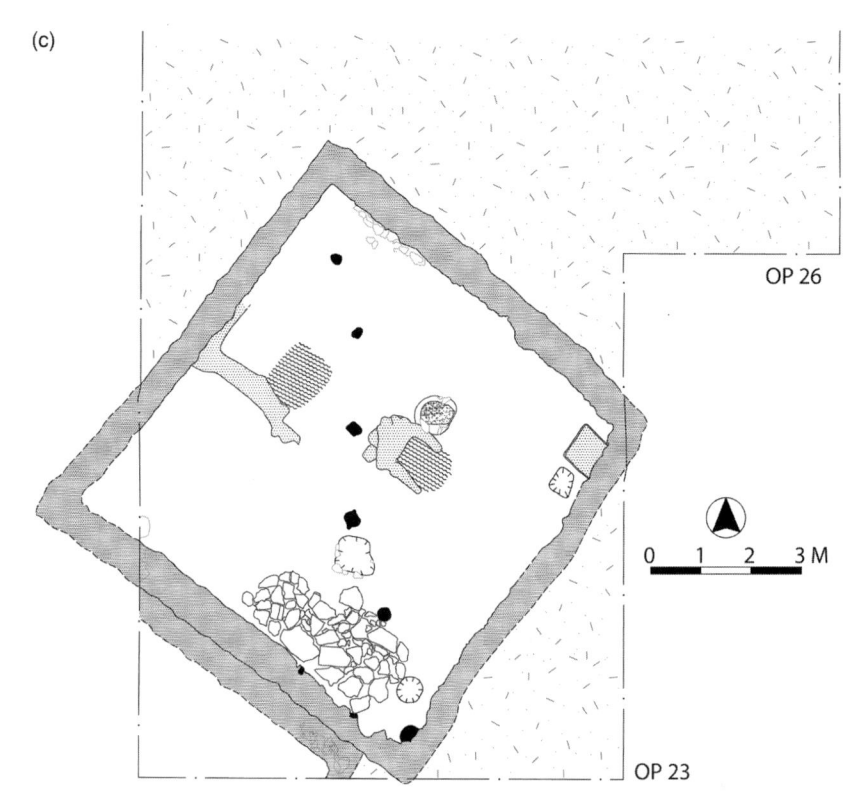

OP 26

OP 23

Fig. 9.6 (*cont.*) (c) The DLW structure is the largest LP house excavated in the Lower Town, cut down through a MP house. The walls have a stone foundation (height 0.70 m), with a mudbrick superstructure; a row of posts set diagonally from north to south supported what must have been a flat roof. The use of space is documented by a series of well-preserved features. The northeastern half of the building was used for cooking and storage, with a hearth set against a short partition wall, and a domed oven adjacent to the southeast. Next to the oven was a round bin with packed mud walls that contained two lydions, and in the eastern corner was a low mud plaster platform, perhaps for a storage vessel. The southwestern part of the building was disturbed by later pits and Roman burials, but a stone paved area was preserved. A second contemporary pithouse to the southwest lay outside the excavation area.

Sources: *9.6a*, image no. 95-1014:34 M. Voigt; *9.6b–c* S. Jarvis; courtesy University of Pennsylvania Museum, Gordion Project Archives.

structure), the most elaborate LP structure excavated in this area (Fig. 9.6c; Voigt and Young 1999:232–233, figs. 31–35). Based on a preliminary study of the pottery, this house dates from the second half of the fifth to the fourth century BCE.

The Outer Town preserves evidence of fairly densely packed domestic housing, constructed with substantial stone foundations built at ground level (Sams and Voigt 1996). Two unique vessels found in the Outer Town have strong parallels to pottery from northwestern Iran, suggesting at least the possibility of Achaemenid resettlement of Iranian groups in the area (Fig. 9.7a and b; Voigt et al. 1997:18, figs. 24, 30e, i).

All four excavated LP tumuli (in chronological order C, R, E and A) date to the beginning of the LP/Achaemenid period, the late sixth century BCE (540–500 BCE; Kohler and Dusinberre 2022). Tumulus C was used for several inhumations and tumuli E, R and A for cremations. The main burial was a child in a coffin placed inside a relatively elaborate stone and wood chamber (Kohler 1995; Kohler and Dusinberre 2022). A small and limited repertoire of associated burial goods included imported ceramics (lydions), knuckle-bones or gaming pieces, an (imported?) alabastron and some animal-shaped ceramic vessels. The latest tumulus known in the immediate vicinity of Gordion is Tumulus A, currently dated to 525 BCE; it contained the cremated

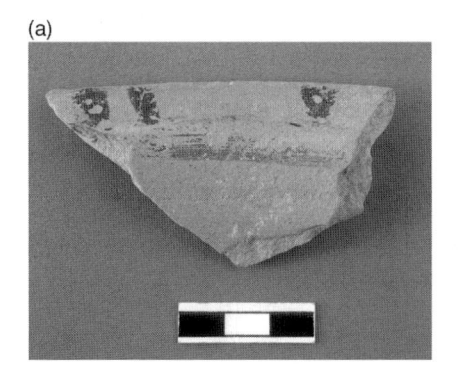

Fig. 9.7 YHSS 4 Late Phrygian pottery from Outer Town Trench (Op 32, see Fig. 3.6a for location). Identified by Henrickson as northwest Iranian on the basis of style and fabric.
(a) "Triangle Ware" bowl (YH 42141).
(b) Two-handled jug with irregular vertical burnishing (YH 38247), rim diameter = 8 cm.
Source: 9.7a–b image nos. 95-1065:22, 94-1053:28, W. Pratt; courtesy University of Pennsylvania Museum, Gordion Project Archives.

remains of a young woman interred with pieces of a vehicle or cart, horse trappings, and silver and gold jewelry (Kohler and Dusinberre 2022).

These LP burials are informative in a variety of ways. They occur at a time when we otherwise have little evidence of occupation in the city, and we might expect local elites to have been in some disarray after the Persian conquest. Also potentially significant is that at least two of the four included females. Prior to the LP, females are rarely identified in comparable funerary settings, suggesting the emergence of new social and political relations in the LP, such as Phrygian elite females as the wives or offspring of Achaemenid elites or as high-status in their own right. Despite the current lack of direct evidence for occupation of the city in the second half of the sixth century BCE, and the less elaborate character of these LP tumuli in comparison to earlier phases, their dating suggests that elites maintained some logistical capacity to assemble and manage a local labor force.

Excavation Summary

Late Phrygian Gordion is no longer viewed as a small and shabby remnant of earlier Phrygian glory, its importance documented by two forms of recent research. First, new excavation has shown that the size of the LP city remained very similar to that of the preceding MP period based on surface survey and the distribution of domestic architecture in the Lower and Outer Town as well as on the Eastern and Western Mounds (Voigt and Young 1999). Second, the fifth century BCE evidence from the Young excavations presented by Dusinberre (2019a, 2019b) and Fields (2010) has implications for what appears to be a more complex transition of place and power. Construction and remodeling of multiple structures in the elite zone suggest that while power may have been practiced differently, the continued use of MP elite space and place into the fifth century BCE appears to be a purposeful legitimation strategy of local elites under Achaemenid rule. The installation of craft activities in the fourth century BCE (if not earlier), in the midst of what had previously been a highly politically charged elite zone, and the partial removal of the wall separating the Inner and Outer Courts (begun in the fifth century), suggests an administrative disjuncture in the community at this time (Fields 2010). What had been the MP political center became a zone of nonelite housing and manufacturing producing smoke, ash and fumes (Rademakers et al. 2018). Fields (2010) argues that this major break in the use of space represents a decline in Persian political power at the site.

Gordion remained a "second-tier" city within the Achaemenid Empire but still retained some significance, perhaps reflecting its strategic location astride major routes of trade and transportation. Integration of both elite and nonelite members of LP communities into the empire is documented by the use of seals that display "a taste for Achaemenid visual culture" (Dusinberre 2013:71), the adoption of ceramic types associated with the Persians (Achaemenid or "tulip" bowls), and the striking polychrome image of a Persian with a crenelated headdress on a single potsherd found in a pit in the industrial zone on the EM (Voigt and Young 1999:fig. 1).

Overview of Late Phrygian Ceramics

As with other periods, multiple ceramic specialists have worked on the LP assemblage. The Greek and imported ceramics for both MMV and RSY excavations have been studied by DeVries, Lynch and Lawall, while local ceramics have been studied by Henrickson for Voigt's excavations. Toteva (2007) worked through a sample of 618 vessels from Young's excavations, selected from six LP contexts dated ca. 400–325 BCE. While the RSY descriptions of excavation contexts are variable, limited and at times uninformative in relation to function, the ceramic finds that Toteva described in her groups 1–4 and 6 suggest mainly domestic deposits involving household "industries," food preparation and storage. Her group 5, from contexts in the Painted House, is an exception that potentially reflected ritual activities.

Forming and Finishing Techniques

Henrickson (1993:141) notes that LP production sequences and finishing techniques were very similar to those used in the late Middle Phrygian period (Chapter 8), with a few notable technological changes. Forming now includes increased use of the wheel. For example, ring bases were cut off the wheel, rather than applied to the bottom of bowls (Henrickson in Voigt et al. 1997). One of the main changes in pyrotechnology was the gradual phasing out of reduction firing.

Forms

Both Toteva (2007) and Henrickson (1993) note strong continuities between the Middle Phrygian wares and forms and the local LP ceramic traditions, particularly among common wares (Fig. 9.8). Cooking pot shapes remained relatively unchanged from the EP to LP periods. Bearing in mind that common (relatively coarse undecorated) and nondiagnostic ceramics were rarely retained from the RSY excavations, Toteva found the fourth century RSY assemblage dominated by bowls and basins (40%). Additional forms included jugs (four types), various

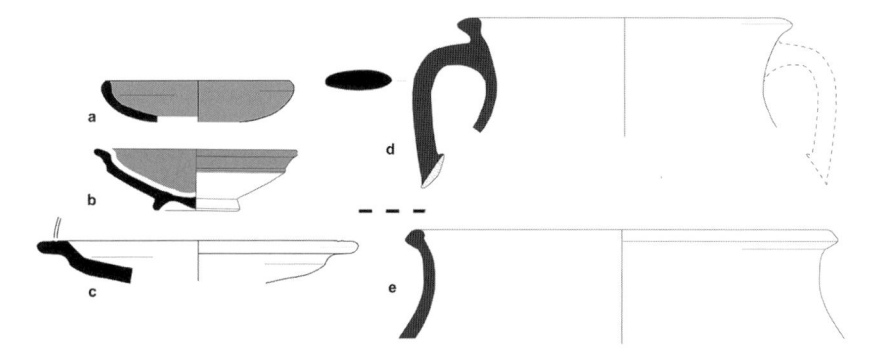

Fig. 9.8 YHSS 4 Late Phrygian vessel forms from across the settlement.
a. bowl with incurved rim, black slipped (Toteva 2007 Pl 2 #14)
b. bowl with carinated rim, red slipped (YH22985; comp T Pl 1 #9)
c. bowl with ledge rim (Toteva 2007 Pl 3 #26)
d. large amphora (Toteva 2007 Pl 8 # 72)
e. large storage jar (Toteva 2007 Pl 7 #67)
Source: G. Toteva and D. Hoffman; courtesy Galya Toteva [Bacheva] and University of Pennsylvania Museum, Gordion Project Archives.

other cooking vessels, and a range of open and closed (jar) forms. Several new shape variants were introduced at this time (e.g. bowl rims that were ledged, flat or internally thickened; Fig. 9.8a). Among the jug types, trefoil forms remain the most popular over the EP to LP periods. Large storage jars and amphora (a late addition to the Phrygian assemblage and identified as both local and imported), now comprise nearly 25% of the closed-vessel assemblage.

Fine-ware forms show the greatest change, with the adoption of Greek and Achaemenid shapes (Plate 12; see also late MP Greek forms in Plate 11; Henrickson 1993). Two new introductions, common across the Persian Empire, are "Achaemenid bowls" (relatively rare at Gordion, <1% of her sample; Toteva 2007) and flared-neck pots. Both grey and buff wares include new shapes: Grey wares tend to include more Achaemenid forms (e.g. Plate 12a) while the buff ware includes more Greek and East Greek forms (e.g. lekythoi and lydions, Plate 12c).

Decoration

In addition to strong continuities in form, the decorative repertoire for the majority of the LP assemblage remains similar to that of MP, although the popularity of specific styles shifted. From 600 BCE black glazed vessels first appeared in small numbers in YHSS 5A, and become more common in YHSS 4. New decorative treatments in the fifth

Fig. 9.9 YHSS 4 Late Phrygian pottery from the Eastern Mound. Two Achaemenid-style vessels from a pit in the Upper Trench Sounding. Jar with sintered slip to left (YH31524), polychrome painted head to right (YH 31538).
Source: Image no. 89-1074:20, L. Foos, courtesy University of Pennsylvania Museum, Gordion Project Archives.

century BCE include black glazing with stamped palmettes on bowls. Some local grey wares were also embellished with stamped palmettes. Western Anatolian styles, including Black on red ware, continued in use. By the fourth century BCE, simplified decorative treatments became increasingly popular, a trend already evident in the late MP.

Continuities in the ceramic repertoire are particularly evident for both fine and coarse grey wares. The main changes include an overall reduction in the percentage of grey ware (to 50–60%) in relation to buff ware (ca. 20% of the assemblage) (Henrickson 1993; Toteva 2007). As defined by Henrickson, grey common ware still makes up the bulk of the grey ware assemblage, while grey fine wares (grey burnished, polished and slipped fine wares) decrease. Similarly, buff ware, dominated by common buff, carries a greater variety of styles, including buff fine, banded (usually red), Phrygian bichrome, and a few West Anatolian Black on red, Greek black glaze types, and painted wares. For the fourth century, Toteva (2007) found that typically buff ware is minimally decorated with a single painted band (orange to red or brown; Plate 13a, b). Decoration was most common on smaller vessels used for food consumption and containers for oil or perfume.

Of the local decorative styles that were popular during the MP, some continue to be produced and used during the LP (grey ware, brown on X and bichromes). "Pattern burnishing" (closely packed fine burnish lines used to create decorative elements on grey or black wares), a decorative technique that was relatively rare in the MP, gains popularity in the first phase of the LP (Plate 13c). While surface burnishing was still typically for grey ware, the coverage becomes more variable (Plate 12a; Henrickson 1993; Toteva 2007). In the second phase of the LP local styles, associated with modeling and burnishing (often in black or grey), become uncommon.

Imports and Emulation

In terms of imports and emulation, lydions and lekythoi occur in EM contexts, as do western Anatolian styles (banded and marbleizing decoration). Greek-style, black glazed and painted wares (both imports and emulations) steadily increased into the fourth century BCE, as did local emulations in grey and buff fabrics (fish plates, two-handled cup/goblets or kantharoi, palmette-stamped bowls; Henrickson 1993:147).

While the earliest Greek imports recovered from the Eastern Mound are from MP 5B contexts (seventh century), imports and emulations are more common in LP YHSS 4. Toteva noted that ca. 10% of her RSY sample was stylistically "non-Phrygian." On the other hand, only 1% of the less biased MMV sample from the UTS consisted of Attic and Lydian imports (Henrickson 1994:113). Excavation of other areas of the site by MMV recovered a slightly higher percentage of Attic ware (ca. 2%). Dusinberre suggests that Attic imports at Gordion during the fourth to fifth century are "ten times greater" than at Sardis, representing the greatest abundance of Attic ceramics transported this far inland (Dusinberre 2019b:226). Amphoras imported from a range of sources are also present (see "Ceramics and Distribution").

NAA Ceramic Assemblage

Sample and Sampling Issues

Most of the assemblage analyzed for the LP period (70%) was recovered from the Eastern Mound, from both MMV (UTS) and RSY excavations (Table 9.1). A comparatively small sample comes from other domestic and craft production contexts excavated by Voigt (Eastern Mound 18%; off mound 12%).

The bias in this sample is colorfully reflected in its sources: the vast majority of the LP NAA sample from the RSY excavations and AIA

Table 9.1. *Late Phrygian YHSS 4 NAA assemblage by excavated sector (see Figs. 3.5a, 3.6).*

(a) Counts by sector with number of NAA groups and percentages.

	A	A1	A2	A11	B	B1	B2	B3	B4	B5	B6	B8	B9	B11	B12	C	C2	C6	D	E	E1	F	G	H	I	J	K	K1	L02	Total	%	# groups
East mound	47	4	2	1	56	5	8	10	5	2	5	5	1	0	2	11	4	2	2	14	1	21	8	3	1	5	2	1	2	230	70	28
West mound NWZ	5	0	1	0	11	0	0	0	0	2	1	0	0	0	0	3	0	0	0	4	0	5	3	0	2	0	0	1	1	39	12	10
West mound SWZ	1	1	0	0	2	3	0	2	0	1	0	0	0	0	0	1	0	0	0	0	0	4	1	2	0	1	0	0	0	19	6	11
Lower Town	1	2	0	0	3	0	0	0	0	0	0	1	0	1	0	0	1	0	0	0	0	1	2	4	0	0	0	0	0	17	5	10
Kucuk Huyuk	0	0	0	0	3	0	0	0	0	0	0	0	0	0	0	0	0	0	0	0	0	1	1	1	1	0	0	0	9	16	5	6
Other/UNID	0	0	0	0	2	0	0	0	0	0	4	0	0	0	0	0	0	0	0	0	0	0	0	0	0	1	0	0	1	8	2	2
Total	54	7	3	1	77	8	8	12	5	5	11	5	2	1	2	15	5	2	2	18	1	32	15	10	5	6	2	2	13	329	100	29
%	16	2	1	0	23	2	2	4	2	2	3	2	1	0	1	5	2	1	1	5	0	10	5	3	2	2	1	1	4	100		

(b) Percentages of compositional groups across sectors.

	A	A1	A2	A11	B	B1	B2	B3	B4	B5	B6	B8	B9	B11	B12	C	C2	C6	D	E	E1	F	G	H	I	J	K	K1	L02	Total
East mound	20	2	1	0	24	2	3	4	2	1	2	2	0	0	1	5	2	1	1	6	0	9	3	1	0	2	1	0	1	100
West Mound NWZ	13	0	3	0	28	0	0	0	0	5	3	0	0	0	0	8	0	0	0	10	0	13	8	0	5	0	0	3	3	100
West Mound SWZ	5	5	0	0	11	16	0	11	0	5	0	0	0	0	0	5	0	0	0	0	0	21	5	11	0	5	0	0	0	100
Lower Town	6	12	0	0	18	0	0	0	0	0	0	6	0	6	0	0	6	0	0	0	0	6	12	24	0	0	0	0	0	100
Kucuk Huyuk	0	0	0	0	19	0	0	0	0	0	0	0	0	0	0	0	0	0	0	0	0	6	6	6	6	0	0	0	56	100
Other/UNID	0	0	0	0	29	0	0	0	0	0	43	0	0	0	0	0	0	0	0	0	0	0	0	0	0	14	0	0	14	100

sampling is buff ware, while all of the undecorated grey wares are from Henrickson's more utilitarian MMV assemblage. Overall, the reduction-fired grey component of Henrickson's NAA ceramic sample is smaller than in previous periods (ca. 25% of the LP assemblage); but it is also much smaller than the 50–60% grey ware component of the MMV *excavated* LP assemblage.

In light of the substantial sampling bias inherent in these data, we focus on the EM and the functional and symbolic transformation that took place as the elite area became a domestic residential area and production zone.

Late Phrygian Results

Of the 341 sherd samples from the RSY ($n = 153$) and MMV excavations ($n = 188$), 329 have NAA results (12 proved too small to be analytically viable). The forms identified in this sample include LP versions of MP forms (jars, cups and various bowls; Table 9.2). Among the identified forms, bowls and jars dominate. Just over 20% of the sample is composed of a range of Greek and western Anatolian-influenced forms (e.g. cups, stemmed bowls, bottles/lekythoi, lydions, lamps, plates), and a few Achaemenid types (Plates 12 and 13; Table 9.2; Achaemenid bowl, flaring-rim jar; cf. Henrickson 1993). Note that that this sample of exotic forms is larger than the 10% estimate for the overall LP excavated assemblage.

About 25% of the LP NAA sample is undecorated body sherds (vs. 70–80% of the excavated assemblage; Table 9.3). West Anatolian decorative styles comprise ca. 50% of the assemblage, with banded and orange/red decorative variants the most frequent (ca. 30%; Plate 13). Banded styles are typically decorated with red but can range in hue from orange to brown on a ground of either buff or white. Western imports, or western-influenced decorative styles, include streaky and marbleizing (or "Lydianizing") slips (Plate 13) and paint, and black glazed wares.

In the LP sample we have the first matches with black glazed Attic wares (group B6). At a gross scale the compositional range of this group, comprising multiple Attic forms, appears to overlap a margin of the larger local/regional cluster B (see discussion in Chapter 4). However, finer-grained comparisons show clear compositional matches with Attic reference datasets, also confirmed by stylistic matches.

Pattern burnishing, a newly popular local style, but a very small component of the NAA sample ($n = 13$), is distributed evenly across both grey and black fabrics (combined into black and grey various styles). MP styles that continue in the LP NAA assemblage include bichromes, brown on X, and black and/or burnished variants (Table 9.3). In general,

Table 9.2. *Late Phrygian YHSS 4 forms and compositional group. Percentage sums for local and nonlocal groups in far right columns. "Local" includes cluster A and local/regional clusters B–D. Sorted by total form count.*

	A	A1	A2	A11	B	B1	B2	B3	B4	B5	B6	B8	B9	B11	B12	C	C2	C6	D	E	E1	F	G	H	I	J	K	K1	L02	Total	%	% Local	% Nonlocal
Body	15	5	1	0	15	2	3	1	3	0	1	1	1	0	0	3	2	1	2	2	1	4	4	0	0	0	0	0	1	68	21	82	18
Jar	11	1	0	0	10	1	4	1	0	2	0	0	1	0	0	3	2	1	0	2	0	4	2	2	1	1	1	1	0	50	15	74	26
Bowl	7	1	0	0	17	2	0	3	0	1	0	0	0	1	0	2	0	0	3	0	0	0	2	1	1	2	0	1	1	46	14	76	24
Cup	5	0	0	0	7	0	0	0	0	0	3	0	0	0	0	0	1	0	0	0	0	11	2	2	0	1	0	0	0	32	10	50	50
Storage vessels (various)	1	0	0	0	5	0	0	2	0	2	0	0	0	0	0	0	0	0	0	3	0	3	1	2	0	1	1	0	0	21	6	48	52
Vessel parts	2	0	0	0	4	0	0	3	0	1	0	0	0	0	0	1	1	0	0	0	0	4	1	0	0	0	0	0	0	18	5	72	28
Lydion	1	0	0	0	5	0	0	0	0	0	0	0	0	0	0	1	0	0	0	0	0	1	1	0	0	0	0	0	6	15	5	40	60
Bowl – shallow	1	0	1	0	2	0	0	0	0	0	0	0	0	0	0	3	0	0	0	3	0	0	0	0	0	0	0	0	0	11	3	64	36
Jug	1	0	0	0	3	1	0	0	0	0	0	0	0	0	0	0	0	0	0	1	0	3	0	0	0	0	0	0	0	10	3	50	50
Pot	4	0	0	0	3	1	0	1	0	0	0	0	0	0	0	0	0	0	0	0	0	0	0	1	0	0	0	0	0	10	3	90	10
Bottle	0	0	1	0	1	0	0	0	0	0	0	0	0	0	0	0	0	0	0	0	1	0	0	0	0	0	0	0	3	8	2	38	63
Crater	2	0	0	0	0	0	0	0	0	0	1	0	0	0	0	0	0	0	2	0	0	0	0	1	0	0	0	0	0	7	2	71	29
Tile	0	0	0	0	0	0	0	0	2	0	0	4	0	0	0	0	0	0	0	0	0	0	0	0	0	0	0	0	0	6	2	100	0
Plate	0	0	0	0	2	0	0	1	0	0	0	0	0	0	0	0	0	0	0	0	0	0	0	0	0	1	0	0	0	6	2	83	17
Bowl – stemmed	2	0	0	0	0	0	0	0	0	0	0	0	0	0	0	0	0	0	0	0	0	0	1	1	1	0	0	0	0	5	2	40	60
Lamp	0	0	0	0	0	0	0	0	0	0	0	0	0	0	0	0	0	0	0	0	0	0	0	0	0	0	0	0	2	4	1	50	50
Bowl – Achaemenid	0	0	0	0	1	0	0	0	0	0	0	0	0	0	0	1	0	0	0	0	0	0	0	0	1	0	0	0	0	3	1	33	67
Jar/jug	2	0	0	0	0	0	0	0	0	0	0	0	0	0	0	0	0	0	0	1	0	0	0	0	0	0	0	0	0	3	1	67	33
Juglet	0	0	0	0	0	1	0	0	0	1	0	0	0	0	0	0	0	0	0	0	0	0	0	0	0	0	0	0	0	2	1	100	0
Basin	0	0	0	0	0	0	0	0	0	0	0	0	0	1	0	0	0	0	0	1	0	0	0	0	0	0	0	0	0	2	1	50	50
Plastic decoration – foot/shoe	0	0	0	0	1	0	0	0	0	0	0	0	0	0	0	1	0	0	0	0	0	0	0	0	0	0	0	0	0	2	1	100	0
Total	54	7	3	1	77	8	8	12	5	5	11	5	2	2	1	15	5	2	2	18	1	32	15	10	5	6	2	2	13	329	100	68	32
%	16	2	1	0	23	2	2	4	2	2	3	2	1	1	0	5	2	1	1	5	0	10	5	3	2	2	1	1	4	100			

Table 9.3. Late Phrygian YHSS 4 ceramic decorative styles and compositional groups. Summary statistics in right-hand columns. "Local" includes cluster A and local/regional clusters B–D. Sorted by total decorative style count.

	A	A1	A2	A11	B	B1	B2	B3	B4	B5	B6	B8	B9	B11	B12	C	C2	C6	D	E	E1	F	G	H	I	J	K	K1	L02	Total	%	# groups	% Local	% Nonlocal
Bands	5	0	1	0	20	1	0	4	0	4	0	0	0	0	0	0	0	0	0	5	0	5	1	2	1	0	0	0	1	50	15.2	12	70	30
None – grey	9	3	1	0	15	3	3	0	2	0	0	1	1	0	0	4	1	1	2	0	1	2	0	1	0	0	0	0	0	49	15	15	94	6
Orange/red various	11	1	0	0	11	0	1	2	0	1	0	0	1	0	1	0	1	0	0	2	0	3	2	2	2	0	0	0	2	43	13	15	70	30
Black glaze	0	0	0	0	10	0	0	1	0	11	0	0	0	0	0	1	0	0	0	1	0	10	2	1	0	0	0	1	3	41	12	10	56	44
None	4	0	1	0	5	0	0	4	3	0	4	0	0	0	0	2	1	0	0	3	0	4	1	0	0	0	0	0	1	34	10	13	74	26
Brown on X	5	2	0	0	5	0	0	0	0	0	0	0	0	0	0	0	1	1	0	0	0	4	2	0	1	0	1	0	0	22	7	9	64	36
Streaky	2	0	0	0	1	3	0	0	0	0	0	0	0	0	0	0	0	1	0	0	0	0	0	2	1	0	3	0	5	17	5	7	35	65
Bichrome	4	0	0	0	3	1	1	0	0	0	0	0	0	0	0	0	0	0	2	0	0	0	0	1	1	1	1	1	0	15	5	9	67	33
Black – various	1	0	0	0	0	0	0	2	0	0	0	0	0	0	0	4	0	0	0	3	0	0	0	1	0	0	0	0	1	12	4	6	58	42
Marbleizing	0	0	0	0	1	0	0	1	0	0	0	0	0	0	0	0	0	0	0	0	0	1	3	1	1	2	0	0	0	10	3	7	20	80
Black/brown on red	2	0	0	0	0	0	0	0	0	0	0	0	0	1	0	0	0	0	0	0	0	3	1	2	0	0	0	0	0	9	3	5	33	67
Grey – various	5	0	0	0	2	0	0	0	0	0	0	0	0	0	0	2	0	0	0	0	0	0	0	0	0	0	0	0	0	9	3	3	100	0
Stamped	4	1	0	0	2	0	0	0	0	0	0	0	0	0	0	0	0	0	0	2	0	0	0	0	0	0	0	0	0	9	3	4	78	22
Brown glaze	0	0	0	1	1	0	0	0	0	0	0	0	0	0	0	2	0	0	0	0	0	0	0	0	0	0	0	0	0	4	1	3	100	0
Cord impressed	0	0	0	0	1	0	0	1	0	0	0	0	0	0	0	0	0	0	0	0	0	0	0	0	0	0	0	0	0	2	1	2	100	0
Modeled	1	0	0	0	0	0	0	0	0	0	0	0	0	0	0	0	0	0	0	0	0	0	0	1	0	0	0	0	0	2	1	2	50	50
Burnished	1	0	0	0	0	0	0	0	0	0	0	0	0	0	0	0	0	0	0	0	0	0	0	0	0	0	0	0	0	1	0	1	100	0
Total	54	7	3	1	77	8	8	12	5	11	5	2	1	2	2	15	5	2	2	18	1	32	15	10	5	6	2	2	13	329	100	29	68	32
%	16	2	1	0	23	2	2	4	2	3	2	1	0	1	1	5	2	1	1	5	0	10	5	3	2	2	1	1	4	100				

325

as in the larger excavated assemblage studied by Henrickson, the NAA sample reflects a greater number and diversity of decorated buff ware in the LP compared to the MP (Henrickson 1993, 1994, 2005).

The NAA LP sample exhibits considerable geochemical diversity (29 NAA clusters). Well over half (68%) the assemblage matches local A (20%) or local/regional clusters (48%) (Table 9.3). In addition, while most periods are dominated by local cluster A and variants, in the LP local/regional cluster B and its variants form the largest (40%) compositional cluster. This suggests significant reorganization in production in this period. While representing fewer sources than in the MP, the number of local and local/regional sources remains relatively large (19).

NAA Results for Decoration and Forms

A strong linear relationship is evident between the number of NAA groups and the number of LP forms (Fig. 9.10a), suggesting that our sample is not exhaustive in terms of the potential range of compositional diversity (e.g. a larger sample of forms such as jugs or lydions would likely also increase the number of compositional groups). Cups are the exception, as the only form that does not follow this linear trend, reflecting a smaller (possibly more specialized) range of local and nonlocal sources.

The distribution of compositional clusters across the best-represented forms (jars, bowls, cups and pots) appears to reflect differences in sources or production. While two NAA local and local/regional source clusters (A and B) account for most of the local samples (Table 9.2), forms are not equally distributed between the two, again suggesting potential production specialization in relation to sources and forms.

In terms of overall percentages, cups, storage vessels, jugs and lydions are most likely to be nonlocal, with bowls and jars most often local (Table 9.2). Pots are the only form that is almost exclusively local (pots include a range of open vessels). If we look at diversity of local vs. nonlocal sources, bowls and jars show the greatest diversity of nonlocal sources (Fig. 9.10b). This suggests a wide exchange network for both goods exchanged in storage vessels and particular types of tablewares. Jugs, not common in the LP sample ($n = 10$), are equally local and nonlocal. As in other assemblages across Anatolia, diagnostic Persian types remain relatively rare (1% "Achaemenid" or tulip bowls, including both local and imported), and it is probably significant that the nonlocal Achaemenid bowls in our sample are compositional matches with Lydian sources. The sample size for other forms is too small to reliably identify patterning. While the Attic component remains a small percentage of the assemblage, it includes a variety of forms (cups, bottles, craters, lamps and small storage vessels).

Identities in Flux　　　　　　　　　　　　　　　　327

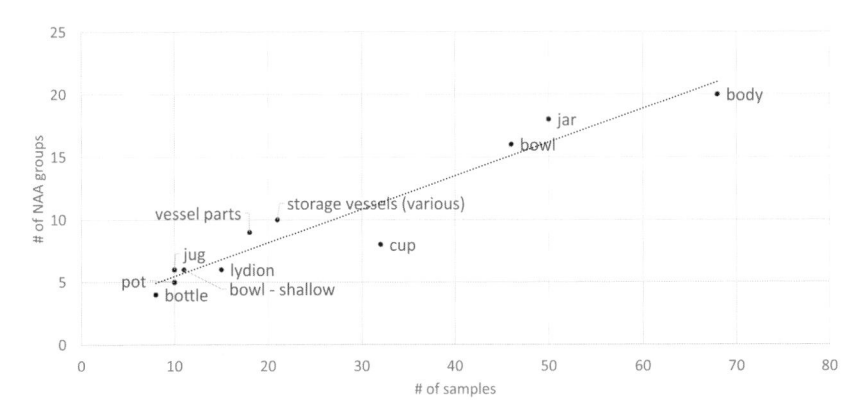

Fig. 9.10 YHSS 4 Late Phrygian NAA pottery assemblage.
(a) Relationship between compositional groups and sample size (forms). Form distribution in relation to the trendline suggests likelihood that more groups would be identified with larger sample sizes for all forms.

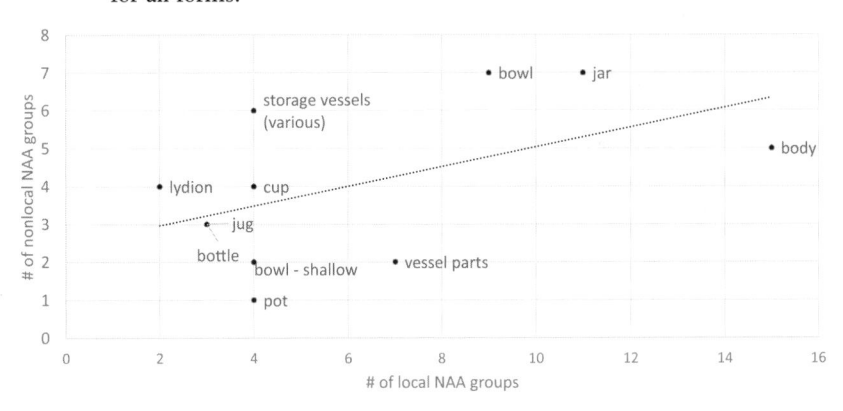

(b) Number of nonlocal vs. local compositional groups for forms. Note that bowls and jars have more nonlocal sources and pots, shallow bowls and other vessel parts have more local sources than the average (trendline).

A strong linear relationship also exists between the number of NAA groups and the number of LP decorative styles (Fig. 9.11a), again indicating that a greater range of compositional diversity is likely. Orange/red decorated styles have a somewhat greater than expected source diversity, both local and nonlocal. Black glazed styles, on the other hand, show relatively low compositional diversity.

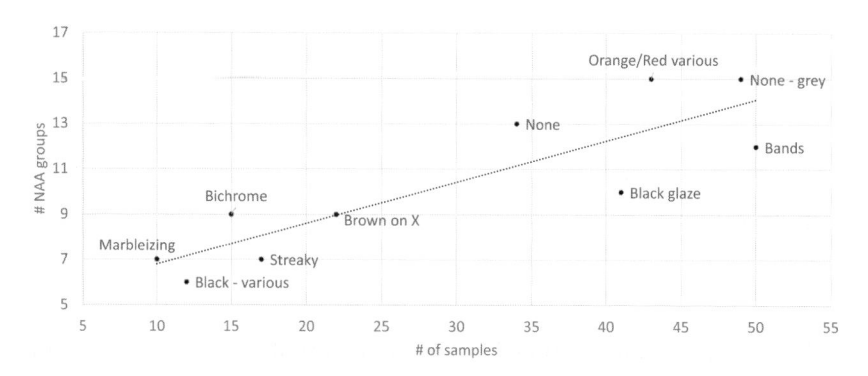

Fig. 9.11 YHSS 4 Late Phrygian pottery decorative styles. NAA assemblage.
(a) Relationship between number of compositional groups and sample size for decorative styles. Trendline suggests likelihood that more groups would be identified with larger sample sizes for all style. Source diversity is low for black glaze and banded styles and high for orange/red various styles relative to the sample population.

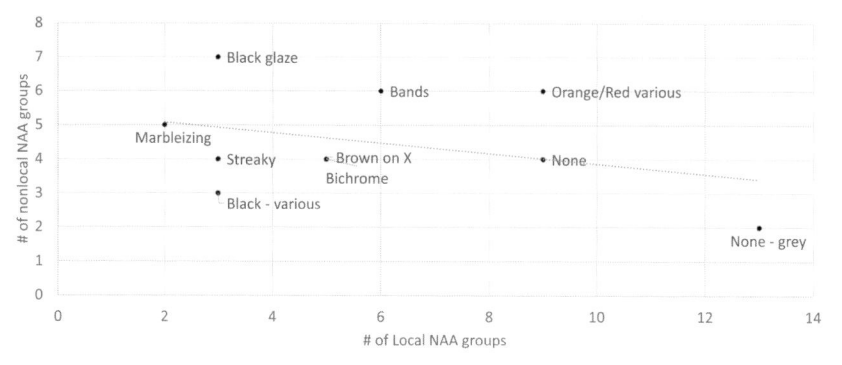

(b) YHSS 4 Late Phrygian decorative styles comparing number of local groups (x-axis) vs. number of nonlocal groups (y-axis) for each style. Note bands, black glazed and orange/red various styles have more nonlocal groups than expected. Undecorated grey wares are mostly local. (Styles type represented by >10 sherds).

The undecorated component of our sample is small relative to the excavated assemblage (see Henrickson 1993) (25% vs. 60%), and is mostly grey ware. Unsurprisingly, most of the undecorated ware is compositionally local (Fig. 9.11b; bottom right).

The three most commonly imported styles are streaky, Black/brown on red and marbleizing (>50% match nonlocal, west Anatolian sources;

Table 9.3). Together, west Anatolian emulations and imports represent the most common decorative styles. Just under one-third of the LP assemblage consists of local emulations of Greek and west Anatolian styles (e.g. orange/red decoration, banded, black glazed styles). Styles most common in the MP and EP period, such as brown on X and bichromes, make up less than 10% each of the LP assemblage. Another third of the LP samples similar to local Phrygian styles (brown on X, bichromes) also match nonlocal sources, while grey various and stamped styles are typically local. A wide range of styles were imported from east-central Anatolia, including bands and red/orange various, bichromes, black various and stamped ware, but overall, imports from this direction decrease.

The increase in black glazed styles from the MP to the LP is striking. In the late MP, the handful of black glazed samples included both local and western Anatolian sources. In the LP assemblage, about 25% of the black glazed sample is locally produced, while all brown glazed versions are local. Attic black glazed samples account for another 25%, and most of the remaining sample is East Greek and west Anatolian (Fig. 9.12).

Notwithstanding the strong sampling bias toward decorated ceramics curated during the RSY phase of excavations, our sample of this assemblage highlights the local influence of Greek, East Greek and western Anatolian styles. While Greek styles are common at Achaemenid sites across the larger region, the increasing preference for western Anatolian styles at Gordion suggests a more complex local set of choices and relationship preferences. The range of styles imported from further afield reveals the expansion of trade networks in this period, and their local emulation shows both their popularity and the responsiveness of local potters to new trends.

Change over Time

As we have noted, comparison of workshop/source diversity over time is generally a linear function of sample size. Slight divergences from this linear trend place the EP as a more diverse period (i.e. it has the largest number of NAA groups relative to sample size; Fig. 9.13a), the LBA and MP as the least diverse and the LP as intermediate. This suggests some shift in the organization of production and source use during periods of centralization (LBA and MP). The intermediate position of workshop or source diversity of the LP potentially reflects the distinct pattern of Achaemenid administration in terms of resource use and organization.

In order to better evaluate this diversity, we can assess the extent to which it reflects local differentiation or extended interaction (regional

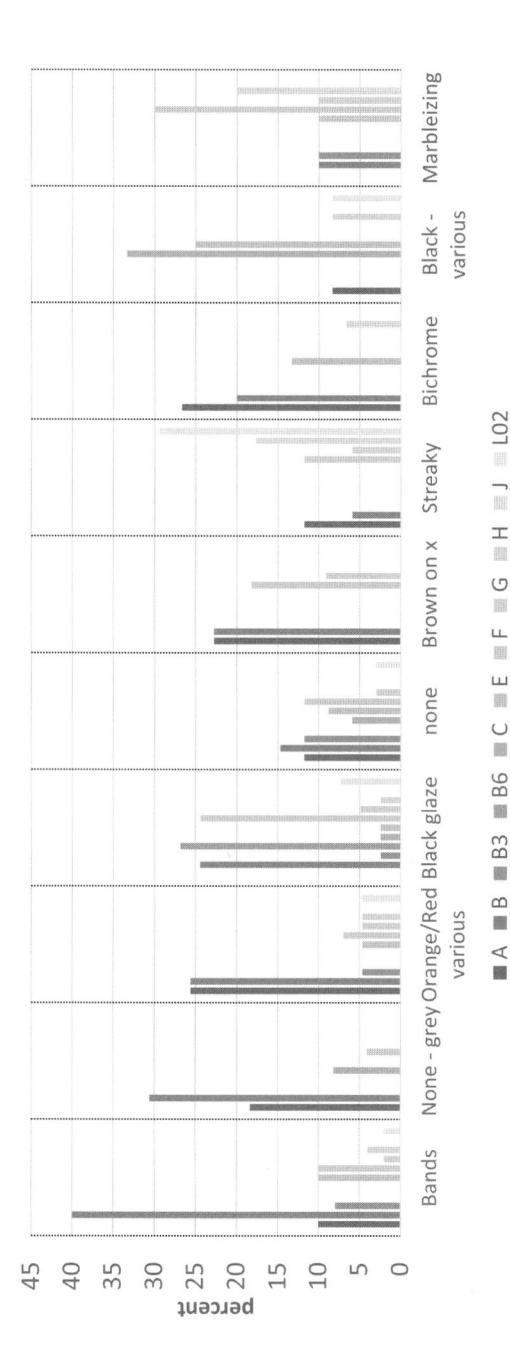

Fig. 9.12 YHSS 4 Late Phrygian distribution of most common NAA groups in percentages by decorative style ($n = \geq 10$). Clusters A–D local to local/regional; clusters E–L nonlocal. B6 however is Attic (see black glaze in graph).

Identities in Flux 331

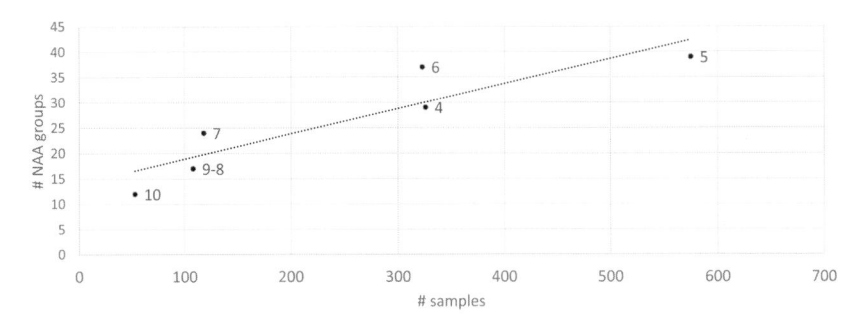

Fig. 9.13 Comparison of all YHSS phases in relation to NAA groups. (a) Compositional diversity (number of NAA groups, y-axis) relative to sample size. Note EP (YHSS 6) has the greatest compositional diversity relative to sample size, while both the LBA (YHSS10 – 9/8) and MP (5) are somewhat less diverse.

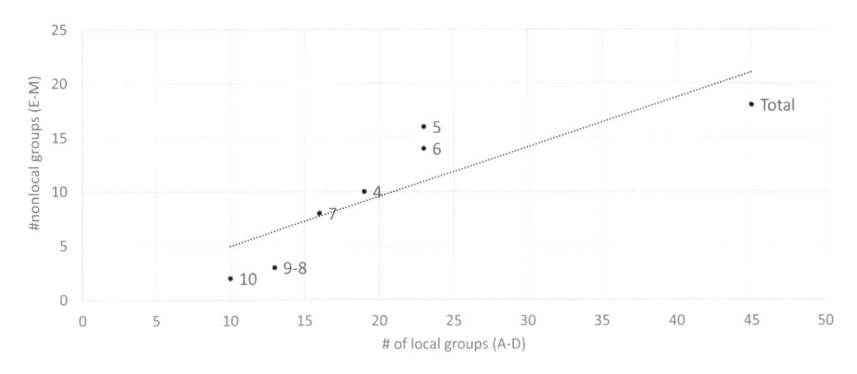

(b) Number of local (x-axis) vs. nonlocal (y-axis) compositional groups by phase. Note slightly higher proportion of EP and MP nonlocal compositional groups.

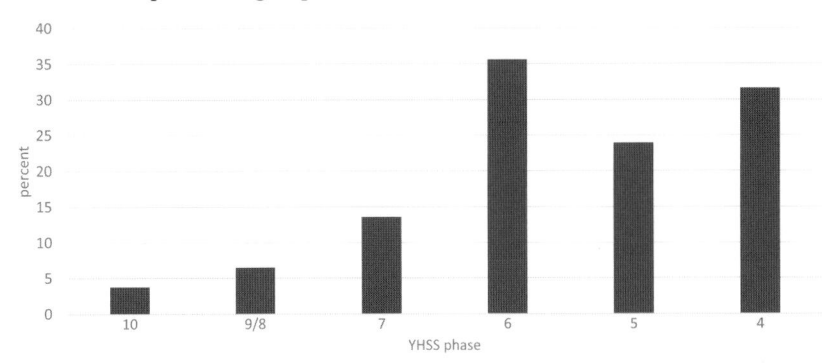

(c) Percentage of nonlocal (groups E–L, x-axis) by YHSS phase.

exchange) through comparisons of the patterning of local vs. nonlocal compositional sources. While biases are inherent in our constituent sample populations, to some extent the Henrickson utilitarian component of the sample balances the Young bias toward the exotic or decorated. While patterning in terms of overall assemblage diversity is similar, the proportion of nonlocal groups is highest in the MP, followed by the EP (Fig. 9.13b). On the other hand, comparison of the overall percentages of nonlocal vs. local samples shows that both the EP and LP have the largest nonlocal assemblages across all periods (Fig. 9.13c). Imports were common during the LP, but came from fewer sources than in the EP. This is also a change from the MP, with a lower relative abundance of imports (with more nonlocal group diversity).

Comparison of local resource use reveals the complexity of changing patterns of supply over time (Fig. 9.14). LP use of local cluster A is low relative to the MP and LBA, apparently with preference shifting to local/regional cluster B and variants (40%). The changes may well reflect technological choices that allowed the LP potters to use resources that better corresponded to the appearance and styles of increasingly popular west Anatolian imports.

These data reveal a multifaceted trajectory of production and interaction. During the LP period, communities at Gordion once again benefited from long-distance exchange networks, as well as promoting

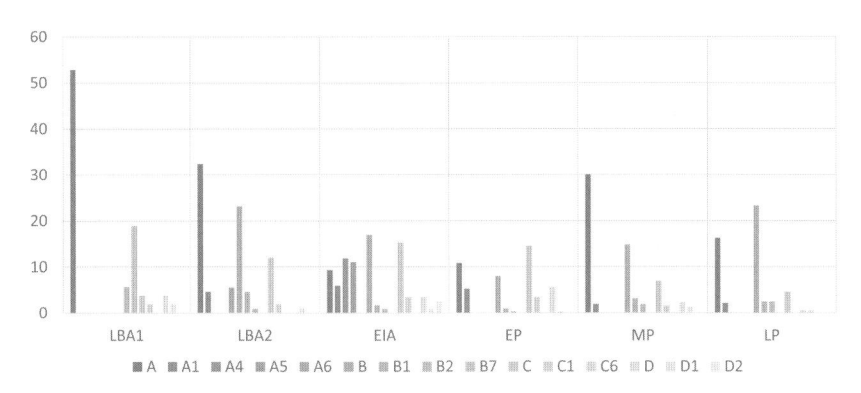

Fig. 9.14 Local resource use pattern (percentage for each NAA group, y-axis) over all analyzed phases.
Note LBA1 (YHSS 10) focused resource use, similarities in LBA2 (YHSS 9-8, Empire period) and MP resource use, and complex shifts in the use of local regional sources (e.g. group B) particularly from the EIA to the LP (sources >5%). Group B may reflect technological similarities in LBA2 and EP.

local emulation of popular cosmopolitan styles. These patterns and practices suggest these communities were actively redefining identities, and engaging with a much larger economic (and possibly social) network than during the MP period through the production, use and exchange of new forms and styles of household ceramics, and likely other imported goods.

NAA Results: Late Phrygian Patterns in Relation to Other Sites
Two other sites in western Anatolia with excavated material contemporary with LP Gordion provide compositional data for comparison: Seyitömer, a small regional center typical of inland west-central Anatolia ca. 200 km to the southwest, and Sardis, an Achaemenid satrapal capital of the coastal hinterland ca. 400 km to the southwest (Fig. 9.1). Our previous work at Seyitömer focused on the composition of Achaemenid-period ceramics from domestic contexts (n = 208) (Grave et al. 2016; Kealhofer et al. 2018). Given its relatively small size and inland location, the ceramic sample analyzed from Seyitömer proved remarkably diverse in both composition and style when compared with either Gordion or Sardis. In contrast, our Sardis sample had surprisingly few imports, with most local ceramic production traceable to a highly specific local resource zone (Kealhofer et al. 2013). While both sample selection and regional geochemistry undoubtedly played a role in the differences in NAA between these three sites, we have suggested that the compositional and typological diversity of ceramics at Seyitömer likely reflects an expanded pattern of local intraregional exchange under the Achaemenids. Similarly, the ceramic diversity present in LP Gordion appears to represent an expansion of long-distance exchange and emulation. Substantial differences in the ceramic sample from these two sites highlight the complexity of local interactions and exchange networks enabled by the regional Persian political economy at this time.

Given the relatively intensive interactions between Lydian communities and Phrygian Gordion, reflected not only in the historical record but in a range of Lydian and Lydian-style artifacts including ceramics, we might expect to see a relatively high frequency of imports from Sardis. Comparison of the local compositional signatures for Sardis and Gordion indicates that during the LP Lydian-style ceramics from other, as yet unidentified, Lydian regional production centers are more common than those from the main, compositionally highly diagnostic Sardis sources. This pattern potentially reflects the expansion and diversification of production centers in line with the evolving political landscape of Achaemenid western Anatolia.

Production, Consumption and Distribution

The processes involved in group formation and transformation are explored in the following sections, making use of data from LP material culture, while emphasizing how ceramic production, distribution and consumption in particular contribute to our understanding of these processes.

Group Formation and Production

Nonceramic Evidence for Production

LP production processes at Gordion inform us about the nature of contemporary community groups. Somewhat fortuitously, this period provides more evidence for production than any other in the Gordion archaeological sequence, representing a diverse range of materials including stone, bone, antler, ivory and especially metal. Only the EP activities in the Terrace Complex provide equally substantial, if very different, types of production evidence. Currently, most of the LP industrial activity, recovered predominantly from the EM (e.g. 272 of 288 pieces of metallurgical debris in the UTS), appears to date to the later phase of the Achaemenid period in the fourth century BCE. This situation contrasts with suggestions in previous chapters that, following ethnographic parallels, earlier production areas were likely located off the EM or at least at its periphery (as with the small MP updraft kiln).

The largest component of the productive sector undoubtedly remained in agriculture, but the balance between farming and pastoralism shifted substantially during the LP. After the particularly intensive farming regime established in the MP period, sheep/goat pastoralism increased in importance in the LP, and this continued into the subsequent Hellenistic period (N. F. Miller et al. 2009). The Late Phrygian agricultural economy still maintained a marginally higher than average mix of cereals and cattle and pigs than in periods prior to the MP. Hunting patterns remained similar to the MP period, with minor increases in deer and decreases in hare, suggesting exploitation across a larger resource region.

While attempts to ameliorate impacts of pasture degradation at this time may have played a role in such shifts, the fifth to fourth century BCE is also a period of lowered environmental stress (slightly wetter conditions). This suggests groups at Gordion had a socioeconomic rationale behind their agricultural management choice to shift back to mixed food production strategies, rather than turning to pastoralism as a response to new climate related environmental risks (N. Roberts et al. 2016). Arguably, the imposition of a very different system of management through taxation and tribute by Achaemenid administrators may also have contributed to a shift in agro-pastoral strategies. Taking into account both the faunal remains and the evidence for pasture degradation, Dusinberre suggests that Gordion became a center for large-scale herding of caprines during the LP period in response to such obligations, with live animals, meat and/or textiles moving along the Persian road system to imperial coffers (Dusinberre 2019a). As current evidence is limited, these changes in agro-pastoralism may equally reflect shifts in local conditions and repercussions of MP land management.

Direct evidence for production of goods other than ceramics was found in a wide range of excavated contexts. Metal working of both bronze and iron is well-documented on the EM, and potentially on the WM (Op. 36). As noted, slag and a large number of crucible remains were found in the "Foundry," a fourth century BCE context that lay above the fifth century BCE Painted House in what had been the MP "Outer Court" (Figs. 3.5b, 9.15; Plate 14; Fields 2010:42). Additional evidence, including crucibles, molds and slag, was recovered by Voigt in an area that had been the Middle Phrygian Terrace Complex (Rademakers et al. 2018). Rademakers and colleagues (2018) suggest current evidence is consistent with small-scale, *ad hoc* workshop production (smelting and smithing), that also made use of recycled copper for bronze production. The proximity of both iron and bronze working slags and debris suggests both were worked in simple pit installations. As yet we know little about ore sources, although Rademakers and colleagues suggest potential local sources for copper and possibly tin.

Elsewhere on the EM, fragments of debris from the production of alabaster/gypsum vessels, including unfinished stone bowls and alabastrons, document local production of a range of goods (e.g. Building H, Floor S House and the Upper Trench Sounding (UTS); Fig. 3.5b, "other workshops"; Zouck 1974). Manufacturing debris for artifacts made of bone, antler, horn and ivory have been recovered primarily from the NWZ on the WM, but also from the Voigt UTS sounding on the EM. Additional production evidence includes chert tesserae in the WM SWZ and ivory working in the Lower Town.

Two possible kilns have been identified, one in the Lower Town (Area A) and another above Building M on the EM (Fields 2010), but in the absence of kiln wasters, their outputs remain uncertain. Similarly, while apparently industrial, the function of the large feature in the NWZ, with

Fig. 9.15 YHSS 4 Late Phrygian evidence of metallurgy.
During the fourth century, the Eastern Mound became the site of small-scale metallurgical production (see Fig. 3.5b, Foundry and area of MP Building I:2). Pits in the Upper Trench Sounding often contained metallurgical debris including charcoal, crucibles, slag, and mold fragments. Illustrated here is a stratigraphic unit in Operation 7, showing many pits cut into outside surfaces and stone walls. Two partially excavated pits to the right show common attributes of the YHSS 4 pyrotechnic features: round or oval plan and a fill rich in ash, charcoal, and often small chunks of rock. In the center foreground is a sub-rectangular pit that has been partially cleared, exposing the reddened face of the truncated stone wall. The two pits in the background contained charcoal but no metallurgical debris.
Source: Image no. 89-1045:31, L. Foos; courtesy University of Pennsylvania Museum, Gordion Project Archives.

steeply sloping plastered surfaces and evidence of burning, remains ambiguous (Voigt and Young 1999).

During the LP at Gordion widespread craft activities attest to relatively vibrant, small-scale local industries consistent with the presence of proficient, independent specialist groups. This is a significant change from the MP (and EP) period when production in the EM not only focused on food, drink and textiles, but was spatially entangled with elite administration. Most of the LP production evidence, primarily for servicing local consumption, must have also included some goods tapped for taxation or tribute.

The early LP tumuli, of more modest dimensions than those of the MP period (Kohler 1995), provide limited and indirect evidence for the scope of production. The construction of the tumuli documents ongoing elite capacity for labor coordination in the late sixth century BCE. In the Tumulus C inhumation, local and imported ceramics and an alabastron (identified as imported by Kohler 1995:31) could be directly associated with this interment.

Production of new architecture and infrastructure was limited in the LP and confined to the fifth century BCE. However, several installations may reflect activities related to Achaemenid occupation, including the possible barracks building in the NWZ. Construction of the Mosaic Building and the partial renovation of Building A, as well as construction of the large stone structures in the NWZ, would still have required skilled craftsmen, specialized work groups and logistical management. Except for the Mosaic Building–Building A complex, LP structures had relatively short life spans. The Citadel wall and gates were renovated, but there is no evidence of major earthmoving projects comparable in scale to those of earlier periods (Rose 2017; Voigt 2013).

If we view the production of large-scale architecture or infrastructure as the materialization of elite power, then Achaemenid elites at Gordion were less invested in exclusionary statements of kingly or elite power (e.g. tumuli, stone structures) than their predecessors. Instead, they appear to have focused more on projects of social and economic utility for both the populace and elites (e.g. maintenance of roads and walls; cf. DeMarrais and Earle 2017). This can be seen as part of a deliberate strategy to reorganize participation in ritual/political events and realign social groups (see also Thonemann 2013 for a discussion of "de-stratification"). More specifically, during the LP phase elite architecture takes on a different form, creating new types of processional access to the rulers or administrators, as exemplified in the construction of the Mosaic Building with its large courtyard and reception space.

Ceramic Production and Groups

As a framework for making inferences about work group composition, scale of production, and the nature and extent of group cooperation we use the relationships Rice (2015:356) defined between the organization of production and specialization (skill level, kinds/quantity of output, uniformity of output and consumer/producer spatial relationships).

Scale of production This is a key measure of the potential size of groups engaged in a particular domestic or larger-scale industry. Henrickson (1993) defined the general scale of production for all of the Phrygian periods (YHSS 6-4) as "workshop" level involving a relatively small number of specialized potters – intermediate between household and industrial production. We evaluate the scalar aspect of workshop production in two ways, using Henrickson's analysis of production style and compositional data.

Late Phrygian production sequences Henrickson's (1993) assessment of LP ceramic production suggests limited change from the MP period. Use of fast-wheel increased and was extended to larger vessels and vessel parts (Henrickson 1993:146). Henrickson noted a shift toward more oxidation firing (i.e. more buff common and fine ware). However, reduction-fired grey wares, generally more highly elaborated (e.g. with labor-intensive polishing and pattern burnishing) than buff ware, still dominate the assemblage. Henrickson (1993:129) posits little change from the MP to the LP in terms of scale of production, the (relatively small) number of workshops, or in technological processes (e.g. firing temperatures/kilns). However, formal and stylistic elements did change, and two new Persian fine-ware forms (i.e. Achaemenid bowls and flared-rim jars) were introduced into the LP repertoire as both imports and emulations.

NAA data For evidence of the pattern and scale of production we turn to compositional data to define local, regional and nonlocal compositional groups. In analyzing both decoration and form, the number of sources remains proportional to sample size, again indicating that our sample is not exhaustive (Figs. 9.10a and 9.11a).

From Henrickson's predictions, we would expect a limited number of workshops for local ceramic production. More elaborate styles and forms requiring more labor or advanced skills might be expected to reflect specific workshops, along with distinct compositions and different recipes. Given the general continuity in most forming sequences, and to a certain extent finishing, we might also expect local producers to make use of an established style palette.

Instead, while two clusters account for almost 60% of local and local/regional production (clusters A and B), a total of 19 sources are identified. The change in preference from local cluster A to B suggests a realignment and elaboration of resource use (11 B subgroups; Table 9.1). However, the number of LP local sources, while less diverse than the EP period (Fig. 9.14), would seem to still exceed the number needed to support local consumption. This pattern of resource use may also suggest that multiple scales of production were in play.

If potters were specializing in particular styles of pottery or vessels, we might expect to see relationships between styles and sources. While

Identities in Flux 339

there are clear preferences for groups within cluster A or B, all styles, including undecorated wares, were produced using multiple sources. Within the subset of decorated wares produced locally, emulations are more common than local styles (Table 9.3). Source representation for both local and nonlocal styles appears a function of the size of our sample rather than evidence of patterns of production. Similarly, comparisons of the number of sources relative to the number of forms provides scant evidence of producer specialization, except perhaps with cups (Rice 2015). Nevertheless, while the number of compositional groups appears largely a function of sample size, the LP pattern is clearly very different from that of the MP period, highlighting major shifts in local and local/regional resource use between the two periods (Tables 8.3a, 9.2 and 9.3).

Production location/numbers/spatial proximity Lack of evidence for ceramic work areas means we can only speculate about production location and organization during Late Phrygian times. In terms of firing, two possible (small) kilns have been noted, one on the EM and one in the Lower Town (Area A). If used for ceramic production then their location would support a shift in production location as identified for other industries in the LP.

If we equate compositional groups with work groups, comparison of MP to LP production shows the overall assemblage diversity (number of sources relative to sample population, Fig. 9.13a) is similar between the two periods. During the MP there is greater diversity in *nonlocal sources* (Fig. 9.13b), while in the LP there is a greater overall abundance of *nonlocal pottery* (Fig. 9.13c). The shift toward more ceramic imports in the LP may be part of a larger transition to economic diversification and specialization under an expanding Persian interaction sphere.

Skill level Evidence for changes in skills from the MP to the LP period includes potters' greater use of fast-wheel production. During the MP black glazed wares were imported (with one apparent exception in 5A), by the fourth century local emulation commences (see locally produced exotic styles, Fig. 9.12). This reflects local improvements in specialized skills for both ceramic production (e.g. glazing, source preparation) and control over kiln conditions (i.e. firing temperature and atmosphere).

Changes in source preference and reduced source diversity may reflect a shift to greater expediency in production and decorative techniques for local production of decorated buff ware (i.e. fewer sources would be expected with expedient larger-scale production). The decorative palette moves from EP elaborate painted buff ware, through finely finished and modeled black and grey decorated wares in the MP. By the later LP period the preference is for using simple, wheel-applied slipped and banded decoration, although some labor-intensive decoration continued through the early LP (e.g. pattern burnishing). The overall decrease in finishes such as burnishing, as a measure of energy expenditure, further supports our suggested shift to production expedience in the LP period. The types of skills needed for production clearly shifted. Locating and modifying local/regional sources, in this case the B subgroups, may also reflect greater technical demands and more skill in clay sourcing and processing.

Technological investment The evidence for increasing use of the fast wheel indicates both developments in production efficiency (and outputs) and new infrastructural capacity. As noted, evidence from other production spheres suggests that relatively small-scale workshops across a diverse range of industries are common on both the Eastern and Western Mounds. To this we would add ethnographic data where craft producers, particularly those using pyrotechnologies, preferentially locate outside of residential zones (Rice 2015). If this preference operated in earlier phases at Gordion, then the shift in location in the LP to craft and workshop zones within what had been a core elite area of the city reflects both a major spatial reorganization of technological investment and dramatic changes in elite and domestic functions in the LP period.

Producing Groups: Summary

Except for a few tableware forms, the overall production sequence and general range of LP forms have much in common with MP potting practices and repertoire. However, within the context of the political changes that overtook Gordion following the Persian conquest in the mid sixth century BCE, there are also clear shifts in ceramic production. This includes greater investment in production infrastructure (i.e. fast wheel), more expedient forming and decoration and the appearance of new decorative styles and forms, along with changes in preferred sources and likely clay preparation. Given the general spatial reorganization of craft production in the city, and increases in imported ceramics with concurrent shifts toward emulated decorative styles, the production of conservative forms in the LP seems somewhat anomalous. These dynamics in LP ceramic production seem more likely to reflect internal change within potting groups, rather than, for example, the arrival of new potters.

As the size of the city itself changed little, the social and economic milieu of the LP seems likely to have created a local ceramic production sphere similar in scale to that of the MP period. However, major changes for producers in Achaemenid Gordion included shifts in production groups, their locations and political context. The production of elaborated fine wares is no longer as relied on for materializing elite identity. Under Achaemenid rule, fine tableware ceramics, including imports, became widely available. The mix of more focused resource use (clusters A and B) with lower diversity across all stages of production may reflect a similarly complex mix of local and Achaemenid economic strategies.

If we compare ceramic production to evidence for other types of local production, a pattern of change in group size, composition and distribution is apparent. Lack of monumental construction as well as changes in agricultural production signal a reorganization of both food acquisition and craft activities. Elite association with large-scale production also declines during the LP. Given the vibrant economy of the fifth century BCE, it seems likely this decline tracks larger shifts over several spheres. In the Achaemenid political economy this involved local changes in power relations (e.g. from competition between local elites to a more integrated hierarchy under Achaemenid rule), as well as reorganization of production and labor (e.g. agriculture, metal working). Changes in the spatial distribution of production also suggest both commoner and elite households negotiated their place in this new economy very differently than during the MP period.

Group Formation and Consumption

Nonceramic Evidence for Consumption

During the LP period at Gordion, within the same excavated areas on the Eastern and Western Mounds, the balance of consumption contexts shifted from elite (political and/or administrative) to domestic and craft production areas. Evidence for elite consumption derives mainly from the handful of elite or administrative contexts identified on the EM, including the large Mosaic Building (ca. 475–450 BCE to ?late fourth/early third century BCE) and smaller structures such as the Yellow House (Inner Court; post-475 BCE), the Painted House (possibly early fifth to early fourth century BCE), and the Building with Columns (second quarter of the fifth century; Dusinberre 2019a). The elite nature of these buildings is evident in the unusual range of elaborated decoration, use of diverse types of wood and stone, decorative terracotta roof tiles, painted murals, ceramic cone mosaics and pebble mosaic floors. Of these features, only pebble mosaic floors (EP and MP) and roof tiles (early sixth century) were used prior to the LP period (Glendinning 2005). Although EP and MP elite building complexes, composed of groups of large megarons, covered a much greater area of the EM, the Mosaic Building remains one of the largest single structures excavated at Gordion (B. Burke 2012) and, as previously noted, has generally been interpreted as a place for Persian administrative, political and potentially ritual functions. A cylinder seal showing kings worshipping the Persian god Ahuramazda, dated to the fifth century BCE, recovered from a robbed foundation trench, was potentially associated with this structure (Dusinberre 2005; Young 1953). In addition to the presence of consumables in these buildings, the buildings themselves established different types of spaces for consumption.

The polychrome decoration of the Painted House provides direct visual evidence for the character of LP consumption (Dusinberre 2019a:119, fig. 7), with figures depicted dining and drinking in what is interpreted as a ritual setting (Mellink 1980). The clothing, while generally East Greek in style, also includes apparently local styles of headdress and shawls (Fig. 9.16). However, given its small size, location and access limitations, the proposed ritual function of this building would have been "consumed" by an elite few.

One significant change in consumption is the abundant evidence of a diverse range of imported seals, often with Persian iconography (Dusinberre 2005, 2019b:227). Prior to this period, seals are rarely recovered. While not made of semiprecious materials, the LP seals nevertheless flag participation of groups at Gordion in broader Achaemenid patterns of consumption and administration.

Material statements about new ways of practicing identity and power include changes in both dining and grooming practices (use of perfumes, oils), along with construction of the most elaborate structure in Late Phrygian Gordion at some distance from earlier MP courts. Most LP glass vessels (core-formed) likely held perfume or oils and were imported from the Aegean or Eastern Mediterranean (J. D. Jones 2020). Similarly, evidence for local ivory working required the import of raw material, and an ivory seal that bears a common Achaemenid image apparently originated in Egypt (Dusinberre 2005:58). Together, exotic items and architecture, both in style and materials, distinguish Achaemenid from earlier Phrygian practices.

Ongoing construction of tumuli, and "consumption" or deposition of funerary goods in the burials, reveals some continuity in elite mortuary practices. However, from the late MP (5A) burial practices changed with the introduction of cremations that are typical of most of the excavated 5A and LP 4 tumuli. The one exception appears to be the looted Tumulus C (ca. 540 BCE) with the main burial of a (?)female child in a coffin (an identification based on grave goods). For this burial, the association with a combination of lydions and black polished pottery, along with the

Identities in Flux 343

Fig. 9.16 YHSS 4 Late Phrygian Eastern Mound. Painted House wall paintings, reconstructions by Piet de Jong.
Source: Dusinberre 2019:fig. 7; courtesy University of Pennsylvania Museum, Gordion Project Archives and *Anatolian Studies*.

construction of the tumulus itself, suggests the maintenance of older MP funerary and consumption practices during a tumultuous time.

Beyond politically charged elite contexts, our analysis of consumption patterns in Gordion's LP households indicates that they run counter to earlier phases, where imports were largely confined to better-built residential structures and elite households. An expanded LP interaction sphere engaged groups other than elites. More widespread access to consumable trade goods during the LP is reflected in the pattern of household consumption of Greek and East Greek-style pottery (Voigt 2013). Botanical data for the LP period also document household consumption preferences for fuel. From the species of plants burned, Miller (2010) suggested notable environmental degradation had developed by this time, resulting in the use of secondary regrowth species for charcoal (Marston 2017).

Socioeconomic differences in a heterogeneous mix of elite and commoner households are evident in the variability of size, quality and building techniques in residential structures across the site (e.g. Figs. 9.5, 9.6 and 9.17). This variability is seen both in adjacent residential structures and between excavation sectors. For example, if the more elaborate structures either remodeled or still in use in the area of the EM Inner and Outer Courts were residential, adjacent "cellars" cut into the MP Terrace Complex were small and poorly built. Similarly, on the WM, large stone-built structures in the NWZ contrast with small pithouses in the SWZ. Difference in size and quality is also evident in houses within the relatively large area exposed in the southern Lower Town, where a large pithouse with wooden supports, an oven and hearth contrasts with adjacent pithouses that were small and less well built (Voigt and Young 1999).

Foodways provide another perspective on consumption patterns across the city that highlight differences between neighborhoods rather than households. A study of LP animal bone recovered in the Upper Trench Sounding of the EM and in both the NWZ and SWZ on the WM reveals statistically significant differences in domestic animal remains between topographic zones (Dandoy and Zeder 2011). Whether or not the NWZ housed a military garrison, the people living there consumed more cattle than sheep/goat in relation to the other two zones sampled, with the SWZ households consuming the least. Higher beef consumption may reflect higher status and/or cultural differences. Additional support for differences between zones is provided by the distribution of wild animal remains. Residents of the EM consumed more venison and birds than those on the WM; and on the WM, those in the SWZ ate more fish and those in the NWZ ate venison along with hare and birds. These food preferences might possibly be an indication of ethnic diversity, a characteristic of some Achaemenid settlements (e.g. Babylon, Persepolis), where texts refer to individuals and groups assembled

Fig. 9.17 YHSS 4 Late Phrygian Eastern Mound. Houses and a workshop dating to the fifth century BCE, excavated in the Upper Trench Sounding.
(a) House or "cellar" cut into YHSS 5 Building I:2, with slabs from the MP building used to line the rough rubble of I:2 foundations. This simple structure had a full range of ceramics typical of YHSS 4 along with loom weights and a spindle whorl.

from geographically distant areas (M. Stolper personal communication 2019). Compared with earlier periods, however, sheep and goats return to importance in the LP, though not as prominently as in the EP (N. F. Miller et al. 2009). This shift can be attributed to multiple potential factors, singly or together, such as changes in political-economic demand, consumption preferences, aridification, or pasture and soil degradation.

Consumption and Ceramics

The widespread consumption of imported ceramics in households in most sectors reveals a uniformity of practices that apparently crosscut differences between neighborhood patterns of food consumption and domestic architecture. As noted, LP consumption of ceramic imports is not restricted to elite households or administrative areas. In the UTS on

Fig. 9.17 (*cont.*) (b) The semisubterranean structure between Buildings I:2 and J was more elaborate, with a neatly constructed wall of reused MP blocks. Set beneath the floor was a drain leading from a second workshop room excavated by R. S. Young.
Sources: *9.17a* image no. 89-1009:032, L. Foos; *9.17b* 89-001:028 M. Voigt; courtesy University of Pennsylvania Museum, Gordion Project Archives.

the EM, an early fifth century cellar contained nearly complete vessels that included a fine example of pattern burnished black polished ware (Plate 13*c*), a lekythos tentatively identified as Lydian, fragments of a Chian transport amphora and, beneath a wall, a nearly complete Attic black figure lekythos stylistically attributed to the Athena painter (Figs. 9.17a, (9.18; Kathleen Lynch personal communication 2018). An adjacent cellar produced fragmentary Attic and East Greek cups, and lekythoi of the same date (Kathleen Lynch personal communication 2018). Imports are also commonly recovered from the area within the UTS given over to metallurgical workshops during the fourth century BCE. This pattern is repeated on the WM, with imports widespread in both the NWZ stone structures and SWZ pithouses. In the Lower Town the situation is somewhat different: very few imports were found in Area A, where architecture is poorly preserved, but in Area B the largest house (Fig. 9.6c) also has the greatest number of imports, including a fourth century Attic black glazed skyphos, an Achaemenid bowl and three lydions.

Fig. 9.18 YHSS 4 Late Phrygian Attic lekythos by the Athena painter, early fifth century BCE. This vessel was deposited beneath the foundations of cellar cut into I:2 in the Upper Trench Sounding. Height 20.5 cm (YHSF 89-130).
Source: Image no. 90-1028:16, L. Foos; courtesy University of Pennsylvania Museum, Gordion Project Archive.

The evidence for consumption from the NAA ceramic sample comes primarily from the central EM and to a lesser extent the WM NWZ. General functional types, including cups, bowls, jars, change little from the MP to the LP, but styles of tableware change substantially. New styles of forms continued to enter the ceramic repertoire during the LP; mostly tablewares, these included Greek (e.g. cups/skyphoi, lekythoi, kraters, kantharoi, rhytons), Lydian (lydions, tall pedestal bowls/fruitstands) and Persian styles (Achaemenid bowls and jars). Nonlocal styles of vessels, either actual imports or emulations, represent at least 25% of the overall NAA LP assemblage. A surprisingly high percentage of forms, compositionally nonlocal but not recognizably exotic in style (Table 9.2), highlight preferences for importing a broad range of tablewares and storage vessels. The addition of Greek-styled forms highlights shifts in both the manner of consumption and perhaps in what is being consumed. These forms, both imported and emulated, are found widely across the city.

The use of exotic goods reflects both changing habits and status. For example, a decrease in the quantity of jugs combined with a slight increase in cups potentially represents a real shift in Achaemenid-period drinking habits, as noted by both Lynch and DeVries (DeVries 1977; Lynch 2016). Social or communal drinking (e.g. wine) among Persians made use of a range of vessels (including rhyta) that are distinct from previous Phrygian practices. The contexts of recovered drinking vessels, as well as the vessels themselves, point to changes in elite/political practices in this period (see also Khatchadourian 2016), and reveal new access to imports, as well as reorganization of household practices.

These new decorative styles and forms suggest more fundamental alterations in expressions of identity. One of the more visible shifts in LP ceramics is the increase in buff ware with simplified decoration, perhaps indicating a change in the function of decoration, with sets of more standardized vessels and imports marking households rather than individualized identities during consumption (compared with the EP and MP).

While the distribution of amphoras changes from the MP through the LP, less is known about changes in consumption of the goods they carried. The diversity of local and nonlocal amphora sources point to consumption and transportation of a range of local and imported liquid products (Lawall 2012). Given the increased proportion of drinking cups in the LP, it seems likely that wine (transported in amphoras) was one of the imported goods (DeVries 1990).

Discussion: Consumption and Groups

Other Gordion scholars have noted cultural influences on styles of consumption in this period, in particular the strong impact of Greek practices (DeVries 1997; Lynch 2016). However, it is apparent that LP consumers at Gordion, while highly selective in materializing identity, drew upon a much larger and more cosmopolitan interaction sphere that extended west to Greece and the Aegean and to Lydia, east to central Anatolia, and east and south to the Levant. Very specific elements were selected, from Attic cups to Attic, East Greek and western Anatolian/Lydian perfume bottle forms and styles (lekythoi, lydions and alabastrons) along with Eastern Mediterranean coreform glass vessels for perfumed oils (J. D. Jones 2020). These imports reveal changes not only in drinking habits and food consumption, but also in grooming practices. Despite the elements of Greek culture adopted and emulated in LP Gordion, the combination of styles and vessel types used is unique. These patterns of preference speak to ongoing negotiation of local elite and nonelite households with the Achaemenid ruling elite.

The patterning of different types of consumption reveals a substantial increase in the heterogeneity of households and groups across the city. At the same time, neighborhood patterning in foodways, and possibly craft production, indicates that the nature of household groups also changed. Broader access to a wider range of trade goods shifted the ways in which individuals and groups constructed their identities. As discussed in Chapter 2, these changes in the patterning of groups provide insights into the nature of community transformation in the LP.

Group Formation and Distribution

How goods are distributed provides insights into group formation. Acts of trade and exchange establish social and economic networks; the spatial distribution of goods can express the social practices involved in the creation, scale and maintenance of group identities. As noted earlier, a diverse range of material culture was transported to Gordion during the LP period.

Nonceramic Evidence for Distribution

By at least the Late Bronze Age an east–west road connected central Anatolia to the coast. This seems likely to have been improved under Phrygian hegemony (Young 1963). In the era of Achaemenid rule, the Persian Royal Road served to formalize and extend the route east and south toward the Persian core (Fig. 9.1). Further, Koçak-Yaldır (2011) suggests that by the sixth century BCE an additional route west to the Hellespont became as important as the better known route southwest to Sardis and the coast. It seems likely that goods were moving overland to the southeast (for tribute and trade), as well as both west and north (to the Black Sea) for exchange and transshipment. Imported items were made of glass, ivory, semiprecious stones, seals and gold; more ephemeral imports included oil, wine, perfume and other high-value goods (based on the presence of containers such as lydions and core-formed glass vessels). Stylistically, many elite items reflect interaction with the Near East. The use of seals across the Achaemenid Empire, from Afghanistan to Egypt, also documents engagement in the broader administrative and exchange system (Dusinberre 2010).

At Gordion the use of imported materials in local production may reflect this increase in the movement of raw materials as well as finished products. The copper/bronze and ivory used in local craft industries could have come from either primary or recycled imported materials.

Some building materials were also likely imported. Wood for construction (in foundations as well as walls, roofs and columns) must have been brought from stands that were at least 30–40 km distant (N.F. Miller 2010). In terms of the potential goods that Gordion inhabitants may have exchanged for these items, locally produced wool products including textiles are likely to have been important, as were the sheep and perhaps goats themselves (Dusinberre 2019a).

Ceramics and Distribution

The distribution of nonlocal goods and the emulation of nonlocal styles and forms provide independent perspectives on group dynamics. At a local level, the distribution of goods within the site and across the local hinterland represents interaction between groups and the formation of networks. During the LP period, imported ceramics increase significantly, along with clear evidence of reorganization of local production. Together these changes mark a substantial restructuring of MP period practices. As the distribution of nonlocal ceramics in the city is discussed in the sections on consumption, here we focus on exchange patterns.

Long distance exchange Greek ceramics were transported into the wider region beginning in the early sixth century (5A) and continued into the fourth century BCE when this trade contracted (DeVries 1977). An upsurge in Greek imports at the end of MP (5A), and during the early phase of the LP (fifth century), undoubtedly reflected greater availability as well as changing consumption patterns at this time. Imported Attic forms most commonly included drinking and dining vessels, while west Anatolian forms were often cups. The expanded presence of Attic black glazed wares at Gordion reflects the unique place of Attic production in an extensive and relatively sophisticated Mediterranean-wide network of production, consumption and distribution that extended deep into inland Anatolia.

In the LP period nonlocal ceramics make up nearly one-third of the NAA assemblage, compared with ~25% in the MP period, reflecting an uptick in long-distance exchange under Achaemenid rule (this is much greater than in the excavated assemblage, but see Dusinberre 2019b). At the same time, the diversity of nonlocal sources decreased, suggesting a realignment of exchange networks. However, even with a decrease in the number of nonlocal sources, most imported styles have a variety of compositional sources indicating a relatively dense network of interaction. While western Anatolian import frequency was similar to that of the EP and MP periods, Attic imports increased in the LP as east-central Anatolia imports declined.

Studies of amphoras provide evidence not only of where the vessels were made but also the routes used to transport them. Lawall (2012) identified a range of potential sources and transport routes for Gordion's amphorae. The origins of amphorae varied over time, but most came from across the Aegean with a Levantine import a possible exception (Lawall 2010). In terms of trade routes, as the pattern and frequency of imported amphora types within the Gordion assemblage appears to match that found in the Pontic region, Lawall (2010) reasoned that such vessels came to Gordion via a shorter north–south overland route from the Black Sea, rather than by the longer overland route from the Aegean or Hellespontine coasts.

It seems likely that smaller lidded or sealed jars were used to transport goods prior to the appearance of transport amphorae in the LP. The NAA sample of amphorae is relatively small, although in contrast to the Lawall study the samples reveal evidence for local production of amphorae that implies transport of locally produced (?liquid) goods.

Lynch (2016) compared the distribution of Attic table and banqueting forms in Sardis and Gordion and concluded that Attic ware may have initially been imported to Gordion from Sardis. By the end of the fifth century the distribution at the two sites diverged, with Gordion more likely obtaining Attic ware from the Hellespont. The particular abundance of Attic forms at Gordion, relative to Sardis, may also speak to Gordion's place in this network. These lines of evidence highlight the diverse and dynamic character of supply routes during the LP, as well as historically documented fluctuations in regional politics.

Emulation Emulation provides a window on the movement and exchange of ideas, indicating direction and change in consumption patterns. At Gordion, virtually all nonlocal styles were locally emulated. Nonlocal banded ware and orange/red-style variants were most frequently emulated, but black (and brown) glazed wares as well as other exotic types also tended to be locally reproduced using a wide range of local resources. In previous periods Black/brown on red-style pottery was primarily imported, but in the LP most are locally produced. During the LP over half of the total count of western Anatolian styles in the NAA sample were local or local/regional emulations. A few nonlocal utilitarian forms, such as Greek/East Greek lamps and censers, were not commonly emulated.

Discussion: Distribution and Groups

During the LP Gordion was integrated into a larger and more complex political and economic system marked by new levels of exchange in ideas as well as goods. This exchange reflects actions and interactions between groups, moving goods and learning new ideas and skills, all of which had the potential to change group composition and power structures within local communities. However, these data also raise questions as to why both emulation and imported wares increase during the Achaemenid period, and how these patterns relate to the formation of group identities. It is tempting to view these strategies as evidence of greater diversity in groups as well as a new means of negotiating identity.

While both administrative and perhaps military activities can be documented within the Mosaic Building and in the NWZ, there is no direct evidence (DNA or textual) for ethnic Persian administrators or military at Gordion. Despite this, the contextual use of goods and the styles of goods still suggests a Persian presence. The broad adoption of both imports and emulations, as well as a significant shift in patterns of local production, consumption and exchange, signal significant LP cultural changes whoever the consumers were.

Tensions between locals and Persian elites and military, who ruled through local groups, are perhaps most evident in the multifaceted combinations of preferences and practices of nonelites in LP Gordion. For example, groups continued using traditional local ceramic forms but rapidly adopted Persian cosmopolitan material culture, including art and architecture. If fine-ware styles and consumption patterns of the MP period reflect the internal sociopolitical structures of power at that time, then LP groups would be likely not only to have actively acquired Achaemenid trade goods, but also to have moved away from the economic and social strategies of previous local elites through new materializations of style, symbols and identity.

Achaemenid actions, through initial military disruption or destruction as well as subsequent civil administration, changed patterns of both ceramic production and exchange across western Anatolia. The network of long-established trade routes was also disrupted and realigned in order to link places where Persians set up administrative centers and military camps. Reorganization of trade, along with changed administration, clearly enhanced the flow of goods into (and probably out of) Gordion. Consequently, patterns of exchanged and emulated ceramics at Gordion reflect both changes in trade networks as well as the creation of new local group identities with the adoption of different ways of drinking, dressing and negotiating relationships in new architectural settings.

Conclusions: Groups in Flux

At Gordion the political and social turmoil of the sixth century BCE created an arena in which identities were redefined and groups reconfigured. The loss of Phrygian political hegemony in the late MP period opened the door to wide-ranging interaction in all directions, while subsequent Achaemenid preferences (including Greek styles) clearly influenced patterns of consumption and production in the city. Adoption and emulation of Greek and western Anatolian styles seem to have been part of renegotiating identity both locally and within the larger Achaemenid social and political world. Cooperation between and among local groups with Achaemenid power brokers presented new opportunities, and distanced earlier, politically obsolete alliances (e.g. groups in east-central Anatolia). The distribution of goods, particularly fine wares related to individual consumption, changed substantially, signaling a major change in practices of power. Cultural shifts are also marked by differences between houses, the patterns of neighborhood food consumption, and the common use of imported ceramics. Households across the city adopted aspects of Achaemenid-style consumption patterns, and domestic organization shifted to smaller households (particularly in the LT). Some aspects of group practices remained, particularly those related to ceramic production techniques, forms and, to a lesser extent, styles (e.g. grey wares).

Local innovations in decorative styles suggest that groups at Gordion adapted to the Achaemenid political and social sphere by producing new markers of identity (e.g. pattern burnished vessels used for drink and drinking as well as local styles of seals). The reconfigurations of production – in terms of both expediency and declines in workshop diversity – also suggest a shift away from some modes and loci that were used to create Phrygian identity during the MP period, as other modes allowed greater engagement with Persian practices and likely social capital (e.g. use of perfumes, drinking styles).

In the preceding chapter, we argued that the expansion in local workshop production, combined with a decline in nonlocal exchange, reflected intentional strategies by Phrygian elites as they constructed local power relationships. The LP period is marked by changes in both strategies: local source/workshop diversity decreases, while the quantity of nonlocal exchange increases (Fig. 9.19). It seems likely that Persian hegemony, in particular the extraction of resources in the form of tribute and labor, promoted the shift away from what had been a political economy focused on mainly local elite production and consumption. Resources that could serve as tribute were likely smaller and more

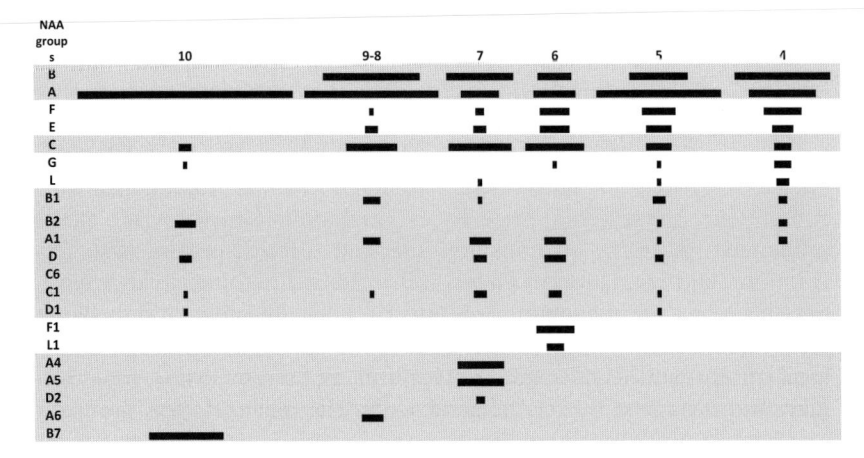

Fig. 9.19 Changing source use (y-axis) over Late Bronze Age to Late Phrygian period (YHSS 10-4, x-axis). Local and local/regional groups highlighted in grey. (Groups >5%).

transportable (e.g. textiles and meat from caprines, possibly metal and stone artifacts) than those previously heavily invested in as part of the production of the Phrygian elite ritual economy (e.g. intensive agriculture, massive elite construction). In terms of collective action, reorientation from internal labor to external tribute is also consistent with a more hierarchical local economy (DeMarrais and Earle 2017). The shape and operation of this new LP political economy is evident in changes that we see across the site, where groups reconfigured their practices (e.g. agricultural production, crafts).

If we recast the LP evidence from Gordion in terms of Hirth's (1996) four types of redistribution (elite redistribution, interregional exchange, world system linkages and tribute-mobilization systems), the MP elite appear to have focused on only two of these (resource mobilization and elite redistribution). In contrast, the LP Achaemenid elite (administrative and military?) effectively expanded their economic reach using all four types of redistribution. Exploring how local urban households negotiated and created new cooperative structures at this time remains a challenge to be met in ongoing archaeological exploration of the city.

10 Conclusion
The Dynamics of Groups and Power at Gordion

This book has sought to address the formation and transformation of social groups at the site of ancient Gordion, as a means to understand the complex processes of social change across the region during the highly dynamic period between the LBA and the conquest of Alexander the Great in the fourth century BCE. Sequences and patterns of group dynamics can provide critical insights into these processes of cultural transformation. In the introduction we proposed the idea that key societal transformations are likely to be driven by innovative and novel modes of group formation. Such transformations include substantial realignment of relationships between kin groups, religious affiliations, political organization and manipulations of ancient social media. In subsequent chapters we explored the nature of social groups chronologically, as a foundation for identifying novel features of Iron Age group formation. In this final chapter we bring together the key insights of this study of Phrygian Gordion and Iron Age societies in this region, to juxtapose and reframe previous explanations for the transformation of ancient societies more generally.

Social Groups at Gordion

Using a generalized definition of groups has enabled us to consider the many different types of groups beyond those conventionally focused on by archaeologists (e.g. elites, commoners). To go beyond the boundaries of functional groups, such as households, we also acknowledged that different types of groups may be ephemeral, intermittent, cross-cutting, as well as enduring. Groups can also be defined by materialized daily practices of social reproduction that are entangled with production, use, consumption and exchange. Such practices create communities and networks that serve to link groups over time and space. Here, our lens on the materialization of daily practices has been through archaeological ceramics for the multifaceted contextual, functional, stylistic, technological and compositional evidence they provide.

In Chapter 2, we argued that a focus on the creation and elaboration of groups over time provided a means to articulate the social and political dynamics of the communities who lived at Gordion. Groups are considered in many different contexts, but here we specifically addressed group in relation to production, distribution and consumption (use and disposal), recognizing that individuals at any one time were also likely to be members of multiple groups. Greater group differentiation is commonly assumed to reflect greater societal complexity. How this complexity is configured, however, is contingent on how groups articulate and become politically salient (through structuration). The elaboration of groups related to production, consumption and distribution characterizes the fluidity of ongoing construction of power in a society. As *loci* for social competition and manipulation, large-scale social contexts, such as feasting, create moments and places where groups and individuals negotiate and reinforce these relationships. More broadly, the creation of polities involves strategies critical for connecting ritual, politics and economy such as large-scale construction projects (e.g. building settlements, walls, monuments) (Pauketat 2007).

Groups are archeologically identified in multiple, overlapping ways including spatial contexts and style (e.g. decorative, technological, consumption patterns). Style, as both reflexive and actively constructed, does the work of creating group identities as well as allowing us to identify the interactions that lead to stylistic/group distributions. The distribution of goods and styles provides insights into when specific styles of things (or styles of practices) are actively being used to negotiate power. The ubiquity and complexity of ceramics, and how they can be used to look at spatial distributions of production, consumption and distribution, is key to their use as a proxy for studying groups.

The Late Bronze Age

Gordion's community in the LBA provides a foundation for studying how groups changed during the Iron Age. The excavated footprint of the LBA is relatively small and subsequent aggrandizing activities during the Early Phrygian period likely destroyed the central part of the Bronze Age settlement. However, while limited, excavated contexts still provide insights into LBA domestic practices. The evidence suggests the LBA community at Gordion operated within the sphere of Hittite influence. Reaching beyond household groups, administrative artifacts, including a bulla, seals and sealings, link Gordion's inhabitants to Hittite bureaucratic practices.

Ceramics currently provide the most compelling evidence for the nature of groups at this time. While we can marshal historical evidence in addition to the administrative artifacts to support Hittite engagement with groups at Gordion (Barjamovic 2017), ceramics are the clearest signal that the otherwise predominantly domestic scale of evidence is somewhat misleading. Households at Gordion were clearly part of the larger North Central Anatolian community; the LBA ceramics sit easily within the NCA assemblage, which is homogenous, simplified and relatively uniform (Glatz 2009). For Gordion at least, this assemblage has been described as mass-produced, representing a specialized economy reliant on workshop production (Henrickson and Blackman 1996). The LBA assemblage stands out from household-scale ceramic traditions at Gordion both before and after this period, which were much more variable, diverse and heterogeneous in form, style and composition.

Daily practices of household food consumption in LBA Gordion were constructed around a shared repertoire of uniform household vessels. These ceramics materialize the presence of different types of groups, not only those involved in producing ceramics outside the household, but groups involved in oversight and management. While virtually all of the LBA ceramics in the NAA sample were produced locally at or near Gordion, the mechanisms underpinning the creation of this unusually uniform and regionally styled assemblage remain poorly understood (e.g. was management of work groups indirect or direct?). Differences between the two LBA assemblages (YHSS 10 and 9/8) suggest that interactions between the Hittite core area and Gordion's community increased during the Empire period. Both use and production of ceramics at Gordion appear closely entangled with Hittite ritual economic processes.

Despite the evidence from ceramics for extra-household-scale groups, there is limited additional evidence for group elaboration in other productive sectors. A few tokens of administrative oversight – seals, sealings – do establish links to extra-local administration. All other evidence, however, suggests the household group at Gordion was a robust domestic unit, with relatively attenuated influence from larger additional groups or larger networks. On the other hand, the ubiquity of the LBA ceramic assemblage style suggests thorough integration into the wider regional NCA community. Given the limited evidence for imports or higher-status goods, we proposed a scenario where, in return for tribute/offerings (e.g. animals, textiles) as required by Hittites of subject populations, groups at Gordion benefited from inclusion in Hittite rituals and protection (e.g. Cammarosano 2018).

The Early Iron Age: Emergent Power

Lack of breadth and depth in group structure within the LBA community at Gordion may have made it more vulnerable to dissolution and/or fragmentation. This makes some sense when we look at the transformation represented by the EIA community, whose practices were very different from their LBA predecessors. The causes of very rapid transformation at the end of the LBA have been discussed and disputed by archaeologists over the past two decades, but most archaeologists working at Gordion agree that small migrant groups from the Balkans moved into central Anatolia and settled at Gordion during the EIA. Continuities in practices, such as production of buff wheelmade pottery, also suggest that local groups continued to live at or near Gordion, confronting and negotiating a complex landscape of political, economic and social change.

Extending over a 250-year period, the EIA at Gordion (1150–900 BCE) has been defined on the basis of stratigraphy and material culture as two distinct phases. Occupation during the first phase (7B) was by highly self-sufficient household groups. Production, consumption and distribution practices were concentrated within household contexts (e.g. foodways, textile production). Phase 7B ceramics reveal little investment in infrastructure or technology, as they are highly variable, low-fired and mostly handmade, with individualized decorative elements (incision, fingernail imprints). This variability can be seen not only in the lack of clear formal types, but also in a relative diversity in local/regional resource use, a pattern that may be capturing family relationships among communities within the local hinterland. During phase 7B there is clear evidence of one feasting event, including a large array of animal remains and drinking vessels that may reflect a multifamily event, but there is no other evidence of elaboration, or of disparate types of social groupings (status, community-related, etc.). Ceramic production in the EIA, very different from LBA practices (workshops), represents a rapid technological transition to household production. Alongside its reduction-fired, handmade ceramic technology, however, there is a very small component of contemporary buff wheelmade pottery, that while distinct from LBA types, potentially points to a continued presence of groups familiar with earlier local technologies.

In the second phase of the EIA, 7A, ceramics once again provide evidence for group transformation. Patterns of diet and pastoral food production remain very similar to those of 7B, as does the evidence for household textile production, but other trends point to groups emerging within the community beyond household and extended kin groups. The earliest Phrygian wall, identified by Young, was built to enclose this differentiating 7A community. The shift in ceramic production to a greater abundance of more uniform wheelmade forms suggests a resurgence of production by work groups. At the same time, household work groups remain important in the continued production of handmade forms. It is unclear if the persistent use of handmade ceramics represents heirlooming (unlikely) or exchange/gifting between local families/groups with disparate practices. Source use changed, including both the addition of imports in 7A and the realignment in local and local/regional source use. The decorative palette is simplified for wheelmade wares, indicating the individualized styles that marked household groups no longer appear salient.

Establishment of work groups, however, had significant social implications, creating new types of groups and contexts for both social competition and social integration: spatially separated work groups likely included non-kin members, and included specialized activities and production of surplus. Expanded use of technologies (kilns, potting wheels and associated tools) both changed behaviors and further differentiated individuals and groups. Similarly, wheel use likely increased outputs for some vessels, expanding the scale of distribution and exchange for local interaction. Practices of social transmission also changed. The elaboration of vessel forms for serving drinks (cups, jugs, juglets, craters), suggests new practices of consumption and social display. By the end of the EIA we see the emergence of the types of groups that we argue were critical for the rapid transformations that mark the Early Phrygian period.

The trigger for this pattern of group integration may have been the arrival of new peoples, ideas or strategies for bringing people together (singly or in some combination). However, the combination of novel and traditional practices across the 7B/7A and subsequent 6A transitions suggest that establishing new group identities and relationships was complex and multifaceted. During the 50-year period from 950 to 900 BCE (7A), rapid social changes and group consolidation occurred, with exchange networks expanding east and west. It seems likely that elements of this process were intentionally managed by factions within the community.

The Early Phrygian Period: Creating Power

The recent addition of a new radiocarbon framework for the EIA at Gordion (Kealhofer et al. 2019) has underscored not only the speed of the transformation of the LBA community (ca. 1150 BCE), but also the rapidity of the consolidation of power in the Early Phrygian period, within a decade or two of 900 BCE. The LBA–EIA transition also involved reducing the scale of organization to individual households. However, this type of entropic change from highly organized to less organized is easier to account for than the speed with which emergent groups expanded and elaborated from household-scale to the more energetic, labor-intensive level of organization that characterized the first few decades of the EP period.

In the earliest EP phase (6B), even our limited evidence reveals the construction of monumental fortifications and points to the involvement of large work groups. Contemporary ceramic data underscore a rapid differentiation of style and group definition across consumption and production contexts. The development and elaboration of groups (and places of group performance) in the better-known EP 6A phase played out in the large-scale architectural creation of a new political landscape of city walls, courtyards, elite building complexes and tumuli, establishing more formal public stages for group activities. Over the course of the next ca. 100 years, the pace of transformation increased as spaces were built, renovated and reorganized several times, with increasing investment in materials and labor, finessing the setting for practice and performance and creating increasingly segregated and elaborated spaces. Those who designed and used these spaces drew selectively on the cultural repertoires of groups both to the southeast (Syro-Hittite zone) and to the west (coastal Anatolia). This, along with the substantial labor investment represented in the walls and buildings of Gordion, were arguably critical components in the creation of a coherent Phrygian ideology to construct their unique version of power.

In each of the spheres of production, consumption and distribution, group elaboration is evident: from *production* areas associated with the new Terrace Complex buildings (textiles, food and drink) to *consumption* arenas in the Outer and Inner Courts (replicated in the tumuli/elite burials), and the expansion of *interaction* both regionally and across western Anatolia (recognizing that these arenas were not solely production or consumption contexts). Despite this clear elaboration of power, only the tumuli provide us with direct evidence that Phrygian practices of power included a hierarchically organized elite and individual ruler. Even there, most of the tumuli of the EP are both variable in contents and size and which, in terms of labor and materials, reflect the resource capacity of elite factions. Only Tumulus W stands above the rest, pointing to a more aggrandizing ruler ca. 850 BCE. However, the core elite areas of the site lack specific evidence for palaces, temples or any other spaces with a specific ritual focus, contrasting strongly with LBA Hittite elite practices in their capital and across their regional centers.

Early Phrygian ceramic evidence reveals an equally complex series of changing and evolving contexts for group elaboration through the ninth century BCE. All ceramics were produced in work groups engaged in the large-scale production of both tournette and wheelmade forms, and control over firing conditions improved (Henrickson and Blackman 1996). The undecorated buff wheelmade assemblage of the late EIA diversified into a wider range of forms; grey wares became increasingly common, and a small but highly elaborated buff ware assemblage emerged during the EP.

Changing social networks are signaled by two new distribution patterns: expansion and diversification of imported ceramics and an increased diversity of local/regional sources. As the most common import, jars may have been at least as valued for their contents as for their form. Western Anatolia is the main source of both imported vessels and emulated forms (e.g. Miletos A), while groups also looked eastward mainly to emulate styles (e.g. Silhouette ware). The increased diversity in sources in the EP period appears to run counter to expectations for increases in workshop/mass production (i.e. a decrease in source diversity), and suggests that nonutilitarian factors shaped the role the ceramic sphere played in a ritual economy. This seems to be the case particularly for the considerable elaboration (e.g. distinctive fine decoration and multiple form variants) of specific buff ware forms related to food/drink consumption (Sams 1994).

The typological and compositional character of the EP ceramic assemblage in conjunction with the large suite of Terrace Complex buildings devoted to food storage and preparation points not only to group activities related to drinking and eating, but also provides a strong indication of the kinds of participants in these groups (both distant and local regional producers). The effectiveness of Phrygian practices of power in pulling together disparate communities is reflected in the material patterns of these places. Feasting practices, while taking on a wide range of forms, nonetheless predominantly perform similar roles: to integrate groups and reify power relationships (Dietler and Hayden 2010). The evidence from Gordion reveals the rapid elaboration of many different types of groups, undoubtedly including individuals with cross-cutting group memberships. Evidence from both tumuli and ceramics suggest these groups formed competing factions (Stephens 2018). Their effective articulation likely required an ideology of both integration and performance, drawing on connections across Anatolia for legitimation.

The success of EP elites was only possible through the development of a highly effective ideology to support both the precocious rate of construction and the political coherence for the Phrygian polity. In stark contrast to previous Hittite, as well as contemporary Neo-Hittite, practices of power, ideological practices at Gordion are evident in group activities, rather than in the elaboration of symbols (statues, temples, palaces).

The Middle Phrygian Period: Reconfiguring Power

During the earlier part of the MP period (800–550 BCE), Phrygian influence expanded over much of central Anatolia. Notwithstanding singular events, like the destruction of the core elite area of the Eastern Mound that provides a division between Early and Middle Phrygian periods, elite aggrandizing activities across this boundary appear to have been continuous. Massive fill and leveling works, terracing, as well as building city walls and tumuli continued unabated over the course of the eighth century BCE (5C-B). In this period, the settlement became a city, expanding with a newly fortified Lower Town that included houses and roads and an Outer Town that is also apparently residential. Rather than representing a new phase of Phrygian political development, these monumental construction projects appear to be more of the ongoing materialized performance and extension of power by Phrygian elites.

Aside from the continuous character of urban expansion and aggrandizing activities, other significant changes occur through the eighth century BCE. These include a shift in the agricultural economy toward more intensive farming of wheat, husbandry of cattle and pigs, and probably the development of a water management system for both the town and crops (N. F. Miller 2010; N. F. Miller et al. 2009). This intensification is contemporary with – rather than preceding – political expansion.

External references to Phrygia and its kings seem to reflect escalating engagement west with Ionia and Greece, and east to southeast toward Assyria (d'Alfonso 2019; Summers 2018). Initially, MP Phrygian rulers engaged politically with Assyrian allies; later, during the seventh century, when Phrygian Gordion itself was in decline, Phrygian influence is evident in the southwest at Midas City, and in the east at Kerkenes, the site of a rapidly constructed but short-lived, large fortified hilltop settlement (Summers 2018). The power of Phrygian elites is also inscribed on Gordion's landscape with the construction of numerous tumuli (including the largest, MM, dated ca. 740 BCE), and the expansion of nearby settlements (Kealhofer 2005b). Investment in craft specialists in the MP is apparent in the production of elaborate grave goods (feasting vessels, furniture, textiles) (Simpson 2010; Young 1981). Together, the diversity of these projects, from water management to monumental construction and craft elaboration, marks the MP as a period of progressively more complex interplay between different modes of production and disparate types of groups.

Changes in ceramic decoration and production also point to ongoing modifications to the nature of social groups and the ritual economy. Somewhat counterintuitively, Phrygian identity formation appears increasingly internalized. Local MP work groups and their ceramic sources played a more important role than in the preceding EP period, with multiple local and regional sources tied to a wide range of vessel forms and decorative styles. These patterns suggest that definitions and negotiations of identity played out within a culturally self-sufficient worldview, in contrast to the more cosmopolitan EP period. Ceramic elaboration develops a uniquely Phrygian palette and style (e.g. bichromes, black polished, black variously decorated). That engagement with regional elites through feasting remained a core Phrygian strategy, despite changes in feasting practices, is suggested in the greater diversity of sources (for jugs, jars, bowls) within elite Eastern Mound contexts. However, as the pattern of high local diversity is not restricted to elite contexts and is also found across the site in phase 5B, it appears that factors beyond elite consumption strategies drove elaboration by local workshops. The internally factionalized competition first evident in the EP period appears more pronounced during the MP, with an increasing number and diversity of local sources in play, and a decrease in imported ceramics or emulation of imported styles (west or east). The commemorative landscape, with more elite burial mound construction in the late eighth century, also supports this interpretation.

Power dynamics changed during the eighth century BCE. Groups appear to constantly realign or renegotiate relationships, and elaborate their status within a highly local landscape of intensive production. As one of multiple lines of archaeological evidence, ceramic data reinforce the changing character of the organization and practices of power toward the end of the eighth century BCE. Historical evidence for larger regional political and potentially military engagement contrasts with contemporary Phrygian group identity that appears largely defined by a local, endogenous cultural landscape (e.g. Osborne 2020). The use of ceramics in dining/feasting and the patterns of local production both suggest intentional, ritualized practices were central in the ongoing creation of new forms of Phrygian identity.

Sometime during the early seventh century BCE this situation changes. At that time, large storage areas (the PPB, South Cellar) were abandoned and filled with artifacts that had formerly been markers of high status. These included a large number of elaborate black polished vessels, drinking bowls with graffiti (possibly indicating the identity of the owner), high-status clothing such as bronze belts and fibulae (both prominent tomb gifts) and two ivory items: an image and a stamp seal. Also in the seventh century, there is the dramatic reduction in the number of tumuli constructed. Together these events suggest a decline in the status investment by elite groups. If so, these changes would also correspond with the end of Midas' reign (DeVries 2011a).

Toward the end of the seventh century and in the first half of the sixth century BCE (5A), further changes in the ceramic sphere are linked to changes elsewhere in the community (e.g. the roofing of buildings in the Outer and Inner Courts with Lydian-style roof tiles). Imports assumed greater importance, but their diversity, along with that of local ceramics, decreases. An emphasis on imports highlights the renewed importance of distribution networks at this time. Elites returned to supporting emulation, particularly of western Anatolian/East Greek patterns of consumption. A strong Lydian influence on drinking vessel forms, as well as small storage vessels such as lydions and lekythoi, in both emulations and imports, redefine consumption behavior and production styles. The decorative palette of these wares is commonly red/orange on buff, often as bands, with a slowly increasing use of black glazed table wares. The groups using these vessels may have been both Lydian and local, but the patterns of use suggest the performance space for signaling status and identity formation was household or extended household contexts of consumption, rather than public arenas. The complexity of the community occupying Gordion after 600 BCE is reflected in the two affluent areas excavated on the Western Mound, which show quite disparate patterns of ceramic consumption in style and form, one more traditional than the other.

Historical references to Kimmerian incursions and Lydian expansion, as well as a recent inscription from Karahöyük (Osborne 2020), provide some indication of potential challenges to Phrygian power in the seventh century BCE. Excavations at Gordion have yet to produce any direct evidence of conflict or hostilities from this period, a situation that contrasts with later (LP) destruction of residential, administrative and ritual spaces on the EM.

The Late Phrygian Period

The arrival of a Persian military force in the mid sixth century BCE brings Phrygian Gordion, along with much of Anatolia, under Achaemenid rule (550–330 BCE). Persian siege ramps and arrow heads remain *in situ* in the MP Lower Town fortification walls, vividly illustrating this event (Voigt and Young 1999). While Achaemenid control led to major economic and political reorganization at Gordion (Dusinberre 2019a), late sixth century tumuli near the city highlight continuities in some elite practices, if not the elite groups themselves.

Conclusion

On the Eastern Mound, Achaemenid remodeling of the city and its political landscape followed a gap of nearly 50 years during which we have little evidence for activities at Gordion. When changes in the use of space began ca. 500 BCE, the buildings most affected were within the Eastern Mound core zone, where Phrygian political performance had been most concentrated. A series of urban renovations in the early fifth century BCE demonstrate the redefinition of cultural and political practices under the Achaemenids: the construction of a new administrative and perhaps residential structure (the Mosaic Building), the Painted House with distinctive but poorly understood images, several new structures with new decorative and architectural elements, and an overall realignment of walls, streets and buildings. At the same time, many of the stone megarons around what had been the MP Inner Court and in the area of the service building in the Terrace Complex were destroyed as new "cellars" were constructed. Nevertheless, through the fifth century at least part of the area around the Outer Court remained elite-controlled.

While some of the new buildings appear to last into the fourth century BCE, an earthquake dating to ca. 400 BCE has been suggested as a key moment in the transformation of the previous elite area of the Eastern Mound. The entire zone became a manufacturing area for metal working and small-scale production groups (e.g. bronze, iron, stone, bone, ivory; Rademakers et al. 2018). Beyond these activities, there is some evidence for domestic construction (or renovation/reconstruction) of the city in the fourth century BCE. While the elite core on the EM was repurposed, people living on the Western Mound and southern Lower Town apparently prospered from the start of the fifth century until the conquest by Alexander. In these areas, a varied range of house styles and potential production areas reveal ongoing activities through the Achaemenid period, likely by an equally diverse population.

Overall, imprinting Achaemenid power relationships on the Phrygian settlement appears to have had limited impact on the household economies of the larger urban community. On the other hand, LP elite households occupied only a small fraction of the city used by their MP predecessors. Arguably, the breadth and depth of group elaboration that occurred in the MP period became less salient as the structures of power turned to servicing Achaemenid interests rather than the projects of producing local power. Limited, smaller-scale construction occurred, and the agricultural economy returned to a predominantly pastoral base, potentially servicing Achaemenid tribute requirements (Dusinberre 2019a).

Changes in ceramic consumption and production evident in the early sixth century BCE continue in the LP period, as groups returned to negotiating identity within a more cosmopolitan and often Greek-influenced style. Fine ceramic and glass imports highlight the wealth of the fifth century community (Dusinberre 2019a). Greek styles (both decoration and vessel types) were common components of LP consumption practices, particularly for food and drink, with only a few distinctive Persian ceramic types (e.g. Achaemenid bowls and jugs). Black decorated wares became less common, but grey wares (particularly common ware) continued. A few new styles were introduced, but there is limited evidence for new ceramic production practices. Certain forms, previously associated with more communal feasting contexts (e.g. jugs), are rare in the LP assemblage. Late Phrygian exchange patterns reveal a more focused supply chain for ceramics, from fewer sources.

Some modes and loci used to create Phrygian identity during the early MP period (elaboration of local ceramic producers and styles) shifted as other modes allowed greater engagement with Persian power and elites (imports, perfumes, elaboration of household tablewares, drinking styles). The types of vessels, both for consuming foods and for perfumes and oils, suggest significant changes in personal practices and identities. What is most striking is that these new practices are found across the settlement, even in households living in fairly rudimentary pithouses.

More generally, there are major changes in the LP political economy. One key change affecting both groups and the practices of power was the cessation of communal-scale construction projects. The level of investment in construction waned significantly, suggesting a much flatter distribution of power and status. Rather than elaborate hierarchies of local power, Achaemenid investment served to connect and redistribute goods and services at Gordion. Utilitarian industries, such as textiles, food and ceramics, appear to have continued at a scale comparable to the MP period given that they supplied a comparable population. However, large-scale production and the highly materially differentiated groups of the MP are less evident. Fragmentation and downsizing of groups under Achaemenid administration, with fewer cross-cutting linkages (ritual, power and economy) seems likely to have been part of the changing satrapal politics of the fourth century BCE in Anatolia. Thoneman (2013) suggests that local Phrygians intentionally downsized production to minimize payment of tribute. While Dusinberre (2019a) proposes that the key shift at Gordion occurred with the collapse of the Achaemenid Empire, this later event may have consolidated a transformation set in motion some decades earlier. Subsequently, local opportunities for group elaboration, and reconstruction of power, further ebbed.

Groups and the Dynamics of Iron Age Economies

Scholars have suggested that the first millennium BCE was an "Axial Age" when the world was transformed by the emergence of universalizing religions, egalitarian ethics and new political approaches (Eisenstadt 2012; Jaspers 1949). While this era in the Gordion region was clearly a period of rapid transformation, few of the material changes align with a posited, fundamental and broad-based ideological transformation by the fourth century BCE, when our study ends. For Phrygian Gordion, the processes appear inherently more complex and contradictory, as both political organization and religious traditions integrate new relationships while maintaining aspects of the old (e.g. the goddess Matar; Roller 1991, 2011).

At a regional scale, the transition from the LBA to the IA in the eastern Mediterranean has long caught scholars' attention as a key moment of cultural transformation, affecting the organization of economies, polities and religions (Frank 1993; Knapp and Manning 2016; Liverani 1987). Several scholars, particularly Mann (1986) and Sherratt and Sherratt (1993), have grappled with the radical societal changes that occurred as Late Bronze Age political economies dissolved in the eastern Mediterranean and Middle East. Mann (1986) suggested that the sources of social power that emerged in the Early Iron Age were tied to innovations in iron technology. Iron tools and weaponry "democratized" societies across the northern Middle East and further north (Mann 1986:185–186). In areas with a strong centralized political history (e.g. the core Middle East) the repercussions played out differently than in regions that were less politically integrated. There are many advantages to iron tools, but Mann argues that iron agricultural tools critically allowed peasants to expand into rainfall agriculture zones (better plows), and gain more economic and political power. Groups such as the Phoenicians, and possibly Cypriot traders (Sherratt and Sherratt 1993), negotiated directly with producers and exchanged value-added goods (e.g. wine, perfumes). Interstitial groups were empowered, at least temporarily, even in areas with previously centralized power.

Sherratt and Sherratt (1993) also argued that the end of the second millennium BCE marked a transformation of eastern Mediterranean societies into a "new order." Several patterns characterize this "new order" (Sherratt and Sherratt 1993: 361–363): *first*, a shift from palace-based bureaucratic economies to mercantile city states, with temples more important places of power than palaces; *second*, iron became increasingly important, not only technologically but also because its adoption displaced and undercut those who controlled the bronze economy; *third*, new forms of power emerged as rulers lost direct control over the (exchange) economy, with increasing importance attached to territorial control and new military technology and organization; and *fourth*, social group boundaries were elaborated, in terms of both ethnicity and slavery (chattel vs. household) for political projects. Phrygia, they suggest, was a secondary state developing on the periphery of the Assyrian Empire, enriched by expanding east–west (northern) exchange networks (Sherratt and Sherratt 1993: 366–367).

At the scale of changing frameworks of social power in the Iron Age, Gordion offers new insights into these transformations. For Gordion (and greater Phrygia), the larger regional transformation in the political/-ritual economy after Hittite collapse opened up spaces and places for local and migrant groups to reorganize economies around new ideologies. While a major ideological change is obvious in this transition (e.g. no images of a pantheon of gods), there is no evidence that special-purpose ritual buildings or temples become an articulating feature of Phrygian society. We have argued instead that elaboration of social groups is one of the principal developments of the EP and MP periods. By extension, as physical walls and boundaries were elaborated we think it likely that social boundaries were also increasingly delineated. However, the operating mode for Phrygian integration seems to better fit a model of factionalized competition between elites and communities than chattel slavery. Evidence for military expansion can be seen in the immense investment in fortifications as well as external historical references, but it is unclear whether territorial control was the goal. Communal, possibly corvée, labor projects were practices of polity building rather than enslavement. Phrygians were initially engaged in long distance trade and emulation, but did not develop as a secondary state on the vast expansion of trade networks. If anything, movement of (some) goods was less during the period of Phrygia's maximum power (eighth century BCE).

At Gordion, the use of iron tools and technology was widespread by the ninth century BCE, both domestically and for agriculture. The breadth and speed of adoption and integration of this technology into daily life undoubtedly created new group relationships, particularly as the meaning and uses of copper/bronze and other materials changed with the adoption of iron. The role of iron tools at Gordion appears to have expanded in line with intensification of agricultural and water management practices, rather than simply in the expansion of rainfall agriculture. If the environmental evidence for drier conditions during the EP and into the MP holds for this area, a scenario of expanding rainfall agriculture is unlikely. While limited in the EIA, evidence for the expansion of iron use in EP elite contexts is not consistent with a link between expanding iron use and the democratization of power. Currently, there is little to suggest that iron technology was the critical factor in societal transformation in this region.

Both perspectives, Mann (1986) and Sherratt and Sherratt (1993), are top-down approaches to understanding the large-scale regional transformations of the Early and Middle Iron Age. As such, neither quite captures the nature of local polities as they emerged into what was a rapidly changing milieu. While many of the factors identified may be significant elsewhere (e.g. the Levant), the emergence of the Phrygian polity appears as an endogenous, albeit carefully constructed, use of a highly specific cosmopolitan lexicon of power and authority. Phrygian ideology, devoid of overt symbolism, appears deeply embedded in social group action: ritualized actions in the construction of a political center, of mortuary mounds and of feasting. Iconography is most salient at smaller scales – consuming and producing groups within the larger community (see, for example, Hubert 2016). Surprisingly, the Phrygian ceramic assemblage provides one of the clearest windows on the practices and material culture of identity formation. In comparison with the prolonged formation of Hittite power over the course of several centuries in the mid second millennium BCE (Seeher 2006), Phrygian ideological practice represents highly dynamic, creative and effective innovations in political technology that revolutionized the operation of local power for about 200 years. It is clear too that these practices created a relatively fragile and ultimately unsustainable balance of power during the conflicts of the seventh century BCE.

Political and Ritual Economies

In Chapter 2 we presented and discussed the relevance of Hirth's (1996) approaches to political economy, or how elites mobilize resources to support their political power. He identified four strategies commonly used in combination: elite redistribution; interregional exchange; "world system" linkages; and tribute-mobilization systems. Over the course of this book, we have highlighted the changing salience of each of these strategies. For example, the practices of feasting in both the EP and MP served as a strategy of elite redistribution. Interregional exchange and emulation – as seen through the lens of pottery – appears to have played a critical role in the formation of the Phrygian polity, but was supplanted during the early MP period when the elaboration of local styles and vessels blossomed. The importance of *interregional exchange* as a strategy played out uniquely during Hittite and Achaemenid hegemony as well:

the Hittites underplayed interregional exchange, while the Persians actively promoted both redistribution and exchange. In terms of *world system linkages*, only the Achaemenid period at Gordion provides such evidence, although it is clear that LBA Hattuša engaged in interpolity interaction and engagement. We argue, however, that *resource mobilization*, particularly labor mobilization, was the most significant strategy enacted during the Phrygian period. That said, it seems unlikely that it could have operated independently of systems of redistribution.

Each phase at Gordion provides evidence of a unique combination of strategies for mobilizing resources. While the Phrygian combination of strategies was evidently effective, it appears that changes in the way both redistribution and resource mobilization were practiced potentially had unintended consequences for the balance of power. On the redistribution side, fragmentation and realignment of the urban core during the MP period suggests that communal practices of feasting were no longer in play in the same way. In other words, the integrative significance of feasting redistribution may have declined. On the other hand, in terms of resource mobilization, Phrygian elites made heavy demands on labor and work groups for massive, ongoing construction projects, culminating in the construction of the MM tumulus. The combination of declining practices of social integration and increasing labor demands, along with region-wide political instability, may have inadvertently increased the vulnerability of the regime.

Another theoretical perspective identifies ritual economies, which focuses on the study of the economic underpinnings of ritual and how it is materialized (McAnany and Wells 2008; G. L. Miller 2015). The materiality of ritual captures the places where political and social relationships are repeatedly defined and redefined (Swenson 2015). Community production of items or places for ritual consumption and performance becomes part of the ritual process and the construction of social relations (Swenson and Warner 2012). Recent discussions of the archaeology of ritual have also recognized the entanglement of political, economic and social components in ritual practices.

If we view Phrygian groups through the lens of ritual economy, then a more conventional focus on the extraction of resources clearly neglects the relevance of agency and engagement of groups that are deeply entangled in the effective practices of power, along with the tensions that likely existed among them. As ritual activities, both feasting and monument construction provided communal arenas for defining political and social relationships as groups are constructed, configured and contested within these arenas. Tracking developments across the late tenth to the eighth century BCE, we can see the emergence of communal ritual activities in foodways, consumption and construction, as well as in the ways that other products were used, consumed and distributed. While we cannot reconstruct in any detail the ideological frames that were used for these ritual activities, we can catch their reflections in the contextual patterning of materials. For example, the late EIA elaboration of undecorated drinking vessels and communal events becomes, during the EP period, events staged within monumental architecture and practiced with much more individually elaborated drinking vessels. The shift from unmarked communal consumption to communal production and stratified marked consumption signals a significant shift in ideology as ritual practices move from commensal to productive.

While the elaboration of production groups plays out most obviously in the construction of commemorative monuments and fortifications, the ceramic sphere provides more quotidian insights. Several threads in particular can be traced through production, consumption and distribution relationships. In terms of production, we see a trajectory of increasingly localized production through the period of Phrygian development (MP). In terms of consumption, there is an elaboration of new distinctive styles across the EP to MP (5B). And finally, in terms of distribution, there are differential practices of interaction and exchange among elites with groups both east and west of Gordion enacting regional communities. Daily practices of increased local ceramic production and the creation of autochthonous styles of goods for use during consumption also underpinned the ritual economy. Elite ritual practices may have engaged in exchange relationships with groups both to the east and west as a critical part of identify formation, but the ritual economy was articulated through the formation and maintenance of local identity and groups.

Concluding Thoughts

The millennium of social, economic and political development at Gordion studied here offers broader insights into group dynamics. The entangled lines of evidence we have described provide a relatively detailed picture of the breadth of group formation in the settlement. During the LBA the formation of groups appears to have been limited but closely integrated into a deep Hittite hierarchy, given the pace of community transformation in the aftermath of Hittite collapse. From 1150 to 925 BCE (EIA 7B) there is little evidence for group elaboration, but beginning ca. 925 BCE (7A), an accelerating rate of change is evident in the emergence of communal spaces and activities, creating new groups. Within 50 years, some of these groups established a sufficiently robust ideological framework to orchestrate large-scale projects and commensurately scaled work groups that extended and expanded across the local landscape for the next 200 years. There are clear indications that the ideology and practices of power shifted continuously, as patterns of production, exchange and consumption realigned within a field of competing factions. The peak of this competitive interplay is most evident in the construction of the massive MM tumulus in the third quarter of the eighth century BCE. By the early seventh century, competitive and aggrandizing activities had equally dramatically declined. By the end of that century elite strategies are once more evident in the intentional shaping of styles of production and consumption across the city, now under strong external influence or leadership. Subsequent negotiations among groups and conquerors, both Lydian and Achaemenid, reshaped both the urban landscape and the configuration of households and groups in the city.

Without downplaying the potential importance of shifts and impacts of both climate and agriculture on the local economy, the speed and scale of group formation remains surprising. The construction of power through group actions, as communal practices, seems only possible within a broader historical and regional framework of memory. The "language" and meaning of symbols of power created by the Hittites, for example, must have been both referential and foundational for the construction of Phrygian ideology, which at the same time rejected their every symbolic tenet. However, the innovations and experiments of Phrygian groups appear to be only one example of many that were underway in the early first millennium BCE across Anatolia, including those of Urartu and Lydia. The rapidity of these developments as well as their volatility and short duration limited their legitimacy in many cases, and left them vulnerable to other groups with more successfully crafted ideologies and practices of power that integrated past ideological heritage with future aspirations.

Appendix   Eski Çağ'da Gordion: Demir Çağı Anadolu'sunda Seramik Üretimi ve Sosyal Grup Oluşumu

Türkçe Özet*

Güneybatı Asya'da yaklaşık olarak M.Ö. 1150–M.Ö. 540 arasına tarihlenen Demir Çağı, kayda değer ekonomik, siyasi ve teknolojik dönüşümlerin yaşandığı dinamik bir dönemdir. Bu kitapta, özgün kültürel çerçeveleri bağlamında değerlendirilen bu toplumsal dönüşümlerin sosyal grup oluşumu üzerindeki etkileri irdelenmiştir. Çalışmanın odağı İç Anadolu bölgesinde yer alan Gordion'un Demir Çağı yerleşimidir. Erken Tunç Çağı'ndan itibaren yerleşim gören Gordion, Orta Demir Çağı'nda (yak. M.Ö. 850–yak. M.Ö. 675) İç Anadolu'da etkin bir siyasi güç haline gelen Frig Devleti'nin başkentliğine yükselerek gelişiminin ve şöhretinin doruğuna ulaşır.

Tunç ve Demir Çağlarında Güneybatı Asya ve Doğu Akdeniz'in siyasi ve ekonomik dönüşümleri üzerine incelemeler, çoğunlukla, elit tabakalardan kaynaklı değişimlere odaklı çerçevelere dayanır. Oysa kanımızca, Gordion ve çevresinin siyasi rejimlerinde yaşanan dönüşümler, ancak, elit kesim kadar halkın günlük yaşamına ait maddi kültürün de etraflıca değerlendirilmesiyle aydınlanabilir. Bu doğrultuda çalışmamızın odağındaki inceleme konusu, sosyal kaynaşma sürecinde yaşanan değişimlerde maddi kültürün oynadığı roldür. Sosyal grup oluşumunu biçimlendiren kaynaşma süreci kompleks toplumların yapısını temelden etkiler. Bu çalışmada prensip olarak, maddi kültürün toplumsal davranışların edilgen bir göstergesi değil, sosyal yeniden üretim sürecinin aracı, malzemesi ve ürünü olduğu kabul edilmiştir (Soja 1989). Öyle ki maddi kültür, toplumun her ölçeğinde, birey, grup ve topluluk kimliklerinin oluşumunda etkin bir role sahiptir. Kompleks toplumların arkeolojik bağlamda en yaygın karşılaşılan maddi kültür kalıntılarından biri olan seramikler, eski çağlarda sosyal grup oluşum sürecini açıklığa kavuşturma potansiyeline sahip bir bilgi hazinesidir. Ayrıca, kırılganlığı nedeniyle kısa süre kullanılan seramikler, grup oluşum sürecinin dinamizmini arkeolojik

---

* İngilizce'den çeviren: Dr. G. Bike Yazıcıoğlu-Santamaria.

zaman ölçeğinde hassas denebilecek zaman dilimleri (on yıldan fazla) çerçevesinde değerlendirmeye olanak tanır.

Gordion kenti, büyük merkezi bir höyük (İç Kale Höyüğü) ile çevresindeki aşağı kent yerleşimi ve 200'ün üzerinde yığma toprak mezardan (tümülüs) oluşur. Yerleşmede aralıklarla sistematik kazılar yürütülmüştür. İlk olarak İç Kale Höyüğü ve 5 tümülüste açılan sondajlarla önemli bir Demir Çağı yerleşiminin varlığı saptanmış (1900; A. ve G. Körte), ardından, İç Kale Höyüğü'nün elit kesime ait yapılarında, Aşağı Kent'in güney kesiminde ve 31 tümülüste yürütülen geniş çaplı kazılarla Demir Çağı'nın büyük ölçekli mimari ve maddi kültür kalıntıları gün ışığına çıkarılmıştır (1950–1973; R. S. Young). İlerleyen yıllarda, elit kesimin ve halkın yaşadığı alanlarda gerçekleştirilen kazılar sonucunda, yerleşmenin kronolojik gelişimi daha hassas ölçütlerle tekrar araştırılmış ve böylelikle önceki kazı dönemlerinin bulguları çerçeveleri bağlamında daha iyi anlaşılmıştır (1988–2006; M. M. Voigt). Bugün sürmekte olan son dönem Gordion Projesi, şehir surlarının ve İç Kale Höyüğü'nün belirli kesimlerinde jeofizik araştırmalar ve kazılar yürütmektedir (2013-sürüyor; C. B. Rose). Çalışmamızın konusunu oluşturan seramikler Young ve Voigt kazı dönemlerinde ele geçmiştir.

Bugün Yassıhöyük olarak bilinen köyün yakınındaki Gordion'un arkeolojik yerleşim tarihçesi Erken Tunç Çağı'ndan Selçuklu ve erken Osmanlı Dönemi'ne uzanır. Burada sunulan çalışma Geç Tunç Çağı'ndan Akhamenid Dönemi'nin sonuna kadar olan yerleşim evrelerini kapsar (M.Ö. 1500–330). Çalışmada, yaklaşık 680 adet Young dönemi etütlük seramik koleksiyonundan, 900 adet ise Voigt dönemi kazıları buluntularından seçilmiş 1600 kadar seramik parça değerlendirilmiştir. Çalışmaya dahil edilen tüm parçalar biçimsel ve stilistik olarak değerlendirilmiş ve yüksek hassasiyetli Nötron Aktivasyon Analizi (NAA) yöntemiyle kimyasal kompozisyonları saptanmıştır. Voigt dönemi kazılarından elde edilen parçaların tümü ve Young kazılarından elde edilen örneklerin çoğu, net olarak tanımlanmış arkeolojik bağlamlarda bulunmuştur.

1. Bölüm, çalışmanın hedeflerini, yöntemlerini ve içeriğini tanıtır.

2. Bölüm, çalışmamızı şekillendiren temel fikirler ve özellikle de 'maddi kültürün' (burada, seramiklerin) sosyal grup oluşumunda etkin bir rol oynadığını öne süren kuramsal bakış açısı ele alınır. Çeşitli yaklaşımları bağdaştıran bu tartışmada, sosyal kaynaşma ve kimlik oluşumuna dair çıkarsamalara olanak tanıyan ve maddi kültür kalıntılarının arkeolojik dağılım şemalarıyla beraber değerlendirilmesini temel alan metodoloji açıklanır. Tekrarlanan ortak etkinlikler ile sürekli ve düzenli sosyal iletişim, maddi kültür kalıntılarının arkeolojik dağılımında (istemli ve istemsiz) yönelimlerin oluşmasına yol açar. Ayrıca, zaman içinde tekrarlanan grup etkinlikleri, üretim sürecini belirleyen bir dizi kararlar zincirine dönüşerek, özünde bir işi yapmanın farklı yolları olarak da tanımlanabilecek 'kültürel stillerin' ortaya çıkmasıyla sonuçlanır. Kültürel grupların ve siyasi kimliklerin doğuşu ve oluşum süreci, yenilik, kaynaşma, seçici benimseme ve öykünme gibi olguların bir ürünüdür, ki bu olguların her birinin maddi kültür kalıntılarında ölçülebilir göstergeleri vardır. Bu süreçlerin temelinde güç ilişkilerinin ve toplumsal uygulamaların yeniden yapılandırılması yatar. Bu çalışmada temel hedefimiz, siyasi hayat ve ritüel ekonomiye ilişkin kuramsal bir çerçeve kapsamında, teknoloji, stil ve teknolojik stilin ölçülebilir maddi göstergelerini bir arada değerlendirerek bu süreçlerin Gordion kentinin yaşamında nasıl şekillendiğini anlamaktır. Burada, antropolojik arkeoloji literatüründe üretim, tüketim ve dağılım ile ilişkili olarak stil ve grup oluşumuna dair tartışmalar ele alınmış ve antropolojik gözlemlerin Gordion'a özgü sosyokültürel soruları nasıl aydınlatabileceği açıklanmıştır. Bu karşılaştırmalı çalışmada iki strateji izlenmiştir. Öncelikle, her dönem kendi içinde ele alınarak birbiriyle ilişkili farklı grupların ve farklı uygulamaların belirlenmesi hedeflenmiştir. İkinci aşamada, dönemler arası karşılaştırmalar yoluyla sosyal grupların yapısında ve uygulamalarında zamanın siyasi ve ekonomik dönüşümleriyle beraber ortaya çıkan değişimler saptanmıştır.

3. Bölüm Gordion'da sosyal grup oluşumu araştırmalarına temel oluşturan arkeolojik bağlamların ve seramik buluntu gruplarının özellikleri tanımlanmıştır. Young (1950–1973) ve Voigt (1988–2006) dönemlerinin farklı kazı ve buluntu konservasyonu stratejileri ve kazı alanlarının seçimi, kuşkusuz, M.Ö. 2. binyıl sonu ve 1. binyılda Gordion'da yaşayan toplumların kimliğine dair görüşlerimizi derinden şekillendirmiştir. İki kazı döneminin araştırma stratejileri arasındaki farklar, bu çalışmada değerlendirilen örneklem gruplarının niteliklerini de belirler. Farklı kronolojik dönemlerin örneklem grupları sayısal olarak karşılaştırılabilir boyutlardadır; ancak seramiklerin kazıda buluntu alanları oldukça farklıdır. Geç Tunç ve Erken Demir Çağı tabakaları Doğu Höyük'te Young döneminin Ana Kazı Alanı içinde, 126 $m^{2'}$yle sınırlı bir sondajda belgelenmiştir; Orta Frig Dönemi tabakaları ise yaklaşık 2.3 hektarlık bir alana yayılan açmalarda gün ışığına çıkarılmıştır.

4. Bölüm, seramiklerden edinilen farklı tür verilere (kimyasal kompozisyon, teknolojik parametreler, stilistik unsurlar) dayanarak sosyal grupları belirlemekte uyguladığımız metodolojiyi açıklar. İlk olarak, NAA örnek seçimi stratejisini belirleyen arazi metodolojisi tanıtılmıştır. NAA verilerinin sayısal kesinlik ve doğruluk kontrol prosedürleri açıklanmış, istatistiki kümeler olarak 'yerel üretim' ve 'ithal' seramiklerin belirlenmesinde başvurulan analitik protokoller tanımlanmış ve istatistiki kümelerden kültürel gözlemlerin azalma metodolojisi açıklanmıştır. Seramik mal gruplarının etnik gruplarla eşleştirilemeyeceği gibi, her istatistiki kümenin bir kültürel gruba denk olduğu söylenemez. Yorum sürecinin ilk aşamasında, kimyasal kompozisyon verilerinden ortaya çıkan istatistiki kümeler birer 'nesne kümesi' olarak belirlenmiştir (Cowgill 1982). İkinci aşamada, bu kümelerin arkeolojik açıdan güvenilirliği ve tutarlılığı, seramikler üzerinde yürüttüğümüz teknolojik, tipolojik ve stilistik analizlerin ve önceki çalışmaların (teknoloji: bkz. R. Henrickson; biçimsel ve stilistik analizler: bkz. G. K. Sams, K. DeVries, vd.) verileriyle karşılaştırılarak değerlendirilmiştir. Ardından, seramik teknolojisi, biçim ve stile ilişkin gözlemler gibi sayısal olmayan kriterler vasıtasıyla kümelerin tutarlılığı ve güvenilirliği kontrol edilmiştir. Bu yaklaşımın hedefi, jeo-kimyasal değerlere dayanan (*etik*) kümelerin olası kültürel (*emik*) gruplarla ilişkilendirilmesini sağlam bir metodolojiye dayandırmaktır.

İlerleyen bölümlerde, seramik üretim, tüketim ve dağılım verilerinden yola çıkılarak sosyal grup oluşumu ve grup dinamiklerine dair arkeolojik kanıtlar değerlendirilir. Kronolojik düzende ilerleyen bölümlerdeki incelemeler, Demir Çağı'nda ortaya çıkan gelişmelere zemin oluşturan Geç Tunç Çağı (GTÇ) tabakaları ile başlar ve Helenistik Dönem başlarına tarihlenen tabakalarla son bulur.

5. **Bölüm** konusu Gordion'un Geç Tunç Çağı (GTÇ) yerleşmesidir (YHSS 10-8, yak. M.Ö. 1500–1150). Bu ve ilerleyen bölümlerde (*6.–9. Bölüm*), dönemin kazı alanları, seramik buluntu grupları ve NAA örneklemi tanıtılmıştır. GTÇ Gordion maddi kültür kalıntıları, dönemin ortak 'Kuzey İç Anadolu' maddi kültürünü yansıtır (Glatz 2009). Buluntuların niteliği ve dağılım şeması Gordion toplumunun bu dönemde Hitit kültürünün etkisinde olduğunu gösterir. Gordion seramikleri Hitit başkenti Boğazköy'ün çağdaş seramikleri ile karşılaştırılarak 'Kuzey İç Anadolu' seramik gruplarında standartlaşma konusunda yeni gözlemler aktarılmıştır. Bu karşılaştırmaların ötesinde, GTÇ Gordion'unda seramik üretimi, tüketimi ve dağılımı incelenmiş ve seramik analizi verileri geniş çaplı GTÇ bulguları çerçevesinde değerlendirilerek grup oluşumu süreçleri tanımlanmaya çalışılmıştır. Burada üzerinde durulan önemli bir konu, büyük ölçekli atölyelerin seri üretim seramikleri verilerinin, diğer bağlamların konut/küçük atölye ölçeğinde üretilmiş seramiklerine ilişkin verilerle kıyaslanamaz

olduğudur; ki bu ayrım, Gordion'un Hitit Krallığı'nın ritüel ekonomisine ne derece dahil olduğunun çarpıcı bir göstergesidir.

6. Bölüm Gordion'un iki evreli Erken Demir Çağı (YHSS 7B-7A, M.Ö. 1150-900) yerleşmesini kapsar. Kazı alanları, seramik buluntu grupları ve seramik üretimi, kullanımı ve dağılımına dair kanıtlar ile grup oluşumuna dair veriler özetlenir. Ana Kazı Alanı'nın Aşağı Açma Sondajında ulaşılan tabakalarda ekonomileri hayvancılık ağırlıklı tarıma dayalı topluluklara ait konutlarla karşılaşılmıştır. Burada, batıdan gelen göçlere dair kanıtlar ile Gordion'un yerel topluluklarının sürekliliğine dair veriler bir arada değerlendirilir. Hem seramik hem mimari veriler Erken Demir Çağı sonlarına doğru ailelerin dışında sosyal grupların ortaya çıktığını gösterir. Seramik üretiminin çapı ve niteliklerinin de bu yeni grup oluşumlarıyla yakından ilişkili olduğu görülür.

7. Bölüm ise hızla gelişen kültürel ve siyasi değişimlerin damgasını vurduğu Erken Frig (EF) Dönemi (YHSS 6, M.Ö. 900-800) konu edilmiştir. Kazı alanları ve seramik buluntular tanıtıldıktan sonra, Doğu Höyük'te yaşayan grupların devamlı inşaat ve yeniden düzenleme etkinliklerine dair kanıtlar ile karmaşık tüketim ve üretim etkinliklerinin açıkça ortaya koyduğu yeni grup oluşumlarına dair kanıtlar bir arada değerlendirilir. Bu dönemde Gordion'un güç toplayan elit kesimi, bir yandan geniş bir coğrafyada doğu ve batı komşularıyla ticari ilişkiler geliştirip çevre kültürlerin simgelerini ve stillerini benimserken, bir yandan da özgün Frig stilini yaratmıştır. Bu kültürel çeşitliliği, kuşkusuz, yeni değiş-tokuş ilişkileri kadar ziyafet sofralarında kullanılan dokuma, seramik vb. maddi kültür stillerindeki çeşitlilik de gözler önüne serer. Grup oluşumunu perçinleyen ortak üretim ve tüketim etkinliklerinde kültürel farkların vurgulanmış olması, yeni dengelerdeki gruplar arası güç rekabetinin Gordion toplumunda önemli rol oynadığını ortaya koyar. Ölü gömme adetlerinde karşılaşılan gösterişli unsurlar ve elit kesime ait surla çevrili çekirdek alanda devamlı inşaat etkinlikleri de gruplar arası rekabetin ve sosyal kaynaşma süreçlerindeki gerginliklerin altını çizer.

8. Bölüm konusu Frig Devleti'nin İç Anadolu'da gücünün doruğuna ulaştığı Orta Frig (OF) dönemini konu alır (YHSS 5, M.Ö. 800-540). Gordion'un farklı kesimlerinde, İç Kale'deki Doğu ve Batı höyüklerde, Aşağı ve Dış Şehir'de yerleşildiğini gösteren en erken arkeolojik veriler bu döneme tarihlenir ve üç arkeolojik evre ile temsil edilir (YHSS 5C-5A). Kazı alanları ve seramik buluntular tanıtıldıktan sonra, üç OF evresi boyunca grup oluşumlarında, siyasi ve sosyal güç yapılarında gözlenen değişimler ele alınır ve yerleşmenin farklı sektörlerinde sosyal davranışlarda gözlenen farklar değerlendirilir. 5C evresinde, hem İç Kale alanındaki Doğu Höyük ve Batı Höyük, hem de Aşağı Şehir ve Yukarı Şehir kesimlerini çepeçevre kuşatan surlarıyla Gordion, gerçek bir şehir haline gelir. Kentin bu hızlı genişleme sürecine paralel olarak Doğu Höyük çekirdek elit kesim yerleşiminde yapılaşma ve genişleme gözlenir; ancak, EF döneminin sonunda bu kesim yangınla sona erer. 5C evresi, aynı zamanda, kentin çevresindeki en tanınmış (ve arkeolojik olarak araştırılmış) tümülüs mezarların da inşa edildiği dönemdir. İlerleyen evrelerde (5B-5A), M.Ö. 7. yüzyıl ve erken 6. yüzyıl boyunca seramik biçimleri ve stillerinin yanı sıra mimaride görülen belirgin değişimler, Friglerin siyasi gücünün zayıfladığını ve Lydia etkisinin güçlendiğini gösterir. OF evreleri boyunca Gordion'da yerel üretim seramiklerin oranı giderek artar. Geç EF ve erken OF evrelerinde karakteristik olan, her biri özgün biçimde üretilmiş, devetüyü hamurlu, boya bezemeli seramikler, ileri OF evrelerinin elit ziyafet sofralarında giderek daha az tercih edilmiştir. İlk olarak EP Dönemi'nde gözlenen gruplar arası rekabet OF Dönemi 5C evresi sonuna doğru (yak. M.Ö. 740) Tümülüs MM'nin inşa edilmesiyle doruğa ulaşır. Buradaki gözlemler hem maddi kültür unsurlarının hem de mekanların yaratılmasında etkin rol oynayan farklı tür iş ve zanaat gruplarının Frig Krallığı'nın sosyal güç yapılarıyla sıkı bağları olduğunu ortaya koyar.

9. *Bölüm* Geç Frig (GF) / Akhamenid Dönemi'ni (YHSS 4, M.Ö. 540-330) konu alır. Geç Frig dönemi, yak. M.Ö. 5. yüzyıl ve yak. M.Ö. 4. yüzyıla denk gelen iki evreye bölünür. Bu dönemin başlangıcını, M.Ö. 540 civarında kentin uğradığı Pers saldırısı belirler. M.Ö. 6. yüzyılın geç safhasında son tümülüsler inşa edilmiş, M.Ö. 5. yüzyılın başlarında Doğu Höyük çekirdek elit kesimde Dış Avlu'da yoğunlaşan sınırlı mimari düzenlemeler yapılmıştır. OF Dönemi'ne ait büyük bir yapıya (A Yapısı) ek olarak bu dönemde inşa edilen "Mozaikli Yapı"nın idari bir merkez olduğu anlaşılır. GF evresinde, Frig Krallığı'nın erken dönemlerinde gerçekleştirdiği büyük ölçekli inşaat projeleriyle karşılaştırılabilecek bir yapılaşma yoktur. Diğer taraftan, mimari yapı planları, stilleri ve kişisel süs eşyalarında sosyal kimlik ve grup oluşumuna yön veren yeni uygulamalarla karşılaşılır. Yerleşmenin çeşitli kesimlerinde yürütülen kazılar, Geç Frig Dönemi boyunca iskanın kesintisiz sürdüğünü gösterir. M.Ö. 4. yüzyılın yerleşim düzeninde çarpıcı değişimler görülür. Öyle ki, Frig yönetimi boyunca hakimiyeti elinde tutan elit kesimin çekirdek yerleşimi olan sektör, madenciliği de içeren çeşitli endüstriyel etkinliklere ve konutlara ayrılmış bir alana dönüşür. Olasılıkla, höyükler üzerindeki yerleşim düzeninin değiştirilmesine neden olan, M.Ö. 4. yüzyılın başlarında meydana gelen bir depremdir. Akhamenid Dönemi'nin her iki evresi

boyunca, özellikle seramikler ve mühürler, yerleşmenin farklı sektörlerinde yaşayan grupların giderek daha da yoğun biçimde ticarete katıldıklarını, ancak aynı zamanda sektörlerin tüketim biçimlerinin birbirinden çok farklı olduğunu gösterir.

Son olarak *10. Bölüm*, seramik analizleri ve maddi kültüre dayanarak varılan sonuçlar ve sosyal grup oluşumlarına dair kanıtlar, Gordion ve Frigya'nın siyasi tarihi hakkındaki güncel bilgimiz çerçevesinde tartışılır. Bugüne dek GTÇ/EDÇ Güneybatı Asya ve Doğu Akdeniz'de siyasi ve ekonomik dönüşümlere dair kapsamlı sentezleri öne süren çalışmalarda, çoğunlukla, elit kesim stratejilerindeki değişimlere odaklanan ve genelden özele giden perspektifler benimsendiğine tekrar değinilir. Bu çalışmada, farklı olarak hem elit kesim hem de halkın günlük yaşamına ait maddi kültür kalıntılarının analizi yoluyla, Gordion'da yeni siyasi rejimlerin nasıl hayata geçirildiğine ve güç dengelerinin kentin günlük yaşamını nasıl şekillendirdiğine dair nüanslı bir anlayış geliştirilmiştir. Birbirinden farklı tür sosyal grupların oluşumunu belgelemeye odaklanan bu bakış açısı, hem siyasi olarak 'yukarıdan aşağı' ve toplumsal olarak 'aşağıdan yukarı' gelişen değişimlerin bir arada anlaşılmasına hem de siyasi ve sosyal gücün maddi kültürle beraber nasıl vücuda geldiğinin gözlenmesine olanak tanır. Aynı zamanda, ekonomik kaynaklar ve siyasi ekonomiye dair hiyerarşik kuramsal çerçevelere (ör. Hirth) ek olarak ritüel ekonominin toplumsal rolünü de irdeleyen bu bakış açısıyla, ritüel, ekonomi ve siyaset alanlarında örtüşen uygulamaların nitelikleri anlaşılmaya çalışılmıştır. Sonuç olarak, Gordion'da meydana gelen sosyal ve siyasi değişimlerin nitelikleri, M.Ö. 1. binyılın ilk yarısı boyunca akıcı bir süreç içinde maddi kültür öğelerine dönüştürülen semboller, mekanlar ve ortak etkinliklerde izlenebilmektedir.

References

Akça, E., J. Arocena, G. Kelling, et al. 2009 Firing temperatures and raw material sources of ancient Hittite ceramics of Asia Minor. *Transactions of the Indian Ceramic Society* 68(1):35–40.

Akürgal, M., M. Kerschner, H. Mommsen and W.-D. Niemeier 2002 Töpferzentren der Ostägäis. Archäometrische und archäologische Untersuchungen zur mykenischen, geometrischen und archaischen Keramik aus Fundorten in Westkleinasien (mit einem Beitrag von S. Ladstätter). In *Ergänzungsheft der Jahreshefte des Österreichischen Archäologischen Institutes*, vol. 3. Österreichischen Archäologischen Institutes, Wien.

Anderson, Gunlog 2012 In the shadow of Tumulus MM: the common cemetery and the Middle Phrygian houses at Gordion. In *The Archaeology of Phrygian Gordion, Royal City of Midas*, edited by C. B. Rose, pp. 171–188. Gordion Special Studies vol. 7. University of Pennsylvania Museum of Anthropology and Archaeology, Philadelphia.

Appadurai, Arjun 1988 *The Social Life of Things: Commodities in Cultural Perspective*. Cambridge University Press, Cambridge.

Arnold, Dean E. 1985 *Ceramic Theory and Cultural Process*. New Studies in Archaeology. Cambridge University Press, Cambridge.

— 1998 Ceramic ethnoarchaeology at Ticul, Yucatán, Mexico. *Society for Archaeological Sciences Bulletin* 21(1–2):6–7.

— 2008 *Social Change and the Evolution of Ceramic Production and Distribution in a Maya Community*. University Press of Colorado, Boulder.

Arnold, Dean E., Hector Neff, Ronald L. Bishop and Michael D. Glascock 1999 Testing interpretive assumptions of Neutron Activation Analysis: Contemporary pottery in Yucatán, 1964–1994. In *Material Meanings: Critical Approaches to the Interpretation of Culture*, edited by E. S. Chilton, pp. 61–84. University of Utah Press, Salt Lake City.

Arnold, Philip J., Christopher A. Pool, Ronald R. Kneebone and Robert S. Santley 1993 Intensive ceramic production and Classic-Period political economy in the Sierra de los Tuxtlas, Veracruz, Mexico. *Ancient Mesoamerica* 4(2):175–191.

Arthur, John W. 2006 *Living with Pottery: Ethnoarchaeology among the Gamo of Southwest Ethiopia*. University of Utah Press, Salt Lake City.

Aslan, Carolyn C. 2013 *Report on Ceramic Analysis Gordion 2013*. Gordion Archives, University of Pennsylvania Museum of Archaeology and Anthropology.

Aslan, Carolyn C. and Gülşah Günata 2016 Gordion, Troy and Maydos: The Late Bronze to Iron Age transition and the question of migration. Paper presented at the Archaeological Institute of America 117th Annual Meeting, San Francisco.

Aslan, Carolyn C. and Pavol Hnila 2015 Migration and integration at Troy from the end of the Late Bronze Age to the Iron Age. In *Nostoi: Indigenous Culture, Migration and Integration in the Aegean Islands and Western Anatolia during the Late Bronze and Early Iron Ages*, edited by N. Stampolidis, Ç. Maner and K. Kopanias, pp. 185–209. Koç University Press, Istanbul.

Aslan, Carolyn C., Lisa Kealhofer and Peter Grave 2014 The Early Iron Age at Troy reconsidered. *Oxford Journal of Archaeology* 33(3):275–312.

Aydıngün, Şengül and Haldun Aydıngün 2013 Erken Demirçağ'da "Istanbul Boğazı" Üzerinden Trak/Frig Kavimlerinin Anadolu'ya Geçişine Ait ilk Bulgular. *Arkeoloji ve Sanat* 142(January–April):65–78.

Aytaçlar, Nezih 2004 The Early Iron Age at Klazomenai. In *Proceedings of the International Symposium held at the Archaeological Museum of Abdera (Abdera, 20–21 October 2001)*, edited by A. Moustaka, E. Skarlatidou, M.-C. Tzannes and Y. Ersoy, pp. 17–42. 19th Ephorate of Prehistoric and Classical Antiquities of Komotini, Greek Ministry of Culture, Abdera.

Bacheva, Galya 2018 Pretty pots on the table: Dotted Triangle Ware in Late Phrygian Gordion. *Istanbuler Mitteilungen Deutsches Archäologisches Institute* 68:59–86.

Bahar, Hasan 1999 The Konya region in the Iron Age and its relations with Cilicia. *Anatolian Studies* 49:1–10.

Barjamovic, Gojko 2017 A commercial geography of Anatolia: integrating Hittite and Assyrian texts, archaeology and topography. In *Hittite Landscape and Geography*, edited by M. Weeden, L. Z. Ullmann and Z. Homan, pp. 311–318. Brill, Leiden.

Barth, Fredrik 1956 Ecological relationships of ethnic groups in Swat, North Pakistan. *American Anthropologist* 58:1079–1089.

    1969 Introduction. In *Ethnic Groups and Boundaries*, edited by F. Barth, pp. 9–38. Little Brown, Boston.

Bauer, Alexander A. and Owen P. Doonan 2012 Fluid histories: culture, community, and the longue durée of the Black Sea world. In *New Regionalism or No Regionalism? Emerging Regionalism in the Black Sea Area*, edited by R. Ivan, pp. 13–30. Ashgate, Burlington, VT.

Baxter, Michael J., Christian C. Beardah and Richard V. S. Wright 1997 Some archaeological applications of kernel density estimates. *Journal of Archaeological Science* 24(4):347–354.

Beardah, Christian C. 1999 Uses of multivariate kernel density estimates in archaeology. In *Archaeology in the Age of the Internet. CAA97. Computer Applications and Quantitative Methods in Archaeology. Proceedings of the 25th Anniversary Conference, University of Birmingham, April 1997*, edited by L. Dingwall, S. Exon, V. Gaffney, S. Laflin and M. van Leusen, 107-5 to 107-12. BAR International Series 750 CD-ROM Archaeopress, Oxford.

Beckman, Gary 1989 The religion of the Hittites. *Biblical Archaeologist* 52(2/3):98–108.

2000 Royal ideology and state administration in Hittite Anatolia. In *Civilizations of the Ancient Near East, Volume 1*, edited by J. Sasson, J. Baines, G. Beckman and K. S. Rubinson, pp. 529–543. Hendrickson, Peabody, MA.

Berg, Ina 2004 The meanings of standardisation: conical cups in the late Bronze Age Aegean. *Antiquity* 78(299):74–85.

Berlin, Andrea and Kathleen M. Lynch 2002 Going Greek: atticizing pottery in the Achaemenid world. *Studia Troica* 12:167–178.

Bernardini, Wesley 2000 Kiln firing groups: inter-household economic collaboration and social organization in the northern American Southwest. *American Antiquity* 65(2):365–377.

Binford, Lewis R. 1967 Smudge pits and hide-smoking: the use of analogy in archaeological reasoning. *American Antiquity* 32(1):1–12.

Bingöl, Ergüzer 1989 Türkiye Jeoloji Haritasi 1: 2 000 000: Geological Map of Turkey. General Directorate of Mineral Research and Exploration, Ankara.

Blackman, M. James, Gil J. Stein and Pamela B. Vandiver 1993 The standardization hypothesis and ceramic mass production: technological, compositional, and metric indexes of craft specialisation at Tell Leilan, Syria. *American Antiquity* 58(1):60–80.

Blanton, Richard E. 1994 *Houses and Households: A Comparative Study*. Plenum Press, New York.

Blanton, Richard E. and Lane F. Fargher 2008 *Collective Action in the Formation of Pre-Modern States*. Springer, New York.

Blinman, E. and Clint Swink 1997 Technology and organization of Anasazi trench kilns. In *The Prehistory and History of Ceramic Kilns*, edited by P. M. Rice, pp. 85–102. American Ceramic Society, Westerville, OH.

Bourdieu, Pierre 1973 The three forms of theoretical knowledge. *Social Science Information* 12(1):53–80.

 1977 *Outline of a Theory of Practice*. Translated by R. Nice. Cambridge University Press, Cambridge.

 1984 *Distinction: a social critique of the judgement of taste*. Harvard University Press & Routledge and Keagan Paul, Cambridge, MA.

 1990 *The Logic of Practice*. Stanford University Press, Redwood City, CA.

Bouthillier, Christina, Carlo Colantoni, Sofie Debruyne, et al. 2014 Further work at Kilise Tepe, 2007–2011: refining the Bronze to Iron Age transition. *Anatolian Studies* 64:95–161.

Bowser, Brenda J. 2000 From pottery to politics: an ethnoarchaeological study of political factionalism, ethnicity, and domestic pottery style in the Ecuadorian Amazon. *Journal of Archaeological Method and Theory* 7(3):219–248.

 2004 Prologue: toward an archaeology of place. *Journal of Archaeological Method and Theory* 11:1–3.

Braekmans, D., P. Degryse, J. Poblome, et al. 2011 Understanding ceramic variability: an archaeometrical interpretation of the Classical and Hellenistic ceramics at Düzen Tepe and Sagalassos (Southwest Turkey). *Journal of Archaeological Science* 38(9):2101–2115.

Bray, Tamara L. 2003 *The Archaeology and Politics of Food and Feasting in Early Atates and Empires*. Kluwer Academic/Plenum, New York.

Brixhe, Claude 2004 Corpus des inscriptions paléo-phrygiennes: Supplément II. *Kadmos* 43(1):1–130.

Brown, Ian W. 1979 Functional group changes and acculturation: a case study of the French and the Indian in the Lower Mississippi Valley. *Mid-Continental Journal of Archaeology* 4(2):147–165.

Brughmans, Tom 2010 Connecting the dots: towards archaeological network analysis. *Oxford Journal of Archaeology* 29(3):277–303.

Burke, Brendan 1998 From Minos to Midas: the organization of textile production in the Aegean and in Anatolia. PhD thesis, Archaeology, University of California, Los Angeles.

2005 Textile production at Gordion and the Phrygian economy. In *The Archaeology of Midas and the Phrygians: Recent Work at Gordion*, edited by L. Kealhofer, pp. 69–81. University of Pennsylvania Museum of Archaeology and Anthropology, Philadelphia.

2012 The rebuilt citadel at Gordion: Building A and the Mosaic Building Complex. In *The Archaeology of Phrygian Gordion, Royal City of Midas*, edited by C. B. Rose, pp. 203–218. University of Pennsylvania Museum of Archaeology and Anthropology, Philadelphia.

Burke, Heather 2012 *Meaning and Ideology in Historical Archaeology: Style, Social Identity, and Capitalism in an Australian Town*. Springer Science & Business Media, New York.

Cahill, Nicholas 1988 Taş Kule: a Persian-period tomb near Phokaia. *American Journal of Archaeology* 92(4):481–501.

2018 *Newsletter from Sardis, 2018*. Harvard University Press, Cambridge, MA.

2020 *Second Newsletter from Sardis, 2019*. Harvard University Press, Cambridge, MA.

Cammarosano, Michele 2018 *Hittite Local Cults*. Writings from the Ancient World 40. Society of Biblical Literature Press, Atlanta, GA.

Campbell, Colin 1994 Capitalism, consumption and the problem of motives: some issues in the understanding of conduct as illustrated by an examination of the treatment of motive and meaning in the works of Weber and Veblen. In *Consumption and Identity*, edited by J. Friedman, pp. 23–46. Harwood Academic Publishers, Chur, Switzerland.

Campbell, Roderick B. 2009 Toward a networks and boundaries approach to early complex societies. *Current Anthropology* 50(6):821–848.

Carballo, David M. and Gary M. Feinman 2016 Cooperation, collective action, and the archeology of large-scale societies. *Evolutionary Anthropology: Issues, News, and Reviews* 25(6):288–296.

Card, Jeb J. 2013 *The Archaeology of Hybrid Material Culture*. Southern Illinois University Press, Carbondale.

Castellano, L. 2018 Staple economies and storage in post-Hittite Anatolia: considerations in light of new data from Niğde-Kınık Höyük (southern Cappadocia). *Journal of Eastern Mediterranean Archaeology and Heritage Studies* 6(4):259–284.

Childe, V. Gordon 1925 *The Dawn of European Civilization*. Routledge, Trench, Trubner, London.

1942 *What Happened in History*. Pelican Books, Harmondsworth.

1951 *Man Makes Himself*. Mentor Books, New York.

Çilingiroğlu, Altan and David French (editors) 1991 *Anatolian Iron Ages: The Proceedings of the Second Anatolian Iron Ages Colloquium held at Izmir 4–8 May 1987*. British Institute of Archaeology at Ankara and Oxbow Books, Oxford.

1994 *Anatolian Iron Ages 3: The Proceedings of the Third Anatolian Iron Ages Colloquium held at Van, 6–12 August 1990*. British Institute of Archaeology at Ankara, Ankara.

Clunas, Craig 1991 *Superfluous Things: Material Culture and Social Status in Early Modern China*. Polity Press, Cambridge.

Codella, Kim and Mary M. Voigt in press Domestic architecture of Middle Phrygian Gordion. In From Midas to Cyrus and Other Stories. Papers on Anatolia in the Iron Age in honour of Geoffrey and Françoise Summers, edited by C. Draycott, S. Branting, J. Lehner and Y. Özarslan. British Institute of Archaeology at Ankara, Ankara.

Conkey, Margaret Wright and Christine A. Hastorf (editors) 1990 *The Uses of Style in Archaeology*. Cambridge University Press, Cambridge.

Conolly, James 2017 Costly signalling in archaeology: origins, relevance, challenges and prospects. *World Archaeology* 49(4):435–445.

Cordell, Ann S. 2014 Late seventeenth/early eighteenth-century Apalachee Colonoware pottery: a case study in continuity and change. In *Global Pottery 1: Historical Archaeology and Archaeometry for Societies in Contact*, edited by J. B. i Garrigós, M. M. i Fernández and J. G. Iñañez, pp. 165–174. BAR International Series 2761. Archaeopress, Oxford.

Costin, C. L. 1991 Craft specialization: issues in defining, documenting, and explaining the organization of production. *Journal of Archaeological Method and Theory* 3:1–56.

1993 Textiles, women, and political economy in Late Prehispanic Peru. *Research in Economic Anthropology* 14:3–28.

2007 Craft production systems. In *Archaeology at the Millennium: A Sourcebook*, edited by G. M. Feinman and T. D. Price, pp. 273–327. Springer USA, Boston, MA.

2020 What is a workshop? In *Approaches to the Analysis of Production Activity at Archaeological Sites*, edited by A. K. Hodgkinson and C. Lelek Tvetmarken, pp. 177–197. Archaeopress, Oxford.

Costin, C. L. and Timothy Earle 1989 Status distinction and legitimation of power as reflected in changing patterns of consumption in Late Prehispanic Peru. *American Antiquity* 54(4):691–714.

Costin, C. L. and M. B. Hagstrum 1995 Standardization, labor investment, skill and the organization of ceramic production in Late Prehispanic Highland Peru. *American Antiquity* 60(4):619–639.

Cowgill, George L. 1982 Clusters of objects and associations between variables: two approaches to archaeological classification. In *Essays on Archaeological Typology*, edited by R. Whallon and J. A. Brown, pp. 30–55. Center for American Archeology Press, Evanston, IL.

d'Alfonso, Lorenzo 2012 Tabal: an out-group definition in the first millennium BC. In *Leggo! Studies Presented to Frederick Mario Fales on the Occasion of His*

65th Birthday, edited by G. B. Lanfranchi, D. M. Bonacossi, C. Pappi and S. Ponchia, pp. 173–194. Harrassowitz, Wiesbaden.

2019 War in Anatolia in the post-Hittite period: the Anatolian hieroglyphic inscription of Topada revised. *Journal of Cuneiform Studies* 71(1):133–152.

2020 An age of experimentation: new thoughts on the multiple outcomes following the fall of the Hittite Empire after the results of the excavations at Niğde-Kınık Höyük (South Cappadocia). In *Anatolia between the 13th and 12th Century BCE*, edited by S. De Martino and E. Devecchi, pp. 95–116. LoGisma, Florence.

D'Altroy, T. N. and Timothy Earle 1985 Staple finance, wealth finance, and storage in the Inka political economy. *Current Anthropology* 26:187–206.

Dandoy, Jeremiah and Melinda A. Zeder 2011 *The Use of Nonparametric Statistics to Analyze Faunal Remains at Gordion, Turkey*. Gordion Archives, University of Pennsylvania Museum of Archaeology and Anthropology.

David, Nicholas, Judy Sterner and Kodzo Gavua 1988 Why pots are decorated. *Current Anthropology* 29(3):365–389.

DeMarrais, Elizabeth and Timothy Earle 2017 Collective action theory and the dynamics of complex societies. *Annual Review of Anthropology* 46:183–201.

DeVries, Keith 1977 Attic pottery in the Achaemenid Empire. *American Journal of Archaeology* 81(4):544–548.

1980 Greeks and Phrygians in the Early Iron Age. In *From Athens to Gordion: The Papers of a Memorial Symposium for Rodney S. Young, held at the University Museum, May 3rd, 1975*, edited by K. DeVries, pp. 33–49. University Museum of the University of Pennsylvania, Philadelphia.

1990 The Gordion excavation seasons of 1969–1973 and subsequent research. *American Journal of Archaeology* 94:371–406.

1997 The Attic pottery from Gordion. In *Athenian Potters and Painters*, edited by J. Oakley, W. D. E. Coulson and O. Palagia, pp. 447–455. Oxbow Books, Oxford.

2000 Gordion. *Expedition* 42(1):17–19.

2005 Greek pottery and Gordion chronology. In *The Archaeology of Midas and the Phrygians*, edited by L. Kealhofer, pp. 36–55. University of Pennsylvania Museum of Archaeology and Anthropology Press, Philadelphia.

2008 The age of Midas at Gordion and beyond. *Ancient Near Eastern Studies* 45:30–64.

2011a The creation of the old chronology. In *The Chronology of Iron Age Gordion*, edited by C. B. Rose and G. Darbyshire, pp. 13–22. University of Pennsylvania Museum of Archaeology and Anthropology, Philadelphia.

2011b Textual evidence and the Destruction Level. In *The New Chronology of Iron Age Gordion*, edited by C. B. Rose and G. Darbyshire, pp. 49–58. University of Pennsylvania Museum of Archaeology and Anthropology, Philadelphia.

DeVries, Keith, Peter Kuniholm, G. Kenneth Sams and Mary M. Voigt 2003 New dates for Iron Age Gordion. *Antiquity* 77(296): www.antiquity.ac.uk/projgall/devries296/

Dietler, Michael and Brian Hayden 2010 *Feasts: Archaeological and Ethnographic Perspectives on Food, Politics, and Power*. University of Alabama Press, Tuscaloosa.

Dobres, Marcia Anne 2000 *Technology and Social Agency*. Blackwell, Oxford.

Dobres, Marcia Anne and Christopher R. Hoffman 1994 Social agency and the dynamics of prehistoric technology. *Journal of Archaeological Method and Theory* 1(3):211–258.

Dobres, Marcia Anne and John E. Robb 2005 "Doing" agency: Introductory remarks on methodology. *Journal of Archaeological Method and Theory* 12(3):159–166.

Doonan, Owen 2010 Sinop landscapes: towards an archaeology of community in the hinterland of a Black Sea port. *Ancient Civilizations from Scythia to Siberia* 16(1-2):175–187.

Dörfler, W., C. Herking, R. Neef, R. Pasternak and A. von den Driesch 2011 Environment and economy in Hittite Anatolia. In *Insights into Hittite History and Archaeology*, edited by H. Genz and D. P. Mielke, pp. 99–124. Colloquia Antiqua 2. Peeters, Leuven.

Douglas, Mary and Baron Isherwood 1979 *The World of Goods: Towards an Anthropology of Consumption*. Routledge, New York.

Dunnell, Robert C. 1978 Style and function: a fundamental dichotomy. *American Antiquity* 43(2):192–202.

Dusinberre, Elspeth R. M. 1999 Satrapal Sardis: Achaemenid bowls in an Achaemenid capital. *American Journal of Archaeology* 103:73–102.

2003 *Aspects of Empire in Achaemenid Sardis*. Cambridge University Press, Cambridge.

2005 *Gordion Seals and Sealings: Individuals and Society*. Gordion Special Studies 124. University of Pennsylvania Museum of Archaeology and Anthropology, Philadelphia.

2010 Anatolian crossroads: Achaemenid seals from Sardis and Gordion. In *The World of Achaemenid Persia: History, Art and Society in Iran and the Ancient Near East, Proceedings of a conference at the British Museum, London*, edited by J. Curtis and S. J. Simpson, pp. 323–335. I. B. Tauris, London.

2013 *Empire, Authority, and Autonomy in Achaemenid Anatolia*. Cambridge University Press, Cambridge.

2019a The collapse of empire at Gordion in the transition from the Achaemenid to the Hellenistic world. *Anatolian Studies* 69:109–132.

2019b Gordion, on and off the grid. In *Spear-won Land: Sardis from the King's Peace to the Peace of Apamea*, edited by A. M. Berlin and P. J. Kosmin, pp. 220–234. University of Wisconsin, Madison.

Dusinberre, Elspeth R. M., Kathleen M. Lynch and Mary M. Voigt 2019 A mid-6th century BCE domestic deposit from Gordion in Central Anatolia: evidence for feasting and the Persian destruction. *Bulletin of the American School of Oriental Research* 382(7):143–209.

Dusinberre, Elspeth R. M. and Maya Vassileva 2018 The South Cellar: elite feasting at Gordion's Inner Court in the Middle Phrygian Period. In *Middle and Late Phrygian Gordion*, edited by C. B. Rose. Unpublished manuscript, University of Pennsylvania Museum of Archaeology and Anthropology, Philadelphia.

Earle, Timothy 1981 Comment on P. Rice, Evolution of specialized pottery production: a trial model. *Current Anthropology* 22(3):230–231.

2011 Redistribution and the political economy: the evolution of an idea. *American Journal of Archaeology* 115(2):237–244.

Eckert, Suzanne L., Kari L. Schleher and William D. James 2015 Communities of identity, communities of practice: understanding Santa Fe black-on-white pottery in the Española Basin of new Mexico. *Journal of Archaeological Science* 63:1–12.

Edwards, G. Roger 1959 The Gordion campaign of 1958: preliminary report. *American Journal of Archaeology* 63(3):263–268.

Eerkens, Jelmer and Carl P. Lipo 2007 Cultural transmission theory and the archaeological record: providing context to understanding variation and temporal changes in material culture. *Journal of Archaeological Research* 15(3):239–274.

Eisenstadt, Shmuel N. (editor) 2012 *The Origins and Diversity of Axial Age Civilizations*. SUNY Press, Albany.

Ertem, Esen and Şahinde Demirci 1999 Characteristics of Hittite pottery sherds from sites in the Kızılırmak Basin. *Journal of Archaeological Science* 26(8):1017–1023.

Fairbairn, Andrew and Sachihiro Omura 2005 Archaeological identification and significance of ÉSAG (Agricultural Storage Pits) at Kaman-Kalehöyük, Central Anatolia. *Anatolian Studies* 55:15–23.

Farnsworth, Paul 1987 The economics of acculturation in the California missions: A historical and archaeological study of Mission Nuestra Senora de la Soledad. PhD thesis, Archaeology Program, University of California, Los Angeles.

Feinman, Gary M. 2004 Archaeology and political economy: setting the stage. In *Archaeological Perspectives on Political Economies*, edited by G. M. Feinman and L. M. Nicholas, pp. 1–6. University of Utah Press, Salt Lake City.

Fields, Alison L. 2010 The Late Phrygian citadel of Gordion, Turkey: a preliminary study. Master's thesis, Classics, University of Cinncinati.

Fisher, Harl'O M. 1989 *A Nuclear Cross-section Data Handbook*. Los Alamos National Lab., Los Alamos, NM.

Foucault, Michel 1977 *Discipline and Punish: The Birth of the Prison*. Translated by A. Sheridan. Allen Lane, London.

1982 The subject and power. *Critical Inquiry* 8(4):777–795.

Fowles, Severin M. 2005 Historical contingency and the prehistoric foundations of moiety organization among the eastern Pueblos. *Journal of Anthropological Research* 61(1):25–52.

Frank, Andre Gunder 1993 Bronze Age world system cycles. *Current Anthropology* 34(4):383–430.

Fried, Morton H. 1967 *The Evolution of Political Society*. Random House, New York.

Friedman, Jonathan 1994 *Consumption and Identity*. Harwood Academic Publishers, Chur, Switzerland.

Friedrich, Margaret Hardin 1970 Design structure and social interaction: archaeological implications of an ethnographic analysis. *American Antiquity* 35(5):332–343.

Garcia, Margarita Diaz-Andreu, Sam Lucy, Stasa Babic and David N. Edwards 2005 *The Archaeology of Identity: Approaches to Gender, Age, Status, Ethnicity and Religion.* Routledge, London.

Gates, Marie-Henriette 2001 Potmarks at Kinet Höyük and the Hittite ceramic industry. In *La Cilicie: espaces et pouvoirs locaux (2e millenaire avant J.-C. – 4e siecle J.-C.)*, edited by E. Jean, A. M. Dincol and S. Durugonu, pp. 137–157. vol. 13. Institut Français d'Études Anatoliennes Georges Dumézil, Istanbul.

2007 Potters and consumers in Cilicia and the Amuq during the Age of Transformations (13th–10th centuries BC). Paper presented at the Societies in Transition. Evolutionary Processes in the Northern Levant between Late Bronze Age II and Early Iron Age. Papers Presented on the Occasion of the 20th Anniversary of the New Excavations in Tell Afis, Bologna, Italy.

2011 Southern and southeastern Anatolia in the Late Bronze Age. In *The Oxford Handbook of Ancient Anatolia, 10,000–323 BCE*, edited by S. Steadman and G. McMahon, pp. 393–412. Oxford University Press, New York.

Genz, Hermann 2000 The Early Iron Age in central Anatolia in light of recent research. *Near Eastern Archaeology* 63:111.

2003 The Early Iron Age in central Anatolia. In *Identifying Changes: The Transition from Bronze to Iron Ages in Anatolia and Its Neighboring Regions. Proceedings of the International Workshop Istanbul, November 8–9, 2002*, edited by B. Fischer, H. Genz, É. Jean and K. Köroğlu, pp. 179–192. Türk Eskiçağ Bilimleri Enstitüsü, Istanbul.

2005 Thoughts on the origin of the Iron Age pottery traditions in central Anatolia. In *Anatolian Iron Ages V Proceedings*, edited by A. Çilingiroğlu and G. Darbyshire, pp. 75–84. British Institute of Archaeology at Ankara, Ankara.

2007 Late Iron Age occupation on the Northwest Slope at Boğazköy. *Proceedings of the Anatolian Iron Ages 6: The Proceedings of the Sixth Anatolian Iron Ages Colloquium, 16–20 August 2004*:135–152. Peeters, Leuven.

2011 The Iron Age in central Anatolia. In *The Black Sea, Greece, Anatolia and Europe in the First Millennium BC*, edited by G. Tsetskhladze, pp. 331–368. Peeters, Leuven.

Genz, H. 2019 Iron Age burial customs. *Phrygia in Antiquity: From the Bronze Age to the Byzantine Period. Proceedings from the International Conference The Phrygian Lands over Time: From Prehistory to the Middle of the 1st Millennium AD, held at Anadolu University, Eskişehir, Turkey, 2nd–8th November, 2015.* Edited by G. Tsetskhladze, pp. 395–410. Peeters, Leuven.

Giddens, Anthony 1979 *Central Problems in Social Theory: Action, Structure, and Contradictions in Social Analysis.* University of California Press, Berkeley.

1984 *The Constitution of Society: Outline of the Theory of Structuration.* University of California Press, Berkeley.

Glascock, Michael D., Hector Neff and K. J. Vaughn 2004 Instrumental neutron activation analysis and multivariate statistics for pottery provenance. *Hyperfine Interactions* 154(1):95–105.

References

Glatz, Claudia 2009 Empire as network: Spheres of material interaction in Late Bronze Age Anatolia. *Journal of Anthropological Archaeology* 28(2):127–141.

2011 The Hittite state and empire from archaeological evidence. In *The Oxford Handbook of Ancient Anatolia (10,000-323 BCE)*, edited by S. Steadman and G. McMahon, pp. 877–899. Oxford University Press, New York.

2016a Introduction: Plain and simple? Another look at plain pottery traditions in early complex societies. In *Plain Pottery Traditions of the Eastern Mediterranean and Near East: Production, Use, and Social Significance*, edited by C. Glatz, pp. 13–37. Routledge, London.

2016b Plain pots, festivals and feasting in Late Bronze Age Anatolia. In *Plain Pottery Traditions of the Eastern Mediterranean and Near East: Production, Use, and Social Significance*, edited by C. Glatz, pp. 183–214. Routledge, London.

Glatz, Claudia and Roger Matthews 2005 Anthropology of a frontier zone: Hittite-Kaska relations in Late Bronze Age north-central Anatolia. *Bulletin of the American Schools of Oriental Research* (339):47–65.

Glendinning, Matt R. 2005 A decorated roof at Gordion: what tiles are revealing about the Phrygian past. In *The Archaeology of Midas and the Phrygians: Recent Work at Gordion*, edited by L. Kealhofer, pp. 82–100. University of Pennsylvania Museum of Archaeology and Anthropology, Philadelphia.

Goldman, Andrew L. and Mary M. Voigt 2014 Investigating Roman Gordion: report on the 1993–2005 excavations. Unpublished manuscript, University of Pennsylvania Museum of Archaeology and Anthropology Archives.

Goodenough, W. H. 1965 *Rethinking "Status" and "Role": Toward a General Model of the Cultural Organization of Social Relationships. The Relevance of Models for Social Anthropology*. ASA Monographs 1: 1–24. Tavistock, London.

Gosden, Chris and Yvonne Marshall 1999 The cultural biography of objects. *World Archaeology* 31(2):169–178.

Gosselain, Olivier P. 2000 Materializing identity: an African perspective. *Journal of Archaeological Method and Theory* 7:187–217.

Grave, Peter and Lisa Kealhofer 2006 Investigating Iron Age trade at Kaman Kalehöyük. *Anatolian Archaeological Studies XV, Kaman Kalehöyük* 15:139–150.

Grave, Peter, Lisa Kealhofer, Ben Marsh, G. Kenneth Sams, et al. 2009 Ceramic production and provenience at Gordion, Central Anatolia. *Journal of Archaeological Science* 36(10):2162–2176.

Grave, Peter, Lisa Kealhofer, Ben Marsh, Taciser Sivas and Hakan Sivas 2012 Reconstructing Iron Age community dynamics in Eskişehir province, central Turkey. *Journal of Archaeological Method and Theory* 19(3):377–406.

Grave, Peter, Lisa Kealhofer, Ben Marsh, Ulf-Dietrich Schoop, et al. 2014 Ceramics, trade, provenience and geology: Cyprus in the Late Bronze Age. *Antiquity* 88(342):1180–1200.

Grave, Peter, Lisa Kealhofer, Pavol Hnila, et al. 2013 Cultural dynamics and ceramic resource use at Late Bronze Age/Early Iron Age Troy, northwestern Turkey. *Journal of Archaeological Science* 40(4):1760–1777.

Grave, Peter, Lisa Kealhofer, Nejat Bilgen and Ben Marsh 2016 The archaeology of Achaemenid power in regional western Anatolia. *Cambridge Archaeological Journal* 26(4):697–720.

Greaves, Alan M. 2011 The Greeks in western Anatolia. In *The Oxford Handbook of Ancient Anatolia, 10,000–323 BCE*, edited by S. R. Steadman and G. McMahon, pp. 500–514. Oxford University Press, Oxford.

Greenewalt, C. H., Jr. 2011 Sardis: a first millennium C.E. capital in western Anatolia In *The Oxford Handbook of Ancient Anatolia (10,000–323 BCE)*, edited by S. R. Steadman and G. McMahon, pp. 1112–1130. Oxford University Press, Oxford.

Greenwood, Roberta S. 1980 The Chinese on Main Street. In *Archaeological Perspectives on Ethnicity in America*, edited by R. Schuyler, pp. 113–123. Baywood.

Gunter, Ann C. 1991 *The Bronze Age*. Gordion Excavations Final Reports III. University Museum of Archaeology and Anthropology, Philadelphia.

2006 Issues in Hittite ceramic production: a view from the western frontier. *Byzas* 4:349–364.

Gürtekin-Demir, R. Gül 2002 Lydian painted pottery at Daskyleion. *Anatolian Studies* 52:111–143.

2007 Provincial production of Lydian painted pottery. In *Proceedings of the Anatolian Iron Ages 6, The Proceedings of the Sixth Anatolian Iron Ages Colloquium Held at Eskişehir, 16–20 August 2004* Supplement 20:47-78. Peeters, Leuven.

2021 *Lydian Painted Pottery Abroad: The Gordion Excavations, 1950–1973*. University of Pennsylvania Press for the Museum of Archeology and Anthropology, Philadelphia.

Hardin, Margaret Ann 1991 Sources of ceramic variability at Zuni Pueblo. In *Ceramic Ethnoarchaeology*, edited by W. A. Longacre, pp. 40–70. University of Arizona Press, Tucson.

Hawkins, John D. 1982 The Neo-Hittite states in Syria and Anatolia. In *The Cambridge Ancient History*, edited by J. Boardman, I. E. S. Edwards, N. G. L. Hammond and E. Sollberger, pp. 372–441. 2nd ed. vol. 3, Part 1. Cambridge University Press, Cambridge.

Hayden, Brian 2009 The proof is in the pudding: feasting and the origins of domestication. *Current Anthropology* 50(5):597–601.

Hayden, Brian and Suzanne Villeneuve 2011 A century of feasting studies. *Annual Review of Anthropology* 40(1):433–449.

Hegmon, Michelle 1998 Technology, style, and social practices: Archaeological approaches. In *The Archaeology of Social Boundaries*, edited by M. Stark, pp. 264–279. Smithsonian Institution Press, Washington, DC.

1992 Archaeological research on style. *Annual Review of Anthropology* 21:517–536.

Helft, Susan 2010 Patterns of exchange/patterns of power: a new archaeology of the Hittite Empire. PhD thesis, Art and Archaeology of the Mediterranean World, University of Pennsylvania, Philadelphia.

Henrickson, Robert C. 1993 Politics, economics and ceramic continuity at Gordion in the late second and first millennia B.C. In *Social and Cultural Contexts of New Ceramic Technologies*, edited by W. D. Kingery, pp. 86–176. American Ceramic Society, Westerville, OH.

1994 Continuity and discontinuity in the ceramic tradition of Gordion during the Iron Age. In *Anatolian Iron Ages 3: Proceedings of the Third International*

Anatolian Iron Age Symposium at Van, August 6–12, edited by D. French and A. Çilingiroğlu, pp. 95–129. Oxbow Press, Ankara.

1995 A comparison of production of large storage vessels in two ancient ceramic traditions. In *Materials Research Society Symposium Proceedings*, edited by P. B. Vandiver, J. Druzik, J. L. Galvain, et al., pp. 553–571. Vol. 352. Materials Research Society, Pittsburgh, PA.

2001 The craft of the Early Phrygian potter. *Türk Arkeoloji ve Etnografya Dergisi* 2:35–46.

2002 Hittite pottery and potters: the view from Late Bronze Age Gordion. In *Across the Anatolian Plateau: Readings in the Archaeology of Ancient Turkey*, edited by D. Hopkins, pp. 123–132. vol. 57, N. Lapp, general editor. American Schools of Oriental Research, Boston, MA.

2005 The local potter's craft at Phrygian Gordion. In *The Archaeology of Midas and the Phrygians*, edited by L. Kealhofer, pp. 124–135. University of Pennsylvania Museum of Archaeology and Anthropology, Philadelphia.

2010 Ceramic development at Gordion. Gordion Archives, University of Pennsylvania Museum of Archaeology and Anthropology. Manuscript on file.

Henrickson, Robert C. and M. James Blackman 1996 Large-scale production of pottery at Gordion: comparison of the Late Bronze and Early Phrygian Industries. *Paléorient* 22(1):67–87.

1999 Hellenistic production of terracotta roof tiles among the ceramic industries at Gordion. *Oxford Journal of Archaeology* 18(3):307–326.

Henrickson, Robert C. and Mary M. Voigt 1998 The Early Iron Age at Gordion. In *Thracians and Phrygians: Problems of Parallelism. Proceedings of an International Symposium on the Archaeology, History, and Ancient Languages of Thrace and Phrygia, Ankara, 3–4 June 1985, Middle East Technical University*, edited by N. Tuna, Z. Akture and M. Lynch, pp. 79–106. Middle East Technical University, Ankara.

Henrickson, Robert C., Pamela B. Vandiver and M. James Blackman 2002 Lustrous black fine ware at Gordion, Turkey: a distinctive sintered slip technology. In *Materials Research Society Symposium Proceedings*, edited by P. B. Vandiver, M. Goodway and J. L. Mass, pp. 391–400. vol. 712. Materials Research Society, Pittsburgh, PA.

Hicks, Dan and Mary C. Beaudry 2010 Introduction: material culture studies: a reactionary view. In *The Oxford Handbook of Material Culture Studies*, edited by D. Hicks and M. C. Beaudry, pp. 1–21. Oxford University Press, Oxford.

Hirth, Kenneth 1996 Political economy and archaeology: perspectives on exchange and production. *Journal of Archaeological Research* 4(3):203–239.

2008 The economy of supply: modeling obsidian procurement and craft provisioning at a Central Mexican urban center. *Latin American Antiquity* 19(4):435–457.

Hnila, Pavol 2012 Pottery of Troy VIIB. Chronology, classification, context and implications of Trojan ceramic assemblages in the Late Bronze Age/Early Iron Age transition PhD thesis, Ur- und Frühgeschichte, Tübingen University, Tübingen, Germany.

Hodder, Ian 1982 *Symbols in Action: Ethnoarchaeological Studies of Material Culture*. Cambridge University Press, Cambridge.

Holzman, Samuel 2019 Unfolding a geometric textile from 9th-century Gordion. *Hesperia: The Journal of the American School of Classical Studies at Athens* 88(3):527–556.

Hoover, Robert 1989 Spanish-native interaction and acculturation in the Alta California missions. In *Columbian Consequences, Volume 1*, edited by D. H. Thomas, pp. 395–406. Smithsonian Institution Press, Washington, DC.

Hubert, Erell 2016 Figuring identity in everyday life. *Journal of Anthropological Archaeology* 44:1–13.

Imparati, Fiorella 2002 Palaces and local communities in some Hittite provincial seats. In *Recent Developments in Hittite Archaeology and History, Papers in Memory of Hans G. Güterbock*, edited by K. A. Yener and H. A. Hoffner, Jr., pp. 93–100. Eisenbrauns, Winona Lake, IN.

Ingold, Timothy 1993 The temporality of the landscape. *World Archaeology* 25:152–174.

Inomata, Takeshi and Lawrence S. Coben (editors) 2006 *Archaeology of Performance: Theaters of Power, Community, and Politics*. Altamira Press Rowman and Littlefield, Lanham, MD.

Insoll, Timothy 2007 *The Archaeology of Identities: A Reader*. Routledge, Abingdon.

Isbell, William H. 2000 What we should be studying: The "imagined community" and the "natural community". In *The Archaeology of Communities: A New World Perspective*, edited by M. Canuto and J. Yaeger, pp. 243–266. Routledge, London.

Jaspers, Karl 1949 *The Origins and Diversity of Axial Age Civilizations*. State University of New York Press, New York.

Johnston, Robert H. 1970 Pottery practices during the 6th–8th centuries B.C. at Gordion in Central Anatolia: an analytical and synthesizing study. PhD, Fine Arts, Pennsylvania State University, University Microfilms.

Jones, Janet Duncan 2009 Did the Phrygians make glass? Sources of moulded glass at Iron Age and Hellenistic Gordion. In *Annales of the 17th Congress of the International Association for the History of Glass, 2006*, edited by K. Janssens, P. Degryse, P. Cosyns, et al., pp. 21–26. International Association for the History of Glass. University Press Antwerp, Antwerp.

  2020 *The Glass Vessels*. Unpublished manuscript, University Museum of Archaeology and Anthropology, Philadelphia.

Jones, Sian 1997 *Archaeology and Ethnicity: Constructing Identities in the Past and the Present*. Routledge, New York.

Kahya, Tarkan 2002 Patara dark age pottery. *Adalya* 5:35–52.

Kaniewski, David, Joël Guiot and Elise Van Campo 2015 Drought and societal collapse 3200 years ago in the Eastern Mediterranean: a review. *Wiley Interdisciplinary Reviews: Climate Change* 6(4):369–382.

Karacic, Steven 2014 The archaeology of Hittite imperialism and ceramic production in Late Bronze Age IIA Tarsus-Gözlükule, Turkey. PhD thesis, Classical and Near Eastern Studies, Bryn Mawr College.

Kealhofer, Lisa (editor) 2005a *The Archaeology of Midas and the Phrygians: Recent Work at Gordion*. University of Pennsylvania Museum of Archaeology and Anthropology, Philadelphia.

2005b Settlement and land use: the Gordion regional survey. In *The Archaeology of Midas and the Phrygians: Recent Work at Gordion*, edited by L. Kealhofer, pp. 137–148. University of Pennsylvania Museum of Archaeology and Anthropology, Philadelphia.

Kealhofer, Lisa and Peter Grave 2008 Land use, political complexity and urbanism in mainland Southeast Asia. *American Antiquity* 73(2):200–225.

2011 The Iron Age on the central Anatolian plateau. In *The Oxford Handbook of Ancient Anatolia (10,000–323 BCE)*, edited by S. Steadman and G. McMahon, pp. 415–442. Oxford University Press, Oxford.

Kealhofer, Lisa and Ben Marsh 2019 Agricultural impact and political economy: niche construction in the Gordion region, central Anatolia. *Quaternary International* 529:91–99.

Kealhofer, Lisa, Peter Grave, Ben Marsh and Kimiyoshi Matsumura 2008 Analysis of specialized Iron Age Wares at Kaman-Kalehöyük. *Anatolian Archaeological Studies, Kaman-Kalehöyük* 17:201–223.

Kealhofer, Lisa, Peter Grave, Ben Marsh, et al. 2010 Patterns of Iron Age interaction in central Anatolia: three sites in Yozgat province. *Anatolian Studies* 60:71–92.

2013 Scaling ceramic provenience at Lydian Sardis, Western Turkey. *Journal of Archaeological Science* 40(4):1918–1934.

Kealhofer, Lisa, Peter Grave and A. Nejat Bilgen 2018 Economy and power: Achaemenid influence on regional economies in western Anatolia. In *Assyromania and More: In Memory of Samuel M. Paley*, edited by F. Pedde and N. Shelley, pp. 95–104. Zaphon, Munster.

Kealhofer, Lisa, Peter Grave and Mary M. Voigt 2019 Dating Gordion: the timing and tempo of Late Bronze and Early Iron Age political transformation. *Radiocarbon* 61(2):495–514.

Kent, Susan (editor) 1993 *Domestic Architecture and the Use of Space: An Interdisciplinary Cross-cultural Study*. Cambridge University Press, Cambridge.

Khatchadourian, Lori 2011 The Iron Age in eastern Anatolia. In *The Oxford Handbook of Eastern Anatolia (10,000–323 BCE)*, edited by S. Steadman and G. McMahon, pp. 464–499. Oxford University Press, Oxford.

2012 The Achaemenid provinces in archaeological perspective. In *A Companion to the Archaeology of the Ancient Near East, Volume 2*, edited by D. T. Potts, pp. 963–983. Wiley-Blackwell, Chichester.

2016 *Imperial Matter: Ancient Persia and the Archaeology of Empires*. University of California Press, Berkeley.

Kibaroğlu, Mustafa, Antonio Sagona and Muharrem Satir 2011 Petrographic and geochemical investigations of the late prehistoric ceramics from Sos Höyük, Erzurum (Eastern Anatolia). *Journal of Archaeological Science* 38(11):3072–3084.

Knapp, A. Bernard and Sturt W. Manning 2016 Crisis in context: the end of the Late Bronze Age in the eastern Mediterranean. *American Journal of Archaeology* 120(1):99–149.

Knappett, Carl 2011 *An Archaeology of Interaction: Network Perspectives on Material Culture and Society*. Oxford University Press, Oxford.

Koçak-Yaldır, Aylin 2011 Imported trade amphoras in Daskyleion from the seventh and sixth centuries BC and the Hellespontine-Phyrygia route. *World Archaeology* 43(3):364–379.

Kohler, Ellen L. 1980 Cremations of the Middle Phrygian period at Gordion. In *From Athens to Gordion: The Papers of a Memorial Symposium for Rodney S. Young*, edited by K. DeVries, pp. 65–89. University of Pennsylvania Museum of Archaeology and Anthropology, Philadelphia.

1995 *The Lesser Phrygian Tumuli, Part I, The Inhumations*. Gordion Excavations Final Reports II. University of Pennsylvania Museum, Philadelphia.

Kohler, Ellen L. and Elspeth R. M. Dusinberre 2022 *The Lesser Phrygian Tumuli, Part 2: The Cremations*. The Gordion Excavations 1950–1973, Final Reports. University of Pennsylvania Museum of Archaeology and Anthropology, Philadelphia.

Körte, Alfred 1897 Kleinasiatische Studien II: Gordion und der Zug des Manlius gegen die Galater, pp. 1–51. vol. 22. Mitteilungen des Deutschen Archäologischen Instituts, Athenische Abteilung.

Körte, Gustav and Alfred Körte 1904 *Gordion: Ergebnisse der Ausgrabung im Jahre 1900. Jahrbuch des Deutchen Archäologischen Instituts 5*. G. Reimer, Berlin.

Kozal, Ekin 2003 Analysis of the distribution patterns of Red Lustrous wheel-made ware, Mycenaean and Cypriot pottery in Anatolia in the 15th–13th centuries B.C. In *Identiyfing Changes: the Transition from Bronze to Iron Ages in Anatolia and its Neighbouring Regions*, edited by B. Fischer, H. Genz, E. Jean and K. Köroglu, pp. 65–78. Türk Eskiçag Bilimleri Enstitüsü, Istanbul.

Kramer, Carol 1985 Ceramic ethnoarchaeology. *Annual Review of Anthropology* 14:77–102.

Kuijt, Ian 2009 What do we really know about food storage, surplus, and feasting in preagricultural communities? *Current Anthropology* 50(5):641–644.

Kuniholm, Peter, Maryanne Newton and Richard Liebhart 2011 Dendrochronology at Gordion. In *The New Chronology of Iron Age Gordion*, edited by C. B. Rose and G. Darbyshire, pp. 79–122. University of Pennsylvania Museum of Archaeology and Anthropology, Philadelphia.

LaViolette, Adria Jean 2000 *Ethno-archaeology in Jenné, Mali: Craft and Status among Smiths, Potters and Masons*. British Archaeological Reports International Series 838 49. British Archaeological Reports Limited, Oxford.

Lawall, Mark L. 2010 Pontic, Aegean and Levantine amphorae at Gordion. *Publications de l'Institut Français d'Études Anatoliennes* 21(1):159–165.

2012 Pontic inhabitants at Gordion? Pots, people, and plans of houses at Middle Phrygian through Early Hellenistic Gordion. In *The Archaeology of Phrygian Gordion, Royal City of Midas*, edited by C. B. Rose, pp. 219–224. University of Pennsylvania Museum of Archaeology and Anthropology, Philadelphia.

Lechtman, Heather 1977 Style in technology - some early thoughts. In *Material Culture: Styles, Organization, and Dynamics of Technology*, edited by H. Lechtman and R. S. Merrill, pp. 3–20. West Publishing Co., St. Paul, MN.

1984 Andean value systems and the development of prehistoric metallurgy. *Technology and Culture* 25(1):1–36.

1993 Technologies of power: the Andean case. In *Configurations of Power: Holistic Anthropology in Theory and Practice*, edited by J. S. Henderson and P. Netherly, pp. 244–280. Cornell University Press, Ithaca, NY.

1996 Cloth and metal: the culture of technology. In *Andean Art at Dumbarton Oaks*, edited by E. H. Boone, pp. 33–43. vol. 1. Dumbarton Oaks Research Library and Collection, Washington, DC.

Lemonnier, Pierre 1992 *Elements for an Anthropology of Technology*. University of Michigan Museum, Ann Arbor.

1993 *Technological Choices: Transformations in Material Cultures since the Neolithic*. Routledge, New York.

Levi, Margaret 1988 *Of Rule and Revenue*. University of California Press, Berkeley.

Lewis, Oscar 1963 *Life in a Mexican Village: Tepoztlan Restudied*. University of Illinois Press, Urbana, IL.

Liebhart, Richard 2010 The tomb chamber complex in Tumulus MM at Gordion. In *Tartarlı: the Return of Colours*, edited by L. Summerer and A. von Kinlin, pp. 268–279. Yapı Kredi Kültür Sanat Yayıncılık, Istanbul.

Liebhart, Richard, Gareth Darbyshire, Evin Erder and Ben Marsh 2016 A fresh look at the tumuli of Gordion. In *Tumulus as Sema: Space, Politics, Culture and Religion in the First Millennium BC*, edited by O. Henry and U. Kelp, pp. 627–636. vol. 27. DeGruyter, Berlin.

Ligorio, O. and A. Lubotsky 2018 Languages of fragmentary attestation: Phrygian. In *Handbücher zur Sprach-und Kommunikationswissenschaft [Handbooks of Linguistics and Communication Science]*, edited by J. Klein, B. Joseph and M. Fritz, pp. 1816–1831. Walter de Gruyter GmbH, Berlin.

Lipo, Carl P. 2001 *Science, Style and the Study of Community Structure: An Example from the Central Mississippi River Valley*. Oxbow, Oxford.

Liverani, Mario 1987 The collapse of the Near Eastern regional system at the end of the Bronze Age: the case of Syria. In *Centre and Periphery in the Ancient World*, edited by M. Rowlands, M. Larsen and K. Kristiansen, pp. 66–73. Cambridge University Press, Cambridge.

Longacre, William A. 1999 Standardization and specialization: what's the link? In *Pottery and People: A Dynamic Interaction*, edited by J. M. Skibo and G. M. Feinman, pp. 44–58. University of Utah Press, Salt Lake City.

Longacre, William A., Kenneth L. Kvamme and Masashi Kobayashi 1988 Southwestern pottery standardization: an ethnoarchaeological view from the Philippines. *The Kiva* 53:101–112.

Lynch, Kathleen M. 2011 *The Symposium in Context: Pottery from a Late Archaic House Near the Athenian Agora*. Hesperia Supplement 46. American School of Classical Studies at Athens, Athens.

2016 Gordion cups and other Black Figure cups at Gordion in Phrygia. In *The Consumers' Choice. Uses of Greek Figure-Decorated Pottery*, edited by T. Carpenter, E. Langridge-Noti and M. Stansbury-O'Donnell, pp. 41–63. Special Papers in Art and Architecture. Archaeological Institute of America, Boston, MA.

Lyons, Patrick D. and Jeffery J. Clark 2008 Interaction, enculturation, social distance, and ancient ethnic identities. In *Archaeology without Borders: Contact, Commerce, and Change in the US Southwest and Northwestern Mexico*, edited by L. D. Webster and M. McBrinn, pp. 185–207. University Press of Colorado, Boulder.

Mac Sweeney, Naoíse 2011 *Community Identity and Archaeology: Dynamic Communities at Aphrodisias and Beycesultan*. University of Michigan Press, Ann Arbor.

Mann, Michael 1986 *The Sources of Social Power, Volume 1, A History of Power from the beginning to AD 1760*. Cambridge University Press, Cambridge.

Manuelli, Federico 2012 A view from the East. Arslantepe and the Central Anatolian world during the Late Bronze and Iron Ages: interactions and local development. In *Proceedings of the 7th International Congress on the Archaeology of the Ancient Near East, Vol. 1*, edited by R. Matthews and J. Curtis, pp. 447–460. Harrassowitz Verlag, Wiesbaden.

Marsh, Ben 1999 Alluvial burial of Gordion, an Iron Age city in Anatolia. *Journal of Field Archaeology* 26(2):163–175.

— 2005 Physical geography, land use, and human impact at Gordion. In *The Archaeology of Midas and the Phrygians*, edited by L. Kealhofer, pp. 161–171. University of Pennsylvania Museum of Archaeology and Anthropology, Philadelphia.

— 2012 Reading Gordion settlement history from stream sedimentation. In *The Archaeology of Phrygian Gordion, Royal City of Midas*, edited by C. B. Rose, pp. 39–45. Gordion Special Studies 7. University of Pennsylvania Museum of Archaeology and Anthropology, Philadelphia.

Marsh, Ben and Lisa Kealhofer 2014 Scales of impact: settlement history and landscape change in the Gordion region, central Anatolia. *The Holocene* 24(6):689–701.

Marston, John M. 2012 Agricultural strategies and political economy in ancient Anatolia. *American Journal of Archaeology* 116(3):377–403.

— 2017 *Agricultural Sustainability and Environmental Change at Ancient Gordion*. Special Studies 8. University of Pennsylvania Museum of Archaeology and Anthropology, Philadelphia.

Matsumura, Kimiyoshi 2008 The Early Iron Age in Kaman-Kalehöyük: the search for its roots. In *Fundstellen Gesammelte Schriften zur Archäologie und Geschichte Altvorderasiens ad honorem Hartmut Kühne*, edited by D. Bonatz, R. M. Czichon and F. J. Kreppner, pp. 42–51. Harrassowitz Verlag, Wiesbaden.

Matsumura, Kimiyoshi and Mark Weeden 2017 Central West: Archaeology. In *Hittite Landscape and Geography*, edited by M. Weeden, L. Z. Ullmann and Z. Homan, pp. 106–118. Brill, Leiden.

Mauss, Marcel 1967 *The Gift: Forms and Functions of Exchange in Arachaic Societies*. Translated by I. Cunnison. W. W. Norton, New York.

McAnany, Patricia A. and E. Christian Wells 2008 Toward a theory of ritual economy. In *Dimensions of Ritual Economy*, edited by P. A. McAnany and E. C. Wells, pp. 1–16. Emerald Group Publishing Limited, Bingley.

McGovern, Patrick E. 2000 The funerary banquet of "King Midas." *Expedition* 42(1):21–29.

McGovern, Patrick E., Donald L. Glusker, Robert A. Moreau, et al. 1999 A funerary feast fit for King Midas. *Nature* 402:863–864.

Mellaart, James 1955 Iron Age pottery from southern Anatolia. *Belleten (Türk Tarih Kurumu)* 19:115–136.

Mellaart, James and Ann Murray 1995 *Beycesultan Vol. III, Part II: Late Bronze Age and Phrygian Pottery and Middle and Late Bronze Age Small Objects*. Occasional Publication 12. British Institute of Archaeology at Ankara Monograph, London.

Mellink, Machteld J. 1956 *A Hittite Cemetery at Gordion*. Museum Monographs. University of Pennsylvania Museum, Philadelphia, PA.

1959 The city of Midas. *Scientific American* 201(1):100–112.

1980 Archaic wall paintings from Gordion. In *From Athens to Gordion: The Papers of a Memorial Symposium for Rodney S. Young*, edited by K. DeVries, pp. 91–98. University Museum Papers 1. University of Pennsylvania Museum, Philadelphia.

Merton, Robert King 1968 *Social Theory and Social Structure*. Simon and Schuster, New York.

Meskell, Lynn 2007 Archaeologies of identity. In *The Archaeology of Identities: A Reader*, edited by T. Insoll, pp. 23–43. Routledge, New York.

Mielke, Dirk Paul 2006 *Kuşaklı-Sarissa 2: The Pottery From the Western Slope*. Verlag Maria Leidorf, Rahden/Westfalia.

2007 Red Lustrous Wheelmade Ware from Hittite dontexts. In *Lustrous Wares of Cyprus and the Eastern Mediterranean*, edited by I. Hein, pp. 155–168. Austrian Academy of Sciences, Vienna.

2011a Hittite cities: looking for a concept. In *Insights into Hittite History and Archaeology*, edited by H. Genz and D. P. Mielke, pp. 153–194. vol. 2 Colloquia Antiqua. Peeters, Leuven.

2011b Key sites of the Hittite Empire. In *The Oxford Handbook of Ancient Anatolia (10,000–323 BCE)*, edited by S. Steadman and G. McMahon, pp. 1031–1054. Oxford University Press, Oxford.

2016 Produktion und Distribution von Keramik im Rahmen der hethitischen Wirtschaftsorganisation. In *Wirtschaft als Machtbasis* edited by Katja Piesker, pp. 155–185. Byzas 22. Deutchen Archäologischen Instituts, Istanbul.

2017 Hittite settlement policy. In *Places and Spaces in Hittite Anatolia I: Hatti and the East*, edited by M. Alparslan, pp. 13–27. Proceedings of an International Workshop on Hittite Historical Geography. Türk Eskiçağ Bilimleri Enstitüsü, İstanbul.

Miller, Daniel (editor) 1995 *Acknowledging Consumption: A Review of New Studies*. Routledge, London.

Miller, G. Logan 2015 Ritual economy and craft production in small-scale societies: evidence from microwear analysis of Hopewell bladelets. *Journal of Anthropological Archaeology* 39:124–138.

Miller, Naomi F. 2010 *Botanical Aspects of Environment and Economy at Gordion, Turkey*. Gordion Special Studies 5. University of Pennsylvania Museum of Archaeology and Anthropology, Philadelphia.

Miller, Naomi F., Melinda A. Zeder and Suzanne Arter 2009 From food and fuel to farms and flocks: the integration of plant and animal remains in the study of the agropastoral economy at Gordion, Turkey. *Current Anthropology* 50(6):915–924.

Mills, Barbara J. (editor) 2004 *Identity Feasting and the Archaeology of the Greater Southwest, Proceedings of the 2002 Southwest Symposium*. University Press of Colorado, Boulder.

2016 Communities of consumption: Cuisines as constellated networks of situated practice. In *Knowledge in Motion: Constellations of Learning Across Time and Place*, edited by A. P. Roddick and A. B. Stahl, pp. 247–270. University of Arizona Press, Tucson.

Miracle, Preston and Nicky Milner 2002 *Consuming Passions and Patterns of Consumption*. McDonald Institute Monographs. McDonald Institute for Archaeological Research, University of Cambridge, Cambridge.

Mora, Clelia and Lorenzo d'Alfonso 2012 Anatolia after the end of the Hittite Empire: new evidence from Southern Cappadocia. *Origini* 34:385–398.

Morgan, Kathryn R. 2018 A moveable feast: production, consumption, and state formation at Early Phrygian Gordion. PhD thesis, Art and Archaeology of the Mediterranean World, University of Pennsylvania, Philadelphia.

Morgan, Lewis Henry 1877 *Ancient Society*. 1964 ed. Belknap Press, Cambridge, MA.

Müller-Karpe, Andreas 1988 *Hethitische Töpferei der Oberstadt von Hattuša: Ein Beitrag zur Kenntnis spät-grossreichszeitlicher Keramik und Töpferbetriebe unter Zugrundelegung der Grabungsergebnisse von 1978–82 in Boğazköy*. Marburger Studien zur Vor- und Frühgeschichte, Band 10. Hitzeroth, Marburg.

2000 Die Akropolis der hethitischen Stadt Kuşaklı-Sarissa. *Nürnberger Blätter zur Archäologie* 16:91–110.

2009 The rise and fall of the Hittite Empire in the light of dendroarchaeological research. In *Tree-Rings, Kings and Old World Archaeology and Environment: Papers Presented in Honor of Peter Ian Kuniholm*, edited by S. Manning and M. J. Bruce, pp. 253–262. Oxbow Books, Oxford.

Mullins, Paul R. 2011 The archaeology of consumption. *Annual Review of Anthropology* 40(1):133–144.

Muscarella, Oscar W. 1989 King Midas of Phrygia and the Greeks. In *Anatolia and the Ancient Near East. Studies in Honor of Tahsin Özgüç*, edited by K. Emre, M. Mellink, B. Hrouda and N. Özgüç, pp. 333–344. Türk Tarih Kurumu Basımevi, Ankara.

Neff, Hector 1993 Theory, sampling, and analytical techniques in the archaeological study of prehistoric ceramics. *American Antiquity* 58(1):23–44.

Neff, Hector, Ronald L. Bishop and Edward V. Sayre 1989 More observations on the problem of tempering in compositional studies of archaeological ceramics. *Journal of Archaeological Science* 16(1):57–69.

Neupert, Mark A. 2000 Clays of contention: An ethnoarchaeolgoical study of factionalism and clay composition. *Journal of Archaeological Method and Theory* 7:249–272.

Neyt, B., Dennis Braekmans, Jeroen Poblome, et al. 2012 Long-term clay raw material selection and use in the region of Classical/Hellenistic to Early Byzantine Sagalassos (SW Turkey). *Journal of Archaeological Science* 39(5):1296–1305.

Nichols, Deborah L., Elizabeth M. Brumfiel, Hector Neff, et al. 2002 Neutrons, markets, cities, and empires: a 1000-year perspective on ceramic production and distribution in the Postclassic Basin of Mexico. *Journal of Anthropological Archaeology* 21(1):25–82.

Niemeier, Wolf-Dietrich 2005 Minoans, Mycenaeans, Hittites and Ionians in western Asia Minor: new excavations in Bronze Age Miletus-Millawanda. In *The Greeks in the East*, edited by A. Villing, pp. 1–36. British Museum Research Publication vol 157. British Museum Press, London.

Obrador-Cursach, Bartomeu 2019 On the place of Phrygian among the Indo-European Languages. *Journal of Language Relationship* 17(3):233–245.

Odess, Daniel 1998 The archaeology of interaction: Views from artifact style and material exchange in Dorset society. *American Antiquity* 63(3):417–435.

Omura, Sachihiro 2011 Kaman-Kalehöyük excavations in central Anatolia. In *The Oxford Handbook of Ancient Anatolia (10,000–323 BCE)*, edited by S. Steadman and G. McMahon, pp. 1095–1111. Oxford University Press, Oxford.

Ortner, Sherry B. 2006 *Anthropology and Social Theory: Culture, Power and the Acting Subject*. Duke University Press, Durham, NC.

Osborne, James F. 2013 Sovereignty and territoriality in the city-state: a case study from the Amuq Valley, Turkey. *Journal of Anthropological Archaeology* 32(4):774–790.

  2020 The city of Hartapu: results of the Türkmen-Karahöyük Intensive Survey Project. *Anatolian Studies* 70:1–27.

Papadopoulos, John K., James F. Vedder and Toby Schreiber 1998 Drawing circles: experimental archaeology and the pivoted multiple brush. *American Journal of Archaeology* 102(3):507–529.

Parkinson, William A., Dimitri Nakassis and Michael L. Galaty 2013 Crafts, specialists, and markets in Mycenaean Greece. Introduction. *American Journal of Archaeology* 117(3):413–422.

Parzinger, Hermann and Rosa Sanz 1992 *Die Oberstadt von Hattuša. Hethitische Keramik aus dem zentralen Tempelviertel. Funde aus den Grabungen 1982–1987*. Boğazköy-Hattuša: Ergebniss der Ausgrabungen 15. Gebrüder Mann, Berlin.

Pauketat, Timothy R. 2001 Practice and history in archaeology: an emerging paradigm. *Anthropological Theory* 1(1):73–98.

  2007 *Chiefdoms and Other Archaeological Delusions*. Altamira, Lanham, MD.

Peacock, David P. S. 1982 *Pottery in the Roman World: An Ethnoarchaeological Approach*. Longman, London.

Petrie, Cameron A., Peter Magee and M. Nasim Khan 2008 Emulation at the edge of empire: the adoption of non-local vessel forms in the NWFP, Pakistan during the mid-late 1st millennium BC. *Gandharan Studies* 2:1–16.

Pfaffenberger, Bryan 1988 Fetishised objects and humanised nature: towards an anthropology of technology. *Man* 23(2):236–252.

  1992 Social anthropology of technology. *Annual Review of Anthropology* 21:491–516.

  1993 The factory as artifact. In *Technological Choices: Transformations in Material Cultures since the Neolithic*, edited by P. LeMonnier, pp. 338–371. Routledge, New York.

Plog, Stephen 1983 Analysis of style in artifacts. *Annual Review of Anthropology* 12:125–142.

Plourde, Aimée M. 2008 The origins of prestige goods as honest signals of skill and knowledge. *Human Nature* 19:374–388.

Pluckhahn, Thomas 2010 Household archaeology in the southeastern United States: history, trends, and challenges. *Journal of Archaeological Research* 18(4):331–385.

Porter, Benjamin W. 2016 Assembling the Iron Age Levant: the archaeology of communities, polities, and imperial peripheries. *Journal of Archaeological Research* 24(4):1–48.

Postgate, J. Nicholas 2007 The ceramics of centralisation and dissolution: a case study from Rough Cilicia. *Anatolian Studies* 57:141–150.

Preucel, Robert W. 2000 Making pueblo communities: architectural discourse at Kotyiti, New Mexico. In *The Archaeology of Communities: A New World Perspective*, edited by M.-A. Canuto and J. Yaeger, pp. 58–77. Routledge, London.

Rademakers, Frederik W., Thilo Rehren and Mary M. Voigt 2018 Bronze metallurgy in the Late Phrygian settlement of Gordion, Turkey. *Journal of Archaeological and Anthropological Sciences* 10(7):1645–1672.

Redfield, Robert 1947 The folk society. *American Journal of Sociology* 52(4):293–308.

1953 The natural history of the folk society. *Social Forces* 31(3):224–228.

1955 Societies and cultures as natural systems. *Journal of the Royal Anthropological Institute of Great Britain and Ireland* 85(1–2):19–32.

Rice, Prudence M. (editor) 1984 *Pots and Potters: Current Approaches in Ceramic Archaeology*. Institute of Archaeology Monograph XXIV. University of California, Los Angeles.

1987 *Pottery Analysis: A Sourcebook*. University of Chicago Press, Chicago, IL.

1996 Recent ceramic analysis: 2. Composition, production, and theory. *Journal of Archaeological Research* 4(3):165–202.

2015 *Pottery Analysis: A Sourcebook*. 2nd ed. University of Chicago Press, Chicago, IL.

Roberts, Michael 1994 The cultured gentleman: the appropriation of manners by the middle class in British Ceylon. *Proceedings of the Anthropological Forum* 7:55–73.

Roberts, Neil, Samantha L. Allcock, Fabien Arnaud, et al. 2016 A tale of two lakes: a multi-proxy comparison of late glacial and Holocene environmental change in Cappadocia, Turkey. *Journal of Quaternary Science* 31(4):348–362.

Rodman, Margaret C. 1992 Empowering place: multilocality and multivocality. *American Anthropologist* 94(3):640–656.

Roller, Lynn E. 1991 The great mother at Gordion: the Hellenization of an Anatolian cult. *Journal of Hellenistic Studies* 111:128–143.

1999 Early Phrygian drawings from Gordion and the elements of Phrygian artistic style. *Anatolian Studies* 49:143–152.

2008 Early Phrygian sculpture: refining the chronology. *Ancient Near Eastern Studies* 45:188–201.

2011 Phrygia and the Phrygians. In *The Oxford Handbook of Ancient Anatolia (10,000–323 BCE)*, edited by S. Steadman and G. McMahon, pp. 560–578. Oxford University Press, Oxford.

Rose, C. Brian (editor) 2012a *The Archaeology of Phrygian Gordion, Royal City of Midas*. Gordion Special Studies 7. University of Pennsylvania Museum of Archaeology and Anthropology, Philadelphia.

2012b Introduction. In *The Archaeology of Phrygian Gordion, Royal City of Midas*, edited by C. B. Rose, pp. 1–19. Gordion Special Studies. vol. 7. University of Pennsylvania Museum of Archaeology and Anthropology, Philadelphia.

2017 Fieldwork at Phrygian Gordion, 2013–2015. *American Journal of Archaeology* 121(1):135–178.

2018 The architecture and stratigraphy of Middle and Late Phrygian Gordion. In Middle and Late Phrygian Gordion, edited by C. B. Rose. Unpublished manuscript, University of Pennsylvania Museum of Archaeology and Anthropology, Philadelphia.

Rose, C. Brian and Gareth Darbyshire (editors) 2011 *The New Chronology of Iron Age Gordion*. University of Pennsylvania Museum of Archaeology and Anthropology, Philadelphia.

Rose, C. Brian and Ayşe Gürsan-Salzman 2017 *Friends of Gordion Newsletter 2017*. University of Pennsylvania Museum of Archaeology and Anthropology, Philadelphia.

2018 *Friends of Gordion Newsletter 2018*. University of Pennsylvania Museum of Archaeology and Anthropology, Philadelphia.

Ross, Jennifer C. 2010 Çadır Höyük, the upper South Slope 2006–2009. *Anatolica* 36:67–87.

Rotroff, Susan I. 2006 *Hellenistic Pottery, the Plain Wares*. Vol. 33 American School of Classical Studies, Princeton, NJ.

Roux, Valentine 2003 Ceramic standardization and intensity of production: quantifying degrees of specialization. *American Antiquity* 68(4):768–782.

Sackett, James R. 1977 The meaning of style in archaeology: a general model. *American Antiquity* 42(3):369–380.

1990 Style and ethnicity in archaeology: the case for isochrestism. In *The Uses of Style in Archaeology*, edited by M. Conkey and C. Hastorf, pp. 32–43. New Directions in Archaeology. Cambridge University Press, Cambridge.

Sagona, Antonio 1999 The Bronze Age-Iron Age transition in northeast Anatolia: a view from Sos Höyük. *Anatolian Studies* 49:153–157.

Sall, John, Mia L Stephens, Ann Lehman and Sheila Loring 2017 *JMP Start Statistics: A Guide to Statistics and Data Analysis Using JMP*. SAS Institute, Cary, NC.

Sams, G. Kenneth 1974 Phrygian painted animals: Anatolian orientalizing art. *Anatolian Studies* 24:169–196.

1977 Beer in the city of Midas. *Archaeology* 30:108–115.

1978 Schools of painting in Early Iron Age Anatolia. In *Proceedings of the Xth International Congress of Classical Archaeology*, pp. 227–236. Ankara.

1988 The early Phrygian period at Gordion: toward a cultural identity. *Source: Notes in the History of Art* 7(3/4):9–15.

1989 Sculpted orthostates at Gordion. In *Anatolia and the Ancient Near East: Studies in Honor of Tahsin Özgüç*, edited by K. Emre, B. Hrouda, M. Mellink and N. Özgüc, pp. 447–454. Türk Tarih Kurumu Basımevi, Ankara.

1994 *The Early Phrygian Pottery*. Gordion Excavations Final Reports 4. University of Pennsylvania Museum of Archaeology and Anthropology, Philadelphia.

1995 Midas of Gordion and the Anatolian kingdom of Phrygia. In *Civilizations of the Ancient Near East*, edited by J. Sasson, pp. 1147–1159. Charles Scribner and Sons, New York.

1997 Gordion and the kingdom of Phrygia. In *Frigi e Frigio*, edited by R. Gusmani, M. Salvini and P. Vanniecelli, pp. 239–248. Consiglio Nazionale delle Ricerche, Rome.

2005 Gordion: exploration over a century. In *The Archaeology of Midas and the Phrygians: Recent Work at Gordion*, edited by L. Kealhofer, pp. 10–21. University of Pennsylvania Museum, Philadelphia.

2011a Anatolia: the first millennium BC in historical context. In *Oxford Handbook of Ancient Anatolia (10,000–323 BCE)*, edited by S. Steadman and G. McMahon, pp. 604–622. Oxford University Press, Oxford.

2011b Artifacts. In *The New Chronology of Iron Age Gordion*, edited by C. B. Rose and G. Darbyshire, pp. 59–78. Gordion Special Studies 6. University of Pennsylvania Museum of Archaeology and Anthropology, Philadelphia.

2012 The new chronology for Gordion and Phrygian pottery. In *The Archaeology of Phrygian Gordion, Royal City of Midas*, edited by C. B. Rose, pp. 56–66. Gordion Special Studies 7. University of Pennsylvania Museum of Archaeology and Anthropology, Philadelphia.

in press Gordion and Phrygia in the seventh century. In *From Midas to Cyrus and Other Stories: Papers on Anatolia in the Iron Age in Honour of Geoffrey and Françoise Summers*, edited by C. Draycott, S. Branting, J. Lehner and Y. Özarslan. British Institute of Archaeology at Ankara, Ankara.

Sams, G. Kenneth and Brendan Burke 2008 Gordion, 2006. *Kazı Sonuçları Toplantısı* 29 (2):329–342.

Sams, G. Kenneth and Mary M. Voigt 1995 Gordion archaeological activities 1993. *Kazı Sonuçları Toplantısı* 16(1):369–392.

1996 Gordion archaeological activities, 1994. *Kazı Sonuçları Toplantısı* 17(1):433–452.

2011 In conclusion. In *The New Chronology of Iron Age Gordion*, edited by C. B. Rose and G. Darbyshire, pp. 155–168. Gordion Special Studies 6. University of Pennsylvania Museum of Archaeology and Anthropology, Philadelphia.

Sams, G. Kenneth, Brendan Burke and Andrew L. Goldman 2007 Gordion, 2005. *Kazı Sonuçları Toplantısı* 28(2):365–386.

Schaus, Gerald P. 1992 Imported West Anatolian pottery at Gordion. *Anatolian Studies* 42: 151–177.

Schoop, Ulf-Dietrich 2003 Pottery traditions of the later Hittite Empire: problems of definition. In *Identifying Changes: The Transition from Bronze to Iron Ages in Anatolia and its Neighboring Regions. Proceedings of the International Workshop Istanbul, November 8–9, 2002*, edited by B. Fischer, H. Genz,

E. Jean and K. Köroğlu, pp. 167–178. Türk Eskiçağ Bilimleri Enstitüsü, Istanbul.

2006 Dating the Hittites with statistics: ten pottery assemblages from Boğazköy-Hattuša. In *Structuring and Dating in Hittite Archaeology*, edited by D. P. Mielke, U.-D. Schoop and J. Seeher, pp. 215–240. Byzas 4. Deutsches Archäologisches Institut, Istanbul.

2009 Indications of structural change in the Hittite pottery inventory at Boğazköy-Hattuša. In *Central-North Anatolia in the Hittite Period: New Perspectives in Light of Recent Research* edited by F. P. Daddi, G. Torri and C. Corti, pp. 145–168. Studia Asiana 5. Herder, Rome.

2011 Hittite pottery: a summary. In *Insights into Hittite History and Archaeology*, edited by H. Genz and D. P. Mielke, pp. 241–274. Peeters, Leuven.

Schoop, Ulf-Dietrich and Jürgen Seeher 2006 Absolute chronologie in Boğazköy-Hattuša: das potential der radiokarbondaten. In *Structuring and Dating in Hittite Archaeology*, edited by D. P. Mielke, U.-D. Schoop and J. Seeher, pp. 53–75. Deutsches Archäologisches Institut, Istanbul.

Schoop, Ulf-Dietrich, Peter Grave, Lisa Kealhofer and G. Jacobsen 2009 Radiocarbon dates from Chalcolithic Çamlıbel Tarlası. In *Die Ausgrabungen in Boğazköy-Hattuša 2008*, edited by A. Schachner, pp. 66–67. Deutsches Archäologisches Institut, Istanbul.

Schortman, Edward 2014 Networks of power in archaeology. *Annual Review of Anthropology* 43(1):167–182.

Schortman, Edward and Patricia Urban (editors) 1992 *Resources, Power, and Interregional Interaction*. Plenum Press, New York.

2004 Modeling the roles of craft production in ancient political economies. *Journal of Archaeological Research* 12(2):185–226.

Seeher, Jürgen 1995 Die Ausgrabungen in Boğazköy-Hattuša 1994. *Archäologischer Anzeiger* 4:597–625.

2006 Chronology in Hattuša: new approaches to an old problem. In *Structuring and Dating in Hittite Archaeology* edited by D. P. Mielke, U.-D. Schoop and J. Seeher, pp. 197–213. Byzas 4. Deutsches Archäologisches Institut, Istanbul.

2011 The plateau: the Hittites. In *The Oxford Handbook of Ancient Anatolia, 10,000–323 BCE*, edited by S. Steadman and G. McMahon, pp. 376–392. Oxford University Press, New York.

Service, Elman R. 1975 *The Origins of the State and Civilisation*. W. W. Norton, New York.

Shackel, Paul A. and Barbara J. Little 1992 Post-processual approaches to meanings and uses of material culture in historical archaeology. *Historical Archaeology* 26(3):5–11.

Sheftel, Phoebe in press *The Bone and Ivory Objects from Gordion*. Gordion Special Studies. University of Pennsylvania Museum of Archaeology and Anthropology, Philadelphia.

Shennan, Stephen J. (editor) 2003 *Archaeological Approaches to Cultural Identity*. Routledge, New York.

Sherratt, Susan and Andrew Sherratt 1993 The growth of the Mediterranean economy in the early first millennium BC. *World Archaeology* 24(3):361–378.

Sidky, Homayun 1997 Irrigation and the rise of the state in Hunza: a case for the Hydraulic Hypothesis. *Modern Asian Studies* 31(4):995–1017.

Sillar, Bill 2000 Dung by preference: the choice of fuel as an example of how Andean pottery production is embedded within wider technical, social, and economic practices. *Archaeometry* 42(1):43–60.

Simpson, Elizabeth 2010 *The Furniture from Tumulus MM Culture and History of the Ancient Near East 32 The Gordion Wooden Objects, Volume 1*. 2 vols. Brill, Leiden.

Simpson, Elizabeth and Krysia Spirydowicz 1999 *Gordion Wooden Furniture*. Museum of Anatolian Civilizations, Ankara.

Slim, Francesca 2020 The faunal remains from CC-3. In Gordion excavations final reports: the Early Phrygian period. Edited by C. B. Rose, G. K. Sams, M. Vassileva, P. Sheftel and B. Cordivari. Unpublished manuscript, University of Pennsylvania Museum.

Small, David B. 1990 Handmade burnished ware and prehistoric Aegean economics: an argument for indigenous appearance. *Journal of Mediterranean Archaeology* 3(1):3–28.

Smith, Adam T. 2003 *The Political Landscape: Constellations of Authority in Early Complex Polities*. University of California Press, Berkeley, CA.

  2006 Urartian spectacle: authority, subjectivity, and aesthetic politics. In *Spectacle, Performance, and Power in Premodern Complex Society*, edited by T. Inomata and L. Coben, pp. 103–134. Altamira, Walnut Creek, CA.

  2011 Archaeologies of sovereignty. *Annual Review of Anthropology* 40(1):415–432.

Smith, Michael E. 2004 The archaeology of ancient state economies. *Annual Review of Anthropology* 33(1):73–102.

  2011 Empirical urban theory for archaeologists. *Journal of Archaeological Method and Theory* 18(3):167–192.

Soja, Edward 1989 *Postmodern Geographies: The Reassertion of Space in Critical Social Theory*. Verso, London.

Spencer, Christopher J, Chris Yakymchuk and Mahmoudreza Ghaznavi 2017 Visualising data distributions with kernel density estimation and reduced chi-squared statistic. *Geoscience Frontiers* 8(6):1247–1252.

Stahl, Ann B., Maria das Dores Cruz, Hector Neff, et al. 2008 Ceramic production, consumption and exchange in the Banda area, Ghana: insights from compositional analyses. *Journal of Anthropological Archaeology* 27(3):363–381.

Stark, Miriam T. 1992 From sibling to suki: social relations and spatial proximity in Kalinga pottery exchange *Journal of Anthropological Archaeology* 11(2):137–151.

  1998 *Archaeology of Social Boundaries*. Smithsonian Institution Press, Washington, DC.

  2003 Current issues in ceramic ethnoarchaeology. *Journal of Archaeological Research* 11(3):193–242.

Stark, Miriam T., Brenda J. Bowser and Lee Horne (editors) 2008 *Cultural Transmission and Material Culture: Breaking Down Boundaries*. University of Arizona Press, Tucson.

Steadman, Sharon R. and Gregory McMahon 2017 The 2015–2016 seasons at Çadır Höyük on the north central Anatolian plateau. In *The Archaeology of Anatolia Volume II: Recent Discoveries (2015–2016)*, edited by S. R. Steadman and G. McMahon, pp. 94–116. Cambridge Scholars Publishing, Newcastle upon Tyne.

Steadman, Sharon R., T. Emre Şerifoğlu, Gregory McMahon, et al. 2017 Recent discoveries (2015–2016) at Çadır Höyük on the north central plateau. *Anatolica* 43:203–250.

Steadman, Sharon R., Gregory McMahon, T. Emre Şerifoğlu, et al. 2019 The 2017–2018 seasons at Çadır Höyük on the north central plateau. *Anatolica* 45:77–119.

Stephens, Lucas 2018 Monumental routes: movement and the built environment at Iron Age Gordion. PhD thesis, Art and Archaeology of the Mediterranean World, University of Pennsylvania, Philadelphia.

Sterba, Johannes H., Hans Mommsen, Georg Steinhauser and Max Bichler 2009 The influence of different tempers on the composition of pottery. *Journal of Archaeological Science* 36(7):1582–1589.

Stewart, Shannan M. 2010 Gordion after the knot: Hellenistic pottery and culture. PhD thesis, Classics, University of Cincinnati.

Summers, Geoffrey D. 1993 *Tille Höyük 4: The Late Bronze Age and the Iron Age Transition*. Monograph 15. British Institute of Archaeology at Ankara, Ankara.

—— 1994 Grey ware and the eastern limits of Phrygia. In *Anatolian Iron Ages 3: Proceedings of the Third Anatolian Iron Ages Colloquium held at Van, 6–12 August 1990*, edited by A. Çilingiroğlu and D. French, pp. 241–252. British Institute of Archaeology at Ankara, Ankara.

—— 2008 Periodisation and technology in the central Anatolian Iron Age, archaeology, history and audiences. *Ancient Near Eastern Studies* 45:202–217.

—— 2013 East of the Halys: thoughts on settlement patterns and historical geography in the late 2nd millennium and first half of the first millennium BC. In *Proceedings of the L'Anatolie des peuples, des cités et des cultures. Autour du projet d'Atlas historique et archéologique de l'Asie Mineure antique. Actes du colloque international de Besançon, (26–27 novembre 2010)*, pp. 41–51. Institut des Sciences et Techniques de l'Antiquité, Besançon.

—— 2018 Phrygians east of the red river: Phrygianisation, migration and desertion. *Anatolian Studies* 68:99–118.

Sumner, William 1987 The Gordion region: an exploratory survey. Field Report, The Ohio State University, Columbus, OH.

Swenson, Edward 2015 The archaeology of ritual. *Annual Review of Anthropology* 44:329–345.

Swenson, Edward and John P. Warner 2012 Crucibles of power: forging copper and forging subjects at the Moche ceremonial center of Huaca Colorada, Peru. *Journal of Anthropological Archaeology* 31(3):314–333.

Tehrani, Jamshid J. and Felix Riede 2008 Towards an archaeology of pedagogy: learning, teaching and the generation of material culture traditions. *World Archaeology* 40(3):316–331.

Thomas, Nicholas 1991 *Entangled Objects: Exchange, Material Culture and Colonialism in the Pacific*. Harvard University Press, Cambridge, MA.

Thonemann, Peter 2013 Phrygia: an anarchist history, 950 BC–AD 100. In *Roman Phrygia. Culture and Society, Cambridge*, edited by P. Thonemann, pp. 1–40. Cambridge University Press, New York.

Tite, Michael S. 2008 Ceramic production, provenance and use – a review. *Archaeometry* 50:216–231.

Toteva, Galya Dechkova 2007 Local cultures of Late Achaemenid Anatolia. PhD thesis, Classics, University of Minnesota, ProQuest.

Vaessen, Rik 2014 Cultural dynamics in Ionia at the end of the second millennium BCE: new archaeological perspectives and prospects. PhD thesis, Archaeology, University of Sheffield.

Van den Hout, Theo 2011 The Hittite Empire from textual evidence. In *The Oxford Handbook of Ancient Anatolia (10,000–323 BCE)*, edited by S. Steadman and G. McMahon, pp. 900–913. Oxford University Press, Oxford.

Van der Leeuw, Sander E. 1977 Towards a study of the economics of pottery making. In *Ex Horreo, Cingula 4*, edited by B. L. Beek, R. W. Brant and W. Gruenman van Watteringe, pp. 68–76. Albert Egges van Giffen Instituut voor Prae- en Protohistorie, University of Amsterdam, Amsterdam.

Van Dongen, Erik 2014 The extent and interactions of the Phrygian kingdom. In *From Source to History: Studies on Ancient Near Eastern Worlds and Beyond*, edited by S. Gaspa, A. Grico, D. M. Bonacossi, et al., pp. 697–711. Ugarit-Verlag, Munster.

Veblen, Thorstein 1899 [2007] *The Theory of the Leisure Class*. Oxford University Press, Oxford.

Voigt, Mary M. 1994 Excavations at Gordion 1988–89: the Yassıhöyük Stratigraphic Sequence. In *Anatolian Iron Ages 3: Proceedings of the Third Anatolian Iron Ages Colloquium held at Van, 6–12 August 1990*, edited by A. Çilingiroğlu and D. French, pp. 265–293. British Institute of Archaeology at Ankara Monograph 16, Ankara.

1997 Stratigraphic sequence, architecture and settlement plan. In Fieldwork at Gordion 1993–1995, by M. M. Voigt, K. DeVries, R. C. Henrickson, M. Lawall, B. Marsh, A. Gürsan-Salzman, and T. C. Young. *Anatolica* 23:1–59.

2002 Gordion: The rise and fall of an Iron Age capital. In *Across the Anatolian Plateau: Readings in the Archaeology of Ancient Turkey*, edited by D. Hopkins, pp. 187–196, N. Lapp, general editor. American Schools of Oriental Research Volume 57, Boston, MA.

2007 The Middle Phrygian occupation at Gordion. In *Proceedings of the Sixth Anatolian Iron Ages Colloquium held at Eskişehir, 16–20 August 2004*, edited by A. Çilingiroğlu and A. Sagona, pp. 311–333. Peeters, Leuven.

2009 The chronology of Phrygian Gordion. In *Tree-Rings, Kings and Old World Archaeology and Environment: Papers Presented in Honor of Peter Ian Kuniholm*, edited by S. Manning and M. J. Bruce, pp. 219–238. Oxbow, Oxford.

2011 Gordion: the changing political and economic roles of a first millennium city. In *The Oxford Handbook of Ancient Anatolia (10,000–323 BCE)*, edited by S. Steadman and G. McMahon, pp. 1069–1094. Oxford University Press, Oxford.

2012a Human and animal sacrifice at Galatian Gordion: the uses of ritual in a multiethnic community. In *Sacred Killing: the Archaeology of Sacrifice in the Ancient Near East*, edited by A. Porter and G. M. Schwartz, pp. 235–288. Eisenbrauns, Winona Lake, IN.

2012b The Unfinished Project of the Gordion Early Phrygian Destruction Level. In *The Archaeology of Phrygian Gordion, Royal City of Midas*, edited by C. B. Rose, pp. 67–100. Gordion Special Studies 7. University of Pennsylvania Museum of Archaeology and Anthropology, Philadelphia.

2013 Gordion as citadel and city. In *Cities and Citadels in Turkey: From the Iron Age to the Seljuks*, edited by S. Redford and N. Ergin, pp. 161–228. Peeters, Leuven.

Voigt, Mary M. and Keith DeVries 2011 Emerging problems and doubts. In *The New Chronology of Iron Age Gordion*, edited by C. B. Rose and G. Darbyshire, pp. 23–48. Gordion Special Studies 6. University of Pennsylvania Museum of Archaeology and Anthropology, Philadelphia.

Voigt, Mary M. and Robert C. Henrickson 2000a The Early Iron Age at Gordion: the evidence from the Yassıhöyük Stratigraphic Sequence. In *The Sea Peoples and Their World: A Reassessment*, edited by E. D. Oren, pp. 327–360. University of Pennsylvania Museum of Archaeology and Anthropology, Philadelphia.

2000b Formation of the Phrygian state: the Early Iron Age at Gordion. *Anatolian Studies* 50:37–54.

Voigt, Mary M. and Lisa Kealhofer in press Observing change, measuring time: documenting the Late Bronze Age-Iron Age sequence at Gordion. In *Between the Age of Diplomacy and the First Great Empire in Ancient West Asia (1200–900 BC): Moving Beyond the Paradigm of Collapse and Regeneration*, edited by L. D'Alfonso, I. Calini, R. Hawley and M. G. Masetti-Rouault. Institute for the Study of the Ancient World, New York.

Voigt, Mary M. and T. Cuyler Young, Jr. 1999 From Phrygian capital to Achaemenid entrepot: Middle and Late Phrygian Gordion. *Iranica antiqua* 34:191–241.

Voigt, Mary M., Keith DeVries, Robert C. Henrickson, et al. 1997 Fieldwork at Gordion 1993–1995. *Anatolica* 23:1–59.

Washburn, Dorothy K. 2003 The property of symmetry and the concept of ethnic style: Archaeological approaches to cultural identity. In *Archaeological Approaches to Cultural Identity*, edited by S. J. Shennan, pp. 157–173. Routledge, New York.

Weeden, Mark, Lee Z. Ullmann and Zenobia Homan 2017 *Hittite Landscape and Geography*. Brill, Leiden.

Wells, Martin Gregory 2012 A cosmopolitan village: the Hellenistic settlement at Gordion. PhD thesis, Classical and Near Eastern Studies, University of Minnesota.

Wiessner, Polly 1989 Style and changing relations between the individual and society. In *The Meanings of Things*, edited by I. Hodder, pp. 56–63. Unwin Hyman, London.

1990 *Is There a Unity to Style: The Uses of Style in Archaeology*. Cambridge University Press, Cambridge.

Wilk, Richard R. and William Rathje 1982 Archaeology of the household: building a prehistory of domestic life. *American Behavioral Scientist* 25(6):617–724.
Winter, Frederick A. 1973 Late Classical and Hellenistic pottery from Gordion. *American Journal of Archaeology* 77:232–233.
Witcher, Robert E. 2000 Globalisation and Roman imperialism: perspectives on identities in Roman Italy. In *The Emergence of State Identities in Italy in the First Millennium BC*, edited by E. Herring and K. Lomas. Accordia Research Institute, University of London, London.
Wobst, H. Martin 1977 Stylistic behavior and information exchange. In *Papers for the Director: Research Essays in Honour of James B. Griffin*, edited by C. E. Cleland, pp. 317–342. Academic Press, New York.
Yaeger, Jason and Marcello Canuto 2000 Introducing an archaeology of communities. In *Archaeology of Communities: A New World Perspective*, edited by M. Canuto and J. Yaeger, pp. 1–15. Routledge, London.
Yakar, Jak 2011 Anatolian chronology and terminology. In *The Oxford Handbook of Ancient Anatolia (10,000–323 BCE)*, edited by S. Steadman and G. McMahon, pp. 56–93. Oxford University Press, Oxford.
Yoffee, Norman 2005 *Myths of the Archaic State, Evolution of the Earliest Cities, States, and Civilizations*. Cambridge University Press, Cambridge.
Young, Rodney S. 1950 Excavations at Yassıhüyük – Gordion 1950. *Archaeology* 3:196–201.
   1953 Progress at Gordion, 1951–1952. *University Museum Bulletin* 17(4):2–39.
   1955 Gordion: Preliminary Report – 1953. *American Journal of Archaeology* 59(1):1–18.
   1956 The campaign of 1955 at Gordion. *American Journal of Archaeology* 60(3):249–266.
   1962 The Gordion campaign of 1961. *American Journal of Archaeology* 66(2):153–168.
   1963 Gordion on the Royal Road. *Proceedings of the American Philosophical Society* 107(4):348–364.
   1964 The 1963 campaign at Gordion. *American Journal of Archaeology* 68(3):279–292.
   1966 The Gordion campaign of 1965. *American Journal of Archaeology* 70(3):267–278.
   1981 *Three Great Early Tumuli*. The Gordion Excavations Final Reports, vol. 1. University of Pennsylvania Museum of Archaeology and Anthropology, Philadelphia.
Zeder, Melinda A. and Suzanne R. Arter 1994 Changing patterns of animal utilization at ancient Gordion. *Paléorient* 20(2):105–118.
Zimansky, Paul 2011 Urartu and the Urartians. In *The Oxford Handbook of Ancient Anatolia (10,000–323 BCE)*, edited by S. Steadman and G. McMahon, pp. 548–560. Oxford University Press, Oxford.
Zouck, Nina Poe 1974 Hand-carved and lathe-turned alabaster from Gordion. PhD thesis, Classical Archaeology, University of Pennsylvania, ProQuest.

Index

abandonment, 47, 51, 139, 237
accuracy (NAA measurement), 56, 63–64, 78–80
Achaemenid Empire, 43, 317, 349, 366
activities, aggrandizing, 14, 213, 356, 360, 362, 372
administration, 337
  Hittite, 89, 357
  Early Phrygian, 180
  Achaemenid, 302, 304, 329, 342, 352, 366
administrators
  Hittite, 86, 92, 130, 133
  Achaemenid, 302, 304, 335, 337, 352
Aegean Sea, 84, 228, 342, 348, 351
  coast, 138, 224, 227, 351
agriculture, 282, 334, 341, 368, 372. *See also* farming, pastoralism
  intensive agriculture, 233, 354
  rainfall agriculture, 233, 367–368
alabaster, 284, 335. *See also* stone
Alexander the Great, 47, 230, 305, 355, 365
Alişar IV or Silhouette style (pottery), 173, 193, 208, 220, 295, 361
analytical clusters, 55–56, 67–68
Anatolia, east-central, 63, 80
  Late Bronze Age, 132
  Early Iron Age, 151, 155, 167–168
  Early Phrygian, 203–205
  Middle Phrygian, 263, 268–273, 280–281, 292–299
  Late Phrygian, 329, 351–353
animals, 1, 31. *See also* bird, cow, deer, goat, hare, horse, pig, sheep
  dung, 124, 128, 144
  Late Bronze Age, 94, 124, 128–129, 132, 357
  Early Iron Age, 170, 358
  Early Phrygian, 178, 211
  fiber, 213
  game, 129
  Middle Phrygian, 282, 290
  wild, 282, 344
  Late Phrygian, 316, 335, 344
antler, 47, 125, 284, 310, 334–335. *See also* bone, horn, ivory
Aslan, Carolyn, 48, 103, 146–147
Assyrians, 5–7, 227, 229, 362, 368

baking plates, Hittite, 94, 115, 131, 133
Balkan region, 139, 146–147, 167, 183, 190–191, 358
barley, 124, 128, 164, 212, 290. *See also* agriculture, cereal, crops, grain
basalt, 60, 69–72, 283. *See also* stone
beads, 129, 164, 166, 290. *See also* jewelry
  amber, 290
beer, 5. *See also* beverages, brewery, drinks
  Hittite, 115, 128
  Early Iron Age, 164
  Early Phrygian, 212–213
  Middle Phrygian, 237, 284, 290, 293–294
belts, 237, 244, 285, 294, 363. *See also* clothing
beverages, 161, 196, 214, 268, 290, 293. *See also* beer, wine, pouring vessels and various pottery drinking vessel types
bichrome pottery decoration, 80, 190
  Early Phrygian, 203
  Middle Phrygian, 237, 248–249, 254, 256, 259, 263, 266–273, 281, 286, 296, 363
  Late Phrygian, 320–321, 323–329
birds, 129, 344. *See also* animals, fauna
black polished decoration (ceramics), 173, 237, 240–244, 249–252, 342–346, 363. *See also* sintered slips
Black Sea, 138, 221, 349, 351
Blackman, James, 51, 57, 62, 127, 131, 149, 186
Boğazköy, 86–117, 128, 130–135, 173. *See also* Hattuša

409

Index

bone, 47. *See also* fauna, ivory, antler, horn
   decoration, 125
   Late Bronze Age, 125, 128–129, 132
   Early Iron Age, 160, 164
   gaming pieces, 164, 316
   Middle Phrygian, 284, 310
   Late Phrygian, 316, 334–335, 344, 365
   tools, 125
   working, 284, 310, 335, 365
Bonn dataset (Neutron Activation Analysis, NAA), 62, 73–75, 78–80. *See also* Mommsen, Hans
borders and boundaries, 7, 17, 21, 297, 368
   Hittite, 92
   Middle Phrygian, 289
   Late Phrygian, 302
Bourdieu, Pierre, 4, 23–24
bowls, Achaemenid, 304, 319, 323, 326, 338, 346–347, 366
bowls, carinated, 108, 114, 190, 248
brewery, 115. *See also* beer
bronze (metal), 160, 219, 244, 285, 294, 310, 335, 350, 365, 367–368. *See also* metal, metal-working
   belts, 363
   bowls, 184, 213, 218, 221, 249, 290
   fibulae, 222, 284, 290–291
   figurines, 219
   jewelry, 129, 160, 164
   military, 310
   points, 129, 290
   production, 310, 335
   rings, 164
   vessels, 197, 219, 221, 244, 249, 290, 294
Building A, Gordion, 236, 309, 337
bulla(e), 93, 101, 128–129, 133–134, 356. *See also* seals
burials, 29. *See also* inhumations, mortuary practices, tumuli
   Bronze Age, 100
   Early Phrygian, 173, 175, 190, 221–222, 360
   Middle Phrygian, 227, 237, 244, 249
   Late Phrygian, 317, 342

Çadır Höyük, 63, 78, 80, 118, 139, 173, 205, 256, 259, 263
cattle (cow, calf, beef). *See also* animal
   Late Bronze Age, 124, 128–129, 132
   Early Phrygian, 212, 282
   Middle Phrygian, 129, 290, 362
   Late Phrygian, 334, 344
cauldrons, 213, 218, 221, 244

cellars, 249, 305, 308–346, 365
   Building I:2, 236–238, 284, 290
   South Cellar, 232, 236–237, 363
cemetery. *See also* morturary practices, tumuli
   Bronze Age, 86, 100, 104, 115
   Early Phrygian, 173
   Middle Phrygian, 233, 253, 270, 283
ceramics, Attic, 30, 49–50, 305
   Middle Phrygian, 234, 292
ceramics, East Greek, 50, 62, 118, 342–344
   Early Phrygian, 208, 222, 248
   Middle Phrygian, 291, 295, 298, 364
   Late Phrygian, 319, 329, 346, 348, 351
ceramics, glazed, 351
   black, 319–321, 323, 327, 329, 339, 364
   Middle Phrygian, 296, 364
   Late Phrygian, 321, 323–329, 339
   Attic, 346, 350
ceramics, handmade. *See* Chapters 6 and 7
ceramics, wheelmade. *See* wheelthrown pottery
cereals, 100, 160, 233, 240, 282, 334. *See also* agriculture, barley, grain, wheat
charcoal, 123, 164, 218, 344
chert, 60, 124. *See also* lithic tools, stone, stone artifacts
   tesserae, 335
child, 244, 316, 342
Cilicia, 95, 97, 134, 302
city state, 137, 184, 229, 367
clay, 73, 84, 155, 160, 215
   fill, 41, 174, 182, 230–232, 238–239, 299, 307, 310
   preparation, 288, 340
   recipe, 208, 216–217, 256, 287
   samples, 54, 62, 127, 134, 215
   slip, 197
   sources, 69, 81–82, 156–163, 169, 196–197, 224–225, 340
Clay Cut (CC) Buildings, 41, 47, 181, 212. *See also* Terrace Buildings and Terrace Complex
climate, 25, 129, 372. *See also* drought
cloth, 22, 200, 217, 221. *See also* belts, fibulae, pins, textiles
   clothing, 20, 125, 160, 213, 244, 284, 291, 342, 363
coins, 47–48, 304–305, 310
collapse, 1
   Hittite, 7, 12, 28, 51, 92–97, 134–135, 167–170, 222, 368–371
   Achaemenid, 366
collective action, 15–16, 26, 354
commoner, 22, 84, 244–246, 341–344, 355

Index

competing factions or polities, 1, 26, 171, 215, 228, 288–299, 361–363, 368–372
consumption, communal. *See* also feasting
   Early Iron Age, 161
   Early Phrygian, 214, 218–221
   Middle Phrygian, 268, 281, 289, 294, 298, 366, 370–371
   Late Phrygian, 348
consumption, food, 5, 10, 25. *See* also feasting
   Late Bronze Age, 107, 132, 357
   Early Iron Age, 164
   Early Phrygian, 218
   Middle Phrygian, 249, 268, 290–293, 297–300
   Late Phrygian, 320, 348, 353
cooking or culinary practices, 4, 106, 155, 160, 164, 212, 284
cooking pots
   Late Bronze Age, 94–115, 131–132
   Early Iron Age, 153
   Early Phrygian, 196, 248
   Late Phrygian, 318
copper, 160, 164, 290, 335, 350, 368. *See* also bronze, metal, metalworking
corvée labor, 203, 284–285, 299, 368
Costin, Cathy Lynne, 21, 84, 125, 203
craft production, 16, 21–22
   Late Bronze Age, 134
   Middle Phrygian, 285, 299
   Late Phrygian, 317, 321, 336, 340–341, 349–350, 354
craftspeople
   Early Phrygian, 223
   Middle Phrygian, 284, 288, 362
   Late Phrygian, 337–340
crater. *See* also Greek pottery
   Early Iron Age, 153, 166
   Early Phrygian, 131, 190–193, 203, 208, 213–214, 219–222, 359
   Middle Phrygian, 259, 266, 276
   Late Phrygian, 326, 347
cremation, 291, 316, 342. *See* also burials
crops, 125, 128, 160, 212, 362. *See* also agriculture, farming
curation, 29, 48–49, 195, 203
Cyprus or Cypriot, 95, 367

daily practices, 4, 11, 27, 55, 83, 355, 368–371
   Late Bronze Age, 128, 357
   Early Iron Age, 161, 167
   Early Phrygian, 171, 183, 217
   Middle Phrygian, 245, 291, 300
   Late Phrygian, 301
decision-making, 12, 14, 57

deer or venison, 129, 160, 170, 334, 344. *See* also animal, consumption, food
deities. *See* god or goddess
detection limits, 64–67. *See* also Neutron Activation Analysis
DeVries, Keith, 5–7, 30, 48–50, 56, 83
   Early Phrygian, 41, 183, 213, 218, 220–221
   Middle Phrygian, 230, 249
   Late Phrygian, 305–306, 318, 348
diet, 129, 218, 282, 358
dilution factor. *See* also Bonn dataset (NAA), Mommsen, Hans
Discriminant Function Analysis, 68, 73
display, 22
   Early Iron Age, 164
   Early Phrygian, 173, 190, 219–224
   Middle Phrygian, 281, 283, 291
   Late Phrygian, 318
disposal (artifacts or goods), 4, 10, 16–19, 21, 24, 241, 356
Doodle Stones, 213
drinking vessels, 28, 371
   Early Iron Age, 164, 358
   Early Phrygian, 186, 213, 218–225
   Middle Phrygian, 237–244, 268, 290, 294–298, 363–364
   Late Phrygian, 342, 348–350, 353
drought, 125, 129, 136, 160, 212, 233, 282, 345
drying (pottery production), 4, 163, 216, 288
dump (trash), 43, 54
   Early Phrygian, 175
   Late Bronze Age, 95, 129
   Middle Phrygian, 240, 276, 282, 284, 290, 293
   Late Phrygian, 312
dung. *See* animals, dung
Dusinberre, Elspeth, 282, 302, 307, 317, 321, 335, 366

Early Bronze Age, 1, 7, 11, 30, 98
Early Iron Age handmade pottery, 142–151, 161–169, 175, 186, 214
East Gate (Gordion), 180–212, 230, 235–237. *See* also gate
East Greek. *See* also ceramics, East Greek communities, 138, 291, 364
Eastern Mound Gordion, 40–47, 49, 53
   Early Iron Age, 139–140
   Early Phrygian, 174–183, 205, 208, 215, 222
   Middle Phrygian, 228–266, 268–284, 290, 362–363
   Late Phrygian, 304–323, 334–347, 365

412　Index

economic strategies, 12, 25, 133, 341, 352, 369
Egypt, 302, 342, 349
empires, 1, 229
　Achaemenid, 302, 304, 318–319
　Assyrian, 368
　Hittite, 7, 33, 51, 92, 97, 101, 128, 134, 137, 222, 357
environmental evidence, 85, 212, 233, 282, 344, 368
Ephesus, 138, 174
erosion, 60, 125, 230
Eski Depot Gordion, 52
Eskişehir, 63, 75–78
ethnicity, 4, 368
ethnoarchaeology (-ical), 21, 60
ethnography (-ic), 18–19, 160, 162, 251–252, 289, 334, 340
exchange networks, 222, 326, 332, 350, 359, 368
experimental results, 62–64, 67

factions, 2, 13
　Late Bronze Age, 86, 92
　Early Phrygian, 215, 359–361
　Middle Phrygian, 288, 298–300
family, 4, 19
　Late Bronze Age, 92, 110, 124, 128
　Early Iron Age, 164–166, 168, 358
　Middle Phrygian, 244
farming. *See* also agriculture, crops, herding, pastoralism
　Late Bronze Age, 124, 134
　Middle Phrygian, 362
　Late Phrygian, 334
fauna, 129, 218, 335. *See* also animal, bone
Fazli's kiln, 270, 273
feasting, 2, 5, 19–20, 23, 25, 28, 356, 370.
　See food consumption
　Late Bronze Age, 131
　Early Iron Age, 164, 166, 358
　Early Phrygian, 190, 212–213, 217–226, 361
　Middle Phrygian, 237, 241, 268, 289–292, 298, 362–363, 366
fibulae, 222, 237, 244, 284, 291, 363.
　See also bronze, cloth or clothing
figurines, 164, 219, 237
fill, construction, 362. *See* also clay, fill for Middle Phrygian clay fill layer
　Late Bronze Age, 101
　Early Phrygian, 142, 177–178, 183, 195, 211
　Middle Phrygian, 43, 230, 244, 253, 270, 299

　Late Phrygian, 337
　Hellenistic, 47, 175
firing (pottery), 4, 113. *See* also kilns
　Late Bronze Age, 125
　Early Iron Age, 142–144, 161–163
　Early Phrygian, 184–186, 195–196, 215–216, 361
　Middle Phrygian, 246–252, 288
　Late Phrygian, 318, 338–339
firing experiments, 113, 248, 251
fish, 129, 344. *See* also animals
floodplain, 32, 54, 175
food storage, 10. *See* also storage pits
　Late Bronze Age, 93
　Early Phrygian, 361
fortifications, 30–47, 368, 371
　Early Iron Age, 139
　Early Phrygian, 174–180, 210–211, 360
　Middle Phrygian, 232–234, 241, 270, 283
　Late Phrygian, 301, 304, 364
fortress, 30, 43, 138
　Early Phrygian, 217
　Middle Phrygian, 232, 241–243, 245, 259, 283, 296
　Late Phrygian, 301
Foucault, Paul-Michel, 4
foundations, 30, 41–43
　Late Bronze Age, 123
　Early Phrygian, 183, 217
　Middle Phrygian, 234–235, 238–243, 283, 290
　Late Phrygian, 304, 310–316, 342, 350
frit, 129, 290, 294. *See* also glass
fruitstands (stemmed bowls), 249, 259, 266, 273, 276, 286, 295–296, 347
fuel, 4, 124–127
　Late Bronze Age, 129
　Early Iron Age, 163–164
　Early Phrygian, 216–218
　Middle Phrygian, 248–252, 290
　Late Phrygian, 344
funerals, 25, 244, 290, 317, 342–344. *See* burials, inhumations, mortuary practices
furniture, 213, 218–219, 244, 290, 362
　hearth-related, 208

Galatians, 8, 47
gate or gatehouse
　Early Phrygian, 174, 176–186, 210, 217
　Middle Phrygian, 230, 235–238, 283
　Late Phrygian, 306–307, 337

Index

gender, 4, 13, 110, 160, 166, 224, 291
Genz, Hermann, 11, 138–139
geochemistry, 9, 29, 52–54, 60–62, 68–69, 81–82. *See* also Neutron Activation Analysis
  Late Bronze Age, 116, 133–134
  Early Iron Age, 151
  Early Phrygian, 203
  Middle Phrygian, 256, 286–288, 294
  Late Phrygian, 326, 333
geology, 25, 29, 60–61, 69–72, 75, 82, 131
geometric decoration (pottery), 78, 80, 113, 191, 210, 220–223, 249–256, 268. *See* also Protogeometric
geospatial trends, 60, 75, 85, 221
gifts, 208, 229, 359, 363
glacis, 38, 41, 211, 232, 235, 283. *See* also fortification
glass, 52. *See* also frit
  Late Bronze Age, 129
  Early Iron Age, 164, 166
  Early Phrygian, 213
  Middle Phrygian, 284–285, 296
  Late Phrygian, 342, 348–349, 366
Glatz, Claudia, 93, 97–98, 100, 102, 132
goat. *See* also animals, herding, pastoralism
  Late Bronze Age, 124, 128–129
  Early Iron Age, 160, 164–166, 170
  Early Phrygian, 212, 218
  Middle Phrygian, 282, 290
  Late Phrygian, 334, 344–345, 350
god or goddess, 92, 94, 342, 367–368
gold, 218, 229, 284, 291, 294, 317, 349
Gordion Museum, 9, 49, 52. *See* also museum
Gordion Regional Survey (GRS), 5, 52–54, 60, 101, 127, 228
graffiti, 213, 240, 249, 284, 290, 363
grain, 5, 233, 237. *See* also agriculture, barley, cereal, crops, wheat
  production, 210
  silos, 124, 139
grave goods, 285, 342, 362. *See* also funerary, mortuary practices
Greek colonization or colonists, 137–138, 227
Greek pottery, 58, 237, 291–295, 319–321, 329, 350, 353, 366. *See* also craters, ceramics
  alabastron, 316, 337, 348
  forms, 248, 296, 323, 344, 347
  kantharos, 321, 347
  lekythos, 276, 291, 295–297, 305, 319–321, 323, 346–348, 364
  rhyton, 211, 266, 347
  skyphos, 295, 347

grinding stones or groundstone, 124, 160, 211–212, 219, 284, 290, 335
group identity, 5, 13–14, 19, 83, 363
Gunter, Ann C., 100–115
Gürtekin Demir, Gül, 48
gypsum, 235, 283, 335. *See* also stone

habitus, 17, 23–24
Haci Tuğrul, 233
Halys River (Kızılırmak), 7, 171, 208
hare, 129, 282, 334, 344. *See* also animal
harvest, 123–124, 282
Hattuša (Hittite capital), 86, 89, 114, 133, 237, 370
hearth, 47. *See* also ovens
  Early Iron Age, 140
  Early Phrygian, 41, 175
  furniture, 211
  Middle Phrygian, 284
  Late Phrygian, 310, 312, 344
hegemony
  Hittite, 92–93, 98, 133
  Early Phrygian, 226
  Middle Phrygian, 229, 298, 300, 353
  Late Phrygian, 349
  Persian, 353
  Roman, 20
Hegmon, Michelle, 17, 20
Hellenistic, 49–52
  period, 7–10, 30, 47, 57, 175, 304–305, 312, 334
  pottery, 19
  roof tiles, 57
Hellespont, 349, 351
Hellespontine Phrygia, 302
Henrickson, Robert C., 9–10, 31, 48–54, 83
  Late Bronze Age, 93–117, 125–127, 131
  Early Iron Age, 142–160
  Early Phrygian, 184–203, 214–216
  Middle Phrygian, 244–254, 256, 268, 285–288, 295
  Late Phrygian, 306, 318–323, 326, 332, 338
herding, 124, 134, 166. *See* also agriculture, animals, cattle, goats, pastoralism, sheep
  caprine, 128, 335
Hierarchical Cluster Analysis, 68. *See* also multivariate analysis
hierarchy
  Late Bronze Age, 128, 371
  Early Iron Age, 164
  Early Phrygian, 212, 225
  Middle Phrygian, 241, 246, 299
  Late Phrygian, 304, 341

414   Index

high status, 180, 217, 219, 225, 237, 299, 317, 363
Hirth, Kenneth, 25–26, 83, 210, 300, 354, 369
horn, 284, 335. *See* also antler, ivory
horse, 164, 170. *See* also animals
  trappings, 181, 184, 212, 241, 290, 304, 317
house, 16, 47. *See* also Painted House, Polychrome Gatehouse, pithouse, residence, residential structure
  Early Bronze Age, 100
  Late Bronze Age, 101, 115, 123–125, 129
  Early Iron Age, 136, 140–142, 162–164, 170, 175
  Middle Phrygian, 233–234, 238–245, 362
  Late Phrygian, 310–316, 344–346, 353, 365–366
hunting, 129, 160, 170, 334
husbandry, 128, 362. *See* also herding, pastoralism

iconography, 183, 222, 228, 233, 300, 342, 369
ideology, 13, 22, 130, 369, 371–372
  Late Bronze Age, 93, 137
  Early Phrygian, 217, 360–361
  Middle Phrygian, 297–298, 300
incised decoration (pottery), 94, 146, 148, 166–167, 203, 212, 248
inclusions (pottery), 93, 105, 184. *See* also temper (pottery)
infrastructure, 15, 218, 283–284, 337
  ceramic, 83, 162–163, 216, 288, 340, 358
inhumation, 183, 244, 316, 337. *See* also burials, mortuary practices
Inner Court
  Early Phrygian, 41, 49, 180, 213, 218–219, 360
  Middle Phrygian, 235–237, 364–365
  Late Phrygian, 305, 307–310, 341
innovation, 1–2, 12, 162, 216, 226, 353–354, 367–372
inscription, 364. *See* also graffiti, texts
  Phrygian, 7, 171, 227
  Greek, 47
intensification, 173, 368
  agricultural, 212, 214, 282–283, 362
interaction networks, 168, 190, 223, 233, 297
Ionia(n), 73, 138, 200, 203–208, 223–224, 256, 362

iron tools, 367–368
  Early Phrygian, 182, 212
  Middle Phrygian, 290
irrigation, 15, 284–285. *See* also water management
ivory, 47. *See* also antler, horn
  Early Phrygian, 181, 184, 213, 218–219, 221
  Middle Phrygian, 237, 243, 294
  Late Phrygian, 310, 334–335, 342, 349–350, 363–365

jewelry, 219, 290–291, 294, 296, 317. *See* also beads, fibulae, ornaments, pins
jugs. *See* also Greek pottery, pouring vessels
  Late Bronze Age, 93–94, 108, 116, 131
  Early Iron Age, 148, 161, 166, 359
  Early Phrygian, 187–193, 200, 214, 219–222, 224
  Middle Phrygian, 248–256, 259–276, 281, 285–286, 289–293, 295–298, 363
  Late Phrygian, 301–326, 348, 366
juniper (wood), 123, 218

Kaman Kalehöyük, 63, 75–80
  Late Bronze Age, 118
  Early Iron Age, 137
  Early Phrygian, 173, 205, 224
  Middle Phrygian, 263
Karahöyük, 364
Kerkenes, 7, 171, 233, 362
Kernel Density Estimation (KDE), 68–69
Kilise Tepe (Cilicia), 93–97, 134
kilns, 82, 85, 125–127
  Late Bronze Age, 113
  Early Iron Age, 145, 161–163, 359
  Early Phrygian, 213–216
  Middle Phrygian, 233–234, 248–253, 270–273, 287–289
  Late Phrygian, 312, 334–335, 339
Kimmerians, 227, 229, 305, 364
kin group, 110, 166, 355, 358
Kinet Höyük, 96
king, 7
  Late Bronze Age, 92
  Early Iron Age, 137
  Early Phrygian, 212
  King Midas, 5, 7, 30, 229
  Middle Phrygian, 229, 362
  Late Phrygian, 337, 342
Kınık Höyük, 138–139, 173
Kızılırmak (river), 7, 89, 171, 208, 233. *See* also Halys River
Konya, 7

Index

Körte, Alfred and Gustav, 5, 30
Küçük Höyük (KH) (fortress), 30, 51, 232–234, 241–245, 249, 259, 270–296, 301
Kuşaklı, 115

labor force, 211, 245, 284–285, 299, 317
Lawall, Mark, 48, 50, 295, 318, 351
learning, 10, 14, 19, 28, 162, 352
Lechtman, Heather, 19, 22
legacy data sets, 14, 55, 62, 85
lekythos. *See* Greek pottery
lentils, 124, 160, 212, 290
Levant (region), 93, 137, 224, 348, 351, 369
Liebhart, Richard, 183
lithic tools, 123–124, 132, 160. *See also* grinding stones or groundstone
loom weights, 125, 160, 181, 212, 290. *See also* spindle whorls, weaving
Lower Town Gordion, 30, 32–43, 58, 232–234
  Middle Phrygian, 228, 232–243, 245, 249, 253, 270, 283–284, 289–293
  Late Phrygian, 301, 304–306, 312, 335–339, 344–346, 362–365
Lower Trench Sounding (LTS), 31
  Late Bronze Age, 98, 100–101, 116–125
  Early Phrygian, 175–177
Lydia, 118, 208, 223, 280, 299, 302, 333, 348, 372. *See also* Sardis
Lydian sources, 215, 273, 281, 326
Lydianizing pottery decoration, 11, 78, 296, 323
lydions
  Middle Phrygian, 248, 273–276, 292–297, 364
  Late Phrygian, 316, 319–323, 326, 349
Lynch, Kathleen M., 48, 50, 291, 306, 318, 348, 351

Main Excavation Area Gordion, 98, 229, 232
marbleizing pottery decoration, 273, 296, 321, 323, 328. *See also* Lydianizing
marl (rock), 60, 69–72. *See also* stone
Marsh, Ben, 31, 54, 60, 232
mass production (pottery), 83–84, 125, 215, 248, 285, 361
meals, 4–5, 19, 160, 190. *See also* feasting, consumption
Medieval period, 30, 47, 49
Mediterranean region, 8, 20, 89, 138, 227, 342–350, 367

megarons, 41, 175–183, 186, 211–213, 217–220, 223, 230–236, 263, 341, 365
Megaron 2, 178, 213
Megaron 3, 41, 49, 184, 218, 221
Megaron 4, 41
Megaron 10, 98, 178
Megaron 10 Sounding, 124–125
Megaron 12, 98
Mellink, Machteld, 31–34, 51, 100, 103, 232–233, 249, 270
Mesopotamia, 84, 227–229
metal, 166, 190
  metal items, 125, 160, 217, 290–294, 354
  metal production, 22, 284
  metal vessels, 181, 244, 249, 298, 304
  metal working, 123, 160, 335–341, 365
micaceous slip, 95, 105–106, 115, 145, 190
Midas. *See* king, King Midas
Midas City, 362
Middle Bronze Age (MBA), 32, 86, 100–117
migration, 14, 102, 139, 146, 167–170
Miletus, 78, 138, 174, 196
military, 1, 26
  Late Bronze Age, 86, 92
  Middle Phrygian, 241–243, 363
  Late Phrygian, 301, 304, 310–312, 344, 352–354, 364, 368
  Roman, 47
Miller, Naomi F., 124, 166, 218, 344
mobilization
  labor, 370
  resource, 26, 300, 354, 370
  tribute, 25, 354, 369
modeled decoration (pottery), 94, 148, 248–249, 321, 339
Mommsen, Hans, 62–63, 73, 80, 203–205
monument, 25, 356
  Late Bronze Age, 92–93, 98
  Early Phrygian, 139, 171, 174–177, 183–184, 211, 217, 226, 360
  Middle Phrygian, 227–229, 238, 283, 289, 299–300, 362–363
  Late Phrygian, 305, 341, 370–371
Morgan, Kathryn, 41, 212–213, 219
mortuary practices, 25, 369. *See also* burials, grave goods, inhumations
  Late Bronze Age, 123
  Early Phrygian, 183, 212, 220
  Middle Phrygian, 227, 283, 291
  Late Phrygian, 304, 342
Mosaic Building, 43, 307–312, 337, 341–342, 352, 365
mudbrick
  Late Bronze Age, 100, 123
  Early Iron Age, 140

416   Index

mudbrick (cont.)
  Early Phrygian, 178
  Middle Phrygian, 43, 228, 243, 283
  Late Phrygian, 301, 304–312
multivariate analysis, 67, 69, 72–73, 85. *See also* Hierarchical Cluster Analysis, Principal Component Analysis
museum. *See also* Gordion Museum
  Museum of Anatolian Civilizations in Ankara, 50, 52, 59
  Smithsonian Institution, 51
  University of Pennsylvania Museum, 5
Mycenaean, 20, 95, 138

National Institute of Standards and Technology (NIST), 10, 57
Neo-Hittite, 184, 222, 229, 251, 300, 361. *See also* Syro-Hittite
Neutron Activation Analysis (NAA), 10, 56–57, 117, 127
  Late Bronze Age, 118, 131, 357
  Early Iron Age, 149–155
  Early Phrygian, 193–203
  Middle Phrygian, 252–263, 280, 286–287, 293–295
  Late Phrygian, 321–329, 338, 347, 351
non-diagnostic ceramics, 9, 50, 117, 153, 318
non-elite, 5–11, 25, 28, 31
  Early Phrygian, 175, 212
  Middle Phrygian, 244, 293
  Late Phrygian, 317–318, 349, 352
North Central Anatolian (NCA), 89, 121, 357
Northeast Ridge Gordion, 58, 86, 100, 233, 244, 253, 284, 293
Northwest Zone (NWZ) Gordion
  Middle Phrygian, 238–239, 253–254, 259, 276–281, 293
  Late Phrygian, 312–337, 344–347, 352
null hypothesis, 72, 82, 197, 286–287
nuts, hazelnuts, 212, 218, 221

oak (wood), 123, 218
Off Mound (OM) Gordion, 253
  Middle Phrygian, 270–276, 280–281, 293
  Late Phrygian, 321
oil, 291, 320, 342, 348–349, 366
Old Kingdom Hittite, 93–94, 115
open area
  Late Bronze Age, 100
  Early Phrygian, 38, 175, 177, 217, 225
  Middle Phrygian, 41, 230, 238, 244
  Late Phrygian, 307

ore (metal), 123, 160, 166, 335
ornaments. *See also* jewelry
  Early Iron Age, 160
  Early Phrygian, 218, 221
  Middle Phrygian, 237, 241, 284, 290, 293
orthostats, 146, 178, 184, 213, 222, 310
Outer Court Gordion, 41, 43
  Early Phrygian, 180–182, 211–213, 217
  Middle Phrygian, 231, 237
  Late Phrygian, 306–307, 317, 335, 344, 365
Outer Town (OT) Gordion, 30–47, 53, 58
  Middle Phrygian, 228–234, 244–245, 253–254, 259, 270, 283, 362
  Late Phrygian, 306, 316–317
oven, 37. *See also* cooking, hearth
  Late Bronze Age, 115
  Early Iron Age, 140, 160
  Early Phrygian, 212, 219
  Middle Phrygian, 238, 244, 284
  Late Phrygian, 344

painted Buff ware, 174, 186–190, 320, 339
painted decoration. *See also* painted buff ware, ceramics
  Late Bronze Age, 94–97, 105, 113
  Early Phrygian, 174, 186–193, 212, 216
  Middle Phrygian, 244, 248, 276–281, 288
  Late Phrygian, 304, 320–321, 339, 341, 346
Painted House, 306–312, 323, 335, 341–342, 365
palace, 16, 41, 360–361, 367
  economy, 1, 367
pantheon, 92, 300, 368
part-time specialization, 127, 214, 285
pastoralism, 124, 166, 170, 212, 282, 334–335. *See also* agriculture, goat, herding, sheep
pasture, 129, 166, 282, 334, 345
pebble floor, 238–239
  mosaic, 180, 309, 341
performance, 14, 18, 20, 22, 57, 299, 370
  Early Phrygian, 219–220, 360–361
  Middle Phrygian, 226, 238, 362, 364
  Late Phrygian, 365
perfume, 367
  Middle Phrygian, 248, 276
  Late Phrygian, 320, 342, 348–349, 353, 366
Persia(n), 8, 12, 47–49, 370. *See also* Chapter 9
  Middle Phrygian, 229–232, 242–245, 270

Index

Late Phrygian, 364–366
Pfaffenberger, Brian, 15, 22
pig or pork. *See* also animals
   Late Bronze Age, 129, 132
   Early Phrygian, 212, 218
   Middle Phrygian, 282, 290, 362
   Late Phrygian, 334
pine. *See* also timber, wood
   Late Bronze Age, 123
   Early Iron Age, 166
   Early Phrygian, 218
pins. *See* also clothing, fibulae, jewelry
   Late Bronze Age, 125
   Early Iron Age, 160
pithos
   Late Bronze Age, 100, 108, 115, 125, 130
   Early Phrygian, 213
   Middle Phrygian, 240, 290
pithouse, 140, 310–312, 344–346, 366. *See* also houses, semi-subterranean structures
plaques, ivory, 184, 213, 218, 243, 294
plaster, 47, 140, 180, 238, 307, 312, 336
points (weapons)
   Late Bronze Age, 125, 129
   Early Iron Age, 160
   Middle Phrygian, 245, 290, 294
political economy, 13–15, 22, 25–27, 84, 369
   Late Bronze Age, 128, 131–132, 367
   Early Phrygian, 225–226
   Middle Phrygian, 234, 298
   Late Phrygian, 333, 341, 345, 353–354, 366
polychrome decoration, 80, 248, 307, 318, 342. *See* also painted decoration
Polychrome Gatehouse, 178–183, 213
poros, 211. *See* also stone
Post and Poros Building (PAP), 178, 211
"Persian Phrygian Building" (PPB), 232, 236–237, 263, 298, 363. *See* also Greek vessels, jugs
Postgate, Nicholas, 95, 97
pouring vessels, 108, 115, 220, 240, 268, 294
prestige goods, 26, 95, 173, 226
Principal Component Analysis (PCA), 67–69, 73, 78, 80. *See* also multivariate analysis
Protogeometric period, 208, 224
Protogeometric styles, 78
Provenance and provenience, 73–75, 80, 221–222
provisioning, 10, 124, 132, 214, 219, 284
pyrotechnology. *See* technology,

radiocarbon dating, 57
   calibration plateau, 48

Destruction Level (6A), 30
Late Bronze Age, 92, 98
Early Iron Age, 359
rainfall agriculture. *See* agriculture, rainfall
ramp. *See* also Küçük Höyük (KH) fortress
   Early Phrygian, 177–178
   Middle Phrygian, 238
siege, 43, 232, 245, 364
rebuilding, 305. *See* also remodeling, renovation
   Middle Phrygian, 41, 230, 284, 305
   Late Phrygian, 307
Red Lustrous Wheelmade Ware, 84, 93, 95
redistribution, 25–27, 369–370
   Late Bronze Age, 124
   Early Iron Age, 169
   Early Phrygian, 224
   Middle Phrygian, 291, 300
   Late Phrygian, 354
reduction firing (pottery), 149, 186, 196, 225, 246, 288, 318–323, 338, 358. *See* also firing
reference samples, 63, 73, 162, 215, 323
sediments, 60, 225
regional interaction, 134, 168, 173, 190, 226
regional survey, 63. *See* Gordion Regional Survey (GRS)
religion, 300, 367
remodeling (renovation), 40–43, 86. *See* also rebuilding, Unfinished Project
   Early Phrygian, 182–219
   Middle Phrygian, 230–232, 235–243
   Late Phrygian, 306, 317, 337, 344, 365
residence (elite or royal), 41, 180, 218
residential area
   Late Bronze Age, 33, 100
   Middle Phrygian, 233, 245, 283
   Late Phrygian, 323, 340
residential structure, 41, 217, 344, 365. *See* also houses, residence
rhyton. *See* Greek pottery, rhyton
Rice, Prudence, 83, 125, 337
risk, 26, 160, 233, 252, 282, 335
ritual, 20, 27, 83–84, 173, 356, 368–371
   Late Bronze Age, 95, 131–134, 357
   Early Iron Age, 167
   Early Phrygian, 183, 217, 222, 226, 360–361
   Middle Phrygian, 268, 286, 289–291, 297–300, 362–364
   Late Phrygian, 307, 318, 337, 342, 354, 366
ritual economy, 131, 289, 299, 362, 368, 370–371
roads, 25, 349. *See* also streets
   Early Phrygian, 195

418 Index

roads (cont.)
  Middle Phrygian, 233, 238, 244, 362
  Late Phrygian, 302, 335, 337
  Roman, 47
  royal road (Persian), 302
robbing trench (stone foundations), 50, 234, 243, 310–311, 342
Roman, 8, 10, 20, 47, 51, 54
  ceramics, 52
  military, 310
Rose, C. Brian, 31, 232

Sakarya River (Sangarios), 5, 29, 31, 177, 282
sample size, 29, 59, 73, 75, 82
  Late Bronze Age, 117–118
  Early Iron Age, 151, 153, 156–159
  Early Phrygian, 195–196, 214, 224
  Middle Phrygian, 253, 266, 270, 280, 286, 290, 292
  Late Phrygian, 326, 329, 338–339
sampling issues, 9, 20, 29, 213, 329. See discussion Chapters 3 and 4
  Early Phrygian, 195
  Middle Phrygian, 253, 266, 286
  Late Phrygian, 323
Sams, G. Kenneth, 31, 48–49, 52, 56, 83
  Early Iron Age, 142, 145, 148, 161
  Early Phrygian, 184, 186–192, 208–209, 220, 223
  Middle Phrygian, 244
sandstone, 175, 213, 283. See also stone
Sardis, 63, 75–78. See also Lydia
  Early Iron Age, 138
  Early Phrygian, 174, 208
  Middle Phrygian, 227, 273, 276, 293
  Late Phrygian, 301–305, 312, 321, 333, 349–351
scheduling, 84, 161, 211, 214, 233. See also seasonality
Schoop, Ulf-Dietrich, 93, 95, 97–98, 114–115
seals and seal impressions. See also bullae
  Late Bronze Age, 92–93, 98–101, 128–135, 356–357
  Middle Phrygian, 237, 363
  Late Phrygian, 304, 318, 342, 349, 353
seasonality, 84, 124, 213, 216, 289. See also scheduling
sediment samples, 29, 52–54, 60–63, 67, 69–72, 127, 203, 263. See also reference samples
  Kaman Kalehöyük, 118
semi-subterranean houses. See also houses, pithouses
  Late Bronze Age, 100, 123
  Early Iron Age, 37, 137, 140, 142
  Middle Phrygian, 43, 232, 236
  Late Phrygian, 44, 310, 312
serving vessels, 359. See also beverages, drinking vessels, Greek pottery, pouring vessels
  Early Iron Age, 161
  Early Phrygian, 193, 214
  Middle Phrygian, 244, 284, 290, 294
Seyitömer, Eskişehir Province, 63, 75, 213, 333
sheep. See also animal, goat, herding, pastoralism
  Late Bronze Age, 124, 128–129, 132, 135
  Early Iron Age, 160, 164, 166, 170
  Early Phrygian, 213, 218
  Middle Phrygian, 282, 290
  Late Phrygian, 334, 344, 350
siege ramp. See ramp, siege
signaling, 10, 164, 173, 221, 226, 268
Silhouette style pottery. See Alişar IV or Silhouette Style
silver, 284, 310, 317. See also metal
  siglos, 310
sintered slips (pottery), 248, 254, 268
skill level, 83
  Late Bronze Age, 116, 127
  Early Iron Age, 162
  Early Phrygian, 215–216
  Middle Phrygian, 285, 288
  Late Phrygian, 337, 339–340
slag, 123, 125, 160, 310, 335. See also metal
slow wheel. See wheel thrown pottery
social context, 23, 82, 166, 217, 356
social display, 131, 190, 359
social networks, 2, 164, 361
social organization, 21, 136
social relations, 2, 4, 19, 225, 300, 370
social reproduction, 4, 23, 355
socio-political, 129, 137, 170, 213, 352
South Cellar. See cellars
Southwest Zone Western Mound, 47
  Middle Phrygian, 234–240, 248–254, 276–282, 293–296
  Late Phrygian, 312, 335, 344–346
spatial proximity (pottery production), 83
  Late Bronze Age, 127
  Early Iron Age, 162
  Early Phrygian, 215
  Middle Phrygian, 285, 287
  Late Phrygian, 339
specialization (pottery production), 83
  Late Bronze Age, 118, 123, 128, 130, 132, 134

Index

Early Iron Age, 161–163
Early Phrygian, 197, 214, 216
Middle Phrygian, 252, 285–286, 289, 299
Late Phrygian, 326, 337, 339
spindle whorls, 125, 129, 160, 181, 220. *See also* loom weights, textiles, weaving
Square Enclosure (EP Gordion), 178
stamped decoration (pottery)
  Late Bronze Age, 101
  Early Phrygian, 220, 223
  Middle Phrygian, 263
  Late Phrygian, 320–321, 329
Standard Ware (LBA), 95, 115, 128, 132–133
standardization
  Late Bronze Age, 95–97, 104, 125, 133, 135
  Early Iron Age, 146–162, 166, 169, 358
  Early Phrygian, 216
  Middle Phrygian, 268, 285
  Late Phrygian, 348
state, 22, 89, 129, 226–227
  control, 95, 97
  secondary, 368
status, 4, 16–17, 19, 24–25, 82. *See also* high status
  Late Bronze Age, 125, 129–131, 357
  Early Iron Age, 163–164, 166, 358
  Early Phrygian, 171–173, 216–220, 222, 225–226
  Middle Phrygian, 41, 244–245, 281, 291, 293, 299, 363–364
  Late Phrygian, 317, 344, 348, 366
stemmed bowls. *See* fruitstands
stone artifacts. *See also* grinding stones (groundstone)
  Late Bronze Age, 93, 124–125
  Early Iron Age, 160
  Early Phrygian, 212, 217, 219
  Middle Phrygian, 284, 290, 310
  Late Phrygian, 47, 334–335, 349, 365
stone, building or wall
  Late Bronze Age, 33, 100, 123
  Early Iron Age, 140
  Early Phrygian, 38, 177–180, 184, 219
  Middle Phrygian, 41–43, 228, 235, 241–245, 283, 305–310
  Late Phrygian, 47, 312–316, 337, 341–346, 365
storage
  artifact, 9, 50, 52. *See also* Eski Depot
storage buildings, 363
  Late Bronze Age, 115
  Early Phrygian, 41, 173, 212, 219

Middle Phrygian, 232, 236–238, 263, 298
storage pits
  Late Bronze Age, 31, 100, 124–125, 129
  Early Iron Age, 37, 137, 160, 175
storage vessels
  Late Bronze Age, 94, 108, 115, 124, 130
  Early Iron Age, 148, 164
  Early Phrygian, 180, 184, 186
  Middle Phrygian, 239–241, 244, 248, 292, 364
  Late Phrygian, 319, 326, 347
streets. *See also* roads
  Early Phrygian, 180
  Middle Phrygian, 231–232, 238
  Late Phrygian, 365
Structuration (Giddens), 15–16, 356
subsistence, 124, 127, 133, 171
Summers, Geoffrey, 7
surplus production, 124, 134–135, 214
survey, 53. *See* Gordion Regional Survey (GRS)
  Anatolian Iron Age (AIA), 54
  geophysical, 30–31, 43, 174, 232–233
  Gordion, 232, 244, 304, 317
  Niğde, 7
  Sinop, 138
  Thrace, 147
symbols, 12, 25, 139, 222, 249, 352, 361, 372
Syro-Hittite, 137, 178, 360. *See also* Neo-Hittite

Tabal, 7, 229, 299
tableware, 20. *See also* Greek pottery
  Late Bronze Age, 147
  Early Iron Age, 155–156
  Early Phrygian, 219, 224
  Middle Phrygian, 259, 270, 281, 291–295, 364
  Late Phrygian, 326, 340–341, 347, 366
taxes, 15, 26, 300, 302, 335, 337
technological investment, 83
  Late Bronze Age, 127
  Early Iron Age, 162
  Early Phrygian, 216
  Middle Phrygian, 285, 288
  Late Phrygian, 340
technological style, 10, 17, 19, 57, 83, 104, 135
technology, 5, 10, 15–22, 56–57, 82, 367–369
  Late Bronze Age, 98, 116, 133
  Early Iron Age, 156, 169, 358
  Early Phrygian, 208

technology (cont.)
  pyrotechnology, 127, 160, 284, 318, 340
temper (pottery), 106–107, 127, 142, 163, 216. *See* also inclusions (pottery)
temple, 16, 95, 131, 211, 360–361, 367
Terrace Buildings and Terrace Complex, 41, 47. *See* also Clay Cut (CC) Buildings
  Early Phrygian, 180–190, 195, 211–220, 223, 360–361
  Middle Phrygian, 231, 235–237, 263, 284, 290
  Late Phrygian, 307–310, 334–335, 344, 365
territory, 4
  Assyrian, 7
  Phrygian, 7, 171, 300
  Lydian, 227
  Achaemenid, 304
  Tabal, 229
textiles. *See* also cloth
  Late Bronze Age, 124–125, 131, 357
  Early Iron Age, 160
  Early Phrygian, 212–213, 217, 219–221, 235, 360
  Middle Phrygian, 244, 284–285, 290–291, 296, 362
  Late Phrygian, 335–336, 350, 354, 366
texts, 5, 29, 137, 352. *See* also Doodle Stones, graffiti, inscriptions
  Hittite, 86, 92, 124, 131
  Assyrian, 229
  Achaemenid, 344
thermal dynamics, 163, 216, 251. *See* also firing (pottery), kilns
Thessaly, 191, 220
Thrace, 147, 167, 169, 183, 223
tile
  painted, 304
  roof, 43, 57, 232–245, 293, 304–310, 341, 364
timber, 123, 211, 218–219. *See* also juniper, pine, oak, wood
tools, 1, 83, 124, 132, 213. *See* iron tools, lithic tools
  pottery-related, 127, 285, 359
  weaving, 213, 284
topography, 30–31, 68, 232, 282, 306, 344
Toteva, Galya (Bacheva), 318, 320–321
trade, 350, 368. *See* also exchange networks, interaction network
  amphora, 295, 346
  networks, 329, 352, 368

routes, 318, 351–352
trade and exchange, 2, 349
trade goods, 212, 344, 349, 352
transmission, 10–11, 27, 97, 127–133, 162, 216, 288, 359
transportation, 15, 131, 218, 318, 348
trash. *See* dump
treatments (surface or decorative)
  Late Bronze Age, 98, 105, 107, 116–117
  Early Iron Age, 148
  Early Phrygian, 56, 214, 219
  Middle Phrygian, 254, 287–288
  Late Phrygian, 319
trefoil rim, 115, 190, 193, 220, 319
tribute, 7, 25, 369
  Late Bronze Age, 94, 124, 357
  Early Phrygian, 214, 217, 221
  Middle Phrygian, 237, 268, 292, 300
  Late Phrygian, 335, 337, 349, 353, 365–366
Troy, 138, 145–148, 167, 174, 208
tulip bowls. *See* bowls, Achaemenid
tumuli, 5, 8, 29–30, 58, 229. *See* also burials, inhumations, monuments, mortuary practices
  Early Phrygian, 174–175, 183, 193, 212, 360–361
  Middle Phrygian, 233, 237–254, 283–285, 289–299, 362–363
  Late Phrygian, 306, 316–317, 337, 342, 364
Tumulus A, 316
Tumulus C, 316, 337, 342
Tumulus E, 316
Tumulus F, 100
Tumulus G, 183
Tumulus MM, 30, 229, 244, 283, 362, 370, 372
Tumulus P, 244
Tumulus R, 316
Tumulus W, 175, 183, 219–220, 360
Tumulus X, 183
tumulus fill, 253, 270, 337

Unfinished Project (EP), 180, 230–231
uniformity (pottery), 56–57, 83. *See* also standardization
  Late Bronze Age, 95, 118, 121, 125, 131
  Early Iron Age, 161
  Early Phrygian, 209, 214
  Middle Phrygian, 285
  Late Phrygian, 337
University of Pennsylvania, 5, 30–31. *See* also museum, University of Pennsylvania Museum

Upper Trench Sounding (UTS), 31, 230–238, 305–312, 321, 334–335, 344–345
Urartu, 137, 227, 372
urban, 1–2, 8, 27, 41–43, 370–372
  Late Bronze Age, 101, 115, 129
  Middle Phrygian, 227–232, 289, 362
  Late Phrygian, 354, 365
utilitarian pottery, 8, 17
  Late Bronze Age, 92–93
  Early Iron Age, 160
  Early Phrygian, 190
  Middle Phrygian, 248, 285, 287, 289, 295
  Late Phrygian, 323, 332, 351, 366

water management, 368. *See* also agriculture, irrigation
  Late Bronze Age, 93, 124
  Early Phrygian, 212
  Middle Phrygian, 233, 282–283, 362
wealth, 218, 293, 366
weapons, 241, 367. *See* also points (weapons)
weaving, 41, 213, 284. *See* also loom, spindle whorls, textiles
west Anatolian sources (pottery/clay)
  Late Bronze Age, 118
  Early Iron Age, 148, 155
  Early Phrygian, 203, 219–220, 222–223
  Middle Phrygian, 263–266, 273–276, 280–281, 293, 295–296
  Late Phrygian, 328–329, 332
west Anatolian styles (pottery)
  Early Phrygian, 223
  Middle Phrygian, 293, 296
  Late Phrygian, 320, 323, 329, 350
Western Mound (WM), 53. *See* also Northwest Zone (NWZ) Western Mound, Southwest Zone (SWZ) Western Mound
  Early Phrygian, 175, 178
  Middle Phrygian, 43, 228–245, 249–254, 259, 268–284, 290–293, 364
  Late Phrygian, 47, 304–317, 335–337, 340–347, 365
  Hellenistic Period, 47
wheat, 124, 212, 282, 290, 362. *See* also agriculture, cereal, grain
wheel thrown pottery, 82
  Late Bronze Age, 113, 125, 133
  Early Iron Age, 145, 161–162, 359
  Late Phrygian, 338
  Early Phrygian, 184
  fast wheel, 156, 339–340
  slow wheel, 116, 184
Wiessner, Polly, 18
wine, 190, 220, 290–291, 294, 348, 367. *See* also beer, beverages, drinking vessels, pouring vessels
wood. *See* also juniper, oak, pine, timber
  Late Bronze Age, 33, 100, 123
  Early Iron Age, 140
  Early Phrygian, 178, 183, 211, 213, 218
  Middle Phrygian, 244, 249, 284, 290
  Late Phrygian, 316, 341, 344, 350
work areas (pottery), 162, 216, 288, 339
workshop production, 84
  Late Bronze Age, 156, 357
  Early Iron Age, 162, 168
  Middle Phrygian, 285–286
  Late Phrygian, 335, 338, 353
world system, 1, 25, 354, 369

Yassıhöyük (modern village or archaeological site), 5, 9, 29, 52, 104
Young, Rodney S., 5, 9–10, 30–54
  Late Bronze Age, 98–104, 117, 124
  Early Iron Age, 140–149
  Early Phrygian, 175–195, 210
  Middle Phrygian, 230, 234–238, 252
  Late Phrygian, 304–306, 317–318, 332

Zeder, Melinda A., 129, 164, 218, 282
Zincirli, 178